Peterson's

CLEP SUCCESS

9th Edition

Peterson's
CLEP SUCCESS

9th Edition

PETERSON'S

A **nelnet.** COMPANY

PETERSON'S

A ⓝelnet COMPANY

About Peterson's, a Nelnet company

Peterson's (www.petersons.com) is a leading provider of education information and advice, with books and online resources focusing on education search, test preparation, and financial aid. Its Web site offers searchable databases and interactive tools for contacting educational institutions, online practice tests and instruction, and planning tools for securing financial aid. Peterson's serves 110 million education consumers annually.

Credits

Sunflowers, Vincent Van Gogh; National Gallery, London/SuperStock
The Road Seen from the Path to Sevres, Alfred Sisley; Musee d'Orsay, Paris/Bridgeman Art Library, London/SuperStock
Montagne Sainte Victoire–View from the South West, Paul Cézanne; Museum of Modern Western Art, Moscow, Russia/ SuperStock
Parliament & Big Ben, London/SuperStock
Impression: Sunrise, Claude Monet; Musee Marmottan, Paris/A.K.G., Berlin/SuperStock
Self-Portrait, Vincent Van Gogh; Fogg Art Museum, Cambridge, Mass./SuperStock
Notre Dame, Paris/SuperStock
Winchester Cathedral, Winchester, Wiltshire/SuperStock
The Pieta, Michelangelo Buonarroti; St. Peter's Basilica, The Vatican, Rome/Jack Novak/SuperStock
Jeune Fille Nue Au Drape, Aristide Maillol; Christie's Images/SuperStock © 2004 Artist Rights Society (ARS), NY/ASAGP, Paris
Tete/Head, Amedeo Modigliani; Perls Galleries, New York/Lauros-Giraudon, Paris/SuperStock
Cube Sculpture, Isami Noguchi; New York City/Dave Overcash/SuperStock
Mouvement De Danse "A", Auguste Rodin; Christie's Images, New York/SuperStock
Bather With Cloak/Baigneuse Au Voile, Pierre-Auguste Renoir; Christie's Images/SuperStock
Jeune Fille Assise, Aristide Maillol; Christie's Images, New York/SuperStock © 2004 Artist Rights Society (ARS), NY/ASAGP, Paris
Unique Forms of Continuity in Space, Umberto Boccioni; Mattioli Collection, Milan/Bridgeman Art Library, London/SuperStock

For more information, contact Peterson's, 2000 Lenox Drive, Lawrenceville, NJ 08648; 800-338-3282; or find us on the World Wide Web at: www.petersons.com/about.

ISBN-13: 978-0-7689-2479-4
ISBN-10: 0-7689-2479-0

Printed in the United States of America

10 9 8 7 6 5 4 3 2 1   09 08 07

Ninth Edition

Contents

CONTENTS

CONTENTS

Before You Begin

WHAT THIS BOOK WILL DO FOR YOU

This book is for people who have attained the college level of education in "nontraditional ways." It is for those who have gained their education outside the classroom. CLEP examinations give you the opportunity to:

- Have your educational attainment validated, thereby establishing the fact that you possess college-level skills and knowledge

- Attain college credit for the knowledge you have acquired outside the classroom and help you progress toward a degree

- Avoid classroom attendance in subjects you already know and obtain advanced placement in a college curriculum

- Qualify for jobs in an industry that requires college training as a prerequisite for employment or advancement

- Demonstrate for your own satisfaction the college-level ability that you have gained

If you want to take the CLEP exams but are reluctant for fear they may be too difficult, this book is for you. Here you will find out all about the CLEP General Examinations, including:

- How to register for the examinations

- Where and when they are given

- How to prepare for the exams with hundreds of questions and answers typical of those found on the actual tests

- How to interpret your scores and use the results to your best advantage

Used correctly, this "self-tutor" will show you what to expect and will give you a speedy brush-up on the subjects particular to your exam. Even if your study time is very limited, you will:

- Become familiar with the type of examination you can expect

- Improve your general test-taking skill

- Improve your skill in answering questions involving reasoning, judgment, comparison, and evaluation

- Improve your speed and skill in reading and understanding what you read—an important part of your ability to learn and an important part of most tests

- Prepare yourself in the particular fields covered by the CLEP General Examinations

In fact, this guide will tell you exactly what to study by presenting in full every type of question you will get on the actual exam. You will do better merely by familiarizing yourself with them.

It will help you find your weaknesses and find them fast with a pretest before each review section. Once you know where you are weak, you will know how best to use your study time in preparing for your exam.

In addition, this book will give you the feel of the exam. Since previous CLEP exams are not available for inspection, the practice test questions in each posttest are invaluable to you.

Finally, this book will give you confidence now, while you are preparing for the exam. It will build your self-confidence as you proceed and help to ward off the pretest jitters that have undermined so many test-takers.

ABOUT THE CD

You have additional CLEP preparation available to you on the enclosed CD. The CD contains 3 practice tests for each of the CLEP General Tests. We suggest that begin by taking the pretests at the beginning of each section in the book. Once you have an idea of how you want to focus your preparation, review the material. As the final part of your preparation, take the posttests and then the practice tests on the CD.

YOU'RE WELL ON YOUR WAY TO SUCCESS

Remember that knowledge is power. By using *Peterson's CLEP Success*, you will be studying the most comprehensive guide available, and you will become extremely knowledgeable about the exams. We look forward to helping you raise your score.

GIVE US YOUR FEEDBACK

Peterson's, a Nelnet company, publishes a full line of resources to help guide you through the college admission process. Peterson's publications can be found at your local bookstore, library, and high school guidance office, and you can access us online at www.petersons.com.

We welcome any comments or suggestions you may have about this publication and invite you to complete our online survey at www.petersons.com/booksurvey. Or you can fill out the survey at the back of this book, tear it out, and mail it to us at:

Publishing Department
Peterson's, a Nelnet company
2000 Lenox Drive
Lawrenceville, NJ 08648

Your feedback will help us make your educational dreams possible.

Part I

ALL ABOUT THE COLLEGE-LEVEL EXAMINATION PROGRAM (CLEP)

Chapter 1
THE COLLEGE-LEVEL EXAMINATION PROGRAM

Do you have know-how that was gained from other than accredited college training? Have you read widely or had life experiences that qualify you for jobs you can't get because you don't have the college credits? Or are you disqualified for advanced placement in college simply because you don't have the course credits from an accredited institution? If so, you are among the large number of people for whom the College-Level Examination Program is designed.

The College-Level Examination Program (CLEP) offers you an opportunity to show a college admissions officer, or a prospective employer, or just yourself, what you know in a variety of subject areas. Some employers in business, industry, professional groups, and government use the results of CLEP examinations to assess a potential employee's educational level, regardless of the credits listed on his or her resume. Many college admissions officers use CLEP scores to determine where to place college applicants in their traditional four-year programs.

There have long been tests to assess the achievement of students who progress from high school to college in the usual way. However, for those who have gained their education through Internet or correspondence courses, television courses, home-study courses via records or tapes, on-the-job training, or life experiences, no widely recognized evaluation test has been available until the CLEP.

The CLEP Examinations are sponsored by the College Board. The College Board employs the services of the Educational Testing Service (ETS) to develop and administer the exams. ETS is a nonprofit corporation specializing in test development and educational research. The College Board, with the support of the Carnegie Corporation of New York, developed the CLEP program to aid students who wish to gain college credit for achievements outside the classroom. CLEP examinations are open to anyone who desires to demonstrate college-level proficiency no matter how or where that proficiency was gained.

TWO KINDS OF CLEP EXAMS

The College-Level Examination Program comprises two types of examinations: the General Examinations and the Subject Examinations.

The General Examinations measure college-level achievement in five basic areas of the liberal arts: English Composition, Humanities, Mathematics, Natural Sciences, and Social Sciences and History. These examinations test material usually covered in the first two years of college, often referred to as the general or liberal education requirement. The General Examinations are not intended to measure specialized knowledge of a particular discipline, nor are they based on a particular curriculum or course of study. Rather, they are designed to evaluate broad-based ability that can be acquired in a number of ways, through personal reading, employment, television, radio, adult classes, Internet classes, or advanced high school work.

Each General Examination is 90 minutes long and, except for English Composition with Essay, consists entirely of multiple-choice questions presented in two separately timed sections. The content and format of each General Examination is fully detailed in the chapters that follow.

The Subject Examinations measure achievement in specific college courses and are used to grant exemption from and credit for these courses. Like the General Examinations, each Subject Examination is 90 minutes long and consists of multiple-choice questions presented in two separately timed sections. The four Subject Exams in Composition and Literature also include an optional 90-minute essay section. Check with the college you are planning to attend to see if the essay section is required.

Twenty-nine Subject Examinations are offered. More detailed information about the Subject Examinations is available at the College Board Web site: www.collegeboard.com.

WHEN AND WHERE CLEP EXAMS ARE GIVEN

CLEP tests are administered throughout the year at more than 1,200 test centers throughout the United States. These centers, usually located on college and university campuses, are listed in the publication *CLEP Colleges*, which you may obtain

by writing: CLEP, P.O. Box 6600, Princeton, NJ 08541-6600

by e-mailing: clep@info.collegeboard.com

or by calling: (609) 771-7865

When you register, you may ask to take the test at the most convenient location for you. If you live more than 150 miles from the nearest listed test center, the College Board may be able to arrange a special test location that is closer to your home. If you require special arrangements, you must pay an extra fee. Arrangements for a special testing center take about five weeks. If you live outside the United States, you may request a special administration of the CLEP exams. You must list at least three cities where you could be tested, and you must submit your request at least four months before the date on which you wish to be tested.

You may register for one or more examinations on a given testing date. No matter which examination you take, you must arrive at the start of the test session. Late arrivals will usually not be admitted as they may disturb those who have begun to work.

HOW TO REGISTER FOR THE EXAMS

The first thing to do if you are considering the possibility of utilizing your life experiences to obtain college credit is getting the booklets *CLEP Colleges* and *Information for Candidates and Registration Form*. These publications are available at College Board offices or from the Princeton address given on this page.

The Registration Form must be completed and sent with your test fee to the test center no later than three weeks before the test is scheduled. Be sure to send your Registration Form and fee to the test center, not to the College Board. Consult the *Information for Candidates* booklet for detailed instructions on registration procedures and for directions for filling out your application form.

If you wish to obtain college credit for participating in the CLEP program, it is important that you contact your college guidance department to learn what regulations govern the use of the tests at your school. College credit is awarded only by the colleges and universities that participate in the program. Although the tests are

devised and administered by the College Entrance Examination Board, the Board is not a college and does not give college credit. Each college and university has its own policy regarding CLEP scores, and it is up to you to find out the requirements of the school to which you are applying for credit.

COMPUTER-BASED TESTING (CBT)

All CLEP exams are administered on a computer. The exam is preceded by a tutorial that explains how to take the exam on a computer. The CLEP CBT exams are fixed-length exams, like the paper-and-pencil version. There are advantages of the CLEP CBT. Your score report will be generated immediately after taking the test, and you will be able to take those scores with you. The English Composition with Essay test will be separately scored. Once you send your essay electronically to CLEP, you will receive your score within two weeks.

HOW THE TESTS ARE SCORED

In the CLEP CBT version, only the right answers will count toward your score.

Your score is then converted to a scaled score that ranges from 200 to 800 for the General Exams and from 20 to 80 for the Subject Exams. The scaled score provides a uniform indicator of performance no matter which edition of a particular test you take.

There are no passing or failing scores on the General Examinations. Each college or university determines how and to what extent it will use CLEP examinations to award credit, including which tests it recognizes and what scores it requires.

HOW SCORES ARE REPORTED

Your scores will be sent to any institutions you designated at the time of your examination. Test scores are kept on file for twenty years. You may request that your test score reports be sent to any institution at any time during this period by completing the Transcript Request Form included in your score report.

Since the optional essay section of the Subject Examination is graded by the institution receiving the score, there is no transcript service on Subject Examination essay answers.

If, after registering for an exam, you decide not to take it, you may cancel your registration and obtain a refund check for one half of your testing fee. Fill out the appropriate space on the bottom of your Admission Form and send the form to the test center where you were scheduled to take the test. Your request must be mailed no later than two days before the testing date, otherwise you won't receive the refund.

You may retake any CLEP examination provided that six months have elapsed since you last took that examination. If you retake an exam within fewer than six months, your score will be cancelled and your fees will not be refunded.

STUDY HINTS

- **Be confident.** It is important to know that you are not expected to answer every question correctly on the CLEP Examinations. The questions have a range of difficulty and differentiate among several levels of skill.

- **Read each question carefully.** The questions on the General Examinations are not designed to trick you through misleading or ambiguous alternative choices. On the other hand, they are not all direct questions of factual information. Some are designed to elicit responses that reveal your ability to reason or to interpret a fact or idea. It's up to you to read each question carefully so you know what is being asked. The test-makers have tried to make the questions clear. Do not go too far astray in looking for hidden meanings.

- **Become familiar with the test's scope, format, and purpose.** It is important to discover how the test is organized, what material is covered, where the concentration is, and how the questions are phrased.

- **Become familiar with practice tests that are based on the examination.** Test yourself and analyze your strong points as well as your weaknesses. Try to find the underlying reasons for the correct answer to each question.

- **As soon as possible, plan a program to prepare yourself for the test.** Long-range studying is more effective than last-minute cramming.

- **Develop regular study habits.** It is far better to study for an hour three times a week for five weeks than to attempt to study for 15 hours during the two or three days preceding the actual examination.

- **Be an active participant in the study process.** Sitting in a comfortable chair, listening to the stereo, and munching on a cookie may be pleasant, but this is certainly not an effective way to study important material. It is better to sit at a well-lighted desk in a quiet place with pencil and paper, underlining key phrases, taking notes, and recording items that you want to remember.

- **Don't burden yourself with unnecessary material.** Many colored markers, slide rules, and tape can prove to be a distraction if not needed.

- **Analyze the questions carefully.** Sometimes a word such as *never*, *always*, or *not* can change the question and its resulting response. Before you answer a question, you must know what the question is.

- **Be positive!** Approach the examination with an optimistic attitude. Know that your studying will help you to do well.

TEST-TAKING TIPS FOR THE DAY OF THE EXAMINATION

- **Get to the room at least 10 to 15 minutes before exam time.** Allow yourself ample time to settle down so that you are familiar with the room and relatively comfortable.

- **Make certain that the test conditions are favorable.** If there are distractions or any adverse conditions, inform the proctor. Don't be a martyr. The test will require all your energy. Don't be distracted unnecessarily.

- **Follow all the directions given by the proctor.** If you do not understand what to do or are uncertain how to proceed, don't hesitate to ask the proctor for assistance.

- **Budget your time wisely.** Be certain you understand the directions for each examination. Don't spend too much time on any one question. Proceed from question to question without needless worry regarding how you answered a previous question. If a question thoroughly confuses you, omit it and move on to the next one.

- **If you find yourself becoming tense, take a few deep breaths.** Some people close their eyes for a few seconds and then continue to work.

- **If you take the essay component, you should allow yourself 5 or 10 minutes to proofread.** You will probably not have enough time to rewrite the entire essay.

If you use this book wisely, you will be at ease with the general format of the exam and the types of questions asked. As a result, there will be no surprises and you will be free to concentrate on your responses. To get the most out of this book, read each section thoroughly and complete all the exercises. For additional practice, be sure to log on to petersons.com/testprep.

Part II

ENGLISH COMPOSITION

Chapter 2
PRETEST

TIME—45 MINUTES	55 QUESTIONS

PART I

Directions: The following sentences test your knowledge of grammar, diction (choice of words), and idiom. Some sentences are correct. No sentence contains more than one error.

You will find that the error, if there is one, is underlined and lettered. Assume that elements of the sentence that are not underlined are correct and cannot be changed. In choosing answers, follow the requirements of standard written English.

If there is an error, select the one underlined part that must be changed to make the sentence correct, and fill in the corresponding oval on your answer sheet. If there is no error, select answer (E).

1. Here, Mr. President, is all the reports issued by
   A   B   C
   the Executive Committee, which met last month.
                            D
   No error.
   E

2. Are you willing to allow we boys to form a
                     A
   cooking class, even though only girls have taken
              B   C
   cooking in the past? No error.
             D   E

3. Such a comment about anyone who we know to be
   A   B   C
   generous, kind, and thoughtful is unfair. No error.
                      D   E

4. 6 percent of the students voted, although there
   A   B
   had been a militant demonstration for students'
   C   D
   rights. No error.
        E

5. Philip answers the telephone, fell against the
        A   B C
   table, and broke his leg. No error.
           D   E

6. The student thought that the lecturer had
            A   B
   referred to *The Communist Manifesto*. No error.
   C   D   E

7. We were not allowed to skate on the pond until
      A   B
   it had froze to a depth of 10 inches and the red
       C
   signal had been hoisted. No error.
          D   E

8. The meeting was interesting to some people and
           A   B
   to me it was boring. No error.
   C D   E

9. They were probably declining in influence as
           A   B
   values of prestige and status became more
                            C
   dominant in American corporate life. No error.
   D   E

10. It is very dangerous to differ from a superior in
    A   B
    the company unless there is mutual respect.
               C   D
    No error.
    E

11. Steve was the least prepared of the two who
            A   B
    took the examination last Friday. No error.
    C   D   E

12. I am living in New York City for five years now,
     A   B
    and I still feel the excitement of this great city.
            C   D
    No error.
    E

GO ON TO THE NEXT PAGE ➤

13. He <u>has always been</u> negligent <u>about</u> his health,
          A   B
    and he <u>is feeling</u> the <u>effects</u> of his carelessness.
          C   D
    <u>No error.</u>
       E

14. <u>From</u> the statement <u>given to</u> the manager, he
      A   B
    <u>implied</u> that Mr. Korn <u>would</u> resign. <u>No error.</u>
      C   D   E

15. If he <u>would have been</u> there, he would have
      A
    seen for <u>himself</u> the <u>further</u> improvements they
      B   C
    <u>had made.</u> <u>No error.</u>
      D   E

Directions: The following sentences test correctness and effectiveness of expression. In choosing answers, follow the requirements of standard written English; that is, pay attention to grammar, diction (choice of words), sentence construction, and punctuation.

In each of the following sentences, part of the sentence or the entire sentence is underlined. Beneath each sentence you will find five versions of the underlined part. Answer (A) repeats the original; answers (B) through (E) present different alternatives.

Choose the answer that best expresses the meaning of the original sentence. If you think the original is better than any of the alternatives, choose it; otherwise, select one of the other answer choices. Your choice should produce the most effective sentence—one that is clear and precise, without awkwardness or ambiguity.

Example

When the Yankees and the Braves meet again in the World Series, <u>their hitting will be decisive.</u>

(A) their hitting will be decisive.
(B) Braves pitching will not be decisive.
(C) the decisive factor will be their hitting.
(D) the decisive factor will be Yankee hitting.
(E) an important factor will be Yankee hitting.

The correct answer is (D). In choices (A) and (C) "their" lacks a clear antecedent (noun or pronoun to which it refers). Choice (B) is only speculative or inferred. Choice (E) doesn't emphasize "decisive," a term stronger than "important."

16. The prosecution entered <u>the following items into evidence. They were a revolver,</u> a dagger, a ballet ticket, and a lock of a woman's hair.

(A) the following items into evidence. They were a revolver,
(B) the following evidence, a revolver,
(C) the following items into evidence, and a revolver,
(D) the following items into evidence: a revolver,
(E) the following items into evidence; a revolver,

17. He had the lingering impression that the woman had not understood <u>the terms he had used to explain his ideas.</u>

(A) the terms he had used to explain his ideas.
(B) his way of using terms to explain his ideas.
(C) his use of terms in explaining his ideas.
(D) the explanation of his ideas because of his use of terms.
(E) the terms of his explanation.

18. <u>Playing with an intensity appropriate to the piece,</u> her eyes grew moist, and she leaned over the keyboard.

(A) Playing with an intensity appropriate to the piece,
(B) Great intensity called for by the piece,
(C) Although the piece called for great intensity,
(D) The piece called for great intensity,
(E) As she played with the intensity appropriate to the piece,

19. The ballerina bent lithely toward him, <u>leaping away like a startled deer.</u>

(A) leaping away like a startled deer.
(B) who leaped away like a startled deer.
(C) and then she leaped away like a startled deer.
(D) afterward, she leaped away like a startled deer.
(E) deerlike, then, leaping away.

20. <u>The ridiculousness of his predicament</u> occurred to him as he reached the wire.

(A) The ridiculousness of his predicament
(B) The absurdity of his situation
(C) His ridiculous predicament
(D) He was impressed by his absurd predicament, it
(E) The ridicule of his predicament

21. Silent-film actors, <u>because of the very nature of the medium, had to project</u> as much emotion as possible through expression, eyes, and body movement.

    (A) because of the very nature of the medium, had to project
    (B) being forced by the medium to project
    (C) the media being what it was to project
    (D) projecting through the media
    (E) since the medium required them to convey as much as they could through the body, projected

22. <u>The day was cool and calm and bright;</u> this day must die.

    (A) The day was cool and calm and bright;
    (B) Being cool and calm and bright,
    (C) Despite its coolness and calmness and brightness,
    (D) Though cool and calm and bright,
    (E) If not cool and calm and bright,

23. <u>Neither do we wish to delude ourselves, nor do</u> we wish to lessen our effectiveness late in the race.

    (A) Neither do we wish to delude ourselves, nor do
    (B) We wish neither to delude ourselves nor do
    (C) We want to delude ourselves as much as
    (D) Deluding ourselves,
    (E) Not deluding ourselves, nor do

24. In the unconscious, where wishes are omnipotent, <u>people whom we think we love may receive harsh treatment.</u>

    (A) people whom we think we love may receive harsh treatment.
    (B) we may treat even those we love harshly.
    (C) imagining harsh things about those we love.
    (D) we may shock ourselves with our honesty.
    (E) we may love the harsh treatment afforded others.

25. We could withdraw from this foreign entanglement, <u>thereby avoiding a dangerous military situation.</u>

    (A) thereby avoiding a dangerous military situation.
    (B) avoiding a dangerous military situation.
    (C) which included a dangerous military situation.
    (D) and the dangerous military situation they involve.
    (E) endangered by a military situation.

Directions: Each of the following selections is an early draft of a student essay in which the sentences have been numbered for easy reference. Some parts of the selections need to be changed.

Read each essay and then answer the questions that follow. Some questions are about particular sentences or parts of sentences and ask you to improve sentence structure and diction (choice of words). In making these decisions, follow the conventions of standard written English. Other questions refer to the entire essay or parts of the essay and ask you to consider organization, development, and effectiveness of language in relation to purpose and audience.

Questions 26–34 are based on the following draft of a student essay.

(1) *Critics of television argue that watching television lulls the brain, dulling the imagination, and encourages physical inactivity.* (2) *But watching television has hidden benefits these critics may not be aware of.* (3) *In my case, watching television has made me better at finding missing items, and the search for these items keeps me active.*

(4) *I have a big family, and we all watch television.* (5) *Sharing the television paraphernalia, sometimes necessary items are misplaced.* (6) *I can't find T.V. Guide.* (7) *I can't find the remote control.* (8) *I have to search for these items before I get comfortable on the couch.*

(9) *T.V. Guide is relatively easy to find.* (10) *It likes to hide under things like big magazines on the coffee table or under the sofa.* (11) *The remote control is much harder to find.* (12) *It is smaller, and it is used very often.* (13) *Its favorite places to hide are between the pillows of the sofa, under the armchair, and on top of the VCR.* (14) *It also has been found in the kitchen.* (15) *It has even been found outside.* (16) *The dog probably took it outside.*

(17) *I figure out where these objects may be, and then I search for them.* (18) *I bend down to look under the table, stretch to reach the top of the VCR, go from the living room to the kitchen to the backyard.*

GO ON TO THE NEXT PAGE

26. Which of the following is the best version of the underlined portion of sentence 1 (reproduced below)?

    Critics of television argue that watching television lulls the brain, dulling the imagination, and encourages physical inactivity.

    (A) (As it is now)
    (B) is lulling to the brain, dulling to the imagination, and encourages physical inactivity.
    (C) lulls the brain, dulls the imagination, and encourages physical inactivity.
    (D) lulls the brain, dulling the imagination and encouraging physical inactivity.
    (E) lulling the brain, dulling the imagination, and encouraging physical inactivity.

27. In context, the best phrase to replace "a big family" in sentence 4 is

    (A) many brothers and sisters
    (B) a very large family
    (C) a plethora of siblings
    (D) a mother, a father, and an older brother
    (E) two brothers and three sisters

28. In the context of paragraph 2, which is the best version of the underlined portion of sentence 5 (reproduced below)?

    Sharing the television paraphernalia, sometimes necessary items are misplaced.

    (A) Because we share the television paraphernalia,
    (B) As a result of the fact that all of the members of the family share the television paraphernalia,
    (C) Having shared the television paraphernalia,
    (D) The television paraphernalia being shared,
    (E) Sharing things needed to watch television

29. Which of the following is the best way to revise and combine sentences 6 and 7 (reproduced below)?

    I can't find *TV Guide*. I can't find the remote control.

    (A) I can't find *TV Guide*, and I can't find the remote control.
    (B) I can find neither *TV Guide* nor the remote control.
    (C) I can't find *TV Guide*, and the remote control is missing.
    (D) Not finding *TV Guide* and the remote control.
    (E) I can't find *TV Guide* I can't find the remote control.

30. Should the writer add the following sentence after sentence 8?

    Let me give you some examples of the items that I need to find before I can begin to watch television.

    (A) No, because the sentence is unnecessarily wordy.
    (B) No, because the writer addresses the reader directly as "you."
    (C) No, because adequate transition from paragraph 2 to paragraph 3 already exists.
    (D) All of the above
    (E) None of the above

31. Which is the best version of the underlined portion of sentence 10 (reproduced below)?

    It likes to hide under things like big magazines on the coffee table or under the sofa.

    (A) (As it is now)
    (B) under the big magazines on the coffee table or under the sofa.
    (C) under things like big magazines on the coffee table, or it hides under the sofa.
    (D) under the big magazines on the coffee table, or it hides under the sofa.
    (E) under the big magazines on the coffee table and it hides under the sofa.

32. Which of the following is the best way to revise and combine sentences 11 and 12 (reproduced below)?

The remote control is much harder to find. It is smaller, and it is used very often.

(A) Because it is smaller and frequently used, the remote control is much harder to find.

(B) The remote control is much harder to find. Because it is smaller and used very often.

(C) Because it is smaller than *T.V. Guide*, and because it is used very often by anyone in my family who is watching television, the remote control is much more difficult to find.

(D) The remote control is found with difficulty because it is smaller and used very often.

(E) The remote control, smaller and often used and difficult to find.

33. Which of the following is the best way to revise and combine sentences 15 and 16 (reproduced below)?

It has even been found outside. The dog probably took it outside.

(A) It has even been found outside, where the dog probably took it.

(B) It has even been found outside, and the dog probably took it there.

(C) It has even been found outside, but the dog probably took it.

(D) It has even been found outside when the dog probably took it.

(E) It has even been found outside whence the dog probably took it.

34. Which of the following, if put before sentence 17, would best link the conclusion to the rest of the essay?

(A) Who said television turns people into couch potatoes?

(B) Thus it is apparent that television does not lull the brain, dull the imagination, or lead to physical laziness.

(C) Searching for the missing items can be fun.

(D) I enjoy watching television.

(E) Locating missing items makes me use my mind and my body.

Questions 35–43 are based on a draft of a book about basic cooking techniques.

(1) Homemade chicken broth requires some care by the cook, but for the most part the soup just sits and simmers all by itself and you don't have to do anything. (2) The small amount of effort is worthwhile, because the homemade broth is more flavorful and better for you than commercial products.

(3) You will need about two pounds of chicken backs, necks, and giblets. (4) You will also need one sliced onion and two sliced carrots. (5) Heat a heavy five-quart pot, such as a dutch oven, over medium heat. (6) Put two tablespoons of vegetable oil into the pot. (7) Add the onions and carrots, and saute until the onion is translucent. (8) Then add the chicken pieces. (9) They may not fit in one layer. (10) Turn the chicken until the skin loses its raw color. (11) Then pour eight cups of cold water over the chicken and vegetables. (12) Raise the heat to high, and as the broth comes to a boil, scum will start to rise. (13) Using a slotted spoon, skim it from the surface. (14) When the scum almost appears to stop coming, turn the heat down so that the broth simmers slowly. (15) Then add the seasonings: $\frac{1}{4}$ teaspoon of dried parsley flakes, one bay leaf, $\frac{1}{4}$ teaspoon of dried thyme, and twelve black peppercorns. (16) Cover the pot. (17) Leave the lid partially askew so that the broth simmers but does not boil. (18) Cook for $1\frac{1}{2}$ hours.

(19) Straining the broth into a large bowl, discard the vegetables. (20) The cooked chicken can be reserved for use in a chicken salad or casseroles. (21) When the broth is cold, the fat will have risen to the top, and it can be easily removed. (22) The broth can keep in the refrigerator for up to a week, or it may be frozen. (23) This salt-free broth can be used as the base for a vegetable soup, to make sauces and gravies, and for flavoring foods cooked in it such as rice or potatoes.

GO ON TO THE NEXT PAGE

35. Which of the following is the best way to revise the underlined portion of sentence 1 (reproduced below)?

    Homemade chicken broth requires some care and attention by the cook, but for the most part the soup just sits and simmers all by itself and you don't have to do anything.

    (A) but mostly the soup takes care of itself.
    (B) but the soup can cook unattended for most of the time it is cooking.
    (C) but while it is simmering, it needs no attention.
    (D) but the cook doesn't have to watch it all of the time while it is cooking.
    (E) but then the soup watches itself.

36. In context, the best phrase to replace "more flavorful and better for you" in sentence 2 is

    (A) tastier and healthier
    (B) tastes better and has less fat
    (C) contains less calories and fat
    (D) tastes richer and fatless
    (E) has richer taste and less fat

37. Which of the following is the best way to revise and combine sentences 8 and 9 (reproduced below)?

    Then add the chicken pieces. They may not fit in one layer.

    (A) Then add the chicken pieces, they may not fit in one layer.
    (B) Then add all the chicken pieces not fitting in one layer.
    (C) Then add the chicken pieces, which may not fit in one layer.
    (D) Then adding the chicken pieces which may not fit in one layer.
    (E) Then add the chicken pieces they may not fit in one layer.

38. In context, the best phrase to replace "appears to stop coming" in sentence 14 is

    (A) stops coming
    (B) doesn't rise to the top surface of the soup any longer
    (C) stops foaming up from the bottom
    (D) no longer accumulates at the top
    (E) ceases to accumulate

39. The author can best improve paragraph 2 by doing which of the following after sentence 14?

    (A) Telling how to gauge the temperature of the soup
    (B) Describing the soup's color at this point in the cooking process
    (C) Explaining the chemistry of soup making
    (D) Describing how one knows the soup is simmering slowly
    (E) All of the above

40. Which of the following is the best way to revise the underlined portions of sentences 16 and 17 (reproduced below) so that the two sentences are combined into one?

    Cover the pot. Leave the lid partially askew so that the soup simmers but does not boil.

    (A) the pot, leave
    (B) the pot, but then one leaves
    (C) the pot, leaving
    (D) the pot, and then you leave
    (E) the pot, while you are leaving

41. Which of the following is the best version of sentence 19 (reproduced below)?

    Straining the broth into a large bowl, discard the vegetables.

    (A) Straining the broth into a large bowl while discarding the vegetables.
    (B) Straining the broth into a large bowl, then you discard the vegetables.
    (C) Strain the broth into a large bowl and then you discard the vegetables.
    (D) Strain the broth into a large bowl; then discard the vegetables.
    (E) While straining the broth into a large bowl, discard the vegetables.

42. The best phrase to replace "in a chicken salad or casseroles" in sentence 20 is

    (A) in chicken salads or casseroles
    (B) in chicken salads or a casserole
    (C) for chicken salads and for a casserole
    (D) for chicken salad and when you are making a casserole.
    (E) when making a casserole and chicken salads

43. To best improve paragraph 3, the writer should add which of the following sentences after sentence 20?

    (A) Refrigerate the soup.
    (B) Put the soup in jars that have covers on them.
    (C) The soup should be poured into covered jars and refrigerated.
    (D) Transfer the soup to covered containers and refrigerate it.
    (E) The soup is then poured into covered jars and refrigerated.

Directions: The following sentences test correctness and effectiveness of expression. In choosing answers, follow the requirements of standard written English; that is, pay attention to grammar, diction (choice of words), sentence construction, and punctuation.

In each of the following sentences, part of the sentence or the entire sentence is underlined. Beneath each sentence you will find five versions of the underlined part. Answer (A) repeats the original; answers (B) through (E) present different alternatives.

Choose the answer that best expresses the meaning of the original sentence. If you think the original is better than any of the alternatives, choose it; otherwise, select one of the other answer choices. Your choice should produce the most effective sentence—one that is clear and precise, without awkwardness or ambiguity.

Example

When the Yankees and the Braves meet again in the World Series, their hitting will be decisive.

(A) their hitting will be decisive.
(B) Braves pitching will not be decisive.
(C) the decisive factor will be their hitting.
(D) the decisive factor will be Yankee hitting.
(E) an important factor will be Yankee hitting.

The correct answer is (D). In choices (A) and (C) "their" lacks a clear antecedent (noun or pronoun to which it refers). Choice (B) is only speculative or inferred. Choice (E) doesn't emphasize "decisive," a term stronger than "important."

44. In recent years, many high schools have replaced traditional English courses with complex elective programs; critics consider that this prompted many to think that it has contributed to the decline in SAT scores.

    (A) critics consider that this prompted many to think that it has contributed to the decline in SAT scores.
    (B) contributing to the decline in SAT scores.
    (C) a movement that has contributed, as many critics believe, to the decline in SAT scores.
    (D) this movement has contributed to the decline in SAT scores.
    (E) a contribution to the decline in SAT scores.

45. The student respected and momentary anger at her professor.

    (A) respected and momentary anger at
    (B) felt respect for and momentary anger in
    (C) though momentarily anger by, admired
    (D) felt respectful and momentarily angered at
    (E) for a moment felt both anger and admiration for

46. The two poets were antithetical—T. S. Eliot, a pious classicist, and W. B. Yeats, a self-obsessed romantic.

    (A) a pious classicist, and W. B. Yeats, a self-obsessed romantic.
    (B) a pious classicist, and W. B. Yeats, shaping a lifelong self-portrait.
    (C) a pious classic, and W. B. Yeats, a selfish romancer.
    (D) being a classicist and Christian, and W. B. Yeats, who was a pagan and romantic.
    (E) a solemn Christian conservative, and W. B. Yeats, who was a wide-eyed romantic portrait painter.

GO ON TO THE NEXT PAGE

47. Allowing high school students a large elective program is a way of saying that they have reached the apex of their intellectual developments.

   (A) Allowing high school students a large elective program is a way of saying that they

   (B) The allowance to let high school students take what they want leading to the assumption that they

   (C) By allowing high school students a large elective program, we assume that they

   (D) Allowing high school students a large elective program, they

   (E) Permission given to high school students to take a large, elective program to suggest that they

48. Sensationalism, not responsible reporting, was used to sell papers.

   (A) Sensationalism, not responsible reporting,

   (B) Not responsible reporting and sensationalism

   (C) Responsible reporting was thrown out, sensationalism

   (D) Reporting events in a responsible way rather than sensationalism

   (E) If responsible reporting were thrown out, sensationalism

49. The SATs did not evoke Helen's interest, either when she prepared for them nor when she was taking them.

   (A) The SATs did not evoke Helen's interest, either when she prepared for them nor when she was taking them.

   (B) Helen was not interested in the SATs, taking them or preparing them.

   (C) Helen did not show interest in preparing the SATs nor taking them.

   (D) Helen was not interested in preparing for taking the SATs, but she did it.

   (E) Helen was not interest when she was preparing for the SATs nor in their taking.

50. Television not only wastes a student's time, but I also feel that much of what is shown on TV is noneducational.

   (A) but I also feel that much of what is shown on TV is noneducational.

   (B) but also giving him much that is noneducational.

   (C) but it also submits him to much that is noneducational.

   (D) but submitting him also to much that is noneducational.

   (E) but noneducational programs also predominate.

51. He quoted all the teachers as being reluctant to teach Shakespeare.

   (A) He quoted all the teachers as being reluctant to teach Shakespeare.

   (B) He cited all the teachers, and they were reluctant to teach Shakespeare.

   (C) He cited all the teachers for whom teaching Shakespeare was a reluctance.

   (D) He quoted all the teachers, who said they were reluctant to teach Shakespeare.

   (E) Being reluctant to teach Shakespeare, he quoted all the teachers.

52. Exposure to neutron radiation from nuclear reactors has gone unstudied because of the inadequacy of measuring techniques and insufficient knowledge of this field.

   (A) because of the inadequacy of measuring techniques and insufficient knowledge of this field.

   (B) because they don't use adequate measuring techniques, not having adequate knowledge of the field.

   (C) because their measuring techniques are inadequate and their knowledge of the field insufficient.

   (D) measuring techniques being bad and knowledge in the field as it is.

   (E) can it be helped if measuring devices in the field are inadequate and knowledge insufficient?

53. Gone are the days when a music director could hire or fire players at will, thanks to union protection and self-governing player committee.

   (A) Gone are the days when a music director could hire or fire players at will,

   (B) Hiring and firing music players at will is a thing of the past for a music director,

   (C) No longer can a music director hire or fire players at will,

   (D) Once when a music director hired or fired players at will,

   (E) A music director, who hires or fires players at will, a thing of the past,

54. <u>Not getting backstage, they wept, the fans of Barry Manilow</u> stood at the theater entrance.

- (A) Not getting backstage, they wept, the fans of Barry Manilow
- (B) Because they were weeping because they could not get backstage the fans of Barry Manilow
- (C) The fans of Barry Manilow wept because they could not get backstage and
- (D) Because they could not get backstage, the fans of Barry Manilow wept while they
- (E) The fans of Barry Manilow could not go backstage and they wept and they

55. Take, for example, the four major tragedies of Shakespeare, <u>which are central to every educated person's understanding of the range and power of the English language.</u>

- (A) which are central to every educated person's understanding of the range and power of the English language.
- (B) being central to every English teacher's and person's grasp of its range and power.
- (C) they are central to the educated person's understanding of the English language's range and power.
- (D) because being central to every educated man's understanding of the range and power of the English language.
- (E) although they are central to every educated person's understanding of the range and power of the English language.

STOP If you finish before the time is up, you may check your work on this section only. Do not turn to any other section in the test.

TIME—45 MINUTES	45 QUESTIONS

PART II

ENGLISH COMPOSITION WITHOUT ESSAY TEST

Directions: Each of the following selections is an early draft of a student essay in which the sentences have been numbered for easy reference. Some parts of the selections need to be changed.

Read each essay and then answer the questions that follow. Some questions are about particular sentences or parts of sentences and ask you to improve sentence structure and diction (choice of words). In making these decisions, follow the conventions of standard written English. Other questions refer to the entire essay or parts of the essay and ask you to consider organization, development, and effectiveness of language in relation to purpose and audience.

Questions 56–64 are based on the following draft of a student essay.

(1) *Working and going to school at the same time is difficult.* (2) *It's hard to find time to do schoolwork, and there's no time for goofing off, leisure, relaxing, and enjoying yourself.* (3) *What makes the situation worse is that as a young person, the only jobs available are usually boring or unpleasant.*

(4) *When I worked at the movie complex, I was getting paid minimum wage.* (5) *I had to run from theater to theater to clean each as quickly as possible.* (6) *Picking up garbage was not only disgusting, it was also exhausting.* (7) *Spilled drinks made the seats and floors sticky.* (8) *Popcorn that was dropped and stepped on became a mushy pulp.*

(9) *The video rental store wasn't much better.* (10) *I always had a manager looking over my shoulder to make sure that I did everything right.* (11) *I was constantly being threatened with losing my job, and the customers have been the rudest people I ever met.* (12) *They would take pleasure in making my life as difficult as possible.*

(13) *Working the buffet line at Soupserve depressed me also.* (14) *But it was the rude customers who made the job unpleasant.* (15) *Sweating from the high*

temperatures, the customers complained the food was not warm enough, while I served them standing between the warming ovens and the steam table.

(16) *Having these jobs has convinced me that I need to complete my education.* (17) *I'm looking forward to completing my degree in my chosen field, business, and going to work as an accountant, which won't be as boring and unpleasant as the jobs I've held while in school.*

56. Which of the following is the best version of the underlined portion of sentence 2 (reproduced below)?

    It's hard to find time to do schoolwork, and there's no time <u>for goofing off, leisure, relaxing, and enjoying yourself.</u>

    (A) to goof off, leisure, relax, and enjoy yourself.
    (B) for goofing off, relaxing, and enjoying yourself.
    (C) to enjoy your leisure time.
    (D) to relax and enjoy yourself.
    (E) for messing around.

57. Which of the following is the best revision of sentence 3 (reproduced below)?

    What makes the situation worse is that as a young person, the only jobs available are usually boring or unpleasant.

    (A) What makes the situation worse is that because you are a young person, the only jobs available are boring or unpleasant.
    (B) Usually, the jobs available to young people are boring or unpleasant, which makes the situation worse.
    (C) Worsening the situation, the jobs available to young people are usually boring or unpleasant.
    (D) Boring and unpleasant jobs available to young people make the situation worse.
    (E) Worsening the situation, available jobs are boring and unpleasant.

18

58. In the context of paragraph 2, which is the best version of the underlined portion of sentence 6 (reproduced below)?

Picking up garbage <u>was not only disgusting, it was also exhausting.</u>

(A) was not only disgusting; it was also exhausting.
(B) was disgusting, also exhausting.
(C) wasn't only exhausting, it was also disgusting.
(D) was disgusting and exhausting.
(E) disgusting and exhausting.

59. Which of the following is the best way to revise the underlined portions of sentences 7 and 8 (reproduced below) so that the two sentences are combined into one?

Spilled drinks made <u>the seats and floors sticky. Popcorn</u> that was dropped and stepped on became a mushy pulp.

(A) the seats and floors sticky, and popcorn
(B) the seats and floors sticky and popcorn
(C) the seats and floors sticky; popcorn
(D) the seats and floors sticky, but popcorn
(E) the seats and floors sticky; however, popcorn

60. Which is the best way to revise the underlined portion of sentence 11 (reproduced below)?

I was constantly being threatened with losing my job, and the customers <u>have been the rudest people</u> I ever met.

(A) are the rudest people
(B) are being the rudest people
(C) had been the rudest people
(D) were among the most rude
(E) were the rudest people

61. Which of the following would best replace *But* at the beginning of sentence 14?

(A) Now
(B) However
(C) And
(D) There
(E) Again

62. Which of the following would be the best revision of sentence 15 (reproduced below)?

Sweating from the high temperatures, the customers complained the food was not warm enough, while I served them standing between the warming ovens and the steam table.

(A) While I sweated from the high temperatures, the customers complained the food was not warm enough while I served them standing between the warming ovens and the steam table.
(B) While I stood between the warming ovens and the steam table on the serving line and sweated, the customers complained the food was not warm enough.
(C) The customers complained the food was not warm enough, sweating from the high temperatures on the serving line standing between the warming ovens and the steam table.
(D) The warming ovens and the steam table surrounded the serving line where I stood, and so I sweated, but the customers complained the food was not warm enough.
(E) I sweated while the customers complained.

63. Which of the following is the best way to revise the underlined portion of sentence 17 (reproduced below)?

I'm looking forward to <u>completing my degree in my chosen field, business, and going to work as an accountant,</u> which won't be as boring and unpleasant as the jobs I've held while in school.

(A) completing my degree in business and beginning to work as an accountant
(B) completing my business degree and working as an accountant
(C) finishing school and going into accounting
(D) finishing school and beginning work at an accounting firm
(E) starting to be an accountant

64. Which of the following is the major strategy used to support the main idea of this passage?

(A) Describing a process
(B) Narrating incidents
(C) Providing examples
(D) Comparing similar situations
(E) Analyzing causes

GO ON TO THE NEXT PAGE

Directions: Effective revision requires choosing among the many options available to a writer. The following questions test your ability to use these options effectively.

Revise each of the sentences below according to the directions that follow it. Some directions require you to change only part of the original sentence; others require you to change the entire sentence. You may need to omit or add certain words in constructing an acceptable revision, but you should keep the meaning of your revised sentence as close to the meaning of the original sentence as the directions permit. Your new sentence should follow the conventions of standard written English and should be clear and concise.

Look through answer choices (A), (B), (C), (D), and (E) under each question for the exact word or phrase that is included in your revised sentence and fill in the corresponding oval on your answer sheet. If you have thought of a revision that does not include any of the words or phrases listed, try to revise the sentence again so that it does include the wording in one of the answer choices.

Example

Having been close to the master all his life, keeping files and writing correspondence, John was the natural choice to write the catalog for the exhibit.

Start with John was.

(A) exhibit, which was
(B) exhibit because he had
(C) exhibit being
(D) exhibit being that
(E) exhibit although he

The correct answer is (B). Your sentence would read: "John was the natural choice to write the catalog for the *exhibit because he had* been close to the master, keeping files and writing correspondence. Choice (A) introduces a clause that could not exist. Choice (C) introduces a present participle that must refer to John, who is too far away. Choice (D) does the same. Choice (E) changes the meaning of the sentence.

65. One is less likely to feel happy when one is passive than when one is active.

    Start with Being active.

    (A) then passivity
    (B) than being active
    (C) than being passive is
    (D) than being passive
    (E) than when one is passive

66. The poet sought to rid himself of the responsibility for the fantasy of her death by accounting for it metaphorically.

    Start with His metaphorical account.

    (A) is an
    (B) are an
    (C) was an
    (D) were a
    (E) were an

67. He tried to save the tree, which was a rare species in that state; he had the trunk bolted, cleaned, and supported.

    Start with The tree.

    (A) supported in
    (B) supported with
    (C) supported and
    (D) supported being
    (E) supported when

68. The negligence of the tree surgeons in leaving a major limb unsupported had led to the death of the tree.

    Start with The tree surgeons.

    (A) neglecting of
    (B) neglecting to
    (C) neglect to
    (D) negligence to
    (E) avoiding

69. The papers recently became concerned about this suspect's guilt or innocence.

    Start with Whether.

    (A) guilty has
    (B) guilt was
    (C) guilt became
    (D) guilty being
    (E) guilty man

20

70. The ridicule he endured in her presence was less painful than his fear she might not open her door to him again.

    Start with The fear.

    (A) was as
    (B) was the
    (C) was more
    (D) was less
    (E) being than

71. She had done some very clever acting; the ambassador was charmed, and the Hungarian linguist was stymied.

    Start with She charmed.

    (A) linguist by
    (B) linguist of
    (C) linguist being
    (D) linguist doing
    (E) linguist with

72. The lyrics of praise in the Bethlehem scene do not have the tone of the opening of the play but do reflect a similar lack of dramatic action and sophistication.

    Start with The Bethlehem scene.

    (A) but not
    (B) but having
    (C) but do
    (D) but that do
    (E) but reflect

73. The final scene appeals to our sense of the ultimate insignificance of what can be contained in fiction or on a stage, making us seek a new level of reality in our own lives.

    Change making to makes.

    (A) scene, appeals
    (B) scene, by appealing
    (C) scene, and it appeals
    (D) scene, if it appeals
    (E) scene, that it appeals

74. Little is known of the food's generation or of its life-giving powers.

    Start with No one.

    (A) or it
    (B) or if
    (C) or how
    (D) or life-preservation
    (E) or life-preserving

Directions: Each of the following passages consists of numbered sentences. Because the passages are part of longer writing samples, they do not necessarily constitute a complete discussion of the issues presented.

Read each passage carefully and answer the questions that follow it. The questions test your awareness of a writer's purpose and of characteristics of prose that are important to good writing.

Questions 75–83 refer to the following paragraphs.

(1) *The second decade of motion pictures, from 1903–1913, witnessed the creation of a new narrative medium.* (2) *At the beginning, even the most advanced story films still retained much of the method of animated lantern slides.* (3) *The nickelodeon explosion in the early twentieth century provided a significant impetus.* (4) *The demand for new films was insatiable and audiences made it plain that what they wanted was stories.* (5) *The interest films and travel films and one-point gags persisted, but as time went on the well-balanced show was expected to provide a melodrama, a comedy, and a western.* (6) *From the magic-lantern era, early film exhibitors had inherited the lecturer, who would link and explain the films.* (7) *In time the lecturer was replaced by explanatory titles either projected by a separate lantern or included in the film itself.*

(8) *Showmen and public alike began to recognize that the best films were those which told their stories so clearly through the pictures that no extraneous explanation was required.* (9) *One obvious way to achieve this goal was to tell stories that everyone already knew; but with the daily program change the supply of familiar tales was soon to run out.* (10) *Filmmakers had to find original stories—or at least to disguise the old ones—and learn to tell them lucidly and expressively.* (11) *This task was easiest if the story was simple to tell and simple to follow; and these conditions were ideally fulfilled by the chase film, which flourished internationally as a genre in its own right in the years 1903–1906.*

GO ON TO THE NEXT PAGE

75. Which of the following most accurately describes what happens in paragraph 2?

    (A) The speaker tries to describe the self-explanatory film genre.
    (B) The speaker attempts to explain the needs that created the new medium.
    (C) The speaker gives examples of how the self-explanatory film genre gained popularity.
    (D) The speaker addresses the problems inherent in creating a familiar tale.
    (E) The speaker tries to clarify the films of that era.

76. The purpose of paragraph 1 is primarily to

    (A) describe the earlier developments and needs of film
    (B) explain the specific methods used in animated lantern slides
    (C) exemplify the types of films that were popular
    (D) discuss the narrative media available
    (E) link lecturers to the clarity of the narrative form

77. Which of the following pairs of words best describes the speaker's approach to the subject?

    (A) Logical and methodical
    (B) Orderly and unvarying
    (C) Informal and reasonable
    (D) Sequential and logical
    (E) Sensible and uncomplicated

78. The speaker ordered the presentation of the material to provide the reader with

    (A) a logical understanding of film development
    (B) background for the development of the narrative film medium
    (C) an explanation of each film genre
    (D) historical background on the early lantern era
    (E) a knowledge of the demands placed on the film industry

79. Which of the following best describes the relationship of sentence 1 to the two paragraphs?

    (A) It establishes the basis for comparisons later between paragraphs 1 and 2.
    (B) It indicates the author's authority on the subject.
    (C) It presents the central focus for the next two paragraphs.
    (D) It establishes the organization for paragraph 1 and introduces paragraph 2.
    (E) It describes the central idea that will be refuted later on.

80. In sentence 9, the effect of using the expression *One obvious way* is to

    (A) stress an evident solution to the problem presented, which could then be contradicted
    (B) reveal the writer's certainty about the details of the sequence of events
    (C) indicate an aforementioned conclusion
    (D) prepare the reader for the following two statements
    (E) reinforce the reader's previous knowledge

81. Which of the following best describes the relationship between the two paragraphs in this passage?

    (A) Paragraph 2 answers the assumption in paragraph 1.
    (B) Paragraph 2 clarifies the problems stated at the end of paragraph 1.
    (C) Paragraph 2 offers concrete illustrations of the information in paragraph 1.
    (D) Paragraph 2 clarifies the needs that developed after paragraph 1.
    (E) Paragraph 2 generalizes the problems presented in paragraph 1.

82. The function of sentence 3 is primarily to

    (A) indicate the original stimulus for a change in the medium
    (B) give an example of the animated lantern slides in sentence 2
    (C) indicate a change in the paragraph to detailed description
    (D) illustrate more advanced story films and their methods
    (E) prepare for the mentioning of the audiences in sentence 4

83. Which of the following best describes the function of sentence 9?

    (A) It indicates an insufficient solution based on an aforementioned need.
    (B) It demonstrates the requirements of the audience.
    (C) It alludes to the difficulties of clearly presenting stories.
    (D) It forces the reader to acknowledge the problem presented.
    (E) It gives an example of what can happen when the lecturer is replaced.

Questions 84–92 refer to the following paragraphs written in 1990.

(1) *It has become a cliché to note the revolutionary impact of information technology, but the real developments lie just ahead.* (2) *While number-based mainframe computers of the 1970s formed this revolution and the popularity of the personal computer in the 1980s brought it to fruition, one needs to ask what the future holds.* (3) *Everyone is racing to the starting lineup to join the bandwagon when perhaps the race began two hours earlier.* (4) *A new social order is evolving in which homes, businesses, educational facilities, and towns are becoming interwoven into a web of intelligent services with incredible opportunities for development in all areas.* (5) *As a society, we are reaching forward to use the computer's ability to store and process information to form a new unit of informational technological pathways.*

(6) *The creation of the optical computer, which would operate with light waves, will revolutionize the industry.* (7) *Such a machine could boost computing power by several orders of magnitude.* (8) *Most of the scientific community is skeptical whether this technology will be available to our present generation.* (9) *I personally believe that its creation is inevitable and will be much sooner than anticipated.* (10) *If one considers the rapidity of personal computing advances in the past ten years, the inevitability becomes clear.* (11) *Small, cheap computer chips will soon be embedded in cars, home appliances, and elsewhere.* (12) *Stationary personal computers will continue to serve a technical function, but more and more we will see the small multifunctional laptop.* (13) *This technology will provide data, word processing, newspapers, TV, and even present movies.* (14) *The American public has never wanted to know how something works, only that it does what it's supposed to do.* (15) *Our society craves instant and simple.* (16) *Life will take place in a living landscape of interacting, intelligent machines that help us through our daily chores and pleasures.*

84. The purpose of paragraph 1 is primarily to
    (A) present the developments of computer-based technology in the 1970s and 1980s
    (B) discuss the impact of computers on the world
    (C) explain the new social order
    (D) clarify the past and present revolution in technology that will affect the future
    (E) discuss the impact of the personal computer on American society

85. Which of the following most accurately describes what happens in paragraph 2?
    (A) It predicts the future technology in the industry of multifunctional computers.
    (B) It explains the mechanics and uses of a cheap, smaller computer chip.
    (C) It predicts the early creation of the optical computer.
    (D) It cites examples of computer power being boosted.
    (E) It provides reasons that technology will increase and progress rapidly.

86. Which of the following sets of words best describes the speaker's opinion of future technology?
    (A) Logical, revolutionary, and inevitable
    (B) Orderly, informal, and rapid
    (C) Multifunctional, revolutionary, and rapid
    (D) Sequential, multifunctional, and simple
    (E) Reasonable, inevitable, and complex

87. The speaker ordered the presentation of the material to provide the reader with
    (A) a logical understanding of technological developments
    (B) background for the development of the optical computer
    (C) a framework for the opinion held by the scientific community
    (D) historical background of the mainframe and personal computers
    (E) historical evidence and substantiation for his opinions

GO ON TO THE NEXT PAGE

88. Which of the following best describes the relationship of sentence 1 to the two paragraphs?

    (A) It establishes the basis for comparisons later between paragraphs 1 and 2.
    (B) It indicates the author's authority on the subject.
    (C) It presents the central focus for paragraph 1.
    (D) It establishes the organization for paragraph 1 and introduces paragraph 2.
    (E) It describes the central idea that will be refuted later on.

89. In sentence 10, the effect of using the expression *If one considers* is to

    (A) reveal the writer's certainty about the details he will be presenting
    (B) draw the reader into a future prediction based on prior knowledge
    (C) indicate an aforementioned conclusion
    (D) prepare the reader for the following two statements
    (E) reinforce the reader's previous knowledge of computer technology

90. Which of the following best describes the relationship between the two paragraphs in this passage?

    (A) Paragraph 2 projects the possible prospects based on paragraph 1.
    (B) Paragraph 2 clarifies the problems stated at the end of paragraph 1.
    (C) Paragraph 2 offers concrete illustrations of the information in paragraph 1.
    (D) Paragraph 2 predicts the needs that will develop after paragraph 1.
    (E) Paragraph 2 generalizes the problems presented in paragraph 1.

91. The function of sentence 2 is primarily to

    (A) provide a historical context for future suppositions
    (B) give examples of technology in the 1970s and 1980s
    (C) indicate a change in the development of computers in those years
    (D) illustrate the advances that have been made in technology
    (E) prepare for the analogy in sentence 3

92. Which of the following best describes the function of sentence 15?

    (A) It indicates a solution based on the afore-mentioned need.
    (B) It demonstrates what was explained in sentence 14.
    (C) It connects sentences 14 and 16 together.
    (D) It forces the reader to acknowledge the problem presented.
    (E) It gives examples of what our society wants.

Directions: The following sentences test your knowledge of grammar, diction (choice of words), and idiom.

Some sentences are correct. No sentence contains more than one error. You will find that the error, if there is one, is underlined and lettered. Assume that elements of the sentence that are not underlined are correct and cannot be changed. In choosing answers, follow the requirements of standard written English.

If there is an error, select the one underlined part that must be changed to make the sentence correct and fill in the corresponding oval on your answer sheet. If there is no error, select answer (E).

93. His method of doing business is hardly appreci-
    ated; he feels inferior than others. No error.

94. It was the worse storm that the inhabitants of
    the island could remember. No error.

95. Johnson has scarcely no equal as a salesman; his
    commissions are larger than those made by
    almost any other salesman. No error.

96. He had no interest toward music, art, or the
    theater, since his time was spent in making
    money. No error.

97. As they <u>listened</u> to his <u>fabulous</u> statistics, the
            A   B
board members <u>became</u> more and more
              C
<u>incredible</u>. <u>No error.</u>
 D   E

98. If people <u>had helped</u> solve the energy crisis, <u>it</u>
A   B   C
might <u>of</u> been a lesson to humanity. <u>No error.</u>
     D   E

99. The actors <u>were</u> <u>already</u> to perform long <u>before</u>
             A   B   C
the curtain <u>went</u> up. <u>No error.</u>
           D   E

100. He <u>had</u> the privilege <u>to be</u> absent <u>whenever</u> he
       A   B   C
had an asthma attack. <u>No error.</u>
D   E

STOP   If you finish before the time is up, you may check your work on this section only. Do not turn to any other section in the test.

PRETEST ANSWER KEY AND EXPLANATIONS

PART I

1. B	12. A	23. A	34. E	45. E
2. A	13. B	24. B	35. C	46. A
3. B	14. C	25. A	36. E	47. C
4. A	15. A	26. D	37. C	48. A
5. A	16. D	27. E	38. E	49. D
6. C	17. E	28. A	39. D	50. C
7. C	18. E	29. C	40. C	51. D
8. B	19. C	30. D	41. D	52. C
9. E	20. B	31. D	42. A	53. C
10. B	21. A	32. A	43. D	54. D
11. A	22. D	33. A	44. C	55. A

PART II: ENGLISH COMPOSITION WITHOUT ESSAY TEST

56. D	65. C	74. C	83. A	92. C
57. B	66. C	75. C	84. D	93. D
58. C	67. A	76. A	85. A	94. B
59. A	68. B	77. D	86. C	95. B
60. E	69. A	78. B	87. E	96. A
61. E	70. C	79. C	88. D	97. D
62. B	71. E	80. A	89. B	98. D
63. B	72. D	81. D	90. A	99. B
64. C	73. B	82. A	91. A	100. B

PART I

1. **The correct answer is (B).** A plural form of the verb is needed because the subject *reports* is plural. *Are* is correct.

2. **The correct answer is (A).** The nominative pronoun *we* should not be used. *Us* is correct because the pronoun is used as the subject of the infinitive *to form*. The infinitive phrase is used as an adverb to modify *willing*.

3. **The correct answer is (B).** The objective case is needed. *Whom* is the object of *we know*.

4. **The correct answer is (A).** Numbers that begin a sentence must be written out. *Six percent* is correct.

5. **The correct answer is (A).** All the verbs in this sentence should be in the past tense. *Answered* is the correct word.

6. **The correct answer is (C).** *Referred* means *mentioned directly. Alluded* is a better choice because it means *suggested indirectly*.

7. **The correct answer is (C).** The correct form of the past-perfect tense of *freeze* is *had frozen*.

8. **The correct answer is (B).** The coordinating conjunction *but* should be used because it contrasts the elements in the sentence.

9. **The correct answer is (E).** There are no errors in this sentence.

10. **The correct answer is (B).** *Differ from* means *to stand apart from because of unlikeness. Differ with*, which is the correct expression, means *to disagree*.

11. **The correct answer is (A).** *Less* is correct because we are comparing only two people.

12. **The correct answer is (A).** The present-perfect tense, *I have been living*, shows the action started and is continuing.

13. **The correct answer is (B).** The idiom is *negligent of*.

14. **The correct answer is (C).** *Implied* means *suggested without stating. Inferred* is correct because it means *reached a conclusion based on evidence*.

15. **The correct answer is (A).** Do not use the past-conditional tense in a dependent clause starting with *if*. Instead, use *If he had been*.

16. **The correct answer is (D).** A colon introduces a series.

17. **The correct answer is (E).** This choice is simple and avoids the awkward phrasing and wordiness of the others.

18. **The correct answer is (E).** Choice (A) creates a dangling participle, which is a participle with nothing logical to modify. Choice (B) is floating grammatically. In choice (C), *although* is contradictory. Choice (D) creates a comma splice, a serious error in which two independent clauses are joined by a comma.

19. **The correct answer is (C).** Choices (A), (B), and (E) confuse the sentence by suggesting that *him* does the leaping. Choice (D) creates a comma splice.

20. **The correct answer is (B).** *Ridiculousness* is a hopelessly awkward word, especially when teamed with *predicament*. Choices (C) and (E) create the wrong subject for the verb *occurred*. Choice (D) creates a comma splice.

21. **The correct answer is (A).** This choice catches the meaning simply and directly. Choices (B), (C), and (D) create sentence fragments because they lack complete predicates. Choice (E) is hopelessly redundant.

22. **The correct answer is (D).** The semicolon implies that even special days are like all days in that they must end. Choices (A) and (B) suggest that the very beauty of the day causes its death. Choice (E) loses the meaning completely. Choice (C) uses long words unnecessarily.

23. **The correct answer is (A).** This choice completes the implied parallelism between the two independent clauses. Choice (B) puts *neither* in the wrong place. Choice (C) creates ambiguity. Choices (D) and (E) destroy the meaning entirely.

24. **The correct answer is (B).** Choices (D) and (E) distort the meaning of the original. Choice (C) creates a sentence fragment because it lacks a complete predicate.

25. **The correct answer is (A).** This clarifies the cause-effect relationship with the use of *thereby*. Choice (B) sets up a misplaced modifier. *Avoiding* cannot logically modify *entanglement*. Choice (C) employs the wrong tense, implying that the military threat is over. In choice (D), *they* is the wrong pronoun. Choice (E) is nonsensical.

26. **The correct answer is (D).** Choices (A) and (B) have errors in parallel construction. Choice (C) has parallel construction, but choices (C), (A), and (B) do not make clear that dulling the imagination and encouraging physical inactivity are descriptions of what happens when the brain is lulled. Choice (E) creates a sentence fragment.

27. **The correct answer is (E).** Choices (A) and (B) are as general as the original phrase. The language of choice (C) is inappropriately formal. Choice (D) would not be considered a big family.

28. **The correct answer is (A).** Choice (B) is wordy, and choices (C), (D), and (E) are dangling modifiers because they cannot logically modify anything in the sentence.

29. **The correct answer is (C).** The conjunction *and* in choice (A) is weak. Choice (B) is too formal in tone. Choice (D) creates a sentence fragment. Choice (E) is a run-on sentence because it presents two sentences joined without an appropriate conjunction and/or punctuation.

30. **The correct answer is (D).** Choice (A) is needlessly wordy. Choice (B) offers a shift in perspective from first (*I*) to second (*you*) person. Choice (C) points out that sufficient transition already exists (in sentence 8). Choice (E) fails to recognize any error.

31. **The correct answer is (D).** Choices (A) and (B) are ambiguous. It is not clear whether the magazines or the remote control is under the sofa. Choice (C) adds unnecessary wording. Choice (E) is a run-on sentence because there is no comma preceding the conjunction *and* that joins the clauses.

32. **The correct answer is (A).** Choice (B) contains a sentence fragment. Choice (C) is wordy. Choice (D) uses an unnecessary passive construction in *is found*. Choice (E) is a sentence fragment.

33. **The correct answer is (A).** The other sentences use words that are not logical in context to connect the two ideas.

34. **The correct answer is (E).** It unifies the selection by referring to the criticism of television in paragraph 1 without directly restating it in words.

35. **The correct answer is (C).** Choices (A) and (E) have unnecessary personification; the soup cannot be regarded as human. Choices (B) and (D) are wordy.

36. **The correct answer is (E).** It is the most precise choice. Choice (A) misuses *healthier*; the appropriate word is *healthful*. *Healthful* means *causing good health*. Choice (B) needlessly sets up a compound predicate. Choice (C) misuses *less*, which refers to matter that can be measured; *fewer* refers to items that can be counted. Choice (D) has an illogical predicate adjective in *fatless*.

37. **The correct answer is (C).** Choices (A), (B), (D), and (E) have errors in grammar and sentence construction. Choice (A) contains a comma splice because it contains only a comma to join two clauses. Choices (B) and (D) are sentence fragments because they lack a complete subject and predicate. Choice (E) is a run-on sentence.

38. **The correct answer is (E).** Choices (A) and (C) are vague. Choices (B) and (D) are wordy.

39. **The correct answer is (D).** The other answers are not relevant to explaining how to make the soup.

40. **The correct answer is (C).** Choice (A) is a comma splice because it contains only a comma to join two clauses. Choices (B), (D), and (E) add unnecessary words. Choice (B) shifts from second person (*you*) to third person (*one*).

41. **The correct answer is (D).** Choice (A) is a sentence fragment because it lacks a complete subject and predicate. Choice (B) contains a dangling modifier in *straining the broth*. Choice (C) contains an unnecessary pronoun. Choice (E) tells the reader to do things at the same time.

42. **The correct answer is (A).** It is the best parallel construction. Both objects of the preposition *in* are plural. Choices (B), (C), and (D) do not offer parallel forms. Choice (E) presents a dangling modifier.

43. **The correct answer is (D).** It explains what needs to be done and is consistent with the tone of the rest of the draft.

44. **The correct answer is (C).** This is the only answer with an unambiguous reference to the rest of the sentence. Choice (A) has a dangling modifier. Choice (B) also has a dangling modifier. Choice (D) has a comma splice. Choice (E) contains a change in the meaning of the sentence.

45. **The correct answer is (E).** This is both idiomatic and complete. Choice (A) has an incomplete predicate. Choice (B) is not idiomatic: *momentary anger in*. Choice (C) has the incorrect form of *angered*. Choice (D) omits a necessary preposition *respectful of*.

46. **The correct answer is (A).** This choice, using appositive phrases to follow each name, achieves parallelism. Choices (B), (D), and (E) are not parallel. Choice (C) is not meaningful.

47. **The correct answer is (C).** This choice keeps the correct meaning and avoids the dangling participle in choices (B) and (D). Choice (E) contains a sentence fragment because it lacks a complete subject and predicate.

48. **The correct answer is (A).** This choice practices subordination properly. Choice (B) presents a choice that lacks parallelism. Choice (C) includes a comma splice. Choice (D) is wordy and also lacks parallelism. Choice (E) incorrectly sets up an "if then" relationship.

49. **The correct answer is (D).** Choice (A) includes the idiomatic form of pertinent verbs *interested* in *preparing* for. Choice (B) contains a dangling modifier: *taking them or preparing them*. Choice (C) lacks parallel structure. Choice (E) offers the present form of *interest*, when the past participle *interested* is needed.

50. **The correct answer is (C).** Of the choices given, choice (C) is the best answer; it changes the verb and thus avoids the faulty use of the participle that is presented in choices (B) and (D). Choice (A) offers an awkward shift to *I*, and choice (E) has an equally awkward shift to *programs*.

51. **The correct answer is (D).** This choice keeps the meaning of the original and avoids the truly awkward usage in choices (A) and (C), the boring coordination of choice (B), and the dangling participle of choice (E).

52. **The correct answer is (C).** This choice maintains parallelism and meaning, which the others do not.

53. **The correct answer is (C).** This choice keeps the meaning and avoids the awkward word order of the others. Choice (B) is wordy. Choices (D) and (E) make fragments of the sentence.

54. **The correct answer is (D).** This choice arranges the various ideas in correct order by using *while* and a subordinate clause. Choice (A) is wordy, with an awkward appositive phrase. Choice (B) is a sentence fragment. Choices (C) and (E) are both run-on sentences.

55. **The correct answer is (A).** The others introduce unwanted complexities as well as wordiness.

PART II: ENGLISH COMPOSITION WITHOUT ESSAY TEST

56. **The correct answer is (D).** *Goofing off* is inappropriately colloquial in choices (A) and (B), as is *messing around* in answer choice (E). Choice (C) causes an awkward repetition of the word *time*.

57. **The correct answer is (B).** It places the important idea in the emphatic position at the end of the sentence. Choice (D) needs a modifying word for *boring and unpleasant*. Choice (A) is wordy. Choices (C) and (E) have a dangling modifier.

58. **The correct answer is (C).** *Disgusting* should be the last word in the sentence because it describes the examples in the next sentence.

59. **The correct answer is (A).** The ideas are coordinate; thus, using the conjunction *and* is a better way to join them than using a semicolon as in choice (C). Choices (D) and (E) use illogical connecting words. Choice (B) is a run-on sentence.

60. **The correct answer is (E).** Choices (A), (B), and (C) shift tenses, and choice (D) is an incorrect form of the comparative.

61. **The correct answer is (E).** It provides coherence by connecting the idea with the same idea in paragraph 2.

62. **The correct answer is (B).** Choices (A) and (C) are confusing and contain dangling modifiers. Choice (D) is grammatically correct, but it is a compound sentence that links clauses without indicating their relationship to each other. Choice (E) leaves out important information.

63. **The correct answer is (B).** Choices (A) and (D) are wordy, and choices (C) and (E) are imprecise.

64. **The correct answer is (C).**

65. **The correct answer is (C).** This sounds a little awkward but avoids ambiguity: Being active is more likely to make one feel happy *than being passive is*.

66. **The correct answer is (C).** His metaphorical account of her death *was an* attempt to rid himself of responsibility for the fantasy of her death. Choices (A) and (B) shift from past to present tense. Choices (D) and (E) have plural verbs.

67. **The correct answer is (A).** The tree, a rare species in his state, was bolted, cleaned, and *supported in* his attempt to save it.

68. **The correct answer is (B).** The tree surgeons had killed the tree by *neglecting to* support one of the major limbs. Choices (A) and (E) offer gerunds (*neglecting* and *avoiding*), which must be modified by the possessive form of a noun or pronoun. Since *surgeons* is not in the possessive form, you have to figure out another approach.

69. **The correct answer is (A).** Whether the suspect is innocent or *guilty has* become a concern of the papers.

70. **The correct answer is (C).** The fear that she might not open the door to him again *was more* painful than the ridicule he endured in her presence.

71. **The correct answer is (E).** She charmed the ambassador and stymied the Hungarian *linguist with* her very clever acting.

72. **The correct answer is (D).** The Bethlehem scene provides the lyrics of praise that do not have the tone of the opening of the play *but that do* reflect a similar lack of dramatic action and sophistication.

73. **The correct answer is (B).** The final *scene, by appealing* to our sense of the ultimate insignificance of what can be contained in fiction or on a stage, makes us seek a new level of reality in our own lives.

74. **The correct answer is (C).** No one knows where the food comes from *or how* it preserves life.

75. **The correct answer is (C).** The author introduces in paragraph 1 the original genre of film and in paragraph 2 explains why this new narrative medium was created. Choices (A), (D), and (E) are too narrow, and choice (B) is too general to be acceptable.

76. **The correct answer is (A).** The introductory sentence is the main idea of the entire paragraph, and the dates indicate the order of sequence. The other answers are too narrow in scope.

77. **The correct answer is (D).** The author's writing is logical and fairly sequential in order. The speaker begins in the early 1903 period and progresses through the various stages of need, problematic situations, etc., to arrive at the narrative medium of the chase scene. Choice (A) is incorrect because the sentence structure varies (this follows for choice (B) as well). Choice (C) is incorrect because the writing is not informal in nature. Choice (E) is incorrect because the adjectives describe a more descriptive/narrative writing form, not an expository one.

78. **The correct answer is (B).** This answer states exactly what paragraph 1 is about. Choices (A) and (C) are too general, while choices (D) and (E) are too specific.

79. **The correct answer is (C).** The first sentence is an introductory sentence, which states the main interest/focus of the essay. Choice (A) is inaccurate because the essay doesn't compare, but explains. Choices (B) and (E) are inaccurate because the author is not involved in the expository sentence and this information will not be refuted. Choice (D) is false because both paragraphs deal with the same subject.

80. **The correct answer is (A).** This answer is a restatement of the wording. Choice (B) is incorrect because the expression does express certainty, but not about details. Choice (C) is incorrect since there is no conclusion beforehand. Choice (D) is incorrect since the word *obvious* states a clear understanding, not an indication of preparation. Choice (E) cannot be true since this information was not presented before.

81. **The correct answer is (D).** Choice (A) is incorrect because there was no assumption. Choice (B) is wrong because there wasn't any problem stated at the end of paragraph 1. Choice (C) is incorrect because the information in the second paragraph is not a series of illustrations based on paragraph 1. Choice (E) is false because there are specific details in paragraph 2, not generalizations.

82. **The correct answer is (A).** The word *impetus* indicates a form of stimulus to create change. Choice (B) is incorrect because the nickelodeon explosion is not an example. Choice (C) is false because the wording does not indicate a change in the structure of the passage. Choice (D) is incorrect because the sentence does not illustrate, but states. Choice (E) would be correct if the word *audiences* was replaced with "demands" or "new stories." The audiences' demands are the central issue in sentence 4.

83. **The correct answer is (A).** The need is for clear stories that require no explanation. Choice (B) is limited to the audience, not showmen and public, as indicated in sentence 8. Choice (C) is incorrect because there is no alluding—it is stated clearly. Choice (D) is false because the reader knows the problem presented—the reader is not forced. Choice (E) is incorrect because *lecturer* is taken completely out of context.

84. **The correct answer is (D).** This choice clearly sums up the purpose of paragraph 1. Choices (A) and (B) are incorrect because they are too specific. Choice (C) is incorrect because it is too general. Choice (E) is incorrect because the reader is making an assumption that the writer is writing about American society.

85. **The correct answer is (A).** This answer states the main idea of the second paragraph. Choices (B), (C), and (D) are too specific, while choice (E) is too general.

86. **The correct answer is (C).** This answer incorporates most of the main points in paragraph 2. Choice (A) is incorrect because *logical* and *revolutionary* are often used as antonyms; something revolutionary rarely follows a logical path. Choice (B) is incorrect because something orderly is rarely informal. Choice (D) is false since the creation of the optical computer referred to at the beginning of the paragraph would not be due for many years; it is not following a proper sequence. Choice (E) is false because the author's opinion may be reasonable to himself, but a reader may not see it as reasonable. Also, the author states that he believes that the future technology will be simplified, not complex.

87. The correct answer is (E). Though this appears to be a data-expository essay, in truth, it is an essay of opinion. Choice (C) states an opinion; however, it is not in concurrence with the author's opinion. Choice (A) is incorrect because it is too general, and the material isn't just about technological developments. Choices (B) and (D) are too specific.

88. The correct answer is (D). This answer is correct because paragraph 1 covers the changes in information technology, and paragraph 2 discusses future developments. Choice (A) is false because paragraph 1 gives background and reasoning to use as a basis in paragraph 2. Choice (B) is false because it does not indicate in any way the author's authority. Choice (C) is incorrect because it is too limited. Paragraph 1 is not about the future. Choice (E) is incorrect because the central idea is clarified, not refuted.

89. The correct answer is (B). Choice (A) is incorrect because he will not be presenting details. Choice (C) is incorrect because the conclusion was not mentioned before. Choice (D) is false because the writer doesn't wish to prepare the reader, but include the reader in his reasoning. Choice (E) is incorrect because the purpose of the writing is not to reinforce, but to convince.

90. The correct answer is (A). This essay is an essay of opinion, based on the author's opinion of what will happen in the future. Therefore, choices (B), (C), and (D) are incorrect because they do not deal with the future. Choice (E) deals with the future, but the author is not discussing the needs of the future as much as the possibilities.

91. The correct answer is (A). It gives the most direct function. Choices (B), (C), and (D) are what the sentences say but are not about their function in relation to the rest of the paragraph. Choice (E) is nonsensical because sentence 2 has very little relation to the analogy presented in sentence 3.

92. The correct answer is (C). Choice (A) is incorrect because sentence 15 does not provide a solution. Choice (B) is incorrect because it gives only part of the answer. Choice (D) is false because the writing is stated as fact, not persuasion. Choice (E) is incorrect because it restates the sentence but doesn't give us the function of the sentence.

93. The correct answer is (D). It is correct to say *inferior to*.

94. The correct answer is (B). *Worst* is correct; the superlative is needed because more than two are being compared.

95. The correct answer is (B). *Scarcely no* acts as a double negative. It should be *scarcely any*.

96. The correct answer is (A). *Interest in* is the correct idiom.

97. The correct answer is (D). *Incredible* means *too extraordinary to be believed*. It is correct to say that the board becomes *incredulous*, meaning *inclined not to believe*.

98. The correct answer is (D). *Might have been* is the correct form.

99. The correct answer is (B). *Already* is an adverb meaning *previously*. *All ready* is correct; it means *all prepared*.

100. The correct answer is (B). The correct form is *privilege of being*.

Chapter 3
OVERVIEW

This section will give you an overview of the material that will appear on the General Examination in English Composition. There are two versions of the exam that are given: the *English Composition without Essay* and the *English Composition with Essay*. The version without the essay contains 100 multiple-choice questions, presented in two 45-minute sections. The second version has one 45-minute multiple-choice section with 55 questions and one 45-minute essay question.

The essay section represents 50 percent of the test, and you are expected to present a point of view in response to a topic that is given to you. You are also expected to support your position or point of view by presenting clearly written, logical arguments and appropriate evidence. If you can write a decent essay, it makes sense to choose this version of the exam. The complete multiple-choice version of the test is very tricky and presents some complicated types of grammatical questions. However, because the *English Composition with Essay* is given only a few times a year, you might need to take the CLEP on a different schedule; therefore, you will also need to be familiar with all of the multiple-choice–type questions.

Because of the complexity of these questions, and because this is the version that is more frequently available, this book will focus on the *English Composition without Essay* version of the tests. All of the sample tests in this book present this version of the exam.

The English Composition without Essay features five different question types:

1. **Identifying Sentence Errors** This type of question appears in both Section I and Section II of this version of the exam.

2. **Restructuring Sentences** This type of question appears only in Section II of this test.

3. **Improving Sentences** This type of question appears only in Section I of this version of the test.

4. **Revising Work in Progress** This type of question appears in both Section I and Section II of this version of the exam.

5. **Analyzing Writing** This type of question appears only in Section II of this test.

The following sections give you an overview and explanation of the different types of questions that will appear on both sections of this exam. We suggest that you carefully memorize the directions for each type of question so that you will not have to spend additional time trying to understand what you are being asked to do when you take the actual examination. Following each set of sample questions and their explanations are several additional questions for practice. And, of course, this book contains numerous exams for further review and practice.

IDENTIFYING SENTENCE ERRORS

The directions and practice questions that follow will give you a good idea of what Sentence Error questions are like. The directions given here are similar to those used on the actual test and are given so that you will be familiar with them on the day of the examination.

Directions: The following sentences will test your knowledge of English grammar, usage, diction (choice of words), and idiom. Some of the sentences with which you will be presented are correct. No sentence with which you are presented contains more than one error.

You will find that the one error, if there is one, is underlined and lettered. You must assume that elements of the sentence NOT underlined are correct and cannot be changed. When you choose your answer, follow the requirements of standard written English.

If there is an error, select the one underlined part that must be changed to make the sentence correct. Indicate that letter on your answer sheet. If the sentence has no error, select answer (E).

Example 1

1. Many themes considered <u>sacrilegious</u> in the
   A
   <u>nineteenth</u> century are treated <u>casually</u> on
   B C
   today's stage. <u>No error.</u>
   D E

The correct answer is (E). There is no error in this sentence.

Example 2

2. The history teacher <u>whom</u> I think was the
    A

    best teacher I ever had told us that he had
    B C D

    served in the Korean War. <u>No error.</u>
    E

The correct answer is (A). The pronoun, *whom*, should be the pronoun, *who*. In this sentence, the pronoun is in the subjective case: *who* is the subject of the verb, *was*. The pronoun, *whom*, can be used only in the objective case as a direct object, indirect object, or object of a preposition.

IDENTIFYING SENTENCE ERRORS: REVIEW QUESTIONS

The following sentences will give you a chance to practice. Read each sentence carefully, mark your answers, and then check them with the answers and explanations that appear at the end of the Overview section.

1. <u>Surely</u> <u>between</u> the three of <u>us</u>, we <u>have</u> enough
    A B C D

    money to buy a dozen doughnuts. <u>No error.</u>
    E

2. We were <u>suppose</u> to <u>accept</u> his apology <u>for</u>
    A B C

    <u>interrupting</u> our private conversation. <u>No error.</u>
    D E

3. <u>Gathering my courage</u>, this <u>car</u> seemed to be the
    A B

    best choice among those for <u>sale</u>. <u>No error.</u>
    C D E

4. Pam had just <u>laid</u> down on the couch <u>for a nap</u>
    A B

    <u>when</u> she <u>heard</u> the doorbell. <u>No error.</u>
    C D E

5. <u>Children</u> and their <u>dogs, played</u> gleefully at the
    A B

    <u>new</u> park <u>in their</u> neighborhood. <u>No error.</u>
    C D E

6. Although my <u>Grandmother</u> was born in the
    A

    <u>South</u>, her family moved to <u>Detroit</u> where her
    B C

    father and brothers worked in a factory.
    D

    <u>No error.</u>
    E

7. I was <u>instructed</u> by <u>my</u> coach <u>to swim</u> ten laps;
    A B C

    after I had <u>swam</u> that long, I was tired. <u>No error.</u>
    D E

8. After the game <u>is</u> over, let's you and <u>I</u> begin
    A B C

    to <u>work</u> on that jigsaw puzzle. <u>No error.</u>
    D E

9. How <u>many</u> people <u>were</u> <u>effected</u> by the flash
    A B C

    floods <u>in</u> Central America? <u>No error.</u>
    D E

10. <u>Sam's</u> photos of <u>Hawaii</u> entertained their family,
    A B

    <u>which</u> <u>was</u> a surprise to his brother. <u>No error.</u>
    C D E

11. For the graduation party, <u>either</u> the students or
    A B

    the class sponsor <u>have</u> to find chaperones
    C

    <u>because</u> the parents will attend another party.
    D

    <u>No error.</u>
    E

12. My <u>sister</u> is <u>one</u> of those people who <u>like</u> to send
    A B C

    funny birthday cards <u>and</u> gag gifts. <u>No error.</u>
    D E

13. The <u>stench</u> of noxious fumes coming from the
    A

    lab <u>aggravated</u> our eyes <u>despite</u> the <u>safety</u> glasses.
    B C D

    <u>No error.</u>
    E

14. A retired historian <u>himself</u>, Dad is <u>still</u> reading
    A B

    Winston <u>Churchill's</u> account of the Norman
    C

    Conquest <u>on the front porch</u>. <u>No error.</u>
    D E

15. The audience was sure the cattle rustler would

    be <u>hung</u> as soon as the <u>marshal</u> caught him and
    A B

    <u>transported</u> the man <u>back</u> to Laredo. <u>No error.</u>
    C D E

16. My best <u>friend Marcia</u> wishes that she <u>was</u> able
    A B

    to <u>narrow</u> her college choices to a <u>handful</u>.
    C D

    <u>No error.</u>
    E

17. Mr. Gunter, the <u>closest</u> witness, remembers <u>only</u>
             A   B

    seeing two men <u>leave</u> the bank <u>on</u> the day of the
                  C   D

    robbery. <u>No error.</u>
             E

18. <u>According to</u> historical records in the
        A

    <u>Library of Congress,</u> the cornerstone for the
          B

    White House <u>was lain</u> on October <u>13, 1792.</u>
              C   D

    <u>No error.</u>
      E

19. <u>To reach</u> our seats <u>in the top tier</u> of the small
       A   B

    theater, we had to climb a <u>steep</u> flight of stairs,
                            C

    <u>which were surprisingly comfortable.</u> <u>No error.</u>
                  D   E

20. So that <u>you</u> can plan <u>efficiently,</u> a hiker on a new
          A   B

    <u>trail</u> must study the maps <u>carefully.</u> <u>No error.</u>
     C   D   E

21. <u>Those</u> Ashby twins <u>are</u> the students <u>who,</u> I think,
      A   B   C

    will <u>collect</u> tickets at the gate. <u>No error.</u>
        D   E

22. As the Olympic <u>athletes</u> <u>continued</u> their march
                   A   B

    <u>into</u> the stadium, the crowd <u>applauded.</u> <u>No error.</u>
     C   D   E

23. Before returning the <u>students'</u> test papers, the
        A   B

    professor <u>inferred</u> that this class was not well
            C   D

    prepared. <u>No error.</u>
          E

24. Overloaded with boxes, the <u>pothole</u> was likely
            A   B

    <u>to be hit</u> by the <u>speeding</u> car. <u>No error.</u>
      C   D   E

25. Even though the running back <u>tried</u> not to <u>loose</u>
                        A   B

    the football, he fumbled <u>and</u> gave the other team
                     C

    a chance to score. <u>No error.</u>
            D   E

RESTRUCTURING SENTENCES

Effective sentence revision requires you to choose among the many options available to a writer. The questions test your ability to use these options effectively.

> **Directions:** Revise each of the following sentences according to the directions that follow it. Some directions require you to change only part of the original sentence, while others require you to change the entire sentence. You may need to omit or add words in constructing an acceptable revision, but you should keep the meaning of your revised sentences as close to the meaning of the original sentence as the directions permit. Your new sentences should follow the conventions of standard written English and should be clear and concise. One way to approach this kind of question is to try to use each option in a restructuring of the sentence. The correct answer will NOT simply be a rearrangement of the words in the original. Sometimes you must change the verb from passive to active voice, or change a noun or pronoun to the possessive form.

Example 1

1. Graduates of the Harvard Law School are more likely to be hired by large Wall Street firms than graduates of a small Midwestern law school.

   Substitute <u>have fewer chances</u> for <u>are more likely</u>.

   (A) of being hired
   (B) by being hired
   (C) with being hired
   (D) instead of being hired
   (E) as well as being hired

The correct answer is (A). The sentence should read: Graduates of a small Midwestern law school have fewer chances *of being hired* by large Wall Street firms than graduates of the Harvard Law School. The rewriting of the entire sentence is necessary to keep the meaning of the sentence.

Example 2

2. Since there were too many books on the weak table, Mary removed two of them and put them on the shelf.

Begin with Mary removed.

(A) on the weak table
(B) by the weak table
(C) from the weak table
(D) upon the weak table
(E) onto the weak table

The correct answer is (C). The sentence should read: Mary removed two of the books *from the weak table* and placed them on the shelf.

RESTRUCTURING SENTENCES: REVIEW QUESTIONS

The following sentences will give you a chance to practice. Read each sentence carefully, mark your answers, and then check them with the answers and explanations that appear at the end of the Overview section.

1. In their support of rising minority-group aspirations, large corporations are not only evidencing true altruism in improving the lot of minorities, but also producing social changes within the communities in which their plants are located.

Substitute both for not only.

(A) and
(B) but
(C) and so
(D) as much as
(E) for

2. No depression in American history has ever lasted as long as the one that began in 1929; it is ironic that only the beginning of World War II in Europe brought prosperity to the United States.

Begin with It is ironic, and substitute ended for brought.

(A) the lasting depression
(B) the longest depression
(C) the 1929 beginning depression
(D) no prosperity in the United States
(E) no depression in American history

3. According to an American Medical Association report, male psychiatrists should be aware that certain types of female patients will attempt to seduce them.

Begin with An American Medical Association.

(A) bewares psychiatrists
(B) arouses psychiatrists
(C) defends psychiatrists
(D) declares psychiatrists
(E) warns psychiatrists

4. African American activists charge that a corporation that hires minority-group workers and then lays them off during a recession is actually intensifying the frustrations of minority workers rather than helping them.

Substitute a corporation's for a corporation.

(A) actually intensifying
(B) intensifies minority workers
(C) actually intensifies
(D) must actually intensify
(E) actually brings on

5. The average laborer with no income except his monthly wages is frequently hard-pressed for immediate cash to pay his or her personal bills.

Substitute whose only for with.

(A) no income except his
(B) income except his
(C) income accepts his
(D) income is his
(E) no income but

6. The truck driver, tired after 40 hours on the highway without rest, took a pep pill; he knew that just one would keep him awake and alert for about 3 hours.

Begin with The truck driver knew.

(A) hours; so tired
(B) hours; therefore, tired
(C) hours, moreover, tired
(D) hours; tired
(E) hours, therefore, tired

7. Anyone's first flight is always a unique experience, no matter how many times he has seen pictures of planes flying or heard tales about the first flight of others.

Begin with No matter and substitute anyone for he.

(A) anyone's own
(B) a person's own
(C) his own
(D) their own
(E) theirs

8. Members of that loose coalition of groups calling themselves the "New Left" believe that the only solution for the nation's problems is the overthrow, through violence, if necessary, of both corrupt capitalism and a corrupt governmental system.

   Substitute advocate for believe.

   (A) system for the only
   (B) system through the only
   (C) system as well as the only
   (D) system as the only
   (E) system by the only

9. He was trapped into a loveless marriage by an overly anxious girl; therefore, he was already weary of her chattering before a month had passed.

   Begin with Trapped into.

   (A) girl, he
   (B) girl; he
   (C) girl, therefore, he
   (D) girl, so he
   (E) girl; therefore, he

10. Certain specialized drugs have been used with remarkable success by doctors treating some mental disorders, particularly the manic-depressive syndrome, which thirty years ago, would have required the patient to be hospitalized indefinitely.

    Begin with Thirty years ago some mental.

    (A) patient, now these disorders
    (B) patient, and now these disorders
    (C) patients, for these disorders
    (D) patient, with these disorders
    (E) patient; now these disorders

11. The old man was tired of listening to his children's complaints; therefore, he disconnected his hearing aid.

    Begin with Tired.

    (A) complaints, and he
    (B) complaints, and the old man
    (C) complaints, the old man
    (D) complaints, he
    (E) complaints, so the old man

12. The waitress was discharged from her position at the restaurant because she refused to wear the uniform required for anyone serving food.

    Begin with The waitress refused.

    (A) food; therefore, she was discharged
    (B) food, and was discharged
    (C) food, so she was discharged
    (D) food and was discharged
    (E) food as a result of which she was discharged

13. Concerned about a fast-spreading influenza epidemic, the company's health officials suggested the plant be closed for two weeks.

    Begin with A fast-spreading influenza.

    (A) provoked company's health officials to recommend a two-week hiatus for all personnel.
    (B) led the company's health officials to recommend the plant's closing for a fortnight.
    (C) caused the company's health officials to recommend a two-week closing of the plant.
    (D) concerning health officials, leading them to suggest a two-week closing of the plant.
    (E) was the cause of recommendation for company health officials to close the plant for two weeks.

14. The Bayeux Tapestry, an embroidery using wool of various colors on linen fabric, presents a historical record of the conquest of England by William the Conqueror in the Battle of Hastings in 1066.

    Begin with William the Conqueror.

    (A) conquered England in the Battle of Hastings, depicted in the Bayeux Tapestry, an elaborate embroidery.
    (B) led the Normans to victory in the Battle of Hastings in 1066 over the English, which is recorded in the Bayeux Tapestry.
    (C) led the Normans to victory in the Battle of Hastings in 1066, a battle preserved by the Bayeux Tapestry.
    (D) was victorious in the 1066 Battle of Hastings, which is recorded in the Bayeux Tapestry.
    (E) led the Normans to victory over the English in the Battle of Hastings, an historical event recorded in the Bayeux Tapestry.

15. Although the original movie *The Wizard of Oz* follows Frank Baum's book reasonably well, Dorothy Gale's shoes are silver, not red.

Begin with Dorothy Gale's shoes.

(A) in Frank Baum's *The Wizard of Oz* are silver in the movie, not red as they are in the movie.

(B) that are red in the famous *The Wizard of Oz* movie are actually silver in Frank Baum's book.

(C) are not supposed to be red as they are in *The Wizard of Oz* movie because in Frank Baum's book, they are silver.

(D) "ruby-red slippers" in *The Wizard of Oz* movie, are silver in Frank Baum's book.

(E) in the original movie are red, which is not the silver color they are in Frank Baum's book *The Wizard of Oz*.

16. The decision to develop the interstate highway system from coast to coast gave the government the right to buy citizens' property at a fair price.

Begin with The government.

(A) bought citizens' property at a fair cost from coast to coast as a result of the development of the interstate highway.

(B) bought citizens' property at a fair price across the country to develop the interstate highway system.

(C) developed the interstate highway system by purchasing citizen's property.

(D) developed the interstate highway system after buying citizens' property.

(E) has the power of eminent domain which played a key role in the interstate highway system.

17. Many people have chosen new lasik surgery to correct their vision so that they no longer have to wear glasses.

Begin with Lasik eye surgery.

(A) works for some people whose vision is flawed because of cataracts.

(B) is a new choice for many people to correct their vision who are delighted with the improvement.

(C) corrects vision in many myopic people who do not need glasses or even contact lenses anymore.

(D) can benefit many people who need to have their vision corrected because they are tired of wearing glasses.

(E) improves vision for many people who do not have to wear glasses anymore.

IMPROVING SENTENCES

Items included in this section test a student's ability to discern what is incorrect about the structure of a sentence. The student must determine, as a writer, what problems might exist in the sentence that would interfere with logical communication.

Directions: In each of the following sentences, part of the sentence or the entire sentence is underlined. Beneath each sentence you will find five versions of the underlined part of the sentence. Answer (A) repeats the original; answers (B) through (E) present different alternatives.

You should choose the answer that best expresses the meaning of the original sentence. If you think the original is better than any of the alternatives, choose answer (A); otherwise, select one of the other answer choices. Whatever your choice, it should produce the most effective sentence—a clear and precise sentence without awkwardness or ambiguity.

Example 1

1. The reason the company failed was because the president spent too much money.

(A) The reason the company failed was because
(B) The company failed because
(C) Because the company failed
(D) Because the reason was the company failed
(E) The company failed was because

The correct answer is (B). The other choices are wordy or create illogical sentences. *Was because* is an error because it is a mixed construction that attempts to use an adverb clause ("because the president spent too much money") as a predicate nominative, which renames the subject.

Example 2

2. When four years old, my father died.

(A) When four years old
(B) When four year's old
(C) When he was four years old
(D) When I was four years old
(E) At the age of four

The correct answer is (D). The underlined section in the original sentence is a dangling modifier; only answer (D) solves that problem. A dangling modifier is more accurately called a lapse in logic on the part of the writer, but it can be defined as the use of a modifier—a phrase or clause—that does not have a specific word in the rest of the sentence to modify. In this sentence, When four years old, cannot logically modify my father. Therefore, answer (D) is correct.

IMPROVING SENTENCES: REVIEW QUESTIONS

The following sentences will give you a chance to practice. Read each sentence carefully, mark your answers, and then check them with the answers and explanations that appear at the end of the Overview section.

1. Driving around the corner, <u>a glimpse of the mountains was caught.</u>

   (A) a glimpse of the mountains was caught.
   (B) a glimpse of the mountains were caught.
   (C) we caught a glimpse of the mountains.
   (D) the mountains were caught a glimpse of.
   (E) we caught a glimpse of the mountains' view.

2. Sitting around the dinner table, <u>family stories were told by each of us.</u>

   (A) family stories were told by each of us.
   (B) family stories were told by all of us.
   (C) each of us told family stories.
   (D) stories of the family were told by each of us.
   (E) there were told family stories by each of us.

3. The loud music of my neighbors and their friends <u>annoys people visiting from England.</u>

   (A) annoys people visiting from England.
   (B) annoys English people.
   (C) annoys persons from England.
   (D) annoy English people.
   (E) annoys people who come from England.

4. <u>After he graduated college,</u> he entered law school.

   (A) After he graduated college,
   (B) After he graduated from college,
   (C) When he graduated college,
   (D) After he graduated school
   (E) As he was graduated from college,

5. When my husband <u>will come home,</u> I'll tell him you called.

   (A) will come home,
   (B) will come home
   (C) will have come home,
   (D) comes home,
   (E) has come home,

6. Gloria was neither in favor of or opposed to capital punishment.

   (A) Gloria was neither in favor of or opposed to capital punishment.
   (B) Gloria was not in favor of or opposed to the plan.
   (C) Gloria was neither in favor of capital punishment or opposed to it.
   (D) Gloria was neither in favor of capital punishment or opposed to capital punishment.
   (E) Gloria was neither in favor of nor opposed to capital punishment.

7. I don't do well in those kinds of tests.

   (A) I don't do well in those kinds of tests.
   (B) I don't do well in those kind of tests.
   (C) I don't do good in those kinds of tests.
   (D) I don't do good in those kind of tests.
   (E) I don't do good in tests like those.

8. We were amazed to see the <u>amount of people waiting in line to see the Clintons.</u>

   (A) amount of people waiting in line to see the Clintons.
   (B) number of people waiting in line to see the Clintons.
   (C) amount of persons waiting in line to see the Clintons.
   (D) amount of people waiting in line to see the Clinton's.
   (E) amount of people waiting to see the Clintons in line.

9. Football teams pay athletes tremendous sums of money each <u>year, the fans pay large sums</u> for seats in the stadium.

   (A) year, the fans pay large sums
   (B) year, the fans paying large sums
   (C) year, for the fans pay large sums
   (D) year; the fans paying large sums
   (E) year, when the fans pay large sums

10. People who attend baseball games often do not know enough about the fine points of offense and defense to enjoy them.

    (A) People who attend baseball games often do not know enough about the fine points of offense and defense to enjoy them.

    (B) People who attend baseball games do not know a sufficient amount about the fine points of offense and defense to appreciate them.

    (C) Some people who attend baseball games do not know enough about the fine points of offense and defense to enjoy the skill of the players.

    (D) People who attend baseball games often do not know enough about them to enjoy the fine points of offense and defense.

    (E) People who attend baseball games do not understand the fine points of offense and defense.

11. Covered in several layers of paint, I was not eager to refinish this old kitchen table.

    (A) Covered in several layers of paint,

    (B) Covered with paint colors in layers,

    (C) Because it was covered with several layers of paint,

    (D) Covered in old layers,

    (E) With a covering of several of old paint layers,

12. My aunt is a long-time admirer of Emily Dickinson, who still attends poetry readings at the bookstore.

    (A) My aunt is a long-time admirer of Emily Dickinson, who still attends poetry readings at the bookstore.

    (B) Readings at the bookstore, my aunt is a long-time admirer of Emily Dickinson.

    (C) My aunt, a fan of Emily Dickinson, still loves reading poetry.

    (D) My aunt, a long-time admirer of poetry readings at the bookstore, owns no poetry books by Emily Dickinson.

    (E) My aunt who is a long-time admirer of Emily Dickinson still attends poetry readings at the bookstore.

13. The students hoping to attend a playoff game, stood in line, bought their tickets, and then they stopped for food.

    (A) hoping to attend a playoff game, stood in line, bought their tickets, and then they stopped for food.

    (B) were standing in line, buying their tickets, and then they stopped for food hoping to attend a playoff game.

    (C) stood in line, bought their tickets, and then they stopped for food, hoping to attend a playoff game.

    (D) stood in line, bought their tickets, and then stopped for food.

    (E) bought their tickets, stood in line, and then they bought some food, hoping to attend a playoff game.

14. The reason that I am happy is because I have won another scholarship.

    (A) The reason that I am happy is because I have won another scholarship.

    (B) The reason I am happy is because I have won another scholarship.

    (C) I am happy because I have won another scholarship.

    (D) The reason that I am happy is because of the fact that I have won another scholarship.

    (E) The reason for my happiness is because of winning another scholarship.

15. While driving back home from the beach, the idea occurred to me that I had left my clothes hanging in the condo closet.

    (A) While driving back home from the beach, the idea occurred to me that I had left my clothes hanging in the condo closet.

    (B) While I was driving home from the beach, I realized I had left clothes in the condo closet.

    (C) While I was driving home from the beach, the idea occurred to me that I had left clothes hanging in the condo closet.

    (D) The idea that I had left clothes occurred to me while driving home in the condo closet from the beach.

    (E) While on my way home from the beach, the clothes I left in the condo closet occurred to me.

16. Ask whomever is at the registration desk what time the banquet begins.

   (A) Ask whomever is at the registration desk what time the banquet begins.
   (B) At the registration ask whomever is there what time the banquet begins.
   (C) At the registration ask whomever is there what time the banquet begins at.
   (D) Ask whoever is at the registration desk what time the banquet begins.
   (E) To learn what time the banquet begins, ask whomever is at the registration desk.

17. Sam admitted that during the spring quarter how challenging carrying an overload was going to be.

   (A) Sam admitted that during the spring quarter how challenging carrying an overload was going to be.
   (B) Carrying an overload was going to be a challenge in the spring quarter was the fact that Sam had admitted.
   (C) Sam admitted that carrying an overload during spring quarter was going to be a challenge.
   (D) Sam admitted in the spring quarter that carrying an overload was going to be a challenge.
   (E) In the spring quarter Sam admitted that carrying an overload was going to be a challenge.

18. Our destination for summer vacation lies about a day's drive from our home.

   (A) lies about a day's drive
   (B) lays about a day's drive
   (C) lies about a drive of days
   (D) lays about one days drive
   (E) lies about a days drive

19. Stan is one of those kind of people who enjoys crossword puzzles.

   (A) one of those kind of people who enjoys
   (B) one of those people who enjoy
   (C) one of those people who enjoys
   (D) one of those peoples who enjoy
   (E) one of those kinds of people who enjoy

20. After my sister had left home, she spends the next five years earning her degree in pharmacy.

   (A) she spends the next five years
   (B) she spended the next five years
   (C) she spent the next five years
   (D) she spent the next five year's
   (E) she will spend the next five years

REVISING WORK IN PROGRESS

In this section, you will find an early draft of a student essay in which the sentences have been numbered for easy reference. Some parts of each selection need to be changed or improved. You will be instructed to read the draft and then answer the multiple-choice questions. In essence, you are being tested on coherence, grammar knowledge, sentence-combining technique, linking sentences to each other, linking sentences to the rest of the paragraph, and improving on the work within specific sentences. As you read the draft, look for any inconsistencies or problem areas. Carefully consider any sentences that sound awkward or repetitive. Consider yourself the writer. What areas would you change?

There are basically seven kinds of questions on the exam. Let's review the typical questions and how they should be answered. Then there is a sample draft essay to read and some sample questions to try.

TYPES OF QUESTIONS

1. SENTENCE COMBINING AND REVISING

This question will typically read:

   Which of the following is the best way to revise and combine sentences x and y?

Sometimes if the two sentences are very long, the question will ask you to combine the underlined portions of each sentence. Here, the testers are looking for your ability to use words in a grammatical fashion and for proper use of mechanics (commas, colons, semicolons, etc.). Assume that these two sentences can be combined. As in all multiple-choice tests, pick the obvious incorrect answers first and discard them. Try to narrow down your choices to two. You want to make sure that the combined sentence contains all the information, is grammatically correct, and uses proper mechanics.

2. ADDING BEFORE OR AFTER A SENTENCE— to link the paragraphs or link the sentence to the rest of the essay

This question will typically read:

   Which of the following sentences, if added after (or before) sentence x, would best link that sentence to the rest of the paragraph?

This question is designed to test for coherence. You must demonstrate that you have understood the passage. You need to figure out what is missing or what would best improve the preceding and following sentences. Try to imagine this as a puzzle. You have the top piece and the bottom piece, but now you need the middle. Go back to the draft and carefully reread the preceding and following sentences. Imagine you were the writer; what would you have put in there? Go back to the choices and eliminate the obvious bad ones. Once you have narrowed down your choices, reread the sentences, putting in the choices that you have made. Which one sounds best to you? Make sure that it is grammatically correct and not repetitive of either the preceding or following sentences. Make sure that it connects or links, but does not repeat, information. Remember the image of the puzzle. You don't want the same of either thing, but something that bridges and unites the two.

3. CHANGING PART OF A SENTENCE WITHIN THE CONTEXT OF THE PARAGRAPH

This question will typically read:

> Which of the following is the best version of the underlined portion of sentence x?

Often the sentence will be reproduced below the question. You need to go back and refer to the sentences preceding and following the sentence you are asked to revise. You will need a context in order to judge whether the sentence section needs to be changed. In the answer choices, often one answer will be *leave as written*. Another answer may be to delete the entire section of the sentence. For the deletion answer, simply read the sentence and determine if that section is needed. The part of the sentence that is being changed needs to correlate with all the other information in the paragraph. In this question you are being tested on your grammar knowledge (correct tenses, correct usage, etc.). Once again, throw out any answers that are in the wrong tense, change the information, use words improperly, or sound awkward. Limit your choices to two or three. Then study those to determine which sounds the best within the sentence itself. Before making a final choice, make sure that the answer will not only fit well within the sentence but will also fit within the entire paragraph.

4. DETERMINING THE STRATEGIES USED BY THE AUTHOR

The question will typically read:

> All of the following strategies are used by the writer of the passage EXCEPT

Four of the answers will be correct, and one will be wrong. This is probably one of the easier questions on the test. First, you need to determine what kind of draft essay is before you. Each kind of writing needs certain things. For example, if the draft is a descriptive piece, it will contain lots of adjectives, a narrowed topic, supporting sentences to convey attitude, and visual cues.

If the draft is an expository one (such as an essay of opinion), it will have examples, adverbs of frequency, and sequential supportive sentences. If the draft is a process essay (telling you how to do something), it will use the second-person voice (you), sequential adverbs (first, second, etc.), and a narrowed topic. To answer this question, you need to ask yourself these questions: (1) What type of essay draft is this? Then, (2) What is NOT required for that kind of writing? If you can't answer this second question (because that will be the answer to the test question), then ask yourself: What does a writer need for this kind of writing? Narrow down your answer to two things that the writer might not have done, and then (after having referred back to the draft) choose the one the writer DIDN'T use. Remember, for this question you are looking for the lump of coal in the diamonds. Concentrate on the wrong one—the one the writer NEVER really used.

5. REPLACING PART OF A SENTENCE WITH DIFFERENT WORDS OR LEAVING IT THE SAME

This question would typically read:

> Which of the following would be the best replacement for "word or phase" at the beginning (or end) of the sentence?

This question resembles question 3 a great deal. While in question 3 you were asked to replace part of the sentence in the context of the entire paragraph, here you will be asked to replace part of the sentence within the sentence itself. The tester wants to see if you can clarify and edit material correctly within a sentence. Here you do not need to consider the entire passage and its content. Now, you need to concentrate on the sentence itself. It isn't necessary to look back in the draft and reread the preceding and following sentences.

In the answer choices, often one answer will be *leave as written*. Another answer may be to delete the entire section of the sentence. For the deletion answer, simply read the sentence and determine if that section is needed in the sentence. Try to establish the problem in the sentence. If you truly can't find one, then the answer is to leave the sentence alone. If the sentence needs something (thus deletion is incorrect) and what is there is not quite right (thus leaving alone is incorrect), you are left with three possible answers. Try to identify the problem (e.g., grammar tense, improper use of word, too wordy, etc.) that will narrow down your choice among the three.

6. CHANGING SENTENCES BY MOVING THEM, COMBINING THEM, ETC.

This question would typically read:

> **The writer of the passage could best improve sentences x and y by:**

The tester is trying to determine your organizational skills, editing skills, and sequential comprehension of the written material. Typically, the answers will include the moving of one of the sentences, the moving of the other sentence, combining them, or moving them both. The fifth choice will be stylistic, such as choosing less specific adjectives or changing the tone. To answer this question, you must go back to the original sentences. Can they be combined together in order to improve the entire essay? Try, then, to see whether moving one or both of the sentences would change the meaning. If the meaning of the draft would change by the movement, then that is an incorrect answer. It is best to approach this question by eliminating the impossibilities first. Once you have eliminated at least three of the worst ones, you can proceed to pick which of the last two is a possibility. Leave the style answer for last; they are the hardest to discern. Concentrate on comprehending the flow and structure of the entire draft. You are truly being tested here on whether or not you can organize information and place it in the correct order. Since that is the case, concentrate on the order first, then on the style.

7. IMPROVING A SENTENCE

This question would typically read:

> **The writer of the passage could best improve sentence x by:**

Here, you are being asked to demonstrate your ability to improve on writing as well as to edit. When you read the sentence, think about it carefully. The tester chose this sentence because something is lacking in it. You need to discern what is lacking. Often, the sentence is weak and needs more examples. Other times, the sentence needs more defining, discussion, acknowledging, or inclusion of personal examples. To determine the correct answer, reread the sentence each time you look at the possible answers. Think of yourself as the editor. What would be the item that stands out to you? Many times it helps to label the draft's writing basis. For example, if the draft is expository in nature, most likely the sentence will require more examples or acknowledging of examples. If the writing is narrative in form, it may need inclusion of more personal examples. By knowing the kind of essay, you can limit your choices. Once again, it would be prudent to eliminate the obvious wrong answers and narrow the field.

REVISING WORK IN PROGRESS: REVIEW QUESTIONS

Now let's try a passage. This is an early draft of a student essay in which the sentences have been numbered for easy reference. Some parts of the selection need to be changed. Read the selection and try to answer the questions. If you find that you are having difficulty answering a question or you get a different answer, refer back to the prior section concerning that type of question. Check your answers with the answers and explanations that appear at the end of the Overview section.

Passage 1

(1) *When I think about my childhood in Mexico, the most vivid memory was our visit to my paternal grandmother's home in the state of Michoacán.* (2) *She was a tiny dark woman with long gray-black braids.* (3) *She lived in a tiny dirt-floored shack off the center square of a small village.* (4) *Our mother came from a wealthy family in the capital.* (5) *My father, a self-made man, never spoke of his roots.* (6) *He had never introduced us to his family.* (7) *When I was five, his father died.* (8) *Usually on the Day of the Dead holiday, we went to the cemetery and laid flowers on the graves.* (9) *That fall, my father informed us that we would be going that holiday to his mother's house.* (10) *My father seemed almost embarrassed to take us there.*

(11) *Imagine my surprise when we accompanied my grandmother to the cemetery the evening before the first of November.* (12) *Everywhere the graves were decorated with orange and yellow flowers.* (13) *People surrounded each grave and placed the deceased's favorite foods, clothing, and drinks there.* (14) *People strolled about selling things while families held their nightlong vigils.* (15) *Card games, drunken brawls, and singing were common.* (16) *There were no artificial lights, only thousands of candles.* (17) *When I asked what we were doing, my grandmother told me we were remembering those who had died and sharing that night with them.* (18) *One would think that a 5-year-old would find that a creepy thought, but I just thought it was great to stay up all night and party.*

1. Sentence combining: Which of the following is the best way to revise and combine sentences 4 and 5 (reproduced below)?

   Our mother came from a wealthy family in the capital. My father, a self-made man, never spoke of his roots.

   (A) My father, a self-made man, never spoke of his roots to my mother's wealthy family in the capital.

   (B) My mother came from a wealthy family in the capital, while my father, a self-made man, never spoke of his roots.

   (C) My father, a self-made man, never came from a wealthy family like my mother, so he never talked about his past.

   (D) Our mother came from a wealthy family in the capital, and my father, as a self-made man, never spoke of his roots.

   (E) My mother was very different from my father because she came from a wealthy family in the capital, and my father was a self-made man who never talked about his family.

2. Adding a sentence: Which of the following sentences, if added after sentence 10, would best link that sentence to the next paragraph?

   (A) In my grandmother's village, there was to be a larger, more traditional ceremony.

   (B) My father felt very uncomfortable going back home.

   (C) I was surprised by what I saw at my grandmother's house.

   (D) Holidays are supposed to be unusual.

   (E) This holiday would be celebrated in a different place and in a different way.

3. Changing part of a sentence: Which of the following is the best version of the underlined portion of sentence 13 (reproduced below)?

   People surrounded each grave and placed the deceased's favorite foods, clothing, and drinks there.

   (A) (leave as is)

   (B) sat around

   (C) encircled

   (D) stood around

   (E) stood by

4. Strategies used by author: All of the following strategies are used by the writer of the passage EXCEPT

   (A) descriptive adjectives

   (B) sensory details

   (C) adverbs of place

   (D) logical examples

   (E) narrowed topic

5. Replacing part of a sentence: Which of the following would be the best replacement for the underlined portion of sentence 16 (reproduced below)?

   There were no artificial lights, only thousands of candles.

   (A) (leave as is)

   (B) (delete)

   (C) the light of thousands of candles.

   (D) many candles with their light.

   (E) the glow of thousands of candles.

6. Changing sentences: The writer of the passage could best improve sentences 2 and 3 by:

   (A) moving sentence 2, but leaving sentence 3 alone

   (B) moving them both to the beginning of paragraph 2

   (C) combining them

   (D) moving sentence 3, but leaving sentence 2 alone

   (E) adding more details

7. Improving a sentence: The writer of the passage could best improve sentence 8 by:

   (A) defining the Day of the Dead

   (B) including personal opinions

   (C) discussing the family's traditions in greater detail

   (D) acknowledging her father's family

   (E) providing more examples

Here is another passage to try.

Passage 2

(1) In the early 1950s, American science fiction movies, such as the original "Invasion of the Body Snatchers," transferred the pervasive fear of Communism and the Cold War to a fantasy world where aliens invaded earth. (2) Following the end of World War II, which was brought to a close by the dropping of the atomic bomb, Americans developed a fear of Josef Stalin, who had been a few years earlier an American ally. (3) The beginning of the Cold War had its origins in the use of nuclear possibilities to defeat Americans. (4) We had nuclear arms, but so did the Soviets. (5) We were afraid that some hasty decision could be the end of not only the United States but also much of the world.

(6) The transfer of these fears about the Soviets led to the creation of U.S. Senator Joseph McCarthy's Un-American Activities Committee. (7) McCarthy accused the Department of State in 1950 of harboring Communists. (8) Even though President Harry Truman and Secretary of State Dean Acheson denied the assertions, the American public began to believe McCarthy's charges. (9) Some of the anxiety developed as a result of the frustrations of the Korean War, the Chinese Communist conquest of mainland China, and the arrest and conviction of several Americans such as Alger Hiss and the Rosenbergs as Soviet spies. (10) The term "McCarthyism" described the widespread accusations and investigations of suspected Communist activities in the U.S. during the 1950s.

(11) This fear of "a communist hiding under every bed" was terrifying to many Americans because of their uncertainty of identifying these so-called Communists. (12) Given that some Americans had been convicted of being Soviet spies, Americans were apprehensive because these spies looked like ordinary American citizens. (13) The fear of infiltration of enemies focused some attention especially on public figures, such as college professors, journalists, and entertainers. (14) Some companies blacklisted those accused.

(15) As a result of the alarm that spread quickly throughout the U.S., the movie industry quickly shifted the fear of Communists to a fear of aliens. (16) This version of the enemy led to even more dread because aliens could supposedly adopt human form. (17) While it was doubtful, of course, that such an alien invasion could occur, apprehension only grew when these "bug-eyed monster" movies were released. (18) UFOs often played prominent roles in these films.

(19) Some movies focused on the effects of nuclear fallout, for instance, mutations like those experienced in "The Fly" and "Attack of the Fifty-Foot Woman." (20) The American public could cope with aliens in unrealistic films better than they could deal with possibly real Communists infiltrating American society. (21) "The Invasion of the Body Snatchers" perfectly depicts this fear because in this movie aliens arrive in "pods" and eventually take over the bodies of humans who die, of course. (22) These "body snatchers" look like the people their friends and family knew; this invasion is accomplished in short order, too quickly for most people to realize before it is too late for them to fight back. (23) Thus the ubiquitous fear of Communists sparked a new interest in science fiction movies.

8. Sentence combining: Which of the following is the best way to revise and combine sentences 4 and 5 (reproduced below)?

   We had nuclear arms, but so did the Soviets. We were afraid that some hasty decision could be the end of not only the U.S. but also much of the world.

   (A) Both the U.S. and the U.S.S.R. had nuclear arms, but we feared a thoughtless decision would bring an end to our world.
   (B) Both the U.S. and the U.S.S.R. had nuclear arms; we all feared the disastrous result of careless use.
   (C) Because the U.S. and the U.S.S.R. had nuclear arms, our entire world was in danger.
   (D) Knowing the U.S.S.R. also had weapons exacerbated our fears about the results of nuclear war.
   (E) Imprudent use of nuclear arms was a strong fear because the U.S.S.R. had the same capability.

9. Adding a sentence: Which of the following sentences, if added after sentence 14, would best link that paragraph to the next paragraph?

   (A) The U.S. was experiencing another "witch hunt" like the one in Salem earlier in American history.
   (B) Freedom of speech was denied to those accused.
   (C) Americans were fearful of shadows everywhere.
   (D) Some actors never worked again; their careers were gone.
   (E) The careers of many actors, however, skyrocketed when they portrayed Communists in movies.

10. Strategies used by the author: Which of the following strategies does the writer of the passage use?
    - (A) Sensory details
    - (B) Descriptive adjectives
    - (C) Narrowed topic
    - (D) Logical examples
    - (E) All of the above

11. Replacing part of a sentence: Which of the following would be the best replacement of the underlined portion of the sentence reproduced below?

    This fear of a "communist hiding under every bed" was terrifying to many Americans because of their uncertainty of identifying these so-called Communists.
    - (A) (leave as is)
    - (B) alarmed
    - (C) was frightful to
    - (D) was frightening to
    - (E) irritated

12. Changing part of a sentence: Which of the following is the best version of the underlined portion of the sentence reproduced below?

    Some companies blacklisted those accused.
    - (A) (leave as is)
    - (B) blackballed
    - (C) dismissed
    - (D) fired
    - (E) blacklisted, or refused to hire,

ANALYZING WRITING

In this section, you will be given a set of passages in which the sentences are numbered for easy reference. Usually, the passages will be part of a longer writing sample, but you will not see the entire sample. Therefore, the samples you will read do not constitute a complete discussion of the issues presented in the passage. This requires that you often project or infer how the original essay was presented. You are being tested on your ability to analyze a writing sample and determine the key components of it: main idea or thesis statement, content, style of the author, the inner organization of the paragraph based on sentence relationship, functions of specific sentences to the piece as a whole, and general revising. Think of yourself more as a reader and less as an editor. Initially, you will need to be a careful reader—looking for the integral features. After you can describe the functions of the writing sample, you will be asked to edit only a small portion. Therefore, concentrate on the specific aspects of the essay.

There are basically seven kinds of questions that will be asked on this part of the test. Let's review what they are and then discuss strategies for answering them. After that, there is a practice test with questions and answers.

TYPES OF QUESTIONS

1. MAIN IDEA
Typically this question is written like this:

> **The main idea of the passage is that:**

The question may also be broken down into paragraph/main idea, to read:

> **Which of the following most accurately describes what happens in the second paragraph?**

Here, you are being tested on your comprehension and ability to summarize. When you read the passage for the first time, think about the main idea. Can you say in one or two words what the general theme of the essay is? Can you narrow down that paragraph into a specific phrase that clarifies what the writing sample is talking about? It is best to think about this WHILE you are reading the passage. When reading, you need to focus on the central issue of the writer. As in all multiple-choice questions, eliminate the obvious incorrect choices and try to narrow down your options to two. Make sure that the key points are in your final choice. Don't be tricked by wording that has been borrowed from the writing sample. Watch out for ideas that are too general and too specific.

2. PURPOSE
Typically this question is written like this:

> **The purpose of this passage (or paragraph x) is primarily to:**

This question resembles question 1 a great deal. While question 1 deals with the "what" of the passage, now you're being tested to see if you can discern the "why." Often, the main idea and purpose become confusing to the reader. Purpose requires clarification. This question requires you to explain why the author has written this passage. For example, the passage may be about the death penalty (the main idea), but why did the author write about that specific subject? Was he trying to convince the reader of his ideas (as in an essay of opinion)? Was the author presenting facts (as in a factual expository essay)? Or was the author relating a story (as in a narrative version)?

In order to determine purpose, you need to determine what kind of writing sample is before you. This is where you need to project or infer what the entire essay looks like. Once you have decided what kind of writing it is, you need to think about why someone writes that kind of essay. The answer to that question will identify the author's purpose.

3. DESCRIPTION OF CONTENT

This question is typically written:

> **Which of the following pairs of words best describes the speaker's reaction to the experience?**

The tester is interested in finding out if you (after having read the entire passage) understand what was written and can now summarize in two or three words how the writer felt. This tests your ability to infer feelings and grasp the reactions of the author from the style used in the passage. Now the tester is asking for the "how" of the writing sample. How did the author feel? Often, you will find that one of the answers is how the reader would feel after having read the sample. Don't be fooled into believing this is the actual reaction of the writer. Sometimes it is, and sometimes it isn't. Look within the passage for examples and facts that indicate the writer's reaction. As always, eliminate the obvious poor choices and concentrate on limiting your choice. Look for similar vocabulary, word usage, and descriptive adjectives for feelings.

4. STYLE

Typically the question is written like this:

> **The descriptive details in sentence x (or in sentences x, y, and z) provide a:**

OR

> **The order of presentation provides:**

Here, the tester is looking for a more in-depth response than in question 3. The tester wants to know if you can identify why the writer organized her ideas, details, and sentences the way she did. By doing what the author did, what happened? As we know, writing doesn't always come from instant inspiration—there is work involved. Specific choices are made. Why did this author make those choices? Try to put yourself in the author's shoes. If you can determine why those choices were made, you can answer the question easily. Think about the motivation of the writer. Did she want to make the image clearer, represent something differently, give a different view, distort something, or bring in another image? The way the material is presented or specific details within a sentence are there for a reason. Eliminate, once again, obvious things that the author would not be doing. Center on key characteristics of the sample.

5. RELATIONSHIPS

These questions are phrased one of two ways:

> **The relationship of sentence x to the rest of the paragraph is:**

OR

> **The relationship of the two paragraphs to each other is:**

You need to determine the organization of the paragraph(s). When answering the first type of question, consider the main idea of the paragraph. Where does this sentence fall in the paragraph? Its actual physical location can lend a great deal of insight. Consider the sentences prior to and after this sentence. What kind of bridge does this sentence provide between those two sentences? Why is this sentence necessary? What does it provide that the others don't?

If you are answering the second type of question, determine what the main ideas are in both paragraphs. Usually, they are different but somehow related. What is that relationship? If the first paragraph talks about a trip to the Bahamas and the second talks about the trip home, the key underlying theme that they share is taking a trip. Imagine a key word or phrase that would apply for both paragraphs. That word or phrase is the relationship that they share. The next step is to determine what kind of relationship that is. Let's look at our example of the trip to the Bahamas. The theme is the trip, but how is the trip different in each paragraph? Perhaps in the first, the writer discusses the trip there; the second paragraph discusses the trip home. This would be an essay of contrast. Therefore, the relationship is the contrast between going and coming. Try to determine the underlying theme, then what the function of the paragraph is to that theme.

6. FUNCTIONS OF SENTENCES

This question is usually written like this:

> **The function of sentence x is primarily to:**

Once again, you are being tested on your comprehension of the writer's organization and style. Now you're being tested to see if you can identify why *sentence x* is in the form it is and the effect of that form. Go back and read the prior sentence, the test-question sentence, and the following sentence. Try to determine what function the middle sentence has relative to the other two. Usually, there is a link to one of the sentences in the paragraph, and the link is normally physically fairly close by. If you have decided that there is no bridge or connection to those two sentences, you have narrowed down your answers to three. Of the three answers left, try to eliminate the one that is obviously incorrect. With the two remaining answer possibilities, you can go back and test them against the sentence in the paragraph. Which answer best responds to the question: why is this sentence here?

7. REVISING

This question is typically phrased:

Which treatment of sentence x is most needed?

Now, you can change from being a reader to being an editor. The tester wishes to know (after you have analyzed the style, organization, and coherence of the writing sample) how you would, as an editor, improve on a specific sentence. First, consider the purpose of the original sentence. Is the sentence needed to further explain, clarify, describe, or express something in particular? Eliminate any answers that change the information or do not serve the same purpose. This approach will usually help you narrow down your choices. Now it will be much easier to choose the correct answer. Stay focused on the objective. You want to improve the writing of the sentence without changing any of its internal structure or information. Oftentimes, this requires restyling or correcting a grammatical error. Sometimes it requires clarification or greater details.

ANALYZING WRITING: REVIEW QUESTIONS

Now, let's try a passage. The sentences have been numbered for easy reference. Remember, this passage was probably part of a larger essay. Consider why the sample was written, what it is primarily about, and what kind of sample it is, and pay attention to the organization. Answer the questions that follow. If you have problems answering the questions or answer them incorrectly, refer back to the previous pages concerning that specific question. Check your answers with the answers and explanations at the end of the Overview section.

(1) *Perhaps one of the most life-altering events for Chicago was the arrival of the World's Columbian Exposition in 1893.* (2) *Compared to today with television and computers, this may appear as a paltry event for mankind.* (3) *This exposition in reality was quite earth-shattering, altering the life of the citizens and institutions at that time.* (4) *The Art Institute building, which was constructed to provide several exhibitions, was left after the closure of the fair.* (5) *The structure became the modern Art Institute of today in Chicago.* (6) *The original Art Institute of Chicago had never had adequate space or lighting.* (7) *This new building provided them*

with both. (8) *With large gallery space, the founders set out to establish an excellent collection of modern art.*

(9) *During the Exposition of 1893, several famous art exhibits were mounted.* (10) *Among these exhibits was one that centered on American art from 1876–1893.* (11) *Another featured American impressionists.* (12) *There were also European artists represented.* (13) *The reaction to these exhibits was astounding.* (14) *People changed their views on art.* (15) *There was a greater interest in seriously collecting American art of that time.* (16) *Chicago, which had been perceived as a crass commercial center with dirt roads and slaughterhouses, became an important center for the visual arts.*

1. Main idea: The main idea of this passage is that
   - (A) the World's Fair of 1893 changed the institutions and citizens of Chicago
   - (B) the Art Institute needed more space and lighting
   - (C) the American artists were finally being recognized
   - (D) the World's Fair exhibitions and the acquiring of a building created an interest in art
   - (E) Chicago changed in the eyes of the world and became an important center

2. Purpose: The purpose of paragraph 2 is primarily to
   - (A) explain why the people changed their interest in the visual arts
   - (B) discuss what kinds of exhibits were mounted
   - (C) offer a different perception of Chicago
   - (D) tell why American art became popular
   - (E) offer examples of different kinds of art

3. Description of content: Which of the following pairs of words best describes the speaker's reaction to the World's Columbian Exposition?
   - (A) Clinical and bored
   - (B) Ecstasy and fear
   - (C) Dismay and surprise
   - (D) Delight and wonder
   - (E) Contentment and satisfaction

4. Style: The descriptive details in sentence 6
   - (A) provide a precise visual image
   - (B) provide a background on which to base a future comparison
   - (C) represent the author's interpretation
   - (D) provide a view of the entire building
   - (E) distort the aforementioned idea

5. Relationships: Which of the following best describes the relationship of sentence 3 to the rest of the paragraph?

   (A) It illustrates the changes that took place in Chicago.
   (B) It establishes the importance of the World's Columbian Exposition.
   (C) It presents the main ideas in each of the paragraphs.
   (D) It demonstrates the insignificance in comparison to modern-day technology.
   (E) It describes the exhibitions that would later provide the building for the Art Institute.

6. Functions of sentences: The function of sentence 14 is primarily to

   (A) present the form that the reaction took
   (B) illustrate the excitement that people felt
   (C) give an example to support sentence 13
   (D) indicate the amount of interest
   (E) prepare the reader for sentence 16

7. Revising: Which treatment of sentence 7 is most needed?

   (A) Leave it as it is.
   (B) It should be placed before sentence 6.
   (C) It should be omitted.
   (D) *Them* should be changed to *the Exposition*.
   (E) *Them* should be changed to *the people of Chicago*.

HOW TO WRITE AN ESSAY

An essay is a way to express your ideas in writing rather than by speaking. To do so effectively, you need to focus on a specific topic, roughly organize your ideas, and write as clearly and logically as possible in the time allotted. A good essay contains the following elements:

- Content
- Cogency
- Clarity
- Coherence
- Correctness

Let's discuss each element separately.

CONTENT

People read an article to the end only if they find it interesting, surprising, or informative. However, in the context in which you are writing an essay, and the fact that the readers must read each essay to the end, use your common sense. Don't try too hard to be unique in your perspective or reasoning, but, on the other hand, avoid clichés and well-worn expressions. Try to avoid melodrama and understatement. In other words, take the subject seriously, respond honestly, and use examples from your own experience, the experience of people you know personally, or your reading. This approach will take care of ensuring both the individuality of your essay and the reader's interest.

COGENCY

If you express your thoughts and point of view about the subject in the context of what you know and believe at the time of writing, you will have no difficulty in being convincing. Remember, no one expects you to be an expert on the subject of the topic since you will have no prior knowledge of what the topic will be. If you use a voice that is not yours, not only will the reader find it difficult to understand you, but also the quality of your writing will suffer.

CLARITY

Time is important here, for both you and the readers. Avoid vague, general words, such as *thing*, and try to use concrete, specific examples and language to avoid wordiness.

COHERENCE

Even though you explore several ideas in your essay, they should all be related or connected. It is important, therefore, that as you move from one idea to another, you make clear the connecting link between them. These connecting links can express opposition or contrast, addition or amplification, cause or effect, relations in time or place, and time sequence, to name a few. Coherence focuses on the importance of transitional words and phrases, which you need to link or connect paragraphs effectively.

CORRECTNESS

If you are taking a test like CLEP, chances are that you have more than a basic command of the English language. You must, however, write under the pressure of time, and it is likely that you will make some mistakes in your essay. Sometimes, as you read over the essay, you will discover that you can express the same idea or information more succinctly. In other instances, you will find that you have inadvertently made an error in grammar or punctuation. Try to familiarize yourself with the more common sentence errors.

RECOGNIZING AND CORRECTING ERRORS IN SENTENCE STRUCTURE

FRAGMENTS

This error occurs when a writer attempts to use only a partial sentence in place of a complete sentence.

> *The baseball player leaped as high as he could to catch the ball. Although his effort was useless.*

In this example, *although his effort was useless* is a sentence fragment because *although* sets up a dependent clause. To correct the error, simply connect this fragment to the first sentence.

> *The baseball player leaped as high as he could to catch the ball although his effort was useless.*

EXAMPLE OF ERROR AND CORRECTION

> *How to avoid sentence fragments*

This phrase is not a complete sentence; it lacks a proper subject and predicate.

> *Learning how to avoid sentence fragments helped me become a more confident writer.*

In this sentence the subject is "learning" and the predicate is "helped."

COMMA SPLICES

This error occurs when a writer attempts to join two or more independent clauses without proper punctuation.

> *When the gentleman entered the room, he quietly moved to the corner, he watched the other guests carefully.*

Here the comma between the clauses is not strong enough to connect the independent clauses. To correct the error, change the second comma to a semicolon, add a conjunction such as *and*, or begin a new sentence.

EXAMPLE OF ERROR AND CORRECTION

> *Ben Franklin wanted the United States bird to be a turkey, fortunately his peers disagreed.*

This construction has two independent clauses, which are the same as simple sentences, connected by only a comma, a form of punctuation that is not strong enough to connect these clauses.

> *Ben Franklin wanted the United States bird to be a turkey, but fortunately his peers disagreed.* Adding a conjunction can correct the error.

> *Ben Franklin wanted the United States bird to be a turkey; fortunately his peers disagreed.* Changing the comma to a semicolon can also correct the error.

> *Ben Franklin wanted the United States bird to be a turkey. Fortunately, his peers disagreed.* Another way to correct this error is to separate the two clauses into two separate sentences.

RUN-ON SENTENCES

This error occurs when a writer attempts to connect too many clauses, which results in a stringy sentence.

> *John and Mary wanted to leave, but their hostess asked them to stay, so they sat down again with the Johnsons to have another cup of coffee, and John even had another piece of the apple pie that Rita had made.*

There are simply too many clauses; the sentence goes on too long. Try treating some of these clauses as separate sentences.

> *John and Mary wanted to leave, but their hostess asked them to stay. So they sat down again with the Johnsons to have another cup of coffee. John even had another piece of the apple pie that Rita Johnson had made.*

Run-on sentences typically have no comma or conjunction to connect the clauses.

EXAMPLE OF ERROR AND CORRECTION

> *Our new neighbors have three children who have three dogs that live in the house fortunately larger than my house across the street that I bought five years ago for my family and our one dog.*

Our new neighbors, in the house across the street, have three children and three dogs. Their house is larger than mine, which I bought five years ago, but we have only one dog.

ANOTHER VERSION OF A RUN-ON SENTENCE

> *When the sun rose the sky was painted pink and blue we were amazed at the colors.*

This sentence error typically has no comma or conjunction to separate clauses.

> *When the sun rose the sky was painted pink and blue, we were amazed at the colors.*

This sentence has an introductory adverb clause, which is always followed by a comma.

RECOGNIZING AND CORRECTING ERRORS IN SENTENCE STRUCTURE: REVIEW QUESTIONS

Determine which kind of error appears in the following sentences and then correct each error, keeping in mind that you probably have more than one option to correct the error. No sentences are correct. Check your answers with the answers and explanations that appear at the end of the Overview section.

1. Analysis of the story demanded careful attention to details many parts were complicated.

2. When I finished reading the story.

3. The story seemed to me to be confusing and needlessly long, reading it required several hours.

4. But I finished reading it.

5. At the beginning the author describes the setting in a frontier cabin in the West a cast iron pot of stew bubbled over an open fire.

6. In a rough fireplace of stones collected for just that purpose.

7. Only one room, the cabin was snug and warm, the children slept in a loft while their parents had the only bed.

8. Heat rising from the fireplace ensured the children's warmth a ladder extended from the cabin floor to their loft.

9. Patchwork quilts folded near their pallets.

10. With no neighbors in sight this family struggled on their own to stay alive they had to grow some vegetables like potatoes and eat game in their area the primary target was deer.

11. Other animals rabbits, squirrels, even prairie dogs whatever the father could find.

12. The meat provided sustenance, the hides were sold or traded for staples like flour and corn meal.

13. Their own livestock, a cow, some chickens, and a few pigs were also sources of food and so the family survived by managing their resources carefully winter was the hardest time.

14. This frontier family worked hard, they kept their hope and determination to succeed in this new territory.

15. By various tactics they made the best of what they had, they did not acknowledge defeat, which only spurred greater effort.

THE PROCESS OF WRITING THE ESSAY

You will be provided with a "prompt"—or topic—about which to write. Be sure that you read the topic carefully, preferably twice. Then take a few minutes to organize your ideas and begin to write. Don't spend too much time on organizing a rough outline; more ideas may occur to you as you write. While the CLEP readers realize that you have a limited amount of time in which to write, you are expected to write logically and clearly.

Four basic steps to writing an essay to follow:

1. Read (about 2-3 minutes)

2. Plan (about 3-4 minutes)

3. Write (about 20-25 minutes)

4. Proofread and edit (about 5 minutes)

Typically, an essay has three parts: introduction, body, and conclusion. Writing the introduction is sometimes the most difficult part of the writing process. Professional writers often write the introduction *after* they have completed the body and conclusion of a piece of writing. You may want to leave some blank space at the top of the page when you write your CLEP essay so that you can come back after finishing your essay and write an effective introduction.

INTRODUCTION

This part of the essay introduces your topic and establishes your focus—that is, the point you want to prove about this topic. While it is possible to write any number of different kinds of opening paragraphs, given the time limit you will have for this CLEP essay, you should strive to be concise and clear. You may want to let your thesis serve as your introduction. In that case, the introduction will be brief, perhaps only a sentence or two. Be sure that your first sentence responds *directly* to the topic. You should begin your discussion as quickly as possible.

BODY

This is the substance, or main content, of your essay. In this section of your essay, you will discuss the topic, offer supporting examples, and draw conclusions—in other words, prove your point. In this main part of your essay, you must be careful to develop your ideas as logically and smoothly as possible.

Fluency of expression and sentence variety are two areas the CLEP readers will evaluate when they read your essay. These skills are best developed by practicing; the more you write, the better you will become at expressing your ideas clearly and effectively. Another important quality necessary for a successful essay is sufficient evidence. Be sure that you have included enough support to prove your point. Each of these supporting details requires discussion to show its significance. You must demonstrate the worth of each point or piece of information. A brief explanation, then, of every supporting example is necessary.

Another very important consideration involves demonstrating your mastery of the basics of English composition. Try to avoid major composition errors such as comma splices and sentence fragments. Comma splices occur when a writer attempts to connect two independent clauses with only a comma to join them. To connect these independent clauses correctly, a writer must use a coordinating conjunction, such as *and* or *but*, and a comma, or the writer may use a semicolon instead of a comma. Of course, a third choice is to treat the two independent clauses as two separate, complete sentences. The CLEP readers will not unduly penalize you for careless mistakes, such as a few spelling errors, but you must strive to write as well as you can.

CONCLUSION

This is the final section of your essay, the place in which you remind your reader of the point you set out to prove. This last part may be only a sentence, or it could be several sentences. Just as there are a number of ways to write the opening paragraph or introduction, the conclusion can take many forms. Reemphasizing your focus is the main purpose of this section.

STEP-BY-STEP

1. **Read the topic or question "prompt."** Read it at least twice. Be sure that you understand the topic. Do not write on any other topic.

2. **Take a few minutes to generate some ideas.** This process is sometimes called "brainstorming." Your goal here is to think of as many possibly relevant ideas as you can. Think quickly, but carefully consider your ideas. Choose one idea that appeals the most to you and about which you know the most.

3. **Compose a thesis, which is a statement of the topic and your focus**—that is, the point you are setting out to prove in your essay. For instance, if the topic is the value of single-sex education, you may choose to agree or to disagree with this approach. Your thesis, then, could be one of these: Single-sex education benefits students more than it limits them. In this thesis, your focus is "benefits." In your essay, you are setting out to prove that the benefits outweigh the limitations. You could, however, write an essay that supports the opposite position. Here is a possible thesis for such an essay: Single-sex education is not beneficial to either gender.

4. **Begin the introduction (or save it for last).** Give an overview of the topic; include your thesis in this opening section. Try to move into the body as quickly as possible.

5. **Write the body of the essay.** While other forms of exposition are touted today, the five-paragraph theme is still alive and well. You can choose to compose three body paragraphs, but you are not restricted to three. *The actual number of paragraphs is not as important as the content in the body.* Each of these body paragraphs should include a strong topic sentence that clearly establishes the main idea of the paragraph; each paragraph is designed to help you build an effective discussion of your topic and focus.

6. **Write the conclusion or closing section of your essay.** Remind the reader of what you set out to prove—your focus. Did you succeed in defending your approach?

7. **Take a few minutes to review and proofread your essay.** Next to planning, this is perhaps the most critical part of the process of writing your essay. Read the essay carefully; check for grammar errors and misspellings. Change any words or phrases that you do not think express your ideas clearly.

Now, try part of this process with a sample topic.

TOPIC OR QUESTION PROMPT

With all of the choices available today in secondary education, each student can decide whether a small college or a large university is the right choice for him or her. Choose to defend one position: small colleges are better for students or large universities are better for students. Develop your response into a well-written essay.

SAMPLE 1—REASONS FOR LARGE UNIVERSITY

Large universities offer students more for their money today. Because the cost of higher education rises dramatically every year, more students are choosing large universities.

In recent years, more college students seem to flock to large universities because of a number of important factors. The multiplicity of offerings or opportunities, both academic and social, is attractive. At a large university, a student often has contact with outstanding educators, nationally recognized experts, such as poets or scientists, who are on the faculty at the university. The library holdings are extensive; usually, the school plant is spacious and well maintained. Security is provided so that students feel safe on campus. A large endowment and operating budget provide access to well-equipped labs for science and languages. A student has many opportunities to be involved in campus life—from social clubs to civic organizations to intramural sports. College athletics for schools at this level are tremendously popular and competitive. Attending a large college or university provides a better value for the dollar. Students concerned about costs and expenses, however, are best advised to determine which qualities in a college or university are the most important to them. The tuition and fees are just one aspect of a much larger whole.

In this sample paragraph, the writer offers a quick overview of some important benefits of attending a large university. The first, underlined sentence in the opening serves as the thesis, with *more* as the focus.

On the other hand, a student can argue in favor of small colleges.

SAMPLE 2—REASONS FOR SMALL COLLEGE

Small colleges offer more benefits to students eager to enter the job market. Because of the competitiveness in the job market today, more students are coming to value the benefits of attending a small college instead of a large university. At a small college, a student finds the enrollment more limited in his or her classes, so that regular participation in class discussions is possible. The instructor or professor actually knows each student by name. A small college provides more opportunities for students to gain the confidence necessary to polish their speaking and writing skills, both of which are essential for successful job applications and interviews.

Campus life is rewarding because the size of the enrollment increases the possibility of close friendships. Although a large university library provides a virtually endless source of information, with the world practically at our fingertips because of the Web and cyberspace, students can access information from almost anywhere, not just in their college library. Students who choose small colleges contend that their choice stems from a desire to be more than a number or a face in the crowd. They believe they will be better prepared to face today's job market because they will have gained the composure and confidence that participating in small classes insures.

In this part of the essay, the first sentence serves as the thesis, with *more benefits* as the focus.

SAMPLE ESSAY TOPICS

Choose one of these and write a practice essay:

The role of technology in our lives today: Have we become too dependent?

The censorship of books and music (the rating of TV shows and movies): Is it ever appropriate?

"Education means developing the mind, not stuffing the memory." (Anon.) Respond to this quotation. Do you agree or disagree? Why?

Single-sex education: Is it more beneficial than coed education?

Qualities of a hero: What are the most important? Why?

The aging of America: What problems are we facing?

Role of violence in society today: How can we reduce the level?

USAGE REVIEW—PARTS OF SPEECH

NOUN

A NOUN is the name of a person, place, or thing.

actor   *city*   *lamp*

There are three kinds of nouns, according to the type of person, place, or thing the noun names.

1. A *common* noun refers to a general type: girl, park, army.

2. A *proper* noun refers to a particular person, place, or thing, and always begins with a capital letter: Mary, Central Park, U.S. Army.

3. A *collective* noun signifies a number of individuals organized into one group: team, crowd, Congress.

SINGULAR/PLURAL

Every noun has number. That means every noun is either singular or plural. The singular noun means only one; the plural noun means more than one. There are four ways to form the plurals of nouns:

1. by adding *s* to the singular (horses, kites, rivers)

2. by adding *es* to the singular (buses, churches, dishes, boxes, buzzes)

3. by changing the singular (*man* becomes *men*, *woman* becomes *women*, *child* becomes *children*, *baby* becomes *babies*, *alumnus* becomes *alumni*)

4. by leaving the singular as it is (*moose*, *deer*, and *sheep* are all plural as well as singular)

Note: When forming the plural of letters and numbers, add *s*: As, 150s.

CASE

Nouns also have case, which indicates the function of the noun in the sentence. There are three cases—the nominative case, the objective case, and the possessive case.

1. NOMINATIVE CASE

A noun is in the nominative case when it is the subject of a sentence: The *book* fell off the table. The *boys* and *girls* ran outside.

The subject of a sentence is the person, place, or thing that the sentence is about. Thus, the *book* fell off the table is about the book.

A noun is in the nominative case when it is a predicate noun. This is a noun used after a linking verb. In such cases, the predicate noun means the same as the subject.

Einstein was a *scientist*. (Einstein = scientist)

Judith was a brilliant *scholar* and gifted *teacher*. (Judith = scholar and teacher)

A noun is in the nominative case when it is used in direct address. A noun in direct address shows that someone or something is being spoken to directly. This noun is set off by commas.

Claudel, please answer the phone.

Go home, *Fido*, before you get hit by a car.

A noun is in the nominative case when it is a nominative absolute. This is a noun with a participle (see verbs) that stands as an independent idea but is part of a sentence.

The *rain* having stopped, we went out to play.

The *bike* having crashed, the race was stopped.

A noun is in the nominative case when it is a nominative in apposition. This is one of a pair of nouns. Both nouns are equal in meaning and are next to each other. The noun in apposition is set off from the rest of the sentence by commas.

Steve, *my son*, is going to college.

That man is Syd, the *musician*.

2. OBJECTIVE CASE

A noun is in the objective case when it is the direct object of a verb. A direct object is the receiver of the action of a verb. A verb that has a direct object is called a transitive verb.

The team elected *David*.

The team won the *game*.

A noun is in the objective case when it is the indirect object of a verb. This is a noun that shows *to* whom or *for* whom the action is taking place. The words *to* and *for* may not actually appear in the sentence, but they are understood. An indirect object **must** be accompanied by a direct object.

Pedro threw *Mario* the ball. (Pedro threw the ball to Mario).

Anya bought her *mother* a gift. (Anya bought a gift for her mother).

A noun is in the objective case when it is an objective complement. An objective complement is a noun that explains the direct object. The word *complement* indicates that this noun *completes* the meaning of the direct object.

The team elected Terry *captain*.

A noun is in the objective case when it is an objective by apposition. An objective by apposition is very much like a nominative in apposition. Again we have a pair of nouns that are equal in meaning and are next to each other. The noun in apposition explains the other noun, but now the noun being explained is in the objective case. Therefore, the noun in apposition is called the objective by apposition. The objective by apposition is set off from the rest of the sentence by commas.

The bully pushed Steve, the little *toddler*, into the sandbox.

He gave the money to Sam, the *banker*.

A noun is in the objective case when it is an adverbial objective. This is a noun that denotes distance or time.

The storm lasted an *hour*.

The troops walked five *miles*.

A noun is in the objective case when it is an object of a preposition.

The stick fell into the *well*. (*Into* is the preposition.)

The picture fell on the *table*. (*On* is the preposition.)

See the section on prepositions.

3. POSSESSIVE CASE

A noun is in the possessive case when it shows ownership. The correct use of the possessive case is often tested on the exam. The following seven rules will help you answer such questions correctly.

1. The possessive case of most nouns is formed by adding an apostrophe and *s* to the singular.

   > The *boy's* book
   >
   > *Emile's* coat

2. If the singular ends in *s* add an apostrophe, or apostrophe *s*.

   > The *bus's* wheels
   >
   >   or
   >
   > The *bus'* wheels
   >
   > *Charles'* books
   >
   >   or
   >
   > *Charles's* books

3. The possessive case of plural nouns ending in *s* is formed by adding just an apostrophe.

   > The *dogs'* bones

   Note: If *dog* was singular, the possessive case would be *dog's*.

4. If the plural noun does not end in *s* then add an apostrophe and *s*.

   > The *children's* toys
   >
   > The *men's* boots

5. The possessive case of compound nouns is formed by adding an apostrophe and *s* to the last word if it is singular, or by adding an *s* and an apostrophe if the word is plural.

   > My *brother-in-law's* house
   >
   > My *two brothers'* house

6. To show individual ownership, add an apostrophe and *s* to each owner.

   > *Joe's* and *Jim's* boats (They each own their own boat.)

7. To show joint ownership, add an apostrophe and *s* to the last name.

   > Joe and *Jim's* boat (They both own the same boat.)

PRONOUNS

A pronoun is used in place of a noun. The noun for which a pronoun is used is called the *antecedent*. The use of pronouns, particularly the relationship between a pronoun and its antecedent, is one of the most common items found on the test. Always make sure a pronoun has a clear antecedent.

John had a candy bar and a cookie. He ate *it* quickly. (Ambiguous) (What is the antecedent of *it—candy bar* or *cookie*?)

The boy rode his bike through the hedge, *which* was very large. (Ambiguous) (What was very large—the *bike* or the *hedge*?)

The captain was very popular. *They* all liked him. (Ambiguous) (Who liked him? *They* has no antecedent.)

There are ten kinds of pronouns:

1. Expletive pronoun. The words *it* and *there* followed by the subject of the sentence are expletive pronouns.

   > *There* were only a few tickets left.
   >
   > *It* was a long list of chores.

   When using an expletive, the verb agrees with the subject.

   > There *remains* one *child* on the bus.
   >
   > There *remain* many *children* on the bus.

2. Intensive pronoun. This is a pronoun, ending in *self* or *selves*, which follows its antecedent and emphasizes it.

   > He *himself* will go.
   >
   > The package was delivered to the boys *themselves*.

3. A reflexive pronoun. This is a pronoun, ending in *self* or *selves*, which is usually the object of a verb or preposition or the complement of a verb.

   > I hate *myself*.
   >
   > They always laugh at *themselves*.

   Myself, yourself, himself, herself, and *itself* are all singular. *Ourselves, yourselves*, and *themselves* are all plural. There is no such pronoun as hisself or theirselves. Do not use *myself* instead of *I* or *me*.

4. Demonstrative pronoun. This is used in place of a noun and points out the noun. Common demonstrative pronouns are *this, that, these*, and *those*.

   > I want *those*.

5. Indefinite pronoun. This pronoun refers to any number of persons or objects. Following is a list of some singular and plural indefinite pronouns.

   SINGULAR

   anybody, anyone, each, everybody, everyone, no one, nobody, none, somebody, someone

   PLURAL

   all, any, many, several, some

   If the singular form is used as a subject, the verb must be singular.

   Everyone of *them* sings. (One person sings.)

   If the singular form is used as an antecedent, its pronoun must be singular.

   Did *anybody* on any of the teams lose *his* sneakers? (One person lost *his* sneakers.)

6. Interrogative pronoun. This pronoun is used in asking a question. Such pronouns are *who, whose, whom, what,* and *which. Whose* shows possession. *Whom* is in the objective case. *Whom* is used only when an object pronoun is needed.

7. Reciprocal pronoun. This pronoun is used when referring to mutual relations. The reciprocal pronouns are *each other* and *one another*.

   They love *one another*.

   They often visit *each other's* houses.

   Note that the possessive is formed by an *'s* after the word *other*.

8. Possessive pronoun. This pronoun refers to a noun that owns something. The possessive pronouns are as follows:

   SINGULAR

   mine (my), yours, his, hers, its

   PLURAL

   ours, yours, theirs

   Notice that possessive pronouns do not use an *'s. It's* is a contraction meaning *it is*; *its* denotes possession.

9. Relative pronoun.

   Nominative case—who, that, which

   Objective case—whom, that, which

   Possessive case—whose

   A relative pronoun used as the *subject* of a dependent clause is in the nominative case.

   I know *who* stole the car.

   Give the prize to *whoever* won it.

   A relative pronoun used as the *object* of a dependent clause is in the objective case.

   He is the thief *whom* I know. (Object of verb *know*)

   Note that the difficulty always comes between choosing *who* or *whom*. Remember that *who* is in the nominative case and is used for the appropriate situations discussed under nominative case in the section on nouns. *Whom* is in the objective case and is used for the appropriate situations discussed under objective case in the section on nouns.

   Who is coming? (*Who* is the subject.)

   Whom are you going with? (*Whom* is the object of the preposition *with*.)

   The relative pronoun in the possessive case is *whose*. Notice there is no apostrophe in this word. The contraction *who's* means *who is*.

   I know *whose* book it is. (Denotes possession)

   I know *who's* on first base. (*Who's* means *who is*.)

10. Personal pronoun.

	SINGULAR	PLURAL
NOMINATIVE CASE		
First person	I	we
Second person	you	you
Third person	he, she, it	they
OBJECTIVE CASE		
First person	me	us
Second person	you	you
Third person	him, her, it	them
POSSESSIVE CASE		
First person	mine (my)	ours (our)
Second person	yours (your)	yours (your)
Third person	his, hers, its (his, her, its)	theirs (their)

Personal pronouns denote what is called *person*. First-person pronouns show the person or thing that is speaking.

> I am going. (First person speaking)

Second-person pronouns show the person or thing being spoken to.

> *You* are my friend. (Second person spoken to)

Third-person pronouns show the person or thing being spoken about.

> Bea did not see *her*. (Third person spoken about)

IMPORTANT FOR THE EXAM

Pronouns must agree with their antecedents in person, number, and gender.

Who refers to persons only.

Which refers to animals or objects.

That refers to persons, animals, or objects.

> I don't know *who* the actor is. (Person)
>
> They missed their dog, *which* died. (Animal)
>
> I finished the book, *which* (or *that*) you recommended. (Object)
>
> They are the people *who* started the fight. (Person)
>
> That is the tiger *that* ran loose. (Animal)
>
> The light *that* failed was broken. (Object)

Note that the singular indefinite antecedents always take a singular pronoun.

> *Everyone* of the girls lost *her* hat.
>
> *None* of the boys lost *his*.
>
> *Someone* left *his* bike outside.

Note that collective singular nouns take singular pronouns; collective plural nouns take plural pronouns.

> The choir sang *its* part beautifully.
>
> The choirs sang *their* parts beautifully.

Note that two or more antecedents joined by *and* take a plural pronoun.

> Dave *and* Steve lost *their* way.

Note that two or more singular antecedents joined by *or* or *nor* take a singular pronoun.

> Tanya *or* Charita may use *her* ball.
>
> Neither Tanya *nor* Charita may use *her* ball.

If two antecedents are joined by *or* or *nor*, and if one is plural and the other is singular, the pronoun agrees in number with the nearer antecedent.

> Neither the *ball* nor the *rackets* were in *their* place.

CASE

Remember that pronouns must also be in the correct case: nominative, objective, or possessive.

1. A pronoun must be in the nominative case when it is the subject of a sentence.

> James and *I* went to the airport.
>
> *We* freshmen helped the seniors.
>
> Peter calls her more than *I* do.
>
> Peter calls her more than *I*. (Here, the verb *do* is understood, and *I* is the subject of the understood verb *do*.)

2. A pronoun is in the objective case when it is a direct object of the verb.

> Leaving James and *me*, they ran away.
>
> John hit *them*.
>
> The freshmen helped *us* seniors.

A pronoun is in the objective case when it is the indirect object of a verb.

> Give *us* the ball.

A pronoun is in the objective case when it is an object of a preposition.

> To Ben and *me*
>
> With Sheila and *her*
>
> Between you and *them*

3. A pronoun is in the possessive case when it shows ownership.

> *Her* car broke down.
>
> *Theirs* did also.

A pronoun is in the possessive case when it appears before a gerund (see verbals).

> *His* going was a sad event.

For a more detailed analysis of the three cases, see the section on the cases of nouns.

ADJECTIVES

An adjective describes or modifies a noun or a pronoun. An adjective usually answers the question *which one*? Or *what kind*? Or *how many*? There are a number of types of adjectives you should know. Here are five.

1. Articles (a, an, the) must agree in number with the noun or pronoun they modify.

> *A* boy
>
> *An* apple
>
> *The* girls

If the noun or pronoun begins with a consonant, use *a*. If the noun or pronoun begins with a vowel, use *an*.

> *A* pear
>
> *An* orange

2. Limiting adjectives point out definite nouns or tell how many there are.

> *Those* books belong to John.
>
> The *three* boys didn't see *any* birds.

3. Descriptive adjectives describe or give a quality of the noun or pronoun they modify.

> The *large* chair
>
> The *sad* song

4. Possessive, demonstrative, and indefinite adjectives look like the pronouns of the same name. However, the adjective does not stand alone. It describes a noun or pronoun.

> *This* is *mine*. (Demonstrative and possessive pronouns)
>
> *This* book is *my* father's. (Demonstrative and possessive adjectives)

5. Interrogative and relative adjectives look the same, but they function differently. Interrogative adjectives ask questions.

> *Which* way should I go?
>
> *Whose* book is this?
>
> *What* time is John coming?

Relative adjectives join two clauses and modify some word in the dependent clause.

> I don't know *whose* book it is.

IMPORTANT FOR THE EXAM

An adjective is used as a predicate adjective after a linking verb. If the modifier is describing the verb (a nonlinking verb), we must use an adverb.

> The boy is *happy*. (Adjective)
> Joe appeared *angry*. (Adjective)
> The soup tasted *spicy*. (Adjective)
> Joe looked *angrily* at the dog. (Adverb—*angrily* modifies *looked*)

POSITIVE, COMPARATIVE, AND SUPERLATIVE ADJECTIVES

The *positive* degree states the quality of an object.

The *comparative* degree compares two things. It is formed by using *less* or *more* or adding *er* to the positive.

The *superlative* degree compares three or more things. It is formed by using *least* or *most* or adding *est* to the positive.

POSITIVE	COMPARATIVE	SUPERLATIVE
Easy	easier; more easy; less easy	easiest; most easy; least easy
Pretty	prettier; more pretty; less pretty	prettiest; least pretty; most pretty

DO NOT USE TWO FORMS TOGETHER

She is the most prettiest. (Incorrect)

She is the prettiest. (Correct)

She is the most pretty. (Correct)

VERBS

A verb either denotes action or a state of being. There are four major types of verbs: transitive, intransitive, linking, and auxiliary.

1. Transitive verbs are action words that must take a direct object. The direct object, which receives the action of the verb, is in the objective case.

> Joe *hit* the ball. (*Ball* is the direct object of *hit*.)
> Joe *hugged* Rita. (*Rita* is the direct object of *hugged*.)

2. Intransitive verbs denote action but do not take a direct object.

> The glass *broke*.
> The boy *fell*.

IMPORTANT FOR THE EXAM

Set, *lay*, and *raise* are always transitive and take an object. *Sit*, *lie*, and *rise* are always intransitive and do not take a direct object.

> *Set* the book down, *lay* the pencil down, and *raise* your hands. (*Book, pencil*, and *hands* are direct objects of *set, lay*, and *raise*.)
> *Sit* in the chair.
> She *lies* in bed all day.
> The sun also *rises*.

The same verb can be transitive or intransitive, depending on the sentence.

> The pitcher *threw* wildly. (Intransitive)
> The pitcher *threw* the ball wildly. (Transitive)

3. Linking verbs have no action. They denote a state of being. Linking verbs mean "equal." Here are some examples: *is, are, was, were, be, been, am* (any form of the verb *to be*), *smell, taste, feel, look, seem, become,* and *appear.*

> Sometimes, these verbs are confusing because they can be linking verbs in one sentence and action verbs in another. You can tell if the verb is a linking verb if it means "equal" in the sentence.

> > He felt nervous. (*He* equals *nervous.*)
> > He felt nervously for the door bell. (*He* does not equal *door bell.*)

> Linking verbs take a predicate nominative or predicate adjective. (See sections on nouns, pronouns, and adjectives.)

> > It *is I.*
> > It *is she.*

4. Auxiliary verbs are sometimes called "helping" verbs. These verbs are used with an infinitive verb (*to* plus *the verb*) or a participle to form a verb phrase.

> The common auxiliary verbs are:

> > All forms of *to be, to have, to do,* and *to keep.*
> > The verbs *can, may, must, ought to, shall, will, would,* and *should.*
> > He *has to go.* (Auxiliary *has* plus the infinitive *to go*)
> > He *was going.* (Auxiliary *was* plus the present participle *going*)
> > He *has gone.* (Auxiliary *has* plus the past participle *gone*)

> There is no such form as *had ought.* Use *ought to have* or *should have.*

> > He *ought to have gone.*
> > He *should have gone.*

Every verb can change its form according to five categories. Each category adds meaning to the verb. The five categories are: *tense, mood, voice, number,* and *person.*

TENSE

Tense indicates the *time,* or *when,* the verb occurs. There are six tenses. They are:

present	past	future
present perfect	past perfect	future perfect

Three principal parts of the verb—the present, the past, and the past participle—are used to form all the tenses.

The *present tense* shows that the action is taking place in the present.

> The dog *sees* the car and *jumps* out of the way.

The present tense of a regular verb looks like this:

	SINGULAR	PLURAL
First person	I jump	We jump
Second person	You jump	You jump
Third person	He, she, it jumps	They jump

Notice that an *s* is added to the third-person singular.

The *past tense* shows that the action took place in the past.

> The dog *saw* the car and *jumped* out of the way.

The past tense of a regular verb looks like this:

	SINGULAR	PLURAL
First person	I jumped	We jumped
Second person	You jumped	You jumped
Third person	He, she, it jumped	They jumped

Notice that *ed* is added to the verb. Sometimes just *d* is added, as in the verb *used,* for example. In regular verbs the past participle has the same form as the past tense, but it is used with an auxiliary verb.

> The dog *had jumped.*

The *future tense* shows that the action is going to take place in the future. The future tense needs the auxiliary verbs *will* or *shall.*

> The dog *will see* the car and *will jump* out of the way.

The future tense of a regular verb looks like this:

	SINGULAR	PLURAL
First person	I shall jump	We shall jump
Second person	You will jump	You will jump
Third person	He, she, it will jump	They will jump

Notice that *shall* is used in the first person of the future tense.

To form the three *perfect tenses,* the verb *to have* and the past participle are used.

> The present tense of *to have* is used to form the *present perfect.*

>> The dog *has seen* the car and *has jumped* out of the way.

The present perfect tense shows that the action has started in the past and is continuing or has just been implemented in the present.

The past tense of *to have* is used to form the *past perfect.*

>> The dog *had seen* the car and *had jumped* out of the way.

The past perfect tense shows that the action had been completed in the past.

The future tense of *to have* is used to form the *future perfect.*

>> The dog *will have seen* the car and *will have jumped* out of the way.

The future perfect tense shows that an action will have been completed before a definite time in the future.

The following table shows the present, past, and future tenses of *to have.*

PRESENT TENSE		
	SINGULAR	PLURAL
First person	I have	We have
Second person	You have	You have
Third person	He, she, it has	They have

PAST TENSE		
	SINGULAR	PLURAL
First person	I had	We had
Second person	You had	You had
Third person	He, she, it had	They had

FUTURE TENSE		
	SINGULAR	PLURAL
First person	I shall have	We shall have
Second person	You will have	You will have
Third person	He, she, it will have	They will have

The perfect tenses all use the past participle. Therefore, you must know the past participle of all the verbs. As we said, the past participle usually is formed by adding *d* or *ed* to the verb. However, there are many irregular verbs. Following is a table of the principal parts of some irregular verbs.

PRESENT	PAST	PAST PARTICIPLE
arise	arose	arisen
awake	awoke, awaked	awoke, awaked, awakened
awaken	awakened	awakened
be	was	been
bear	bore	borne
beat	beat	beaten
become	became	become
begin	began	begun
bend	bent	bent
bet	bet	bet
bid (command)	bade, bid	bidden, bid
bind	bound	bound
bite	bit	bitten
bleed	bled	bled
blow	blew	blown
break	broke	broken
bring	brought	brought
build	built	built
burn	burned	burned, burnt
burst	burst	burst

PRESENT	PAST	PAST PARTICIPLE
buy	bought	bought
catch	caught	caught
choose	chose	chosen
come	came	come
cost	cost	cost
dig	dug	dug
dive	dived, dove	dived
do	did	done
draw	drew	drawn
dream	dreamed	dreamed
drink	drank	drunk
drive	drove	driven
eat	ate	eaten
fall	fell	fallen
fight	fought	fought
fit	fitted	fitted
fly	flew	flown
forget	forgot	forgotten, forgot
freeze	froze	frozen
get	got	got, gotten
give	gave	given
go	went	gone
grow	grew	grown
hang (kill)	hanged	hanged
hang (suspended)	hung	hung
hide	hid	hidden
hold	held	held
know	knew	known
lay	laid	laid
lead	led	led
lend	lent	lent
lie (recline)	lay	lain
lie (untruth)	lied	lied
light	lit	lit
pay	paid	paid
raise (take up)	raised	raised
read	read	read
rid	rid	rid
ride	rode	ridden
ring	rang	rung
rise (go up)	rose	risen
run	ran	run
saw (cut)	sawed	sawed
say	said	said
see	saw	seen
set	set	set
shake	shook	shaken
shine (light)	shone	shone
shine (to polish)	shined	shined
show	showed	shown, showed
shrink	shrank	shrunk, shrunken
sing	sang	sung

PRESENT	PAST	PAST PARTICIPLE
sit	sat	sat
slay	slew	slain
speak	spoke	spoken
spend	spent	spent
spit	spat, spit	spat, spit
spring	sprang	sprung
stand	stood	stood
steal	stole	stolen
swear	swore	sworn
swim	swam	swum
swing	swung	swung
take	took	taken
teach	taught	taught
tear	tore	torn
throw	threw	thrown
wake	waked, woke	waked, woken
wear	wore	worn
weave	wove, weaved	woven, weaved
weep	wept	wept
win	won	won
write	wrote	written

Another aspect of tense that appears on the test is the *correct sequence* or *order of tenses*. Be sure if you change tense you know why you are doing so. Following are some rules to help you.

When using the perfect tenses remember:

The present perfect tense goes with the present tense.

present
As Dave *steps* up to the mound,

present perfect
the pitcher *has thrown* the ball to

present perfect
first, and I *have caught* it.

The past perfect tense goes with the past tense.

past
Before Dave *stepped* up to the

past perfect
mound, the pitcher *had thrown*

past perfect
the ball to first, and I *had caught* it.

The future perfect goes with the future tense.

> future
> Before Dave *will step* up to the mound, the pitcher
>
> future perfect
> *will have thrown* the ball to first,
>
> future perfect
> and I *shall have caught* it.

The present participle (verb + *ing*) is used when its action occurs at the same time as the action of the main verb.

> John, *answering* the bell, *knocked* over the plant. (*Answering* and *knocked* occur at the same time.)

The past participle is used when its action occurs before the main verb.

> The elves, *dressed* in costumes, will *march* proudly to the shoemaker. (The elves dressed *before* they will march.)

MOOD

The mood or mode of a verb shows the manner of the action. There are three moods.

1. The *indicative mood* shows the sentence is factual. Most of what we say is in the indicative mode.

2. The *subjunctive mood* is used for conditions contrary to fact or for strong desires. The use of the subjunctive mood for the verb *to be* is a test item.

Following is the conjugation (list of forms) of the verb *to be* in the subjunctive mood:

PRESENT TENSE

	SINGULAR	PLURAL
First person	I be	We be
Second person	You be	You be
Third person	He, she, it be	They be

PAST TENSE

	SINGULAR	PLURAL
First person	I were	We were
Second person	You were	You were
Third person	He, she, it were	They were

If I *be* wrong, then punish me.
If he *were* king, he would pardon me.

Also, *shall* and *should* are used for the subjunctive mood.
> If he *shall* fail, he will cry.
> If you *should* win, don't forget us.

3. The *imperative mood* is used for commands.

> Go at once!

If strong feelings are expressed, the command ends with an exclamation point. In commands, the subject *you* is not stated but is understood.

VOICE

There are two voices of verbs. The active voice shows that the subject is acting upon something or doing something *to* something else. The active voice has a direct object.

> subject   object
> The *car* hit the *box*.

The passive voice shows that the subject is acted upon *by* something. Something was done *to* the subject. The direct object becomes the subject. The verb *to be* plus the past participle is used in the passive voice.

> subject
> The *box* was hit by the car.

NUMBER

This, as before, means singular or plural. A verb must agree with its subject in number.

> The *list was* long. (Singular)
> The *lists were* long. (Plural)

Nouns appearing between subject and verb do not change subject/verb agreement.

> The *list* of chores *was* long. (Singular)
> The *lists* of chores *were* long. (Plural)

Subjects joined by *and* are singular if the subject is one person or unit.

> My *friend and colleague has* decided to leave. (Singular)
> *Five and five is* ten. (Singular)
> *Tea and milk is* my favorite drink. (Singular)

Singular subjects joined by *or, either-or,* and *neither-nor* take singular verbs.

> Either Alvin or Lynette *goes* to the movies.

If one subject is singular and one is plural, the verb agrees with the nearer subject.

> Either Alvin or the girls *go* to the movies.

The use of the expletive pronouns *there* and *it* do not change subject/verb agreement.

> There *is no one* here.
> There *are snakes* in the grass.
> Think: No one is there; snakes are in the grass.

A relative pronoun takes a verb that agrees in number with the pronoun's antecedent.

> It is the *electrician who suggests* new wiring. (Singular)
> It is the *electricians who suggest* new wiring. (Plural)

Singular indefinite pronouns take singular verbs.

> Everybody *buys* tickets.

It is hard to tell if some nouns are singular. Following is a list of tricky nouns that take singular verbs.

> Collective nouns—*army, class, committee, team*
> Singular nouns in plural form—*news, economics, mathematics, measles, mumps, politics*
> Titles, although plural in form, refer to a single work—The *New York Times*, Henry James's *The Ambassadors*
> The *army is* coming.
> *News travels* fast.
> *Jaws is* a good movie.

Don't (do not) is incorrect for third-person singular. *Doesn't (does not)* is correct.

> He *doesn't* agree.

PERSON

Person, as before, refers to first person (speaking), second person (spoken to), and third person (spoken about). A verb must agree with its subject in person.

> I study. (First person)

> He studies. (Third person)

Intervening nouns or pronouns do not change subject/verb agreement.

> *He* as well as she *is* going. (Third person)

If there are two or more subjects joined by *or* or *nor*, the verb agrees with the nearer subject.

> Either John or *we are* going. (First-person plural)

ADVERBS

An adverb describes or modifies a verb, an adjective, or another adverb. Adverbs usually answer the questions *why?, where?, when?, how?* and *to what degree?* Many adverbs end in *ly*. There are two types of adverbs similar in use to the same type of adjective.

1. *Interrogative adverbs* ask questions.

   > *Where* are you going?
   > *When* will you be home?

2. *Relative adverbs* join two clauses and modify some word in the dependent clause.

   > No liquor is sold *where* I live.

As with adjectives, there are three degrees of comparison for adverbs and a corresponding form for each.

1. The *positive* degree is often formed by adding *ly* to the adjective.

   She was *angry*. (Adjective)
   She screamed *angrily*. (Adverb)

2. The *comparative* is formed by using *more* or *less* or adding *er* to the positive.

3. The *superlative* is formed by using *most* or *least* or adding *est* to the positive.

   Here are two typical adverbs:

POSITIVE DEGREE	COMPARATIVE DEGREE	SUPERLATIVE DEGREE
easily	easier, more easily, less easily	easiest, most easily, least easily
happily	happier, more happily, less happily	happiest, most happily, least happily

CONJUNCTIONS

Conjunctions connect words, phrases, or clauses. Conjunctions can connect equal parts of speech.

> and
> but
> for
> or

Some conjunctions are used in pairs:

> either . . . or
> neither . . . nor
> not only . . . but also

Here are some phrases and clauses using conjunctions:

> John *or* Mary (Nouns are connected.)

> On the wall *and* in the window (Phrases are connected.)

> Mark had gone, *but* I had not. (Clauses are connected.)

> *Either* you go, *or* I will. (Clauses are connected.)

If the conjunction connects two long clauses, a comma is used in front of the coordinating conjunction:

> Julio went to the game in the afternoon, but Pedro decided to wait and go to the evening game.

Some conjunctions are transitional:

therefore
however
moreover
finally
nevertheless

These conjunctions connect the meaning of two clauses or sentences.

IMPORTANT FOR THE EXAM

Be aware of *comma splices*. Comma splices occur when one connects two independent clauses with a comma rather than with a semicolon or with a comma followed by a coordinating conjunction. An independent clause is a clause that can stand alone as a complete sentence.

> His bike was broken; therefore, he could not ride. (Correct)

> His bike was broken. Therefore, he could not ride. (Correct)

> His bike was broken, and, therefore, he could not ride. (Correct)

> His bike was broken, therefore, he could not ride. (Incorrect)

> He found his wallet, however he still left the auction. (Incorrect)

The last two sentences are comma splices and are incorrect. *Remember, two independent clauses cannot be connected by a comma.*

PREPOSITIONS

A preposition shows the relationship between a noun or pronoun and some other word in the sentence.

The following are all prepositions:

about	for	through
above	in	to
across	inside	under
around	into	up
behind	of	upon
beneath	off	within
during	over	without

Sometimes groups of words are treated as single prepositions. Here are some examples:

according to
ahead of
in front of
in between

The preposition, together with the noun or pronoun it introduces, is called a prepositional phrase.

> *Under* the table
> *In front of* the oil painting
> *Behind* the glass jar
> *Along* the waterfront
> *Beside* the canal

Very often on the test, idiomatic expressions are given that depend upon prepositions to be correct. Following is a list of idioms showing the correct preposition to use:

Abhorrence of: He showed an *abhorrence of* violence.

Abound in (or *with*): The lake *abounded with* fish.

Accompanied by (a person): He was *accompanied by* his friend.

Accompanied with: He *accompanied* his visit *with* a house gift.

Accused by, of: He was *accused by* a person *of* a crime.

Adept in: He is *adept in* jogging.

Agree to (an offer): I *agree to* the terms of the contract.

Agree with (a person): I *agree with* my son.

Agree upon (or *on*) (a plan): I *agree upon* that approach to the problem.

Angry at (a situation): I was *angry at* the delay.

Available for (a purpose): I am *available for* tutoring.

Available to (a person): Those machines are *available to* the tenants.

Burden with: I won't *burden* you *with* my problems.

Centered on (or *in*): His efforts *centered on* winning.

Compare to (shows similarity): An orange can be *compared to* a grapefruit.

Compare with (shows difference): An orange can't be *compared with* a desk.

Conform to (or *with*): He does not *conform to* the rules.

Differ with (an opinion): I *differ with* his judgment.

Differ from (a thing): The boss's car *differs from* the worker's car.

Different from: His book is *different from* mine. (Use *different than* with a clause.)

Employed at (salary): He is *employed at* $25 a day.

Employed in (work): He is *employed in* building houses.

Envious of: She is *envious of* her sister.

Fearful of: She is *fearful of* thunder.

Free of: She will soon be *free of* her burden.

Hatred of: He has a *hatred of* violence.

Hint at: They *hinted at* a surprise.

Identical with: Your dress is *identical with* mine.

Independent of: I am *independent of* my parents.

In search of: He went in *search of* truth.

Interest in: He was not *interested in* his friends.

Jealous of: He was *jealous of* them.

Negligent of: He was *negligent of* his responsibilities.

Object to: I *object to* waiting so long.

Privilege of: He had the *privilege of* being born a millionaire.

Proficient in: You will be *proficient in* grammar.

Wait for: We will *wait for* them.

Wait on (service): The maid *waited on* them.

Like is used as a preposition. He wanted his dog to act *like* Lassie.

VERBALS

Sometimes verbs can change their form and be used as nouns, adverbs, or adjectives. These forms are called verbals.

1. The infinitive is formed by adding *to* in front of the verb. The infinitive may act as a noun, adjective, or adverb.

> I love *to sing*. (Noun)
> Music *to sing* is my favorite kind. (Adjective)
> He went *to sing* in the choir. (Adverb)

An infinitive phrase is used as a noun, adjective, or adverb.

> I love *to sing songs*. (Noun)
> Music *to sing easily* is my favorite. (Adjective)
> He went *to sing very often*. (Adverb)

2. The participle can be either present or past. The present participle is usually formed by adding *ing* to a verb. The past participle is usually formed by adding *n, en, d,* or *ed* to a verb. The participle is used as an adjective.

> The *swaying* crane struck the *fallen* boy.
> (*Swaying* is a present participle; *fallen* is a past participle.)

A participle phrase is used as an adjective.

> *Blowing the crane fiercely*, the wind caused much danger.

IMPORTANT FOR THE EXAM

Beware of dangling participle phrases.

> *Blowing the crane fiercely*, the crowd ran.
> (The wind is blowing the crane, not the crowd.)

The gerund is formed by adding *ing* to a verb. Although the gerund may look like a present participle, it is used only as a noun.

> *Seeing* clearly is important for good *driving*.
> (*Seeing* is the subject; *driving* is the object of the preposition *for*.)

A participle phrase is used as a noun.

> *Seeing traffic signals* is important for good driving.

PHRASES

A prepositional phrase begins with a preposition. A prepositional phrase can also be a noun phrase, an adjective phrase, or an adverbial phrase.

> *"Over the hill"* was the slogan of the geriatric club. (Noun phrase)
> The top *of the statue* was broken. (Adjective phrase)
> The owl sat *in the nest*. (Adverbial phrase)

See the previous section on *verbals* for infinitive phrases, participle phrases, and gerund phrases.

IMPORTANT FOR THE EXAM

A dangling or misplaced modifier is a word or phrase acting as a modifier that does not refer clearly to the word or phrase it modifies.

> A bright light blinded his eyes *over the door*. (Misplaced modifier—his eyes were not over the door.)
> *Blowing the crane fiercely*, the crowd ran. (Misplaced participle phrase—the crowd was not blowing the crane.)

Watching television, cookies were eaten. (Dangling gerund phrase—cookies were not watching television.)

Not able to stop, the man jumped out of my way. (Dangling infinitive phrase—is it the man who could not stop?)

The following modifying phrases clearly show what they modify.

A bright light over the door blinded his eyes.

Because the wind was blowing the crane fiercely, the crowd ran.

Watching television, Laura ate the cookies.

Since I was not able to stop, the man jumped out of my way.

CLAUSES

Clauses are groups of words that contain a subject and a predicate (verb part of the sentence). There are two main kinds of clauses. One kind is the *independent clause*, which makes sense when it stands alone. Independent clauses are joined by coordinating conjunctions.

I know how to clean silver, *but* I never learned how to clean copper.

(The two independent clauses could stand alone as complete sentences.)

I know how to clean silver. I never learned how to clean copper.

The other kind of clause is a *dependent* or *subordinate clause*. Although this type of clause has a subject and a predicate, it cannot stand alone.

When I learn to clean copper, I will keep my pots sparkling.

When I learn to clean copper, by itself, does not make sense. Dependent clauses are always used as a single part of speech in a sentence. They function as nouns or adjectives or adverbs. When they function as nouns, they are called *noun clauses*. When they function as adjectives, they are called *adjective clauses*. When they are adverbs, they are called *adverbial clauses*. Since a dependent or subordinate clause cannot stand alone, it must be joined with an independent clause to make a sentence. A *subordinating conjunction* does this job. A relative pronoun (*who, that, which, what, whose,* and *whom*) may act as the subordinating conjunction. For adjective and adverbial clauses, a relative adverb (*while* and *when*) may act as the subordinating conjunction.

I noticed *that he was very pale*.

That he was very pale is a noun clause—the object of the verb *noticed*. *That* is the subordinating conjunction.

Who was guilty is not known.

Who was guilty is a noun clause—the subject of the verb *is*. *Who* is the subordinating conjunction.

She lost the belt, *which was a present*.

Which was a present is an adjective clause describing *belt*. *Which* is the subordinating conjunction.

She lost the belt *when she dropped the bag*.

When she dropped the bag is an adverbial clause answering the question *when* about the predicate. *When* is the subordinating conjunction.

Clauses should refer clearly and logically to the part of the sentence they modify.

We bought a dress at Bloomingdale's, *which was expensive*.

(Misplaced adjective clause. Did the writer mean Bloomingdale's was expensive?)

Correct: We bought a dress, *which was expensive,* at Bloomingdale's.

When finally discovered, not a sound was heard.

(Misplaced adverbial clause. Who or what is discovered?)

Correct: *When finally discovered*, the boys didn't make a sound.

SENTENCES

A sentence is a group of words that expresses a complete thought. An independent clause can stand by itself and may or may not be a complete sentence.

Beth and Terry rode the Ferris wheel; they enjoyed the ride. (Two independent clauses connected by a semicolon)

Beth and Terry rode the Ferris wheel. They enjoyed the ride. (Two independent clauses—each is a sentence)

1. A simple sentence has one independent clause. A dependent clause is never a sentence by itself. Here are some simple sentences:

   John and Fred played.

   John laughed and sang.

   John and Fred ate hot dogs and drank beer.

The following is not an independent clause:

   Fred said. (Incorrect—*said* is a transitive verb. It needs a direct object.)

   Fred said hello. (Correct)

2. A compound sentence has at least two independent clauses.

> *Darryl bought the meat*, and *Laverne bought the potatoes*.

3. A complex sentence has one independent clause and at least one dependent clause.

> Because she left early, she missed the end.
>
> (*Because she left early* is the dependent clause. *She missed the end* is an independent clause.)

4. A compound-complex sentence has two independent clauses and one or more dependent clauses.

> You prefer math, and I prefer music, although I am the math major.
>
> (*You prefer math* and *I prefer music* are the independent clauses. The dependent clause is *although I am a math major*.)

COMMON SENTENCE ERRORS

SENTENCE FRAGMENTS

These are parts of sentences that are incorrectly written with the capitals and punctuation of a sentence.

> Around the corner.
> Because she left early.
> Going to the movies.
> A terrible tragedy.

Remember that sentences must have at least a subject and a verb.

RUN-ON SENTENCES

These are sentences that are linked incorrectly.

> The rain was heavy, lightning was crackling he could not row the boat. (Incorrect)
>
> Because the rain was heavy and lightning was crackling, he could not row the boat. (Correct)
>
> The rain was heavy. Lightning was crackling. He could not row the boat. (Correct)

FAULTY PARALLELISM

Elements of equal importance within a sentence should have parallel structure or similar form.

> To sing, *dancing*, and to laugh make life happy. (Incorrect)
>
> To sing, to dance, and to laugh make life happy. (Correct)
>
> He wants health, wealth, and *to be happy*. (Incorrect)
>
> He wants health, wealth, and happiness. (Correct)

WATCH ARBITRARY TENSE SHIFTS

> He *complained* while his father *listens*. (Incorrect)
>
> He *complained* while his father *listened*. (Correct)

WATCH NOUN-PRONOUN AGREEMENTS

> A *person* may pass if *they* study. (Incorrect)
>
> A *person* may pass if *he* studies. (Correct)

WATCH THESE DON'TS

> DON'T use *being that*; use *since* or *because*.
>
> DON'T use *could of, should of, would of*; use *could have, should have, would have*.
>
> DON'T use the preposition *of* in the following: off *of* the table, inside *of* the house.
>
> DON'T use *this here* or *that there*; use just *this* or *that*.
>
> DON'T misuse *then* as a coordinating conjunction; use *than* instead.
>
> > He is better *than* he used to be. (Correct)
> >
> > He is better *then* he used to be. (Incorrect)

CAPITALIZATION

Capitalize all proper nouns.

> Capitalize names of specific people, places, things, peoples, and their languages: Americans, America, Spanish. Note: Henry takes Spanish three times a week. Henry takes math three times a week.

Capitalize religions and holy books.

> Islam
> Koran
> Bible

Capitalize calendar words.

> Monday
> April

Capitalize historical periods and events.

> Renaissance
> Civil War

Always capitalize the first word in a sentence

> It is Henry.

Capitalize the first word in a letter salutation.

> Dear John,
> Dear Sir,

Capitalize the first word of a letter closing.

> Very truly yours,

Capitalize the first word in a direct quote.

> He said, "Go away."

Capitalize the first, last, and important words in titles.

> *The Man Without a Country*

Note: *A, an, and,* and *the* are usually not capitalized unless they are the first word.

Note also that conjunctions and prepositions with less than five letters are usually not capitalized.

Capitalize words used as part of a proper noun.

> Hudson Street
> Uncle Fritz

Capitalize specific regions.

> I want to move to the South.

Capitalize abbreviations of capitalized words.

> D. B. Edelson

Capitalize acronyms formed from capitalized words.

> NASA
> NATO

Capitalize the pronoun *I.*

> I beseech you to hear my prayer.

Note that capitals are not used for seasons (summer, winter).

Note that capitals are not used for compass directions (east, northeast).

Note that capitals are not used for the second part of a quote: "I see," she said, "how smart Henry is."

PUNCTUATION

THE PERIOD

Use the period to end full sentences.

> Harry loves candy.

> Although John knew the course was difficult, he did not expect to fail.

Use the period with abbreviations.

> Mr.

> Ph.D.

THE QUESTION MARK

Use the question mark to end a direct question.

> Are you going to the store?

Note that indirect questions end with a period.
> He asked how Sue knew the right answer.

THE EXCLAMATION POINT

Use the exclamation point to denote strong feeling.
> Act now!

THE COLON

The colon can introduce a series or an explanation, but it must always follow an independent clause.

> The following sciences are commonly taught in college: biology, chemistry, and physics. (Correct)

> The sciences are: biology, chemistry, and physics. (Incorrect)

> *The sciences are* is not an independent clause.

The colon is used after the salutation in a business letter.

> Dear Sir:

The colon is used to express the time.

> It is 1:45.

THE SEMICOLON

The semicolon is used to link related independent clauses not linked by *and, but, or, nor, for, so,* or *yet.*

> No person is born prejudiced; prejudice must be taught.

The semicolon is used before conjunctive adverbs and transitional phrases placed between independent clauses.

> No person is born prejudiced; however, he has been taught well.

No person is born prejudiced; nevertheless, he has always appeared bigoted.

The semicolon is used to separate a series that already contains commas.

> The team had John, the pitcher; Paul, the catcher; and Peter, the shortstop.

THE COMMA

The comma is used before long independent clauses linked by *and, but, or, nor, for, so,* or *yet.*

> No person is born prejudiced, but some people learn quickly.

The comma is used following clauses, phrases, or expressions that introduce a sentence.

> As I was eating, the waiter cleared the table.

> In a great country like ours, people enjoy traveling.

The comma is used with nonrestrictive, or parenthetical, expressions (not essential to the meaning of the main clause).

> He pulled the ice-cream sundae, topped with whipped cream, toward him.

> John is afraid of all women who carry hand grenades. *Notice there is no comma.* John is not afraid of all women. He is afraid of all women who carry hand grenades (restrictive clause).

Use commas between items in a series.

> Beth loves cake, candy, cookies, and ice cream.

Use the comma in direct address.

> Pearl, come here.

Use the comma before and after terms in apposition.

> Give it to Pearl, our good friend.

Use the comma in dates or addresses.

> June 3, 1996

> Freeport, Long Island

Use the comma after the salutation in a friendly letter.

> Dear Henry,

Use the comma after the closing in letters.

> Sincerely yours,

Use a comma between a direct quotation and the rest of the sentence.

> "Our fudge," the cook bragged, "is the best in town."

Be sure to use two commas when needed.

> A good dancer, generally speaking, loves to dance.

Do not separate subjects and verbs with a comma.

> Students and teachers, receive rewards. (Incorrect)

Do not separate verbs and their objects with a comma.

> He scolded and punished, the boys. (Incorrect)

THE APOSTROPHE

Use the apostrophe to denote possession (see nouns).

> John's friend

Use the apostrophe in contractions.

> Didn't (did not)

> There's (there is)

Do not use an apostrophe with *his, hers, ours, yours, theirs,* or *whose.* Use an apostrophe with *its* if *its* is a contraction.

> The dog chewed *its* bone; *it's* hard for a little dog to chew such a big bone. (*It's* means it is; *its* is a pronoun that denotes possession.)

QUOTATION MARKS

Use quotation marks in direct quotes.

> "Get up," she said.

Use single quotes for a quote within a quote.

> Mark said, "Denise keeps saying 'I love you' to Ralph."

PARENTHESES

Use parentheses to set off nonrestrictive or unnecessary parts of a sentence.

> This book (an excellent review tool) will help students.

THE DASH

Use the dash instead of parentheses.

> This book—an excellent review—will help students.

Use the dash to show interruption in thought.

> There are eight—remember, eight—parts of speech.

RHETORICAL REVIEW

STYLE

Good writing is clear and economical.

AVOID AMBIGUOUS PRONOUN REFERENCES

> Tom killed Jerry. I feel sorry for *him.* (Who is *him?* Tom? Jerry?)

> Burt is a nice man. I don't know why *they* insulted him. (Who does *they* refer to?)

AVOID CLICHÉS

Betty is *sharp as a tack*.

The math exam was *easy as pie*.

It will be *a cold day in August* before I eat dinner with Louisa again.

AVOID REDUNDANCY

Harry is a man who loves to gamble. (Redundant—we know that Harry is a man.)

Harry loves to gamble. (Correct)

Claire is a strange one. (Redundant—one is not necessary.)

Claire is strange.

This July has been particularly hot in terms of weather. (Redundant—*in terms of weather* is not necessary.)

This July has been particularly hot. (Correct)

AVOID WORDINESS

The phrases on the left are wordy. Use the words on the right.

WORDY	PREFERABLE
the reason why is that	because
the question as to whether	whether
in a hasty manner	hastily
be aware of the fact that	know
due to the fact that	because
in light of the fact that	since
regardless of the fact that	although
for the purpose of	to

AVOID VAGUE WORDS OR PHRASES

It is always preferable to use specific, concrete language rather than vague words and phrases.

The reality of the situation necessitated action. (Vague)

Bill tied up the burglar before the burglar could tie up him. (Specific)

BE ARTICULATE—use the appropriate word or phrase

The following are words or phrases that are commonly misused:

Accept: to receive or agree to (verb)
I *accept* your offer.

Except: preposition that means to leave out
They all left *except* Dave.

Adapt: to change (verb)
We must *adapt* to the new ways.

Adopt: to take as one's own, to incorporate (verb)
We will *adopt* a child.

Affect: to influence (verb)
Their attitude may well *affect* mine.

Effect: result (noun)
What is the *effect* of their attitude?

Allusion: a reference to something (noun)
The teacher made an *allusion* to Milton.

Illusion: a false idea (noun)
He had the *illusion* that he was king.

Among: use with more than two items (preposition)
They pushed *among* the soldiers.

Between: use with two items (preposition)
They pushed *between* both soldiers.

Amount: cannot be counted (noun)
Sue has a large *amount* of pride.

Number: can be counted (noun)
Sue bought a *number* of apples.

Apt: capable (adjective)
She is an *apt* student.

Likely: probably (adjective)
We are *likely* to receive the prize.

Beside: at the side of (preposition)
He sat *beside* me.

Besides: in addition to (preposition)
There were others there *besides* Joe.

Bring: toward the speaker (verb)
Bring that to me.

Take: away from the speaker (verb)
Take that to him.

Can: to be able to (verb)
I *can* ride a bike.

May: permission (verb)
May I ride my bike?

Famous: well known (adjective)
He is a *famous* movie star.

Infamous: well known but not for anything good (adjective)
He is the *infamous* criminal.

Fewer: can be counted (adjective)
I have *fewer* pennies than John.

Less: cannot be counted (adjective)
I have *less* pride than John.

Imply: the speaker or writer is making a hint or suggestion (verb)
He *implied* in his book that women were inferior.

Infer: to draw a conclusion from the speaker or writer (verb)
The audience *inferred* that he was a woman-hater.

In:	something is already there (preposition)
	He is *in* the kitchen.
Into:	something is going there (preposition)
	He is on his way *into* the kitchen.
Irritate:	to annoy (verb)
	His whining *irritated* me.
Aggravate:	to make worse (verb)
	The soap *aggravated* his rash.
Teach:	to provide knowledge (verb)
	She *taught* him how to swim.
Learn:	to acquire knowledge (verb)
	He *learned* how to swim from her.
Uninterested:	bored (adjective)
	She is *uninterested* in everything.
Disinterested:	impartial (adjective)
	He wanted a *disinterested* jury at his trial.

ORGANIZATION

A paragraph, like an essay, must have some organization plan. Each paragraph should represent the development of some point the author is making. Learn to recognize topic sentences, which often come at the beginning or end of a paragraph. Topic sentences tell the reader the main point of the paragraph.

Here are some sample topic sentences:

De Tocqueville is also concerned with the conflict between individual liberty and equality.

Another of the social institutions that leads to disaster in *Candide* is the aristocracy.

The Fortinbras subplot is the final subplot that points to Hamlet's procrastination.

Read the following paragraph and answer the appropriate questions.

(1) *Throughout history, writers and poets have created countless works of art.* (2) *The result is Paul's failure to pursue Clara and establish a meaningful relationship with her.* (3) *Paul's mother loves him, but the love is smothering and overprotective.* (4) *Although Paul feels free to tell his mother almost everything, he fails to tell her he is sexually attracted to Clara.* (5) *His feelings for Clara obviously make him feel he is betraying his mother.* (6) *Paul Morel's relationship with his mother in Sons and Lovers interferes with his relationship with Clara.*

1. Which sentence does not belong in the above paragraph?
   (A) 3, 6
   (B) 1
   (C) 4, 5
   (D) 2

The correct answer is (B). The first sentence is inappropriate to the idea of the paragraph, which concerns Paul's relationship with his mother and with Clara. The first sentence is also vague and virtually meaningless. Obviously, many works of art have been created throughout history.

2. Unscramble the above paragraph and put the sentences in the correct order.
   (A) 2, 4, 3, 6, 5
   (B) 6, 5, 2, 4, 3
   (C) 3, 4, 5, 6, 2
   (D) 6, 3, 4, 5, 2

The correct answer is (D). Obviously, sentence 1 does not fit the paragraph. Sentence 6 mentions Paul by his full name, the name of the work, and his relationships with both women, all of which are covered in the paragraph. It is the topic sentence. Sentence 2 sums up the paragraph; the clue is in the phrase "the result is." Logically, sentence 2 should end the paragraph. Since the paragraph concerns Paul's relationship with his mother and its effect on his relationship with Clara, the other sentences should fall in place.

SUMMARY

This section has covered a lot of the basic rules of grammar. It is primarily a reference section, and you will not be expected to know everything on the exam. However, we suggest you use this section as a handy guide to help you understand many of the answers that might involve certain grammar principles with which you may not be familiar. Feel free to highlight certain portions of these principles so you can go back to them from time to time, especially when confronted with more difficult explanations of some of the problems both in the Strategy section and in any of the exams in the book.

REVIEW ANSWERS AND EXPLANATIONS

IDENTIFYING SENTENCE ERRORS

1. **The correct answer is (B).** *Between* is used for only two; *among* is the correct preposition.

2. **The correct answer is (A).** Because the verb in this sentence is in passive voice and past tense, the past participle is used. *Supposed* is needed.

3. **The correct answer is (A).** The participial phrase *Gathering my courage* is located in a position to modify *the car*; therefore, this sentence is an example of a dangling participle. To correct the sentence, one would insert a suitable subject such as the following: *Gathering my courage, I decided this car was the best among those on sale.*

4. **The correct answer is (A).** The verb *laid* is a transitive verb; it must have a direct object. *Lay* and *lie* are confusing unless you use a strategy to differentiate them. *Lay* means "to put" or "to place" and *lay* requires a direct object; on the other hand, *lie* means "to rest" or "to recline" and *lie* is a verb that takes no object.

5. **The correct answer is (B).** A comma should not separate sentence subject and predicate.

6. **The correct answer is (A).** Because in this sentence, *Grandmother* follows a possessive pronoun (*my*), *Grandmother* should not be capitalized. If, however, that word is the way you address your grandmother, the word and others that refer to relatives, such as Mother, Uncle Bob, Dad, and Aunt Martha, should be capitalized.

7. **The correct answer is (D).** The principal parts of the verb "to swim" are *swim, swam, swum*. This sentence requires the use of the past principal *swum*.

8. **The correct answer is (C).** The construction "let's" is a contraction for "let us." Since the pronouns following it in the sentence serve as appositives, they should also be in the objective case: *you and me.*

9. **The correct answer is (C).** *Effect* and *affect* are words sometimes confused. Remember that *effect* is usually a noun while *affect* is always a verb.

10. **The correct answer is (C).** The relative pronoun *which* has no antecedent; that is, it replaces or refers to no single noun or pronoun. Revising this sentence will require rewriting rather than merely replacing a word. Here is one way to revise it: *Because Sam's photos of Hawaii entertained their family, his brother was surprised.* Notice *which* has been omitted.

11. **The correct answer is (C).** In a compound subject joined by *either-or* or *neither-nor*, you must choose the number of the verb (singular or plural) by making it agree with the subject closer to the verb. *Sponsor* is a singular subject.

12. **The correct answer is (E).** There is no error in this sentence. Although your ear may tell you that the verb in the adjective clause should be *tells*, the antecedent for *who* is *people*, not *one of*.

13. **The correct answer is (B).** *Aggravated* means "to intensify a pre-existing condition." *Irritate*, on the other hand, means "to cause to become sore or inflamed."

14. **The correct answer is (D).** *On the front porch* is a misplaced modifier; the Norman Conquest did not occur on the porch.

15. **The correct answer is (A).** The word *hang* refers to two different verbs; you have to decide which form to use. *Hang* can mean to fasten something, like placing a picture on a wall; the principal parts of this verb are *hang, hung, hung*. Another form of *hang* refers to a type of capital punishment; the principal parts of this verb are *hang, hanged, hanged*. Simply put, pictures are *hung*, while criminals are *hanged*.

16. **The correct answer is (B).** This sentence requires the use of subjunctive mood because it states a condition contrary to fact or a wish. The correct form here is *were*.

17. **The correct answer is (B).** Be careful when a sentence contains *only* because this adverb can modify many other words. In this sentence, you can ask yourself, "Did he only see them?" or "Did they only leave the bank?" or "Did he see only two men?" The first of these questions is patterned after the test question. Perhaps he also heard them? Or did he run into them? Try asking yourself questions like these to determine the correct placement for *only*.

18. **The correct answer is (C).** The verb required for this sentence means "to put" or "to place" so the correct form for passive voice, past tense is *laid*, not *lain*, which means "to rest" or "to recline."

19. **The correct answer is (D).** This clause seems to modify *the stairs*, which have already been described as *steep*. *Seats*, however, is the word correctly described by the adjective clause.

20. **The correct answer is (A).** The problem in this sentence involves a pronoun without an antecedent (*you*). Because *hiker* must study the maps, the correct pronoun in the introductory adverb clause should be *he* or *she* or *one*.

21. **The correct answer is (E).** This sentence has no error. *Who* is the correct form because it serves as the subject of the adjective clause: *who will collect tickets at the gate*. The interrupter *I think* does not affect this adjective clause.

22. **The correct answer is (E).** This sentence has no error. *Into* is the correct preposition because it shows movement into an area, while *in* means "within."

23. **The correct answer is (C).** *Infer* and *imply* are often confused. *Imply* means "to suggest something" while *infer* means "to interpret."

24. **The correct answer is (A).** Here is a misplaced modifier. The participle phrase *overloaded with boxes* describes the *speeding car*, not the *pothole*.

25. **The correct answer is (B).** The correct spelling in this sentence should be "lose."

RESTRUCTURING SENTENCES

1. **The correct answer is (A).** The sentence should read: *In their support of rising minority-group aspirations, large corporations are both evidencing true altruism in improving the lot of minorities <u>and</u> producing social changes within the communities in which their plants are located.*

2. **The correct answer is (B).** The sentence should read: *It is ironic that only the outbreak of World War II ended <u>the longest depression</u> in American history and brought prosperity to the United States.*

3. **The correct answer is (E).** The sentence should read: *An American Medical Association report <u>warns psychiatrists</u> that certain types of female patients will attempt to seduce them.*

4. **The correct answer is (C).** The sentence should read: *African American activists charge that a corporation's hiring minority-group workers and then laying them off during a recession <u>actually intensifies the frustration</u> of minority workers rather than helps them.*

5. **The correct answer is (D).** The sentence should read: *The average laborer whose only <u>income is his monthly wages</u> is often hard-pressed for immediate cash to pay his personal bills.*

6. **The correct answer is (B).** The sentence should read: *The truck driver knew that one pep pill would keep him awake and alert for about 3 <u>hours; therefore, tired</u> after 40 hours on the highway without rest, he took one.*

7. **The correct answer is (B).** The sentence should read: *No matter how many times anyone has seen pictures of planes flying or heard tales about the first flights of others, <u>a person's own</u> first flight is always a unique experience.*

8. **The correct answer is (D).** The sentence should read: *Members of that loose coalition of groups calling themselves the "New Left" advocate the overthrow, through violence, if necessary, of both corrupt capitalism and a corrupt governmental <u>system as the only</u> solution for the nation's problems.*

9. **The correct answer is (A).** The sentence should read: *Trapped into a loveless marriage by an overly anxious <u>girl, he</u> was already weary of her chattering before a month had passed.*

10. **The correct answer is (E).** The sentence should read: *Thirty years ago, some mental disorders would have required the indefinite hospitalization of <u>the patient; now these disorders</u> respond to treatment by certain specialized drugs.*

11. **The correct answer is (C).** The sentence should read: *Tired of listening to his children's <u>complaints, the old man</u> disconnected his hearing aid.*

12. **The correct answer is (A).** The sentence should read: *The waitress refused to wear the uniform required of anyone serving <u>food; therefore, she was discharged</u> from her position in the restaurant.*

13. **The correct answer is (C).** This choice is the most concise option. Choice (A) offers a version that is somewhat wordy; the word *hiatus* is not synonymous with a plant closing. Choice (B) is also wordy; *fortnight* is an archaic term, no longer used in modern English. Choice (D) is actually a sentence fragment; it lacks a complete predicate. Choice (E) is the most verbose of the choices.

14. **The correct answer is (E).** Choice (A) omits the year of the battle. Choice (B) includes a misplaced modifier, *over the English*, which needs to be placed after *victory*. Choice (C) is wordy, and the prepositional phrase *In 1066,* should be closer to *led* or *to victory*. Although choice (D) is more concise, it omits entirely any reference to the Bayeux Tapestry.

15. **The correct answer is (D).** It is the only choice that concisely and accurately states the information.

16. **The correct answer is (C).** Choice (A) reverses the cause-effect relationship between buying the land and developing the interstate system. Choice (B) offers a possibly correct answer, but choice (C) is better because it presents the sequence of events accurately. Choice (D) is not entirely correct; buying the property was just the first step in developing the interstate system. Choice (E) presents a new term, *eminent domain*, that is used correctly, but the original sentence does not include any reference to this legal term.

17. **The correct answer is (E).** Choice (A) is not correct because it limits patients to those with cataracts. Choice (B) presents a sentence in which the ideas are not arranged logically and effectively. Choice (C) also incorrectly limits the patients to those who are myopic. Choice (D) includes reference to patients who choose this kind of surgery because they are tired of wearing glasses, but the original sentence has no mention of this idea.

IMPROVING SENTENCES

1. **The correct answer is (C).** Choice (A) is awkward because *glimpse* becomes the subject of the sentence and *was caught* is the verb. The implication of physical action makes this incorrect. Choice (B) is incorrect because *glimpse* is singular, but the verb *were caught* is plural. Also, *driving around the corner* has nothing to modify logically. Was *a glimpse driving around the corner*? Choice (D) is incorrect because the subject becomes *mountains*, and the verb *were caught* makes the mountains responsible for the action. Choice (E) is incorrect because *mountain's* is possessive.

2. **The correct answer is (C).** Choices (A), (B), (D), and (E) are incorrect because they do not include anything logical for *Sitting around the dinner table* to modify.

3. **The correct answer is (E).** Choice (A) indicates that people are annoyed from England (leave the country) because of the music. Choice (B) indicates that ONLY English people are annoyed by the music. Choice (C) is awkwardly stated in the *persons from England*. Choice (D) is incorrect because *music* is the subject of the sentence and is singular; however, the verb *annoy* is plural.

4. **The correct answer is (B).** Choices (A) and (C) are incorrect because the word *from* is omitted. Choice (D) is incorrect because there is no comma following the word *school*, which is necessary for an introductory phrase. Choice (E) is incorrect because the word *As* indicates that the two events occurred at the same time.

5. **The correct answer is (D).** Choice (A) is incorrect because of the future tense of the verb. Choice (B) is incorrect because of the future tense of the verb and the lack of a comma following an introductory adverb clause. Choice (C) is incorrect because of the use of the future perfect verb tense. Choice (E) is incorrect because of the perfect verb tense.

6. **The correct answer is (E).** Choice (A) is incorrect because parallel construction, when linked by correlative conjunctions expressing similar ideas, must carry conjunctions that match. *Neither* and *or* do not match. Choice (B) is incorrect for the same reasons. *Not* and *or* do not match. Choices (C) and (D) are incorrect because *neither* and *or* do not match.

7. **The correct answer is (A).** Choice (B) is incorrect because *those* is a plural pronoun and requires a plural noun; *kind* is singular. Choice (C) is incorrect because of the word choice *good*. Choice (D) is incorrect for the same reasons as both choices (B) and (C). Choice (E) is incorrect because of the word choice *good*.

8. **The correct answer is (B).** *Amount* is used to describe something that can be measured, such as *the amount of water from the flood has receded. Number* is used for items or people that can be counted. Choices (A) and (C) are incorrect because of the word choice *amount*. Choice (D) is incorrect because of the word choice *amount* and the placement of the apostrophe, indicating possession. Choice (E) is incorrect because of the word choice *amount*.

9. **The correct answer is (C).** The original sentence contains a comma splice, and only choice (C) corrects the problem logically. A comma splice is an error that occurs when a comma by itself joins independent clauses. The only time that a comma is correct between two independent clauses is when the comma is followed by a coordinating conjunction. The word *splice* means *to fasten ends together*. The end of one independent clause and the beginning of another should not be fastened together with a comma alone.

10. **The correct answer is (C).** Choices (A) and (B) use *them*, which is a vague pronoun. Choice (D) has the same problem, even though *them* is moved within the sentence. Choice (E) changes the meaning of the original too much.

11. **The correct answer is (C).** The other choices are wordy, and they create illogical constructions. Choices (A), (B), and (D) are dangling modifiers introduced by participles; none can logically modify *I*. The final option, choice (E), opens with a prepositional phrase that cannot logically modify *I* either because an introductory prepositional phrase usually modifies the predicate.

12. **The correct answer is (E).** The original error presents a misplaced modifier. Emily Dickinson, a poet, is long dead. The other choices offer similar modifier problems, or they change the meaning of the sentence.

13. **The correct answer is (D).** The original sentence lacks parallelism. The structure is based on a compound predicate, but the final part of the sentence is an independent clause. The only choice that provides a three-part predicate is (D).

14. **The correct answer is (C).** The original sentence offers a mixed construction. *The reason . . . is because* . . . uses a subordinate clause as a predicate nominative; "because" is a subordinate conjunction. Choice (C) is the only choice that avoids a mixed construction or wordiness.

15. **The correct answer is (B).** Again the errors involve misplaced modifiers, and wordiness. Choice (B) is the only choice that offers a concise, logical sentence.

16. **The correct answer is (D).** The correct relative pronoun in the noun clause should be *whoever* because it serves as the subject of the clause. *Whomever* is an objective case relative pronoun.

17. **The correct answer is (C).** This is the only option that places the prepositional phrase, *during the spring quarter* in its proper position so that it modifies *carrying an overload*.

18. **The correct answer is (A).** The potential traps are the "lay/lie" choice and the correct form of "day's." "Lie" and "lay" are often troublesome because of their overlapping forms. The principal parts of "lie" are *lie, lay, lain* while the principal parts of "lay" are *lay, lay, laid*. The other error focuses attention on the correct form of "days." The phrase, "lies about a day's drive," uses the possessive form of *day* to replace the phrase "drive of a day."

19. **The correct answer is (B).** In this sentence two errors pose a problem. First, "these" and "those" are plural forms so they must modify a plural noun. "Those kinds of people" is a correct form; the error is wordiness. Is "kinds of" necessary? No. Choice (B) offers a more concise statement.

20. **The correct answer is (C).** The tense of the verb in the introductory adverb clause, "had left," indicates that this action occurred before the predicate in the independent clause. "Spent" is the past tense of "spend." "Year's" is another error because the plural form of "year," not the possessive form, is what you need.

REVISING WORK IN PROGRESS

1. **The correct answer is (B).** Choice (B) combines all the information together in the correct grammatical format. Choice (A) is incorrect because it adds extra information that was not present in the original two sentences (the father speaking to the mother's family). Choice (C) is false because it deletes the information about the father speaking of his roots. Choice (D) is wrong since these two sentences are intended by the writer to juxtapose two separate lifestyles. The use of *and* is incorrect stylistically because its use indicates the joining of equal ideas. Choice (E) is wrong because it is too wordy.

2. **The correct answer is (A).** It would be a good transition here to bring a word from sentence 11 up to the first paragraph. In this case *grandmother* works well. Also, it prepares the reader for a discussion in the next paragraph of the holiday traditions. Choice (B) is not good because it repeats sentence 10. Choice (C) is incorrect because it repeats the information of sentence 11. Choice (D) is too general and does not relate well to the next paragraph. Choice (E) could be reworked to sound good, but, in its present form, it sounds awkward and doesn't provide the necessary bridge to paragraph 2.

3. **The correct answer is (C).** Choice (A) is an acceptable answer, but choice (C) is better. The image the writer wishes to give is a group of people around all the sides of a grave. Choices (B) and (D) are wrong because we don't know if the people were sitting or standing. Later in the paragraph, the writer speaks of *drunken brawls*, etc., so sitting was probably not an option. Choice (E) is incorrect because it neglects to project the image of making a circle around something.

4. **The correct answer is (D).** This is a descriptive narrative essay. Choices (A), (B), (C), and (E) are all parts of that kind of essay. Choice (D) is part of an expository essay.

5. **The correct answer is (E).** Choice (A) is not as clear a picture as choice (E). Choice (B) is incorrect since there must be opposition here. Choice (C) is not good because it repeats the word *light* too much. Choice (D) is incorrect for the same reason, and it does not improve the image.

6. **The correct answer is (B).** The problem here is that the information on the grandmother should come later, when she is being discussed. Therefore, choices (A) and (D) are not sufficient. Also, choice (C) is incorrect; though possible, it will not improve the passage. Choice (E) could always be true, but it is not what is necessary here.

7. **The correct answer is (A).** It is not clear until later when and what this holiday is. Choices (B), (C), (D), and (E) are not necessary to improve the sentence. The problem with the sentence is a lack of prior knowledge of when this holiday actually takes place and why. Choice (C) is the only other possible answer, but, in this case, it is less necessary than choice (A).

8. **The correct answer is (C).** Choice (A) connects the two clauses with a coordinate conjunction "but," which typically sets up a contrast; no contrast is needed in these sentences. Choice (B) has a focus on the "disastrous results," which are not specified in the original sentences. In choice (D), the word "exacerbates" is an extreme verb; the implication in this sentence is that our fears were intensified by the knowledge of the Soviet arsenal. Choice (E), on the other hand, seems too mild with "imprudent."

9. **The correct answer is (A).** With the emphasis on persecuting certain public figures, the writer seeks to remind the reader that McCarthyism was similar to the Salem Witch Trials, in which citizens had only to be accused. They were guilty until proven innocent. Choice (B) has no basis in fact. Choice (C) offers "fearful of shadows," yet there is nothing in the passage to support that interpretation. In choice (D), the statement is true, but it is not a good choice to link paragraphs. Choice (E) offers an assumption with no basis in fact either.

10. **The correct answer is (E).** All of the above. This piece of writing is expository; the details are offered logically with description and visual cues. The writer wants the reader to see and experience the details as clearly as possible.

11. **The correct answer is (A).** "Terrifying" is the best choice to describe the citizens' fears about Communists infiltrating America. The other choices offer milder verbs that do not convey the intensity of the fears.

12. **The correct answer is (E).** "Blacklisted, or refused to hire" clarifies how those accused suffered regardless of their innocence. The other choices do not offer the depth of their ostracism.

ANALYZING WRITING

1. **The correct answer is (D).** Choices (A) and (E) are too general. Questions still remain: What institutions changed, or What kind of a center? These are broad aspects of the main idea, but not necessarily the main idea itself. Choices (B) and (C) are too specific. They are details of the sample.

2. **The correct answer is (A).** Choices (B) and (C) are incorrect because they tell what was actually done in the paragraph not WHY it was done. Choice (D) is wrong because the paragraph doesn't really touch on this subject, it only infers it. Choice (E) is too general and does not go with the paragraph at all.

3. **The correct answer is (D).** The use of the adjective *astounding* in sentence 13 indicates "happily surprised." Choice (A) is incorrect because the writer's style is not dry. Choice (B) is incorrect because the writer never expresses fear. Choice (C) is wrong because the sample ends on a positive note, so one can infer that the writer is not dismayed. Choice (E) is incorrect because it indicates a kind of complacency that the writer does not reflect.

4. **The correct answer is (B).** The details in sentence 6 are used as a basis for contrast to the later building that was adopted. Choice (A) is incorrect because this may be what the sentence does, but it is not the purpose of the sentence. Choices (C) and (E) are incorrect since they have no correlation to the paragraph. Choice (D) is wrong because the details don't describe the entire building, and this isn't the purpose of the details in the first place.

5. **The correct answer is (C).** Sentence 3 presents the idea of the building itself and how the citizens would respond (the themes of paragraphs 1 and 2). Choice (A) is incorrect because it is too general and simply restates the sentence. Choice (B) is false because, while the sentence does establish somewhat the importance of the exposition, that is not sentence 3's key relationship. Choice (D) is incorrect because it restates sentence 2. Choice (E) is incorrect because it restates sentence 4.

6. **The correct answer is (A).** Sentence 14 is the consequence to what happened in sentence 13. Choice (B) is incorrect because this sentence doesn't illustrate the excitement; it states what form the excitement took. Choice (C) is false since sentence 14 gives a consequence, not an example. Choice (D) is false since no amount is stated. Choice (E) is wrong because sentence 16 is based on sentence 15.

7. **The correct answer is (E).** Choice (A) is unclear; who is *them*? Choice (B) is incorrect because changing the placement before sentence 6 will disrupt the organization of the writing. Choice (C) is wrong because a contrasting sentence must be stated. Choice (D) is wrong since *them* does not refer to the exposition itself.

RECOGNIZING AND CORRECTING ERRORS IN SENTENCE STRUCTURE

1. This is a run-on sentence; two independent clauses are joined without a conjunction (like because) or a semicolon, which is a mark of punctuation that can connect these clauses. It is also correct to separate the two clauses into two separate simple sentences.

2. This item is a sentence fragment; that is, it is not a complete sentence. To correct this kind of error, you need to add some words to make a complete sentence. Here you can correct the error by writing "When I finished reading the story, I was confused." Notice, too, that you can connect this fragment to the sentence that follows, provided that the error there is corrected.

3. This item is an example of a comma splice. The term "splice" means that the writer is trying to connect independent clauses by using only a comma. You can add a conjunction to connect the clauses such as "because." Another way to correct the comma splice is to change the comma into a semicolon. Of course, you can also correct the error by separating the two clauses and make two separate sentences.

4. This item is a sentence fragment because "but" is a coordinate conjunction. You can eliminate the conjunction or add another independent clause.

5. This item is a run-on sentence. Some break should appear after "West." Insert a semicolon, add a conjunction such as "while," or separate the two clauses into two sentences.

6. This item is a sentence fragment. It lacks a complete predicate or verb. To correct this error you can eliminate "of" and insert "were." The resulting construction is an inverted sentence; the typical subject-verb arrangement is reversed. Such a construction can provide effective sentence variety.

7. This item has a comma splice. The comma following "room" is correct because that introductory phrase acts as an appositive for "cabin." The comma error follows "warm." Here you can insert a conjunction such as "and" or "so that." Another way to correct the error is to change the comma to a semicolon. Finally, you have the option to separate the two clauses into two sentences.

8. This item is a run-on sentence. The independent clauses have nothing to separate them or to connect them properly. To correct this error you can insert a semicolon after "warmth," insert a conjunction such as "because" or "since," or you can separate the two clauses to make two separate sentences.

9. This item is a sentence fragment because it lacks a complete predicate or verb. It may look like a complete sentence, perhaps, if you read "collected" as the predicate, but that reading is not logical. The "quilts" are not "folding"; someone has folded them. To correct this error you can add details to the fragment to make a complete sentence. You can add "Visitors saw patchwork quilts . . ." or you can add "were" immediately after "quilts."

10. This item is another example of a run-on sentence slightly different from the previous examples. This construction offers a series of "stringy sentences" with the result that too much information is offered without suitable breaks or subordination. You can separate these clauses to create these sentences: "With no neighbors in sight, this family struggled on their own to stay alive. They had to grow some vegetables like potatoes and eat game. In their area the primary target was deer."

11. This item is a sentence fragment because the construction lacks a complete predicate. You can correct the error by providing a predicate such as "dogs were sources of food, whatever. . . ."

12. This item is an example of a comma splice with a comma used to connect two independent clauses. You can correct the error by changing the comma to a semicolon, inserting a conjunction such as "and" after "sustenance," or separating the two clauses into two sentences.

13. This item is an example of a run-on sentence with a series of clauses strung together without sufficient punctuation or conjunctions. You can correct this sentence error by placing a period after "food" and beginning a new sentence with "The family. . . ." Omit "so" or you will create a sentence fragment.

14. This item is an example of a comma splice. You can correct this error by changing the comma after "hard" to a semicolon, adding a conjunction such as "and," or beginning a new sentence with "They."

15. This item is a comma splice. You can correct this error by changing the comma after "had" to a period, adding a conjunction such as "but" after "had," or separating the clauses into two separate sentences.

Chapter 4
POSTTEST

TIME—45 MINUTES	55 QUESTIONS

PART I

Directions: The following sentences test your knowledge of grammar, diction (choice of words), and idiom. Some sentences are correct. No sentence contains more than one error.

You will find that the error, if there is one, is underlined and lettered. Assume that elements of the sentence that are not underlined are correct and cannot be changed. In choosing answers, follow the requirements of standard written English.

If there is an error, select the one underlined part that must be changed to make the sentence correct and fill in the corresponding oval on your answer sheet. If there is no error, select answer (E).

1. The tests <u>tell</u> us many <u>things one</u> of them <u>is</u> how
       A   B   C
   fast the students <u>read</u>. <u>No error.</u>
                 D   E

2. <u>When</u> you go to the store, please <u>bring</u> this item
      A   B
   to the salesman <u>at</u> the refund counter; <u>this</u> lamp
                C   D
   must be returned, since it doesn't work.

   <u>No error.</u>
     E

3. <u>Examination of the data</u> <u>discloses</u> a number <u>of</u>
        A   B   C
   reasons <u>for</u> an involuntary termination. <u>No error.</u>
        D   E

4. If he <u>had had</u> the <u>forethought to arrange</u> an
          A   B
   appointment, his interview <u>would have been</u>
                          C   D
   more productive. <u>No error.</u>
                  E

5. The train <u>having stopped</u> <u>continuously</u> during the
             A   B
   night, we couldn't even <u>lie</u> down <u>to</u> sleep.
                     C   D
   <u>No error.</u>
    E

6. He was <u>filled with</u> anger <u>against</u> those <u>whom</u> he
            A   B   C
   <u>believed</u> had hurt or humiliated him. <u>No error.</u>
      D   E

7. Admirers of American television <u>have made</u> the
                           A
   claim that <u>its</u> programs are <u>as good</u> or <u>better than</u>
           B   C   D
   the British programs. <u>No error.</u>
                 E

8. <u>Rather than</u> <u>going</u> with her to the movies, Steve
       A   B
   decided to stay <u>home</u>. <u>No error.</u>
     C   D   E

9. <u>You</u> telling the truth <u>in the face of such dire con-</u>
     A   B
   sequences <u>required</u> great <u>moral courage</u>. <u>No error.</u>
           C   D   E

10. <u>Every</u> sheet of graph paper and <u>every</u> sheet of
      A   B
    ruled paper <u>is</u> <u>examined</u> by three proctors.
             C   D
    <u>No error.</u>
     E

11. The baby's hair is black <u>as</u> his father's, and his
                        A
    eyes <u>are</u> blue <u>like</u> his <u>mother's</u>. <u>No error.</u>
        B   C   D   E

12. His speech covered all the topics <u>in regards to</u>
                                 A
    <u>obtaining</u> permission <u>to serve</u> liquor <u>in a bar</u>.
      B   C   D
    <u>No error.</u>
     E

GO ON TO THE NEXT PAGE

13. Half of the roadways in the city are disintegrating
    $\underline{}$ $\underline{}$
    A   B
    because of the severe winter weather. No error.
    $\underline{}$ $\underline{}$ $\underline{}$
    C   D   E

14. The automobile, as well as our luggage and our
    $\underline{}$ $\underline{}$
    A   B
    hats and coats, were stolen. No error.
    $\underline{}$ $\underline{}$ $\underline{}$
    C   D   E

15. He is one of those persons who is never satis-
    $\underline{}$ $\underline{}$ $\underline{}$ $\underline{}$
    A   B   C   D
    fied. No error.
    $\underline{}$
    E

Directions: The following sentences test correctness and effectiveness of expression. In choosing answers, follow the requirements of standard written English; that is, pay attention to grammar, diction (choice of words), sentence construction, and punctuation.

In each of the following sentences, part of the sentence or the entire sentence is underlined. Beneath each sentence you will find five versions of the underlined part. Choice (A) repeats the original; answers (B) through (E) present different alternatives.

Choose the answer that best expresses the meaning of the original sentence. If you think the original is better than any of the alternatives, choose it; otherwise select one of the other answer choices. Your choice should produce the most effective sentence—one that is clear and precise, without awkwardness or ambiguity.

Example

When the Yankees and the Braves meet again in the World Series, their hitting will be decisive.

(A) their hitting will be decisive.
(B) Braves pitching will not be decisive.
(C) the decisive factor will be their hitting.
(D) the decisive factor will be Yankee hitting.
(E) an important factor will be Yankee hitting.

The correct answer is (D). Choices (A) and (C) lack clear antecedents (nouns or pronouns to which they refer). Choice (B) is only speculative, or inferred. Choice (E) doesn't emphasize *decisive*, a term stronger than *important*.

16. If good writing is desired, allow sentences to be shaped by thought and feeling in a forceful way.

(A) If good writing is desired, allow sentences to be shaped by
(B) If you want to write good, allow sentences to shape your
(C) If one wants to write good, allow your mind to shape your
(D) In good writing, the sentences shape
(E) In writing well means to let the sentences shape

17. Without wishing to call for a serious moratorium in the arms race, the prospects for peace are not good.

(A) Without wishing to call for a serious moratorium in the arms race,
(B) Most nations are unwilling to call for a serious moratorium to the arms race,
(C) Although most nations are unwilling to call for a serious moratorium in the arms race,
(D) Most nations not being willing to call for a serious moratorium in the arms race,
(E) If most nations really want war,

18. Rather than decline precipitously as they threatened to do ten years ago, symphony orchestras have flourished and are receiving more federal and state aid.

(A) Rather than decline precipitously as they threatened to do ten years ago,
(B) Instead of declining precipitously as they threatened to do ten years ago,
(C) More than fall into the precipitous decline threatened ten years ago,
(D) Instead of falling into the precipitous decline which they threatened to fall into ten years ago,
(E) They did not fall into the precipitous decline that was forecast for them ten years ago,

19. Because we had duplicated the Japanese cipher machine and had broken their secret military code, we were able to win a number of victories against enormous odds.

(A) Because we had duplicated the Japanese cipher machine and had broken their secret military code,
(B) Had we duplicated their cipher machine and broken their secret code,
(C) We had duplicated the Japanese cipher machine and had broken the secret code,
(D) Building the Japanese cipher machine and breaking their code,
(E) Having duplicated the Japanese cipher machine and broken their secret military code,

20. Either school curricula or television is to blame, declining SAT scores are a problem.

(A) Either school curricula or television is to blame,

(B) If either school curricula or television are to blame,

(C) Blaming either television or school curricula,

(D) Although either school curricula or television is to blame,

(E) Whether we blame school curricula or television,

21. The decision to build the gym on top of the cliff was the Board of Trustees', not the president's.

(A) The decision to build the gym on top of the cliff was the Board of Trustees', not the president's.

(B) By building the gym on top of the cliff, it implied the Board of Trustees, not the president.

(C) The Board of Trustees, not the president, decided to build the gym on top of the cliff.

(D) If the gym was built on top of the cliff, that was the Board of Trustees' fault, not the president.

(E) The gym was built on top of the cliff, being the fault of the Trustees and the president.

22. The agricultural community is dependent on the oil industry because chemical fertilizers are a petroleum product.

(A) because chemical fertilizers are a petroleum product.

(B) artificial fertilizers are made from oil.

(C) by reason of its making fertilizers from oil.

(D) because of artificial fertilizers, which are petroleum products.

(E) in that it makes fertilizers from oil.

23. Investigators have shown that a nonsmoker will inhale the equivalent of a pack of cigarettes just by breathing for one afternoon the air of a bar where twenty people are smoking.

(A) will inhale the equivalent of a pack of cigarettes just by breathing for one afternoon the air of a bar where twenty people are smoking.

(B) in a bar with twenty smokers in an afternoon inhaling the equivalent of a pack of cigarettes.

(C) will inhale the equivalent of a pack of cigarettes if twenty people are smoking in a bar.

(D) will inhale the equivalent of a pack of cigarettes just by breathing the air of a bar for an afternoon with twenty smokers in it.

(E) spending an afternoon in a bar where twenty smokers are smoking, inhaling the equivalent of a pack of cigarettes.

24. The cherry trees are in blossom now; the winter weather has been prolonged.

(A) now; the winter weather has been prolonged.

(B) now because the winter weather had been prolonged.

(C) only now because of the lingering winter weather.

(D) now, and the winter weather lingered.

(E) now, being that the winter weather lingered.

25. The basic conflict in the epic poem is between the hero's desire for personal honor and the inexorable presence of death.

(A) The basic conflict in the epic poem is between

(B) The epic poem basically shows

(C) The epic poem basically juxtaposes

(D) Basically, the epic poem tenses

(E) Basic to the epic poem is the conflict between

GO ON TO THE NEXT PAGE

Directions: Each of the following selections is an early draft of a student essay in which the sentences have been numbered for easy reference. Some parts of the selections need to be changed.

Read each essay and then answer the questions that follow. Some questions are about particular sentences or parts of sentences and ask you to improve sentence structure and diction (choice of words). In making these decisions, follow the conventions of standard written English. Other questions refer to the entire essay or parts of the essay and ask you to consider organization, development, and effectiveness of language in relation to purpose and audience.

Questions 26–34 are based on a draft of an editorial in a school newspaper.

(1) For the last five years, less than ten percent of the student population has voted in the Student Government Association election. (2) Most students do not know who the candidates are. (3) They don't know what they stand for. (4) When some students were surveyed last Thursday during lunch hour, many of them did not know anything about the election. (5) And the election was held on Friday. (6) It is not surprising that only 8 percent of the students voted. (7) This is not the fault of the students.

(8) The problem is in the campaign process. (9) Everything must be approved and stamped, from the campaign posters to flyers and buttons. (10) Limits are placed on where posters can be hung and the times when candidates may talk with students. (11) A pile of paperwork must be filled out in order for those running to distribute flyers. (12) The colorful posters may have the candidate's names in pretty colors, but that does little to educate students about the candidates' positions on issues that are important to the interest and welfare and well-being of the students.

(13) Candidates are only given one week to campaign. (14) This is not enough time to present a cohesive platform. (15) The campaign process should be changed. (16) Allowing three weeks for campaigning, and dropping some of the cumbersome and unnecessary rules and procedures would permit the candidates to get their message across to the students. (17) And then maybe more of them would vote.

26. Which of the following is the best way to revise the underlined portions of sentences 2 and 3 (reproduced below) so that the two sentences are combined into one?

Most students do not know who the <u>candidates are. They don't know</u> what they stand for.

   (A) candidates are, and they don't know
   (B) candidates are; they don't know
   (C) candidates are, so they don't know
   (D) candidates are, nor do they know
   (E) candidates are and they don't know

27. The writer could best improve sentence 4 by:

   (A) quoting the question asked in the survey
   (B) specifying how many students were surveyed and how many of them did not know about the election
   (C) naming some of the students who were asked the survey question
   (D) specifying where the questioners were when they asked the students the question about the election
   (E) giving Thursday's date

28. Which of the following is the best word to add to begin sentence 6?

   (A) Thusly
   (B) Hence
   (C) Consequently
   (D) Accordingly
   (E) Therefore

29. Which of the following is the best way to revise sentence 7 (reproduced below)?

This is not the fault of the students.

   (A) This is not the student's fault.
   (B) This is not the students' fault.
   (C) The low voting rate is not the student's fault.
   (D) The low voting rate is not the students' fault.
   (E) That is not the fault of the students.

30. Which of the following is the best phrase to replace *that does* in sentence 12?

   (A) it does
   (B) they do
   (C) it has
   (D) they have
   (E) they does

31. In context, which of the following is the best revision for <u>are important to the interest and welfare and well-being of the students,</u> which appears at the end of sentence 12?

    (A) are relevant to students' welfare
    (B) are interesting to students
    (C) effect the interests of the students
    (D) affect students' interests
    (E) connect to students' interests

32. Which of the following is the best version of the underlined portion of sentence 13 (reproduced below)?

    Candidates <u>are only given one week to campaign.</u>

    (A) only are given one week to campaign.
    (B) are given one only week to campaign.
    (C) are given one week to only campaign.
    (D) are given one week to campaign only.
    (E) are given only one week to campaign.

33. In context, the best phrase to replace *present a cohesive platform* in sentence 14 is:

    (A) cohere their platforms and explain them.
    (B) explain the issues and their positions on them.
    (C) explain the many issues affecting students and discussing their positions.
    (D) explain and discuss their positions on the issues in the campaign.
    (E) present a coherent platform and explain and discuss issues.

34. Which of the following is the best revision of sentence 17 (reproduced below)?

    And then maybe more of them would vote.

    (A) That change should result in more students voting in the elections.
    (B) That change would result in more students voting in the elections.
    (C) Then more students will want to vote in these important elections.
    (D) As a result, more students would be ready, willing, and able to vote.
    (E) More students will then vote.

Questions 35–43 refer to the following paragraph.

(1) *I have visited this place many times and I am always happy to return there.* (2) *An ancient, pretty town in the Ukraine, it consists of two-storied houses.* (3) *In a cozy, peaceful valley, it is surrounded by tall beautiful trees and a wonderful landscape.* (4) *What truly makes the town unique is the monastery.* (5) *Located on the edge of town, it hangs off a wall of rock.* (6) *The white walls tower above everything.* (7) *The abbey and monastery can be seen from any place in the borough.* (8) *Some parts of its mountain are covered with forest or barren rocks.* (9) *Different than most Slavic churches with their twisted spires, colorful colors, and stained-glass windows, the monastery is a contrast of white and black.* (10) *Its simplicity and starkness draw the eye more than anything else.* (11) *I can't describe the actual structure since it is more about the feelings that it evokes for me.* (12) *I feel rapture, respect, and peace.* (13) *A stream quietly winds its way at the foot of the monastery's base.* (14) *All is still with no people around—only water, trees, rocks, stately walls, and a deep blue sky.*

35. Which of the following is the best way to revise sentences 5 and 6 (reproduced below) so that the two sentences are combined into one?

    Located on the edge of town, it hangs off a wall of rock. The white walls tower above everything.

    (A) Located on the edge of town, its white walls tower above the village.
    (B) Hanging from a wall of rock at the edge of town, it towers above everything.
    (C) Located and hanging from a wall of white rock, it towers above the town.
    (D) On the edge of town, it hangs off a wall of rock, its white walls towering above.
    (E) Its white walls towering over the edge of the town; it hangs there.

36. Which of the following sentences, if added after sentence 13, would best link that sentence to the rest of the paragraph?

    (A) Like the winding water, a serene harmony exists.
    (B) The water is cool yet gentle in its movements.
    (C) One can only hear the murmuring of the water as it descends the rocks.
    (D) The monastery's base is washed by the water.
    (E) Peacefully, the water moves.

GO ON TO THE NEXT PAGE

37. Which of the following is the best way to revise and combine sentences 11 and 12 (reproduced below)?

I can't describe the actual structure since it is more about the feelings that it evokes for me. I feel rapture, respect, and peace.

(A) Clearer to me are my feelings of rapture, respect, and peace than what the structure looked like.
(B) When I think of the monastery I can't describe it except to say my feelings that are of peace, rapture, and respect.
(C) The building itself isn't important, but the feelings it evokes are: peace, rapture, and respect.
(D) The feelings of rapture, respect, and peace are more vivid than the real building itself.
(E) The rapture, respect, and peaceful feelings evoked by the monastery are easier to describe than its actual structure.

38. Which of the following is the best version of the underlined portion of sentence 8 (reproduced below)?

Some parts of its mountain are covered with forest or barren rocks.

(A) (leave as it is now)
(B) ; other parts are barren rock.
(C) , barren rocks, etc.
(D) yet other parts can be seen as barren rocks.
(E) and barren rocks.

39. All of the following strategies are used by the writer of the passage EXCEPT:

(A) descriptive adjectives.
(B) sequential development of examples.
(C) visual cues.
(D) narrowed topic.
(E) supporting sentences that convey attitude.

40. Which of the following would be the best replacement for *different than* at the beginning of sentence 9?

(A) Unlike most
(B) In contrasting to
(C) In comparison
(D) (delete it completely)
(E) (keep it the same)

41. The writer of the passage could best improve sentences 7 and 13 by:

(A) moving sentence 7 and leaving sentence 13 alone.
(B) moving sentence 13 and leaving sentence 7 alone.
(C) combining them.
(D) using less specific adjectives and details.
(E) moving them to the beginning of the paragraph.

42. In context, the best phrase to replace *anything else* in sentence 10 would be:

(A) (keep it the same)
(B) the village.
(C) the other pretty things.
(D) the tall green mountains.
(E) the other structures.

43. Which is the best version of the underlined portion of sentence 1 (reproduced below)?

I have visited this place many times and I am always happy to return there.

(A) (leave as it is now)
(B) (name of the town)
(C) that place
(D) (delete it altogether)
(E) the monastery

Directions: The following sentences test correctness and effectiveness of expression. In choosing answers, follow the requirements of standard written English; that is, pay attention to grammar, diction (choice of words), sentence construction, and punctuation.

In each of the following sentences, part of the sentence or the entire sentence is underlined. Beneath each sentence you will find five versions of the underlined part. Choice (A) repeats the original; answers (B) through (E) present different alternatives.

Choose the answer that best expresses the meaning of the original sentence. If you think the original is better than any of the alternatives, choose it; otherwise select one of the other answer choices. Your choice should produce the most effective sentence—one that is clear and precise, without awkwardness or ambiguity.

Example

When the Yankees and the Braves meet again in the World Series, their hitting will be decisive.

- (A) their hitting will be decisive.
- (B) Braves pitching will not be decisive.
- (C) the decisive factor will be their hitting.
- (D) the decisive factor will be Yankee hitting.
- (E) an important factor will be Yankee hitting.

The correct answer is (D). In choices (A) and (C) *their* lacks a clear antecedent (noun or pronoun to which it refers). Choice (B) is only speculative, or inferred. Choice (E) doesn't emphasize *decisive*, a term stronger than *important*.

44. The new model, with its low gas mileage and roomy interior, will answer the major critics of our company as much as it will satisfy the needs of our customers.
- (A) will answer the major critics of our company as much as it will satisfy the needs of our customers.
- (B) will more than answer the major critics of our company than the needs of our customers.
- (C) answering the major critics of our company and satisfying the needs of our customers.
- (D) will satisfy both our major critics and our customers.
- (E) it will answer the major critics of our company and the needs of our customers.

45. A strenuous sport, such as long-distance running, cycling, or tennis singles, if practiced consistently and wisely through middle age, can protect the heart against disease.
- (A) if practiced consistently and wisely through middle age, can protect the heart against disease.
- (B) is important for middle-aged men as a protection against heart disease, which is practiced through middle age.
- (C) is suggested for men who have heart problems because it can protect the heart against disease well into middle age if practiced consistently and wisely.
- (D) should be played well into middle age as a protection for the heart against heart disease, which comes with middle age.
- (E) sports that will protect the heart against heart disease if practiced steadily and wisely into middle age.

46. By writing well, we express better what we think we know and we begin to understand what we could know.
- (A) we express better what we think we know and we begin to understand what we could know.
- (B) we express better our acquired knowledge and our suspected knowledge.
- (C) we articulate our knowing and what of us is becoming.
- (D) we express our conscious knowledge more precisely than others, and we give form to ideas only beginning to form.
- (E) we articulate more clearly our acquired knowledge and we give a tentative shape to new ideas.

47. Given his radical leanings, his speech was rather moderate.
- (A) Given his radical leanings,
- (B) Having radical leanings,
- (C) Though having radical leanings,
- (D) Compared to his radical leanings,
- (E) If his opinions were radical,

GO ON TO THE NEXT PAGE

48. Existentialists confront death with <u>anguish; many writers have depicted the same anguish without recourse to formal philosophy.</u>

   (A) anguish; many writers have depicted the same anguish without recourse to formal philosophy.

   (B) anguish, which many nonexistential writers have also depicted.

   (C) anguish, many writers have also depicted it without recourse to formal philosophy.

   (D) the same anguish that many modern writers who are not existentialists have also depicted.

   (E) anguish, depicting it much as many writers who are not existentialists have depicted it.

49. The pro taught her <u>how she should hold the racket, how she should step into each shot, and how she should prepare herself mentally for a match.</u>

   (A) how she should hold the racket, how she should step into each shot, and how she should prepare herself mentally for a match.

   (B) racket holding, shot addressing, and mental preparation.

   (C) how to hold the racket, how to step into a shot, and how to prepare for a match.

   (D) racket holds, shot steps, and match preparation.

   (E) how to hold the racket, stepping into each shot, and preparing for a match.

50. The Leakeys discovered the footprint of a humanlike ape in East Africa's Great Rift <u>Valley; radioactive carbon dating placed the print at 3.59 to 3.75 million years ago.</u>

   (A) Valley; radioactive carbon dating placed the print at 3.59 to 3.75 million years ago.

   (B) Valley, which radioactive carbon dating has placed 3.59–3.75 million years ago.

   (C) Valley, and radioactive carbon dating has placed it between 3.59 and 3.75 million years ago.

   (D) Valley, but radioactive carbon dating has placed it between 3.59 to 3.75 million years ago.

   (E) Valley, being dated by radioactive carbon means to between 3.59 and 3.75 million years ago.

51. This book <u>belongs to the Joneses, not to Jane.</u>

   (A) belongs to the Joneses, not to Jane.

   (B) is to the Joneses, not to Jane.

   (C) is the Joneses', not Jane's.

   (D) is the Jonese's, not Janes'.

   (E) is the Joneses's, not Janes's.

52. Unlike his predecessors, John <u>has adjusted well to the new position.</u>

   (A) has adjusted well to the new position.

   (B) has adjusted better than them to the new position.

   (C) has adjusted into the new position more smoothly.

   (D) has found the new position adjustable to.

   (E) has had no trouble adjusting to the new position.

53. In *The Last of the Mohicans*, James Fenimore Cooper <u>developed a contrast between Alice and Cora.</u>

   (A) developed a contrast between Alice and Cora.

   (B) developed, of Alice and Cora, a contrast.

   (C) contrasted Alice and Cora.

   (D) developed two contradicting stereotypes in Alice and Cora.

   (E) developed two opposites: Alice versus Cora.

54. During the office celebration, the president <u>ascribed the success</u> of the new sales campaign to everyone's hard work.

   (A) ascribed the success

   (B) contributed the success

   (C) attributed the success

   (D) resolved the success

   (E) considered the success

55. The article was written <u>in order to raise money for the boy's treatment, not to satisfy the readers' taste for the macabre.</u>

   (A) in order to raise money for the boy's treatment, not to satisfy the readers' taste for the macabre.

   (B) in the treatment of the boy, not for the readers' macabre tastes.

   (C) for the sake of the raising of the money for the boy's treatment and not for the sake of the tastes of the macabre on the part of the readers of the paper.

   (D) to help raise money for treatment of the boy and not to satisfy the macabre tastes of the readers.

   (E) because money needed to be raised for the boy's treatment, not for the macabre tastes of the readers.

STOP If you finish before the time is up, you may check your work on this section only. Do not turn to any other section in the test.

TIME—45 MINUTES	45 QUESTIONS

PART II

ENGLISH COMPOSITION WITHOUT ESSAY TEST

Directions: Each of the following selections is an early draft of a student essay in which the sentences have been numbered for easy reference. Some parts of the selections need to be changed.

Read each essay and then answer the questions that follow. Some questions are about particular sentences or parts of sentences and ask you to improve sentence structure and diction (choice of words). In making these decisions, follow the conventions of standard written English. Other questions refer to the entire essay or parts of the essay and ask you to consider organization, development, and effectiveness of language in relation to purpose and audience.

Questions 56–64 refer to the following paragraph.

(1) *It is true that Nelson Mandela is a real hero.* (2) *The main reason I admire him is that he fought for equal rights in his country and didn't give up until he had achieved his goal.* (3) *His courage and civil disobedience landed him in one of the toughest prisons where he was held for twenty-six years.* (4) *He was a young man when he demonstrated against the government's policy of apartheid.* (5) *He led a group in prison and witnessed to the world about the injustices in South Africa.* (6) *He was released from prison in 1990.* (7) *He took over the leadership of the opposition party.* (8) *Mandela pushed the government to represent all the citizens.* (9) *Finally in 1994, apartheid ended and his dream was fulfilled.* (10) *In America, we often confuse heroes with popular idols.* (11) *A basketball player who takes drugs and scores a lot of points in the game is not a hero.* (12) *Nelson Mandela is a hero because he stayed true to his cause and never gave up his ideals.*

56. Which of the following is the best way to revise sentences 6 and 7 (reproduced below) so that the two sentences are combined into one?

    He was released from prison in 1990. He took over the leadership of the opposition party.

    (A) He took over the leadership of the opposition as he was released from prison in 1990.
    (B) After release from prison in 1990, he took over the leadership of the opposition party.
    (C) He was released from prison in 1990, and he took over the leadership of the opposition party.
    (D) While he was being released in 1990, he took over leadership of the opposition party.
    (E) He took over the leadership of the opposition party soon after being released from prison.

57. Which of the following sentences, if added after sentence 9, would best link that sentence to the rest of the paragraph?

    (A) His dreams made him a hero.
    (B) Luckily, America had long given up its version of apartheid.
    (C) Nelson Mandela truly exemplifies the ideal of a hero.
    (D) A hero is someone who has a dream.
    (E) This marked the year that we acknowledged a hero.

58. Which of the following is the best revision of the underlined portion of sentence 5 (reproduced below)?

    He led a group in prison and witnessed to the world about the injustices in South Africa.

    (A) (leave as it is now)
    (B) Nelson Mandela led a group in prison and witnessed
    (C) Mandela in prison witnessed to the world
    (D) While Nelson Mandela was in prison, he led a group and continued witnessing
    (E) When he led a group in prison, he witnessed

GO ON TO THE NEXT PAGE

59. Which of the following is the best revision of the underlined portion of sentence 4?

He was a young man when he demonstrated against the government's policy of apartheid.

(A) (leave as it is now)
(B) As a young man, he
(C) A young man like himself often
(D) As young as he was, he
(E) In his younger years, he

60. All of the following strategies are used by the writer of the passage EXCEPT

(A) descriptive adjectives
(B) sequential development of examples
(C) logical support of thesis statement
(D) narrowed topic
(E) statements that provide information

61. Which of the following would be the best replacement for "It is true that Nelson Mandela is" at the beginning of sentence 1?

(A) Nelson Mandela is considered by many to be
(B) Many believe that it is true that Nelson Mandela is
(C) The world considers that Nelson Mandela is
(D) (delete all except for the name)
(E) (keep it the same)

62. The writer of the passage could best improve sentences 3 and 4 by

(A) moving sentence 3 and leaving sentence 4 alone
(B) moving both sentences 3 and 4
(C) combining them
(D) using less specific adjectives and details
(E) moving sentence 4 before sentence 3

63. The writer of the passage could best improve sentence 4 by

(A) providing examples of the demonstrations
(B) including a personal opinion
(C) discussing the ramifications of this
(D) defining the word *apartheid*
(E) acknowledging the difficulties involved

64. Which of the following is the best way to revise the underlined portion of sentence 2 (reproduced below)?

The main reason I admire him is that he fought for equal rights in his country and didn't give up until he had achieved his goal.

(A) (leave as it is now)
(B) I admire him greatly because
(C) I admire him for many reasons such as
(D) (delete it altogether)
(E) The many reasons that I admire him are that

Directions: Effective revision requires choosing among the many options available to a writer. The following questions test your ability to use these options effectively. Revise each of the sentences below according to the directions that follow it. Some directions require you to change only part of the original sentence; others require you to change the entire sentence. You may need to omit or add certain words in constructing an acceptable revision, but you should keep the meaning of your revised sentence as close to the meaning of the original sentences as the directions permit. Your new sentence should follow the conventions of standard written English and should be clear and concise.

Look through answer choices (A) through (E) under each question for the exact word or phrase that is included in your revised sentence and fill in the corresponding space on your answer sheet. If you have thought of a revision that does not include any of the words or phrases listed, try to revise the sentence again so that it does include the wording in one of the answer choices.

Example

Having been close to the master all his life, keeping files and writing correspondence, John was the natural choice to write the catalog for the exhibit.

Start with John was.

(A) exhibit, which was
(B) exhibit because he had
(C) exhibit being
(D) exhibit being that
(E) exhibit although he

The correct answer is (B). Your sentence should read: "John was the natural choice to write the catalog for the *exhibit because he had* been close to the master, keeping files and writing correspondence." Choice (A) introduces a clause that could not exist. Choice (C) introduces a present participle that must refer to John, who is too far away; choice (D) does the same. Choice (E) changes the meaning of the sentence.

65. The bell tolled slowly for the burial of the stranger, but the poet realized that the bell also tolled for himself and for all of mankind.

    Start with The poet realized.

    (A) which was tolling
    (B) which had been tolling
    (C) which tolls
    (D) which tolling
    (E) that tolling

66. The opponents of the new airport drove slowly around the approach roads and succeeded in shutting it down.

    Begin with By driving slowly.

    (A) down, the opponents
    (B) roads the opponents
    (C) airport, the opponents
    (D) roads, the opponents
    (E) succeeded, the opponents

67. Some teachers do not care about their students; they give erratic grades and do not hold office hours.

    Begin with Some teachers give.

    (A) hours, because they
    (B) hours, and they
    (C) hours because some teachers
    (D) hours because they
    (E) hours although

68. How George could break his engagement with the charming Ms. Banister is hard for most people in our circle to comprehend.

    Start with Most people in our circle.

    (A) find it comprehendible
    (B) find it uncomprehendable
    (C) comprehensible
    (D) find it incomprehensible
    (E) find it incredulous

69. Not only did he appreciate her personal generosity and her concern for his theater, but he also sensed in her a potential for greatness.

    Eliminate the not only . . . but also construction.

    (A) and he
    (B) but he
    (C) theater he
    (D) if
    (E) when

GO ON TO THE NEXT PAGE

70. That the chairman disliked the committee was not immediately apparent but dawned on us slowly as his expression grew more dour every day.

Start with His expression.

(A) apparent, and
(B) apparent, but
(C) apparent, the
(D) apparent: the
(E) apparent because

71. Some people inhabit industrial areas where the water and air are not healthy; they must demand more protection from the industries and the government.

Start with Demanding.

(A) right of people
(B) salvation of people
(C) way for people
(D) need of people
(E) obligation of people

72. John learned less Greek from Professor Whitman than he did from his tutor, who had just finished his dissertation.

Start with John's tutor.

(A) than did
(B) and less from
(C) compared to
(D) less than
(E) and the

73. According to Ernest Jones, Hamlet hesitates in his pursuit of Claudius because he associates himself subconsciously with Claudius's actions.

Start with Hamlet's subconscious association.

(A) is Ernest Jones's idea why
(B) are Ernest Jones's explanations for
(C) is Ernest Jones's theory as to why
(D) is Ernest Jones's explanation for
(E) is Ernest Jones's description of

74. Given the limited musicianship and the bad taste of many new rock groups, music lovers have begun to listen to the Beatles again.

Start with The limited musicianship.

(A) has forced music
(B) have innovated music
(C) have made the Beatles
(D) has stampeded music
(E) has turned music lovers back

Directions: Each of the following passages consists of numbered sentences. Because the passages are part of longer writing samples, they do not necessarily constitute a complete discussion of the issues presented.

Read each passage carefully and answer the questions that follow it. The questions test your awareness of a writer's purpose and of characteristics of prose that are important to good writing.

Questions 75–83 refer to the following paragraphs.

(1) *For the past few centuries women's employment outside of the home has said to be responsible for the breakdown of society and the central family structure.* (2) *Before considering any such ramifications, one must reflect upon the history of women's employment.* (3) *During the nineteenth century, the outside system replicated the gender divisions of the household in the new setting of metropolitan industry.* (4) *There had always been a clear division of labor based primarily on outwork; trades like clothing that relied on put-out work became women's trades, while those that did not—mostly remained closed to women.* (5) *The consequence was a segmentation of industry that limited women in the cities to a few trades.* (6) *By 1860, three or four dozen industries employed more than 90 percent of the city's workwomen.*

(7) *To understand the importance of women to "metropolitan industrialization" as Sean Wilentz has termed it, we must first rethink older conceptions of the role of outwork (now referred to as piecework).* (8) *Historians and economists have always viewed this kind of labor as a transition, a precursor to the average industrial form of the factory.* (9) *Dispersing a workforce and having general piecework accountability during the Victorian age often proved wasteful as soon as a centralized factory system was developed.* (10) *Sweatshops that worked under one roof and were well supervised generated greater production than the individual in the home.* (11) *In New York City, for example, material conditions did not favor the rise of factories, but other conditions proved propitious.* (12) *Of great advantage to employers was the city's proximity to the port and an enormous pool of cheap labor.* (13) *By expanding their markets and tapping this labor pool, employers transformed the home-based craft system.* (14) *Employers could expand their production outside their shop walls until the centralized factory model took hold.*

75. Which of the following most accurately describes what happens in paragraph 2?

(A) The writer explains the rise of factories from outwork and cheap labor.

(B) The writer attempts to explain the causes for the rise in piecework.

(C) The writer gives examples of the various conditions that created outwork.

(D) The writer addresses the problems of dispersing a workforce.

(E) The writer tries to describe how historians and economists viewed women's labor.

76. The purpose of paragraph 1 is primarily to

(A) describe the earlier developments in gender divisions

(B) explain the specific examples of women-based work

(C) exemplify the types of roles women assumed

(D) discuss the trades available to men and women

(E) link the gender roles in the home to women's trade labor roles

77. Which of the following words best describes the speaker's approach to the subject?

(A) Logical and methodical

(B) Orderly and unvarying

(C) Logical and orderly

(D) Sequential and informal

(E) Sensible and uncomplicated

78. The speaker ordered the presentation of the material to provide the reader with

(A) a logical understanding of the development of gender-based trades

(B) background for the development of the factory or sweatshop

(C) an explanation of outwork.

(D) historical background of outwork in New York City

(E) a knowledge of the demands placed on the working women of the nineteenth century

79. Which of the following best describes the relationship of sentence 2 to the two paragraphs?

(A) It establishes the basis for later comparisons between paragraphs 1 and 2.

(B) It indicates the author's authority on the subject.

(C) It presents the central focus for the next two paragraphs that will be refuted later.

(D) It establishes the organization for paragraph 1 and introduces paragraph 2.

(E) It introduces the central idea that will be elaborated and used as a reference later.

80. In sentence 7, the effect of using the expression *To understand the importance* is to

(A) stress an evident solution to the problem presented, which could then be contradicted

(B) prepare the reader for the following statement

(C) to indicate an aforementioned conclusion

(D) reveal the writer's certainty about the details of the sequence of events

(E) prepare the reader with logical reasoning and support

81. Which of the following best describes the relationship between the two paragraphs in this passage?

(A) Paragraph 2 answers the assumption in paragraph 1.

(B) Paragraph 2 clarifies the problems stated at the end of paragraph 1.

(C) Paragraph 2 offers concrete illustrations of the information in paragraph 1.

(D) Paragraph 2 clarifies specifically the developments from paragraph 1.

(E) Paragraph 2 generalizes the problems presented in paragraph 1.

82. The function of sentence 3 is primarily to

(A) provide a bridge from the household to the labor force

(B) give an example of the ramifications stated in sentence 2

(C) indicate a change in the paragraph to detailed description

(D) illustrate the setting of the metropolitan industry

(E) prepare for the mentioning of outwork in sentence 4

83. Which of the following best describes the function of sentence 11?

(A) It indicates an insufficient solution based on an aforementioned need.

(B) It demonstrates an example of how women were moved from outwork to factories.

(C) It alludes to the possibility of another reason factories developed.

(D) It forces the reader to acknowledge the problem presented.

(E) It gives an example of another reason factories increased.

GO ON TO THE NEXT PAGE

Questions 84–92 refer to the following paragraph.

(1) *With a faint rending noise, the tires came loose from the frozen earth of the barn ramp. (2) The resistance of the car's weight diminished; sluggishly it began gliding downhill. (3) We both hopped in, the doors slammed, and slowly the car picked up speed, rolling, dipping, and rumbling over the gravel. (4) The stones crackled like slowly crumbling ice under our tires. (5) With a dignified yet determined acceleration, the car lurched forward down the incline of the hill. (6) My father let in the clutch, the motor jerked, and suddenly we were aloft. (7) We floated seemingly across the meadow: a brown-and-white carpet at the base of the hill. (8) The fallow, flat fields loomed ahead, and off in the distance the silhouette of the town rose in the crisp air. (9) I fervently prayed that the entire town would rise up like the dead and rush forward, no longer to laugh at my father's folly, but to cheer his triumphant descent. (10) Soon we bumped and shuffled onto our road, so little traveled that in the center remained weeds long dead and partially covered with snow. (11) If we stalled now, we would be out of luck, for we were on level land and no amount of coasting could reinvent the acceleration of the land behind us. (12) My father pushed the choke in halfway and muttered a mild prayer. (13) Through the clear margins of the sheet frost on the front window, I could see forward as we approached the end of our land. (14) To the right, a battered red mailbox saluted our attempts at freedom, while behind us, the road weeds bent in humble dismay at our passing.*

84. The main implication of this passage is that

   (A) the car was difficult yet exciting to start
   (B) the town didn't approve of the car
   (C) the weather caused difficulties when starting the car
   (D) the owners lived on a farm
   (E) the hill was required to start the car

85. The purpose of the passage is primarily to

   (A) describe the countryside and her father's farm
   (B) explain the steps involved in starting the car
   (C) narrate the adventures in her father's car
   (D) discuss the movements the car made
   (E) describe the process of starting her father's car

86. Which of the following words best describes the speaker's style?

   (A) Whimsical and melancholy
   (B) Interested and excited
   (C) Amused and exasperated
   (D) Frustrated and studious
   (E) Aloof and sarcastic

87. The writer ordered the presentation of the material to provide the reader with

   (A) a logical understanding of how to start the car
   (B) a background of the car's functions
   (C) an explanation of a typical day trip in the car.
   (D) an understanding of the excitement and difficulty of starting the car
   (E) a knowledge of the various steps required to start a car

88. Which of the following best describes the relationship of sentence 1 to the paragraph?

   (A) It establishes the organization of the paragraph as a whole.
   (B) It contrasts the motionlessness of the car with the later movement.
   (C) It demonstrates the first steps toward the ultimate goal.
   (D) It opens the paragraph and begins the movement.
   (E) It sets up the environment and seasonal aspects of the paragraph.

89. In sentence 9, the effect of using the expression *I fervently prayed* is to

   (A) create an understanding of the next sentence
   (B) indicate the hopes of the speaker
   (C) sarcastically respond to prior criticism
   (D) show the fear of the speaker
   (E) attest to the religious leanings of the author

90. Which of the following best describes the relationship of sentence 11 to the rest of the passage?

   (A) It presents the crucial moment or the culmination.
   (B) It establishes the tension and explains the outcome.
   (C) It presents the excitement of the final accomplishment.
   (D) It establishes the organization for the rest of the passage.
   (E) It refutes the idea that the car will continue to run.

91. The function of sentence 14 is primarily to

   (A) indicate the surrounding environment
   (B) give the reader an appreciation of the area
   (C) indicate the success of starting the car
   (D) illustrate the acceptance by inanimate objects
   (E) prepare the reader for the next paragraph

92. What is the author trying to imply by her wording in sentence 9?

(A) The characters lived near a ghost town.
(B) The car was considered inoperable by the townsfolk.
(C) The town was very close to the farm.
(D) The car was considered an extravagance.
(E) The townspeople would now see the usefulness of the car.

Directions: The following sentences test your knowledge of grammar, diction (choice of words), and idiom. Some sentences are correct. No sentence contains more than one error.

You will find that the error, if there is one, is underlined and lettered. Assume that elements of the sentence that are not underlined are correct and cannot be changed. In choosing answers, follow the requirements of standard written English.

If there is an error, select the one underlined part that must be changed to make the sentence correct and fill in the corresponding oval on your answer sheet. If there is no error, select answer (E).

93. The Board of Aldermen choose a president
A
after all the other officers of the town have been
B   C   D
chosen. No error.
E

94. After her long and serious illness, the woman
A
was grateful for any hour when she felt at all
B   C
good. No error.
D   E

95. It says in this morning's newspaper that much
A   B
wheat has been grown on the plains in the
C
Middle West in spite of severe windstorms.
D
No error.
E

96. The judges wanted to see only witnesses whom
A   B   C
they knew were honest. No error.
D   E

97. It was she who determined the policy of the
A   B
board of directors, not them, the members who
C
were selected by popular vote. No error.
D   E

98. The atmosphere in his classroom is different than
A   B   C
that in his home. No error.
D   E

99. Several times, the women have risen desperate
A
and given their assistance, without, however, any
B   C
resulting effect upon the males in the audience.
D
No error.
E

100. His abhorrence to violence was widely
A   B
recognized among his peers. No error.
C   D   E

STOP If you finish before the time is up, you may check your work on this section only. Do not turn to any other section in the test.

POSTTEST ANSWER KEY AND EXPLANATIONS

PART I

1. B	12. A	23. A	34. A	45. A
2. B	13. E	24. C	35. D	46. E
3. E	14. D	25. E	36. A	47. D
4. E	15. D	26. A	37. E	48. D
5. B	16. D	27. B	38. B	49. C
6. C	17. D	28. E	39. B	50. C
7. C	18. B	29. D	40. A	51. C
8. B	19. E	30. B	41. E	52. E
9. A	20. E	31. D	42. D	53. C
10. C	21. C	32. E	43. B	54. C
11. A	22. D	33. B	44. D	55. D

PART II: ENGLISH COMPOSITION WITHOUT ESSAY TEST

56. B	65. A	74. C	83. E	92. B
57. C	66. D	75. A	84. A	93. A
58. D	67. D	76. E	85. E	94. D
59. B	68. D	77. C	86. B	95. A
60. A	69. A	78. B	87. D	96. C
61. A	70. D	79. E	88. D	97. C
62. E	71. E	80. E	89. B	98. C
63. D	72. A	81. D	90. A	99. A
64. B	73. D	82. A	91. C	100. A

PART I

1. **The correct answer is (B).** This is a run-on sentence. To correct it, we can write *things; one* or *things. One.*

2. **The correct answer is (B).** *Bring* means "to carry toward the person who is speaking." *Take* would be the correct word.

3. **The correct answer is (E).**

4. **The correct answer is (E).**

5. **The correct answer is (B).** *Continuously* means "without pause." *Continually* would be correct. It means "at recurrent intervals."

6. **The correct answer is (C).** The pronoun *who* is correct, since a nominative pronoun is needed as the subject for the verb *had hurt.*

7. **The correct answer is (C).** The correct form is *as good as.*

8. **The correct answer is (B).** The gerund *going* is incorrect; *go* is the correct verb form.

9. **The correct answer is (A).** The gerund *telling* used as a noun takes a possessive pronoun. *Your* is correct.

10. **The correct answer is (C).** This sentence has a compound subject (*sheet* and *sheet*), which takes a plural verb. *Are* is correct.

11. **The correct answer is (A).** *Like* is a preposition and should be used here.

12. **The correct answer is (A).** *In regards to* is the incorrect form for *in regard to.*

13. **The correct answer is (E).** Although the subject *half* seems to be singular, *half* is one of a few words whose number is determined by the prepositional phrase that follows. *Roadways* is plural.

14. **The correct answer is (D).** The subject of the sentence is singular—*automobile.* The verb must be singular—*was.*

15. **The correct answer is (D).** The number of the pronoun *who* in a relative clause is determined by the number of the antecedent, *persons,* which is plural. Therefore, the verb should be *are.*

16. The correct answer is (D). This avoids the awkwardness in gerunds, pronouns, and passive voice that the other answer choices exhibit.

17. The correct answer is (D). This introduces an absolute phrase that is correct. Choice (A) is a dangling modifier because it cannot logically modify anything. Choice (B) is a comma splice, a serious error in which a comma is used to join two independent clauses. *Although* in choice (C) has the wrong sense. Choice (E) distorts the original.

18. The correct answer is (B). This alone preserves the meaning and the complete construction.

19. The correct answer is (E). This is the right tense and choice of verb.

20. The correct answer is (E). Note the dangling participle in choice (C). The others are meaningless.

21. The correct answer is (C). This avoids the ambiguity of the other sentences.

22. The correct answer is (D). This is clear. Choice (A) has a dangling participle. Choice (B) would create a fused or run-on sentence. Choices (C) and (E) have ambiguous pronouns.

23. The correct answer is (A). This arranges the groups of phrases and clauses correctly. Choice (B) is a sentence fragment because it lacks a complete predicate. Choices (C), (D), and (E) include problems with correct placement of phrases and clauses.

24. The correct answer is (C). The other choices have trouble with the tense or form of the verb.

25. The correct answer is (E). The others misuse the verb and *basically*.

26. The correct answer is (A). It provides the smoothest transition between the two clauses of the new sentence.

27. The correct answer is (B). The other answers do not provide relevant or necessary information.

28. The correct answer is (E). The other choices mean the same thing, but they are too formal for the context.

29. The correct answer is (D). *This* in choices (A) and (B) is ambiguous, as is *that* in choice (E). Choice (C) incorrectly uses the singular possessive form of student.

30. The correct answer is (B). The pronoun refers to the posters, so it must be plural. *Has* or *have*, as in choices (C) and (D), is a vague verb in context. Choice (E) has an agreement error because *they* is plural, while *does* is singular.

31. The correct answer is (D). The other answers are less precise. Choice (A) focuses solely on welfare. Choice (B) changes the meaning of the original. Choice (C) presents a misspelling in *effect*, which is usually a noun. Choice (E) changes the meaning of the sentence.

32. The correct answer is (E). *Only* modifies *one week*, so it should appear directly before that phrase.

33. The correct answer is (B). Choice (A) misuses *cohere* and choices (C), (D), and (E) are wordy.

34. The correct answer is (A). Choices (B), (C), and (E) are poor choices because they state an effect is certain, when it is only a possibility. Choice (D) is wordy and contains a cliché.

35. The correct answer is (D). It is correct because it combines all the components of both sentences. Choice (A) is incorrect because it deletes the wall of rock. Choice (B) is incorrect because now the color is absent. Choice (C) is incorrect because the writer intended the walls of the monastery to be white above a rock face—the rock face is not white itself. Choice (E) is incorrect because *there* means nothing. Where is "there"?

36. The correct answer is (A). It introduces the last sentence, which is based on the word "still"—matched by serene and harmony. Choice (B) is incorrect because this is outside information that does not fit the description. Choice (C) is wrong because it does not connect with the stillness of the next sentence. Choice (D) is not good because it repeats the word *monastery*. Choice (E) is not good because it simply restates sentence 13.

37. The correct answer is (E). It is the best answer because it combines all the elements. Choice (A) is incorrect because it changes the time frame and uses too many pronouns. Choice (B) is not good because it is awkward with the word *that*. Choice (C) is incorrect because the first part of the statement is inaccurate. Choice (D) is not the best answer because it changes the word *structure* for *building*, and the writer was referring to the actual building composition. What is *real*?

38. The correct answer is (B). It doesn't change the context and it clarifies the *other parts*. Choice (A) is incorrect because the reader is left asking what the other parts are covered with. Choice (C) is incorrect because what is *etc.*? Choice (D) is too verbose, and choice (E), once again, doesn't indicate what the rest of the land is supposed to be.

39. The correct answer is (B). This is a requirement of expository writing. This is a descriptive piece, of which choices (A), (C), (D), and (E) are components.

40. The correct answer is (A). It is a synonym for *different than* and sounds less awkward. Choice (B) is incorrect because it changes time (using the present progressive form). Choice (C) is incorrect because the author is contrasting the objects involved, not comparing them. Choice (D) would not work because the reader needs to know that a contrast is being made. Choice (E) is awkward and not specific.

41. The correct answer is (E). It is correct since these sentences deal with the initial visual description of the monastery. Choices (A) and (B) are not complete. Choice (C) is a possibility, but not the central problem. Choice (D) is incorrect because the writer doesn't use many descriptive adjectives and details in these two sentences.

42. **The correct answer is (D).** It gives the most vivid picture. Starkness indicates a juxtaposition of color. Since the prior sentence deals with colors, sentence 10 must connect with color. Choice (A) provides too general a basis for contrast. Choice (B) is incorrect since *town* was the word used originally, not *village*. Choice (C) is incorrect since *stark* does not indicate *pretty*. *Pretty* also is not a clear adjective. Choice (E) is incorrect as it repeats the word *structure* from sentence 11, and the writer doesn't mention any other structures except the houses.

43. **The correct answer is (B).** It would be more accurate and clear. Choice (A) is too vague. Choice (C) is incorrect because the demonstrative adjective indicates prior knowledge. Choice (D) is incorrect because some object is required for the verb. Choice (E) is incorrect because it narrows the subject too quickly. The writer begins with the town and then narrows to the monastery.

44. **The correct answer is (D).** *Both . . . and* keeps the emphasis of *as much as*.

45. **The correct answer is (A).** This choice practices subordination correctly and avoids wordiness and ambiguity.

46. **The correct answer is (E).** This choice keeps it simple and parallel.

47. **The correct answer is (D).** The first three choices contain dangling participles. None of these participles modifies the subject *speech*. Choice (E) changes the meaning.

48. **The correct answer is (D).** This keeps the emphasis correct and the diction smooth.

49. **The correct answer is (C).** This keeps a sensible parallelism within the series; the others do not.

50. **The correct answer is (C).** The force of the semicolon here is *and*.

51. **The correct answer is (C).** This has the correct punctuation for plural of *Jones* and singular possessive for *Jane*.

52. **The correct answer is (E).** This avoids the ambiguity or unidiomatic expressions of the others. Choice (A) offers an incomplete ambiguous comparison: *better than predecessors liked* or *likes his position better than he likes his predecessors?* Choice (B) has *them* as the subject of an elliptical clause: *than they have adjusted.* Choice (C) misuses *into,* and choice (D) is awkward.

53. **The correct answer is (C).** The others are either unidiomatic or examples of jargon. Only choice (C) concisely and accurately revises the original. Choice (A) is wordy. Choice (B) is awkward. Choices (D) and (E) are also wordy.

54. **The correct answer is (C).** The preposition *to* requires *attributed*. The other verb choices change the meaning of the sentence.

55. **The correct answer is (D).** This is idiomatic and keeps parallel structure. It avoids the wordiness of the other answer choices.

PART II: ENGLISH COMPOSITION WITHOUT ESSAY TEST

56. **The correct answer is (B).** Choice (A) is untrue because he took over the party after being released. Choice (C) is not good because the writer is now just joining the two sentences and not improving them. Choice (D) is false because the word *while* is used incorrectly. *While* indicates a period of time, and being released from prison is a singular event. Choice (E) is not a good choice because now the date is missing, and there is a supposition that the leadership control happened soon after.

57. **The correct answer is (C).** In sentence 9, the author is concluding the historical documentation for his thesis statement. Suddenly, with sentence 10, he appears to change the subject. A bridge is needed here. Choice (A) is false because of the repetitive use of *his* and *him*. Choice (B) is off the subject and doesn't link to the next sentence. Choice (D) links to sentence 10 but doesn't follow sentence 9 any better. Choice (E) is perhaps untrue—we have no proof or knowledge that this statement is fact.

58. **The correct answer is (D).** Choice (A) is incorrect since the word *he* is overused. Choice (B) is not good since it really doesn't create sentence variation. Choice (C) is false since it omits the information about leading a group. Choice (E) is not good because it indicates that his witnessing occurred only when he led the group in prison.

59. **The correct answer is (B).** Choice (A) is incorrect since the use of the word *he* is redundant. Choice (C) is false since the use of *like himself* indicates perhaps the subject is not the same. Choices (D) and (E) are incorrect—each gives the reader the impression of judgment, which may not be accurate.

60. **The correct answer is (A).** This is an expository essay of opinion and therefore requires choices (B), (C), (D), and (E). Choice (A) is not absolutely necessary and not found extensively throughout.

61. **The correct answer is (A).** Choice (B) is repetitive with the word *that*. Choice (C) is false since the assumption that the entire world believes this is a generalization is too broad. Choice (D) is acceptable, but very simplistic. Choice (E) is wrong since the word *it* is too general.

62. **The correct answer is (E).** Choice (A) is false since the order is disrupted more by sentence 4 than sentence 3. Choice (B) is false because both sentences do not need to be moved. Choice (C) is incorrect because these are two opposite points that should not be combined. Choice (D) is false because the problem is sequencing, not sentence structure or use of adjectives.

63. **The correct answer is (D).** There is an assumption by the writer that the reader knows what this word means. Choice (A) is false. It would be interesting to add a sentence about this after sentence 4 but within the sentence would make it awkward and too long. Choice (B) is incorrect since this statement is factual information, not opinion. Choices (C) and (E) are false because the answers are too vague.

64. The correct answer is (B). Choice (A) is not a good way to begin and sounds very awkward. Choice (C) is awkward with the use of *many reasons* followed with the singular *such as*. Choice (D) would work, but then there would be the constant repetition of the use of the word *he*. Choice (E) is not good because it too is awkward and repeats the word *that*.

65. The correct answer is (A). The poet realized that the bell, *which was tolling* for the burial of the stranger, also tolled for himself and for all humankind. This choice maintains tense consistency. Choices (B) and (C) shift tenses. Choice (D) is nonsensical. Choice (E) would set up repetition of *tolling*.

66. The correct answer is (D). By driving slowly around the approach *roads, the opponents* succeeded in shutting down the new airport. This answer sets up a logical sequence of events.

67. The correct answer is (D). Some teachers give erratic grades and do not hold office *hours because they* do not care about their students. No comma is required before this adverb clause.

68. The correct answer is (D). Most people in our circle *find it incomprehensible* that George could break his engagement with the charming Ms. Banister. *Incomprehensible* is the correct word choice to maintain the meaning of the sentence.

69. The correct answer is (A). He appreciated her generosity and her concern for his theater, *and he* sensed in her a potential for greatness. Choice (B) sets up an incorrect contrast. Choice (C) will set up a fused or run-on sentence. Choices (D) and (E) change the basic premise.

70. The correct answer is (D). His expression, growing more dour by the day, indicated something to us that had not been immediately *apparent: the* chairman disliked the committee. Choices (A), (B), and (E) offer illogical relationships. Choice (C) includes a comma splice, which occurs when you try to link independent clauses with a comma. Choice (D) presents an independent clause after a colon to explain the first clause.

71. The correct answer is (E). Demanding more protection from industry and government is the obligation of people who live near polluted industrial areas. *Obligation* is the best choice to correspond to *must demand*.

72. The correct answer is (A). John's tutor, who had just finished his dissertation, taught him more Greek *than did* the professor. This answer is the only one that conveys the correct comparison.

73. The correct answer is (D). Hamlet's subconscious association with Claudius's actions *is Ernest Jones's explanation for* Hamlet's hesitation in pursuit of Claudius. Choices (A) and (C) imply that Jones has insufficient evidence. Choice (B) sets up a subject-verb agreement problem. Choice (E) is off-topic.

74. The correct answer is (C). The limited musicianship and the bad taste of many new rock groups *have made the Beatles* popular again. Choices (A), (D), and (E) have singular verbs; a plural verb is needed. Choice (B) changes the meaning of the sentence.

75. The correct answer is (A). Choice (B) is false since it does not concern itself with the rise of piecework, but the factories. Choice (C) is inaccurate and does not address the material covered in paragraph 2. The conditions didn't create the "outwork"; they created factories. Choice (D) is too specific. Choice (E) is an incorrect restatement of sentence 8.

76. The correct answer is (E). Choice (A) is too general, and paragraph 1 does not speak generally of all the possible roles. Choice (B) is incorrect because there are not any specific examples. Choice (C) is false; once again, no examples are offered. Choice (D) is incorrect because men are not even mentioned specifically, only implied.

77. The correct answer is (C). It is correct because the author begins with the division of labor in the home and proceeds to apply that to trades. In paragraph 2, he speaks of outwork and cheap labor as its correlation to the growth of factories. Choice (A) is incorrect because the sentence structure varies—this follows for choice (B) as well. Choice (D) is incorrect because the writing is not informal in nature. Choice (E) is incorrect because the adjectives describe a more descriptive/narrative writing form—not an expository one.

78. The correct answer is (B). Choice (A) is incorrect because the essay does not discuss only gender-based trades (drawing a comparison between women's and men's jobs). Choice (C) is incorrect because the explanation is handled in parentheses. Choice (D) is false because it is too specific. Choice (E) is wrong because there is no discussion on the demands of the workwomen.

79. The correct answer is (E). This choice is correct because these two paragraphs seem to be part of a larger text that will discuss the supposition stated in sentence 1. Choice (A) is false because paragraph 1 gives information and background that is continued in paragraph 2. Choice (B) is false because it does not indicate in any way the author's authority. Choice (C) is incorrect because the central idea is clarified, not refuted. Choice (D) is incorrect because the sentence applies to both the paragraphs as they both pertain to historical information.

80. The correct answer is (E). The author wishes for the reader to understand a future thesis, so he is stating that he is going to provide the prerequisite information. Choice (A) is incorrect because he will not be presenting a solution. Choice (B) is false because the writer wishes to prepare the reader, but not just for the next sentence. Choice (C) is incorrect because the conclusion was not mentioned before. Choice (D) is incorrect because the purpose of the writing is not to reinforce but to provide knowledge.

81. **The correct answer is (D).** Choice (A) is incorrect because there was no assumption. Choice (B) is wrong because, though the last sentence implied a problem, it did not specifically state the problems. Choice (C) is incorrect because the information in paragraph 2 is not a series of illustrations based on paragraph 1. Choice (E) is false because paragraph 2 does not generalize but gives a clarification.

82. **The correct answer is (A).** Choice (B) is incorrect because sentence 3 does not give an example. Choice (C) is incorrect because sentence 3 introduces the historical background; it does not indicate a change. Choice (D) is false because this describes part of the sentence but not its function. Choice (E) is partially true in the sense that the author is preparing the reader to understand outwork's place in the employment of women; however, it is not the entire function of the sentence.

83. **The correct answer is (E).** Choice (A) is nonsensical and doesn't speak to the issue of an example. Choice (B) is incorrect because the example used concerns itself with cheap labor not outwork. Choice (C) is wrong because there is no alluding. Choice (D) is false because there is no forcing the reader; the author is giving an example of a different situation.

84. **The correct answer is (A).** Choices (B), (C), and (D) are false because these are specific details, not the main idea. Choice (E) is also a detail.

85. **The correct answer is (E).** This is a descriptive, narrative essay. Choice (A) is incorrect because it is too specific. Choices (B) and (D) are incorrect because they would deal with an expository theme. Choice (C) is false because the narrative is not about the adventures in the car.

86. **The correct answer is (B).** The author is looking ahead out the window, and she is noting all the various things that are happening. Choice (A) is incorrect because there is no sadness attached to this writing. Choices (C) and (D) are false because, though the author may be amused and interested, she does not sound frustrated. Choice (E) is wrong because the author wishes for the reader to be as engaged as she is.

87. **The correct answer is (D).** Choices (A) and (E) are from a process essay, and the speaker did not order the information so that it could be recreated. Choice (B) is false because the speaker was not interested in providing historical information. Choice (C) is untrue because this paragraph does not describe an entire day trip.

88. **The correct answer is (D).** Choice (A) is untrue because this is a narrative that doesn't follow a specific organizational style. Choice (B) is false because the sentence does not set up a contrast—it introduces. Choice (C) is incorrect because it shows the first steps, but this is not a process essay in which there is a demonstration. Choice (E) is too specific because it concentrates on the weather only.

89. **The correct answer is (B).** Choice (A) is false because the words have no correlation to the next sentence. Choice (C) is wrong because there is no sarcasm. Choice (D) is incorrect because the speaker is not afraid, but hoping the town will see. Choice (E) is incorrect because the references are not specifically centered on the religion of the author.

90. **The correct answer is (A).** The writer will now continue the trip if the car runs. Choice (B) is the wrong answer. Though there is tension, sentence 11 doesn't state the outcome. Choice (C) is incorrect because the writer doesn't lead the reader to a final accomplishment yet. Choice (D) is wrong because, in a narrative essay, the organization depends on the story line, and this passage is not completely based on this sentence. Choice (E) is false because there is no refuting.

91. **The correct answer is (C).** Choice (A) is false because that isn't the purpose of the sentence. Choice (B) may give the reader an appreciation, but, again, that is not the function. Choice (D) is an aspect of the sentence but not its complete purpose. Choice (E) is partially true but unknown and unclear to the reader.

92. **The correct answer is (B).** The fact that the writer speaks of pushing it down a hill and starting it indicates that the car was considered inoperable. Choice (A) is an incorrect application of the metaphor. Choice (C) is incorrect because this aspect deals with a detail that does not apply to the sentence. Choice (D) is false because it does not state who viewed it as an extravagance, the owner or the town. Choice (E) is wrong because that is what the author actually hoped for.

93. **The correct answer is (A).** This choice is the correct answer because *Board* is the singular subject. *Chooses* would be the singular verb.

94. **The correct answer is (D).** Felt is a linking verb. Here, *well* pertains to a state of good health.

95. **The correct answer is (A).** *It* is an unjustified indefinite pronoun. The sentence should read, *This morning's newspaper says.*

96. **The correct answer is (C).** The relative pronoun *whom* is the subject of a clause, "whom were honest." The answer should be in the nominative case—*who.*

97. **The correct answer is (C).** If the predicate compliment of the linking verb is a pronoun, it must be in the nominative case—*they.* The construction of the sentence actually is *It was she, not they who determined. . . . They* is a negative opposite for *she,* a predicate nominative.

98. **The correct answer is (C).** The expression is *different from. Different than* is often misused.

99. **The correct answer is (A).** An adverb, *desperately,* is needed to modify *have risen.*

100. **The correct answer is (A).** The idiomatic expression is *abhorrence of.*

Part III

COLLEGE MATHEMATICS

Chapter 5
PRETEST

PART I

Directions: Answer the following questions. Do not spend too much time on any one question.

Note:
1. Unless otherwise specified, the domain of any function f is assumed to be the set of all real numbers x for which $f(x)$ is a real number.
2. i will be used to denote $\sqrt{-1}$.
3. Figures that accompany the following problems are intended to provide information useful in solving the problems. They are drawn as accurately as possible EXCEPT when it is stated in a specific problem that its figure is not drawn to scale. All figures lie in a plane unless otherwise indicated.

1. If A and B are disjoint sets, and A contains 5 elements, while B contains 7, how many elements are in the union of A and B?

   (A) 2
   (B) 12
   (C) 35
   (D) The answer cannot be determined from the information given.

2. If A is the set of values of x at which $f(x) = 0$, and B is the set of values of x at which $g(x) = 0$, what can you say about the set of values of x at which $f(x)g(x) = 0$?

   (A) It is the intersection of A and B.
   (B) It is the union of A and B.
   (C) It is a proper subset of the union of A and B.
   (D) It is the Cartesian product of A and B.

3. If A = {1, 2, 3} and B = {3, 4, 5}, how many elements are in the intersection of A and B?

   (A) 0
   (B) 1
   (C) 3
   (D) 5

4. There are 93 students in a class; 42 like math, while 41 like English. If 30 students don't like either subject, how many students like both?

   (A) 10
   (B) 20
   (C) 41
   (D) The answer cannot be determined from the data given.

5. What is the complement of the union of A and B?

   (A) The intersection of the complements of A and B
   (B) The union of the complements of A and B
   (C) The complement of the intersection of A and B
   (D) The complement of the Cartesian product of A and B

6. There are 25 members of the student council. Twelve of them are boys, 8 are seniors, and 10 are honors students. Exactly 3 of the girls are not honors students, and 6 of the seniors are not honors students. How many senior girls are honors students?

   (A) 0
   (B) 1
   (C) 2
   (D) 3

GO ON TO THE NEXT PAGE

7. Which of the following is the logical equivalent of "If Sally loves me, she will marry me"?

    (A) "If Sally marries me, she loves me."
    (B) "If Sally does not love me, she won't marry me."
    (C) "If Sally loves me, she won't marry Bill."
    (D) "If Sally doesn't marry me, she doesn't love me."

8. Here is a "Truth Table":

p	q	r
T	T	T
T	F	F
F	T	T
F	F	T

    According to this truth table, which of the following statements describes *r*?

    (A) *p* and *q*
    (B) *p* implies *q*
    (C) *p* or *q*
    (D) *p* or not *q*

9. Which of the following is a counter-example to the assertion "All primes are odd numbers"?

    (A) 2
    (B) 5
    (C) 9
    (D) the Mersenne primes

10. Which of the following is the converse to "All men are liars"?

    (A) "Women never lie."
    (B) "No men tell the truth."
    (C) "Someone who doesn't lie is not a man."
    (D) "All liars are men."

11. Consider the following two statements. A: "X and Y are both even numbers." B: "X + Y is an even number." What can be said about statements A and B?

    (A) A is a necessary and sufficient condition for B.
    (B) A is necessary but not a sufficient condition for B.
    (C) A is not necessary but is a sufficient condition for B.
    (D) A is neither necessary nor sufficient for B.

12. Given that not (A and B) implies C, what does (not C) imply?

    (A) A and B
    (B) (not A) or (not B)
    (C) (not A and B) or (A and not B)
    (D) A or B

13. Which of the following illustrates the transitive property of implication?

    (A) (A implies B) and (B implies A) means that A and B are logically equivalent.
    (B) Not A or B is the same as A implies B.
    (C) (A implies B) and (B implies C) implies (A implies C).
    (D) The transitive property does not apply to implication.

14. What are the prime factors of 18?

    (A) 1, 2, 3, 6, 9, and 18
    (B) 1, 2, 3, 6, and 9
    (C) 2, 3, 6, and 9
    (D) 2 and 3

15. Which of the following numbers is a composite?

    (A) 7
    (B) 31
    (C) 103
    (D) None of the above

16. Each of the following numbers is written in binary notation. Which of them is a prime?

    (A) 111111
    (B) 1101011010
    (C) 11101
    (D) None of the above

17. What is the greatest real number less than 10?

    (A) There is no greatest real number less than 10.
    (B) 9
    (C) 9.999....
    (D) 10 minus epsilon

18. If $a < b$, which of the following statements is always true?

    (A) $|a| < |b|$ if $a > 0$
    (B) $|a| < |b|$
    (C) $a^2 < b^2$
    (D) None of the above

19. Which of the following is an irrational number?

    (A) 67
    (B) The least root of $x^2 + 3x - 7 = 0$
    (C) $-\dfrac{3}{2}$
    (D) $\dfrac{22}{7}$

20. A number is said to be "perfect" if it is the sum of its proper factors. Which of the following numbers is perfect?

(A) 6
(B) 28
(C) Both 6 and 28
(D) None of the above

21. If A = {$x: x < 2$} and B = {$x: x > -2$}, which of the following expressions describes the intersection of A and B?

(A) $|x| < 2$
(B) {$x: x < 2$ or $x > -2$}
(C) The complement of the intersection of the complements of A and B
(D) The null set

22. If a number is expressed in binary, which of the following is a necessary and sufficient condition to test whether it is divisible by 3?

(A) If the number does not end in 0
(B) If the alternating sum of the digits is 0 or divisible by 3
(C) If the number includes an even number of 1s and an even number of 0s
(D) If the number, when rewritten in decimal form, has the sum of its digits divisible by 3

23. If A and B are both odd numbers, what can be said about $A^2 + 4AB + B^2$?

(A) It is always odd.
(B) It is sometimes odd and sometimes even.
(C) It is always even.
(D) It is divisible by 4.

24. Let A be a non-empty set of rational numbers such that all elements of A are negative. Which of the following is always true?

(A) There is a unique real number that is greater than or equal to every element of A and less than any other real number that is greater than or equal to every element of A.
(B) There is an element of A that is greater than every other element of A.
(C) There is a one-to-one correspondence between the elements of A and those rational numbers that are greater than every element of A.
(D) There is a (possibly very small) positive number x such that, for any rational number a greater than 0, $a - x$ is greater than every element of A.

25. Which of the following sets includes all the others?

(A) Integers
(B) Rational numbers
(C) Irrational numbers
(D) Real numbers

26. Which of the following numbers is irrational?

(A) The roots of $x^2 + 30x + 221 = 0$

(B) $\dfrac{\sqrt{2}}{1 - \sqrt{2}} + \sqrt{2}$

(C) $-\sqrt{81}$

(D) The roots of $x^2 - 4x + 6 = 0$

27. If $y = x^2$ has the set of all real numbers as its domain, what is its range?

(A) {$y: y \geq 0$}
(B) The set of all real numbers
(C) {$y: y > 0$}
(D) The set of perfect squares

28. Consider the system

$ax + by = c$

$dx + ey = f$

where the constants a, b, c, d, e, and f are all different. How many pairs of values of x and y can satisfy the system?

(A) 0
(B) 1
(C) 0 or 1
(D) 0, 1, or an infinite number

29. Given an equation $ax^2 + bx + c = 0$, with $b^2 = 4ac$, how many real values of x satisfy the equation?

(A) 0
(B) 1
(C) 2
(D) The question cannot be answered without more information.

GO ON TO THE NEXT PAGE

Questions 30 and 31 are based on the following figure.

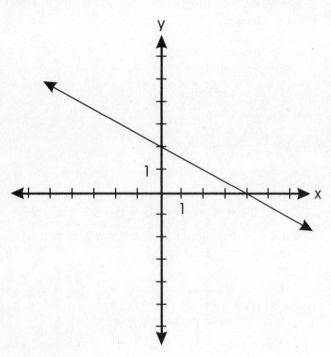

31. What is the equation of a line passing through the point $(-1, -2)$ that is perpendicular to the line shown in the illustration?

   (A) $2y + 3 = x$
   (B) $y = 2x + 3$
   (C) $y = 2x$
   (D) None of the above

32. What are the asymptotes of $y = \dfrac{x^2 - 1}{x - 2}$?

   (A) $x = 2$, $x = 1$, and $x = -1$
   (B) $x = 2$ and $y = 2x$
   (C) $y = x + 2$
   (D) $y = x + 2$ and $x = 2$

33. Where does the line $y = 2x + 1$ intersect the curve $y = x^2 - 4x + 6$?

   (A) There are no real points of intersection.
   (B) $x = 5$, $y = 11$, and $x = 1$, $y = 3$
   (C) $x = 1$, $y = 3$, and $x = -1$, $y = 11$
   (D) $x = 1$, $y = 3$ is a point of tangency between the line and the curve.

30. What is the equation of the line shown in the accompanying figure?

   (A) $y + 8 = 2x$
   (B) $y + 2x = 8$
   (C) $2y + 4 = x$
   (D) $2y + x = 4$

STOP If you finish before the time is up, you may check your work on this section only. Do not turn to any other section in the test.

TIME—45 MINUTES	32 QUESTIONS

PART II

Directions: Answer the following questions. Do not spend too much time on any one question.

Note:
1. Unless otherwise specified, the domain of any function f is assumed to be the set of all real numbers x for which $f(x)$ is a real number.
2. i will be used to denote $\sqrt{-1}$.
3. Figures that accompany the following problems are intended to provide information useful in solving the problems. They are drawn as accurately as possible EXCEPT when it is stated in a specific problem that its figure is not drawn to scale. All figures lie in a plane unless otherwise indicated.

34. For what values of k is the line $y = kx - 1$ tangent to the parabola defined by $y = x^2 + 2x + 3$?

    (A) There are no real values of k that accomplish this.
    (B) 2 and −7
    (C) −2 and 6
    (D) −14

35. What are the x- and y-intercepts of the equation $2x + 3y - 6 = 0$?

    (A) $x = \dfrac{3}{2}$ and $y = \dfrac{2}{3}$
    (B) $x = 3$ and $y = 2$
    (C) $x = 6$ and $y = -2$
    (D) $-3x + 2y = 0$

36. What are the maximum and minimum values achieved by $y = x^3 + 3x^2 + 3x + 10$ over the domain $\{x \mid -2 \le x \le 2\}$?

    (A) 36 and 9
    (B) The minimum is 9, and it does not achieve any maximum over that domain.
    (C) 36 and 8
    (D) 42 and 9

37. Lemon drops are 2 cents each, and chocolate kisses are 5 cents each. Sally spent $1 and got 35 pieces of candy. How many lemon drops did she get?

    (A) 10
    (B) 25
    (C) 35
    (D) 50

38. Arc tan(x) is the inverse of the tangent function. What is the inverse of the function $f(x) = \dfrac{ax + b}{cx + d}$?

    (A) $g(x) = \text{Arc sin}(x)$
    (B) $g(x) = \dfrac{cx + d}{ax + b}$
    (C) $g(x) = \dfrac{-dx + b}{cx - a}$
    (D) $g(x) = \dfrac{a + bx}{c + dx}$

39. If you have two ellipses with different eccentricities but the same center, how many points of intersection will they have?

    (A) 0
    (B) 2
    (C) 4
    (D) It is impossible to answer from the given data.

40. How many different ways can you make up a committee of 5 people from a group of 9 people?

    (A) 126
    (B) 512
    (C) 15,120
    (D) None of the above

41. If you draw 2 cards from a standard deck of 52 cards, what is the probability they will both be spades?

    (A) $\dfrac{1}{15}$
    (B) $\dfrac{1}{16}$
    (C) $\dfrac{1}{17}$
    (D) None of the above

GO ON TO THE NEXT PAGE

42. If you draw 4 M&Ms from a bag containing 4 red, 4 yellow, 4 green, and 4 brown ones, what is the probability that you will get 1 of each color?

(A) $\dfrac{48}{455}$

(B) $\dfrac{64}{455}$

(C) $\dfrac{128}{1,365}$

(D) $\dfrac{24}{256}$

43. Nellie likes to keep her 6 school books in a neat row on her shelf. How many different ways can she line up her 6 books?

(A) 720
(B) 64
(C) 36
(D) 216

44. If you flip 10 pennies all at the same time, what is the probability that exactly 3 will come up heads and 7 will come up tails?

(A) $\dfrac{3}{10}$

(B) $\dfrac{21}{100}$

(C) $\dfrac{15}{128}$

(D) None of the above

45. Consider the following set of numbers: {3, 5, 6, 7, 14}. What is the relation between the mean and the median of this set?

(A) The median is greater than the mean.
(B) The median is exactly the same as the mean.
(C) The mean is greater than the median.
(D) More information is required to answer this question.

46. If you roll two standard dice, what is the probability that the sum of their spot values will be a prime number?

(A) $\dfrac{7}{18}$

(B) $\dfrac{13}{36}$

(C) $\dfrac{1}{4}$

(D) $\dfrac{5}{12}$

47. If you draw two cards from a standard deck, and they are not a pair (that is, they are not both kings, or both tens, and so on), what is the probability that they are of the same suit?

(A) $\dfrac{4}{17}$

(B) $\dfrac{1}{4}$

(C) $\dfrac{3}{11}$

(D) None of the above

48. What is the probability that, if you roll a single standard die four times, you will roll four different numbers?

(A) $\dfrac{5}{18}$

(B) $\dfrac{240}{1,296}$

(C) $\dfrac{1}{3}$

(D) None of the above

49. If each team has a 50 percent chance of winning each game, what is the probability that the World Series will go 7 games? (Note for non-baseball fans: the series ends when one team or the other has won 4 games.)

(A) $\dfrac{4}{7}$

(B) $\dfrac{5}{16}$

(C) $\dfrac{35}{64}$

(D) None of the above

50. What is the sum of the 10 binomial coefficients of the form C(9, k)?

(A) 45
(B) 362,880
(C) 512
(D) 1,729

51. If you have 1 pair of red and 1 pair of blue socks in your drawer, what is your chance of getting a matching pair if you draw 2 socks at random?

    (A) $\dfrac{2}{3}$

    (B) $\dfrac{1}{2}$

    (C) $\dfrac{1}{4}$

    (D) $\dfrac{1}{3}$

52. A certain disease afflicts 5 percent of the population. There is a diagnostic test for the disease that gives a positive result 90 percent of the time for those who have the disease and 10 percent of the time for those who do not. Your results are positive. In the absence of any other evidence, what is the probability you have the disease?

    (A) $\dfrac{1}{20}$

    (B) $\dfrac{9}{28}$

    (C) $\dfrac{11}{19}$

    (D) $\dfrac{9}{10}$

53. Carlos is ten years older than Angelo. Five years ago, Carlos was three times as old as Angelo. How old is Angelo now?

    (A) 5
    (B) 10
    (C) 20
    (D) 12

54. Given that log(2) = .30103 and log(3) = .47712, what is log(160)?

    (A) 2.20412
    (B) 2.20951
    (C) 2.22185
    (D) 2.77815

55. Henry can paint the house in 4 hours, and Gretchen can paint the house in 3 hours. How long would it take the two of them to do the job together?

    (A) $3\dfrac{1}{2}$ hours

    (B) 2 hours

    (C) $1\dfrac{3}{4}$ hours

    (D) $1\dfrac{5}{7}$ hours

56. What is the cube root of -1?

    (A) -1

    (B) $1 + i\dfrac{\sqrt{3}}{2}$

    (C) $1 - i\dfrac{\sqrt{3}}{2}$

    (D) All of the above

57. A rectangular field, with area 4,800 square yards, has a perimeter of 280 yards. What is the length of the diagonal of this field?

    (A) $40\sqrt{3}$ yards
    (B) $70\sqrt{2}$ yards
    (C) 100 yards
    (D) It cannot be determined from the data given.

58. Which of the following expressions is NOT equal to the other three?

    (A) $-i^2 + i^4 - i^6 + i^8$
    (B) $i + i^3$
    (C) $\dfrac{2}{1-i} - (i+1)$
    (D) $i + i^2 + i^3 + i^4$

59. If $\ln(4) + \ln(x) = \ln(20)$, what does $\ln(x)$ equal?

    (A) $2e - 4$
    (B) $\ln(16)$
    (C) $\ln(5)$
    (D) 16

60. Five bags of gold coins are weighed two at a time. The weights obtained are 8, 9, 11, 12, 14, 15, 15, 17, 18, and 21 pounds. What is the median weight of the five bags of coins?

    (A) 14.5 pounds
    (B) 7 pounds
    (C) 6 pounds
    (D) It cannot be determined without knowing which bag was in each weighing.

GO ON TO THE NEXT PAGE

61. The set of positive even integers is closed under which of the following operations?

(A) Addition
(B) Subtraction
(C) Division
(D) None of the above

62. If $10^x = y$, which of the following statements is true?

(A) $\log(x) = y$
(B) $x = \log(y)$
(C) $\log(x) + \log(10) = \log(y)$
(D) $10\left(\dfrac{x}{y}\right) = 1$

63. Santa Evita and Casa de Cafe, two towns in California, are 100 miles apart. Sally starts pedaling her bicycle from Santa Evita toward Casa de Cafe at a speed of 12 miles per hour. One hour later, Henry leaves Casa de Cafe, pedaling toward Santa Evita at a speed of 10 miles per hour. How far from Casa de Cafe will the two cyclists meet?

(A) 10 miles
(B) 22 miles
(C) 40 miles
(D) $45\dfrac{4}{9}$ miles

64. What is the sum of the roots of $x^3 + 6x^2 - 7x + 10 = 0$?

(A) 10
(B) -7
(C) 6
(D) -6

65. If each year you deposit $5,000 in an account that earns 8 percent each year, compounded annually, how much will you have after 30 years? Hint: $(1.08)^{30} = 10.06$.

(A) Approximately $1,500,000
(B) Approximately $1,000,000
(C) Approximately $500,000
(D) Approximately $250,000

STOP If you finish before the time is up, you may check your work on this section only. Do not turn to any other section in the test.

PRETEST ANSWER KEY AND EXPLANATIONS

PART I

1.	B	8.	B	15.	D	22.	C	28.	D
2.	B	9.	A	16.	C	23.	C	29.	B
3.	B	10.	D	17.	A	24.	A	30.	D
4.	B	11.	C	18.	A	25.	D	31.	C
5.	A	12.	A	19.	B	26.	D	32.	D
6.	C	13.	C	20.	C	27.	A	33.	B
7.	D	14.	D	21.	A				

PART II

34.	C	41.	C	48.	A	54.	A	60.	C
35.	B	42.	B	49.	B	55.	D	61.	A
36.	C	43.	A	50.	C	56.	D	62.	B
37.	B	44.	C	51.	D	57.	C	63.	C
38.	C	45.	C	52.	B	58.	A	64.	D
39.	D	46.	D	53.	B	59.	C	65.	C
40.	A	47.	B						

PART I

1. **The correct answer is (B).** *Disjoint* means *having no elements in common,* and *union* is *the set of all elements in one set or the other.*

2. **The correct answer is (B).** If x is a zero of either $f(x)$ or $g(x)$, it will be a zero of $f(x)g(x)$ and conversely.

3. **The correct answer is (B).** The only element in both sets is 3, and *intersection* means *the set of elements in both sets.*

4. **The correct answer is (B).** There are 63 students who like either English or math, and that number must equal the sum of the students who like English and the students who like math, minus the number who like both.

5. **The correct answer is (A).** This is a well-known duality principle for sets.

6. **The correct answer is (C).** Since there are only 13 girls, and 3 of them are not honors students, all of the 10 honors students must be girls. Only 2 of the seniors are honors students, and they must both be girls. So 2 of the senior girls are honors students.

7. **The correct answer is (D).** This is the contrapositive, sometimes called *modus tollens.* The other statements are not logical equivalents of the given statement.

8. **The correct answer is (B).** $p \rightarrow q$ is the same as q or not p (in symbols, $q \lor \sim p$).

9. **The correct answer is (A).** 2 is a prime but not an odd number. It is the only counter-example to the given statement.

10. **The correct answer is (D).** The converse to A $\rightarrow$ B is B $\rightarrow$ A. "Women never lie" is not the same as "All liars are men" because institutions (newspapers, for example) may be liars and are neither women nor men.

11. **The correct answer is (C).** A certainly implies B, but if X and Y were both odd, then X + Y would be an even number, so A is not a necessary condition for B.

12. **The correct answer is (A).** This is just the contrapositive, or *modus tollens,* applied to the given statement.

13. **The correct answer is (C).** Foils A and B are true but are not the transitive property.

14. **The correct answer is (D).** The other three lists are all factors of 18 but include numbers that are not primes.

15. **The correct answer is (D).** A composite is a number that is not prime, and all three of the given numbers are primes.

16. **The correct answer is (C).** This number is 29, a prime. Foil A is 63, or 9 times 7, and Foil B is divisible by 2 (since it ends in zero).

17. **The correct answer is (A).** For any number X, the set of reals (or rationals, for that matter) less than X has no greatest member. The greatest real number less than or equal to 10 is, of course, 10.

18. **The correct answer is (A).** The example, $a = -2$, $b = 1$, shows that choices (B) and (C) are not correct.

19. **The correct answer is (B).** Since the discriminant ($3^2 + 28 = 37$) is not a perfect square, the roots are irrational. All other possibilities are rational numbers.

20. The correct answer is (C). $6 = 1 + 2 + 3$, and $28 = 1 + 2 + 4 + 7 + 14$.

21. The correct answer is (A). The definition of absolute value shows that this is the proper answer.

22. The correct answer is (C). Answer choice (D) works, but it can hardly be called "quick and easy." The reason choice (C) works is that the remainder of 11 divided by 10 is 1.

23. The correct answer is (C). $A^2 + 4AB + B^2 = (A + B)^2 + 2AB$. Since $(A + B)$ must be even, $(A + B)^2$ is divisible by $4j$, but $2AB$ is divisible just by 2, so foil D is not correct.

24. The correct answer is (A). This is almost the definition of a real number.

25. The correct answer is (D).

26. The correct answer is (D). The discriminant of the equation in (A) is a perfect square (16), and so the roots are rational. The quantity in (B) is equal to 2, and 81 is a perfect square, so only (D) is a truly irrational number (the discriminant is 40).

27. The correct answer is (A). There are no negative numbers in its range, and 0 must be included since $0^2 = 0$.

28. The correct answer is (D). The example $x + 2y = 3$ and $5x + 10y = 15$ shows that there can be an infinite number of solutions—in this case, all number pairs of the form $(1 + 2t, 1 - t)$.

29. The correct answer is (B). The one solution is $x = -\dfrac{b}{2a}$. This result is a direct consequence of the quadratic formula.

30. The correct answer is (D). Note that the y-intercept is 2 and the x-intercept is 4.

31. The correct answer is (C). The slope of the line in question 30 is $-\dfrac{1}{2}$, so the slope of this line must be 2. $y = 2x$ passes through $(-1, -2)$.

32. The correct answer is (D). There is a vertical asymptote at $x = 2$, and dividing shows that $y = x + 2$ is an oblique asymptote.

33. The correct answer is (B). Just set the two functions of x equal to each other and solve the quadratic.

PART II

34. The correct answer is (C). The discriminant of $kx - 1 = x^2 + 2x + 3$ is $(2 - k)^2 - 16$, which is equal to 0 if, and only if, $k = -2$ or 6. The discriminant being 0 is a necessary and sufficient condition for the equation to have just one root, which means the line is tangent to the parabola.

35. The correct answer is (B). Just set $y = 0$ and then set $x = 0$ to find the two intercepts.

36. The correct answer is (C). The function is the same as $(x + 1)^3 + 9$, which has a point of inflection at $x = -1$, and is increasing throughout the given interval. Therefore, the minimum is achieved at $x = -2$ and the maximum at $x = 2$. The values of the minimum and maximum are 8 and 36.

37. The correct answer is (B). Let x be the number of lemon drops and y the number of chocolate kisses. Then $2x + 5y = 100$, and $x + y = 35$. Simply solve those two equations and you get $x = 25$ and $y = 10$.

38. The correct answer is (C). Simply solve $y = \dfrac{ax + b}{cx + d}$ for x in terms of y, and you have the inverse function.

39. The correct answer is (D). There can be 0, 2, or 4 points of intersection, depending on the eccentricities and sizes of the ellipses. If it were not specified that the ellipses have the same center, it would also be possible to have 1 or 3 points of intersection.

40. The correct answer is (A). This is the binomial coefficient C(9,5).

41. The correct answer is (C). There are $\dfrac{13(12)}{2} = 78$ ways to get two spades, and $\dfrac{52(51)}{2}$ different draws you can make. $\dfrac{13(12)}{52(51)} = \dfrac{3}{51} = \dfrac{1}{17}$.

42. The correct answer is (B). The chance the second one drawn will be a different color from the first one is $\dfrac{12}{15}$, and, given that the first two are of different colors, the chance that the third one won't match either of them is $\dfrac{8}{14}$. Given that the first three are all different colors, the probability that the fourth one drawn will be of the fourth color is $\dfrac{4}{13}$. So the total probability of drawing three nonmatchers is $\dfrac{12 \times 8 \times 4}{15 \times 14 \times 13} = \dfrac{384}{2,730} = \dfrac{64}{455}$.

43. The correct answer is (A). There are 6 choices for the first book, 5 for the second, 4 for the third, 3 for the fourth, 2 for the fifth, and 1 for the sixth. That makes $6 \times 5 \times 4 \times 3 \times 2 \times 1 = 720$ possibilities all together.

44. The correct answer is (C). This is C(10,7) times $\dfrac{1}{2^{10}}$. C(10,7) $= \dfrac{10 \times 9 \times 8}{1 \times 2 \times 3} = 120 = 15 \times 2^3$, so the answer is $\dfrac{15 \times 2^3}{2^{10}} = \dfrac{15}{2^7} = \dfrac{15}{128}$.

45. The correct answer is (C). The median is 6 (the middle number in the set). The mean is $\dfrac{3 + 5 + 6 + 7 + 14}{5} = 7$.

46. The correct answer is (D). There are 36 possible rolls, and 1 of these gives 2, 2 give 3, 4 give 5, 6 give 7, and 2 give 11, for a $\dfrac{15}{36} = \dfrac{5}{12}$ probability of rolling a prime number.

47. **The correct answer is (B).** There are 13 spades you can get on the first draw (out of 52 cards all together) and 12 you can get on the second (out of 48 cards that are different in spot value from the first one). So there is $\frac{1}{16}$ chance of getting 2 spades, and the same probability for each of the other four suits, so the total chance of having the first two cards of the same suit, given that they don't have the same spot value, is $\frac{1}{4}$.

48. **The correct answer is (A).** The second roll has a $\frac{5}{6}$ chance of not matching the first one. Given that the first two rolls are different, the third roll has a $\frac{2}{3}$ chance of being different. Given that the first three rolls are all different, the fourth roll has a $\frac{1}{2}$ chance of being different. Therefore, the total chance of not rolling the same number twice is $\frac{5}{18}$.

49. **The correct answer is (B).** If two teams play 7 games, there are 70 out of 128 outcomes that end in a 4 - 3 split. Of these 70 cases, $\frac{4}{7}$ have the "winning" team winning the last game. Therefore, the chances that a world series will go 7 games ought to be $\left(\frac{4}{7}\right)\left(\frac{70}{128}\right) = \frac{5}{16}$.

50. **The correct answer is (C).** The 10 binomial coefficients of the form $C(9, k)$ are the coefficients of terms in the expansion of $(x + y)^9$. Set $x = y = 1$, and the indicated result follows.

51. **The correct answer is (D).** Say you pick 1 blue sock first. Then there are only 1 blue sock and 2 red socks left in the drawer, so your chance of a match is only $\frac{1}{3}$.

52. **The correct answer is (B).** Suppose 200 people are chosen at random. One hundred ninety of these people do not have the disease, and 10 do. If they are each given the test, you will have 19 well people getting a positive, and 9 sick people getting a positive. Therefore, if you have a positive test, in the absence of any other evidence, your chance of having the disease is $\frac{9}{28}$.

53. **The correct answer is (B).** Angelo is 10, and Carlos is 20. Five years ago, they were 5 and 15, respectively.

54. **The correct answer is (A).** $\text{Log}(16) = \log(2^4) = 4\log(2) = 1.20412$. $\text{Log}(10) = 1$, so $\log(160) = 2.20412$.

55. **The correct answer is (D).** Henry paints $\frac{1}{4}$ of the house each hour, and Gretchen paints $\frac{1}{3}$ of the house each hour. Therefore, solve $\frac{h}{4} + \frac{h}{3} = 1$ for h and get $h = 1\frac{5}{7}$.

56. **The correct answer is (D).** All three of the given quantities are cube roots of -1, as direct computation will prove.

57. **The correct answer is (C).** Let L be the length and W be the width of the field. Then L + W = 140, and LW = 4,800. Solve these equations to find L = 80, W = 60, and, thus, the diagonal of the field (by the Pythagorean Theorem) is 100 yards.

58. **The correct answer is (A).** All the expressions equal 0 except (A).

59. **The correct answer is (C).** $\ln(20) - \ln(4) = \ln\left(\frac{20}{4}\right) = \ln(5)$.

60. **The correct answer is (C).** Adding all the weights together and dividing by 4 (since each bag was weighed four times) shows that the total weight of all five bags is 35 pounds. The two lightest bags weigh 8 pounds together, and the two heaviest bags weigh 21 pounds together. So, the middle bag must weigh 6 pounds.

61. **The correct answer is (A).** It is not closed under subtraction because $4 - 6 = -2$, which is not a positive integer.

62. **The correct answer is (B).** $\text{Log}(y) = \log(10^x) = x \log(10) = x$.

63. **The correct answer is (C).** They are 88 miles apart when Henry starts pedaling, and they are closing at 22 miles per hour. So, they meet in four hours, after Henry has pedaled 40 miles from Casa de Cafe.

64. **The correct answer is (D).** The sum of the roots of a polynomial of degree n, whose leading coefficient is 1, is the negative of the coefficient of $x^{(n-1)}$.

65. **The correct answer is (C).** The exact expression is $\dfrac{5{,}000((1.08)^{30} - 1)}{.08}$.

Chapter 6
OVERVIEW

WHOLE NUMBERS

The set of numbers {1, 2, 3, 4, . . .} is called the set of *counting numbers* or natural numbers and sometimes, the set *of positive integers.* (The notation, { }, means "set" or collection, and the three dots after the number 4 indicate that the list continues in the same pattern without end.) *Zero* is not considered one of the counting numbers. Together, the counting numbers and zero make up the set of *whole numbers.*

CONSECUTIVE WHOLE NUMBERS

Numbers are consecutive if each number is the successor of the number that precedes it. In a consecutive series of whole numbers, an odd number is always followed by an even number and an even number by an odd. If three consecutive whole numbers are given, either two of them are odd and one is even or two are even and one is odd.

Example 1

7, 8, 9, 10, and 11 are consecutive whole numbers.

Example 2

8, 10, 12, and 14 are consecutive even numbers.

Example 3

21, 23, 25, and 27 are consecutive odd numbers.

Example 4

21, 23, and 27 are *not* consecutive odd numbers because 25 is missing.

THE NUMBER LINE

A useful method of representing numbers geometrically makes it easier to understand numbers. It is called the *number line.* Draw a horizontal line, considered to extend without end in both directions. Select some point on the line and label it with the number 0. This point is called the *origin.* Choose some convenient distance as a unit of length. Take the point on the number line that lies one unit to the right of the origin and label it with the number 1. The point on the number line that is one unit to the right of 1 is labeled 2, and so on. In this way, every whole number is associated with one point on the line, but it is not true that every point on the line represents a whole number.

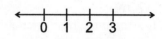

Number line

ORDERING OF WHOLE NUMBERS

On the number line, the point representing 8 lies to the right of the point representing 5, and we say $8 > 5$ (read *8 is greater than 5*). One can also say $5 < 8$ (*5 is less than 8*). For any two whole numbers a and b, there are always three possibilities:

$$a < b, \quad a = b, \quad \text{or} \quad a > b.$$

If $a = b$, the points representing the numbers a and b coincide on the number line.

OPERATIONS WITH WHOLE NUMBERS

The basic operations on whole numbers are addition ($+$), subtraction ($-$), multiplication ($\cdot$ or $\times$), and division ($\div$). These are all *binary* operations—that is, one works with two numbers at a time in order to get a unique answer.

ADDITION

If addition is a binary operation, how are three numbers—say, 3, 4, and 8—added? One way is to write:

$$(3 + 4) + 8 = 7 + 8 = 15$$

Another way is to write:

$$3 + (4 + 8) = 3 + 12 = 15$$

The parentheses merely group the numbers together. The fact that the same answer, 15, is obtained either way illustrates the *associative property* of addition:

$$(r + s) + t = r + (s + t)$$

The order in which whole numbers are added is immaterial—that is, $3 + 4 = 4 + 3$. This principle is called the *commutative property* of addition. Most people use this property without realizing it when they add a column of numbers from the top down and then check their result by beginning over again from the bottom. (Even though there may be a long column of numbers, only two numbers are added at a time.)

If 0 is added to any whole number, the whole number is unchanged. Zero is called the *identity element* for addition.

SUBTRACTION

Subtraction is the inverse of addition. The order in which the numbers are written is important; there is no commutative property for subtraction.

$$4 - 3 \neq 3 - 4$$

The $\neq$ is read *not equal*.

MULTIPLICATION

Multiplication is a commutative operation:

$$43 \cdot 73 = 73 \cdot 43$$

The result or answer in a multiplication problem is called the *product*.

If a number is multiplied by 1, the number is unchanged; the *identity element* for multiplication is 1.

Zero times any number is 0:

$$42 \cdot 0 = 0$$

Multiplication can be expressed with several different symbols:

$$9 \cdot 7 \cdot 3 = 9 \times 7 \times 3 = 9(7)(3)$$

Besides being commutative, multiplication is *associative*:

$$(9 \cdot 7) \cdot 3 = 63 \cdot 3 = 189$$

and

$$9 \cdot (7 \cdot 3) = 9 \cdot 21 = 189$$

A number can be quickly multiplied by 10 by adding a zero at the right of the number. Similarly, a number can be multiplied by 100 by adding two zeros at the right:

$$38 \cdot 10 = 380$$

and

$$100 \cdot 76 = 7600$$

DIVISION

Division is the inverse of multiplication. It is not commutative:

$$8 \div 4 \neq 4 \div 8$$

The parts of a division example are named as follows:

$$\frac{\text{quotient}}{\text{divisor}) \overline{\text{dividend}}} \qquad 4\overline{)8}^{\,2} \qquad 8 \div 4 = 2$$

If a number is divided by 1, the quotient is the original number.

Division by 0 is not defined (has no meaning). Zero divided by any number other than 0 is 0:

$$0 \div 56 = 0$$

DIVISORS AND MULTIPLES

The whole number b divides the whole number a if there exists a whole number k such that $a = bk$. The whole number a is then said to be an integer *multiple* of b, and b is called a *divisor* (or *factor*) of a.

Example 1

3 divides 15 because $15 = 3 \cdot 5$. Thus, 3 is a divisor of 15 (and so is 5), and 15 is an integer multiple of 3 (and of 5).

Example 2

3 does not divide 8 because $8 \neq 3k$ for any whole number k.

Example 3

Divisors of 28 are 1, 2, 4, 7, 14, and 28.

Example 4

Multiples of 3 are 3, 6, 9, 12, 15, ...

WHOLE NUMBERS: REVIEW QUESTIONS

The following problems will give you a chance to practice. Read each problem carefully, write down your answers, and then check them with the answers and explanations that appear at the end of the Overview section.

1. Find the first seven multiples of 6.

2. Find all of the divisors of 72.

3. Find all of the factors of 47.

4. Which property is illustrated by the following statement?

   $$(3 + 7) + 8 = 3 + (7 + 8)$$

5. Which property is illustrated by the following statement?

   $$11 \times (7 \times 5) = 11 \times (5 \times 7)$$

6. Find all of the common factors of 30 and 105.

7. Give an example to show that subtraction on the set of real numbers is not commutative.

8. Which property is illustrated by the following statement?

   $$(9 \times 7) \times 5 = 9 \times (7 \times 5)$$

9. Which property is illustrated by the following statement?

   $$(16 + 18) + 20 = (18 + 16) + 20$$

10. In each of the statements below, replace the # with either <, >, or = to make a true statement.

  a. −12 # 13

  b. $\frac{1}{16}$ # 0.0625

  c. $3\frac{1}{2}$ # $3\frac{2}{5}$

FRACTIONS

If a and b are whole numbers and $b \neq 0$, the symbol $\frac{a}{b}$ (or a/b) is called a fraction. The upper part, a, is called the *numerator,* and the lower part, b, is called the *denominator.* The denominator indicates into how many parts something is divided, and the numerator tells how many of these parts are represented. A fraction indicates division:

$$\frac{7}{8} = 8\overline{)7}$$

If the numerator of a fraction is 0, the value of the fraction is 0. If the denominator of a fraction is 0, the fraction is not defined (has no meaning):

$$\frac{0}{17} = 0 \qquad \frac{17}{0} \text{ is not defined (has no meaning)}$$

If the denominator of a fraction is 1, the value of the fraction is the same as the numerator:

$$\frac{18}{1} = 18$$

If the numerator and denominator are the same number, the value of the fraction is 1:

$$\frac{7}{7} = 1$$

EQUIVALENT FRACTIONS

Fractions that represent the same number are said to be *equivalent.* If m is a counting number and $\frac{a}{b}$ is a fraction, then:

$$\frac{m \times a}{m \times b} = \frac{a}{b}$$

because $\frac{m}{m} = 1$ and $1 \times \frac{a}{b} = \frac{a}{b}$.

Example

$$\frac{2}{3} = \frac{4}{6} = \frac{6}{9} = \frac{8}{12}$$

These fractions are all equivalent.

INEQUALITY OF FRACTIONS

If two fractions are not equivalent, one is smaller than the other. The ideas of "less than" and "greater than" were previously defined and used for whole numbers.

For the fractions $\frac{a}{b}$ and $\frac{c}{b}$:

$$\frac{a}{b} < \frac{c}{b} \text{ if } a < c.$$

That is, if two fractions have the same denominator, the one with the lesser numerator has the lesser value.

If two fractions have different denominators, find a common denominator by multiplying one denominator by the other. Then use the common denominator to compare numerators.

Example
Which is less, $\frac{5}{8}$ or $\frac{4}{7}$?

$8 \cdot 7 = 56 = $ the common denominator.

$$\frac{5}{8} \times \frac{7}{7} = \frac{35}{56} \text{ and } \frac{4}{7} \times \frac{8}{8} = \frac{32}{56}.$$

Since $32 < 35$,

$$\frac{32}{56} < \frac{35}{56} \text{ and } \frac{4}{7} < \frac{5}{8}.$$

SIMPLIFYING TO SIMPLEST FORM

The principle that

$$\frac{m \times a}{m \times b} = \frac{a}{b}$$

can be particularly useful in simplifying fractions to simplest form. Fractions are expressed in *simplest form* when the numerator and denominator have no common factor except 1. To simplify a fraction to an equivalent fraction in simplest form, express the numerator and denominator as products of their prime factors. Each time a prime appears in the numerator and the same prime is the denominator, $\frac{p}{p}$, substitute its equal value, 1.

Example
Simplify $\frac{30}{42}$ to an equivalent fraction in simplest form:

$$\frac{30}{42} = \frac{2 \cdot 3 \cdot 5}{2 \cdot 3 \cdot 7} = 1 \cdot 1 \cdot \frac{5}{7} = \frac{5}{7}.$$

In practice, this can be done even more quickly by dividing numerator and denominator by any number, prime or not, which will divide both evenly. Repeat this process until there is no prime factor remaining that is common to both numerator and denominator:

$$\frac{30}{42} = \frac{15}{21} = \frac{5}{7}.$$

PROPER FRACTIONS, IMPROPER FRACTIONS, AND MIXED NUMBERS

A *proper fraction* is a fraction whose numerator is less than its denominator. Proper fractions always have a value less than 1:

$$\frac{3}{4} \quad \frac{5}{8} \quad \frac{121}{132} \quad \frac{0}{1}$$

An *improper fraction* is a fraction with numerator equal to or greater than the denominator. Improper fractions always have a value equal to or greater than 1:

$$\frac{3}{2} \quad \frac{17}{17} \quad \frac{9}{1} \quad \frac{15}{14}$$

A *mixed number* is a number composed of a whole number and a proper fraction. It is always greater than 1 in value:

$$3\frac{7}{8} \quad 5\frac{1}{4} \quad 11\frac{3}{14}$$

The symbol $3\frac{7}{8}$ means $3 + \frac{7}{8}$ and is read *three and seven-eighths.*

TO RENAME A MIXED NUMBER AS AN IMPROPER FRACTION

Multiply the denominator by the whole number and add this product to the numerator. Use the sum so obtained as the new numerator, and keep the original denominator.

Example

Rename $9\frac{4}{11}$ as an improper fraction:

$$9\frac{4}{11} = \frac{(9 \times 11) + 4}{11} = \frac{99 + 4}{11} = \frac{103}{11}$$

Note: In any calculations with mixed numbers, first rename the mixed numbers as improper fractions.

TO RENAME AN IMPROPER FRACTION AS A MIXED NUMBER

Divide the numerator by the denominator. The result is the whole-number part of the mixed number. If there is a remainder in the division process because the division does not come out evenly, write the remainder as the numerator and keep the original denominator. This gives the fractional part of the mixed number:

$$\frac{20}{3} = 3\overline{)20} \quad = 6\frac{2}{3}$$
$$\underline{18}$$
$$2 \text{ remainder}$$

MULTIPLICATION

PROPER AND IMPROPER FRACTIONS

Multiply the two numerators and then multiply the two denominators. If the numerator obtained is greater than the denominator, divide the numerator of the resulting fraction by its denominator:

$$\frac{3}{8} \times \frac{15}{11} = \frac{45}{88} \qquad \frac{3}{8} \times \frac{22}{7} = \frac{66}{56} = 1\frac{10}{56}$$

Multiplication of fractions is commutative.

Three or more fractions are multiplied in the same way; two numerators are done at a time and the result multiplied by the next numerator.

The product in the multiplication of fractions is usually expressed in simplest form.

DIVIDING COMMON FACTORS

In multiplying fractions, if any of the numerators and denominators have a common divisor (factor), divide each of them by this common factor and the value of the fraction remains the same.

Example

$$\frac{27}{18} \times \frac{90}{300} = ?$$

$$\frac{27}{18} \times \frac{90}{300} = \frac{27}{18} \times \frac{9}{30}$$
Divide the numerator and denominator of the second fraction by 10.

$$= \frac{\overset{3}{\cancel{27}}}{\underset{2}{\cancel{18}}} \times \frac{\overset{1}{\cancel{9}}}{\underset{10}{\cancel{30}}}$$
Divide: 18 and 9 each divisible by 9; 27 and 30 each divisible by 3

$$= \frac{9 \times 1}{2 \times 10} = \frac{9}{20}$$
Multiply numerators; multiply denominators

Another method:

$$\frac{\overset{3}{\cancel{27}}}{\underset{2}{\cancel{18}}} \times \frac{\overset{3}{\cancel{9}}}{\underset{10}{\cancel{30}}} = \frac{3 \times 3}{2 \times 10} = \frac{9}{20}$$
Divide: 27 and 18 have common factor 9; 9 and 30 have common factor 3

Note: Dividing can take place only between a numerator and a denominator, in the same or a different fraction, never between two numerators or between two denominators.

MIXED NUMBERS

Mixed numbers should be renamed as improper fractions before multiplying. Then multiply as described above.

Example

To multiply

$$\frac{4}{7} \times 3\frac{5}{8}$$

rename $3\frac{5}{8}$ as an improper fraction:

$$3\frac{5}{8} = \frac{(3 \times 8) + 5}{8} = \frac{24 + 5}{8} = \frac{29}{8}$$

Multiply

$$\frac{\overset{1}{\cancel{4}}}{7} \times \frac{29}{\underset{2}{\cancel{8}}} = \frac{29}{14}$$

The answer should be renamed as a mixed number:

$$2\frac{1}{14}$$

FRACTIONS WITH WHOLE NUMBERS

Rename the whole number as a fraction with a denominator of 1 and then multiply:

$$\frac{3}{4} \times 7 = \frac{3}{4} \times \frac{7}{1} = \frac{21}{4} = 5\frac{1}{4}$$

Note: When any fraction is multiplied by 1, its value remains unchanged. When any fraction is multiplied by 0, the product is 0.

DIVISION

RECIPROCALS

Division of fractions involves reciprocals. One fraction is the *reciprocal* of another if the product of the fractions is 1.

Example 1

$\frac{3}{4}$ and $\frac{4}{3}$ are reciprocals since

$$\frac{\overset{1}{\cancel{3}}}{\underset{1}{\cancel{4}}} \times \frac{\overset{1}{\cancel{4}}}{\underset{1}{\cancel{3}}} = \frac{1 \times 1}{1 \times 1} = 1$$

Example 2

$\frac{1}{3}$ and 3 are reciprocals since

$$\frac{1}{\underset{1}{\cancel{3}}} \times \frac{\overset{1}{\cancel{3}}}{1} = 1$$

To find the reciprocal of a fraction, interchange the numerator and denominator—that is, "invert the fraction," or "turn it upside down."

PROPER AND IMPROPER FRACTIONS

Multiply the first fraction (dividend) by the reciprocal of the second fraction (divisor). Simplify if possible. Rename the answer to a mixed number when possible:

Example

$$\frac{9}{2} \div \frac{4}{7} = \frac{9}{2} \times \frac{7}{4}. \quad \text{The reciprocal of } \frac{4}{7} \text{ is } \frac{7}{4} \text{ because}$$

$$\frac{4}{7} \times \frac{7}{4} = 1$$

$$= \frac{63}{8}$$

$$= 7\frac{7}{8}$$

MIXED NUMBERS AND/OR WHOLE NUMBERS

Both mixed numbers and whole numbers must first be renamed as improper fractions. Then proceed as described above.

Note: If a fraction or a mixed number is divided by 1, its value is unchanged. Division of a fraction or a mixed number by 0 is not defined. If a fraction is divided by itself or an equivalent fraction, the quotient is 1:

$$\frac{19}{7} \div \frac{19}{7} = \frac{19}{7} \times \frac{7}{19} \quad \text{Reciprocal of } \frac{19}{7} \text{ is } \frac{7}{19}$$

$$= 1 \times 1 = 1$$

ADDITION

Fractions can be added only if their denominators are the same (called the *common denominator*). Add the numerators; the denominator remains the same. Simplify the sum to simplest form:

$$\frac{3}{8} + \frac{2}{8} + \frac{1}{8} = \frac{3+2+1}{8} = \frac{6}{8} = \frac{3}{4}$$

When the fractions have different denominators, you must find a common denominator. One way of doing this is to find the product of the different denominators.

Example

$$\frac{5}{6} + \frac{1}{4} = ?$$

A common denominator is $6 \cdot 4 = 24$.

$$\frac{5}{6} \times \frac{4}{4} = \frac{20}{24} \quad \text{and} \quad \frac{1}{4} \times \frac{6}{6} = \frac{6}{24}$$

$$\frac{5}{6} + \frac{1}{4} = \frac{20}{24} + \frac{6}{24}$$

$$= \frac{20+6}{24}$$

$$= \frac{26}{24}$$

$$= \frac{13}{12}$$

$$= 1\frac{1}{12}$$

LEAST COMMON DENOMINATOR

A denominator can often be found that is less than the product of the different denominators. If the denominator of each fraction will divide into such a number evenly, and it is the *least* such number, it is called the *least common denominator*, abbreviated as LCD. Finding a least common denominator may make it unnecessary to simplify the answer and enables one to work with lesser numbers. There are two common methods.

First Method: By Inspection

$$\frac{5}{6} + \frac{1}{4} = ?$$

LCD = 12 because 12 is the least number divisible by both 6 and 4. Therefore:

$$12 \div 6 = 2 \qquad \text{multiply } \frac{5}{6} \times \frac{2}{2} = \frac{10}{12}$$

$$12 \div 4 = 3 \qquad \text{multiply } \frac{1}{4} \times \frac{3}{3} = \frac{3}{12}$$

Then:

$$\frac{5}{6} + \frac{1}{4} = \frac{10}{12} + \frac{3}{12}$$

$$= \frac{13}{12}$$

$$= 1\frac{1}{12}$$

Second Method: By Factoring

This method can be used when the LCD is not recognized by inspection. Factor each denominator into its prime factors. The LCD is the product of the greatest power of each separate factor, where *power* refers to the number of times a factor occurs.

Example

$$\frac{5}{6} + \frac{1}{4} = ?$$

Factoring denominators gives:

$$6 = 2 \cdot 3 \quad \text{and} \quad 4 = 2 \cdot 2$$

$$\text{LCD} = 2 \cdot 2 \cdot 3$$

$$= 12$$

Rename with LCD:

$$\frac{5}{6} \times \frac{2}{2} = \frac{10}{12} \qquad \frac{1}{4} \times \frac{3}{3} = \frac{3}{12}$$

$$\frac{5}{6} + \frac{1}{4} = \frac{10}{12} + \frac{3}{12}$$

$$= \frac{13}{12}$$

$$= 1\frac{1}{12}$$

The denominators 4 and 6 factor into $2 \cdot 2$ and $2 \cdot 3$, respectively. Although the factor 2 *appears* three times, its power is 2^2 from factoring 4. The factor 3 appears once, so its power is 3^1. Therefore, the LCD as a *product* of the *greatest power of each separate factor* is $2 \times 2 \times 3$.

The factoring method of adding fractions can be extended to three or more fractions.

Example

$$\frac{1}{4} + \frac{3}{8} + \frac{1}{12} = ?$$

Factoring denominators gives:

$$4 = 2 \cdot 2 \qquad 8 = 2 \cdot 2 \cdot 2 \qquad 12 = 2 \cdot 2 \cdot 3$$

$$LCD = 2 \cdot 2 \cdot 2 \cdot 3$$
$$= 24$$

Renaming with LCD:

$$\frac{1}{4} \times \frac{6}{6} = \frac{6}{24} \qquad \frac{3}{8} \times \frac{3}{3} = \frac{9}{24} \qquad \frac{1}{12} \times \frac{2}{2} = \frac{2}{24}$$

$$\frac{1}{4} + \frac{3}{8} + \frac{1}{12} = \frac{6}{24} + \frac{9}{24} + \frac{2}{24}$$

$$= \frac{6 + 9 + 2}{24}$$

$$= \frac{17}{24}$$

ADDITION OF MIXED NUMBERS

Rename any mixed numbers as improper fractions. If the fractions have the same denominator, add the numerators. If the fractions have different denominators, find the LCD of the several denominators and then add the numerators. Simplify the answer if possible. Write the answer as a mixed number if you wish.

Example

$$2\frac{2}{3} + 5\frac{1}{2} + 1\frac{2}{9} = ?$$

Factoring denominators gives:

$$3 = 3 \qquad 2 = 2 \qquad 9 = 3 \cdot 3$$

$$LCD = 2 \cdot 3 \cdot 3$$
$$= 18$$

Renaming with LCD:

$$\frac{8}{3} \times \frac{6}{6} = \frac{48}{18} \qquad \frac{11}{2} \times \frac{9}{9} = \frac{99}{18} \qquad \frac{11}{9} \times \frac{2}{2} = \frac{22}{18}$$

$$2\frac{2}{3} + 5\frac{1}{2} + 1\frac{2}{9} = \frac{8}{3} + \frac{11}{2} + \frac{11}{9}$$

$$= \frac{48}{18} + \frac{99}{18} + \frac{22}{18}$$

$$= \frac{48 + 99 + 22}{18}$$

$$= \frac{169}{18} = 9\frac{7}{18}$$

SUBTRACTION

Fractions can be subtracted only if the denominators are the same. If the denominators are the same, find the difference between the numerators. The denominator remains unchanged.

Example

$$\frac{19}{3} - \frac{2}{3} = ?$$

$$= \frac{19 - 2}{3}$$

$$= \frac{17}{3}$$

$$= 5\frac{2}{3}$$

When fractions have different denominators, find equivalent fractions with a common denominator and then subtract numerators.

Example

$$\frac{7}{8} - \frac{3}{4} = ?$$

Factoring denominators gives:

$$8 = 2 \cdot 2 \cdot 2 \qquad 4 = 2 \cdot 2$$

$$LCD = 2 \cdot 2 \cdot 2$$
$$= 8$$

Renaming with LCD:

$$\frac{7}{8} = \frac{7}{8} \qquad \frac{3}{4} \times \frac{2}{2} = \frac{6}{8}$$

$$\frac{7}{8} - \frac{3}{4} = \frac{7}{8} - \frac{6}{8}$$

$$= \frac{7 - 6}{8} = \frac{1}{8}$$

MIXED NUMBERS

To subtract mixed numbers, rename each mixed number as an improper fraction. Find the LCD for the fractions. Rename each fraction as an equivalent fraction whose denominator is the common denominator. Find the difference between the numerators.

Example

$$3\frac{3}{8} - 2\frac{5}{6} = ?$$

$$LCD = 24$$

$$3\frac{3}{8} - 2\frac{5}{6} = \frac{27}{8} - \frac{17}{6}$$

$$= \frac{81}{24} - \frac{68}{24}$$

$$= \frac{13}{24}$$

If zero is subtracted from a fraction, the result is the original fraction:

$$\frac{3}{4} - 0 = \frac{3}{4} - \frac{0}{4} = \frac{3}{4}$$

FRACTIONS: REVIEW QUESTIONS

The following problems will give you a chance to practice. Read each problem carefully, write down your answers, and then check them with the answers and explanations that appear at the end of the Overview section.

1. $\frac{2}{15} + \frac{2}{3} =$

2. $\frac{4}{5} - \frac{2}{13} =$

3. $\frac{3}{8} \times \frac{4}{21} =$

4. $\frac{2}{3} \div \frac{5}{6} =$

5. $9\frac{1}{5} - 3\frac{1}{4} =$

6. $6\frac{2}{3} \times 1\frac{4}{5} =$

7. $\frac{2}{3} \times \frac{12}{8} =$

8. $\frac{3}{4} \div \frac{7}{8} =$

9. $2\frac{3}{5} + 7\frac{3}{5} =$

10. $\frac{6}{7} \times \frac{3}{4} \times \frac{2}{3} =$

11. $6 \times \frac{2}{3} \times 2\frac{5}{6} =$

12. $2\frac{2}{3} \div 1\frac{7}{9} =$

DECIMALS

The system of whole numbers, or the decimal system, can be extended to fractions by using a period called a *decimal point*. The digits after a decimal point form a *decimal fraction*. Decimal fractions are smaller than 1—for example, .3, .37, .372, and .105. The first position to the right of the decimal point is called the *tenths' place* since the digit in that position tells how many tenths there are. The second digit to the right of the decimal point is in the *hundredths' place*. The third digit to the right of the decimal point is in the *thousandths' place,* and so on.

Example 1

.3 is a decimal fraction that means

$$3 \times \frac{1}{10} = \frac{3}{10},$$

read "three-tenths."

Example 2

The decimal fraction of .37 means

$$3 \times \frac{1}{10} + 7 \times \frac{1}{100} = 3 \times \frac{10}{100} + 7 \times \frac{1}{100}$$

$$= \frac{30}{100} + \frac{7}{100} = \frac{37}{100},$$

read "thirty-seven hundredths."

Example 3

The decimal fraction .372 means

$$\frac{300}{1000} + \frac{70}{1000} + \frac{2}{1000} = \frac{372}{1000},$$

read "three hundred seventy-two thousandths."

Whole numbers have an understood (unwritten) decimal point to the right of the last digit (i.e., 4 = 4.0). Decimal fractions can be combined with whole numbers to make *decimals*—for example, 3.246, 10.85, and 4.7.

Note: Placing zeros to the right of a decimal after the last digit does not change the value of the decimal.

ROUNDING OFF

Sometimes a decimal is expressed with more digits than desired. As the number of digits to the right of the decimal point increases, the number increases in accuracy, but a high degree of accuracy is not always needed. Depending on how accurate the number must be, the number can be "rounded off" to a certain decimal place.

To round off, identify the "place" to be rounded off. If the digit to the right of it is 0, 1, 2, 3, or 4, the round-off place digit remains the same. If the digit to the right is 5, 6, 7, 8, or 9, add 1 to the round-off place digit.

Example 1

Round off .6384 to the nearest thousandth. The digit in the thousandths' place is 8. The digit to the right, in the ten-thousandths' place, is 4, so the answer is .638.

Example 2

.6386 rounded to the nearest thousandth is .639, rounded to the nearest hundredth is .64, and rounded to the nearest tenth is .6.

After a decimal fraction has been rounded off to a particular decimal place, all the digits to the right of that place will be 0.

Note: Rounding off whole numbers can be done by a similar method. It is less common but is sometimes used to get approximate answers quickly.

Example

Round 32,756 to the nearest *hundred*. This means, to find the multiple of 100 that is nearest the given number. The number in the hundreds' place is 7. The number immediately to the right is 5, so 32,756 rounds to 32,800.

DECIMALS AND FRACTIONS

REWRITING A DECIMAL AS A FRACTION

Place the digits to the right of the decimal point over the value of the place in which the last digit appears and simplify if possible. The whole number remains the same.

Example

Rewrite 2.14 as a fraction or mixed number. Observe that 4 is the last digit and is in the hundredths' place.

$$.14 = \frac{14}{100} = \frac{7}{50}$$

Therefore:

$$2.14 = 2\frac{7}{50}$$

REWRITING A FRACTION AS A DECIMAL

Divide the numerator of the fraction by the denominator. First put a decimal point followed by zeros to the right of the number in the numerator. Add and divide until there is no remainder. The decimal point in the quotient is aligned directly above the decimal point in the dividend.

Example 1

Rewrite $\frac{3}{8}$ as a decimal.

```
     .375
  8)3.000
    24
    ‾‾
     60
     56
     ‾‾
      40
      40
      ‾‾
```

Example 2

Rewrite $\frac{5}{6}$ as a decimal.

```
     .833
  6)5.000
    48
    ‾‾
     20
     18
     ‾‾
      20
      18
      ‾‾
       2
```

The 3 in the quotient will be repeated indefinitely. It is called a *repeated decimal* and is written .833… .

ADDITION

Addition of decimals is both commutative and associative. Decimals are simpler to add than fractions. Place the decimals in a column with the decimal points aligned under each other. Add in the usual way. The decimal point of the answer is also aligned under the other decimal points.

Example

$43 + 2.73 + .9 + 3.01 = ?$

```
  43.
   2.73
    .9
   3.01
  ‾‾‾‾‾
  49.64
```

SUBTRACTION

For subtraction, the decimal points must be aligned under each other. Place zeros to the right of the decimal point if desired. Subtract as with whole numbers.

Examples

21.567	21.567	39.00
−9.4	−9.48	−17.48
12.167	12.087	21.52

MULTIPLICATION

Multiplication of decimals is commutative and associative:

$$5.39 \times .04 = .04 \times 5.39$$

$$(.7 \times .02) \times .1 = .7 \times (.02 \times .1)$$

Multiply the decimals as if they were whole numbers. The total number of decimal places in the product is the sum of the number of places (to the right of the decimal point) in all of the numbers multiplied.

Example

$$8.64 \times .003 = ?$$

8.64	2 places to right of decimal point
×.003	+ 3 places to right of decimal point
.02592	5 places to right of decimal point

A zero had to be placed to the left of the product before writing the decimal point to ensure that there would be five decimal places in the product.

Note: To multiply a decimal by 10, simply move the decimal point one place to the right; to multiply by 100, move the decimal point two places to the right; and so on.

DIVISION

To divide one decimal (the dividend) by another (the divisor), move the decimal point in the divisor as many places as necessary to the right to make the divisor a whole number. Then move the decimal point in the dividend (expressed or understood) a corresponding number of places, placing additional zeros if necessary. Then divide as with whole numbers. The decimal point in the quotient is placed above the decimal point in the dividend after the decimal point has been moved.

Example

Divide 7.6 by .32.

$$.32\overline{)7.60} = 32\overline{)760.00}$$
$$23.75$$

Note: "Divide 7.6 by .32" can be written as $\frac{7.6}{.32}$. If this fraction is multiplied by $\frac{100}{100}$, an equivalent fraction is obtained with a whole number in the denominator:

$$\frac{7.6}{.32} \times \frac{100}{100} = \frac{760}{32}$$

Moving the decimal point two places to the right in both divisor and dividend is equivalent to multiplying each number by 100.

SPECIAL CASES

If the dividend has a decimal point and the divisor does not, divide as with whole numbers and place the decimal point of the quotient above the decimal point in the divisor.

If both dividend and divisor are whole numbers but the quotient is a decimal, place a decimal point after the last digit of the dividend and place additional zeros as necessary to get the required degree of accuracy. (*See* Rewriting a Fraction as a Decimal, page 117).

Note: To divide any number by 10, simply move its decimal point (understood to be after the last digit for a whole number) one place to the left; to divide by 100, move the decimal point two places to the left; and so on.

DECIMALS: REVIEW QUESTIONS

The following problems will give you a chance to practice. Read each problem carefully, write down your answers, and then check them with the answers and explanations that appear at the end of the Overview section.

1. Rewrite the following fractions as decimals.

   a. $\dfrac{5}{8}$

   b. $\dfrac{1}{6}$

2. Rewrite the following decimals as fractions and simplify.

   a. 2.08
   b. 13.24

In the following problems, perform the indicated operations.

3. $31.32 + 3.829$

4. $2.567 - 0.021$

5. 0.7×3.1

6. $0.064 \div 0.04$

7. Rewrite the following decimals as fractions and simplify.

   a. 17.56
   b. 21.002

In the following problems, perform the indicated operations.

8. $5.746 + 354.34$

9. $3.261 - 2.59$

10. $73 - .46$

11. 9.2×0.003

12. $5.43 + .154 + 17$

13. $0.033 \div 0.11$

14. Which of the three decimals, .09, .769, and .8, is the least?

PERCENTS

Percents, like fractions and decimals, are ways of expressing parts of whole numbers, as 93%, 50%, and 22.4%. Percents are expressions of hundredths—that is, of fractions whose denominator is 100. The symbol for percent is "%".

Example

$$25\% = \text{twenty-five hundredths} = \frac{25}{100} = \frac{1}{4}$$

The word *percent* means *per hundred*. Its main use is in comparing fractions with equal denominators of 100.

RELATIONSHIP WITH FRACTIONS AND DECIMALS

REWRITING A PERCENT AS A DECIMAL

Divide the percent by 100 and "drop" the symbol for percent. Place zeros to the left when necessary:

$$30\% = .30 \qquad 1\% = .01$$

Remember that the short method of dividing by 100 is to move the decimal point two places to the left.

REWRITING A DECIMAL AS A PERCENT

Multiply the decimal by 100 by moving the decimal point two places to the right, and "add" the symbol for percent:

$$.375 = 37.5\% \qquad .001 = .1\%$$

REWRITING A PERCENT AS A FRACTION

"Drop" the percent sign. Write the number as the numerator over a denominator of 100. If the numerator has a decimal point, move the decimal point to the right the necessary number of places to make the numerator a whole number. Place the same number of zeros to the right of the denominator as you moved places to the right in the numerator. Simplify where possible.

Examples

$$20\% = \frac{20}{100} = \frac{2}{10} = \frac{1}{5}$$

$$36.5\% = \frac{36.5}{100} = \frac{365}{1000} = \frac{73}{200}$$

REWRITING A FRACTION AS A PERCENT

Use either of two methods.

First Method: Rewrite the fraction as an equivalent fraction with a denominator of 100. "Drop" the denominator (equivalent to multiplying by 100) and "add" the % sign.

Example

Express $\dfrac{6}{20}$ as a percent.

$$\frac{6}{20} \times \frac{5}{5} = \frac{30}{100} = 30\%$$

Second Method: Divide the numerator by the denominator to get a decimal with two places (express the remainder as a fraction if necessary). Rewrite the decimal as a percent.

Example

Express $\dfrac{6}{20}$ as a percent.

$$\frac{6}{20} = 20\overline{)6.00}^{\,.30} = 30\%$$
$$\underline{60}$$

PERCENTS: REVIEW QUESTIONS

The following problems will give you a chance to practice. Read each problem carefully, write down your answers, and then check them with the answers and explanations that appear at the end of the Overview section.

1. Rewrite the following decimals as percents:

   a. 0.374
   b. 13.02

2. Rewrite the following percents as decimals:

   a. 62.9%
   b. 0.002%

3. Rewrite the following fractions as percents:

   a. $\dfrac{5}{8}$

   b. $\dfrac{44}{100}$

4. Rewrite the following percents as fractions:

   a. 37.5%
   b. 0.04%

5. Rewrite $12\frac{1}{4}\%$ as a decimal.

6. Write .07% as both a decimal and a fraction.

7. Write $\dfrac{11}{16}$ as both a decimal and a percent.

8. Write 1.25 as both a percent and a fraction.

9. Which of the following is the greatest: $\dfrac{5}{8}$, 62%, or .628?

PERCENT WORD PROBLEMS

When doing percent problems, it is usually easier to rewrite the percent as a decimal or a fraction before computing. When we take a percent of a certain number, that number is called the *base*, the percent we take is called the *rate*, and the result is called the *percentage* or *part*. If we let B represent the base, R the rate, and P the part, the relationship between these quantities is expressed by the following formula:

$$P = R \cdot B$$

All percent problems can be done with the help of this formula.

Example 1

In a class of 24 students, 25% received an A. How many students received an A? The number of students (24) is the base, and 25% is the rate. Rewrite the rate as a fraction, for ease of handling, and apply the formula.

$$25\% = \frac{25}{100} = \frac{1}{4}$$

$$P = R \times B$$

$$= \frac{1}{\cancel{4}} \times \frac{\cancel{24}^{\,6}}{1}$$

$$= 6 \text{ students}$$

To choose between rewriting the percent (rate) as a decimal or a fraction, simply decide which would be easier to work with. In Example 1, the fraction was easier to work with because simplification was possible. In Example 2, the situation is the same except for a different rate. This time the decimal form is easier.

Example 2

In a class of 24 students, 29.17% received an A. How many students received an A? Rewriting the rate as a fraction yields

$$\frac{29.17}{100} = \frac{2917}{10,000}$$

You can quickly see that the decimal is the better choice.

$$29.17\% = .2917$$

$$P = R \times B$$
$$= .2917 \times 24$$
$$= 7 \text{ students}$$

$$\begin{array}{r} .2917 \\ \times\ 24 \\ \hline 1.1668 \\ 5.834 \\ \hline 7.0008 \end{array}$$

Example 3

What percent of a 40-hour week is a 16-hour schedule?

40 hours is the base and 16 hours is the part.

$$P = R \cdot B$$
$$16 = R \cdot 40$$

Divide each side of the equation by 40.

$$\frac{16}{40} = R$$
$$\frac{2}{5} = R$$
$$40\% = R$$

Example 4

A woman paid $15,000 as a down payment on a house. If this amount was 20% of the price, what did the house cost?

The part (or percentage) is $15,000, the rate is 20%, and we must find the base. Rewrite the rate as a fraction.

$$20\% = \frac{1}{5}$$
$$P = R \times B$$
$$\$15,000 = \frac{1}{5} \times B$$

Multiply each side of the equation by 5.

$$\$75,000 = B = \text{cost of house}$$

PERCENT OF INCREASE OR DECREASE

This kind of problem is not really new but follows immediately from the previous problems. First calculate the *amount* of increase or decrease. This amount is the P (percentage or part) from the formula $P = R \cdot B$. The base, B, is the original amount, regardless of whether there was a loss or gain.

Example

By what percent does Mary's salary increase if her present salary is $20,000 and she accepts a new job at a salary of $28,000?

Amount of increase is:

$$\$28,000 - \$20,000 = \$8000$$

$$P = R \cdot B$$
$$\$8000 = R \cdot \$20,000$$

Divide each side of the equation by $20,000. Then:

$$\frac{\overset{40}{\cancel{8000}}}{\underset{100}{\cancel{20,000}}} = \frac{40}{100} = R = 40\% \text{ increase}$$

DISCOUNT AND INTEREST

These special kinds of percent problems require no new methods of attack.

Discount: The amount of discount is the difference between the original price and the sale, or discount, price. The rate of discount is usually given as a fraction or as a percent. Use the formula of the percent problems, $P = R \cdot B$, but now P stands for the *part* or *discount*, R is the *rate*, and B, the *base*, is the original price.

Example 1

A table listed at $160 is marked 20% off. What is the sale price?

$$P = R \cdot B$$
$$= .20 \cdot \$160 = \$32$$

This is the amount of discount or how much must be subtracted from the original price. Then:

$$\$160 - \$32 = \$128 \text{ sale price}$$

Example 2

A car priced at $9000 was sold for $7200. What was the rate of discount?

$$\text{Amount of discount} = \$9000 - \$7200$$
$$= \$1800$$
$$\text{Discount} = \text{rate} \cdot \text{original price}$$
$$\$1800 = R \cdot \$9000$$

Divide each side of the equation by $9000. Then:

$$\frac{\overset{20}{\cancel{1800}}}{\underset{100}{\cancel{9000}}} = \frac{20}{100} = R = 20\%$$

Successive Discounting: When an item is discounted more than once, it is called successive discounting.

Example 1

In one store, a dress tagged at $40 was discounted 15%. When it did not sell at the lower price, it was discounted an additional 10%. What was the final selling price?

$$\text{Discount} = R \cdot \text{original price}$$
$$\text{First discount} = .15 \cdot \$40 = \$6$$
$$\$40 - \$6 = \$34 \text{ selling price after first discount}$$

$$\text{Second discount} = .10 \cdot \$34 = \$3.40$$
$$\$34 - \$3.40 = \$30.60 \text{ final selling price}$$

Example 2

In another store, an identical dress was also tagged at $40. When it did not sell, it was discounted 25% all at once. Is the final selling price lower or higher than in Example 1?

Discount = $R \cdot$ original price

$\qquad = .25 \cdot \$40$

$\qquad = \$10$

$40 - 10 = \$30$ final selling price

This is a lower selling price than in Example 1, where two successive discounts were taken. Although the two discounts from Example 1 add up to the discount of Example 2, the final selling price is not the same.

Interest: Interest problems are similar to discount and percent problems. If money is left in the bank for a year and the interest is calculated at the end of the year, the usual formula $P = R \cdot B$ can be used, where P is the *interest*, R is the *rate*, and B is the *principal* (original amount of money borrowed or loaned).

Example 1

A certain bank pays interest on savings accounts at the rate of 4% per year. If a man has $6700 on deposit, find the interest earned after 1 year.

$$P = R \cdot B$$

Interest = rate · principal

$$P = .04 \cdot \$6700 = \$268 \text{ interest}$$

Interest problems frequently involve more or less time than 1 year. Then the formula becomes:

Interest = rate · principal · time

Example 2

If the money is left in the bank for 3 years at simple interest (the kind we are discussing), the interest is

$3 \cdot \$268 = \$804$

Example 3

Suppose $6700 is deposited in the bank at 4% interest for 3 months. How much interest is earned?

Interest = rate · principal · time

Here the 4% rate is for 1 year. Since 3 months is

$$\frac{3}{12} = \frac{1}{4}$$

Interest = $.04 \cdot \$6700 \cdot \dfrac{1}{4} = \$67$

PERCENT WORD PROBLEMS: REVIEW QUESTIONS

The following problems will give you a chance to practice. Read each problem carefully, write down your answers, and then check them with the answers and explanations that appear at the end of the Overview section.

1. Susan purchased a new refrigerator priced at $675. She made a down payment of 15% of the price. Find the amount of the down payment.

2. Sales volume at an office supply company climbed from $18,300 last month to $56,730 this month. Find the percent of increase in sales.

3. A men's clothing retailer orders $25,400 worth of outer garments, and receives a discount of 15%, followed by an additional discount of 10%. What is the cost of the clothing after these two discounts?

4. A self-employed individual places $5,000 in an account that earns 8% simple annual interest. How much money will be in this account after two years?

5. Janet receives a 6% commission for selling boxes of greeting cards. If she sells 12 boxes for $40 each, how much does she earn?

6. After having lunch, Ian leaves a tip of $4.32. If this amount represents 18% of the lunch bill, how much was the bill?

7. Before beginning her diet, Janet weighed 125 pounds. After completing the diet, she weighed 110 pounds. What percent of her weight did she lose?

8. If a $12,000 car loses 10% of its value every year, what is it worth after 3 years?

9. Peter invests $5000 at 4% simple annual interest. How much is his investment worth after 2 months?

10. A small business office bought a used copy machine for 75% of the original price. If the original price was $3500, how much did they pay for the copy machine?

11. A lawyer who is currently earning $42,380 annually receives a 6.5% raise. What is his new annual salary?

12. An industrial plant reduces its number of employees, which was originally 3,760, by 5%. How many employees now work at the plant?

SIGNED NUMBERS

The set of *integers* is the set of all positive and negative whole numbers and zero. It is the set $\{..., -4, -3, -2, -1, 0, 1, 2, 3, 4, ...\}$.

The first three dots symbolize the fact that the negative integers go on indefinitely, just as the positive integers do. Integers preceded by a negative sign (called *negative integers*) appear to the left of 0 on a number line.

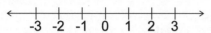

Decimals, fractions, and mixed numbers can also have negative signs. Together with positive fractions and decimals, they appear on the number line in this fashion:

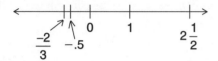

All numbers to the right of 0 are called *positive numbers*. They have the sign +, whether it is actually written or not.

Business gains or losses, feet above or below sea level, and temperature above and below zero can all be expressed by means of signed numbers.

ADDITION

If the numbers to be added have the same sign, add the numbers (integers, fractions, decimals) as usual and use their common sign in the answer:

$$+9 + (+8) + (+2) = +19 \text{ or } 19$$
$$-4 + (-11) + (-7) + (-1) = -23$$

If the numbers to be added have different signs, add the positive numbers and then the negative numbers. Ignore the signs and subtract the lesser total from the greater total. If the greater total was positive, the answer will be positive; if the greater total was negative, the answer will be negative. The answer may be zero. Zero is neither positive nor negative and has no sign.

Example

$$+3 + (-5) + (-8) + (+2) = ?$$

First, add the positive numbers:

$$+3 + (+2) = +5$$

Then, add the negative numbers:

$$-5 + (-8) = -13$$

Subtract the lesser total from the greater total:

$$13 - 5 = 8$$

Since the greater total (13) had a negative sign, the answer is −8.

SUBTRACTION

The second number in a subtraction problem is called the *subtrahend*. In order to subtract, change the sign of the subtrahend and then continue as if you were *adding* signed numbers. If there is no sign in front of the subtrahend, it is assumed to be positive.

Examples

Subtract the subtrahend (bottom number) from the top number.

15	5	−35	−35	42
5	15	−42	42	35
10	−10	7	−77	7

MULTIPLICATION

If two and only two signed numbers are to be multiplied, multiply the numbers as you would if they were not signed. Then, if the two numbers have the *same sign*, the product is *positive*. If the two numbers have *different signs*, the product is *negative*. If more than two numbers are being multiplied, proceed two at a time in the same way as before, finding the signed product of the first two numbers, then multiplying that product by the next number, and so on. The product has a positive sign if all the factors are positive or there is an even number of negative factors. The product has a negative sign if there is an odd number of negative factors.

Example

$$-3 \cdot (+5) \cdot (-11) \cdot (-2) = -330$$

The answer is negative because there is an odd number (three) of negative factors.

The product of a signed number and zero is zero. The product of a signed number and 1 is the original number. The product of a signed number and −1 is the original number with its sign changed.

Examples

$$-5 \cdot 0 = 0$$
$$-5 \cdot 1 = -5$$
$$-5 \cdot (-1) = +5$$

DIVISION

If the divisor and the dividend have the same sign, the answer is positive. Divide the numbers as you normally would. If the divisor and the dividend have different signs, the answer is negative. Divide the numbers as you normally would.

Examples

$$-3 \div (-2) = \frac{3}{2} = 1\frac{1}{2}$$
$$8 \div (-.2) = -40$$

If zero is divided by a signed number, the answer is zero. If a signed number is divided by zero, the answer is undefined. If a signed number is divided by 1, the number remains the same. If a signed number is divided by -1, the quotient is the original number with its sign changed.

Examples

$$0 \div (-2) = 0$$

$$-\frac{4}{3} \div 0 \qquad \text{not defined}$$

$$\frac{2}{3} \div 1 = \frac{2}{3}$$

$$4 \div -1 = -4$$

SIGNED NUMBERS: REVIEW QUESTIONS

The following problems will give you a chance to practice. Read each problem carefully, write down your answers, and then check them with the answers and explanations that appear at the end of the Overview section. Perform the indicated operations:

1. $+12 + (-10) + (+2) + (-6) =$

2. $-(-8) - 10 - (+12) + (-4) =$

3. $-2 \times (-3) \times (+4) \times (-2) =$

4. $15 \div (-0.5) =$

5. $+7 + (-2) + (-8) + (+3) =$

6. $-3 - (-7) - (+4) + (-2) =$

7. $-6 \times (+2) \times (-1) \times (-7) =$

8. $\dfrac{+12 \times -2}{-4} =$

9. $(3)(2)(1)(0)(-1)(-2)(-3) =$

10. $\dfrac{(-8)(+3)}{(-6)(-2)(5)} =$

11. $\dfrac{6}{15} \div \left(\dfrac{-12}{5}\right) =$

12. $\dfrac{(+5) - (-13)}{(-4) + (-5)} =$

POWERS, EXPONENTS, AND ROOTS

POWERS AND EXPONENTS

The product $10 \cdot 10 \cdot 10$ can be written 10^3. We say 10 is raised to the *third power*. In general, $a \times a \times a \ldots a$ n times is written a^n. The *base, a,* is raised to the nth power, and n is called the *exponent.*

Examples

$$3^2 = 3 \cdot 3 \qquad \text{read } 3 \text{ squared}$$
$$2^3 = 2 \cdot 2 \cdot 2 \qquad \text{read } 2 \text{ cubed}$$
$$5^4 = 5 \cdot 5 \cdot 5 \cdot 5 \quad \text{read } 5 \text{ to the fourth power}$$

If the exponent is 1, it is usually understood and not written; thus, $a^1 = a$.

Since

$$a^2 = a \times a \qquad \text{and} \qquad a^3 = a \times a \times a$$

then

$$a^2 \times a^3 = (a \times a)(a \times a \times a) = a^5$$

There are three rules for exponents. In general, if k and m are any numbers, and a is any number, not equal to 0:

Rule 1: $a^k \times a^m = a^{k+m}$
Rule 2: $a^m \cdot b^m = (ab)^m$
Rule 3: $(a^k)^n = a^{kn}$

Examples

Rule 1: $2^2 \cdot 2^3 = 4 \times 8 = 32$
and $2^2 \times 2^3 = 2^5 = 32$

Rule 2: $3^2 \times 4^2 = 9 \times 16 = 144$
and $3^2 \times 4^2 = (3 \times 4)^2 = 12^2 = 144$

Rule 3: $(3^2)^3 = 9^3 = 729$
and $(3^2)^3 = 3^6 = 729$

ROOTS

The definition of roots is based on exponents. If $a^n = c$, where a is the base and n the exponent, a is called the nth *root* of c. This is written $a = \sqrt[n]{c}$. The symbol $\sqrt{}$ is called a *radical sign*. Since $5^4 = 625$, $\sqrt[4]{625} = 5$, and 5 is the fourth root of 625. The most frequently used roots are the second (called the *square*) root and the third (called the *cube*) root. The square root is written $\sqrt{}$, and the cube root is written $\sqrt[3]{}$.

SQUARE ROOTS

If c is a positive number, there are two values, one negative and one positive, which, when multiplied together, will produce c.

Example

$$+4 \cdot (+4) = 16 \quad \text{and} \quad -4 \cdot (-4) = 16$$

The positive square root of a positive number c is called the *principal* square root of c (briefly, the *square root of c*) and is denoted by $\sqrt{c}$:

$$\sqrt{144} = 12$$

If $c = 0$, there is only one square root, 0. If c is a negative number, there is no real number that is the square root of c:

$$\sqrt{-4} \text{ is not a real number}$$

CUBE ROOTS

Both positive and negative numbers have real cube roots. The cube root of 0 is 0. The cube root of a positive number is positive; that of a negative number is negative.

Examples

$$2 \cdot 2 \cdot 2 = 8$$

Therefore $\sqrt[3]{8} = 2$

$$-3 \cdot (-3) \cdot (-3) = -27$$

Therefore $\sqrt[3]{-27} = -3$

Each number has only one real cube root.

FRACTIONAL EXPONENTS

The values of k, m, and n from the three exponent rules can be expanded to include positive and negative fractions. In particular, roots can be expressed as fractional exponents. In Rule 3, $(a^k)^n = a^{kn}$. Let $k = \dfrac{1}{n}$. Then $(a^{\frac{1}{n}})^n = a^1 = a$ and $a^{\frac{1}{n}}$ is the nth root of a. Rule 2, $a^m \times b^m = (a \times b)^m$, which is true when a and b are any numbers and n is an integer, can be extended to include the case in which the exponent is a fraction. Suppose $m = \dfrac{1}{k}$. Then:

$$a^{\frac{1}{k}} \times b^{\frac{1}{k}} = (a \times b)^{\frac{1}{k}}$$

$$\text{or } \sqrt[k]{a \times b} = \sqrt[k]{a} \times \sqrt[k]{b}$$

This last formulation justifies the simplification of square roots. If the number under the radical sign is a square number, the process will terminate in a number without the radical sign. If the number is not square, the process should terminate when the number remaining under the radical sign no longer contains a square.

Example 1

Simplify $\sqrt{98}$

$$\sqrt{98} = \sqrt{2 \times 49}$$
$$= \sqrt{2} \times \sqrt{49},$$

where 49 is a square number

$$= \sqrt{2} \times 7$$

Therefore, $\sqrt{98} = 7\sqrt{2}$, and the process terminates because there is no whole number whose square is 2. $7\sqrt{2}$ is called a radical expression or simply a *radical*.

Example 2

Which is greater, $\left(\sqrt{96}\right)^2$ or $\sqrt{2^{14}}$?

$$\left(\sqrt{96}\right)^2 = \sqrt{96} \times \sqrt{96} = \sqrt{96 \times 96} = 96$$

$$\sqrt{2^{14}} = 2^7 = 128 \quad \text{because } 2^{14} = 2^7 \times 2^7 \text{ by}$$

Rule 1 or because $\sqrt{2^{14}} = (2^{14})^{1/2} = 2^7$ by Rule 3.

Since $128 > 96$, $\sqrt{2^{14}} > \left(\sqrt{96}\right)^2$

Example 3

Which is greater, $2\sqrt{75}$ or $6\sqrt{12}$?

These numbers can be compared if the same number appears under the radical sign. Then the greater number is the one with the greater number in front of the radical sign.

$$\sqrt{75} = \sqrt{25 \times 3} = \sqrt{25} \times \sqrt{3} = 5\sqrt{3}$$

Therefore:

$$2\sqrt{75} = 2(5\sqrt{3}) = 10\sqrt{3}$$

$$\sqrt{12} = \sqrt{4 \times 3} = \sqrt{4} \times \sqrt{3} = 2\sqrt{3}$$

Therefore:

$$6\sqrt{12} = 6(2\sqrt{3}) = 12\sqrt{3}$$

Since $12\sqrt{3} > 10\sqrt{3}$, $6\sqrt{12} > 2\sqrt{75}$

Note: Numbers such as $\sqrt{2}$ and $\sqrt{3}$ are called *irrational* numbers to distinguish them from *rational* numbers, which include the integers and the fractions. Irrational numbers also have places on the number line. They may have positive or negative signs. The combination of rational and irrational numbers, all the numbers we have used so far, make up the *real* numbers. Arithmetic, algebra, and geometry deal with real numbers. The number π, the ratio of the circumference of a circle to its diameter, is also a real number; it is irrational, although it is approximated by 3.14159....

Radicals can be added and subtracted only if they have the same number under the radical sign. Otherwise, they must be simplified to expressions having the same number under the radical sign.

Example 1

Solve $2\sqrt{18} + 4\sqrt{8} - \sqrt{2}$.

$\sqrt{18} = \sqrt{9 \times 2} = \sqrt{9} \times \sqrt{2} = 3\sqrt{2}$;

therefore, $2\sqrt{18} = 2(3\sqrt{2}) = 6\sqrt{2}$,

and $\sqrt{8} = \sqrt{4 \times 2} = \sqrt{4} \times \sqrt{2} = 2\sqrt{2}$;

therefore, $4\sqrt{8} = 4(2\sqrt{2}) = 8\sqrt{2}$,

giving $2\sqrt{18} + 4\sqrt{8} - \sqrt{2}$

$= 6\sqrt{2} + 8\sqrt{2} - \sqrt{2} = 13\sqrt{2}$

Radicals are multiplied using the rule that

$$\sqrt[k]{a \times b} = \sqrt[k]{a} \times \sqrt[k]{b}$$

Example 2

$\sqrt{2}(\sqrt{2} - 5\sqrt{3}) = \sqrt{4} - 5\sqrt{6} = 2 - 5\sqrt{6}$

A quotient rule for radicals similar to the product rule is:

$$\sqrt[k]{\frac{a}{b}} = \frac{\sqrt[k]{a}}{\sqrt[k]{b}}$$

Example 3

$$\sqrt{\frac{9}{4}} = \frac{\sqrt{9}}{\sqrt{4}} = \frac{3}{2}$$

POWERS, EXPONENTS, AND ROOTS: REVIEW QUESTIONS

The following problems will give you a chance to practice. Read each problem carefully, write down your answers, and then check them with the answers and explanations that appear at the end of the Overview section.

1. Simplify
   $\sqrt{180}$

2. Combine
   $2\sqrt{20} + 6\sqrt{45} - \sqrt{125}$

3. Find the difference
   $8\sqrt{12} - 2\sqrt{27}$

4. Simplify
   $\sqrt{7}(2\sqrt{7} - \sqrt{3})$

5. Divide and simplify
   $\frac{12\sqrt{75}}{4\sqrt{108}}$

6. Calculate $3^2 \times 2^4$

7. Find the sum of $\sqrt{45} + \sqrt{125}$

8. Simplify $(3\sqrt{32})(7\sqrt{6})$

9. Simplify $\frac{20\sqrt{96}}{5\sqrt{4}}$

10. Evaluate $-3^2 + (3^2)^3$

11. Simplify $(\sqrt{15})^2$

12. Simplify $\sqrt{6}\sqrt{3}\sqrt{2}$

ALGEBRA

Algebra is a generalization of arithmetic. It provides methods for solving problems that cannot be done by arithmetic alone or that can be done by arithmetic only after long computations. Algebra provides a shorthand way of simplifying long verbal statements to brief formulas, expressions, or equations. After the verbal statements have been simplified, the resulting algebraic expressions can be simplified. Suppose that a room is 12 feet wide and 20 feet long. Its perimeter (measurement around the outside) can be expressed as:

$12 + 20 + 12 + 20$ or $2(12 + 20)$.

If the width of the room remains 12 feet but the letter l is used to symbolize length, the perimeter is:

$12 + l + 12 + l$ or $2(12 + l)$.

Further, if w is used for width, the perimeter of *any* rectangular room can be written as $2(w + l)$. This same room has an area of 12 feet by 20 feet or $12 \cdot 20$. If l is substituted for 20, any room of width 12 has an area equal to $12l$. If w is substituted for the number 12, the area of any rectangular room is given by wl or lw. Expressions such as wl and $2(w + l)$ are called *algebraic expressions*. An *equation* is a statement that two algebraic expressions are equal. A *formula* is a special type of equation.

EVALUATING FORMULAS

If we are given an expression and numerical values to be assigned to each letter, the expression can be evaluated.

Example

Evaluate $2x + 3y - 7$, if $x = 2$ and $y = -4$.

Substitute the given values:

$2(2) + 3(-4) - 7 = ?$

Multiply the numbers using the rules for signed numbers:

$4 + -12 - 7 = ?$

Collect the numbers:

$4 - 19 = -15$

We have already evaluated formulas in arithmetic when solving percent, discount, and interest problems.

Example

The formula for temperature conversion is:

$$F = \frac{9}{5}C + 32$$

where C stands for the temperature in degrees Celsius and F for degrees Fahrenheit. Find the Fahrenheit temperature that is equivalent to 20°C.

$$F = \frac{9}{5}(20°C) + 32 = 36 + 32 = 68°F$$

ALGEBRAIC EXPRESSIONS

FORMULATION

A more difficult problem than evaluating an expression or formula is to translate from a verbal expression to an algebraic one:

Verbal	Algebraic
Thirteen more than x	$x + 13$
Six less than twice x	$2x - 6$
The square of the sum of x and 5	$(x + 5)^2$
The sum of the square of x and the square of 5	$x^2 + 5^2$
The distance traveled by a car going 50 miles an hour for x hours	$50x$
The average of 70, 80, 85, and x	$\dfrac{70 + 80 + 85 + x}{4}$

SIMPLIFICATION

After algebraic expressions have been formulated, they can usually be simplified by means of the laws of exponents and the common operations of addition, subtraction, multiplication, and division. These techniques will be described in the next section. Algebraic expressions and equations frequently contain parentheses, which are removed in the process of simplifying. Brackets, [ ], which are often used instead of parentheses, are treated the same way. If an expression contains more than one set of parentheses (and/or brackets), remove the inner set first and then the outer set. Parentheses are used to indicate multiplication. Thus $3(x + y)$ means that 3 is to be multiplied by the sum of x and y. The *distributive law* is used to accomplish this:

$$a(b + c) = ab + ac$$

The expression in front of the parentheses is multiplied by each term inside. Rules for signed numbers apply.

Example

Simplify $3[4(2 - 8) - 5(4 + 2)]$.

This can be done in two ways.

Method 1: Combine the numbers inside the parentheses first:

$$\begin{aligned} 3[4(2 - 8) - 5(4 + 2)] &= 3[4(-6) - 5(6)] \\ &= 3[-24 - 30] \\ &= 3[-54] = -162 \end{aligned}$$

Method 2: Use the distributive law:

$$\begin{aligned} 3[4(2 - 8) - 5(4 + 2)] &= 3[8 - 32 - 20 - 10] \\ &= 3[8 - 62] \\ &= 3[-54] = -162 \end{aligned}$$

If there is a (+) before the parentheses, the signs of the terms inside the parentheses remain the same when the parentheses are removed. If there is a (−) before the parentheses, the sign of each term inside the parentheses changes when the parentheses are removed.

Once parentheses have been removed, the order of operations is exponentiation first, then multiplication and division from left to right, then addition and subtraction from left to right.

Example

$(-15 + 17) \cdot 3 - [(4 \cdot 9) \div 6] = ?$

Work inside the parentheses first:

$(2) \cdot 3 - [36 \div 6] = ?$

Then work inside the brackets:

$2 \cdot 3 - [6] = ?$

Multiply first, then subtract, proceeding from left to right:

$6 - 6 = 0$

The placement of parentheses and brackets is important. Using the same numbers as above with the parentheses and brackets placed in different positions can give many different answers.

Example

$$-15 + [(17 \cdot 3) - (4 \cdot 9)] \div 6 = ?$$

Work inside the parentheses first:

$$-15 + [(51) - (36)] \div 6 = ?$$

Then work inside the brackets:

$$-15 + [15] \div 6 = ?$$

Since there are no more parentheses or brackets, proceed from left to right, dividing before adding:

$$-15 + 2\frac{1}{2} = -12\frac{1}{2}$$

OPERATIONS

When letter symbols and numbers are combined with the operations of arithmetic $(+, -, \cdot, \div)$ and with certain other mathematical operations, we have an *algebraic expression*. If an algebraic expression is made up of two or more parts connected by an addition or subtraction sign; each of those parts are called a *term*. Terms with the same variable part are called *like terms*. Since algebraic expressions represent numbers, they can be added, subtracted, multiplied, and divided.

When we defined the commutative law of addition in arithmetic by writing $a + b = b + a$, we meant that a and b could represent any number. The equation $a + b = b + a$ is an *identity* because it is true for all numbers. The equation $n + 5 = 14$ is not an identity because it is not true for all numbers; it becomes true only when the number 9 is substituted for n. Letters used to represent numbers are called *variables*. If a number stands alone (the 5 or 14 in $n + 5 = 14$), it is called a *constant* because its value is constant or unchanging. If a number appears in front of a variable, it is called a *coefficient*. Because the letter x is frequently used to represent a variable, or *unknown*, the times sign $\times$, which can be confused with it in handwriting, is rarely used to express multiplication in algebra. Other expressions used for multiplication are a dot, parentheses, or simply writing a number and letter together:

$$5 \cdot 4 \text{ or } 5(4) \text{ or } 5a$$

Of course, 54 still means fifty-four.

ADDITION AND SUBTRACTION

Only like terms can be combined. Add or subtract the coefficients of like terms, using the rules for signed numbers.

Example 1

Add $x + 2y - 2x + 3y$.

$$x - 2x + 2y + 3y = -x + 5y$$

Example 2

Perform the subtraction:

$$\begin{array}{r} -30a - 15b + 4c \\ - (-5a + 3b - c + d) \end{array}$$

Change the sign of each term in the subtrahend and then add, using the rules for signed numbers:

$$\begin{array}{r} -30a - 15b + 4c \\ \underline{5a - 3b + c - d} \\ -25a - 18b + 5c - d \end{array}$$

MULTIPLICATION

Multiplication is accomplished by using the *distributive property*. If the multiplier has only one term, then

$$a(b + c) = ab + bc.$$

Example

$$9x(5m + 9q) = (9x)(5m) + (9x)(9q)$$
$$= 45mx + 81qx$$

When the multiplier contains more than one term and you are multiplying two expressions, multiply each term of the first expression by each term of the second and then add like terms. Follow the rules for signed numbers and exponents at all times.

Example

$$(3x + 8)(4x^2 + 2x + 1)$$
$$= 3x(4x^2 + 2x + 1) + 8(4x^2 + 2x + 1)$$
$$= 12x^3 + 6x^2 + 3x + 32x^2 + 16x + 8$$
$$= 12x^3 + 38x^2 + 19x + 8$$

If more than two expressions are to be multiplied, multiply the first two, then multiply the product by the third factor, and so on, until all factors have been used.

Algebraic expressions can be multiplied by themselves (squared) or raised to any power.

Example 1

$$(a + b)^2 = (a + b)(a + b)$$
$$= a(a + b) + b(a + b)$$
$$= a^2 + ab + ba + b^2$$
$$= a^2 + 2ab + b^2$$

since $ab = ba$ by the commutative law.

Example 2

$$(a + b)(a - b) = a(a - b) + b(a - b)$$
$$= a^2 - ab + ba - b^2$$
$$= a^2 - b^2$$

FACTORING

When two or more algebraic expressions are multiplied, each is called a factor, and the result is the *product*. The reverse process of finding the factors when given the product is called *factoring*. A product can often be factored in more than one way. Factoring is useful in multiplication, division, and solving equations.

One way to factor an expression is to remove any single-term factor that is common to each of the terms and write it outside the parentheses. It is the distributive law that permits this.

Example

$$3x^3 + 6x^2 + 9x = 3x(x^2 + 2x + 3)$$

The result can be checked by multiplication.

Expressions containing squares can sometimes be factored into expressions containing variables raised to the first power only, called *linear factors*. We have seen that

$$(a + b)(a - b) = a^2 - b^2.$$

Therefore, if we have an expression in the form of a difference of two squares, it can be factored as:

$$a^2 - b^2 = (a + b)(a - b).$$

Example

Factor $4x^2 - 9$.

$$4x^2 - 9 = (2x)^2 - (3)^2 = (2x + 3)(2x - 3).$$

Again, the result can be checked by multiplication.

A third type of expression that can be factored is one containing three terms, such as $x^2 + 5x + 6$. Since

$$\begin{aligned}(x + a)(x + b) &= x(x + b) + a(x + b) \\ &= x^2 + xb + ax + ab \\ &= x^2 + (a + b)x + ab\end{aligned}$$

an expression in the form $x^2 + (a + b)x + ab$ can be factored into two factors of the form $(x + a)$ and $(x + b)$. We must find two numbers whose product is the constant in the given expression and whose sum is the coefficient of the term containing x.

Example 1

Find factors of $x^2 + 5x + 6$.

First find two numbers which, when multiplied, have $+6$ as a product. Possibilities are 2 and 3, -2 and -3, 1 and 6, -1 and -6. From these, select the one pair whose sum is 5. The pair 2 and 3 is the only possible selection, and so:

$$x^2 + 5x + 6 = (x + 2)(x + 3) \quad \text{written in either order.}$$

Example 2

Factor $x^2 - 5x - 6$.

Possible factors of -6 are -1 and 6, 1 and -6, 2 and -3, -2 and 3. We must select the pair whose sum is -5. The only pair whose sum is -5 is $+1$ and -6, and so

$$x^2 - 5x - 6 = (x + 1)(x - 6).$$

In factoring expressions of this type, notice that if the last sign is positive, both a and b have the same sign, and it is the same as the sign of the middle term. If the last sign is negative, the numbers have opposite signs.

Many expressions cannot be factored.

DIVISION

Write the division example as a fraction. If numerator and denominator each contain one term, divide the numbers using laws of signed numbers, and use the laws of exponents to simplify the letter part of the problem.

Example

Method 1: Law of Exponents

$$\frac{36mx^2}{9m^2x} = 4m^1x^2m^{-2}x^{-1}$$

$$= 4m^{-1}x^1 = \frac{4x}{m}$$

Method 2: Division of Common Factors

$$\frac{36mx^2}{9m^2x} = \frac{\overset{4}{\cancel{36}}mx\cancel{x}}{\cancel{9}m\cancel{m}x} = \frac{4x}{m}$$

This is acceptable because

$$\frac{ac}{bc} = \frac{a}{b}\left(\frac{c}{c}\right) \text{ and } \frac{c}{c} = 1, \text{ where } c \neq 0$$

so that $\dfrac{ac}{bc} = \dfrac{a}{b}$.

If the divisor contains only one term and the dividend is a sum, divide each term in the dividend by the divisor and simplify as you did in Method 2.

Example

$$\frac{9x^3 + 3x^2 + 6x}{3x} = \frac{\overset{3x^2}{\cancel{9x^3}}}{\cancel{3x}} + \frac{\overset{x}{\cancel{3x^2}}}{\cancel{3x}} + \frac{\overset{2}{\cancel{6x}}}{\cancel{3x}}$$

$$= 3x^2 + x + 2$$

This method cannot be followed if there are two or more terms in the denominator since

$$\frac{a}{b + c} \neq \frac{a}{b} + \frac{a}{c}.$$

In this case, write the example as a fraction. Factor the numerator and denominator if possible. Then use the laws of exponents or divide by common factors.

Example

Divide $x^3 - 9x$ by $x^3 + 6x^2 + 9x$.

Write as:

$$\frac{x^3 - 9x}{x^3 + 6x^2 + 9x}.$$

Both numerator and denominator can be factored to give:

$$\frac{x(x^2 - 9)}{x(x^2 + 6x + 9)} = \frac{\cancel{x}\cancel{(x+3)}(x-3)}{\cancel{x}\cancel{(x+3)}(x+3)} = \frac{x-3}{x+3}.$$

ALGEBRA: REVIEW QUESTIONS

The following problems will give you a chance to practice. Read each problem carefully, write down your answers, and then check them with the answers and explanations that appear at the end of the Overview section.

1. Simplify: $3[4(6 - 14) - 8(-2 - 5)]$

2. Add and subtract: $(5x^2 - 5x + 2) - (-2x^2 + 3x - 7) + (-4x^2 + 2x - 3)$

3. Multiply: $(x - 2)(x^2 + 3x + 7)$

4. Factor completely: $4x^2 - 36$

5. Factor completely: $6x^2 - 3x - 18$

6. Simplify: $\dfrac{x^2 - 4x - 21}{x^2 - 9x + 14}$

7. Add: $(a - b - c) + (a - b - c) - (a - b - c)$

8. Multiply: $(a + 1)^2 (a + 2)$

9. Multiply: $(2x + 1)(3x^2 - x + 6)$

10. Factor completely: $12x^2 + 14x + 4$

11. Factor completely: $6x^4 - 150x^2$

12. Factor completely: $4a^2b + 12\,ab - 72b$

13. Multiply: $\dfrac{x^2 - x - 6}{x^2 - 9} \times \dfrac{x^2 + 4x + 3}{x^2 + 5x + 6}$

EQUATIONS

Solving equations is one of the major objectives in algebra. If a variable x in an equation is replaced by a value or expression that makes the equation a true statement, the value or expression is called a *solution* of the equation. (Remember that an equation is a mathematical statement that one algebraic expression is equal to another.)

An equation may contain one or more variables. We begin with one variable. Certain rules apply to equations, whether there are one or more variables. The following rules are applied to give equivalent equations that are simpler than the original:

Addition: If $s = t$, then $s + c = t + c$.
Subtraction: If $s + c = t + c$, then $s = t$.
Multiplication: If $s = t$, then $cs = ct$.
Division: If $cs = ct$ and $c \neq 0$, then $s = t$.

To solve for x in an equation in the form $ax = b$ with $a \neq 0$, divide each side of the equation by a:

$$\frac{ax}{a} = \frac{b}{a} \quad \text{yielding} \quad x = \frac{b}{a}.$$

Then, $\dfrac{b}{a}$ is the solution to the equation.

Example 1

Solve $4x = 8$.

Write $\dfrac{4x}{4} = \dfrac{8}{4}$.

$x = 2$.

Example 2

Solve $2x - (x - 4) = 5(x + 2)$ for x.

$2x - (x - 4) = 5(x + 2)$

$2x - x + 4 = 5x + 10$	Remove parentheses by distributive law.
$x + 4 = 5x + 10$	Combine like terms.
$x = 5x + 6$	Subtract 4 from each side.
$-4x = 6$	Subtract $5x$ from each side.
$x = \dfrac{6}{-4}$	Divide each side by -4.
$= -\dfrac{3}{2}$	Simplify fraction to simplest form. Negative sign now applies to the entire fraction.

Check the solution for accuracy by substituting in the original equation:

$$2(-\frac{3}{2}) - (-\frac{3}{2} - 4) \overset{?}{=} 5\,(-\frac{3}{2} + 2)$$

$$-3 - \left(-\frac{11}{2}\right) \overset{?}{=} 5\left(\frac{1}{2}\right)$$

$$-3 + \frac{11}{2} \overset{?}{=} \frac{5}{2}$$

$$-\frac{6}{2} + \frac{11}{2} \overset{?}{=} \frac{5}{2} \quad \text{check}$$

EQUATIONS: REVIEW QUESTIONS

Solve the following equations for x and then check your work with the answers and explanations that appear at the end of the Overview section:

1. $6 + 4x = 6x - 10$

2. $8 - 2x = 2(4x + 3)$

3. $3x - 4(3x - 2) = -x$

4. $6 + 8(8 - 2x) = 14 - 8(4x - 2)$

5. $-5x + 3 = x + 2$

6. $x + 3(2x + 5) = -20$

7. $4(x + 2) - (2x + 1) = x + 5$

8. $3(2x + 5) = 10x + 7 + 2(x - 8)$

9. $\dfrac{2x + 3}{5} - 10 = \dfrac{4 - 3x}{2}$

10. $3(2x + 1) + 2(3x + 1) = 17$

11. $(x - 5)^2 = 4 + (x + 5)^2$

WORD PROBLEMS INVOLVING ONE UNKNOWN

In many cases, if you read a word problem carefully, assign a letter to the quantity to be found, and understand the relationships between known and unknown quantities, you can formulate an equation for one unknown.

NUMBER PROBLEMS AND AGE PROBLEMS

These two kinds of problems are similar to each other.

Example

One number is 3 times another, and their sum is 48. Find the two numbers.

Let x = second number. Then the first number is $3x$. Since their sum is 48,

$$3x + x = 48$$
$$4x = 48$$
$$x = 12$$

Therefore, the first number is $3x = 36$.

$36 + 12 = 48$ check

DISTANCE PROBLEMS

The basic concept is:

Distance = rate · time

Example

In a mileage test, a man drives a truck at a fixed rate of speed for 1 hour. Then he increases the speed by 20 miles per hour and drives at that rate for 2 hours. He then reduces that speed by 5 miles per hour and drives at that rate for 3 hours. If the distance traveled was 295 miles, what are the rates of speed over each part of the test?

Let x be the first speed, $x + 20$ the second, and $x + (20 - 5) = x + 15$ the third. Because distance = rate · time, multiply these rates by the time and formulate the equation by separating the two equal expressions for distance by an equals sign:

$$1x + 2(x + 20) + 3(x + 15) = 295$$
$$x + 2x + 3x + 40 + 45 = 295$$
$$6x = 210$$
$$x = 35$$

The speeds are 35, 55, and 50 miles per hour.

CONSECUTIVE NUMBER PROBLEMS

This type usually involves only one unknown. Two numbers are consecutive if one is the successor of the other. Three consecutive numbers are of the form x, $x + 1$, and $x + 2$. Since an even number is divisible by 2, consecutive even numbers are of the form $2x$, $2x + 2$, and $2x + 4$. An odd number is of the form $2x + 1$.

Example

Find three consecutive whole numbers whose sum is 75.

Let the first number be x, the second $x + 1$, and the third $x + 2$. Then:

$$x + (x + 1) + (x + 2) = 75$$
$$3x + 3 = 75$$
$$3x = 72$$
$$x = 24.$$

The numbers whose sum is 75 are 24, 25, and 26. Many versions of this problem have no solution. For example, no three consecutive whole numbers have a sum of 74.

WORK PROBLEMS

These problems concern the speed with which work can be accomplished and the time necessary to perform a task if the size of the work force is changed.

Example

If Joe can type a chapter alone in 6 days, and Ann can type the same chapter in 8 days, how long will it take them to type the chapter if they both work on it?

We let x = number of days required if they work together, and then put our information into tabular form:

	Joe	Ann	Together
Days to type chapter	6	8	x
Part typed in 1 day	$\dfrac{1}{6}$	$\dfrac{1}{8}$	$\dfrac{1}{x}$

Since the part done by Joe in 1 day plus the part done by Ann in 1 day equals the part done by both in 1 day, we have:

$$\frac{1}{6} + \frac{1}{8} = \frac{1}{x}$$

Next we multiply each member by $48x$ to clear the fractions, giving:

$$8x + 6x = 48$$
$$14x = 48$$
$$x = 3\frac{3}{7} \text{ days}$$

WORD PROBLEMS INVOLVING ONE UNKNOWN: REVIEW QUESTIONS

The following problems will give you a chance to practice. Read each problem carefully, write down your answers, and then check them with the answers and explanations that appear at the end of the Overview section.

1. One integer is two more than a second integer. The first integer added to four times the second is equal to 17. Find the values of the two integers.

2. The sum of three consecutive even integers is 84. Find the least of the integers.

3. One pump working continuously can fill a reservoir in 30 days. A second pump can fill the reservoir in 20 days. How long would it take both pumps working together to fill the reservoir?

4. In a recent local election with two candidates, the winner received 372 more votes than the loser. If the total number of votes cast was 1,370, how many votes did the winning candidate receive?

5. Mrs. Krauser invested a part of her $6,000 inheritance at 9% simple annual interest, and the rest at 12% simple annual interest. If the total interest earned in one year was $660, how much did she invest at 12%?

6. If 6 times a number is decreased by 4, the result is the same as when 3 times the number is increased by 2. What is the number?

7. The lesser of two numbers is 31 less than three times the greater. If the numbers differ by 7, what is the lesser number?

8. Mike is 3 years older than Al. In 9 years the sum of their ages will be 47. How old is Mike now?

9. At the Wardlaw Hartridge School Christmas program, student tickets cost $3, and adult tickets cost twice as much. If a total of 200 tickets were sold, and $900 was collected, how many student tickets were sold?

10. Working together, Brian, Peter, and Jared can shovel the driveway in 12 minutes. If Brian alone can shovel the driveway in 21 minutes, and Peter alone can shovel the driveway in 84 minutes, how long would it take Jared to shovel the driveway alone?

11. Jimmy is now three years older than Bobby. If seven years from now the sum of their ages is 79, how old is Bobby now?

12. A freight train and a passenger train leave the same station at noon, and travel in opposite directions. If the freight train travels 52 mph and the passenger train travels 84 mph, at what time are they 680 miles apart?

LITERAL EQUATIONS

An equation may have other letters in it besides the variable (or variables). Such an equation is called a *literal equation*. An illustration is $x + b = a$, with x the variable. The solution of such an equation will not be a specific number but will involve letter symbols. Literal equations are solved by exactly the same methods as those involving numbers, but we must know which of the letters in the equation is to be considered the variable. Then, the other letters are treated as constants.

Example 1

Solve $ax - 2bc = d$ for x.

$$ax = d + 2bc$$

$$x = \frac{d + 2bc}{a} \text{ if } a \neq 0$$

Example 2

Solve $ay - by = a^2 - b^2$ for y.

$y(a - b) = a^2 - b^2$ Factor out the common term.

$y(a - b) = (a + b)(a - b)$ Factor the expression on the right side.

$y = a + b$ Divide each side by $a - b$ if $a \neq b$.

Example 3

Solve for S:

$$\frac{1}{R} = \frac{1}{S} + \frac{1}{T}$$

Multiply every term by RST, the LCD:

$$ST = RT + RS$$

$$ST - RS = RT$$

$$S(T - R) = RT$$

$$S = \frac{RT}{T - R} \qquad \text{If } T \neq R$$

QUADRATIC EQUATIONS

An equation containing the square of an unknown quantity is called a *quadratic* equation. One way of solving such an equation is by factoring. If the product of two expressions is zero, at least one of the expressions must be zero.

Example 1

Solve $y^2 + 2y = 0$.

$y(y + 2) = 0$ Factor out the common factor.

$y = 0$ or $y + 2 = 0$ Since the product is 0, at least one of the factors must be 0.

$y = 0$ or $y = -2$

Check by substituting both values in the original equation:

$$(0)^2 + 2(0) = 0$$

$$(-2)^2 + 2(-2) = 4 - 4 = 0$$

In this case there are two solutions.

Example 2

Solve $x^2 + 7x + 10 = 0$.

$$x^2 + 7x + 10 = (x + 5)(x + 2) = 0$$

$$x + 5 = 0 \quad \text{or} \quad x + 2 = 0$$

$$x = -5 \quad \text{or} \quad x = -2$$

Check:

$$(-5)^2 + 7(-5) + 10 = 25 - 35 + 10 = 0$$

$$(-2)^2 + 7(-2) + 10 = 4 - 14 + 10 = 0$$

Not all quadratic equations can be factored using only integers, but solutions can always be found by means of a formula. A quadratic equation may have two real solutions, one real solution, or occasionally no real solutions. If the quadratic equation is in the form $Ax^2 + Bx + C = 0$, x can be found from the following formula:

$$x = \frac{-B \pm \sqrt{B^2 - 4AC}}{2A}$$

Example

Solve $2y^2 + 5y + 2 = 0$ by formula.

Assume $A = 2$, $B = 5$, and $C = 2$.

$$x = \frac{-5 \pm \sqrt{5^2 - 4(2)(2)}}{2(2)}$$

$$= \frac{-5 \pm \sqrt{25 - 16}}{4}$$

$$= \frac{-5 \pm \sqrt{9}}{4}$$

$$= \frac{-5 \pm 3}{4}$$

This yields two solutions:

$$x = \frac{-5 + 3}{4} = \frac{-2}{4} = \frac{-1}{2} \text{ and}$$

$$x = \frac{-5 - 3}{4} = \frac{-8}{4} = -2$$

So far, each quadratic we have solved has had two distinct answers, but an equation may have a single answer (repeated), as in

$$x^2 + 4x + 4 = 0$$
$$(x + 2)(x + 2) = 0$$
$$x + 2 = 0 \text{ and } x + 2 = 0$$
$$x = -2 \text{ and } x = -2$$

The only solution is -2.

It is also possible for a quadratic equation to have no real solution at all.

Example

If we attempt to solve $x^2 + x + 1 = 0$, by formula, we get:

$$x = \frac{-1 \pm \sqrt{1 - 4(1)(1)}}{2} = \frac{-1 \pm \sqrt{-3}}{2}$$

Since $\sqrt{-3}$ is not a real number, this quadratic has no real answer.

REWRITING EQUATIONS

Certain equations written with a variable in the denominator can be rewritten as quadratics.

Example

Solve $-\dfrac{4}{x} + 5 = x$

$$-4 + 5x = x^2 \qquad \text{Multiply both sides by } x \neq 0.$$
$$-x^2 + 5x - 4 = 0 \qquad \text{Collect terms on one side of equals and set sum equal to 0.}$$
$$x^2 - 5x + 4 = 0 \qquad \text{Multiply both sides by } -1.$$
$$(x - 4)(x - 1) = 0 \qquad \text{Factor}$$
$$x - 4 = 0 \quad \text{or} \quad x - 1 = 0$$
$$x = 4 \quad \text{or} \qquad x = 1$$

Check the result by substitution:

$$-\frac{4}{4} + 5 \stackrel{?}{=} 4 \text{ and } -\frac{4}{1} + 5 \stackrel{?}{=} 1$$

$$-1 + 5 = 4 \qquad -4 + 5 = 1$$

Some equations containing a radical sign can also be converted into a quadratic equation. The solution of this type of problem depends on the principle that

$$\text{If } A = B \quad \text{then } A^2 = B^2$$
$$\text{and If } A^2 = B^2 \quad \text{then} \quad A = B \text{ or } A = -B.$$

Example

Solve $y = \sqrt{3y + 4}$.

$$y = \sqrt{3y + 4}$$
$$y^2 = 3y + 4$$
$$y^2 - 3y - 4 = 0$$
$$(y - 4)(y + 1) = 0$$
$$y = 4 \text{ or } y = -1$$

Check by substituting values into the original equation:

$$4 \stackrel{?}{=} \sqrt{3(4) + 4} \text{ and}$$
$$-1 \stackrel{?}{=} \sqrt{3(-1) + 4}$$
$$4 \stackrel{?}{=} \sqrt{16} \qquad -1 \stackrel{?}{=} \sqrt{1}$$
$$4 = 4 \qquad\qquad -1 \neq 1$$

The single solution is $y = 4$; the false root $y = -1$ was introduced when the original equation was squared.

LITERAL EQUATIONS: REVIEW QUESTIONS

Solve the following equations for the variable indicated and then check your work with the answers and explanations at the end of the Overview section:

1. Solve for c: $A = \dfrac{1}{2} b(b + c)$

2. Solve for w: $aw - b = cw + d$

3. Solve for x: $10x^2 = 5x$

4. Solve for x: $2x^2 - x = 21$

5. Solve for x: $2\sqrt{x + 5} = 8$

6. Solve for b_2: $2A = (b_1 + b_2)b$

7. Solve for d: $\left(\dfrac{a}{b}\right) = \left(\dfrac{c}{d}\right)$

8. Solve for x: $3x^2 - 12 = x(1 + 2x)$

9. Solve for x: $5x^2 = 36 + x^2$

10. Solve for x: $4\sqrt{\dfrac{2x}{3}} = 48$

11. Solve for x: $3x^2 - x - 4 = 0$

12. Solve $\dfrac{q}{x} + \dfrac{p}{x} = 1$ *for* x

13. Solve for x: $3x^2 - 5 = 0$

LINEAR INEQUALITIES

For each of the sets of numbers we have considered, we have established an ordering of the members of the set by defining what it means to say that one number is greater than the other. Every number we have considered can be represented by a point on a number line.

An *algebraic inequality* is a statement that one algebraic expression is greater than (or less than) another algebraic expression. If all the variables in the inequality are raised to the first power, the inequality is said to be a *linear inequality*. We solve the inequality by simplifying it to a simpler inequality whose solution is apparent. The answer is not unique, as it is in an equation, since a great number of values may satisfy the inequality.

There are three rules for producing equivalent inequalities:

1. The same quantity can be added or subtracted from each side of an inequality.

2. Each side of an inequality can be multiplied or divided by the same *positive* quantity.

3. If each side of an inequality is multiplied or divided by the same *negative* quantity, the sign of the inequality must be reversed so that the new inequality is equivalent to the first.

Example 1

Solve $5x - 5 > -9 + 3x$.

$5x > -4 + 3x$ Add 5 to each side.
$2x > -4$ Subtract $3x$ from each side.
$x > -2$ Divide by $+2$.

Any number greater than -2 is a solution to this inequality.

Example 2

Solve $2x - 12 < 5x - 3$.

$2x < 5x + 9$ Add 12 to each side.
$-3x < 9$ Subtract $5x$ from each side.
$x > -3$ Divide each side by -3, changing sign of inequality.

Any number greater than -3 (for example, $-2\frac{1}{2}$, 0, 1, or 4) is a solution to this inequality.

LINEAR EQUATIONS IN TWO UNKNOWNS

GRAPHING EQUATIONS

The number line is useful in picturing the values of one variable. When two variables are involved, a coordinate system is effective. The Cartesian coordinate system is constructed by placing a vertical number line and a horizontal number line on a plane so that the lines intersect at their zero points. This meeting place is called the *origin*. The horizontal number line is called the *x*-axis, and the vertical number line (with positive numbers above the *x*-axis) is called the *y*-axis. Points in the plane correspond to ordered pairs of real numbers.

Example

The points in this example are:

x	y
0	0
1	1
3	−1
−2	−2
−2	1

A first-degree equation in two variables is an equation that can be written in the form $ax + by = c$, where *a*, *b*, and *c* are constants. *First-degree* means that x and y appear to the first power. *Linear* refers to the graph of the solutions (x, y) of the equation, which is a straight line. We have already discussed linear equations of one variable.

Example

Graph the line $y = 2x - 4$.

First make a table and select small integral values of x. Find the value of each corresponding y and write it in the table:

x	y
0	−4
1	−2
2	0
3	2

If $x = 1$, for example, $y = 2(1) - 4 = -2$. Then plot the four points on a coordinate system. It is not necessary to have four points; two would do since two points determine a line, but plotting three or more points reduces the possibility of error.

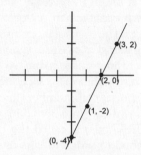

After the points have been plotted (placed on the graph), draw a line through the points and extend it in both directions. This line represents the equation $y = 2x - 4$.

SOLVING SIMULTANEOUS LINEAR EQUATIONS

Two linear equations can be solved together (simultaneously) to yield an answer (x, y) if it exists. On the coordinate system, this amounts to drawing the graphs of two lines and finding their point of intersection. If the lines are parallel and, therefore, never meet, no solution exists.

Simultaneous linear equations can be solved in the following manner without drawing graphs. From the first equation find the value of one variable in terms of the other; substitute this value in the second equation. The second equation is now a linear equation in one variable and can be solved. After the numerical value of the one variable has been found, substitute that value into the first equation to find the value of the second variable. Check the results by substituting both values into the second equation.

Example 1

Solve the system:

$$2x + y = 3$$
$$4x - y = 0$$

From the first equation, $y = 3 - 2x$. Substitute this value of y into the second equation to get:

$$4x - (3 - 2x) = 0$$
$$4x - 3 + 2x = 0$$
$$6x = 3$$
$$x = \frac{1}{2}$$

Substitute $x = \frac{1}{2}$ in the first of the original equations:

$$2\left(\frac{1}{2}\right) + y = 3$$
$$1 + y = 3$$
$$y = 2$$

Check by substituting both x and y values into the second equation:

$$4\left(\frac{1}{2}\right) + -2 = 0$$
$$2 - 2 = 0$$

Example 2

A change-making machine contains $30 in dimes and quarters. There are 150 coins in the machine. Find the number of each type of coin.

Let x = number of dimes and y = number of quarters. Then:

$$x + y = 150$$

Since $.25y$ is the product of a quarter of a dollar and the number of quarters and $.10x$ is the amount of money in dimes,

$$.10x + .25y = 30$$

Multiply the last equation by 100 to eliminate the decimal points:

$$10x + 25y = 3000$$

From the first equation, $y = 150 - x$. Substitute this value in the equivalent form of the second equation.

$$10x + 25(150 - x) = 3000$$
$$-15x = -750$$
$$x = 50$$

This is the number of dimes. Substitute this value in $x + y = 150$ to find the number of quarters, $y = 100$.

Check:

$$.10(50) + .25(100) = 30$$
$$\$5 + \$25 = \$30$$

LINEAR INEQUALITIES AND LINEAR EQUATIONS IN TWO UNKNOWNS: REVIEW QUESTIONS

The following problems will give you a chance to practice. Read each problem carefully, write down your answers, and then check them with the answers and explanations that appear at the end of the Overview section.

1. Solve for x: $108x < 15(6x + 12)$

2. Solve for a: $4a - 9 > 9a - 24$

3. Find the common solution:

   $3x + 2y = 11$
   $5x - 4y = 11$

4. The sum of two numbers is 45 and their difference is 11. What are the two numbers?

5. Three binders and four notebooks cost a total of \$4.32. One binder and five notebooks cost \$3.97. What is the cost of one notebook?

6. Solve for x: $12 - 2x > 4$

7. Solve for x: $\left(\dfrac{x}{6}\right) - \left(\dfrac{x}{2}\right) < 1$

8. Solve for z: $6z + 1 \le 3(z - 2)$

9. Find the common solution:
   $y = 3x + 1$
   $x + y = 9$

10. Find the common solution:
    $2x + y = 8$
    $x - y = 1$

11. Solve for a common solution:
    $5x + 3y = 28$
    $7x - 2y = 2$

12. A printer and monitor together cost \$356. The monitor cost \$20 more than two times the printer. How much do the printer and monitor cost separately?

RATIO AND PROPORTION

Many problems in arithmetic and algebra can be solved using the concept of *ratio* to compare numbers. The ratio of a to b is the fraction $\dfrac{a}{b}$. If the two ratios $\dfrac{a}{b}$ and $\dfrac{c}{d}$ represent the same comparison, we write:

$$\frac{a}{b} = \frac{c}{d}$$

This equation (statement of equality) is called a *proportion*. A proportion states the equivalence of two different expressions for the same ratio.

Example 1

In a class of 39 students, 17 are men. Find the ratio of men to women.

39 students − 17 men = 22 women
Ratio of men to women is 17/22, also written 17:22.

Example 2

A fertilizer contains 3 parts nitrogen, 2 parts potash, and 2 parts phosphate by weight. How many pounds of fertilizer will contain 60 pounds of nitrogen?

The ratio of pounds of nitrogen to pounds of fertilizer is 3 to 3 + 2 + 2 = 3/7. Let x be the number of pounds of mixture. Then:

$$\frac{3}{7} = \frac{60}{x}$$

Multiply both sides of the equation by $7x$ to get:

$$3x = 420$$
$$x = 140 \text{ pounds}$$

COMPUTATIONS

Measures of location describe the "centering" of a set of data; that is, they are used to represent the central value of the data. There are three common measures of central location. The one that is typically the most useful (and certainly the most common) is the *arithmetic mean*, which is computed by adding up all of the individual data values and dividing by the number of values.

Example 1

A researcher wishes to determine the average (arithmetic mean) amount of time a particular prescription drug remains in the bloodstream of users. She examines 5 people who have taken the drug, and determines the amount of time the drug has remained in each of their bloodstreams. In hours, these times are: 24.3, 24.6, 23.8, 24.0, and 24.3. What is the mean number of hours that the drug remains in the bloodstream of these experimental participants?

To find the mean, we begin by adding up all of the measured values. In this case, 24.3 + 24.6 + 23.8 + 24.0 + 24.3 = 121. We then divide by the number of participants (5) and obtain $\frac{121}{5}$ = 24.2 as the mean.

Example 2

Suppose the participant with the 23.8 hour measurement had actually been measured incorrectly, and a measurement of 11.8 hours was obtained instead. What would the mean number of hours have been?

In this case, the sum of the data values is only 109, and the mean becomes 21.8.

This example exhibits the fact that the mean can be greatly "thrown off" by one incorrect measurement. Similarly, one measurement that is unusually large or unusually small can have great impact upon the mean. A measure of location that is not impacted as much by extreme values is called the *median*. The median of a group of numbers is simply the value in the middle when the data values are arranged in numerical order. This numerical measure is sometimes used in the place of the mean when we wish to minimize the impact of extreme values.

Example 3

What is the median value of the data from example 1? What is the median value of the modified data from example 2?

Note that in both cases, the median is 24.3. Clearly, the median was not impacted by the one unusually small observation in example 2.

In the event that there are an even number of data values, we find the median by computing the number halfway between the two values in the middle (that is, we find the mean of the two middle values).

Another measure of location is called the *mode*. The mode is simply the most frequently occurring value in a series of data. In the examples above, the mode is 24.3. The mode is determined in an experiment when we wish to know which outcome has happened the most often.

MEDIAN

If a set of numbers is arranged in order, the number in the middle is called the *median*.

Example

Find the median test score of 62, 80, 60, 30, 50, 90, and 20. Arrange the numbers in increasing (or decreasing) order

20, 30, 50, 60, 62, 80, 90

Since 60 is the number in the middle, it is the median. It is not the same as the arithmetic mean, which is 56.

If the number of scores is an even number, the median is the arithmetic mean of the middle two scores.

SYSTEMS OF NUMBERS

Recall that within the real number system, numbers of various kinds can be identified. The numbers that are used for counting {1, 2, 3, 4, 5, ...} are called the *natural numbers* or *positive integers*. The set of positive integers, together with 0, is called the set of *whole numbers*. The positive integers, together with 0 and the *negative integers* {..., −5, −4, −3, −2, −1}, make up the set of *integers*.

A real number is said to be a *rational number* if it can be written as the ratio of two integers, where the denominator is not 0. Thus, for example, numbers such as $-16, \frac{2}{3}, \frac{-5}{6}, 0, 25, 12\frac{5}{8}$ are rational numbers.

Any real number that cannot be expressed as the ratio of two integers is called an *irrational number*. Numbers such as $\sqrt{3}, -\sqrt{5}$, and π are irrational. Finally, the set of rational numbers, together with the set of irrational numbers, is called the set of *real numbers*.

ODD AND EVEN NUMBERS

Any integer that is divisible by 2 is called an *even* integer. Any integer that is not divisible by 2 is called an *odd* integer. When working with odd and even integers, remember the following properties:

Addition:	Subtraction:	Multiplication:
even + even = even	even − even = even	even × even = even
odd + odd = even	odd − odd = even	odd × odd = odd
odd + even = odd	even − odd = odd	even × odd = even
	odd − even = odd	

There are no set rules for division. For example, an even number divided by an even number may be either odd or even.

PRIME AND COMPOSITE NUMBERS

A whole number n is *divisible* by a whole number m if, when n is divided by m, there is no remainder (that is, it goes in evenly). As an example, since 28 can be evenly divided by 7, we say that 28 is divisible by 7. Further, 7 is said to be a *factor* or a *divisor* of 28, and 28 is said to be a *multiple* of 7. It should be obvious that each whole number has an infinite number of multiples but only a finite number of divisors. For example, the number 15 has multiples 15, 30, 45, 60, 75, 90, ..., but its only divisors are 1, 3, 5, and 15.

A whole number that has only two divisors, itself and 1, is called a *prime number*. A whole number that has more than two divisors is called a *composite* number. Note that 1 and 0 are considered to be neither prime nor composite numbers. Thus, the first seven prime numbers are 2, 3, 5, 7, 11, 13, and 17. On the other hand, the numbers 4, 6, 8, 9, 10, 12, 14, and 15 are composite.

Every composite number can be written as a product of prime numbers in a unique way. For example, the composite number 60 is equal to $2 \times 2 \times 3 \times 5$. This particular factorization of 60 is called its *prime factorization*.

There are several procedures that can be used to prime factor a composite number. Perhaps the easiest technique is simply to make a "factor tree." To begin, write down the number you wish to prime factor. Then, find *any* pair of numbers whose product is the given number, and write this pair of numbers at the end of two branches leading down from the number. Continue this process until every number at the end of each branch is a prime number. The prime factorization consists of all of the numbers at the ends of the branches.

This process is shown below for the number 315:

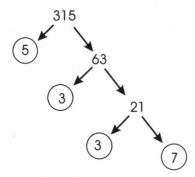

Thus, $315 = 3 \times 3 \times 5 \times 7$.

ABSOLUTE VALUE

The *absolute value* of a number is the value of the number without regard to its sign. It is considered to be the distance from zero on a number line. The absolute value of a number is indicated by placing vertical lines on either side of the number. Thus, for example, $|5| = 5$, and $|-7| = 7$.

Example

Calculate the value of $|-3| - |8| + |-5|\,|-2|$.

$$|-3| - |8| + |-5|\,|-2| = 3 - 8 + (5)(2)$$
$$= 3 - 8 + 10$$
$$= 5$$

THE BINARY NUMBER SYSTEM

The number system that we use to represent the numbers we write is called a *decimal* system, since it represents numbers in terms of powers of 10. For example, $1987 = 1(10)^3 + 9(10)^2 + 8(10) + 7$.

Thus, 1987 represents a number containing 1 "thousand," 9 "hundreds," 8 "tens," and 7 "ones."

Modern computers, instead, make use of the *binary system*. In this system, numbers are expressed in terms of powers of 2, and only two digits, usually 0 and 1, are required. In this system, the rightmost digit of a number represents the number of "ones" that the number contains, the next digit represents the number of "twos" that the number contains, the next digit represents the number of "fours," then "eights," and so on.

For example, the decimal system number 13 can be written in terms of powers of 2 as: $13 = 1(2)^3 + 1(2)^2 + 0(2) + 1$ and is therefore written in the binary system as 1101_2, where the subscript 2 denotes the use of binary digits. The leftmost digit of the figure 1101_2 can be thought of as telling us that the decimal number 13 contains one 8. The next digit of 1101_2 tells us that the figure contains one 4. Similarly, it contains no 2s, and has a remainder of 1.

To write a decimal number in binary, begin by finding the greatest power of 2 that is less than the number. Then, subtract this power of 2 from the original number, and find the greatest power of 2 that is less than the remainder. Continue this process until you end up with a remainder of 1 or 0.

For example, to express the decimal number 27 in binary, begin by determining the greatest power of 2 less than 27. Since the powers of 2 are 1, 2, 4, 8, 16, 32, 64, ..., the greatest power of 2 less than 27 is 16. Put another way, there is one 16 in the number 27. Now, $27 - 16 = 11$, and there is one 8 in 11. Next, look at the number $11 - 8 = 3$. There are no 4s in 3, but there is one 2, and a remainder of 1. Thus, 27 can be written in binary as 11011_2. Again, think of 11011_2 as representing a number that consists of one 16, one 8, no 4s, one 2, and a remainder of 1.

It is very easy to express a binary number in decimal notation. Consider, for example, the number 101110_2. The leftmost digit of this number occupies the "32's place," and, thus, the number contains one 32. It also contains no 16s, one 8, one 4, one 2, and no ones. Thus, $101110_2 = 32 + 8 + 4 + 2 = 46$.

SYSTEMS OF NUMBERS: REVIEW QUESTIONS

The following problems will give you a chance to practice. Read each problem carefully, write down your answers, and then check them with the answers and explanations that appear at the end of the Overview section.

1. If k represents an integer, which of the following must be even integers?

    $2k, 2k + 6, \dfrac{8k}{4}, 3k + 5, 2k - 1$

2. If n represents an odd integer, which of the following must be even integers?

    $2n, 3n, 3n + 1, 3n - 5, 4n + 1$

3. What is the value of $|5| - |-7| - |-4| \, |12|$?

4. a. Express the number 47 as a binary number.
   b. Express the binary number 110111_2 in the decimal system.

5. What is the prime factorization of 120?

In the problems below, classify each of the following numbers as whole, integer, rational, irrational, or real. Use all terms that apply.

6. -7

7. $\dfrac{1}{7}$

8. $5\dfrac{2}{3}$

9. 0

10. $\sqrt{13}$

COMPLEX NUMBERS

Up to this point, the real number system has been sufficient for us to be able to solve all of the algebraic equations that we have seen. However, a simple quadratic equation such as

$$x^2 + 1 = 0$$

has no solution in the real number system. In order to be able to solve such equations, mathematicians have introduced the number i, with the property that

$$i^2 + 1 = 0$$

or

$$i^2 = -1.$$

Thus, i would be the solution to $x^2 + 1 = 0$.

Since $i^2 = -1$, we can write $i = \sqrt{-1}$ and say that i is equal to "the square root of -1." The number i is called the *imaginary unit*.

Note that when you raise i to successive powers, you end up with values repeating in cycles of four, in the pattern $i, -1, -i, 1$. That is,

$$i^1 = i$$
$$i^2 = -1$$
$$i^3 = (-1)i = -i$$
$$i^4 = (-1)(-1) = 1$$
$$i^5 = (i^4)i = (1)i = i$$
$$i^6 = (i^4)i^2 = (1)i^2 = -1$$
$$i^7 = (i^4)i^3 = (1)i^3 = -i$$
$$i^8 = (i^4)i^4 = (1)(1) = 1, \text{ etc.}$$

Also note that, for any real number n,

$$\sqrt{-n} = \sqrt{(-1)n} = \sqrt{(-1)}\sqrt{n} = i\sqrt{n}.$$

Example

Simplify $\sqrt{-25} + \sqrt{-20}$.

$$\sqrt{-25} + \sqrt{-20} = i\sqrt{25} + i\sqrt{20}$$
$$= 5i + 2i\sqrt{5}$$

A number of the form bi, where b is any real number, is called an *imaginary number*. Any number of the form $a + bi$ is called a *complex number*. For any complex number $a + bi$, the number $a - bi$ is called the *complex conjugate*.

OPERATIONS WITH COMPLEX NUMBERS

The following examples show how we perform the fundamental arithmetic operations on complex numbers.

Examples

Perform the indicated operations:

(a) $(3 + 2i) + (2 + 7i)$
(b) $(3 + 2i) - (2 + 7i)$
(c) $(3 + 2i)(2 + 7i)$
(d) $\dfrac{3 + 2i}{2 + 7i}$

Solutions

(a) $(3 + 2i) + (2 + 7i) = 3 + 2i + 2 + 7i = (3 + 2) + (2i + 7i) = 5 + 9i$.

(b) $(3 + 2i) - (2 + 7i) = 3 + 2i - 2 - 7i = (3 - 2) + (2i - 7i) = 1 - 5i$.

(c) $(3 + 2i)(2 + 7i)$. Note that complex numbers are multiplied in exactly the same fashion as binomials. Thus,

$$(3 + 2i)(2 + 7i) = 6 + 3(7i) + 2(2i) + (2i)(7i)$$
$$= 6 + 21i + 4i + 14i^2 = 6 + 21i + 4i + 14(-1)$$
$$= 6 + 21i + 4i - 14 = -8 + 25i.$$

(d) $\dfrac{3 + 2i}{2 + 7i}$. The procedure for dividing complex numbers requires that both the numerator and the denominator of the quotient be multiplied by the *conjugate* of the denominator.

$$\frac{3 + 2i}{2 + 7i} = \frac{3 + 2i}{2 + 7i} \times \frac{2 - 7i}{2 - 7i}$$

$$= \frac{(3 + 2i)(2 - 7i)}{(2 + 7i)(2 - 7i)} = \frac{6 - 21i + 4i + 14}{4 + 49}$$

$$= \frac{20 - 17i}{53}.$$

Note: We can do this because we are just multiplying by 1. Frequently, when solving quadratic equations via the quadratic formula, you will end up with complex solutions.

Example

Solve the equation $x^2 + 3x + 5 = 0$.

Using the quadratic formula, $a = 1$, $b = 3$, and $c = 5$,

$$x = \frac{-b \pm \sqrt{b^2 - 4ac}}{2a} = \frac{-3 \pm \sqrt{3^2 - 4(1)(5)}}{2(1)}$$

$$= \frac{-3 \pm \sqrt{9 - 20}}{2} = \frac{-3 \pm \sqrt{-11}}{2}$$

$$= \frac{-3 \pm i\sqrt{11}}{2},$$

Thus, the solutions are $\dfrac{-3 + i\sqrt{11}}{2}$ and $\dfrac{-3 - i\sqrt{11}}{2}$.

COMPLEX NUMBERS: REVIEW QUESTIONS

The following problems will give you a chance to practice. Read each problem carefully, write down your answers, and then check them with the answers and explanations that appear at the end of the Overview section.

1. Simplify the following expressions:
   a. $7i^2$
   b. $-6i^8$
   c. $8i^7$

2. Perform the indicated operations:
   a. $(5 + 3i) + (3 - 2i)$
   b. $(8 - 2i) - (-2 - 6i)$

3. Perform the indicated operations:
   a. $(5 + 3i)(3 - 2i)$
   b. $\dfrac{(5 + 3i)}{(3 - 2i)}$

4. Find the sum of $5 + 3i$ and its conjugate.

5. Solve for x: $x^2 + x + 4 = 0$.

6. Simplify $\sqrt{-27} + 2\sqrt{-45}$.

7. What is the value of i^{77}?

8. Perform the indicated operation: $(3 - 7i)^2$.

9. Perform the indicated operation: $\dfrac{7 - 4i}{2 + i}$.

10. Solve for x: $3x^2 + 2x + 5 = 0$.

FUNCTIONS AND THEIR GRAPHS

Let D and R be any two sets. Then, we define the *function f from D to R* as a rule that assigns to each member of D one and only one member of R. The set D is called the *domain* of f, and the set R is called the *range* of f. Typically, the letter x is used to represent any element of the domain, and the letter y is used to represent any element of the range.

Note that in the definition above, we have not defined the word "function," but the phrase *function f from D to R.* In order to specify a function, you must not only state the rule, which is symbolized by the letter f, but also the domain D and the range R. However, as you will see, whenever D and R are not specified, there are some generally accepted conventions as to what they are.

In general, the sets D and R can contain any type of members at all. For example, one could define a "telephone number" function in which the domain consists of the names of all of the homeowners in a particular town, the range contains all of the phone numbers in the town, and the rule f associates the homeowner with their phone number. However, in mathematics, the sets D and R are usually sets of numbers.

Once again, the letter x is typically used to represent a value of the domain, and the letter y is used to represent a value of the range. Because the value of x determines the value of y (that is, as soon as x is selected, a unique value of y is determined by the rule f), x is called the *independent variable*, and y is called the *dependent variable*.

The symbol $f(x)$, which is read f of x, is often used instead of y to represent the range value of the function. Often, the rule that specifies a function is expressed in what is called *function notation*. For example, $f(x) = 2x + 3$ specifies a function, which, for each value x in the domain, associates the value $2x + 3$ in the range. For the domain value $x = 7$, we express the corresponding range value as $f(7)$, and compute: $f(7) = 2(7) + 3 = 17$. Thus, this function associates the domain value 7 with the range value 17.

Carefully note that the definition of function requires that, for each domain element, the rule associate one and only one range element. This requirement is made to avoid ambiguities when trying to determine the value that f associates to x. For example, consider a domain that once again contains the names of all of the homeowners in a particular town, and let the range be all of the cars in the town. Let the rule f associate each element x in the domain with an element y in the range whenever x is the owner of y. Then, f is *not* a function from D to R, since there would be several homeowners who own more than one car. That is, if x were a homeowner with more than one car, $f(x)$ would not have a well-defined meaning since we wouldn't know which car $f(x)$ actually represents.

Also note that, in general, if a rule f is given and the domain and range are not specified, then the domain of f is assumed to be the set of all real numbers except for those for which $f(x)$ does not exist. The range of f is then the subset of the set of real numbers, which is obtained by plugging all possible values of x into the rule.

Example 1

If $f(x) = 2x^2 - 5x + 1$, find $f(3)$, $f(0)$, $f(a)$, and $f(b^2)$.

$f(3) = 2(3)^2 - 5(3) + 1 = 18 - 15 + 1 = 4$.

$f(0) = 2(0)^2 - 5(0) + 1 = 1$.

$f(a) = 2a^2 - 5a + 1$.

$f(b^2) = 2(b^2)^2 - 5(b^2) + 1 = 2b^4 - 5b^2 + 1$.

Example 2

Find the domain and range of the following functions:

(a) $f(x) = 5x^2$

(b) $f(x) = \dfrac{1}{x^2}$

For $f(x) = 5x^2$, the domain is the set of all real numbers because the rule produces a real number value for each real value of x. The range is the set of all non-negative real numbers, since, for every value of x, $5x^2 \geq 0$.

For $f(x) = \dfrac{1}{x^2}$, the domain is all real numbers except 0, since the rule is undefined at 0. The range is the set of all positive real numbers since $\dfrac{1}{x^2} > 0$ for all real values of x (except 0).

ARITHMETIC OF FUNCTIONS

Functions can be added, subtracted, multiplied, and divided to form new functions. Let $f(x)$ and $g(x)$ represent two functions. Then, we define the following four functions:

$$(f + g)(x) = f(x) + g(x)$$

This new function is called the *sum* of $f(x)$ and $g(x)$.

$$(f - g)(x) = f(x) - g(x)$$

This new function is called the *difference* of $f(x)$ and $g(x)$.

$$(f \times g)(x) = f(x)g(x)$$

This new function is called the *product* of $f(x)$ and $g(x)$

$$\left(\frac{f}{g}\right)(x) = \frac{f(x)}{g(x)} \text{ where } g(x) \neq 0$$

This new function is called the *quotient* of $f(x)$ and $g(x)$.

Example

Let f and g be functions defined by the rules $f(x) = 2x + 3$ and $g(x) = x - 3$. Find $(f + g)(x)$, $(f - g)(x)$, $(f \times g)(x)$, $\left(\dfrac{f}{g}\right)(x)$, and $\left(\dfrac{g}{f}\right)(x)$.

$(f + g)(x) = (2x + 3) + (x - 3) = 3x$

$(f - g)(x) = (2x + 3) - (x - 3) = x + 6$

$(f \times g)(x) = (2x + 3)(x - 3) = 2x^2 - 3x - 9$

$$\left(\frac{f}{g}\right)(x) = \frac{2x + 3}{x - 3}$$

Note that the domain of this function is all real numbers except 3.

$$\left(\frac{g}{f}\right)(x) = \frac{x - 3}{2x + 3}$$

Note that the domain is all real numbers except $-\dfrac{3}{2}$.

It is also possible to combine two functions f and g in a fifth way, known as the *composite function*, written $f \circ g$. The composite function is defined as $f \circ g = f(g(x))$. The composite function can be thought of as representing a chain reaction, where a domain value is first associated with a range value by the rule g, and then this range value is treated as if it were a domain value for f and is associated with a range value for f.

Example

For the functions $f(x) = 2x + 3$ and $g(x) = x - 3$, find $f \circ g$, $g \circ f$, and $f \circ f$.

$$f \circ g = f(g(x)) = f(x - 3) = 2(x - 3) + 3 = 2x - 3$$

$$g \circ f = g(f(x)) = g(2x + 3) = (2x + 3) - 3 = 2x$$

$$f \circ f = f(f(x)) = f(2x + 3) = 2(2x + 3) + 3 = 4x + 9$$

INVERSE FUNCTIONS

The *inverse* of a function, which is written f^{-1}, can be obtained from the rule for the function by interchanging the values of x and y and then solving for y. The inverse of a function will always "undo" the action of a function; for example, if a function f takes the domain value 3 and associates it with 7, then f^{-1} would take the domain value of 7 and associate it with 3.

Example

Find the inverse of the function $f(x) = 7x - 4$.

Write $f(x) = 7x - 4$ as $y = 7x - 4$. Then, interchange x and y.

$x = 7y - 4$. Solve for y.

$y = \dfrac{(x + 4)}{7}$. Thus,

$f^{-1} = \dfrac{x + 4}{7}$.

GRAPHS OF FUNCTIONS

Functions can be graphed on a coordinate axis by plotting domain values along the x-axis and the corresponding y values along the y-axis. A function of the form $f(x) = c$, where c is any constant, is called a *constant function*, and its graph will always be a horizontal line. A function of the form $f(x) = mx + b$, where m and b are constants, is called a *linear function*. Its graph will always be a straight line that crosses the y-axis at b, and has a slope of m. (This means that for every unit that the graph runs horizontally, it rises m units vertically.) Finally, a graph of the form

$$f(x) = ax^n + bx^{n-1} + cx^{n-2} + \ldots\ldots + kx^2 + mx + p$$

where n is a positive integer, and $a, b, c, \ldots\ldots, k, m, p$ are real numbers, is called a *polynomial function*. If $n = 2$, the function looks like $f(x) = ax^2 + bx + c$. Such a function is called a *polynomial function* of degree 2 or a *quadratic*, and its graph is a parabola.

Examples

Graph the following functions: $f(x) = 3x + 4$, $g(x) = x^2 + 2x + 1$.

The function $f(x) = 3x + 4$ is linear, so we only need 2 values to draw the graph. Since $f(0) = 4$, and $f(1) = 7$, we have

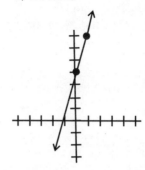

The function $g(x) = x^2 + 2x + 1$ is quadratic, and, thus, the graph will be a parabola. We need to find several points in order to graph the function

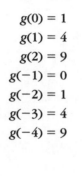

$$g(0) = 1$$
$$g(1) = 4$$
$$g(2) = 9$$
$$g(-1) = 0$$
$$g(-2) = 1$$
$$g(-3) = 4$$
$$g(-4) = 9$$

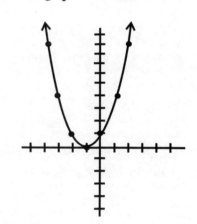

FUNCTIONS AND THEIR GRAPHS: REVIEW QUESTIONS

The following problems will give you a chance to practice. Read each problem carefully, write down your answers, and then check them with the answers and explanations that appear at the end of the Overview section.

1. If $f(x) = 3 - 2x$, find $f(-4)$ and $f(11)$.

2. State the domain and range of the following functions:

   a. $f(x) = 3x^2 - 2x + 1$

   b. $g(x) = \dfrac{1}{x}$

3. If $f(x) = x^2$ and $g(x) = 2x - 6$, find the following functions: $(f + g)(x)$, $(f \times g)(x)$, $(f \circ g)(x)$, $(f \circ f)(x)$, $g^{-1}(x)$.

4. Graph the following functions:
   a. $f(x) = 2x - 3$
   b. $g(x) = x^2 + 2x + 2$

5. If $f(x) = 4 - 3x$, find $f(-5)$ and $f(13)$.

6. What is the domain of the function $y = \sqrt{x + 3}$?

In the problems below, $f(x) = x^2$ and $g(x) = 4x - 2$. Find the following functions:

7. $(f + g)(x)$

8. $(fg)(x)$

9. $(f \circ g)(x)$

10. $(f \circ f)(x)$

11. Find the inverse of $f(x) = 5x + 2$.

EXPONENTS AND LOGARITHMS

When we discussed exponents in the arithmetic review section, all of the exponents we looked at were positive integers. However, meaning can also be given to negative and fractional exponents.

Negative exponents are defined by the definition $a^{-n} = \dfrac{1}{a^n}$. Thus, for example, $5^{-2} = \dfrac{1}{5^2}$.

By definition, we say that $a^0 = 1$. We have thus given meaning to all integral exponents.

There are five rules for computing with exponents. In general, if k and m are integers, and a and b are any numbers:

Rule 1: $a^k \times a^m = a^{k+m}$.

Rule 2: $\dfrac{a^k}{a^m} = a^{k-m}$.

Rule 3: $(a^k)^m = a^{km}$.

Rule 4: $(ab)^m = a^m \times b^m$.

Rule 5: $\left(\dfrac{a}{b}\right)^m = \dfrac{a^m}{b^m}$.

Examples

Rule 1: $2^2 \times 2^3 = 4 \times 8 = 32$, and $2^2 \times 2^3 = 2^5 = 32$.

Rule 2: $\dfrac{3^5}{3^7} = \dfrac{243}{2187} = \dfrac{1}{9} = \dfrac{1}{3^2} = 3^{-2}$,

and $\dfrac{3^5}{3^7} = 3^{5-7} = 3^{-2}$.

Rule 3: $(3^2)^3 = 9^3 = 729$ and $(3^2)^3 = 3^6 = 729$.

Rule 4: $(3 \times 4)^2 = 12^2 = 144$, and $(3 \times 4)^2 = 3^2 \times 4^2 = 9 \times 16 = 144$.

Rule 5: $\left(\dfrac{6}{2}\right)^4 = 3^4 = 81$,

and $\left(\dfrac{6}{2}\right)^4 = \dfrac{6^4}{2^4} = \dfrac{1296}{16} = 81$.

SCIENTIFIC NOTATION

Any number can be written as the product of a number between 1 and 10 and some power of 10. A number written this way is said to be written in *scientific notation*.

To express a number in scientific notation, begin by repositioning the decimal point, so that the number becomes a number between 1 and 10. (That is, place the decimal point so that there is one digit to its left.) Then, the appropriate power of 10 can be determined by counting the number of places that the decimal point has been moved. The examples below will clarify this concept.

Example 1

Write the following numbers in scientific notation:

(a) 640,000

In writing this number as 6.4, the decimal point is moved 5 places to the left. Thus, $640,000 = 6.4 \times 10^5$.

(b) 2,730,000

To change this number to 2.73, the decimal point needs to be moved 6 places to the left. Thus, $2,730,000 = 2.73 \times 10^6$.

(c) .00085

To change this number to 8.5, the decimal point must be moved 4 places to the right. Thus, $.00085 = 8.5 \times 10^{-4}$.

(d) .000000562

To change this number to 5.62, the decimal point needs to be moved 7 places to the right. Thus, $.000000562 = 5.62 \times 10^{-7}$.

Example 2

Write the following numbers without scientific notation:

(a) 3.69×10^3

Since $10^3 = 1,000$, we see that $3.69 \times 10^3 = 3.69 \times 1,000 = 3,690$.

(b) 6.7×10^{-4}

Since $10^{-4} = .0001$, $6.7 \times 10^{-4} = 6.7 \times .0001 = .00067$.

FRACTIONAL EXPONENTS

The definitions of exponents can be extended to include fractional exponents. In particular, roots of numbers can be indicated by fractions with a numerator of 1. For example, $\sqrt{2}$ can be written as $2^{1/2}$. Similarly, $\sqrt[3]{7} = 7^{1/3}$. Using the previous exponent rules, we can also make sense of any negative fractional exponents.

Examples

(a) $8^{-\frac{1}{2}} = \dfrac{1}{\sqrt{8}}$

(b) $7^{-\frac{5}{2}} = (7^{-5})^{\frac{1}{2}} = \left(\dfrac{1}{7^5}\right)^{\frac{1}{2}} = \left(\dfrac{1}{16807}\right)^{\frac{1}{2}}$

$= \dfrac{1}{\sqrt{16807}} \approx .0077$

Note that from Rule 4 we can determine that $(a \times b)^{\frac{1}{k}} = a^{\frac{1}{k}} \times b^{\frac{1}{k}}$. Written in radical notation, this expression becomes $\sqrt[k]{a \times b} = \sqrt[k]{a} \times \sqrt[k]{b}$. This statement justifies the technique we have used for the simplification of square roots.

EXPONENTIAL EQUATIONS

An exponential equation is an equation whose variable appears in an exponent. Such equations can be solved by algebraic means if it is possible to express both sides of the equation as powers of the same base.

Example 1

Solve $5^{2x-1} = 25$.

Rewrite the equation as $5^{2x-1} = 5^2$. Then it must be true that $2x - 1 = 2$. This means that $x = \dfrac{3}{2}$.

Example 2

Solve $9^{x+3} = 27^{2x}$.

Rewrite the left side of the equation as $(3^2)^{x+3} = 3^{2x+6}$. Rewrite the right side of the equation as $(3^3)^{2x} = 3^{6x}$. Then, it must be true that $2x + 6 = 6x$. This means that $x = \dfrac{3}{2}$.

Exponential equations in which the bases cannot both be changed to the same number can be solved by using logarithms.

THE MEANING OF LOGARITHMS

The logarithm of a number is the power to which a given base must be raised to produce the number. For example, the logarithm of 25 to the base 5 is 2, since 5 must be raised to the second power to produce the number 25. The statement *the logarithm of 25 to the base 5 is 2* is written as $\log_5 25 = 2$.

Note that every time we write a statement about exponents, we can write an equivalent statement about logarithms. For example, $\log_3 27 = 3$ since $3^3 = 27$, and $\log_8 4 = \dfrac{2}{3}$, since $8^{\frac{2}{3}} = 4$.

An important byproduct of the definition of logarithms is that we cannot determine values for $\log_a x$ if x is either zero or a negative number. For example, if $\log_2 0 = b$, then $2^b = 0$, but there is no exponent satisfying this property. Similarly, if $\log_2(-8) = b$, then $2^b = -8$, and there is no exponent satisfying this property.

While logarithms can be written to any base, logarithms to the base 10 are used so frequently that they are called common logarithms, and the symbol "log" is often used to stand for "$\log_{10}$".

Example 1

Write logarithmic equivalents to the following statements about exponents:

(a) $2^5 = 32$.

The statement $2^5 = 32$ is equivalent to $\log_2 32 = 5$.

(b) $12^0 = 1$.

The statement $12^0 = 1$ is equivalent to $\log_{12} 1 = 0$.

Example 2

Use the definition of logarithm to evaluate the following:

(a) $\log_6 36$

$\log_6 36 = 2$, since $6^2 = 36$.

(b) $\log_4 \left(\dfrac{1}{16}\right)$

$\log_4 \left(\dfrac{1}{16}\right) = -2$, since $4^{-2} = \dfrac{1}{16}$.

PROPERTIES OF LOGARITHMS

Since logarithms are exponents, they follow the rules of exponents previously discussed. For example, since when exponents to the same base are multiplied, their exponents are added, we have the rule: $\log_a xy = \log_a x + \log_a y$. The three most frequently used rules of logarithms are:

Rule 1: $\log_a xy = \log_a x + \log_a y$.

Rule 2: $\log_a \left(\dfrac{x}{y}\right) = \log_a x - \log_a y$.

Rule 3: $\log_a x^b = b \log_a x$.

Examples

Rule 1: $\log_3 14 = \log_3(7 \times 2) = \log_3 7 + \log_3 2$.

Rule 2: $\log \left(\dfrac{13}{4}\right) = \log 13 - \log 4$.

Rule 3: $\log_7 \sqrt{5} = \log_7(5^{\frac{1}{2}}) = \dfrac{1}{2}\log_7 5$.

By combining these rules, we can see, for example, that $\log \left(\dfrac{5b}{7}\right) = \log 5 + \log b - \log 7$.

EXPONENTS AND LOGARITHIMS: REVIEW QUESTIONS

The following problems will give you a chance to practice. Read each problem carefully, write down your answers, and then check them with the answers and explanations that appear at the end of the Overview section.

1. Express the following equations in logarithmic form:
   a. $3^2 = 9$
   b. $7^{-2} = \dfrac{1}{49}$

2. Express the following equations in exponential form:
   a. $\log_6 36 = 2$
   b. $\log_{10}\left(\dfrac{1}{10}\right) = -1$

3. Find the value of the following logarithms:
   a. $\log_2 8$
   b. $\log_{12} 1$

4. Express as the sum or difference of logarithms of simpler quantities:
   a. $\log 12$
   b. $\log\left(\dfrac{ab}{c}\right)$

5. Solve the following equation for x: $125 = 5^{2x-1}$.

In exercises 6 and 7, write an equivalent exponential form for each radical expression.

6. $\sqrt{11}$

7. $\sqrt[3]{13}$

In exercises 8 and 9, write an equivalent radical expression for each exponential expression.

8. $8^{\frac{1}{5}}$

9. $(x^2)^{\frac{1}{3}}$

In exercises 10 and 11, evaluate the given expressions.

10. $27^{\frac{1}{3}}$

11. $125^{\frac{2}{3}}$

12. Express the following numbers using scientific notation.
    a. 1,234.56
    b. 0.0876

13. Write the following numbers without scientific notation.
    a. 1.234×10^5
    b. 5.45×10^{-3}

14. Solve the following equation for x: $3^{2x} = 4^{x-1}$

SET THEORY

A *set* is a collection of objects. The objects in a particular set are called the *members* or the *elements* of the set. In mathematics, sets are usually represented by capital letters, and their members are represented by lower case letters. Braces, { and }, are usually used to enclose the members of a set. Thus, the set A, which has members a, b, c, d, and e and no other members, can be written as A = {a, b, c, d, e}. Note that the order in which the elements of a set are listed is not important; thus, the set {1, 2, 3} and the set {2, 3, 1} represent identical sets.

The symbol used to indicate that an element belongs to a particular set is $\in$, and the symbol that indicates that an element does not belong to a set is $\notin$. Thus, if B = {2, 4, 6, 8}, we can say $6 \in$ B and $7 \notin$ B. If a set is defined so that it does not contain any elements, it is called the *empty set*, or the *null set*, and can be written as { } or $\varnothing$.

There are several different notational techniques that can be used to represent a set. The simplest one is called *enumeration* or *roster notation*, in which all of the elements of the set are listed within braces. For example, if C is the set of all odd integers between 10 and 20, we can use enumeration to represent the set as C = {11, 13, 15, 17, 19}. The other is called *set-builder notation*. In this notation, a short vertical bar is used to stand for the phrase "such that." For example, the set of all integers less than 15 can be written as:

$$\{ x \mid x < 15, x \text{ is an integer} \}$$

and is read, *The set of all* x, *such that* x *is less than 15, and* x *is an integer.*

A set that contains a finite number of elements is called a *finite* set. A set that is neither finite nor empty is called an *infinite* set. When using the method of enumeration to describe a set, we can use three dots to indicate "and so on." Thus, the infinite set containing all positive integers can be written as {1, 2, 3, 4, ...}. The infinite set containing all of the even integers between 2 and 200 can be enumerated as {2, 4, 6, ..., 200}.

Suppose that J is the set containing everyone who lives in New Jersey, and K is the set of all people living in New Jersey who are older that 65. Then, clearly, all members of K are also members of J, and we say *K is a subset of J*. This relationship is written symbolically as K ⊆ J. In general, A is a subset of B if every element of A is also an element of B. For example, the set A = {2, 4, 6} is a subset of the set B = {0, 2, 4, 6, 8, 10}. By convention, we agree that the null set is a subset of every other set. Thus, we can write ∅ ⊆ A, where A is any set. Also note that if A and B contain exactly the same elements, then A ⊆ B and B ⊆ A. In such a case, we write A = B. If A ⊆ B but A ≠ B, we call A a *proper subset* of B. This is written A ⊂ B. Thus, if A is a subset of B, and B contains at least one element that is not in A, then A is a proper subset of B, and we write A ⊂ B.

In a particular discussion, the *universal set* represents the largest possible set; that is, it is the set that contains all of the possible elements under consideration. All other sets in the discussion must therefore be subsets of the universal set, which is represented by the letter U. If N is a subset of U, then N′, which is called the *complement* of N, is the set of all elements from the universal set that are not in N. For example, if, in a particular problem, U is the set of all integers, and N is the set of negative integers, then N′ is the set of all non-negative integers.

VENN DIAGRAMS, UNION, AND INTERSECTION

Let U be a universal set and N a subset of U. Then, the drawing below, called a *Venn diagram*, illustrates the relationship between U, N, and N′.

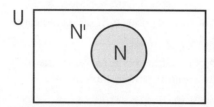

The *union* of two sets A and B, indicated A ∪ B, is the set of all elements that are in either A or B. The intersection of two sets, indicated A ∩ B, is the set of all elements that are in both A and B. Thus, if A = {2, 4, 6, 8, 10} and B = {1, 2, 3, 4}, we have A ∪ B = {1, 2, 3, 4, 6, 8, 10} and A ∩ B = {2, 4}. If A ∩ B = ∅, then A and B are said to be *disjoint*.

The Venn diagrams below represent the operations of union and intersection.

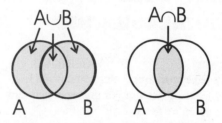

CARTESIAN PRODUCTS

In addition to the operations of union and intersection, there is one other common way of combining two sets. Let A = {1, 2} and B = {3, 4, 5}. Then, the set of all possible ordered pairs (a, b), with a∈A and b∈B, is called the *Cartesian Product* of A and B and is written A × B. Thus, in this case,

$$A \times B = \{(1,3), (1,4), (1,5), (2,3), (2,4), (2,5)\}$$

SET THEORY: REVIEW QUESTIONS

The following problems will give you a chance to practice. Read each problem carefully, write down your answers, and then check them with the answers and explanations that appear at the end of the Overview section.

1. Use set-builder notation to describe the set of all integers greater than 12 and less than 48.

2. List all of the subsets of the set {a, b, c, d}.

3. If A = {2, 4, 6}, B = {1, 3, 5}, and C = {2, 3, 4}, find A ∪ B, A ∪ C, A ∩ C, A ∩ B, A ∩ (B ∪ C).

4. If U = {2, 4, 6, 8, 10, 12, 14, 16, 18, 20}, and W = {2, 6, 12, 18}, find W′.

5. If Q = {2, 6, 9}, and R = {2, 4, 7}, find Q × R.

6. Draw a Venn diagram to represent the set (A ∩ B) ∩ C.

7. Use numeration to describe the set of negative integers.

In problems 8–11, describe the sets listed in terms of D, E, F, and intersections, unions, and complements.

8. {x | x ∈ D and x ∉ E}.

9. {x | x ∈ F or x ∈ E}.

10. {x | x ∈ D and x ∈ E}.

11. {x | x ∈ D and x is not an element of either E or F}.

PERMUTATIONS AND COMBINATIONS

A FUNDAMENTAL COUNTING PRINCIPLE

Consider the following problem. Set A contains 3 elements, A = {2, 4, 6}. Set B contains 2 elements, B = {3, 7}. How many different sets exist containing one element from set A and one element from set B?

In order to answer this question, simply note that for each of the three possible selections from set A, there are two possible corresponding selections from set B. Thus, the sets that can be formed are {2, 3}, {2, 7}, {4, 3}, {4, 7}, {6, 3}, and {6, 7}. This means that there are 2 × 3 = 6 sets that can be formed.

This result can be generalized in the following way: If one experiment can be performed in r possible ways, and a second experiment can be performed in s possible ways, then there are a total of rs possible ways to perform both experiments. This principle can be extended to any number of sets and can be applied in many different situations, as the following examples show.

Example 1

How many two-digit numbers can be formed from the digits 2, 4, 6, 8, and 9 if it is permissible to use the same digit twice?

If it is permissible to use the same digit twice, there are 5 choices for the tens digit, and 5 choices for the units digit. The principle above thus tells us that there are 5 × 5 = 25 ways to form two-digit numbers.

Example 2

How many three-letter sequences can be formed from the letters b, c, d, f, g, and h if it is permissible to use the same letter twice?

There are 6 choices for the first letter of the sequence, 6 choices for the second letter, and 6 choices for the third. Thus, there are 6 × 6 × 6 = 216 possible sequences.

PERMUTATIONS

A *permutation* is any arrangement of the elements of a set in definite order. For example, consider the set C = {p, q, r}. There are six different orders in which the elements of this set can be ordered:

pqr, prq, rpq, rqp, qrp, qpr

Thus, there are six permutations of the set C. Of course, it would have been possible to determine that there were six permutations of the given set without listing them all. Simply note that the first letter listed can be any element of the set, so that there are 3 possible choices for the first element. After a letter has been selected to go first, there are only two possible selections that remain to go second. And, after the first two selections have been made, there is only 1 remaining choice for the final selection. By multiplying together the number of choices at each stage, 3 × 2 × 1 = 6, we obtain the number of permutations.

The product 3 × 2 × 1 can be written in what is called *factorial notation* as 3!, which is read *three factorial*. Similarly, 5! = 5 × 4 × 3 × 2 × 1. And, in general, we have the definition

$$n! = n \times (n-1) \times (n-2) \times \ldots\ldots\ldots \times 3 \times 2 \times 1.$$

The example above illustrates the following fact about permutations: the number of permutations of a set containing n members is $n!$

Now, consider the following problem. Let D = {a, b, c, d, e, f}. How would we count the number of permutations of the six elements from this set taken 3 at a time? Once again, we would reason as follows: there are 6 possible choices for the first element of the permutation, 5 possible choices for the second element of the permutation, and 4 choices for the final element. Thus, there are 6 × 5 × 4 = 120 permutations of 6 objects taken 3 at a time.

This example illustrates the following fact about permutations: The number of permutations of n elements taken r at a time is given by

$$_nP_r = n(n-1)(n-2) \ldots [n - (r - 1)].$$

Example

In how many ways can a president and a vice president be chosen from a club with 8 members?

We are looking for the number of permutations of 8 members taken 2 at a time.

$_nP_r = n(n-1)$ so $_8P_2 = 8 \times 7 = 56$.

COMBINATIONS

A *combination* is any arrangement of the elements of a set without regard to order. For example, consider the set $F = \{a, b, c, d\}$. How many subsets containing 3 elements does this set have? The subsets are $\{a, b, c\}$, $\{a, b, d\}$, $\{a, c, d\}$, and $\{b, c, d\}$. Thus, we say that the number of combinations of 4 objects taken 3 at a time, which is written $_4C_3$, is 4.

In general, the formula for the number of combinations of n objects taken r at a time is given by

$$_nC_r = \frac{n!}{r!\,(n-r)!}.$$

Example

In how many ways can an advisory board of 3 members be chosen from a committee of 10?

We need to find the number of combinations of 10 objects taken 3 at a time.

$$_nC_r = {}_{10}C_3 = \frac{10!}{(3!)(7!)} = \frac{(10 \times 9 \times 8)}{(3 \times 2 \times 1)} = 120.$$

PERMUTATIONS AND COMBINATIONS: REVIEW QUESTIONS

The following problems will give you a chance to practice. Read each problem carefully, write down your answers, and then check them with the answers and explanations that appear at the end of the Overview section.

1. Brian has 5 different shirts, 2 different pairs of pants, and 3 different ties. How many different outfits can Brian wear?

2. In how many different orders can 5 boys stand on a line?

3. In how many different ways can a judge award first, second, and third places in a contest with 13 contestants?

4. A mathematics instructor plans to assign as homework three problems from a set of ten problems. How many different homework assignments are possible?

5. A baseball card dealer has 40 different cards that Brian would like to own. For his birthday, Brian is allowed to pick any 4 of these cards. How many choices does he have?

6. How many permutations are there of six elements from a set taken 3 at a time?

7. In how many ways can a special committee of 3 members be chosen from an association of 10 people?

8. How many three-digit numbers can be formed with the digits 0, 1, 2, 3, 4, 5, 6, 7, 8, and 9 if repetitions of digits *are not* permitted?

9. How many three-digit numbers can be formed with the digits 0, 1, 2, 3, 4, 5, 6, 7, 8, and 9 if repetitions of digits *are* permitted?

10. How many three-digit numbers can be formed with the digits 0, 1, 2, 3, 4, 5, 6, 7, 8, and 9 if repetitions of digits are not permitted, and the last digit must be 7?

PROBABILITY

Probability is the branch of mathematics that gives you techniques for dealing with uncertainties. Intuitively, probability can be thought of as a numerical measure of the likelihood, or the chance, that an event will occur.

A probability value is always a number between 0 and 1. The nearer a probability value is to 0, the more unlikely the event is to occur; a probability value near 1 indicates that the event is almost certain to occur. Other probability values between 0 and 1 represent varying degrees of likelihood that an event will occur.

In the study of probability, an *experiment* is any process that yields one of a number of well-defined outcomes. By this we mean that on any single performance of an experiment, one and only one of a number of possible outcomes will occur. Thus, tossing a coin is an experiment with two possible outcomes: heads or tails. Rolling a die is an experiment with six possible outcomes; playing a game of hockey is an experiment with three possible outcomes (win, lose, tie).

COMPUTING PROBABILITIES

In some experiments, all possible outcomes are equally likely. In such an experiment with, say, n possible outcomes, we assign a probability of $\frac{1}{n}$ to each outcome. Thus, for example, in the experiment of tossing a fair coin, for which there are two equally likely outcomes, we would say that the probability of each outcome is $\frac{1}{2}$. In the experiment of tossing a fair die, for which there are six equally likely outcomes, we would say that the probability of each outcome is $\frac{1}{6}$. (Note: a six-sided die is assumed when we say "fair die.")

How would you determine the probability of obtaining an even number when tossing a die? Clearly, there are three distinct ways that an even number can be obtained: tossing a 2, a 4, or a 6. The probability of each one of these three outcomes is $\frac{1}{6}$. The probability of obtaining an even number is simply the sum of the probabilities of these three favorable outcomes; that is to say, the probability of tossing an even number is equal to the probability of tossing a 2, plus the probability of tossing a 4, plus the probability of tossing a 6, which is $\frac{1}{6} + \frac{1}{6} + \frac{1}{6} = \frac{3}{6} = \frac{1}{2}$.

This result leads us to the fundamental formula for computing probabilities for events with equally likely outcomes:

The probability of an event occurring =

$$\frac{\text{The number of favorable outcomes}}{\text{The total number of possible outcomes}}$$

In the case of tossing a die and obtaining an even number, as we saw, there are six possible outcomes, three of which are favorable, leading to a probability of $\frac{3}{6} = \frac{1}{2}$.

Example 1

What is the probability of drawing one card from a standard deck of 52 cards and having it be a king? When you select a card from a deck, there are 52 possible outcomes, 4 of which are favorable. Thus, the probability of drawing a king is $\frac{4}{52} = \frac{1}{13}$.

Example 2

Human eye color is controlled by a single pair of genes, one of which comes from the mother and one of which comes from the father, called a genotype. Brown eye color, B, is dominant over blue eye color, ℓ. Therefore, in the genotype $B\ell$, which consists of one brown gene B and one blue gene ℓ, the brown gene dominates. A person with a $B\ell$ genotype will have brown eyes.

If both parents have genotype $B\ell$, what is the probability that their child will have blue eyes? To answer the question, we need to consider every possible eye-color genotype for the child. They are given in the table below:

father / mother	B	ℓ
B	BB	Bℓ
ℓ	ℓB	$\ell\ell$

The four possible genotypes for the child are equally likely, so we can use the formula above to compute the probability. Of the four possible outcomes, blue eyes can occur only with the $\ell\ell$ genotype, so only one of the four possible outcomes is favorable to blue eyes. Thus, the probability that the child has blue eyes is $\frac{1}{4}$.

Two events are said to be *independent* if the occurrence of one does not affect the probability of the occurrence of the other. For example, if a coin is tossed and a die is thrown, obtaining heads on the coin and obtaining a 5 on the die are independent events. On the other hand, if a coin is tossed three times, the probability of obtaining heads on the first toss and the probability of obtaining tails on all three tosses are not independent. In particular, if heads is obtained on the first toss, the probability of obtaining three tails becomes 0.

When two events are independent, the probability that they both happen is the product of their individual probabilities. For example, the probability of obtaining heads when a coin is tossed is $\frac{1}{2}$, and the probability of obtaining 5 when a die is thrown is $\frac{1}{6}$; thus, the probability of both of these events happening is

$$\left(\frac{1}{2}\right)\left(\frac{1}{6}\right) = \frac{1}{12}.$$

In a situation where two events occur one after the other, be sure to correctly determine the number of favorable outcomes and the total number of possible outcomes.

Example

Consider a standard deck of 52 cards. What is the probability of drawing two kings in a row, if the first card drawn is replaced in the deck before the second card is drawn? What is the probability of drawing two kings in a row if the first card drawn is *not* replaced in the deck?

In the first case, the probability of drawing a king from the deck on the first attempt is $\frac{4}{52} = \frac{1}{13}$. If the selected card is replaced in the deck, the probability of drawing a king on the second draw is also $\frac{1}{13}$, and, thus, the probability of drawing two consecutive kings would be $\left(\frac{1}{13}\right)\left(\frac{1}{13}\right) = \frac{1}{169}$. On the other hand, if the first card drawn is a king and is not replaced, there are now only three kings in a deck of 51 cards, and the probability of drawing the second king becomes $\frac{3}{51} = \frac{1}{17}$. The overall probability, thus, would be $\left(\frac{1}{13}\right)\left(\frac{1}{17}\right) = \frac{1}{221}$.

PROBABILITY: REVIEW QUESTIONS

The following problems will give you a chance to practice. Read each problem carefully, write down your answers, and then check them with the answers and explanations that appear at the end of the Overview section.

1. A bag contains seven blue marbles, three red marbles, and two white marbles. If one marble is chosen at random from the bag, what is the probability that it will be red? What is the probability that it will *not* be blue?

2. A woman's change purse contains a quarter, two dimes, and two pennies. What is the probability that a coin chosen at random will be worth at least 10 cents?

3. A bag contains four white and three black marbles. One marble is selected, its color is noted, and then it is returned to the bag. Then a second marble is selected. What is the probability that both selected marbles were white?

4. Using the same set up as given in problem 3, what is the probability that both selected marbles will be white if the first marble is *not* returned to the bag?

5. A man applying for his driver's license estimates that his chances of passing the written test are $\frac{2}{3}$, and that his chances of passing the driving test, if he does pass the written test, are $\frac{1}{4}$. What is the probability that he passes both tests?

6. What is the probability of drawing two diamonds from a standard deck of cards if the first card drawn is not replaced?

7. A bag of marbles contains nine marbles in three different colors. There are three marbles to each color. What is the probability of pulling three different colors of marbles if none of the marbles are placed back into the bag once picked?

8. What is the probability of rolling two dice and the sum of the dice being prime?

9. What is the probability of rolling a fair die three times and getting three different numbers?

10. If three kings are removed from a standard deck of cards, what is the probability of drawing the last king from the remaining cards?

LOGIC

Logic is a field of mathematics in which algebraic techniques are used to establish the truth or falsity of statements.

A *statement* or *assertion* is any expression that can be labeled as either true or false. Letters such as p, q, r, s, and t are used to represent statements. *Compound* statements can be formed by connecting two or more statements.

Examples

1. "My dog is a Boston terrier," "My house is a mess," and "My name is Howard," are statements since they are either true or false.

2. "How old are you?" and "Where do you live?" are not statements since they are neither true or false.

3. "My cat is named Nora, and my dog is named Krauser," is a compound statement consisting of the two *substatements,* "My cat is named Nora," and "My dog is named Krauser."

4. "He is a natural musician or he practices a lot," is a compound statement consisting of the two *substatements,* "He is a natural musician," and "He practices a lot."

The truth or falsity of a statement is called its *truth value* (or its logical value). The truth or falsity of a compound statement can be found by determining the truth value of the statements that comprise it and then examining the way in which the statements are connected. We will now consider some of the fundamental ways to connect statements.

CONNECTIVES

If two statements are combined by the word *and*, the resulting compound statement is called the *conjunction* of the two original statements. If *p and q* are statements, the conjunction of *p and q* is written $p \wedge q$. In order to determine whether a particular conjunction is true, we can create what is called a *truth table*. The truth table for this conjunction is:

p	q	$p \wedge q$
T	T	T
T	F	F
F	T	F
F	F	F

This first line of this table tells us, for example, that if statement *p* is true and statement *q* is true, then $p \wedge q$ is true. On the other hand, the second line tells us that if *p* is true but *q* is false, then $p \wedge q$ is false. Note that the table tells us that the only way $p \wedge q$ is true is if both *p* and *q* are true.

Example

Consider the following four compound statements:

1. The capital of the United States is Washington, D. C., and Christmas is on December 25.

2. The capital of the United States is Washington, D. C., and Christmas is on January 25.

3. The capital of the United States is Buffalo, NY, and Christmas is on December 25.

4. The capital of the United States is Buffalo, NY, and Christmas is on January 25.

Of these four statements, only the first one, which consists of two true substatements, is true.

If two statements are combined by the word *or*, the resulting compound statement is called the *disjunction* of the two original statements. If *p* and *q* are the two statements, we indicate the disjunction of *p* and *q* with the symbol $p \vee q$.

The truth table for disjunction is:

p	q	$p \vee q$
T	T	T
T	F	T
F	T	T
F	F	F

Thus, a disjunction is false only when both substatements are false. Note, therefore, that, in logic, the word *or* is used in the sense of *either or both*.

Example

1. The capital of the United States is Washington, D. C., or Christmas is on December 25.

2. The capital of the United States is Washington, D. C., or Christmas is on January 25.

3. The capital of the United States is Buffalo, NY, or Christmas is on December 25.

4. The capital of the United States is Buffalo, NY, or Christmas is on January 25.

Of these four statements, only the last one, which consists of two false substatements, is false.

Given any statement *p*, another statement can be created by inserting the word *not* in *p*. Such a statement is called the *negation* or contradiction of *p*, is symbolized as ∼*p*, and is read *not p*.

The truth table for negation is:

p	∼p
T	F
F	T

Thus, if *p* is true, then ∼*p* is false and vice versa.

For statements *p* and *q*, $p \rightarrow q$ represents the statement *if p, then q*. The statement $p \rightarrow q$ is also read *p implies q*. Such statements are called *implications* or *conditional* statements. The truth table for → is

p	q	$p \rightarrow q$
T	T	T
T	F	F
F	T	T
F	F	T

Another compound statement is the *biconditional* statement, which is written $p \Leftrightarrow q$ and read *p if and only if q*. $p \Leftrightarrow q$ is true if and only if *p* and *q* have the same truth values. Thus, the truth table is:

p	q	$p \Leftrightarrow q$
T	T	T
T	F	F
F	T	F
F	F	T

TRUTH TABLES, TAUTOLOGIES, AND CONTRADICTIONS

By using various combinations of the connectives $\wedge$, $\vee$, ∼, →, and ⇔, we can create compound statements that are much more complicated than those we have considered so far. The truth or falsity of a compound statement can be determined from the truth values of its substatements. A truth table is a simple way to determine the truth or falsity of a compound statement. For example, consider the compound statement $p \lor (q \land \sim q)$. A truth table for this statement would look like:

p	q	~q	q ∧ ~q	p ∨ (q ∧ ~q)
T	T	F	F	T
T	F	T	F	T
F	T	F	F	F
F	F	T	F	F

Note that in the table above, the first two columns contain all possible combinations of truth and falsity for p and q. The third and fourth columns simply help us keep track of the truth or falsity of the components of the compound statement, and the final column lists the truth values for the given compound statement. Note that, for example, if p and q are both true, then $p \lor (q \land \sim q)$ is also true.

Any compound statement that is true for any possible combination of truth values of the statements that form it is called a *tautology*. In the same way, a compound statement is called a *contradiction* if it is false for all possible truth values of the statements that form it.

Example

Construct a truth table to verify that $p \lor \sim (p \land q)$ is a tautology.

p	q	p ∧ q	~(p ∧ q)	p ∨ ~(p ∧ q)
T	T	T	F	T
T	F	F	T	T
F	T	F	T	T
F	F	F	T	T

Since $p \lor \sim (p \land q)$ is true regardless of the truth or falsity of p and q, it is a tautology.

Two statements are said to be logically equivalent if they have the same truth table. For example, look once again at the truth table for $p \lor (q \land \sim q)$. Notice that it has the same values as p. Thus, p and $p \lor (q \land \sim q)$ are logically equivalent.

ARGUMENTS, HYPOTHESES, AND CONCLUSIONS

An *argument* is a claim that a number of statements, called *hypotheses* or *premises,* imply another statement, called the *conclusion*. An argument is said to be valid if the conclusion is true whenever all of the hypotheses are true. A *fallacy* is an argument that is not valid. If the hypotheses are written as p_1, p_2, ..., p_n, and the conclusion is q, then the arguments are written as $p_1, p_2, ..., p_n \perp q$.

Example

Prove that the argument $p \Leftrightarrow q$, $q \perp p$ is valid.

Begin by making a truth table containing p, q, and $p \Leftrightarrow q$.

p	q	p ⇔ q
T	T	T
T	F	F
F	T	F
F	F	T

Note that q and $p \Leftrightarrow q$ are both true only on the first line of the table. On this line, p is also true. Thus, whenever q and $p \Leftrightarrow q$ are both true, p is true also. This means that the argument is valid.

CONVERSE, INVERSE, AND CONTRAPOSITIVE

Once again, let us consider the conditional statement $p \to q$. The statement $q \to p$ is called the *converse* of $p \to q$. Similarly, $\sim p \to \sim q$ is called the *inverse* of $p \to q$, and $\sim q \to \sim p$ is called the *contrapositive* of $p \to q$.

Example

Show that the contrapositive $\sim q \to \sim p$ is logically equivalent to the conditional $p \to q$.

Create the truth tables for the conditional and contrapositive:

p	q	~p	~q	p → q	~q → ~p
T	T	F	F	T	T
T	F	F	T	F	F
F	T	T	F	T	T
F	F	T	T	T	T

Note that the truth tables for the conditional and contrapositive are the same. Therefore, they are logically equivalent.

LOGIC: REVIEW QUESTIONS

The following problems will give you a chance to practice. Read each problem carefully, write down your answers, and then check them with the answers and explanations that appear at the end of the Overview section.

1. Let p be the statement, "I am at work," and let q be the statement "It is snowing." Write in words the meaning of each of the following compound statements:

   a. $p \land q$
   b. $p \lor q$
   c. $p \land \sim q$
   d. $\sim \sim q$
   e. $q \to p$

2. Let r be the statement, "I have a cold," and let s be the statement, "I am at home." Write each of the following using the connective notation discussed in this section.

   a. I have a cold and I am at home.
   b. I have a cold and I am not at home.
   c. I do not have a cold.
   d. I do not have a cold, or I have a cold and am at home.
   e. It is false that I do not have a cold and am at home.

3. Construct the truth table for $\sim(\sim p \vee q)$.

4. Demonstrate that $\sim(\sim p \wedge \sim q)$ is logically equivalent to $p \vee q$.

5. Show that "If I go home, then it rained" is logically equivalent to "If it did not rain, then I did not go home."

In the problems below, $\wedge$ represents conjunction, $\vee$ represents disjunction, and $\sim$ represents negation. A is a true logic variable, and B is a false logic variable. For each problem, determine whether the given compound statement is true or false.

6. $A \wedge (\sim B)$

7. $A \wedge (\sim A)$

8. $\sim(A \wedge B)$

9. $A \vee (B \wedge \sim A)$

10. $B \vee (A \wedge \sim A)$

REVIEW ANSWERS AND EXPLANATIONS

WHOLE NUMBERS

1. 6, 12, 18, 24, 30, 36, 42
2. 1, 2, 3, 4, 6, 8, 9, 12, 18, 24, 36, 72
3. 1 and 47 are the only factors
4. The associative property of addition
5. The commutative property of multiplication
6. 30 can be factored as $2 \times 3 \times 5$. 105 can be factored as $3 \times 5 \times 7$. Thus, the common factors are 1 and 3 and 5 and 15. Don't forget 1 is a factor of every number.
7. $4 - 5 \neq 5 - 4$
8. The associative property of multiplication
9. The commutative property of addition
10. a. $-12 < 13$

    b. $\dfrac{1}{16} = 0.0625$

    c. $3\dfrac{1}{2} > 3\dfrac{2}{5}$

FRACTIONS

1. $\dfrac{2}{15} + \dfrac{2}{3} = \dfrac{2}{15} + \dfrac{10}{15} = \dfrac{12}{15} = \dfrac{4}{5}$

2. $\dfrac{4}{5} - \dfrac{2}{13} = \dfrac{52}{65} - \dfrac{10}{65} = \dfrac{42}{65}$

3. $\dfrac{3}{8} \times \dfrac{4}{21} = \dfrac{\overset{1}{\cancel{3}}}{\underset{2}{\cancel{8}}} \times \dfrac{\overset{1}{\cancel{4}}}{\underset{7}{\cancel{21}}} = \dfrac{1}{2} \times \dfrac{1}{7} = \dfrac{1}{14}$

4. $\dfrac{2}{3} \div \dfrac{5}{6} = \dfrac{2}{\underset{1}{\cancel{3}}} \times \dfrac{\overset{2}{\cancel{6}}}{5} = \dfrac{2}{1} \times \dfrac{2}{5} = \dfrac{4}{5}$

5. $9\dfrac{1}{5} - 3\dfrac{1}{4} = 8\dfrac{6}{5} - 3\dfrac{1}{4} = 8\dfrac{24}{20} - 3\dfrac{5}{20} = 5\dfrac{19}{20}$

6. $6\dfrac{2}{3} \times 1\dfrac{4}{5} = \dfrac{\overset{4}{\cancel{20}}}{\underset{1}{\cancel{3}}} \times \dfrac{\overset{3}{\cancel{9}}}{\underset{1}{\cancel{5}}} = \dfrac{4}{1} \times \dfrac{3}{1} = 12$

7. $\dfrac{2}{3} \times \dfrac{12}{8} = \dfrac{\overset{1}{\cancel{2}}}{\underset{1}{\cancel{3}}} \times \dfrac{\overset{1}{\cancel{12}}}{\underset{1}{\cancel{8}}} = \dfrac{1}{1} \times \dfrac{1}{1} = 1$

8. $\dfrac{3}{4} \div \dfrac{7}{8} = \dfrac{3}{\underset{1}{\cancel{4}}} \times \dfrac{\overset{2}{\cancel{8}}}{7} = \dfrac{6}{7}$

9. $2\dfrac{3}{5} + 7\dfrac{3}{5} = \dfrac{13}{5} + \dfrac{38}{5} = \dfrac{51}{5} = 10\dfrac{1}{5}$

10. $\dfrac{6}{7} \times \dfrac{3}{4} \times \dfrac{2}{3} = \dfrac{6}{7} \times \dfrac{1}{2} \times \dfrac{1}{1} = \dfrac{3}{7} \times \dfrac{1}{1} \times \dfrac{1}{1} = \dfrac{3}{7}$

11. $6 \times \dfrac{2}{3} \times 2\dfrac{5}{6} = \dfrac{6}{1} \times \dfrac{2}{3} \times \dfrac{17}{6} = \dfrac{34}{3} = 11\dfrac{1}{3}$

12. $2\dfrac{2}{3} \div 1\dfrac{7}{9} = \dfrac{8}{3} \div \dfrac{16}{9} = \dfrac{8}{3} \times \dfrac{9}{16} = \dfrac{1}{1} \times \dfrac{3}{2} = \dfrac{3}{2}$

DECIMALS

1. a.
$$
\begin{array}{r}
0.625 \\
8\overline{)5.000} \\
\underline{48} \\
20 \\
\underline{-16} \\
40
\end{array}
$$

   b.
$$
\begin{array}{r}
0.166... \\
6\overline{)1.0000} \\
\underline{6} \\
40 \\
\underline{-36} \\
40
\end{array}
$$

2. a. $2.08 = 2\dfrac{8}{100} = 2\dfrac{2}{25}$

   b. $13.24 = 13\dfrac{24}{100} = 13\dfrac{6}{25}$

3.
$$
\begin{array}{r}
31.32 \\
+\ 3.829 \\
\hline
35.149
\end{array}
$$

4.
$$
\begin{array}{r}
2.567 \\
-0.021 \\
\hline
2.546
\end{array}
$$

5.
$$
\begin{array}{r}
3.1 \\
\times 0.7 \\
\hline
2.17
\end{array}
$$

6. $.04\overline{)0.064}$ rewrite $4\overline{)6.4}$ (quotient 1.6)

7. a. $17.56 = 17\dfrac{56}{100} = 17\dfrac{28}{50} = 17\dfrac{14}{25}$

   b. $21.002 = 21\dfrac{2}{1000} = 21\dfrac{1}{500}$

8.
$$
\begin{array}{r}
5.746 \\
+\ 354.34 \\
\hline
360.086
\end{array}
$$

9. $\begin{array}{r} 3.261 \\ -\ 2.59 \\ \hline 0.671 \end{array}$

10. $\begin{array}{r} 73.00 \\ -\ .46 \\ \hline 72.54 \end{array}$

11. $\begin{array}{r} 9.2 \\ \times\ .003 \\ \hline .0276 \end{array}$ (One digit to the right of the decimal point)
     (Three digits to the right of the decimal point)
     (Four digits to the right of the decimal point)

12. $\begin{array}{r} 5.430 \\ .154 \\ +\ 17.000 \\ \hline 22.584 \end{array}$

13. $.11\overline{)\,.033}$ rewrite $1.1\overline{)\,0.33}$ with quotient 0.3

14. The easiest way to determine the least decimal value is to append 0's to the end of each of the numbers until they all have the same number of digits. Then, ignore the decimal points and see which number is the least. Thus, .09 = .090, .769 = .769, .8 = .800. Clearly, the least number is .09

PERCENTS

1. **a.** 0.374 = 37.4%

    b. 13.02 = 1302%

2. **a.** 62.9% = 0.629

    b. 00.002% = 0.00002

3. **a.** $\dfrac{5}{8} = 8\overline{)5.000}$ with quotient 0.625 = 62.5%

    b. $\dfrac{44}{100} = 100\overline{)44.00}$ with quotient 0.44 = 44%

4. **a.** 37.5% = 0.375 = $\dfrac{375}{1000} = \dfrac{3}{8}$

    b. 00.04% = 0.0004 = $\dfrac{4}{10000} = \dfrac{1}{2500}$

5. $12\dfrac{1}{4}\% = 12.25\% = 0.1225$

6. $.07\% = 0.0007 = \dfrac{7}{10000}$

7. $\dfrac{11}{16} = 16\overline{)11.0000}$ with quotient $.6875$ = 68.75%

8. $1.25 = 125\% = \dfrac{125}{100} = \dfrac{5}{4}$

9. In order to determine the greatest number, we must write them all in the same form. Writing 5/8 as a decimal, we obtain .625. If we write 62% as a decimal, we get .620. Thus, .628 is the greatest of the three numbers.

PERCENT WORD PROBLEMS

1. Amount of down payment = $675 × 15% = $675 × .15 = $101.25

2. Amount of increase = $56,730 − $18,300 = $38,430

    Percent of increase = $\dfrac{\$38,430}{\$18,300}$ = 210%

3. Price after the first markdown = $25,400 × 85% = $21,590

    Price after the second markdown = $21,590 × 90% = $19,431

4. Each year, the amount of interest earned is $5,000 × 8% = $400. Thus, in two years, $800 in interest is earned, and the account has $5,800 in it.

5. Twelve boxes for $40 each cost $480. Since Janet makes a 6% commission, she will receive $480 × 6% = $28.80.

6. Amount of bill = $\dfrac{\text{Amount of tip}}{\text{Percent of tip}} = \dfrac{\$4.32}{0.18}$ = $24.00

7. Amount of weight lost = 125 − 110 = 15 lb.

    Percent of weight lost = $\dfrac{\text{Amount of weight lost}}{\text{Original weight}}$

    $= \dfrac{15}{125}$ = 12%

8. Value of car after 1 year = $12,000 × 0.90 = $10,800
    Value of car after 2 years = $10,800 × 0.90 = $9,720
    Value of car after 3 years = $9,720 × 0.90 = $8,748

9. Value of increase = Principal × Rate × Time = $5,000 × 0.04 × $\dfrac{1}{6}$ = $33.33. Therefore investment = $5,000 + $33.33 = $5,033.33

10. Cost = $3500 × 75% = $2625

11. Amount of raise = $42,380 × 6.5% = $2754.70.
    New Salary = $42,380 + $2754.70 = $45,134.70

12. Number of employees who lost their jobs = 3,760 × 5% = 188
    Number of employees who now work at the plant = 3760 − 188 = 3572

SIGNED NUMBERS

1. $\begin{aligned} +12 + (-10) + (+2) + (-6) &= +2 + (+2) + (-6) \\ &= 4 + (-6) \\ &= -2 \end{aligned}$

2. $\begin{aligned} -(-8) - 10 - (+12) + (-4) &= +8 - 10 - (+12) + (-4) \\ &= -2 - (+12) + (-4) \\ &= -14 + (-4) \\ &= -18 \end{aligned}$

3. $\begin{aligned} -2 \times (-3) \times (+4) \times (-2) &= +6 \times (+4) \times (-2) \\ &= 24 \times (-2) \\ &= -48 \end{aligned}$

4. $15 \div (-0.5) = -30$

5. $+7 + (-2) = +7 - 2 = +5$
$+5 + (-8) = +5 - 8 = -3$
$-3 + (+3) = 0$

6. $-3 - (-7) = -3 + 7 = +4$
$+4 - (+4) = +4 - 4 = 0$
$0 + (-2) = -2$

7. $-6 \times (+2) = -12$
$-12 \times (-1) = +12$
$+12 \times (-7) = -84$

8. $+12 \times (-2) = -24$
$\dfrac{(-24)}{(-4)} = +6$

9. $(3)(2)(1)(0)(-1)(-2)(-3) = 0$, since, if 0 is a factor in any multiplication, the result is 0.

10. $\dfrac{(-8)(+3)}{(-6)(-2)(5)} = \dfrac{-24}{60} = -\dfrac{2}{5}$

11. $\dfrac{6}{15} \div \left(\dfrac{-12}{5}\right) = \dfrac{6}{15} \times \dfrac{5}{-12} = -\dfrac{1}{6}$

12. $\dfrac{(+5) - (-13)}{(-4) + (-5)} = \dfrac{5 + 13}{-9} = \dfrac{18}{-9} = -2$

POWERS, EXPONENTS, AND ROOTS

1. $\sqrt{180} = \sqrt{36 \times 5} = 6\sqrt{5}$

2. $2\sqrt{20} + 6\sqrt{45} - \sqrt{125}$
$= 2\sqrt{4 \times 5} + 6\sqrt{9 \times 5} - \sqrt{25 \times 5}$
$= 4\sqrt{5} + 18\sqrt{5} - 5\sqrt{5}$
$= 17\sqrt{5}$

3. $8\sqrt{12} - 2\sqrt{27} = 8\sqrt{4 \times 3} - 2\sqrt{9 \times 3}$
$= 16\sqrt{3} - 6\sqrt{3}$
$= 10\sqrt{3}$

4. Simplify $\sqrt{7}(2\sqrt{7} - \sqrt{3}) = 2\sqrt{7}\sqrt{7} - \sqrt{7}\sqrt{3}$
$= 2\sqrt{49} - \sqrt{21}$
$= 2(7) - \sqrt{21}$
$= 14 - \sqrt{21}$

5. $\dfrac{12\sqrt{75}}{4\sqrt{108}} = \dfrac{12\sqrt{25 \times 3}}{4\sqrt{36 \times 3}}$
$= \dfrac{12 \times 5\sqrt{3}}{4 \times 6\sqrt{3}}$
$= \dfrac{60\sqrt{3}}{24\sqrt{3}}$
$= \dfrac{60}{24}$
$= \dfrac{5}{2}$
$= 2\dfrac{1}{2}$

6. $3^2 \times 2^4 = 9 \times 16 = 144$

7. $\sqrt{45} + \sqrt{125} = 3\sqrt{5} + 5\sqrt{5} = 8\sqrt{5}$

8. $(3\sqrt{32})(7\sqrt{2}) = 21(\sqrt{64}) = 21(8) = 168$

9. $\dfrac{(20\sqrt{96})}{(5\sqrt{4})} = \left(\dfrac{20}{5}\right)\left(\dfrac{\sqrt{96}}{\sqrt{4}}\right)$
$= 4\sqrt{\left(\dfrac{96}{4}\right)}$
$= 4\sqrt{24}$
$= 8\sqrt{6}$

10. $-3^2 + (3^2)^3 = -9 + 3^6 = -9 + 729 = 720$

11. $(\sqrt{15})^2 = 15$ since squares and roots are inverse operations

12. $\sqrt{6}\sqrt{3}\sqrt{2} = \sqrt{6 \times 3 \times 2} = \sqrt{36} = 6$

ALGEBRA

1. $3[4(6 - 14) - 8(-2 - 5)] = 3[4(-8) - 8(-7)]$
$= 3[-32 + 56]$
$= 3(24)$
$= 72$

2. $(5x^2 - 5x + 2) - (-2x^2 + 3x - 7) + (-4x^2 + 2x - 3)$
$= 5x^2 - 5x + 2 + 2x^2 - 3x + 7 - 4x^2 + 2x - 3$
$= 3x^2 - 6x + 6$

3. $(x - 2)(x^2 + 3x + 7) = x(x^2 + 3x + 7) - 2(x^2 + 3x + 7)$
$= x^3 + 3x^2 + 7x - 2x^2 - 6x - 14$
$= x^3 + x^2 + x - 14$

4. $4x^2 - 36 = 4(x^2 - 9) = 4(x - 3)(x + 3)$

5. $6x^2 - 3x - 18 = 3(2x^2 - x - 6) = 3(2x + 3)(x - 2)$

6. $\dfrac{x^2 - 4x - 21}{x^2 - 9x + 14} = \dfrac{(x + 3)(x - 7)}{(x - 7)(x - 2)} = \dfrac{x + 3}{x - 2}$

7. $(a - b - c) + (a - b - c) - (a - b - c)$
$= a - b - c + a - b - c - a + b + c$
$= a - b - c$

8. $(a + 1)^2 (a + 2) = (a + 1)(a + 1)(a + 2)$
$= (a^2 + 2a + 1)(a + 2)$
$= a^3 + 2a^2 + 2a^2 + 4a + a + 2$
$= a^3 + 4a^2 + 5a + 2$

9. $(2x + 1)(3x^2 - x + 6) = 2x(3x^2 - x + 6) + 1(3x^2 - x + 6)$
$= 6x^3 - 2x^2 + 12x + 3x^2 - x + 6$
$= 6x^3 + x^2 + 11x + 6$

10. $12x^2 + 14x + 4 = 2(6x^2 + 7x + 2) = 2(3x + 2)(2x + 1)$

11. $6x^4 - 150x^2 = 6x^2(x^2 - 25) = 6x^2(x - 5)(x + 5)$

12. $4a^2b + 12ab - 72b = 4b(a^2 + 3a - 18)$
$= 4b(a + 6)(a - 3)$

13. $\dfrac{x^2 - x - 6}{x^2 - 9} \times \dfrac{x^2 + 4x + 3}{x^2 + 5x + 6}$

$= \dfrac{(x-3)(x+2)}{(x-3)(x+3)} \times \dfrac{(x+3)(x+1)}{(x+2)(x+3)}$

$= \dfrac{x+1}{x+3}$

EQUATIONS

1. $6 + 4x = 6x - 10$
   $6 = 2x - 10$
   $16 = 2x$
   $x = 8$

2. $8 - 2x = 2(4x + 3)$
   $8 - 2x = 8x + 6$
   $8 = 10x + 6$
   $2 = 10x$
   $x = \dfrac{1}{5}$

3. $3x - 4(3x - 2) = -x$
   $3x - 12x + 8 = -x$
   $-9x + 8 = -x$
   $8 = 8x$
   $x = 1$

4. $6 + 8(8 - 2x) = 14 - 8(4x - 2)$
   $6 + 64 - 16x = 14 - 32x + 16$
   $70 - 16x = 30 - 32x$
   $16x = -40$
   $x = -\dfrac{40}{16} = -\dfrac{5}{2} = -2\dfrac{1}{2}$

5. $\begin{array}{rcl} -5x + 3 & = & x + 2 \\ +5x & & +5x \\ \hline 3 & = & 6x + 2 \\ -2 & & -2 \\ \hline 1 & = & 6x \end{array}$

   $\dfrac{1}{6} = x$

6. $x + 3(2x + 5) = -20$
   $x + 6x + 15 = -20$
   $7x + 15 = -20$
   $7x = -35$
   $x = -5$

7. $4(x + 2) - (2x + 1) = x + 5$
   $4x + 8 - 2x - 1 = x + 5$
   $2x + 7 = x + 5$
   $x = -2$

8. $3(2x + 5) = 10x + 7 + 2(x - 8)$
   $6x + 15 = 10x + 7 + 2x - 16$
   $6x + 15 = 12x - 9$
   $24 = 6x$
   $x = 3$

9. $\dfrac{2x + 3}{5} - 10 = \dfrac{4 - 3x}{2}$
   $10 \times \dfrac{x + 3}{5} - 10 \times 10 = \dfrac{4 - 3x}{2} \times 10$
   $2(2x + 3) - 100 = 5(4 - 3x)$
   $4x + 6 - 100 = 20 - 15x$
   $4x - 94 = 20 - 15x$
   $4x = 114 - 15x$
   $19x = 114$
   $x = 6$

10. $3(2x + 1) + 2(3x + 1) = 17$
    $6x + 3 + 6x + 2 = 17$
    $12x + 5 = 17$
    $12x = 12$
    $x = 1$

11. $(x - 5)^2 = 4 + (x + 5)^2$
    $x^2 - 10x + 25 = 4 + x^2 + 10x + 25$

    Subtract x^2 from both sides and combine terms:

    $-10x + 25 = 10x + 29$
    $20x = -4$
    $x = -\dfrac{1}{5}$

WORD PROBLEMS INVOLVING ONE UNKNOWN

1. Let $x = $ the first integer.

   Then, $x - 2 = $ the second integer, and
   $x + 4(x - 2) = 17$
   $x + 4x - 8 = 17$
   $5x - 8 = 17$
   $5x = 25$
   $x = 5.$

   The second integer is $x - 2 = 5 - 2 = 3.$

   The integers are 3 and 5.

2. Let $x = $ the least integer. Then,

   $x + 2 = $ the second integer, and
   $x + 4 = $ the greatest integer.
   $x + (x + 2) + (x + 4) = 84$
   $3x + 6 = 84$
   $3x = 78$
   $x = 26.$

   The least of the three integers is 26.

3. Let x = the number of days that it would take both pumps working together to fill the reservoir. In this time, the first pump will fill $\frac{x}{30}$ of the reservoir, and the second pump will fill $\frac{x}{20}$ of the reservoir. Thus,

$$\frac{x}{30} + \frac{x}{20} = 1.$$

Multiply both sides by 60:

$$2x + 3x = 60$$
$$5x = 60$$
$$x = 12.$$

It takes 12 days for both pumps to fill the reservoir together.

4. Let W = the number of votes the winner received. Then, $W - 372$ = the number of votes the loser received.

$$W + (W - 372) = 1,370$$
$$2W - 372 = 1,370$$
$$2W = 1,742$$
$$W = 871.$$

The winner received 871 votes.

5. Let x = the amount invested at 12%. Then, since she invested a total of \$6,000, she must have invested \$6,000 $- x$ at 9%. And, since she received \$660 in interest, we have

$$12\%(x) + 9\%(6,000 - x) = 660 \quad \text{or,}$$
$$.12x + .09(6,000 - x) = 660$$
$$.12x + 540 - .09x = 660$$
$$.03x + 540 = 660$$
$$.03x = 120$$
$$x = \frac{120}{.03} = 4,000.$$

She invested \$4,000 at 12%.

6. Let x = the number. Then,

$$6x - 4 = 3x + 2$$
$$3x = 6$$
$$x = 2. \quad \textit{The number is 2.}$$

7. Let S = the lesser number. Then, the greater number = S + 7, and

$$S + 31 = 3(S + 7)$$
$$S + 31 = 3S + 21$$
$$2S = 10$$
$$S = 5. \quad \textit{The lesser number is 5.}$$

8. Let M = Mike's age now. Then,

$M - 3$ = Al's age. In 9 years, Mike will be $M + 9$ and Al will be $M + 6$. Therefore,

$$M + 9 + M + 6 = 47$$
$$2M + 15 = 47$$
$$2M = 32$$
$$M = 16. \quad \textit{Thus, Mike is 16 now.}$$

9. Let S = the number of student tickets sold. Then,

$200 - S$ = the number of adult tickets sold.

Thus, the money from student tickets is $3S$, and the money received from adult tickets is $6(200 - S)$. Since a total of \$900 was collected,

$$3S + 6(200 - S) = 900$$
$$3S + 1200 - 6S = 900$$
$$3S = 300$$
$$S = 100.$$

Therefore, 100 student tickets were sold.

10. Let J = the time Jared needs to shovel the driveway alone.

In 12 minutes, Brian can shovel $\frac{12}{21}$ of the driveway.

In 12 minutes, Peter can shovel $\frac{12}{84}$ of the driveway.

In 12 minutes, Jared can shovel $\frac{12}{J}$ of the driveway. Therefore,

$$\frac{12}{21} + \frac{12}{84} + \frac{12}{J} = 1. \textit{ Multiply both sides by 84J:}$$

$$48J + 12J + 1008 = 84J$$
$$24J = 1008$$
$$J = 42.$$

Jared can shovel the driveway in 42 minutes.

11. Let B = Bobby's age. Then, $B + 3$ = Jimmy's age. In seven years, Bobby's age will be $B + 7$, and Jimmy's will be $B + 10$. Therefore, in 7 years, we will have

$$(B + 7) + (B + 10) = 79$$
$$2B + 17 = 79$$
$$2B = 62$$
$$B = 31.$$

Bobby is 31 now.

12. Let t = the amount of time each train travels. Then, the distance the freight train travels is $52t$, and the distance the passenger train travels is $84t$. Thus,

$$52t + 84t = 680$$
$$136t = 680$$
$$t = 5.$$

The trains each travel for 5 hours, so they will be 680 miles apart at 5 p.m.

LITERAL EQUATIONS

1.
$$A = \frac{1}{2}b(b + c)$$
$$2A = bb + bc$$
$$2A - bb = bc$$
$$c = \frac{2A - bb}{b}$$

2.
$$aw - b = cw + d$$
$$aw - cw = b + d$$
$$w(a - c) = b + d$$
$$w = \frac{b + d}{a - c}$$

3.
$$10x^2 = 5x$$
$$10x^2 - 5x = 0$$
$$5x(2x - 1) = 0$$
$$x = 0, \frac{1}{2}$$

4.
$$2x^2 - x = 21$$
$$2x^2 - x - 21 = 0$$
$$(2x - 7)(x + 3) = 0$$
$$x = -3, \frac{7}{2}$$

5.
$$2\sqrt{x + 5} = 8$$
$$\sqrt{x + 5} = 4$$
$$(\sqrt{x + 5})^2 = 4^2$$
$$x + 5 = 16$$
$$x = 11$$

6.
$$2A = (b_1 + b_2)b$$
$$2A = b_1 b + b_2 b$$
$$2A - b_1 b = b_2 b$$
$$\frac{(2A - b_1 b)}{b} = b_2$$

7. $\frac{a}{b} = \frac{c}{d}$ *Cross-multiply.*
$$ad = bc$$
$$d = \frac{bc}{a}$$

8.
$$3x^2 - 12 = x(1 + 2x)$$
$$3x^2 - 12 = x + 2x^2$$
$$x^2 - x - 12 = 0$$
$$(x - 4)(x + 3) = 0$$

Thus, $x = -3$ or 4.

9.
$$5x^2 = 36 + x^2$$
$$4x^2 - 36 = 0$$
$$4(x^2 - 9) = 0$$
$$4(x + 3)(x - 3) = 0$$

Thus, $x = +3$ or -3.

10. Begin by dividing both sides by 4 to get $\sqrt{\frac{2x}{3}} = 12$. Then, square both sides:

$$\left(\sqrt{\frac{2x}{3}}\right)^2 = 12^2$$
$$\frac{2x}{3} = 144.$$ Now, *multiply both sides by* 3.
$$2x = 432$$
$$x = 216.$$

11. $3x^2 - x - 4 = 0$. Here, $A = 3$, $B = -1$, and $C = -4$. Using the quadratic formula, we get:

$$x = \frac{-B \pm \sqrt{B^2 - 4AC}}{2A} = \frac{1 \pm \sqrt{1 - 4(3)(-4)}}{6}$$
$$= \frac{1 \pm \sqrt{1 + 48}}{6}$$
$$= \frac{1 \pm \sqrt{49}}{6}$$
$$= \frac{1 \pm 7}{6} = \frac{8}{6}, \frac{-6}{6}$$

Thus, $x = \frac{4}{3}$ or -1. Note that this equation could have been solved by factoring as well. The quadratic formula, however, can be used to solve all quadratic equations, including those that cannot be factored.

12. $\frac{q}{x} + \frac{p}{x} = 1$. Multiply both sides by x to clear the fraction, and obtain $q + p = x$.

13. $3x^2 - 5 = 0$. This equation can easily be solved for x by first solving for x^2 and then taking the square root of both sides.

$$3x^2 = 5$$
$$x^2 = \frac{5}{3}$$
$$\sqrt{x^2} = \pm\sqrt{\frac{5}{3}}.$$

Since $\sqrt{x^2} = x$, we have $x = \pm\sqrt{\frac{5}{3}}$.

LINEAR INEQUALITIES AND LINEAR EQUATIONS IN TWO UNKNOWNS

1. $108x < 15(6x + 12)$
$108x < 90x + 180$
$18x < 180$
$x < 10$

2. $4a - 9 > 9a - 24$
$-5a > -15$ Divide by -5, reverse the inequality sign.
$a < 3$

3. $3x + 2y = 11$
$5x - 4y = 11$

Multiply the first equation by 2.

$2(3x + 2y) = 2(11)$
$5x - 4y = 11$

Add the two equations together.

$6x + 4y = 22$
$\underline{5x - 4y = 11}$
$11x = 33$
$x = 3$

Now, substitute this value for x in the first equation

$3(3) + 2y = 11$
$9 + 2y = 11$
$2y = 2$
$y = 1$

The common solution is (3, 1).

4. Let x = the greater of the two numbers
Let y = the lesser of the two numbers

Then, we have

$x + y = 45$
$x - y = 11$

Add the two equations together.

$x + y = 45$
$\underline{x - y = 11}$
$2x = 56$
$x = 28$

If x is 28, and the numbers differ by 11, $y = 17$.

The numbers are 28 and 17.

5. Let B = the cost of a binder.
Let N = the cost of a notebook.

Then, we have:

$3B + 4N = 4.32$
$1B + 5N = 3.97$

Multiply the second equation by -3:

$3B + 4N = 4.32$
$-3(1B + 5N) = (3.97)(-3)$

or,

$3B + 4N = 4.32$
$\underline{-3B - 15N = 11.91}$
$-11N = -7.59$
$N = 0.69$

Thus, the cost of a notebook is $0.69.

6. $12 - 2x > 4$
$-2x > -8$ Divide by -2,
$x < 4$ reverse the inequality sign.

7. $\left(\dfrac{x}{6}\right) - \left(\dfrac{x}{2}\right) < 1$ *Multiply both sides by 6.*
$x - 3x < 6$
$-2x < 6$ Divide by -2,
$x > -3$ reverse the inequality sign

8. $6z + 1 \leq 3(z - 2)$
$6z + 1 \leq 3z - 6$
$3z \leq -7$
$z \leq -\dfrac{7}{3}$

Note that even though the answer is negative, we do not reverse the inequality sign since we never multiplied or divided by a negative number.

9. $y = 3x + 1$
$x + y = 9$

Begin by substituting $y = 3x + 1$ into the second equation:

$x + (3x + 1) = 9$
$4x + 1 = 9$
$4x = 8$
$x = 2$

If $x = 2$, $y = 3(2) + 1 = 6 + 1 = 7$.

10. $2x + y = 8$
$x - y = 1$

From the second equation, we can see $x = y + 1$. Then, substituting into the first equation:

$2(y + 1) + y = 8$
$3y + 2 = 8$
$3y = 6$
$y = 2$

If $y = 2$, then $x = y + 1 = 2 + 1 = 3$.

11. $5x + 3y = 28$
$7x - 2y = 2$

Multiply the first equation by 2, the second equation by 3:

$$2(5x + 3y) = 2(28)$$
$$3(7x - 2y) = 3(2) \quad \textit{Thus,}$$

$$10x + 6y = 56$$
$$\underline{21x - 6y = 6} \;\; \textbf{\textit{Add the equations together}}:$$
$$31x = 62$$
$$x = 2$$

Now, solve for y by plugging $x = 2$ into, say, the second equation:

$$7(2) - 2y = 2$$
$$14 - 2y = 2$$
$$-2y = -12$$
$$y = 6$$

Thus, the common solution is (2, 6).

12. Let P = the cost of the printer.
Let M = the cost of the monitor. Then,

$$P + M = 356$$
$$M = 20 + 2P$$

Substituting for M in the first equation, we get:

$$P + (20 + 2P) = 356$$
$$3P + 20 = 356$$
$$3P = 336$$
$$P = 112$$

Then, $M = 20 + 2(112) = 244$.

The printer costs \$112, and the monitor costs \$244.

SYSTEMS OF NUMBERS

1. If k represents an integer, then $2k$ is even, since 2 times any integer is even. Further, $2k + 6$ is also even; $\frac{8k}{4} = 2k$, so $\frac{8k}{4}$ is even. Next, $3k$ may be even or odd, so $3k + 5$ may be even or odd. Finally, $2k - 1$ is odd, since 1 less than an even number is odd. Thus, of the numbers given, $2k$, $2k + 6$, and $\frac{8k}{4}$ must be even.

2. If n represents an odd integer, then $2n$ represents an even number times an odd number and is therefore even; $3n$ is the product of two odds and is thus odd; $3n + 1$ is the sum of two odds and is therefore even; $3n - 5$ is the difference of odds and is thus even; $4n + 1$ is the sum of an even and an odd and is thus odd. Overall, then, $2n$, $3n + 1$, and $3n - 5$ are even.

3. $|5| - |-7| - |-4| \,|12| = 5 - (+7) - (4)(12)$
$= 5 - 7 - 48$
$= -50$

4. a. 47 contains one 32. $47 - 32 = 15$. 15 contains no 16s but contains one 8. $15 - 8 = 7$. 7 contains one 4. $7 - 4 = 3$. 3 contains one 2, with a remainder of one. Therefore, $47 = 101111_2$.

b. $110111_2 = 32 + 16 + 4 + 2 + 1 = 55$

5. $2 \times 2 \times 2 \times 3 \times 5$

6. -7 is real, rational, and an integer.

7. $\frac{1}{7}$ is real and rational.

8. $5\frac{2}{3}$ can be written as $\frac{17}{3}$ and is thus real and rational.

9. 0 is real, rational, an integer, and a whole number.

10. $\sqrt{13}$ is real and irrational.

COMPLEX NUMBERS

1. a. $7i^2 = 7(-1) = -7$

b. $-6i^8 = -6(1) = -6$

c. $8i^7 = 8(-i) = -8i$

2. a. $(5 + 3i) + (3 - 2i) = 5 + 3i + 3 - 2i = 8 + i$

b. $(8 - 2i) - (-2 - 6i) = 8 - 2i + 2 + 6i = 10 + 4i$

3. a. $(5 + 3i)(3 - 2i) = 15 - 10i + 9i - (2i)(3i)$
$= 15 - 10i + 9i + 6$
$= 21 - i$

b. $\frac{5 + 3i}{3 - 2i} = \frac{(5 + 3i)(3 + 2i)}{(3 - 2i)(3 + 2i)} = \frac{15 + 10i + 9i - 6}{9 + 4}$
$= \frac{9 + 19i}{13}$

4. The conjugate of $5 + 3i$ is $5 - 3i$. The sum of the two numbers is simply 10.

5. $x^2 + x + 4 = 0$. We must use the quadratic formula to solve this equation.

$a = 1$, $b = 1$, and $c = 4$.

$$x = \frac{-b \pm \sqrt{b^2 - 4ac}}{2a} = \frac{-1 \pm \sqrt{1^2 - 4(1)(4)}}{2(1)}$$
$$= \frac{-1 \pm \sqrt{1 - 16}}{2}$$
$$= \frac{-1 \pm \sqrt{-15}}{2}$$
$$= \frac{-1 \pm i\sqrt{15}}{2}$$

6. $\sqrt{-27} + 2\sqrt{-45} = 3i\sqrt{3} + (2)(3)i\sqrt{5}$
$= 3i\sqrt{3} + 6i\sqrt{5}$

7. $i^{77} = (i^4)^{19}(i) = (1)^{19}(i) = i$

8. $(3 - 7i)^2 = (3 - 7i)(3 - 7i) = 9 - 21i - 21i + 49i^2$
$= 9 - 42i - 49$
$= -40 - 42i$

9. $\dfrac{7-4i}{2+i} = \dfrac{7-4i}{2+i} \times \dfrac{2-i}{2-i}$

$\qquad = \dfrac{14 - 7i - 8i + 4i^2}{4 - i^2}$

$\qquad = \dfrac{14 - 15i - 4}{4 + 1}$

$\qquad = \dfrac{10 - 15i}{5}$

$\qquad = 2 - 3i$

10. In this equation, $a = 3$, $b = 2$, and $c = 5$.

$x = \dfrac{-b \pm \sqrt{b^2 - 4ac}}{2a}$

$\quad = \dfrac{-2 \pm \sqrt{4 - 4(3)(5)}}{6}$

$\quad = \dfrac{-2 \pm \sqrt{-56}}{6}$

$\quad = \dfrac{-2 \pm i\sqrt{56}}{6}$

$\quad = \dfrac{-2 \pm 2i\sqrt{14}}{6}$

$\quad = \dfrac{-1 \pm i\sqrt{14}}{3}$

FUNCTIONS AND THEIR GRAPHS

1. If $f(x) = 3 - 2x$, $f(-4) = 3 - 2(-4) = 3 + 8 = 11$, and $f(11) = 3 - 2(11) = 3 - 22 = -19$.

2. a. $f(x) = 3x^2 - 2x + 1$

The domain and range are the set of all real numbers.

b. $g(x) = \dfrac{1}{x}$

The domain is all real numbers except 0; the range is also all real numbers except 0.

3. If $f(x) = x^2$ and $g(x) = 2x - 6$,
$(f + g)(x) = f(x) + g(x) = x^2 + 2x - 6$;
$(f \times g)(x) = f(x)g(x) = x^2(2x - 6) = 2x^3 - 6x^2$;
$(f \circ g)(x) = f(g(x)) = f(2x - 6) = (2x - 6)^2$
$\qquad\qquad = 4x^2 - 24x + 36$;
$(f \circ f)(x) = f(f(x)) = f(x^2) = x^4$.

To find $g^{-1}(x)$, write $g(x)$ as $y = 2x - 6$. Switch x and y and solve for y.

$x = 2y - 6$

$2y = x + 6$

$y = \dfrac{(x + 6)}{2}$.

Therefore, $g^{-1}(x) = \dfrac{x + 6}{2}$.

4. a. Since $f(x)$ is linear, we only need two points to draw the graph. Let's use $f(0) = -3$, and $f(3) = 3$. Then, the graph is:

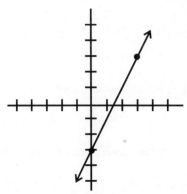

b. $g(x)$ is a quadratic function. We will need to find a series of values until we are able to determine the shape of the graph.

$g(0) = 2$
$g(1) = 5$
$g(2) = 10$
$g(-1) = 1$
$g(-2) = 2$
$g(-3) = 5$
$g(-4) = 10$

Drawing the graph, we can see that it is parabolic in shape:

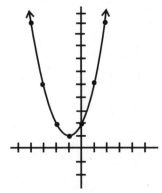

5. $f(-5) = 4 - 3(-5) = 19$

$f(13) = 4 - 3(13) = 4 - 39 = -35$

6. $y = \sqrt{x + 3}$. The domain is $\{x \mid x \geq -3\}$.

7. $(f + g)(x) = x^2 + 4x - 2$

8. $(fg)(x) = x^2 (4x - 2) = 4x^3 - 2x^2$

9. $(f \circ g)(x) = f(4x - 2) = (4x - 2)^2 = 16x^2 - 16x + 4$

10. $(f \circ f)(x) = (x^2)^2 = x^4$

11. Write $f(x) = 5x + 2$ as $y = 5x + 2$. Switch x and y to get $x = 5y + 2$. Solve for y to get $y = \dfrac{(x - 2)}{5}$. Thus, $f^{-1}(x) = \dfrac{(x - 2)}{5}$.

PART III: COLLEGE MATHEMATICS

EXPONENTS AND LOGARITHMS

1. **a.** $3^2 = 9$ is equivalent to $\log_3 9 = 2$.

   b. $7^{-2} = \frac{1}{49}$ is equivalent to $\log_7\left(\frac{1}{49}\right) = -2$.

2. **a.** $\log_6 36 = 2$ is equivalent to $6^2 = 36$.

   b. $\log_{10}\left(\frac{1}{10}\right) = -1$ is equivalent to $10^{-1} = \frac{1}{10}$.

3. **a.** $\log_2 8 = 3$ (The power that 2 must be raised to to equal 8 is 3.)

   b. $\log_{12} 1 = 0$ (The power that 12 must be raised to to equal 1 is 0.)

4. **a.** $\log 12 = \log(2^2 \times 3) = \log(2^2) + \log 3 = 2\log 2 + \log 3$

   b. $\log\left(\frac{ab}{c}\right) = \log(ab) - \log c = \log a + \log b - \log c$

5. $125 = 5^{2x-1}$. Rewrite 125 as 5^3. Then, $5^3 = 5^{2x-1}$.

   Thus, it must be true that $3 = 2x - 1$ or $2x = 4$ so that $x = 2$.

6. $11^{\frac{1}{2}}$

7. $13^{\frac{1}{3}}$

8. $\sqrt[5]{8}$

9. $\sqrt[3]{x^2}$

10. $27^{\frac{1}{3}} = \sqrt[3]{27} = 3$

11. $125^{\frac{2}{3}} = (\sqrt[3]{125})^2 = 5^2 = 25$

12. **a.** $1{,}234.56 = 1.23456 \times 10^3$

    b. $0.0876 = 8.76 \times 10^{-2}$

13. **a.** $1.234 \times 10^5 = 123{,}400$

    b. $5.45 \times 10^{-3} = 0.00545$

14. $\log 3^{2x} = \log 4^{x-1}$

$$2x\log 3 = (x - 1)\log 4$$
$$2x\log 3 = x\log 4 - \log 4$$
$$2x\log 3 - x\log 4 = -\log 4$$
$$x(2\log 3 - \log 4) = -\log 4$$

$$x = \frac{-\log 4}{(2\log 3 - \log 4)}$$

SET THEORY

1. $\{x \mid 12 < x < 48, x \text{ is an integer}\}$

2. $\varnothing$, $\{a\}$, $\{b\}$, $\{c\}$, $\{d\}$, $\{a, b\}$, $\{a, c\}$, $\{a, d\}$, $\{b, c\}$, $\{b, d\}$, $\{c, d\}$, $\{a, b, c\}$, $\{a, b, d\}$, $\{a, c, d\}$, $\{b, c, d\}$, $\{a, b, c, d\}$.

3. $A \cup B = \{1, 2, 3, 4, 5, 6\}$, $A \cup C = \{2, 3, 4, 6\}$, $A \cap C = \{2, 4\}$, $A \cap B = \varnothing$, $A \cap (B \cup C) = \{2, 4\}$.

4. $W' = \{4, 8, 10, 14, 16, 20\}$

5. $Q \times R = \{(2,2), (2,4), (2,7), (6,2), (6,4), (6,7), (9,2), (9,4), (9,7)\}$

6.

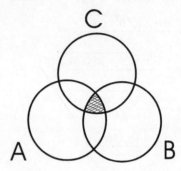

7. $\{ \dots, -4, -3, -2, -1\}$

8. $D \cap E'$

9. $F \cup E$

10. $D \cap E$

11. $D \cap (E \cup F)'$

PERMUTATIONS AND COMBINATIONS

1. By the fundamental counting principle, Brian can wear $5 \times 2 \times 3 = 30$ different outfits.

2. The number of different orders that 5 boys can stand on a line is given by $5! = 5 \times 4 \times 3 \times 2 \times 1 = 120$.

3. There are 13 choices for first place. After that, second place can go to 12 people, and then third place can go to 11 people. Thus, there are $13 \times 12 \times 11 = 1{,}716$ ways to award the prize.

4. Here, we need to count the number of combinations of 10 objects taken 3 at a time. This number is given by

$$_nC_r = \frac{n!}{r!\,(n - r)!}$$

with $n = 10$ and $r = 3$. Thus, we need to evaluate:

$$\frac{n!}{r!\,(n - r)!} = \frac{10!}{3!(7!)} = \frac{10 \times 9 \times 8}{3 \times 2 \times 1}$$
$$= 10 \times 3 \times 4$$
$$= 120.$$

5. We need to count the number of combinations of 40 objects taken 4 at a time. This number is given by

$$_nC_r = \frac{n!}{r!\,(n-r)!}$$

with $n = 40$ and $r = 4$. Thus, we need to evaluate:

$$\frac{n!}{r!\,(n-r)!} = \frac{40!}{4!(36!)}$$
$$= \frac{(40 \times 39 \times 38 \times 37)}{(4 \times 3 \times 2 \times 1)}$$
$$= 10 \times 13 \times 19 \times 37 = 91{,}390.$$

6. We need to find $_6P_3$. By the formula, this is equal to $6 \times 5 \times 4 = 120$ permutations.

7. We need to find the number of combinations of 10 objects taken 3 at a time.

$$_nC_r = \frac{10!}{3!(7!)} = \frac{(10 \times 9 \times 8)}{(3 \times 2 \times 1)} = 120.$$

8. The first digit of the number can be anything other than 0, since a three-digit number cannot begin with a zero. Thus, there are 9 possibilities for the first digit. The second digit of the number can be any one of the 9 digits not used as the first digit. The third digit can be any one of the 8 remaining digits not used for the first two digits. Thus, there are $9 \times 9 \times 8 = 648$ numbers that can be formed.

9. Once again, the first digit can be any of the digits other than 0. Therefore, there are 9 possibilities for the first digit. The second and third digits can be any one of the 10 digits. Thus, there are $9 \times 10 \times 10 = 900$ possible numbers that can be formed.

10. There are 8 possible choices for the first digit, since the first digit can be neither 0 nor 7. There are 8 possibilities for the second digit, since it can be anything other than 7 and the number that was chosen for the first digit. The third digit must be 7; there is no choice here. Therefore, the total number of numbers that can be formed is $8 \times 8 = 64$.

PROBABILITY

1. There are twelve marbles in the bag. Since three of them are red, the probability of picking a red marble is $\frac{3}{12} = \frac{1}{4}$. There are five marbles in the bag that are not blue, so the probability of picking a marble that is not blue is $\frac{5}{12}$.

2. There are 5 coins in the purse, and 3 of them are worth at least 10 cents. Thus, the probability that a coin chosen at random will be worth at least 10 cents is $\frac{3}{5}$.

3. By the fundamental counting principle, there are $7 \times 7 = 49$ ways in which two marbles can be selected. Since there are four ways to select a white marble on the first draw, and 4 ways to select a white marble on the second draw, there are a total of $4 \times 4 = 16$ ways to select a white marble on two draws. Thus, the probability of selecting white on both draws is $\frac{16}{49}$.

4. The two selections can be made in $7 \times 6 = 42$ ways. Two white marbles can be selected in $4 \times 3 = 12$ ways. Thus, the desired probability is $\frac{12}{42} = \frac{2}{7}$.

5. Since these two events are independent, the probability of passing both is $\frac{2}{3} \times \frac{1}{4} = \frac{1}{6}$.

6. The probability of drawing a diamond from the full deck is $\frac{13}{52} = \frac{1}{4}$. After the first diamond has been removed, there are 51 cards in the deck, 12 of which are diamonds. The probability of selecting a diamond from this reduced deck is $\frac{12}{51}$. The probability, thus, of selecting two diamonds is $\frac{1}{4} \times \frac{12}{51} = \frac{1}{17}$.

7. After the first marble is selected, the bag has eight marbles left, six of which are of a different color than that of the first marble selected. Thus, the probability that the second marble is of a different color is $\frac{6}{8}$. If the second marble is different, there are then seven marbles in the bag, three of which are of the color not yet selected. The odds of drawing a marble of the third color is $\frac{3}{7}$. Overall, then, the probability of drawing three different colors is $\frac{6}{8} \times \frac{3}{7} = \frac{18}{56} = \frac{9}{28}$.

8. If two dice are rolled, the possible outcomes for the sums of the two dice are 2 through 12. Of these, 2, 3, 5, 7, and 11 are prime. There is one way to get a sum of two, two ways to get a sum of three, four ways to get a sum of five, six ways to get a sum of seven, and two ways to get a sum of 11. Thus, the probability of rolling a prime sum is $\frac{15}{36} = \frac{5}{12}$.

9. After you roll the die the first time, there is a five out of six chance that the next roll will be different. Then, there is a four out of six chance that the third roll will be different. Thus, the probability of rolling three different numbers is $\frac{5}{6} \times \frac{4}{6} = \frac{5}{9}$.

10. After three cards are selected, there are 49 cards left in the deck, of which only one is a king. Thus, the probability of drawing a king on the fourth draw is $\frac{1}{49}$.

LOGIC

1. **a.** I am at work, and it is snowing.

   b. I am at work, or it is snowing.

   c. I am at work, and it is not snowing.

   d. It is false that it is not snowing.

   e. If it is snowing, then I am at work.

2. **a.** $r \wedge s$

   b. $r \wedge {\sim}s$

   c. ${\sim}r$

   d. ${\sim}r \vee (r \wedge s)$

   e. ${\sim}({\sim}r \wedge s)$

3.

p	q	~p	~p ∨ q	~(~p ∨ q)
T	T	F	T	F
T	F	F	F	T
F	T	T	T	F
F	F	T	T	F

4. First make truth tables for $\sim({\sim}p \wedge {\sim}q)$ and $p \vee q$

p	q	p ∨ q	~p	~q	~p ∧ ~q	~(~p ∧ ~q)
T	T	T	F	F	F	T
T	F	T	F	T	F	T
F	T	T	T	F	F	T
F	F	F	T	T	T	F

Note that the third column is the same as the last column. This establishes that the two statements are logically equivalent.

5. Let p represent the statement, "I go home," and let q represent the statement, "It rained." Then, "If I go home, then it rained," can be represented as $p \to q$. The statement "If it did not rain, then I did not go home," can be represented as ${\sim}q \to {\sim}p$, which is the contrapositive of the given conditional statement. It was shown in a previous problem that the conditional and the contrapositive are logically equivalent.

6. The statement is true. Since B is false, then ~B, the negation of B, is true. Then, true conjuncted with true is true.

7. The statement is false. Since A is true, ~A is false, and the conjunction of a true statement with a false statement is false.

8. The statement is true. $A \wedge B$ is false, since B is false. The negation of a false statement is true.

9. The statement is true. ~A is false, so $(B \wedge {\sim}A)$ is also false. Then, when A, which is true, is disjuncted with a false statement, the result will be true.

10. The statement is false. $(A \wedge {\sim}A)$ is false, and a false statement disjuncted with a false statement is also false.

Chapter 7
POSTTEST

TIME—45 MINUTES   33 QUESTIONS

PART I

Directions: Answer the following questions. Do not spend too much time on any one question.

Note:
1. Unless otherwise specified, the domain of any function f is assumed to be the set of all real numbers x for which $f(x)$ is a real number.
2. i will be used to denote $\sqrt{-1}$.
3. Figures that accompany the following problems are intended to provide information useful in solving the problems. They are drawn as accurately as possible EXCEPT when it is stated in a specific problem that its figure is not drawn to scale. All figures lie in a plane unless otherwise indicated.

1. Let A and B be two sets, with A = {1, 2, 3, 4} and B = {3, 4, 5, 6}. Which of the following sets is the intersection of A and B?

   (A) {1, 2, 3, 4, 5, 6}
   (B) {3, 4}
   (C) The set of natural numbers
   (D) None of the above

2. Let C and D be two sets. What is the intersection of the complement of C with the complement of D?

   (A) The complement of the union of C and D
   (B) The complement of the intersection of C and D
   (C) The union of the complements of C and D
   (D) The null set

3. Let A be the set of all even integers greater than 0, and let B be the set of all prime numbers. What is the intersection of A and B?

   (A) The null set
   (B) {2}
   (C) The set consisting of all even numbers and all prime numbers
   (D) None of the above

4. There are 40 soldiers in the third platoon: 30 of them are qualified as paratroopers, and 20 of them are trained in demolition; 3 of them are not trained in either one. How many qualified paratroopers in the third platoon are trained in demolition?

   (A) 7
   (B) 11
   (C) 13
   (D) 17

5. Which of the following is NOT an element in the union of the set of all numbers divisible by 6 and the set of all numbers divisible by 4?

   (A) 24
   (B) 28
   (C) 36
   (D) 94

6. If R is a relation defined on the elements of the set A, which of the following is always true of R?

   (A) It is a subset of the Cartesian product of A with A.
   (B) It is symmetric, transitive, and idempotent.
   (C) It is a function with domain and range identical to each other.
   (D) None of the above

GO ON TO THE NEXT PAGE ➤

7. If A → B and ~A → C, what does ~C imply?

(A) ~A
(B) B
(C) ~B
(D) It implies a contradiction.

8. What is the logical inverse of "If Betty is smart, Betty studies."

(A) "If Betty is not smart, Betty does not study."
(B) "If Betty does not study, Betty is not smart."
(C) "If Betty studies, then Betty is smart."
(D) "If Betty studies, then Betty is not smart."

9. Suppose $f(x) = x^2 + 3x + 2$. Which of the following correctly completes the statement "For t to satisfy the equation $f(t) = 0$,..."

(A) It is necessary and sufficient that $t = -1$.
(B) It is sufficient but not necessary that $t = -1$.
(C) It is necessary but not sufficient that $t = -1$.
(D) It is neither necessary nor sufficient that $t = -1$.

10. Which of the following is a counter-example to the statement "For all positive integers n, $(2n) + 1$ is a prime number?"

(A) $n = 0$
(B) $n = 1$
(C) $n = 2$
(D) $n = 4$

11. Here is a Truth Table:

p	q	r	s
T	T	T	T
T	F	F	T
F	T	F	T
F	F	F	F

Which of the following describe r and s correctly?

(A) $r = p \rightarrow q, s = p \land q$
(B) $r = p \lor q, s = p \land q$
(C) $r = p \land q, s = p \lor q$
(D) $r = \sim(\sim p \lor \sim q), s = \sim p \rightarrow \sim q$

12. In a complex case of bank fraud, the district attorney has evidence that proves that if Alan is guilty, then Baker is guilty. He also knows that either Alan or Charles is guilty, and if Charles is guilty, then Fran is not guilty. If convincing evidence suddenly appears that indicates Fran is guilty, what does that mean about the other three defendants?

(A) It does not establish their guilt or innocence.
(B) They are all guilty.
(C) Baker and Charles are guilty, and Alan is innocent.
(D) Charles is innocent, and Alan and Baker are guilty.

13. Which of the following is logically equivalent to $p \rightarrow q$?

(A) $\sim p \lor q$
(B) $p \lor \sim q$
(C) $p \lor q$
(D) $\sim p \lor \sim q$

14. Which of the following sets is a subset of the prime numbers?

(A) {2, 5, 13, 29, 41}
(B) {3, 5, 13, 39, 51}
(C) {3, 9, 27, 81, 243}
(D) {7, 29, 61, 103, 221}

15. Which of the following is a composite number?

(A) 31
(B) 41
(C) 51
(D) 61

16. If m is any integer, which of the following must be an odd integer?

(A) $m^2 + 4m + 3$
(B) $3m + 1$
(C) $m^2 - m$
(D) $4m + 5$

17. The number 1101 is written in binary notation. How would it be written in decimal notation?

(A) 9
(B) 11
(C) 13
(D) 25

18. How would the number 68 be written in binary notation?

(A) 1000100
(B) 1001000
(C) 1011000
(D) 1100100

19. What is the greatest common factor of 156 and 204?

    (A) 6
    (B) 8
    (C) 12
    (D) 24

20. Which of the following is a factor of $x^4 - 7x^3 + x^2 + 3x + 2$?

    (A) $x^2 - 3x + 2$
    (B) $x + 1$
    (C) $x - 2$
    (D) $x - 1$

21. If it is given that $x > y$, which of the following must be true?

    (A) $x^2 > y^2$
    (B) $|x| > |y|$
    (C) $|x - y| = x - y$
    (D) $x^2 > y$

22. Which of the following is equal to the set of all x, such that $(x - 1)^2 > 4$?

    (A) All x, such that $x > 3$
    (B) All x, such that $|x-1| > 2$
    (C) The complement to the set of all x, such that $-1 < x < 3$
    (D) The union of the set of all x, such that $x > 3$ and the set of all x, such that $x > -1$

23. Which of the following is a rational number?

    (A) $\sqrt{121}$
    (B) Pi
    (C) The length of the hypotenuse of a right triangle whose legs are of length 3 and 5
    (D) $\sqrt{\dfrac{3}{2}}$

24. Which of the following is true of any rational number?

    (A) It is always the root of an algebraic equation with integer coefficients.
    (B) Its decimal always begins to repeat eventually.
    (C) You can find an integer that, when multiplied by the number, gives another integer.
    (D) All of the above

25. What do you get if you add two distinct irrational numbers together?

    (A) Another irrational number
    (B) A rational number
    (C) A real number
    (D) None of the above

26. Which of the following is a true statement?

    (A) The set of all integers can be put into one-to-one correspondence with the set of all rational numbers.
    (B) The set of all rational numbers can be put into one-to-one correspondence with the set of all real numbers.
    (C) The set of all rational numbers can be put into one-to-one correspondence with the set of all points on a line.
    (D) None of the above

27. What is the slope of the line defined by $2y + 6x = 19$?

    (A) -3
    (B) 2
    (C) 3
    (D) 6

28. Which of the following functions is graphed in below?

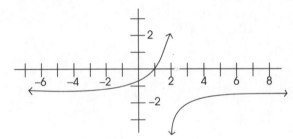

    (A) $y = \dfrac{x^2 - 2x + 4}{x - 2}$
    (B) $y = \dfrac{1 - x}{x - 2}$
    (C) $y = \dfrac{1}{x - 2}$
    (D) $y = \dfrac{-x^2}{x^2 - 4}$

29. What are the x-intercepts of the curve defined by $x^2 + 2xy + y^2 = 3y + 4$?

    (A) $y = +4$ and $y = -1$
    (B) $y = -4$ and $y = +1$
    (C) $x = -2$ and $x = +2$
    (D) $x = -y + \sqrt{3y + 4}$

GO ON TO THE NEXT PAGE

30. Suppose $f(x) = ax + b$ and $g(x) = cx + d$. What is a necessary and sufficient condition for $f(g(x)) = g(f(x))$?

(A) $f(d) = g(b)$

(B) $a = c$ and $b = d$

(C) The slopes must be negative reciprocals of each other.

(D) $ad - bc = 0$

31. How many real roots does the equation $x^3 - 2x^2 - 10x + 1 = 0$ have?

(A) 0

(B) 1

(C) 2

(D) 3

32. What is the equation of the oblique asymptote to the function $y = \dfrac{x^2 + 2x + 5}{x - 1}$?

(A) $x = 1$

(B) $y = -5$

(C) $y = x + 2$

(D) $y = x + 3$

33. Which of the following is the equation of an ellipse?

(A) $\dfrac{x^2}{4} + \dfrac{y^2}{9} = 1$

(B) $\dfrac{x^2}{4} - \dfrac{y^2}{9} = 1$

(C) $y = 4x^2$

(D) $xy = 1$

STOP If you finish before the time is up, you may check your work on this section only. Do not turn to any other section in the test.

TIME—45 MINUTES   32 QUESTIONS

PART II

Directions: Answer the following questions. Do not spend too much time on any one question.

Note:
1. Unless otherwise specified, the domain of any function f is assumed to be the set of all real numbers x for which $f(x)$ is a real number.
2. i will be used to denote $\sqrt{-1}$.
3. Figures that accompany the following questions are intended to provide information useful in solving the problems. They are drawn as accurately as possible EXCEPT when it is stated in a specific problem that its figure is not drawn to scale. All figures lie in a plane unless otherwise indicated.

34. The domain of the function $y = x^2 - 1$ is the set of all real numbers. What is its range?

(A) All real numbers either greater than or equal to 1 or less than or equal to -1

(B) All real numbers greater than -1

(C) All real numbers greater than or equal to -1

(D) All real numbers

35. Find the equation of a line passing through the point (1, 3) that is perpendicular to the line defined by $y = 2x + 5$.

(A) $y - 2x + 5 = 0$

(B) $2y - x - 5 = 0$

(C) $y + 2x - 7 = 0$

(D) $2y + x - 7 = 0$

36. Which of the following is an asymptote of $y = \dfrac{x^2 + 1}{x^2 - 1}$?

(A) $x = -1$

(B) $x = +1$

(C) $y = +1$

(D) All of the above

37. Which of the following is the function graphed below?

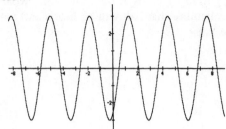

(A) $y = 3 \sin(2x + 1)$

(B) $y = 3 \sin\left(\dfrac{x}{2} + 1\right)$

(C) $y = 3 \sin\left(\dfrac{x}{2} - 1\right)$

(D) $y = 3 \sin(2x - 1)$

38. What are the asymptotes of the curve defined by $\dfrac{y^2}{4} - \dfrac{x^2}{9} = 1$?

(A) $y = 2\sqrt{\dfrac{1 + x^2}{9}}$ and $2\sqrt{\dfrac{1 - x^2}{9}}$

(B) $3y - 2x = 0$ and $3y + 2x = 0$

(C) $x = 0$ and $y = 0$

(D) The curve has no asymptotes.

39. If the curve C defined by $F(x, y) = 0$ defines y as a function of x for all x in the set A, which of the following must be true?

(A) If a is in A, then the curve $x = a$ must intersect C exactly once.

(B) If a is in A, then the curve $y = a$ must intersect C exactly once.

(C) If a is not in A, then $x = a$ must be an asymptote to C.

(D) If a is not in A, then $F(a, y)$ is not equal to zero for any value of y.

GO ON TO THE NEXT PAGE

40. In how many different ways can you make 25 cents, using standard U.S. coins?

   (A) 4 ways
   (B) 9 ways
   (C) 13 ways
   (D) 25 ways

41. If you flip 4 coins at the same time, what is the probability that half will be heads and half will be tails?

   (A) $\dfrac{1}{5}$

   (B) $\dfrac{3}{16}$

   (C) $\dfrac{3}{8}$

   (D) $\dfrac{1}{2}$

42. If you have a class consisting of 10 girls and 20 boys, in how many different ways can you form a committee from the class members such that there will be 2 girls and 2 boys on the committee?

   (A) 50
   (B) 8,550
   (C) 34,200
   (D) None of the above

43. For the class spring dance you have to choose a King and Prince from the boys, and a Queen and Princess from the girls. If there are 10 boys and 20 girls in the class, in how many different ways can you do this?

   (A) 50
   (B) 8,550
   (C) 34,200
   (D) None of the above

44. You draw 4 M&Ms out of a bag containing hundreds of M&Ms colored red, green, or yellow. How many different combinations of colors can you have? Note that 3 reds and 1 yellow counts as a different combination from 2 reds and 2 yellows.

   (A) 7
   (B) 15
   (C) 18
   (D) 81

45. If you roll a pair of fair dice, the spots can total any number from 2 up to 12. Which is more likely, an odd total or an even total?

   (A) An odd total
   (B) An even total
   (C) They are both equally likely
   (D) None of the above

46. Let X be the number of coins that come up heads when you flip 16 fair coins. What is the standard deviation of the random variable X?

   (A) 2
   (B) 2.87...
   (C) 4
   (D) $\sqrt{8}$

47. If you are dealt 5 cards in a game of draw poker, and 3 of them are 5s, what is the probability you will get another 5 if you draw 2 cards?

   (A) $\dfrac{2}{47}$

   (B) $\dfrac{2}{49}$

   (C) $\dfrac{1}{6}$

   (D) $\dfrac{2}{13}$

Questions 48–49 are based on the following railroad map.

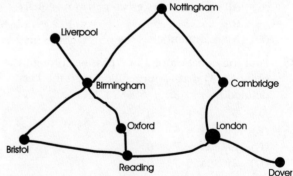

48. If you pick two different cities on this map at random, what is the probability that they will be directly connected by a railroad line, with no intermediate stops?

   (A) $\dfrac{5}{18}$

   (B) $\dfrac{11}{45}$

   (C) $\dfrac{1}{3}$

   (D) None of the above

49. If you pick two cities entirely at random, and at least one of them turns out to have a name beginning with the letter "L," what is the probability the two cities are directly connected?

(A) $\frac{1}{3}$

(B) $\frac{2}{7}$

(C) $\frac{14}{45}$

(D) $\frac{4}{15}$

50. If you flip 7 coins simultaneously, what is the probability that 3 or 4 will come up heads?

(A) $\frac{1}{4}$

(B) $\frac{2}{7}$

(C) $\frac{1}{2}$

(D) $\frac{35}{64}$

51. White and black peas are distributed at random among a number of boxes. There are 2 peas in each box, and one third of the boxes have 2 white peas, one third have 1 white pea and 1 black pea, and one third have 2 black peas. You pick a box at random and draw a white pea from it. What is the probability that the other pea in the box is also white?

(A) $\frac{1}{3}$

(B) $\frac{1}{2}$

(C) $\frac{2}{3}$

(D) None of the above

52. Skilled basketball players make $\frac{3}{4}$ of their free throws. Unskilled players make $\frac{1}{4}$ of their free throws. Half the boys in the gym class are skilled, and half are unskilled. Jimmy, a boy picked at random from the class, steps up to the line and makes 3 out of 5 free throws. What is the probability that he is a skilled basketball player?

(A) $\frac{3}{5}$

(B) $\frac{3}{4}$

(C) $\frac{9}{13}$

(D) None of the above

53. In a certain game, you roll 3 dice and are given one dollar for each 6 that is rolled. So, on each play, you may earn 0, 1, 2, or 3 dollars. What are your expected earnings per play?

(A) Nothing
(B) 50 cents
(C) 1 dollar
(D) 1 dollar and 50 cents

54. Consider the set consisting of the first nine primes {2, 3, 5, 7, 11, 13, 17, 19, 23}. What is the difference between the mean and the median?

(A) 0

(B) $\frac{1}{29}$

(C) $\frac{1}{11}$

(D) $\frac{1}{9}$

55. Let a, b, and c be three distinct positive numbers. What can be said about the difference between the mean and the median of these three numbers?

(A) It is always positive or zero.
(B) It is less than one third of the difference between the greatest and least of the numbers.
(C) It is always negative or zero.
(D) None of the above

GO ON TO THE NEXT PAGE

56. If *a* and *b* are two distinct, positive real numbers, which is greater—the arithmetic mean or the geometric mean?

   (A) They are both equal.
   (B) The geometric mean is greater.
   (C) The arithmetic mean is greater.
   (D) Either could be greater, depending on the particular numbers involved.

57. Alice can paint the house in 5 hours, and Bob can paint it in 7 hours. How long will it take them if they work together?

   (A) 2 hours and 45 minutes
   (B) 2 hours and 55 minutes
   (C) 3 hours exactly
   (D) 3 hours and 10 minutes

58. Traveling from Los Angeles to San Diego, Carlos drove 30 miles at 30 miles per hour, 35 miles at 70 miles per hour, and 40 miles at 60 miles per hour. What was Carlos' average speed for the whole trip?

   (A) 48.46 miles per hour
   (B) 54.76 miles per hour
   (C) 57.97 miles per hour
   (D) 60 miles per hour

59. Betsy invests an amount P at 6% annual interest compounded semi-annually. Which of the following formulas tells how much she will have after 5 years?

   (A) $P(1.06)^5$
   (B) $P(1.30)$
   (C) $P(1.06)(1.12)^2$
   (D) $P(1.03)^{10}$

60. Two years ago, Fred was three times as old as George. Five years from now, Fred will be twice as old as George. What is the sum of their ages right now?

   (A) 21
   (B) 28
   (C) 32
   (D) 42

61. A strip of lawn has an area of 60 square meters and a perimeter of 34 meters. What must be the range of a sprinkler, that, positioned in the center of the strip, covers the entire area?

   (A) 650 centimeters
   (B) 3.87 meters
   (C) 4.25 meters
   (D) $3\sqrt{5}$ meters

62. What is one square root of $1 + i$?

   (A) $\sqrt{\dfrac{1+\sqrt{2}}{2}} + i\sqrt{\dfrac{-1+\sqrt{2}}{2}}$
   (B) $1 - i$
   (C) $\sqrt{2} - i\sqrt{2}$
   (D) $\cos(22.5) + i\sin(22.5)$ (angles are measured in degrees)

63. If $\log(u) = v$, what is the log of $10(u^2)$?

   (A) $2v + 1$
   (B) $10v^2$
   (C) $2(v+1)$
   (D) v^2

64. If $e^x = 5$ and $e^y = 2$, where $e = 2.71828...$ is Euler's constant, what is xy?

   (A) $(\ln(2))(\ln(5))$
   (B) $\ln(10)$
   (C) 25
   (D) 32

65. In Biblical times, 1 talent of copper was worth 1 shekel of gold, while 1 talent of tin was worth 3 shekels of gold. If Solomon bought 500 talents of these metals from the Queen of Sheba and paid 1,000 shekels of gold for them, how many talents of tin did he buy?

   (A) 125
   (B) 200
   (C) 250
   (D) $333\dfrac{1}{3}$

STOP If you finish before the time is up, you may check your work on this section only. Do not turn to any other section in the test.

POSTTEST ANSWER KEY AND EXPLANATIONS

PART I

1. B	8. A	15. C	22. B	28. B
2. A	9. B	16. D	23. A	29. C
3. B	10. D	17. C	24. D	30. A
4. C	11. C	18. A	25. C	31. D
5. D	12. D	19. C	26. A	32. D
6. A	13. A	20. D	27. A	33. A
7. B	14. A	21. C		

PART II

34. C	41. C	48. A	54. D	60. C
35. D	42. B	49. D	55. B	61. A
36. D	43. C	50. D	56. C	62. A
37. D	44. B	51. C	57. B	63. A
38. B	45. C	52. B	58. A	64. A
39. A	46. A	53. B	59. D	65. C
40. C	47. A			

PART I

1. **The correct answer is (B).** The intersection of two sets consists of all the elements that are in both sets.

2. **The correct answer is (A).** The complement of the union is the intersection of the complements, and the complement of the intersection is the union of the complements.

3. **The correct answer is (B).** The only prime number that is even is 2.

4. **The correct answer is (C).** There are 37 who are trained in one or the other, and the sum of the elements in A and B, minus the elements in A union B, is the number of elements in A intersection B. $50 - 37 = 13$.

5. **The correct answer is (D).** 94 is not divisible by either 4 or 6.

6. **The correct answer is (A).** A relation is a set of ordered pairs, and the Cartesian product of A with A is the set of all possible ordered pairs from A.

7. **The correct answer is (B).** ~C implies A by *modus tollens,* and A implies B by *modus ponens.*

8. **The correct answer is (A).** The logical inverse of $A \rightarrow B$ is defined to be $\sim A \rightarrow \sim B$.

9. **The correct answer is (B).** Since $x = -2$ is also a root of the equation, it is not necessary that $t = -1$ for $f(t) = 0$.

10. **The correct answer is (D).** If $n = 4$, then $(2n) + 1 = (2 \times 4) + 1 = 8 + 1 = 9$, which is not a prime number.

11. **The correct answer is (C).** The Truth Tables are actually a definition of what is meant by "$\vee$" and "$\wedge$."

12. **The correct answer is (D).** Since Fran is guilty, by *modus tollens,* Charles is innocent. Therefore, Alan is guilty; so by *modus ponens,* Baker is also guilty.

13. **The correct answer is (A).** If p is true (so that ~p is false), then q must be true.

14. **The correct answer is (A).** $39 = 3 \times 13$. $9 = 3 \times 3$. $221 = 13 \times 17$. So no answer except A is correct.

15. **The correct answer is (C).** $51 = 3 \times 17$.

16. **The correct answer is (D).** $4m$ is even, so $4m + 5$ must be odd.

17. **The correct answer is (C).** $1101_2 = 8 + 4 + 1 = 13$.

18. **The correct answer is (A).** $1000100_2 = (1 \times 64) + (0 \times 32) + (0 \times 16) + (0 \times 8) + (1 \times 4) + (0 \times 2) + (0 \times 1) = 64 + 4 = 68$.

19. **The correct answer is (C).** $156 = 13 \times 12$, and $204 = 17 \times 12$.

20. **The correct answer is (D).** $x = 1$ is obviously a zero of the expression, so $x - 1$ is a factor of it.

21. **The correct answer is (C).** $x - y$ must be positive, so it is equal to its absolute value. A and B won't be true if x is a number less than zero, and D will not hold if $x = \frac{1}{2}$ and $y = \frac{1}{3}$.

22. **The correct answer is (B).** We must either have $x - 1 > 2$ or $x - 1 < -2$ for the inequality to hold. Choice (C) is not a correct response because the set it specifies includes $x = 3$ and $x = -1$, which do not satisfy the inequality.

23. **The correct answer is (A).** $\sqrt{121}$ is 11, which is rational.

24. **The correct answer is (D).** $\frac{a}{b}$ is the root of $bx - a = 0$; decimal expansion will always repeat eventually; and $b\left(\frac{a}{b}\right) = a$, so all three of the alternatives given are correct.

25. **The correct answer is (C).** You always get a real number, but it can be either rational or irrational. $\sqrt{2}$ and $5 - \sqrt{2}$ are both irrational, but their sum is rational.

26. **The correct answer is (A).** The *diagonal* process gives a one-to-one correspondence between the set of all positive rationals and the set of all positive integers. The reals cannot be put into one-to-one correspondence with the rationals, and therefore, the rationals cannot be put into one-to-one correspondence with the points on a line.

27. **The correct answer is (A).** The given equation is equivalent to $y = -3x + 9.5$.

28. **The correct answer is (B).** Note that the function is zero when $x = 1$.

29. **The correct answer is (C).** You find the x-intercepts by setting $y = 0$ and solving for x.

30. **The correct answer is (A).** It is easy to see this by plugging one function into the other and then equating coefficients.

31. **The correct answer is (D).** It is easy to see this, since $f(0) = 1$, $f(1) = -10$, and $f(x)$ is great and positive for great positive x and great and negative for great negative x.

32. **The correct answer is (D).** Simply do the division and you get $y = x + 3 + \dfrac{8}{x - 1}$.

33. **The correct answer is (A).** Choices (B) and (D) are hyperbolas, and choice (C) is a parabola.

PART II

34. **The correct answer is (C).** The function equals -1 when $x = 0$, and the rest of its values are greater than -1.

35. **The correct answer is (D).** The slope must be $\dfrac{-1}{2}$, and choice (D) is the only alternative that satisfies this condition.

36. **The correct answer is (D).** Two of the given asymptotes are vertical asymptotes, and one is a horizontal asymptote.

37. **The correct answer is (D).** The period of the graph is about pi, and the first zero is at about $x = \dfrac{1}{2}$, so the argument of the sine must be $2x - 1$.

38. **The correct answer is (B).** The curve is a hyperbola, and the asymptotes are the lines defined by $9y^2 - 4x^2 = 0$.

39. **The correct answer is (A).** This is the well-known *vertical line test*.

40. **The correct answer is (C).** The 13 ways are: {Q}, {2D,N}, {2D,5P}, {D,3N}, {D,2N,5P}, {D,N,10P}, {D,15P}, {5N}, {4N,5P}, {3N,10P}, {2N,15P}, {N,20P}, and {25P}.

41. **The correct answer is (C).** The formula is $\dfrac{C(4,2)}{[2^4]} = \dfrac{6}{[16]} = \dfrac{3}{8}$.

42. **The correct answer is (B).** There are 45 ways to pick 2 girls, and 190 ways to pick 2 boys, so the total number of committees is $45 \times 190 = 8,550$.

43. **The correct answer is (C).** There are 20×19 ways to pick a Queen and Princess, and 10×9 ways to pick a King and Prince, so there are $20 \times 19 \times 10 \times 9 = 34,200$ ways to do it all together. Note that the difference between this question and question 42 is that the 2 boys are distinguished from each other, and so are the 2 girls. Choosing Julie as Queen and Anne as Princess is not the same as choosing Anne as Queen and Julie as Princess.

44. **The correct answer is (B).** There are 4 basic patterns you can have: all one color; 3 of one color and 1 of another; 2 of one color and 2 of another; or 2 of one color and 1 of each other color. The first of these gives you 3 possibilities (all red, all green, or all yellow), the second gives you 6 possibilities, the third gives you 3 possibilities, and the last gives you 3 possibilities. That makes a total of 15 different possible patterns.

45. **The correct answer is (C).** You can total up the probabilities for the odd and even totals, but an easier way to solve the problem is to note that, after you have rolled one die, there are an equal number of rolls of the other one that will give you an odd or an even total.

46. **The correct answer is (A).** The variance when you flip a single coin is $\dfrac{1}{4}$. Therefore, the variance when you flip 16 coins is $\dfrac{16}{4} = 4$. The standard deviation is the square root of the variance.

47. **The correct answer is (A).** There is only one card left in the deck that is a 5. There are 47 more cards in the deck. If you draw 2 cards, the chance that you will draw the 5 is $\dfrac{2}{47}$.

48. **The correct answer is (A).** There are 9 cities, so $C(9,2) = 36$ possible pairs of cities, and 10 have direct rail links, so there is a $\dfrac{10}{36} = \dfrac{5}{18}$ probability that a pair picked at random will have a direct link.

49. The correct answer is (D). There are 15 pairs that include a city beginning with the letter "L." There are 4 links to cities beginning with the letter "L," so the probability is $\frac{4}{15}$.

50. The correct answer is (D). The probability that 3 heads will come up is $\frac{C(7,3)}{2^7} = \frac{35}{128}$. The probability that 4 heads will come up is the same, so the probability that 3 or 4 heads will come up must be $\frac{70}{128} = \frac{35}{64}$.

51. The correct answer is (C). By Bayes' Theorem, $P(E \mid A) = P(A \mid E)P(E)/P(A)$. In this case, E is "choosing a box with 2 white peas," and A is "drawing a white pea from the box." $P(A) = \frac{1}{2}$, $P(E) = \frac{1}{3}$, and $P(A \mid E)$ is unity. So $P(E \mid A) = \frac{2}{3}$.

52. The correct answer is (B). This is another application of Bayes' Theorem, but with $P(E) = \frac{1}{2}$, $P(A) = \frac{C(5,3)[3^3 + 3^2]}{2^{11}}$, and $P(A \mid E) = \frac{C(5,3)3^3}{4^5}$.

53. The correct answer is (B). The expected earnings are $3\left(\frac{1}{216}\right) + 2\left(\frac{15}{216}\right) + 1\left(\frac{75}{216}\right) = \frac{108}{216} = \frac{1}{2}$ dollar, or 50 cents.

54. The correct answer is (D). The median is 11, and the mean is $\frac{100}{9} = 11\frac{1}{9}$.

55. The correct answer is (B). Let $0 < a < b < c$. The difference between the mean and median is $\frac{a + b + c}{3} - b = \frac{(c - b) - (b - a)}{3}$, which is clearly less than $\frac{c - a}{3}$.

56. The correct answer is (C). $(\sqrt{a} - \sqrt{b})^2 > 0$, so $a - 2\sqrt{ab} + b > 0$, so $\frac{a+b}{2} > \sqrt{ab}$.

57. The correct answer is (B). You want $\frac{b}{5} + \frac{b}{7} = 1$. Solve for b and you get $b = \frac{35}{12} = 2\frac{11}{12}$. $\frac{11}{12}$ of an hour is 55 minutes.

58. The correct answer is (A). The trip of 105 miles took $\frac{13}{6}$ of an hour, so the average speed was $\frac{105}{\frac{13}{6}} = \frac{630}{13} \approx 48.46$ miles per hour.

59. The correct answer is (D). 6 percent annually is the same as 3 percent each half-year, and so the formula is $P(1.03)^{10}$.

60. The correct answer is (C). Solve the equations $F - 2 = 3(G - 2)$ and $F + 5 = 2(G + 5)$ to find the ages of Fred and George now. George is 9, and Fred is 23.

61. The correct answer is (A). It is given that $LW = 60$ and $L + W = 17$. So, $W = 5$ and $L = 12$. By the Pythagorean Theorem, the diagonal is 13 meters, and, with the sprinkler in the middle, it must reach 6.5 meters (650 centimeters) to reach all four corners.

62. The correct answer is (A). You can calculate it by De Moivre's Theorem, but it should be obvious that the other three alternatives don't even have the right magnitude to be a square root of $1 + i$.

63. The correct answer is (A). $\log(10u^2) = \log(10) + 2\log(u) = 1 + 2v$.

64. The correct answer is (A). $x = \ln(5)$ and $y = \ln(2)$, so $xy = (\ln(5))(\ln(2))$.

65. The correct answer is (C). Just solve the equations $c + t = 500$ and $c + 3t = 1,000$.

Part IV

HUMANITIES

Chapter 8
PRETEST

PART I

Directions: Each of the questions or incomplete statements below is followed by five suggested answers or completions. Select the one that is best in each case.

1. Which one of the following plays is NOT taken from a preexisting story?

    (A) *Romeo and Juliet*
    (B) *Macbeth*
    (C) *Henry the Fifth*
    (D) *The Importance of Being Earnest*
    (E) *My Fair Lady*

2. What do Jesus and Socrates have in common?

    (A) They were religious leaders.
    (B) They were fictional characters.
    (C) Neither of them ever wrote anything.
    (D) Both of them committed suicide.
    (E) Each one's father was a carpenter.

3. In what verse form did Shakespeare write his plays?

    (A) Sonnet
    (B) Blank verse
    (C) Free verse
    (D) Ballad
    (E) Epic

4. Proceed, proceed. We will begin these nights
    As we do trust they'll end in true delights

    The passage above from *As You Like It* is best described as

    (A) a heroic couplet
    (B) ironic
    (C) blank verse
    (D) trochee
    (E) didactic

5. Which of the following plays was NOT written by Shakespeare?

    (A) *Two Gentlemen of Verona*
    (B) *The Winter's Tale*
    (C) *The Jew of Malta*
    (D) *Cymbeline*
    (E) *Pericles, Prince of Tyre*

6. Which one of the following poems was written by Sir Walter Scott?

    (A) *To a Skylark*
    (B) *Youth and Age*
    (C) *The Lady of the Lake*
    (D) *Ozymandias*
    (E) *Endymion*

7. All of the following are forms of poetry EXCEPT the

    (A) essay
    (B) ode
    (C) lyric
    (D) song
    (E) sonnet

8. All of the following types of literature may be humorous EXCEPT

    (A) comics
    (B) elegies
    (C) limericks
    (D) novels
    (E) farces

9. All of the following are Nobel Prize winners EXCEPT

    (A) Ernest Hemingway
    (B) Mark Twain
    (C) Czeslaw Milosz
    (D) Saul Bellow
    (E) Pablo Neruda

GO ON TO THE NEXT PAGE

10. A word or idea referring to a generality, state of being, or quality that cannot be attained by the five senses is a definition of

    (A) bildungsroman
    (B) antithesis
    (C) abstract
    (D) epigram
    (E) tone

11. The use of paradoxical, or opposite, words for effect (e.g., "poor little rich girl") is the definition of

    (A) litotes
    (B) malapropism
    (C) paraphrase
    (D) oxymoron
    (E) blurb

12. Each of the following is a *nom de plume* EXCEPT

    (A) Mark Twain
    (B) George Sand
    (C) George Eliot
    (D) Lope de Vega
    (E) Boz

13. All of the following are literary allusions that have become standard in the language EXCEPT

    (A) Catch-22
    (B) Bligh
    (C) Belling the cat
    (D) King
    (E) Byronic

14. Which of the following quotations was written by Alexander Pope?

    (A) "A thing of beauty is a joy forever."
    (B) "A little learning is a dangerous thing."
    (C) "A penny saved is a penny earned."
    (D) "A man's reach should exceed his grasp."
    (E) "But I have promises to keep, and miles to go before I sleep. . ."

15. Thomas Mann wrote all of the following EXCEPT

    (A) *The Magic Mountain*
    (B) *Death in Venice*
    (C) *Buddenbrooks*
    (D) *The Prince*
    (E) *Doctor Faustus*

16. All of the following are characters from Shakespeare EXCEPT

    (A) Brutus
    (B) Grendel
    (C) Falstaff
    (D) Cordelia
    (E) Portia

17. Each of the following pairs are Greek and Roman gods of similar domains EXCEPT

    (A) Eros and Cupid
    (B) Hera and Juno
    (C) Poseidon and Janus
    (D) Zeus and Jupiter
    (E) Helios and Apollo

18. The Boatman who took the souls of the dead across the river Styx into the underworld was

    (A) Charon
    (B) Daedalus
    (C) Electra
    (D) Cereberus
    (E) Circe

19. All of the following are real places EXCEPT

    (A) Parnassus
    (B) Mount Olympus
    (C) Toledo
    (D) Lilliput
    (E) Cairo

20. Mudville is

    (A) a place in *Tom Sawyer*
    (B) the village in *The Legend of Sleepy Hollow*
    (C) the site of *Casey at the Bat*
    (D) one of William Faulkner's fictional towns
    (E) where Little John bested Robin Hood

21. An author associated with the classicism school of criticism was

    (A) John Crowe Ransom
    (B) Jacques Derrida
    (C) Aristotle
    (D) William Hazlitt
    (E) Roland Barthes

22. A novel about the decline of a southern family was

    (A) *The Mosquito Coast*
    (B) *Ordinary People*
    (C) *Lie Down in Darkness*
    (D) *The Joy Luck Club*
    (E) *The Metamorphosis*

23. All of the following are autobiographies EXCEPT

(A) Russell Baker's *Growing Up*
(B) Margaret Mead's *Blackberry Winter*
(C) John Huston's *An Open Book*
(D) George Eliot's *Silas Marner*
(E) Ron Kovic's *Born on the Fourth of July*

24. William F. Buckley Jr., Eric Ambler, John Dickson Carr, and Sir Arthur Conan Doyle have what in common?

(A) They are English.
(B) They are Americans.
(C) They are poets.
(D) They are mystery writers.
(E) They are all women.

25. *One Corpse Too Many, St. Peter's Fair, The Leper of St. Giles,* and *The Pilgrim of Hate* were all written by

(A) Agatha Christie
(B) Raymond Chandler
(C) Ellis Peters
(D) Ngaio Marsh
(E) Ross MacDonald

26. All of the following historical and quasi literary documents are correctly paired EXCEPT

(A) Bill of Rights . . . 1791 C.E.
(B) *Mein Kampf* . . . 1925 C.E.
(C) Magna Carta . . . 1062 C.E.
(D) Koran . . . 640 C.E.
(E) Laws of Solon . . . 590 B.C.E.

27. All of the following are Renaissance epics EXCEPT

(A) *The Odyssey*
(B) *Orlando Furioso*
(C) *Paradise Regained*
(D) *The Faerie Queen*
(E) *Gerusalemme Liberata*

28. All of the following epic novels and authors are correctly paired EXCEPT

(A) *Tom Jones* . . . Henry Fielding
(B) *Ulysses* . . . Herman Melville
(C) *War and Peace* . . . Leo Tolstoy
(D) *Doctor Zhivago* . . . Boris Pasternak
(E) *Don Quixote* . . . Miguel de Cervantes

29. Of the following essay masters, all are from the eighteenth century EXCEPT

(A) Alexander Pope
(B) John Galsworthy
(C) Richard Steele
(D) Jonathan Swift
(E) Oliver Goldsmith

30. The following are all fables of Aesop EXCEPT

(A) *The Bull and the Goat*
(B) *The Fox and the Bramble*
(C) *The Crow and the Pitcher*
(D) *The Armadillo and the Eagle*
(E) *Androcles and the Lion*

31. 1. John Updike; 2. William Faulkner; 3. Ernest Hemingway; 4. Booth Tarkington; and 5. Bernard Malamud . . . each won the Pulitzer Prize. The only one of the following combinations that correctly lists those who won three times is

(A) 1 and 4
(B) 3 and 4
(C) 3 and 5
(D) 1, 3, and 5
(E) 1, 2, 3, 4, and 5

32. Ernest Hemingway wrote all of the following EXCEPT

(A) *A Bell for Adano*
(B) *The Sun Also Rises*
(C) *In Our Time*
(D) *A Farewell to Arms*
(E) *Intruder in the Dust*

33. In *The Great Gatsby*, F. Scott Fitzgerald writes that

(A) Nick is a careless young man
(B) Jordon is the model sports person
(C) Daisy smells like money
(D) Tom works hard for his money
(E) Gatsby doesn't believe in recreating the past

34. What do Leo Tolstoy, Sigrid Undset, Ivan Turgenev, Francois Rabelais, and Franz Kafka have in common?

(A) They were all Americans.
(B) They were all British.
(C) They were all contemporary male authors.
(D) They were neither American nor British.
(E) They were all Russians.

35. The picaresque novel concerns a main character who is born disadvantaged and is often a rogue. By adapting cleverly to events, the hero conforms to the demands of the world. The following paired novels are all picaresque EXCEPT

(A) *Huckleberry Finn* . . . *The Stranger*
(B) *Catch-22* . . . *Don Quixote*
(C) *The Invisible Man* . . . *The Grapes of Wrath*
(D) *Joseph Andrews* . . . *Moll Flanders*
(E) *Comic Romance* . . . *The Pickwick Papers*

GO ON TO THE NEXT PAGE →

36. In Sherwood Anderson's *Winesburg, Ohio*, the unifying thread is the fact that
    (A) the characters are all members of one family
    (B) each story is true
    (C) the characters have the same vocation
    (D) the characters are "grotesque"
    (E) the characters are without dreams

37. The repetition of consonant sounds—usually at the beginning of words, to create smoothness and effect—is
    (A) enjambment
    (B) cinquain
    (C) assonance
    (D) alliteration
    (E) tanka

38. Words that sound like what they represent are
    (A) refrain
    (B) onomatopoeia
    (C) grue
    (D) caesura
    (E) assonance

39. All of the following dramatists are from the nineteenth century EXCEPT
    (A) Alexander Dumas
    (B) Maxim Gorky
    (C) Henrik Ibsen
    (D) Luigi Pirandello
    (E) Edmond Rostand

40. The "Little Book," a common name for *The Elements of Style*, was originally written by
    (A) Richard Lederer
    (B) William F. Buckley Jr.
    (C) William Strunk
    (D) E. B. White
    (E) Tom Wolfe

41. In Emily Dickinson's poem about "a narrow fellow in the grass," she is referring to
    (A) a conservative politician
    (B) a skinny man
    (C) a snake
    (D) a hungry grasshopper
    (E) a tired worker resting

42. Adonis was known for his
    (A) handsome features
    (B) poetry
    (C) wisdom
    (D) morality
    (E) forgetfulness

43. In Robert Frost's poem "Mending Wall," when the narrator says, "I could say elves to him . . ." he means
    (A) they are fairies who plant flowers
    (B) something mystical tumbles the stones from the wall
    (C) they left the gold
    (D) he wants to scare the man
    (E) the elves are a local gang

44. In his Nobel Prize acceptance speech, William Faulkner promised that mankind would
    (A) be doomed
    (B) endure
    (C) prevail
    (D) overcome
    (E) end with a whimper, not a bang

45. What great war leader said, "My armies will be the rocks and the trees and the birds of the sky"?
    (A) Adolf Hitler
    (B) Winston Churchill
    (C) Charlemagne
    (D) Julius Caesar
    (E) Alexander the Great

46. Why did the Ancient Mariner shoot the albatross?
    (A) He needed the feathers.
    (B) He needed to eat.
    (C) He did it as a reward to himself.
    (D) He did it for no reason.
    (E) He wanted to impress the sailors.

47. Which poet ignores the usual rules of capital letters?
    (A) Robert Frost
    (B) T. S. Eliot
    (C) E. E. Cummings
    (D) Richard Armour
    (E) Carl Sandburg

48. "The Gift of The Magi" involves in part
    (A) a killing
    (B) a stone
    (C) a haircut
    (D) mistaken identity
    (E) a lost love

49. The actual villain in *Othello* is
    (A) Othello
    (B) Desdemona
    (C) Iago
    (D) Cassio
    (E) Emilia

50. Who slew the Minotaur?

(A) Zeus
(B) Hercules
(C) Jason
(D) Theseus
(E) Circe

51. Sherlock Holmes lived on

(A) Oak Street
(B) Baker Street
(C) First Avenue
(D) Queen's Road
(E) Canterbury Road

52. All of the following have something in common EXCEPT

(A) *The Red Badge of Courage*
(B) *Born on the Fourth of July*
(C) *War and Peace*
(D) *As I Lay Dying*
(E) *The Red and The Black*

53. Which of the following is NOT one of the "Secret Lives of Walter Mitty"?

(A) Pilot
(B) Sea captain
(C) Doctor
(D) Astronaut
(E) Race-car driver

54. The only rational creature in the land of the Houyhnhnms was the

(A) dog
(B) monkey
(C) cow
(D) man
(E) horse

55. In Eugene O'Neill's *Mourning Becomes Electra*, which of the following does the author use to dramatize his conviction that the Greek concept of fate should be replaced?

(A) Predestination
(B) Accident
(C) Psychological determination
(D) Irony
(E) A vengeful God

56. "The yellow fog that rubs its back upon the window-panes/The yellow smoke that rubs its muzzle on the window-panes"

In "The Love Song of J. Alfred Prufrock," the lines above create a powerful image through a figure of speech known as

(A) metaphor
(B) trope
(C) hyperbole
(D) personification
(E) metonymy

57. "They sat down at the table and the girl looked across at the hills on the dry side of the valley and the man looked at her and at the table."

These words were written by

(A) William Faulkner
(B) John Steinbeck
(C) F. Scott Fitzgerald
(D) Ernest Hemingway
(E) Mark Twain

58. *Arrow of God*, a novel set in an African village, was written by

(A) Alex La Guma
(B) Toni Morrison
(C) Chinua Achebe
(D) Ralph Ellison
(E) Ntozake Shange

59. Considering the cultural background of the authors of the following, which does NOT belong?

(A) *The Year in San Fernando*
(B) *Black Spring*
(C) *Native Son*
(D) *In the Castle of My Skin*
(E) *Soul on Ice*

60. In *Ulysses*, by Lord Alfred Tennyson, "There lies the port the vessel puffs her sail" uses a figure of speech known as

(A) metaphor
(B) simile
(C) hyperbole
(D) personification
(E) oxymoron

61. What is the title of an Ezra Pound poem that opens: "The gilded phaloi of the crocuses/are thrusting at the spring air"?

(A) "The Tea Shop"
(B) "The Encounter"
(C) "Coitus"
(D) "Coda"
(E) "Amities"

GO ON TO THE NEXT PAGE

62. *Canto XIII*: "Kung walked/by the dynastic temple/and into the cedar grove,/and then out by the lower river."

These lines are typical of

(A) W. B. Yeats
(B) John Donne
(C) Robert Frost
(D) Ezra Pound
(E) T. S. Eliot

63. In John Knowles's *A Separate Peace*, the paired friends were

(A) Huck and Tom
(B) Hero and Leander
(C) Brinker and Leper
(D) Quackenbush and Phineas
(E) Gene and Finny

64. ". . . The interpretation of reality through literary representation, or 'imitation,' has occupied me for a long time. . . ."

This quote is from a book by Erich Auerbach, titled

(A) *Theory of Literature*
(B) *Literary Reality*
(C) *Critical Theory*
(D) *Mimesis*
(E) *Art and Life*

65. "so much depends/upon/a red wheel/barrow."

These lines above from William Carlos Williams's "The Red Wheelbarrow" represent what kind of poem?

(A) Elegy
(B) Couplet
(C) Lyric
(D) Concrete
(E) Refrain

66. To say that Madonna was locked out of the audition for *Evita!* because she couldn't find the right key is an example of a(n)

(A) pun
(B) metaphor
(C) simile
(D) oxymoron
(E) hyperbole

67. "Trueblue" and "nineteen" are examples of what poetic foot?

(A) Iamb
(B) Spondee
(C) Trochee
(D) Pentameter
(E) Dactyl

68. "And I have known the arms already . . ."

The line above, from "The Love Song of J. Alfred Prufrock"—in which a part represents the whole—is the trope known as

(A) metonymy
(B) synecdoche
(C) personification
(D) conceit
(E) apostrophe

69. When one is seated in a theater and an actor is on one's extreme right and as close as possible to the edge of the stage, the actor is said to be

(A) upstage
(B) center
(C) right
(D) stage left
(E) down left

70. "As flies to wanton boys, are we to the gods, they kill us for their sport."

This quote is from

(A) *Hamlet*
(B) *King Lear*
(C) *Othello*
(D) *Macbeth*
(E) *Twelfth Night*

71. "How sharper than a serpent's tooth it is to have a thankless child."

This quote is from

(A) *Romeo and Juliet*
(B) *King Lear*
(C) *Julius Caesar*
(D) *As You Like It*
(E) *A Midsummer Night's Dream*

72. What do *Animal Farm, Death in Venice, Everyman, Ship of Fools*, and *Pilgrim's Progress* have in common?

(A) They were written by Nobel authors.
(B) They are allegories.
(C) They describe journeys.
(D) They are realistic novels.
(E) They are dramas.

73. All of the following authors have written something in common EXCEPT

(A) William Faulkner
(B) Walt Morey
(C) Michael Bond
(D) Alice Daigliesh
(E) Ernest Hemingway

74. The following are all Beat writers EXCEPT

(A) Allen Ginsberg
(B) Jack Kerouac
(C) Amrose Bierce
(D) William Burroughs
(E) Gregory Corso

75. Place the following events in chronological order:

1. Johannes Gutenberg printed *Constance Mass Book.*
2. Francis Bacon wrote *Essays, Civil and Moral.*
3. Lord Byron wrote *Don Juan.*
4. *The Picture of Dorian Gray* was written.
5. Johann Goethe wrote *Faust, Part I.*
6. *Moll Flanders* was written.
7. Erasmus published a collection of proverbs.
8. Geoffrey Chaucer was born.
9. Japanese *noh* plays developed.
10. Dante wrote his *Divine Comedy.*

(A) 1, 2, 3, 4, 5, 6, 7, 8, 9, 10
(B) 10, 9, 8, 1, 7, 2, 6, 5, 3, 4
(C) 4, 6, 9, 10, 8, 7, 5, 3, 2, 1
(D) 6, 3, 2, 1, 7, 8, 4, 9, 10, 5
(E) 5, 4, 3, 2, 1, 6, 7, 8, 9, 10

STOP If you finish before the time is up, you may check your work on this section only. Do not turn to any other section in the test.

TIME—45 MINUTES	75 QUESTIONS

PART II

Directions: Each of the questions or incomplete statements below is followed by five suggested answers or completions. Select the one that is best in each case.

76. A recurring musical phrase is called a
    (A) lieder
    (B) driving note
    (C) chorus
    (D) leading motif, or leitmotiv
    (E) sinfonia

77. A combination of three or more tones is a
    (A) chapeau
    (B) turn
    (C) chord
    (D) tarantella
    (E) piccolo

78. A dance in $\frac{6}{8}$ time, which is characterized by a frenzied tempo, is called a
    (A) tarantella
    (B) tattoo
    (C) waltz
    (D) rag
    (E) presto

79. The drumbeat at night recalling soldiers for sleep preceding taps is called a(n)
    (A) zither
    (B) tympani
    (C) atonal
    (D) toccata
    (E) tattoo

80. A musical clause, short passage, or figure is called a
    (A) canon
    (B) crescendo
    (C) phrase
    (D) legato
    (E) presto

81. A gradual increase in volume and intensity is called a
    (A) cue
    (B) courante
    (C) score
    (D) meter
    (E) crescendo

82. To play smoothly and lyrically is to play
    (A) reverie
    (B) cantabile
    (C) tutta
    (D) syncopation
    (E) volante

83. The first, or opening, section of a suite is called a
    (A) finale
    (B) sonata
    (C) prelude
    (D) cantata
    (E) rondo

84. Drama set to music is called
    (A) opera
    (B) chorus
    (C) concerto
    (D) stretch
    (E) chamber music

85. Music composed for a small auditorium and group of instruments, such as a string quartet or a pianoforte trio, is called
    (A) a chorale
    (B) a symphony
    (C) a tone poem
    (D) chamber music
    (E) a concerto

86. When an opera has more lyricism than dramatic action, it is a(n)
    (A) folk song
    (B) elegy
    (C) ballad-opera
    (D) sonnet
    (E) masque

87. Where did spirituals originate?
    (A) At camp meetings in Kentucky
    (B) In the salons of France
    (C) In the meetings of Puritans
    (D) In the dance halls of New Orleans
    (E) In early churches

88. In what country was the piano, or pianoforte, invented?

(A) England
(B) Italy
(C) Spain
(D) Austria
(E) Norway

89. To play in a smooth, even style is to play

(A) legato
(B) lento
(C) syncopated
(D) jazz
(E) choral

90. A Romantic-period composer known for his études is

(A) Hector Berlioz
(B) Frédéric Chopin
(C) Gustav Holst
(D) Francis Poulenc
(E) Richard Wagner

91. An arrangement of the parts of a composition with bars drawn across all the parts to connect the simultaneous measures is called a(n)

(A) book
(B) orchestra
(C) score
(D) step
(E) staccato

92. A study outwardly intended for practice in some special difficulty of technic, often marked with much art, is a(n)

(A) elegy
(B) étude
(C) impromptu
(D) concerto
(E) prelude

93. This word means *to play slowly,* usually considered between andante and largo. What is the term?

(A) Coloratura
(B) Allegretto
(C) Moderato
(D) Lento
(E) Molto

94. A congregational hymn or psalm, or a service in which the entire liturgy is chanted or intoned, is called a(n)

(A) rhapsody
(B) chorale
(C) elegy
(D) minuet
(E) Gregorian chant

95. Who was known as the father of the string quartet and the symphony (not the sonata form), although he crystallized these forms while not originating them?

(A) Sergei Rachmaninoff
(B) Frédéric Chopin
(C) Edvard Grieg
(D) Joseph Haydn
(E) Giuseppe Verdi

96. What does the term *presto* mean?

(A) To play lyrically
(B) To play very fast
(C) An Italian herb
(D) A chorus in unison
(E) To play loudly

97. A gifted composer whose operas include *The Marriage of Figaro* and *The Magic Flute* was

(A) Antonín Dvořák
(B) Gustav Mahler
(C) George Gershwin
(D) Wolfgang Amadeus Mozart
(E) Claude Debussy

98. Ludwig van Beethoven's greatest misfortune was his

(A) deafness
(B) lack of formal education
(C) poor social grace
(D) inability to earn a living
(E) inability to find married happiness

99. A notable composer of romantic lieder who was part of the musical life of Vienna was

(A) Jean Sibelius
(B) Claude Debussy
(C) Igor Stravinsky
(D) Orlando Gibbons
(E) Franz Peter Schubert

100. Sacred music developed during the Gothic or Medieval period, which became popular again in the late twentieth century, is called

(A) lyric
(B) Gregorian chant
(C) madrigal
(D) ocarina
(E) impromptu

GO ON TO THE NEXT PAGE

Questions 101–102 refer to the following illustrations.

A. Sunflowers.

B. The Road Seen from the Path to Sevres.

C. Montagne Sainte Victoire—View from the South West.

101. To which of these paintings was the artist referring when he wrote, "I am trying to find a special brushwork without stippling or anything else, nothing but the varied stroke."

(A) A
(B) B
(C) C
(D) All of the above
(E) None of the above

102. The painter of *Sunflowers* was

(A) Pablo Picasso
(B) Camille Pissaro
(C) Paul Gauguin
(D) Vincent van Gogh
(E) None of the above

103. Which of the following is an etching by James McNeill Whistler?

(A) Above the Castle
(B) Battersea Bridge and Venetian Scene
(C) Bonaparte
(D) Ships at War
(E) Mother

104. *The Singing Boys* was sculpted by what artist?

(A) Heinz Mack
(B) Jean Tinguely
(C) Luca Della Robbia
(D) Otto Piene
(E) Nicolas Schoffer

105. The school of painters that used minute dots in pure color on their canvas was known as

    (A) abstractionist
    (B) pointillist
    (C) absurdist
    (D) cubist
    (E) dotist

106. The Italian metal worker who made a salt-cellar for Francis I was

    (A) Caravaggio
    (B) Alexis Preller
    (C) Benvenuto Cellini
    (D) Auguste Rodin
    (E) Orazio Gentileschi

107. The French artist noted for his paintings of the South Seas islands was

    (A) Vincent van Gogh
    (B) François Mansart
    (C) Paul Gauguin
    (D) Pierre Matisse
    (E) Francisco Goya

108. An accomplished Italian painter and sculptor also known for his sonnets is

    (A) Michelangelo Buonarotti
    (B) Pietro da Cortona
    (C) Guarino Guarini
    (D) Galileo Galilei
    (E) Sandro Botticelli

109. The monument to Admiral Farragut in New York City, the Shaw Memorial in Boston, and the Statue of Lincoln in Chicago were all sculpted by

    (A) Auguste Rodin
    (B) Augustus Saint-Gaudens
    (C) Henry Moore
    (D) Desiderius Erasmus
    (E) Edgar Degas

110. Flat impressions and a unique use of color were two contributions made by which nineteenth-century French artist?

    (A) Georges de La Tour
    (B) Paul Cézanne
    (C) John Galsworthy
    (D) Edouard Manet
    (E) Nicolas Poussin

111. Henry VIII was the patron of which of the following painters?

    (A) Pieter Aertsen
    (B) Joachim Beukelaer
    (C) Christopher Wren
    (D) Hans Holbein
    (E) Pieter Brueghel

112. Which American artist often created lithographs and paintings depicting prizefighters?

    (A) James McNeill Whistler
    (B) George Bellows
    (C) Grant Wood
    (D) Winslow Homer
    (E) Frank Stella

113. Which American painter was also a dry-point artist?

    (A) Jackson Pollock
    (B) James McNeill Whistler
    (C) Grant Wood
    (D) Andrew Wyeth
    (E) Keith Haring

114. *Sherman Led by Victory* is a famous equestrian statue sculpted by

    (A) Henry Moore
    (B) Leonardo da Vinci
    (C) Augustus Saint-Gaudens
    (D) Edward Hopper
    (E) Paul Manship

115. *The Thinker* is a famous statue by

    (A) Paul Gauguin
    (B) Michelangelo Buonarotti
    (C) Auguste Rodin
    (D) Leonardo da Vinci
    (E) Sandro Botticelli

116. *The Discus Thrower* was originally sculpted in what country?

    (A) Italy
    (B) Greece
    (C) France
    (D) Turkey
    (E) Spain

117. Which German artist is known for his engravings and woodcuts of the *Apocalypse* and *Melancholia I*?

    (A) Paul Klee
    (B) Bertolt Brecht
    (C) Albrecht Dürer
    (D) Frans Hals
    (E) Oskar Kokoschka

GO ON TO THE NEXT PAGE

118. This painting by Francisco Goya was made to commemorate a revolt in support of the Spanish king against French suppression. The French retaliated with mass executions. The painting's title is

    (A) *The Family of Charles IV*
    (B) *Saturn Devouring One of His Sons*
    (C) *Third of May 1808*
    (D) *Los Caprichos*
    (E) *Floridablanca*

Questions 119–121 refer to the following illustration.

119. The title of this famous sculpture is

    (A) *Sorrow*
    (B) *Mother's Child*
    (C) *Sleep*
    (D) *The Pièta*
    (E) *The Peace*

120. Who was the artist?

    (A) Sandro Botticelli
    (B) Jacopo Bellini
    (C) Titian
    (D) Michelangelo Buonarotti
    (E) Raphael

121. Where is the permanent home of this sculpture?

    (A) Louvre
    (B) Notre Dame
    (C) London
    (D) St. Peter's
    (E) Florence

122. A grouping of objects, flowers, or foods, usually without obvious stories or people, is called a

    (A) glaze
    (B) tableau
    (C) still life
    (D) landscape
    (E) rococo

123. Which group of artists was known for its interest in American landscapes and the sublime wilderness?

    (A) Colonial Portraitists
    (B) Ashcan School
    (C) Impressionists
    (D) Hudson River School
    (E) Fauvists

124. The Maine coastline was captured in watercolors by what American artist?

    (A) Grant Wood
    (B) Winslow Homer
    (C) George Bellows
    (D) Georgia O'Keeffe
    (E) Barnett Newman

125. All of the following artists were members of an artistic movement called Superrealism EXCEPT

    (A) Philip Pearlstein
    (B) Richard Estes
    (C) Chuck Close
    (D) Roy Lichtenstein
    (E) Duane Hanson

126. Classical ballet is distinguished from other dance forms by the precise foot and arm positions. How many foot positions are considered basic to ballet, today?

    (A) 2
    (B) 4
    (C) 5
    (D) 6
    (E) 7

127. Ballet, meaning *to dance,* is a classic, formalized solo or ensemble dancing of a disciplined, dramatic nature, usually performed to music. Foreshadowed in mummeries and masquerades, ballet emerged as a distinct form in lavish court spectacles in what country?

    (A) Russia
    (B) France
    (C) Italy
    (D) Germany
    (E) Poland

128. Ballet, as a distinct dance-theater form, appeared

(A) in 1300
(B) in the sixteenth century
(C) in the eighteenth century
(D) in 1820
(E) at the court of Henry VIII

129. For what is Sergei Diaghilev known?

(A) He was the first male dancer.
(B) He wrote *Swan Lake*.
(C) With others, he was the founder of the Ballet Russes.
(D) He defected to the West.
(E) He was a contemporary of Pierre Beauchamps.

130. What dance pioneer performed barefoot in a revealing Greek tunic, interpreting great and complex music composed by the likes of Chopin, Beethoven, and Wagner?

(A) Agnes De Mille
(B) Loie Fuller
(C) Isadora Duncan
(D) Martha Graham
(E) Ruth St. Denis

131. A decorative-arts movement that began in Western Europe lasted from the 1880s to World War I. It was characterized by a richly ornamental, asymmetrical style of whiplash linearity, reminiscent of twining plant tendrils. All of the following were exponents EXCEPT

(A) Aubrey Beardsley
(B) Walter Crane
(C) Victor Horta
(D) Frank Lloyd Wright
(E) Louis C. Tiffany

132. In the ballet composed by Igor Stravinsky, Petrouchka is a

(A) puppet
(B) magician
(C) Gypsy
(D) flower girl
(E) bird

133. A polka is a dance in what time?

(A) $\frac{3}{4}$
(B) $\frac{6}{8}$
(C) $\frac{2}{4}$
(D) $\frac{4}{4}$
(E) Polyrhythm

134. A primitive, tribal, or ethnic form of the dance is called a

(A) folk dance
(B) tarantella
(C) polka
(D) waltz
(E) minuet

135. A French dance introduced at Louis XIV's court in 1650 is called a

(A) square dance
(B) minuet
(C) polka
(D) polonaise
(E) Virginia reel

136. The choreographer of *West Side Story* was

(A) Dan Dailey
(B) Gene Kelly
(C) Gower Champion
(D) Bob Fosse
(E) Jerome Robbins

137. Which of the following wrote the ballet *Billy the Kid?*

(A) Richard Rodgers
(B) Irving Berlin
(C) Jerome Kern
(D) Aaron Copland
(E) Lerner and Lowe

138. Which of the following is NOT considered a major choreographer?

(A) George Balanchine
(B) Agnes De Mille
(C) Antony Tudor
(D) Martha Graham
(E) Alicia Alonso

139. Concerning the founding of the American Ballet School, which one of the following pairs is correct?

(A) Gene Kelly . . . 1932
(B) Fred Astaire . . . 1941
(C) George Balanchine . . . 1934
(D) Bob Fosse . . . 1955
(E) Gower Champion . . . 1948

140. Which one of the following was NOT a dancer with the New York City Ballet?

(A) Edward Villella
(B) Maria Tallchief
(C) Suzanne Farrell
(D) Isadora Duncan
(E) Melissa Hayden

GO ON TO THE NEXT PAGE

141. Which one of the following is NOT a part of the American musical-theater scene?

   (A) Tennessee Williams
   (B) Jerome Kern
   (C) William Rodgers
   (D) Oscar Hammerstein
   (E) Stephen Sondheim

142. Which one of the following was NOT written by Andrew Lloyd Webber?

   (A) *Cats*
   (B) *Jesus Christ Superstar!*
   (C) *My Fair Lady*
   (D) *Evita!*
   (E) *Sunset Boulevard*

143. *Porgy and Bess*, a folk opera, was written by which American composer?

   (A) Irving Berlin
   (B) Charles Ives
   (C) George Kauffman
   (D) Leonard Bernstein
   (E) George Gershwin

144. The first primarily African American dance company was called

   (A) Apollo
   (B) Cotton Club
   (C) Dance Theatre of Harlem
   (D) Nigerian Ballet Company
   (E) Ballet Folklorico

145. The dance craze made popular by Chubby Checker in the 1960s was called the

   (A) frug
   (B) bugaloo
   (C) push
   (D) twist
   (E) pony

146. A dance made famous in the 1920s, named for a southern town, was the

   (A) Atlanta
   (B) Charleston
   (C) Mobile
   (D) Orleans Drag
   (E) Chattanooga

147. Teenage dancing was made popular on television by

   (A) *American Bandstand*
   (B) *Philadelphia Dancing*
   (C) *L.A. Stomp Shop*
   (D) *The Big Apple*
   (E) *Peppermint Lounge*

148. Which of the following is NOT a play written by Tennessee Williams?

   (A) *Summer and Smoke*
   (B) *Sweet Bird of Youth*
   (C) *Night of the Iguana*
   (D) *The Glass Menagerie*
   (E) *A Streetcar Named Desire*

149. A film loosely based on the life of Bob Fosse is

   (A) *Singin' in the Rain*
   (B) *Gypsy*
   (C) *Chicago*
   (D) *All That Jazz*
   (E) *Dancin'*

150. Which of the following musicals is set in the United States?

   (A) *Jesus Christ Superstar!*
   (B) *My Fair Lady*
   (C) *Miss Saigon*
   (D) *The King and I*
   (E) *Gypsy*

STOP If you finish before the time is up, you may check your work on this section only. Do not turn to any other section in the test.

PRETEST ANSWER KEY AND EXPLANATIONS

PART I

1.	D	16.	B	31.	A	46.	D	61.	C
2.	C	17.	C	32.	A	47.	C	62.	D
3.	B	18.	A	33.	C	48.	C	63.	E
4.	A	19.	D	34.	D	49.	C	64.	D
5.	C	20.	C	35.	C	50.	D	65.	D
6.	C	21.	C	36.	D	51.	B	66.	A
7.	A	22.	C	37.	D	52.	D	67.	C
8.	B	23.	D	38.	B	53.	D	68.	C
9.	B	24.	D	39.	D	54.	E	69.	E
10.	C	25.	C	40.	C	55.	C	70.	B
11.	D	26.	C	41.	C	56.	A	71.	B
12.	D	27.	A	42.	A	57.	D	72.	B
13.	D	28.	B	43.	B	58.	C	73.	E
14.	B	29.	B	44.	C	59.	B	74.	C
15.	D	30.	D	45.	C	60.	D	75.	B

PART II

76.	D	91.	C	106.	C	121.	D	136.	E
77.	C	92.	B	107.	C	122.	C	137.	D
78.	A	93.	D	108.	A	123.	D	138.	E
79.	E	94.	B	109.	B	124.	B	139.	C
80.	C	95.	D	110.	B	125.	D	140.	D
81.	E	96.	B	111.	D	126.	C	141.	A
82.	B	97.	D	112.	B	127.	C	142.	C
83.	C	98.	A	113.	B	128.	B	143.	E
84.	A	99.	E	114.	C	129.	C	144.	C
85.	D	100.	B	115.	C	130.	C	145.	D
86.	C	101.	D	116.	B	131.	D	146.	B
87.	A	102.	D	117.	C	132.	A	147.	A
88.	B	103.	B	118.	C	133.	C	148.	A
89.	A	104.	C	119.	D	134.	A	149.	D
90.	B	105.	B	120.	D	135.	B	150.	E

PART I

1. **The correct answer is (D).** It was an original play by Oscar Wilde. The others were based on older or mythological stories.

2. **The correct answer is (C).** Both were great teachers who never wrote anything. What we know about them was written by others: in the case of Jesus, the Bible; in the case of Socrates, the works of Plato.

3. **The correct answer is (B).** Except for certain specific dramatic effects in which he used rhymed couplets, his plays do not rhyme.

4. **The correct answer is (A).** The only instances of rhyme in Shakespeare's plays are when he uses iambic pentameter, rhymed couplets called heroic couplets.

5. **The correct answer is (C).** This play has some of the same story elements of *The Merchant of Venice*, but it was not written by Shakespeare.

6. **The correct answer is (C).** The others were written, respectively, by William Wordsworth, Samuel Taylor Coleridge, Percy Bysshe Shelley, and John Keats.

7. **The correct answer is (A).** An essay is almost always a prose form.

8. **The correct answer is (B).** An elegy is a poem of mourning.

9. **The correct answer is (B).** Even though Hemingway and others state that *Huckleberry Finn* was the foundation of American literature, Twain wrote before the Nobel Prize existed.

10. **The correct answer is (C).** The term suggests something that is not concrete.

11. **The correct answer is (D).** The other terms refer in order to: choice (A), an understatement; choice (B), a confusion of similar-sounding words; choice (C), a restatement; choice (E), a short publicity article.

12. **The correct answer is (D).** Lope de Vega was a prolific Spanish writer of more than 150 works.

13. **The correct answer is (D).** King is merely a title that appears in many works. The others have specific reference from a work or a collection of works.

14. **The correct answer is (B).** Alexander Pope wrote this in his *An Essay on Criticism*.

15. **The correct answer is (D).** It was written by Niccolò Machiavelli.

16. **The correct answer is (B).** Grendel was the monster in *Beowulf*.

17. **The correct answer is (C).** Poseidon's Roman counterpoint was Neptune.

18. **The correct answer is (A).** The others were, in order: choice (B), inventor of a maze called the labyrinth; choice (C), Agamemnon's daughter; choice (D), a dog with three heads at the gates of the underworld; choice (E), a sorceress who turned men into swine.

19. **The correct answer is (D).** Lilliput was the fictional name of the island populated by little people and upon which Gulliver was shipwrecked.

20. **The correct answer is (C).** "There was no joy in Mudville. . . ."

21. **The correct answer is (C).** Aristotle wrote that literature should please and instruct.

22. **The correct answer is (C).** Choices (A), (B), and (D) are about families, and choice (E) is about a man who changes. Only choice (C), by William Styron, is correct.

23. **The correct answer is (D).** George Eliot was the pen name of a woman writer (Mary Ann Evans) who wrote about the common people.

24. **The correct answer is (D).** Each writer has written mystery stories in addition to being known for other pursuits.

25. **The correct answer is (C).** While the others are mystery writers, Ellis Peters wrote of medieval crimes involving Brother Cadfael.

26. **The correct answer is (C).** The Magna Carta (King James's guarantee of freedom) was signed in 1265 C.E. The battle of Hastings took place in 1066.

27. **The correct answer is (A).** This is a Classical epic.

28. **The correct answer is (B).** Melville wrote the epic novel *Moby Dick*. *Ulysses* was written by James Joyce.

29. **The correct answer is (B).** John Galsworthy is a twentieth-century essayist who wrote about social change.

30. **The correct answer is (D).** Aesop probably would not have knowledge of the armadillo, a New World animal.

31. **The correct answer is (A).** Although winners, Faulkner, Hemingway, and Malamud did not win three times each.

32. **The correct answer is (A).** John Hersey was the author of this book.

33. **The correct answer is (C).** When the group is preparing to go into town, Jay reveals this opinion of Daisy to Nick.

34. **The correct answer is (D).** These are masters of the novel who are not from England or America.

35. **The correct answer is (C).** While the Joads appear disadvantaged, they are neither rogues nor particularly cunning.

36. **The correct answer is (D).** Anderson calls a belief that is held to be true in all situations and for all times a "grotesque," and the characters in this collection of stories have this in common.

37. **The correct answer is (D).** An intense example is "the sudden sea seizes shore."

38. **The correct answer is (B).** An example is "buzz."

39. **The correct answer is (D).** Pirandello is a modern Italian dramatist from the *theatre of the absurd*.

40. **The correct answer is (C).** William Strunk was a teacher of E. B. White. White heard Professor Strunk refer to his book on style as the "Little Book." White later edited a new edition of the book and added his own name to it.

41. **The correct answer is (C).** The stark poem, about a snake in the grass, was written with intense understatement.

42. **The correct answer is (A).** Any male who is extraordinarily good looking is referred to as an Adonis.

43. **The correct answer is (B).** The narrator is referring to what it is that "doesn't love a wall that wants it down."

44. **The correct answer is (C).** Faulkner spoke of the capacity of the human heart not merely to endure, but to prevail.

45. **The correct answer is (C).** While the others placed great emphasis on overwhelming armies, only Charlemagne placed value in forces other than men.

46. **The correct answer is (D).** He had no reason to shoot the bird, even though he knew it was taboo to kill it.

47. **The correct answer is (C).** This poet signed his name "e. e. cummings."

48. **The correct answer is (C).** The man sells his watch for a comb for his wife's long hair, and she sells her hair to buy him a watch chain.

49. **The correct answer is (C).** Iago creates jealousy and mistrust in Othello, causing him to kill his bride, Desdemona.

50. **The correct answer is (D).** Theseus, in Greek mythology, was the greatest Athenian hero. With the help of Ariadne, the daughter of Minos, king of Crete, Theseus killed the Minotaur, who was confined in a labyrinth under the palace.

51. **The correct answer is (B).** The most famous detective lived on Baker Street.

52. **The correct answer is (D).** All of the others have war in common.

53. **The correct answer is (D).** Mitty lived before the time of space travel, even though Buck Rogers was a fictional contemporary.

54. **The correct answer is (E).** In this stop in *Gulliver's Travels*, only horses were rational.

55. **The correct answer is (C).** O'Neill used the desires of the Mannons to show the material of contemporary tragedy.

56. **The correct answer is (A).** While it is a trope, and although it might seem to be a personification, it is an implied metaphor of an animal, perhaps a cat.

57. **The correct answer is (D).** This sparse, terse passage is found in "Hills Like White Elephants."

58. **The correct answer is (C).** This novel was written by the author of *Things Fall Apart*.

59. **The correct answer is (B).** Written by Henry Miller, this is the only novel not written by an author of African roots.

60. **The correct answer is (D).** Wind may fill a sail, but the use of puffs creates an image of a person breathing.

61. **The correct answer is (C).** The personification of the flowers mating with the air introduces the joy of continuing life.

62. **The correct answer is (D).** Pound used the style and rhythms of the Chinese poets in his cantos.

63. **The correct answer is (E).** Gene and Phineas (Finny) were close friends, although they were often the instruments of failure for each other.

64. **The correct answer is (D).** This book has, in recent times, been the source for critical writing on all matters in literature.

65. **The correct answer is (D).** When placed in lines, each pair of lines of the poem looks like an outline of a wheelbarrow.

66. **The correct answer is (A).** Both doors and music have keys, but to use the word in proximity to *locked* creates a peculiar image in the mind that plays on the various meanings.

67. **The correct answer is (C).** The thump-thump of both syllables stressed is used to provide a change from an iambic to trochaic beat.

68. **The correct answer is (C).** In these lines, the arms represent those of women, and the arms dramatically create a vision of union, hugs, nurturing, etc.

69. **The correct answer is (E).** The stage is sectioned into nine basic areas, with the directions noted as seen from the actors' viewpoint, EXCEPT that toward the audience is "down."

70. **The correct answer is (B).** These words were spoken by the Earl of Gloucester, friend of Lear, commenting on the futility of life.

71. **The correct answer is (B).** King Lear spoke these words to express his hurt and disappointment about his treatment at the hands of his daughters.

72. **The correct answer is (B).** Each of these works uses persons, places, and things as equivalents of abstractions or qualities, in a systematic way.

73. **The correct answer is (E).** The others all wrote stories about bears. In order: choice (A), *The Bear*; choice (B), *Gentle Ben*; choice (C), *A Bear Called Paddington*; and choice (D), *The Bears on Hemlock Mountain*.

74. **The correct answer is (C).** Ambrose Bierce was a local-color author who came several generations before the Beats of the mid-twentieth century.

75. **The correct answer is (B).** The dates and the correct order are as follows: *Divine Comedy*, 1307; *noh*, 1325; Chaucer, ca. 1342; Gutenberg, 1450; Erasmus, 1500; Bacon, 1597; *Moll Flanders,* 1722; Goethe, 1808; Byron, 1818; *Dorian Gray*, 1890.

PART II

76. **The correct answer is (D).** The leading motif, or leitmotiv, is commonly known as the representative theme in a composition.

77. **The correct answer is (C).** A chord is a combination of any notes, usually three or more.

78. **The correct answer is (A).** The tarantella is an Italian dance in $\frac{6}{8}$ time, and it probably takes its name from the dance once performed to cure an individual who had been bitten by the tarantula spider.

79. **The correct answer is (E).** The tattoo, a piece often played with bugles and drums, was used to call soldiers back to camp at night.

80. **The correct answer is (C).** *Phrase* is a musical term used to represent a short section of music, vocal or instrumental. It is an inexact term in that it is also commonly used to signify a short segment that can be sung in one breath.

81. **The correct answer is (E).** The crescendo is a musical marking written by the composer to signify a gradual increase in volume.

82. **The correct answer is (B).** *Cantabile* is an Italian term meaning *singingly* or *lyrically*.

83. **The correct answer is (C).** A prelude is a musical form that precedes another musical form such as a fugue. The prelude can also be the first piece in a suite.

84. **The correct answer is (A).** Opera is a drama set to music in which the singers usually perform in costume.

85. **The correct answer is (D).** Chamber music was not intended to be performed in a church, theater, or large public concert hall. This music was composed for a small ensemble, with one instrument per part.

86. **The correct answer is (C).** A ballad-opera is opera that has spoken words and often uses familiar tunes of the day set with new words.

87. **The correct answer is (A).** The camp meetings began in Kentucky in an effort to spread the religious gospel to all people, which included the slaves in that area. The slaves began mixing the Bible-originated words with their more rhythmic, complex songs from Africa, creating what is known as the spiritual.

88. **The correct answer is (B).** The piano was invented in Florence, Italy, in 1709, by Bartolomeo Cristofori.

89. **The correct answer is (A).** The musical term *legato* means, in terms of technique, to play in a smooth and connected style.

90. **The correct answer is (B).** Chopin composed twenty-seven études. These pieces were short and designed to improve one's technique. Chopin's études are considered masterful and suitable for public performance.

91. **The correct answer is (C).** A score is a complete copy of music that shows all parts appropriate to various instruments or performers.

92. **The correct answer is (B).** An étude is a form of music specifically designed to improve a particular technic.

93. **The correct answer is (D).** *Lento* is a term that indicates a piece should be played at a slow tempo and "fits" between andante, which means to move along, slowish but not slow, and largo, which means to play slowly and broadly.

94. **The correct answer is (B).** The chorale is a hymn or psalm, generally sung in unison. Martin Luther wished to restore the congregational role in the church, thus composing unison congregational songs of familiar melodies (i.e., plainsong).

95. **The correct answer is (D).** Haydn is considered the father of the symphony and string quartets. While he composed a vast number of symphonies and string quartets, he did not originate the forms.

96. **The correct answer is (B).** *Presto* is a musical term referring to tempo. It means to play very fast.

97. **The correct answer is (D).** Mozart was the composer of these two famous comic operas.

98. **The correct answer is (A).** Beethoven began to go deaf at the age of thirty-eight. He considered this the most devastating infirmity that a musician-composer could possibly have.

99. **The correct answer is (E).** Schubert was the most masterful of the lieder (or song) composers in Vienna. His gift for beautiful melodies and subtlety is unsurpassed.

100. **The correct answer is (B).** Gregorian chant (or plainsong) was developed during the medieval period and is a form of music that is made up of a single melody in uneven rhythm. This type of music became popular again in the late twentieth century.

101. **The correct answer is (D).** Van Gogh's unique brushwork is known for its energetic strokes of thickly applied paint.

102. **The correct answer is (D).** Van Gogh painted this subject several times—this particular version of *Sunflowers* was done in 1888.

103. **The correct answer is (B).** Whistler's most famous work is of his mother, but it is an oil painting.

104. **The correct answer is (C).** *The Singing Boys* is a relief from the cantoria, which was the choir gallery for the Florence cathedral, carved in 1431–38.

105. **The correct answer is (B).** The phrase *peinture au point* (painting by dots) was used by a Parisian art critic, and the style became known as pointillism.

106. **The correct answer is (C).** Cellini was trained in Florence and worked for the French king, Francis I, from 1540 to 1545.

107. **The correct answer is (C).** Born in Paris, Gauguin had a yearning for a tropical paradise that led him to live and work in Tahiti and other South Seas islands.

108. **The correct answer is (A).** Michelangelo wrote more than 300 sonnets. Before his death, he nearly completed a project to publish 105 of them. His grandnephew first published them in 1623.

109. **The correct answer is (B).** Saint-Gaudens was the most noted American sculptor of the late nineteenth century.

110. **The correct answer is (B).** Cézanne's landscape and still-life compositions were an intense examination of the possibilities of two-dimensional relationships in painting.

111. **The correct answer is (D).** Born in Germany, Holbein became the court painter to Henry VIII of England in 1536.

112. **The correct answer is (B).** Bellows excelled at painting sports subjects.

113. **The correct answer is (B).** Dry-point is an intaglio printing process used since the sixteenth century.

114. **The correct answer is (C).** The bronze work in New York's Central Park was created from 1892 to 1903.

115. **The correct answer is (C).** *The Thinker* by Auguste Rodin was created for *The Gates of Hell*, a sculpture originally intended for crowning the large doors designed for the Museum of Decorative Arts in Paris.

116. **The correct answer is (B).** The original work in bronze was created in Greece by the sculptor Myron. Today, it is known by the Roman marble copy in the National Museum in Rome.

117. **The correct answer is (C).** Dürer had a flourishing printing business in his hometown of Nuremberg.

118. **The correct answer is (C).** Goya shows the French firing squad in the very early morning in lantern light.

119. **The correct answer is (D).** *Pièta* means "pity" and is traditionally a devotional image of Mary holding her dead son, Christ.

120. **The correct answer is (D).** Michelangelo sculpted this work in 1498, when he was 20 years old.

121. **The correct answer is (D).** St. Peter's is the cathedral in Vatican City.

122. **The correct answer is (C).** A still life is a drawing or painting of a group of inanimate objects.

123. **The correct answer is (D).** Though not actually in an academic school, artists like Asher Durand, Thomas Cole, and Frederic Edwin Church from the Hudson River area became well known in Europe and America.

124. **The correct answer is (B).** Winslow Homer also painted seascapes in oil paints.

125. **The correct answer is (D).** Roy Lichtenstein was a Pop artist, basing his art on the comic book. He took the small frames of the comic and dot-color patterns and enlarged them to huge, imposing images.

126. **The correct answer is (C).** All ballet performed today descends from the five basic positions of the feet and principles of technique established by the French dancing master Pierre Beauchamp in the 1600s. The number of positions is considered to be five, although variations are permissable in the fourth and fifth positions.

127. **The correct answer is (C).** The earliest ballets were intended to display the wealth and generosity of the court, and they were presented as entertainments at royal Italian banquet fêtes.

128. **The correct answer is (B).** Extravagant dance productions did flourish in Renaissance Italy and France, but Italian Catherine de' Medici sponsored the production of the first bona fide ballet in 1581, when she became the new queen of France.

129. **The correct answer is (C).** Under impresario Diaghilev's leadership, the Ballet Russes revitalized the art of ballet in the early 1900s.

130. **The correct answer is (C).** Isadora Duncan is considered to be the first modern dancer because she did not use ballet steps to communicate her artistic vision. She instead rebelled against the confinements of ballet and used her own body timing, gave in to the earth, and insisted on total freedom of expression.

131. **The correct answer is (D).**

132. **The correct answer is (A).**

133. **The correct answer is (C).**

134. **The correct answer is (A).**

135. **The correct answer is (B).**

136. **The correct answer is (E).**

137. **The correct answer is (D).**

138. **The correct answer is (E).** Although considered one of the greatest twentieth-century ballerinas, having danced with Diaghilev's Ballet Russes, American Ballet Theater, and, finally, the Cuban National Ballet, Alicia Alonso is not considered a major choreographer.

139. **The correct answer is (C).** In 1934, George Balanchine, at the invitation of Lincoln Kirstein, founded the School of American Ballet and the American Ballet Company, which eventually became the New York City Ballet in 1948.

140. **The correct answer is (D).** Isadora Duncan, modern dancer and innovator, performed and taught in the early 1900s. The New York City Ballet was formed after her death.

141. **The correct answer is (A).** Tennessee Williams is considered a dramatic playwright. The others are major composers and lyricists of the American musical-theater genre.

142. **The correct answer is (C).** Frederick Loewe wrote the music for *My Fair Lady* and Alan Jay Lerner was responsible for the lyrics and the book.

143. **The correct answer is (E).** Written in 1934, Gershwin's *Porgy and Bess* has been called the greatest American musical drama ever written. Gershwin's inspiration came from a drama written by playwrights DuBose and Dorothy Heyward in 1927.

144. **The correct answer is (C).** The Dance Theatre of Harlem, cofounded by Arthur Mitchell and Karel Shook, provided a performing company for African American ballet dancers. At the same time, the School of the Dance Theatre of Harlem was formed to give the children of Harlem the opportunity to train for the ballet and, ultimately, provide a source of dancers for the company.

145. **The correct answer is (D).** Although the twist is really an old African American folk dance step, it appeared as a new dance craze in the 1960s when Chubby Checker released his single, "The Twist."

146. **The correct answer is (B).** In the jazz age of the 1920s and 1930s, the Charleston was made fashionable by African American showgirl Josephine Baker while she was performing in the French Folies Bergères.

147. **The correct answer is (A).** *American Bandstand* was hosted by Dick Clark.

148. **The correct answer is (A).** Although the subject matter of this work was the South, this was a movie based on some of William Faulkner's stories.

149. The correct answer is (D). In 1980, director Bob Fosse released his film, *All That Jazz*, a treatment in parable and metaphor of the current dilemma of a successful theater personality. The film is considered to be loosely autobiographical. Fosse depicts the life of a director/choreographer in the present, as well as in flashbacks, all with stylized dance sequences.

150. The correct answer is (E). All the rest were set in other countries. *Gypsy* was a musical about Gypsy Rose Lee. It was based on her book about her mother, her sister, and herself in show business. She later became the first lady of burlesque, with a reputation for bringing dignity to striptease.

Chapter 9
OVERVIEW

Because the topic of humanities is so diverse, there is no easy way to cover all the material that one should know in order to score high on this segment of the CLEP tests. We recommend that you read as much as you can from a diverse group of publications. Read local and international newspapers and magazines. Pay attention to the cultural news in these periodicals, since the Humanities test covers the following areas:

Literature (50%)
Drama (5–10%)
Poetry (15–20%)
Fiction (10–15%)
Nonfiction (5–10%)
Philosophy (5%)

Fine Arts (50%)
Visual arts (painting, sculpture, etc.) (25%)
Music (15%)
Performing arts (film, dance, etc.) (5%)
Architecture (5%)

From this breakdown, you will be able to get an idea of where to focus your studies. The test contains 150 multiple-choice questions divided into two separate sections, each 45 minutes long. You will be required to have a knowledge of facts, such as names, specific works, and so on; at least one half of all the questions on the exam will be of this nature.

About 30 percent of the exam will require you to have a knowledge of various techniques, whether they involve poetry (rhyme schemes), painting (medium or style), or even specific periods of literature and/or art.

The last 20 percent of the examination will require an understanding and an ability to interpret literary passages and artwork. There are several pieces of artwork or photographs throughout the test. Some may be familiar to you; however, you may not have seen many of them prior to the exam.

Do not be overwhelmed by all this information. You are not expected to know everything. However, you can certainly help yourself prepare for the test by exposing yourself to as many extracurricular cultural events as possible. Visit museums. Watch public-television programs that deal with the topics covered on the test. Again, read as much as you can about these areas. Talk to your local librarian to get recommendations of popular cultural magazines or good research resources.

If you are computer literate, you may want to explore the Internet for information. Use any of the popular search engines and merely type in what you're looking for. You will undoubtedly be overwhelmed with the amount of material available.

Following is a brief time line, covering many of the areas you will encounter on the exam. While it is certainly not complete, the objective is to present you with some type of "snapshot" of the humanities throughout history. The purpose is also to give you a familiarity with names, places, and cultural movements, so that these will all become somewhat familiar to you before you take the actual examination.

You will find that the time line is a broad, and very general, collection of names and events in chronological order. It is very likely that you will encounter many of these names, events, and artistic or literary movements on the Humanities test. If there are names of people you do not know, spend some time at the library doing some research on them. Make it your business to learn about them and their contributions to their specific fields of endeavor. If, for example, you are not familiar with pop art, you should use a good art encyclopedia. If the Romantic movement in music is a complete mystery to you, again, spending some time in the library will be beneficial.

For each of the fields, there has been an attempt to include some recent events with which you should be familiar. You may have gleaned some of this information by reading the newspapers or watching television throughout the last decade or so. Assign yourself the task of finding out as much as you can about each area of study.

TIMELINE
ARCHITECTURE

2800 B.C.E.–400 B.C.E.
Egyptian pyramids are constructed
Cretan palaces flourish, Knossos being the biggest
Temple at Karnak is built
Ionian Greeks build large temples

The Parthenon, a Doric temple, is finished on Acropolis. The Erechtheum, an Ionic temple, is built at the same site

Roman forums are built. Innovations in use of arch, barrel vault, and groin vault

Romans made copies of Greek sculpture, had a distinct tradition of portrait busts

C.E.: The first 1,000 years:
Colosseum
Forum of Trajan
Temple of Olympian Zeus at Athens
Pantheon
Baths of Caracalla
Old St. Peter's begun
Santa Maria Maggiore begun
Ravenna: Church of St. Apollinaire Nuovo begun
Church of San Vitale begun (center-style)

1000 C.E.–1400 C.E.
St. Etienne and St. Trinité at Caen (Norman style)
Third church at Cluny (Romanesque style)
La Madelaine at Vezelay
St. Denis (Gothic style)
Cathedral of Notre Dame in Paris
Cathedral of Notre Dame in Chartres
Cathedrals of Amiens at Rouen
St. Chapelle started in Paris. Characteristics: pointed arch, cross-vaulting, extensive use of stained glass, greater and greater height of nave attempted, towers, flying buttresses.

1400–1800
1400s
Renaissance style in Florence: Brunelleschi designs the Foundling Hospital
Pazzi Chapel
Leon Alberti, Ruccellai Palace

1500s
Andrea Palladio builds Villa Rotunda

1600s
Wren begins rebuilding St. Paul's in London
Palace at Versailles is finished for Louis XIV

1800–Present
1800s
Joseph Paxton designs Crystal Palace
Alexander Gustave designs Eiffel Tower, Paris

1900s
Frank Lloyd Wright designs American skyscrapers
Le Corbusier, Swiss architect, revolutionizes architectural ideas
Beaubourg Center, Paris

World Trade Center towers built, New York City
Sears Tower constructed, Chicago
East Building of National Gallery built, Washington, D.C.
AT&T Building (Philip Johnson) built
Archaeologists discover 644 miles of the Great Wall of China
SunAmerica Center completed, 1990, Des Moines, Iowa
Nixon Library and Birthplace opens, California, 1990
Legoland, California, opens in San Diego, 1999

Twenty-First Century
Ait Iktel Community (Abadou, Morocco) and Nubian Museum (Aswan, Egypt) winners of Aga Khan Award for Architecture, 2001
Milwaukee Art Museum, 2001
World Trade Center, NYC, destroyed in terrorist attack, September 11, 2001
Jewish Museum Berlin opens Libeskind-designed building to public, 2001
San Diego Padres ballpark opens, 2002
Taipei 101 becomes the tallest buildingin the world, 2003
Construction begins on the Freedom Tower, a replacement for the Word Trade Center, 2006

ART AND SCULPTURE

2000 B.C.E.–100 B.C.E.
Egyptian statuary realistic, ceremonial
Snake goddesses, frescoes, naturalistic painting
Development of realism in Greek sculpture
Various Greek states develop pottery, black-figured ware
Red-figured pots from Athens and Attica dominate
Example of early classical sculpture is Charioteer from Delphi
Poseidon from Artemisium
Praxiteles is late-Classical sculpture
Hellenistic sculpture
Winged victory of Samothrace
Venus de Milo
Laocoon group

1000 C.E.–1400 C.E.
Giotto works on frescoes of St. Francis's life at Assisi

Early Renaissance (1350–1500)
Florence: Donatello sculpts David, free-standing bronze
Ghiberti working on Baptistry doors, Pazzi Chapel
Masaccio, Trinity fresco (first successful use of perspective) and Brancacci Chapel
Brunelleschi experiments with perspective in painting; designs and builds dome of the cathedral
Alberti, in *On Painting,* describes the new perspective
Paolo Uccello practices the new perspective
Piero della Francesco, Pollaiuollo, Verrocchio, and Fra Filippo Lippi are other major innovators in painting and sculpture

High Renaissance (1500–1520)
Botticelli
Michelangelo: Sistine Chapel ceiling, *David*, Medici
    Chapel, *Moses*, architect of St. Peter's
Leonardo da Vinci: *Mona Lisa, St. Anne and the Virgin*,
    anatomical drawings
Raphael

Venetian Renaissance (1500–1600)
Giorgione
Giovanni Bellini
Carpaccio
Parmigianino
Cellini
Bronzino
Vasari—wrote *Lives of the Artists* about his great
    predecessors
Titian
Vernonese
Tintoretto

Baroque (1600–1700)
Rome: Caravaggio
Rome: Bernini, *The Ecstasy of St. Theresa*, the armlike
    colonnades of St. Peter's courtyard
Rome: Borromini
Spain: El Greco
Spain: Velázquez
Flanders: Rubens
France: Poussin
France: Lorraine
Holland: Rembrandt
Holland: Jan Vermeer

Painting—Decadent or Realistic (1720–1800)
Jean Watteau
François Boucher
Fragonard

French Classicism and Romanticism (1800s)
Théodore Géricault
Jacques Louis David
Ingrès
Eugène Delacroix

Impressionism in France (1800s–early 1900s)
Georges Seurat
Pierre Auguste Renoir
Claude Monet
Vincent van Gogh
Paul Gauguin
Paul Cézanne

Cubism (early 1900s)
Pablo Picasso
Georges Braque

Sculpture (early 1900s)
Henry Moore
Constantin Brancusi
Jacques Lipchitz

Expressionism (mid-1900s)
Paul Klee
Vassily Kandinsky
Henri Matisse

American Realism and Regionalism (1930s)
Ben Shahn
Reginald Marsh
Grant Wood
Edward Hopper

Sculpture (mid-1900s–present)
Marcel Duchamp
Alexander Calder
Man Ray (also photography)
Isamu Noguchi
Robert Morris
George Segal
Christo

Abstract Expressionism (1950s)
Jackson Pollock

Pop Art (1950s–1960s)
David Hockney
Claes Oldenburg
Roy Lichtenstein
Andy Warhol
Robert Indiana
Jim Dine

Photorealism (1960s–present)
Linda Bacon
Chuck Close
Richard Estes
Don Eddy
Audrey Flack
Philip Pearlstein

LITERATURE

1500 B.C.E.–100 C.E.
The epic tradition (oral)
"Homer" writes *Iliad* and *Odyssey*
Drama starts
Aeschylus
Sophocles
Euripides
Aristophanes

The Lyric Tradition
Archilochus
Sappho
Solon

Pindar
Tyrtaeus
Greek Oratory, Demosthenes, opposed Philip and
    Alexander

**Golden Age of Roman Literature
    (57 B.C.E.–8 B.C.E.)**
Catullus
Lucretius
Julius Caesar
Cicero
Virgil writes *The Aeneid*, the epic in honor of Augustus
    and the Roman race
Ovid
Horace

Silver Age of Roman Literature (65 C.E.–174 C.E.)
Seneca
Petronius
Tacitus (*Germania*)
Juvenal (*Satires*)
Suetonius (*Lives of the Twelve Caesars*)
Marcus Aurelius (*The Meditations*)

1100–1400
Provençal tradition in lyric poetry flourishes in southern
    France
The Romance form is developed by Chrétien de Troyes
Dante finishes *Divine Comedy* while in exile from
    Florence
Chaucer, *The Canterbury Tales, Troilus and Cressida*.
    Also the Pearl Poets, Langland, and Gower.
The late flowering of the English Middle Ages

English Literature (1500–1700)
Sir Philip Sidney
Christopher Marlowe
William Shakespeare
John Donne
Ben Jonson
John Milton
Andrew Marvell

**Seventeenth-century French Literature—
    Neoclassicism (1650–1700)**
Moliére
Corneille
Racine

**Augustan and Sentimental Poetry in England
    (1700–1800)**
John Dryden
Alexander Pope
Jonathan Swift
Thomas Gray
Samuel Johnson

The Novel (1740–1840)
Samuel Richardson, *Pamela*
Henry Fielding, *Tom Jones*
Jane Austen
Sir Walter Scott

German "Storm and Stress" Movement (late 1800s)
early Goethe
Klinger

1820–1900
Johann Goethe, *Faust*
John Keats
Percy Bysshe Shelley
Lord Byron
William Blake
William Wordsworth
England: Dante Gabriel Rossetti
Charles Baudelaire, *Flowers of Evil*
Gustave Flaubert, *Madame Bovary*
Emily Brontë
James Fenimore Cooper
Nikolai Gogol
Henry David Thoreau
Nathaniel Hawthorne
Charles Dickens
Fyodor Dostoevsky
Ralph Waldo Emerson
Victor Hugo
Robert Browning
Anthony Hopkins
Alfred, Lord Tennyson
Herman Melville
Leo Tolstoy
Charlotte Brontë
Henry James, *Portrait of a Lady, The Ambassadors*
George Eliot
Emile Zola

1900–present
Anton Chekhov
George Meredith
Thomas Mann, *Death in Venice*
Marcel Proust, *Remembrance of Things Past*
William Butler Yeats
James Joyce
E. M. Forster
George Orwell
Evelyn Waugh
W. H. Auden
Henry Green
Samuel Beckett

Modern and Experimental Literature and Poetry
Robert Frost
Ernest Hemingway
Wallace Stevens
Hart Crane

Ezra Pound
F. Scott Fitzgerald
T. S. Eliot
William Faulkner
Günter Grass
Friedrich Dürrenmatt
Heinrich Böll
Allen Silletoe
Graham Greene
Albert Camus
Jean-Paul Sartre
Alexander Solzhenitsyn

Contemporary Authors
Saul Bellow
J. D. Salinger
Robert Penn Warren
Thomas Pynchon
Eudora Welty
Bernard Malamud
Norman Mailer
James Baldwin
Joyce Carol Oates
Toni Morrison
Philip Roth
Chinua Achebe

1900–1999
Wole Soyinka, Nigerian poet, first black African to win Nobel Prize for literature
Howard Nemerov appointed third official Poet Laureate of the United States
Salman Rushdie writes novel, *The Satanic Verses*, and death threats are issued against his life by Muslim fundamentalists in Iran
Mexican poet, Camilo José Cela, wins Nobel Prize for literature
Rabbit at Rest, John Updike, published 1990
All the Pretty Horses, Cormac McCarthy, National Book Critics Circle Award, 1992
The Young Man from Atlanta, Horton Foote, Pulitzer Prize, 1995
Rent, Jonathan Larson, Pulitzer Prize, 1996
Angela's Ashes, Frank McCourt, Pulitzer Prize, 1997
Personal History, Katherine Graham, Pulitzer Prize, 1998
A Beautiful Mind, Sylvia Nasar, National Book Critics Circle Award, 1998
Wit, Margaret Edson, Pulitzer Prize, 1999

2000–Present
Hirohito and the Making of Modern Japan, Herbert Bix, National Book Critics Circle Award, 2000, and Pulitzer Prize, 2001
Gao Xingjian (Chinese), Nobel Prize in Literature, 2000

In America, Susan Sontag, and *In the Heart of the Sea: The Tragedy of the Whaleship Essex*, Nathaniel Philbrick, National Book Awards, 2000
V.S. Naipaul (British), Nobel Prize in Literature, 2001
Austerlitz, W.G. Sebald, National Book Critics Circle Award, 2001
The Corrections, Jonathan Franzen, and *The Noonday Demon: An Atlas of Depression*, Andrew Solomon, National Book Awards, 2001
Three Junes, Julia Glass, and *Master of the Senate: The Years of Lyndon Johnson*, Robert A. Caro, National Book Awards, 2002
Carry Me Home: Birmingham, Alabama: The Climactic Battle of the Civil Rights Revolution, Diane McWhorter, Pulitzer Prize, 2002
Imre Kertész (Hungarian), Nobel Prize in Literature, 2002
Harriet Doerr, American Book Award in 1984 for *Stones for Ibarra*, d. 2002
Taranarive Due, American Book Award in 2002 for *The Living Blood*
John Maxwell Coetzce (South African), Nobel Prize in Literature, 2003
Elfriede Jelinek (Austrian), Nobel Prize in Literature, 2004
Harold Pinter (British), Nobel Prize in Literature, 2005
Ohan Pamuk (Turkish), Nobel Prize in Literature, 2006

PHILOSOPHY

500 B.C.E.–100 B.C.E.
(*The Presocratics*) Thales, Anaximander, Parmenides, Heraclitus
Historian: Thucydides, *The Pelopennesian Wars*
Empedocles
Socrates
Democritus
Plato
Aristotle
Euclid
Epicurus
Zeno (founded Stoicism)
Archimedes

29 C.E.–1000 C.E.
Christianity spreads rapidly after Christ's crucifixion
St. Augustine, *Confessions*
The City of God
Boethius, *The Consolations of Philosophy*
St. Benedict, founded Western monasticism

1000–1500
Boccaccio, *Decameron*
Petrarch dies, leaving letters and sonnets that consummate the courtly love tradition and are forecasts of Renaissance attitudes

Florentine Humanism includes Ficino, who translates all of Plato

Pico della Mirandola, *Oration on the Dignity of Man*

1500–1700

Machiavelli, *The Prince*

Erasmus, *In Praise of Folly*

Copernicus publishes *On the Revolutions of the Heavenly Bodies*, which includes the revolutionary idea that the sun orbits the earth

Condorcet, *Spirit of Laws*

Descartes

Pascal

Thomas Hobbes

Observations and discoveries of Brahe, Kepler, and Galileo support Copernican view; Sir Isaac Newton publishes *Principia Mathematica*, which correctly describes the motion and places of the planets and sun, firmly grounding the idea of gravity

1700–1800 (Enlightenment in France)

John Locke

Diderot edits the *Encyclopedie*

Voltaire, *Candide*

Jean-Jacques Rousseau, *Social Contract*

Thomas Jefferson, *Declaration of Independence*

Immanuel Kant, *Critique of Pure Reason*

Notes on Virginia

1800–1900

Karl Marx and Friedrich Engels, *The Communist Manifesto*

Charles Darwin, *Origin of the Species*

1900–present

Sigmund Freud, *The Interpretation of Dreams*

Friedrich Nietzsche

Albert Einstein, *The General Theory*

Karl Barth

Reinhold Niebuhr

Paul Tillich

Jean-Paul Sartre

Mohandas Gandhi

Martin Luther King Jr.

MUSIC

1400–1600

Guillaume Dufay

Josquin des Prez

1600–1800

Rameau

Lully

Purcell

Classical and Romantic Music

Johann Sebastian Bach

George Frideric Handel, religious music

Wolfgang Amadeus Mozart, *The Marriage of Figaro*, opera

Franz Joseph Haydn

1800–1900 (Classical Music)

Ludwig van Beethoven

Felix Mendelssohn

Modest Mussorgsky, *Boris Godunov*, opera

Richard Wagner, *The Ring of the Nibelungen*, opera

Charles Gounod

1900–1970

Giuseppe Verdi

Richard Strauss

Claude Debussy

George Gershwin

Maurice Ravel

Béla Bartók

Rock 'n' roll is born (1950s)

1970–1999

Igor Stravinsky

John Cage, electronic music

Dmitri Shostakovich

Disco music emerges

Reggae is popularized by Bob Marley

Rock 'n' roll star Elvis Presley

Bruce Springstein

Rap music becomes popular

Merce Cunningham, *Quartets* (dance)

"Live Aid" Rock Concert in London and Philadelphia: produced by Bob Geldof, featuring performances by Status Quo, Dire Straits, U2, David Bowie, Beach Boys, Paul McCartney, Phil Collins, The Who, Madonna, and Bob Dylan; raised more than $60 million for African-famine relief

Beethoven's unfinished Tenth Symphony is performed

Philip Glass, *The Fall of the House of Usher* (opera)

Andrew Lloyd Webber, *Phantom of the Opera* (musical theater)

"Three Tenors' World Cup Concert" begins in Rome, with Luciano Pavarotti, Placido Domingo, José Carreras

1990 Dance Biennial in France, largest-ever gathering of U.S. dance companies

Bastille Opera House, Paris, opens

Dame Margot Fonteyn (ballerina), d. 1991

English National Opera premiers *Clarissa*, by Robin Holloway, 1990

Stringmusic, Morton Gould, 1995 Pulitzer Prize

Morton Gould, composer, d. 1996

Blood on the Fields, Wynton Marsalis, first Pulitzer Prize for jazz, 1997

Santana wins Grammy Award, Album of the Year, 1999

Rolf Liebermann, d. 1999 (Swiss composer)

2000–Present

Life Is a Dream, Opera in Three Acts by Lewis Spratlan, premiers

Faith Hill wins Grammy Award for Best Female Performer

U2 wins Record of the Year for *Walk On*

The Concert For New York City to benefit families of police officers and firefighters killed in the attacks on the World Trade Center featured Paul McCartney, Elton John, The Who, David Bowie, Mick Jagger and Keith Richards, Backstreet Boys, Destiny's Child, Jay-Z, and many others. Top grossing concert of 2001 ($12 million), October 2001

George Harrison, d. 2001 (former Beatle)

Lenny Kravitz wins Grammy Award for Best Male Vocalist

Hairspray, based on the movie by John Waters, opens on Broadway, 2002

Moving Out, based on the music of Billy Joel and choreographed by Twyla Tharp, Broadway hit, 2002

Pure pop and Teen pop music re-enters the mainstream after a three-year break, 2006

James Brown, d. 2006

Chapter 10
POSTTEST

PART I

Directions: Each of the questions or incomplete statements below is followed by five suggested answers or completions. Select the one that is best in each case.

1. A number of important documents with great literary value have been recorded and have influenced the world. Choose the correct chronological order for the following:

   1. Bill of Rights
   2. The Mayflower Compact
   3. Edict of Milan
   4. Koran
   5. Magna Carta
   6. Laws of Solon
   7. Code Napoleon
   8. U.S. Constitution
   9. *Communist Manifesto*
   10. Martin Luther's Theses

   (A) 5, 4, 8, 2, 1, 6, 7, 9, 3, 10
   (B) 6, 3, 4, 5, 10, 2, 8, 1, 7, 9
   (C) 1, 2, 3, 4, 5, 6, 7, 8, 9, 10
   (D) 2, 3, 10, 5, 6, 1, 8, 7, 4, 9
   (E) 6, 3, 4, 5, 10, 2, 1, 8, 7, 9

2. Epics are long works telling what happened in the life of a hero or heroine, usually based on history or folklore. All of the following are epics EXCEPT

   (A) *Orlando Furioso*
   (B) *The Great Gatsby*
   (C) *Don Quixote*
   (D) *The Cid*
   (E) *Mother Courage*

3. The following essays are required reading for all students of literature: Sir Philip Sidney's *The Defense of Poesie*, Thomas de Quincy's *On the Knocking at the Gate in Macbeth*, Thomas Love Peacock's *The Four Ages of Poetry*, and Edmund Wilson's *The Shores of Light*. What do the four essays have in common?

   (A) Literary criticism
   (B) Humor
   (C) Social reform
   (D) Poetic criticism
   (E) Satire

4. If poetry comes not as naturally as leaves to a tree it had better not come at all.

   Who penned the lines above?

   (A) John Donne
   (B) William Carlos Williams
   (C) T. S. Eliot
   (D) John Keats
   (E) Robert Frost

5. Many a rose-lipt maiden/And many a lightfoot lad.

   These lines are from *A Shropshire Lad*, written by

   (A) A. E. Houseman
   (B) John Donne
   (C) Walt Whitman
   (D) Emily Dickinson
   (E) Robert Frost

GO ON TO THE NEXT PAGE

Questions 6–10 refer to the following lines.

A. God so commanded, and left that command
   Sole daughter of his voice; the rest, we live
   Law to ourselves, our reason is our law.

B. I've never seen a Jaguar,
   Nor yet an Armadillo dilloing in his armour
   And I s'pose I never will.

C. A well-written Life is almost as rare as a
   well-spent one.

D. Now sleeps the crimson petal, now the white'
   Nor waves the cypress in the palace walk;
   Nor winks the gold fin in the porphyry font;
   The fire-fly wakens; waken thou with me.

E. So Lord Howard past away with five ships of war
   that day,
   Till he melted like a cloud in the silent summer
   heaven.

6. Which lines contain alliteration?

7. Which lines contain a personification?

8. Which lines were written by John Milton?

9. Which poet wrote two of the sections?

   (A) Alfred, Lord Tennyson
   (B) John Milton
   (C) Rudyard Kipling
   (D) William Shakespeare
   (E) Thomas Carlyle

10. Which was written by Thomas Carlyle?

11. La quinta columna.

   This statement from a radio address by Emilio
   Mola, a general in the Spanish Civil War (1936–
   1939), refers to

   (A) a war tactic
   (B) a Doric structure
   (C) secret subversives
   (D) a democratic party
   (E) a hotel

12. I have shot mine arrow o'er the house/And hurt
   my brother.

   This statement is made by

   (A) Hamlet
   (B) Stanley Kowalsky
   (C) Laertes
   (D) Puck
   (E) Horatio

13. What can be avoided/Whose end is purpos'd by
   the mighty gods?

   This statement from Shakespeare is spoken by

   (A) Hamlet
   (B) Caesar
   (C) Othello
   (D) Lear
   (E) Henry IV

14. Writers James Thurber, Virginia Woolf, Henry
   David Thoreau, Jonathan Swift, Sir Francis Bacon,
   and Thomas Carlyle have what in common?

   (A) They wrote humorous works.
   (B) They wrote serious works.
   (C) They were poets.
   (D) They were feminists.
   (E) They were essayists.

15. *A Fable* by William Faulkner, *The Bridge of San
   Luis Rey* by Thorton Wilder, and *To Kill a
   Mockingbird* by Harper Lee have something in
   common. What common thread unites these
   authors and their respective works?

   (A) Women
   (B) Men
   (C) Nobel Prize
   (D) Pulitzer Prize
   (E) War stories

16. Which one of the following names does NOT
   belong in this list?

   (A) Nellie Bly
   (B) John Henry
   (C) Uncle Remus
   (D) Paul Bunyon
   (E) Pecos Bill

17. Which one of the following does NOT belong in
   this list?

   (A) Lizzie Borden
   (B) Dan McGrew
   (C) Annie Oakley
   (D) Pocahontas
   (E) Casey Jones

18. The fictional Pele was

   (A) a soccer player
   (B) a fire goddess
   (C) Huck's slave friend
   (D) the Indian killed by Jim Bridger
   (E) the dwarf displayed by P. T. Barnum

19. Which writer wrote the nonfiction works *In My Father's Court, A Little Boy in Search of God,* and *Lost in America*?
    (A) Carl Sandburg
    (B) Oliver Wendell Holmes
    (C) Isaac Bashevis Singer
    (D) John Crowe Ransom
    (E) Dorothy Parker

20. Which of the following authors, had any of them lived in current times, might have written something similar to these books by Judy Blume: *Deenie, Blubber, Superfudge, Forever,* and *Tiger Eyes*?
    (A) Pearl S. Buck
    (B) Louisa May Alcott
    (C) Ned Buntline
    (D) Edgar Rice Burroughs
    (E) Stephen Crane

21. Which one of the following authors is British?
    (A) J. R. R. Tolkien
    (B) George Sand
    (C) Harry Martinson
    (D) Carlos Fuentes
    (E) Claude Simon

Questions 22–26 refer to the following nursery rhyme characters.

    A. Bobby Shafto
    B. Little Jack Horner
    C. Old Mother Hubbard
    D. Old King Cole
    E. Simple Simon

22. Who couldn't feed her dog?

23. Who was a merry old soul?

24. Who met a pieman?

25. Who went to sea?

26. Who ate a Christmas pie?

27. What do the following authors have in common: Ray Bradbury, Edgar Rice Burroughs, Arthur C. Clarke, Anthony Burgess, and Isaac Asimov?
    (A) They were feminists.
    (B) They were poets.
    (C) They wrote science fiction.
    (D) They wrote romance stories.
    (E) They wrote youth stories.

28. Which of the following authors wrote *A Clockwork Orange*?
    (A) Ray Bradbury
    (B) Edgar Rice Burroughs
    (C) Arthur C. Clarke
    (D) Anthony Burgess
    (E) Isaac Asimov

29. "The Snows of Kilimanjaro," "The Short Happy Life of Francis Macomber," and "The End of Something" were all written by which short-story master?
    (A) O. Henry
    (B) Washington Irving
    (C) William Faulkner
    (D) Ernest Hemingway
    (E) Ambrose Bierce

30. All sonnets have fourteen lines of
    (A) trochaic tetrameter
    (B) iambic pentameter
    (C) iambic tetrameter
    (D) trochaic pentameter
    (E) dactylic pentameter

31. The usual rhyme scheme of the Petrarchean sonnet is
    (A) abba abba cde cde
    (B) aabb aabb cd cd cd
    (C) abab cbcb efef gg
    (D) abab cdcd cdcd ee
    (E) abab bbcc dd dd ee

32. Which of the patterns in question 30 is a Shakespearean sonnet pattern?

33. Which of the patterns in question 30 is a Spenserian sonnet pattern?

GO ON TO THE NEXT PAGE

Questions 34–38 refer to E. E. Cummings's poem "In Just-."

in Just-
spring when the world is mud-
luscious the little
lame balloonman

whistles far and wee

and eddieandbill come
running from marbles and
piracies and it's
spring

when the world is puddle-wonderful

the queer
old balloonman whistles
far and wee
and bettyandisbel come dancing

from hop-scotch and jump-rope and

it's
spring
and
the

goat-footed

balloonMan whistles
far
and
wee

34. The *balloonman* alludes to

(A) Puck
(B) Peter Pan
(C) Pan
(D) Cupid
(E) Apollo

35. The poem is written in

(A) rhyme
(B) blank verse
(C) slant rhyme
(D) free verse
(E) couplets

36. *mud-luscious* and *puddle-wonderful* make use of

(A) consonance
(B) assonance
(C) alliteration
(D) assonance and consonance
(E) personification

37. *luscious the little/lame balloonman* is an example of

(A) assonance
(B) consonance
(C) alliteration
(D) assonance and consonance
(E) personification

38. The setting of the poem is

(A) England
(B) the woods
(C) urban
(D) the circus
(E) the seaside

Questions 39–41 refer to "The Hound," by Robert Francis.

Line Life the hound
Equivocal
Comes at a bound
Either to rend me
5   Or to befriend me.

I cannot tell
The hound's intent
Till he has sprung
At my bare hand
10 With teeth or tongue.

Meanwhile I stand
And wait the event.

39. With *teeth or tongue* is what figure of speech?

(A) metaphor
(B) simile
(C) synecdoche
(D) metonymy
(E) hyperbole

40. Which lines comprise the only rhyming couplet?

(A) 1 and 2
(B) 1 and 3
(C) 3 and 4
(D) 4 and 5
(E) 6 and 7

41. Although the basic meter of the poem is iambic dimeter, which lines are perfectly regular?

(A) 1, 2, and 3
(B) 2, 7, and 10
(C) 2, 7, and 12
(D) 5, 6, and 7
(E) 8, 9, and 10

Questions 42–46 refer to the following poem by Emily Dickinson.

> A route of evanescence
> With a revolving wheel;
> A resonance of emerald,
> A rush of cochineal;
> And every blossom on the bush
> Adjusts its tumbled head,—
> The mail from Tunis, probably,
> An easy morning's ride.

42. Emily Dickinson did not title her poems, yet later editors titled them as they saw fit. What would be the title created for this poem?

 (A) "Morning's Ride"
 (B) "Mail from Tunis"
 (C) "A Hummingbird"
 (D) "Gem Wheel"
 (E) "Sound and Light"

43. In the entire poem, there is only one

 (A) noun
 (B) predication
 (C) adjective
 (D) metaphor
 (E) metonymy

44. *Route* and *rush* are

 (A) metaphors
 (B) alliterations
 (C) metonymies
 (D) similes
 (E) hyperboles

45. In lines 3-4, *resonance*, *rush*, and *cochineal* are examples of

 (A) metaphor
 (B) metonomy
 (C) synesthesia
 (D) personification
 (E) consonance

46. "An easy morning's ride" is an example of

 (A) metonymy
 (B) personification
 (C) metaphor
 (D) synecdoche
 (E) hyperbole

47. What do the plays *El Hajj Malik, Family Portrait, Sister Son/Ji,* and *We Righteous Bombers* have in common?

 (A) They were written by women.
 (B) They were written in verse.
 (C) They were performed on Broadway.
 (D) They are about the Black experience.
 (E) They are about feminist causes.

48. *The Death of Malcolm X* was written by

 (A) Herbert Stokes
 (B) Sonia Sanchez
 (C) Ben Caldwell
 (D) LeRoi Jones
 (E) Salimu

49. A posthumously published book that dramatized the clash between natural goodness and innocence and unprovoked evil was

 (A) *Huckleberry Finn*
 (B) *Catcher in the Rye*
 (C) *Billy Budd*
 (D) *Franny and Zooey*
 (E) *Catch-22*

50. The cause of the hero's downfall in the book in question 49 was

 (A) Captain Vere
 (B) Lieutenant Ratcliffe
 (C) John Claggert
 (D) the dansker
 (E) the afterguardsman

51. The name of the ship upon which the hero of the book in question 49 sailed was

 (A) *The Eagle*
 (B) *The Hound*
 (C) *Indomitable*
 (D) *Queens Court*
 (E) *Old Ironsides*

52. The author of the book in question 49 was

 (A) Nathaniel Hawthorne
 (B) Henry David Thoreau
 (C) Herman Melville
 (D) Miguel de Cervantes
 (E) Henry James

GO ON TO THE NEXT PAGE

53. In an unfinished allegory, Franz Kafka traced the steps of what has been called a modern *Pilgrim's Progress*. The name of this book was

    (A) *The Castle*
    (B) *The River*
    (C) *Heartbreak*
    (D) *The Dungeon*
    (E) *The Balcony*

54. *Critique of Pure Reason* is a masterpiece in metaphysics designed to answer the question, "How are synthetic *a priori* judgments possible?" Who wrote this groundbreaking work?

    (A) Sören Kierkegaard
    (B) Immanuel Kant
    (C) Jean-Paul Sarte
    (D) Henri Rousseau
    (E) Karl Marx

55. Edmund Rostand wrote what engaging play about the life of a French playwright and soldier?

    (A) *The Three Musketeers*
    (B) *The Cardinal*
    (C) *Cyrano de Bergerac*
    (D) *Don Quixote*
    (E) *The Count of Monte Cristo*

56. What book is considered one of the greatest novels in the Russian language for its characterizations, satiric humor, and style?

    (A) *War and Peace*
    (B) *Dead Souls*
    (C) *Crime and Punishment*
    (D) *The Brothers Karimozov*
    (E) *Anna Karenina*

57. Who wrote the novel *Dead Souls*?

    (A) Leo Tolstoy
    (B) Ivan Turgenev
    (C) Fyodor Dostoyevsky
    (D) Anton Chekhov
    (E) Nikolai Gogol

58. Who wrote *Death Comes for the Archbishop*, a chronicle of historical merging of cultures in New Mexico?

    (A) Mark Twain
    (B) Bret Harte
    (C) Willa Cather
    (D) Sarah Orne Jewett
    (E) Jack London

59. Plato was a pupil of

    (A) Gorgias
    (B) Socrates
    (C) Crito
    (D) Aristotle
    (E) Aristophanes

60. The epic poem *Don Juan* was written by

    (A) Lord Byron
    (B) Percy Shelley
    (C) John Keats
    (D) Alfred, Lord Tennyson
    (E) William Wordsworth

61. In the following list, the only one who is NOT a character in *Don Quixote de la Mancha* is

    (A) Sancho Panza
    (B) Don Quixote
    (C) Christian
    (D) Rocinante
    (E) Rogue Guinart

62. Adam Trask, Aron Trask, Cathy Ames, and Caleb Trask are characters in what novel by John Steinbeck?

    (A) *Tortilla Flat*
    (B) *The Pearl*
    (C) *East of Eden*
    (D) *Of Mice and Men*
    (E) *The Winter of Our Discontent*

63. *Ethan Fromme* was written by

    (A) Willa Cather
    (B) John Steinbeck
    (C) Edith Wharton
    (D) Saul Bellow
    (E) Nathaniel Hawthorne

64. The play *Everyman* is a traditional

    (A) epic
    (B) novel
    (C) moral allegory
    (D) biography
    (E) autobiography

65. *Arf, whiz, rustle, crunch,* and *kerplunk* are all examples of

    (A) hyperbole
    (B) litotes
    (C) onomatopoeia
    (D) paradox
    (E) apostrophe

66. *Slimy, slithering snake* is an example of
    - (A) alliteration
    - (B) assonance
    - (C) metonymy
    - (D) onomatopoeia
    - (E) litotes

67. *She moves about the room* and *eager beaver* are phrases that illustrate
    - (A) assonance
    - (B) alliteration
    - (C) litotes
    - (D) hyperbole
    - (E) onomatopoeia

68. Five lines, unrhymed—specifically twenty-two total syllables divided as follows: first line (2); second line (4); third line (6); fourth line (8); fifth line (2)—are a
    - (A) stanza
    - (B) tercet
    - (C) couplet
    - (D) cinquain
    - (E) octave

69. The following dramatists are listed in the order in which they received the Pulitzer Prize for drama: William Inge, John Patrick, Tennessee Williams, Goodrich/Hackett, Eugene O'Neill. During which of the following periods were the awards made?
    - (A) 1939–1943
    - (B) 1940–1944
    - (C) 1948–1952
    - (D) 1952–1956
    - (E) 1953–1957

70. Washington Irving, James Fenimore Cooper, and William Cullen Bryant are writers known by the group name of
    - (A) Beat writers
    - (B) Black Mountain poets
    - (C) Knickerbockers
    - (D) Concord group
    - (E) Lost Generation

71. Allen Ginsberg, William Burroughs, Jack Kerouac, and Lawrence Ferlinghetti are writers of what group?
    - (A) Knickerbockers
    - (B) Concord group
    - (C) Beat writers
    - (D) Lost Generation
    - (E) Black Mountain poets

72. Ezra Pound, Gertrude Stein, E. E. Cummings, and John Dos Passos belong to what group of writers?
    - (A) Beat writers
    - (B) Fireside Poets
    - (C) Lost Generation
    - (D) Knickerbockers
    - (E) Black Mountain poets

73. Ambrose Bierce, Willa Cather, Kate Chopin, Bret Harte, Sarah Orne Jewett, and Mark Twain were members of what group?
    - (A) Knickerbockers
    - (B) Black Mountain poets
    - (C) Local Color
    - (D) Graveyard Poets
    - (E) Beat writers

74. Henry Wadsworth Longfellow, John Greenleaf Whittier, and Oliver Wendell Holmes were members of what group?
    - (A) New York poets
    - (B) Fireside Poets
    - (C) Graveyard Poets
    - (D) University Wits
    - (E) Local Color

75. Anger, envy, covetousness, gluttony, lust, pride, and sloth are also known as
    - (A) modern rock bands
    - (B) the seven deadly sins
    - (C) rites of passage
    - (D) the Ten Commandments
    - (E) the sins of Paul

STOP If you finish before the time is up, you may check your work on this section only. Do not turn to any other section in the test.

TIME—45 MINUTES	75 QUESTIONS

PART II

Directions: Each of the questions or incomplete statements below is followed by five suggested answers or completions. Select the one that is best in each case.

76. Which of the following musical scores caused a riot in 1913 at its Paris performance?

(A) *The Rite of Spring*
(B) *Afternoon of a Faun*
(C) *The Moldau*
(D) *The Bartered Bride*
(E) *Billy the Kid*

77. The Baroque period was noted for music written in a complex and melodically ornate style. Which of the following terms describes this style?

(A) Chamber
(B) Allegretto
(C) Polyphonic
(D) Sonic
(E) Rigid

78. What is the term for music in which the parts are written in several keys simultaneously?

(A) Positive
(B) Sonata
(C) Classical
(D) Polytonal
(E) Compound

79. What term describes music that is performed by, and features, one artist or musical instrument?

(A) Solo
(B) Oratorio
(C) Suite
(D) Tonic
(E) Tone poem

80. Many of the marches Frédéric Chopin composed came from what Polish dance form?

(A) Interval
(B) Mass
(C) Polonaise
(D) Placido
(E) Skip

81. What term describes a curved line connecting two or more notes that are to be played legato?

(A) Matachin
(B) Bar
(C) Measure
(D) Slur
(E) Staff

82. The "pioneer-oriented" ballets—*Billy the Kid*, *Rodeo*, and *Appalachian Spring*—were composed by which twentieth-century composer?

(A) Sergei Prokofiev
(B) John Williams
(C) Aaron Copland
(D) Maurice Ravel
(E) Gioacchino Rossini

83. What term describes music that suggests the composer's birthplace?

(A) Nationalism
(B) Classicism
(C) Liturgy
(D) Romanticism
(E) Anthem

84. The poet-musician of the eleventh century who was skilled in singing, mostly of love, was a

(A) schisma
(B) juggler
(C) troubadour
(D) coloratura
(E) conductor

85. In musical notation, the five horizontal parallel lines upon which notes are placed are a

(A) transient
(B) tonic
(C) shift
(D) quintet
(E) staff, or stave

86. What term is used for the G clef and the higher voices, or register?

(A) Baritone
(B) Treble
(C) Tenor
(D) Coloratura
(E) Mute

87. The keynote part of a key—i.e., where the scale begins and ends—is called the

(A) treble
(B) shift
(C) tonic
(D) bar
(E) largo

88. The act of changing the pitch of a composition to a lower or higher key is

(A) transposing
(B) magadizing
(C) recurring
(D) bravura
(E) intensity

89. A vocal performance in octaves is called

(A) sextet
(B) magadizing
(C) leader
(D) moderato
(E) symphonic

90. What is the characteristic that describes the height and depth of a tone?

(A) Intensity
(B) Scale
(C) Pitch
(D) String
(E) Duration

91. Which of the following words does NOT describe the quality of a musical tone?

(A) Intensity
(B) Duration
(C) Timbre
(D) Pitch
(E) Moderato

92. A form of music with literal imitation of one voice by a succeeding voice or voices is a(n)

(A) symphony
(B) mass
(C) canon
(D) opera
(E) minuet

93. Nicolo Amati, Joseph Guarneri, Jacob Strainer, and Antonio Stradivari have what in common?

(A) They wrote music.
(B) They worked for musicians.
(C) They lived in the twentieth century.
(D) They were famous violin makers.
(E) They were monks in the Baroque era.

94. Which of the following is NOT a woodwind instrument?

(A) Flute
(B) Piccolo
(C) Clarinet
(D) Tuba
(E) Oboe

95. Which of the following does NOT pertain to pitch?

(A) Staff
(B) Clef
(C) Notes
(D) Accidentals
(E) Score

96. The succession of tones in any key is called

(A) metronome
(B) scale
(C) treble
(D) nass
(E) violin

97. What sign raises the pitch in a semitone?

(A) Slur
(B) Rest
(C) Legato
(D) Sharp
(E) Finale

98. When one note is common to successive chords, it is called a

(A) connecting note
(B) conductor
(C) bar line
(D) modulation
(E) largo

99. What sign lowers the pitch in a semitone?

(A) Bar line
(B) Allegretto
(C) Molto
(D) Canon
(E) Flat

100. The scale that progresses in semitones is called

(A) bass
(B) treble
(C) Beethovian
(D) chromatic
(E) romantic

GO ON TO THE NEXT PAGE

101. Which of the following does NOT belong to the string group of instruments?

    (A) Violin
    (B) Cello
    (C) Double bass
    (D) Contra-bassoon
    (E) Viola

102. Which of the following instruments does NOT belong to the percussion section?

    (A) Kettle drum
    (B) Clarinet
    (C) Tambourine
    (D) Chimes
    (E) Gong

103. The composition *Moment Musicale* (*Moments Musicaux*) was composed by

    (A) Sergei Rachmaninoff
    (B) Jean Sibelius
    (C) Ralph Vaughan Williams
    (D) Robert Schumann
    (E) Franz Schubert

104. The *Clock Symphony* was composed by

    (A) Robert Schumann
    (B) Maurice Ravel
    (C) Wolfgang Amadeus Mozart
    (D) Franz Joseph Haydn
    (E) Johannes Brahms

105. The ballet *Daphnis et Chloë* was composed by what Romantic-period composer?

    (A) Béla Bartók
    (B) Sergei Rachmaninoff
    (C) Ludwig van Beethoven
    (D) Frédéric Chopin
    (E) Maurice Ravel

106. Which of the following composers does NOT belong to the Romantic period?

    (A) Hector Berlioz
    (B) Johannes Brahms
    (C) Franz Liszt
    (D) Aaron Copland
    (E) Frédéric Chopin

107. The Sun Dance—a summer ceremony usually consisting of eight days of ritual smoking, fasting, and penance through self-torture—was practiced by

    (A) Gypsies
    (B) indigenous peoples of the American Plains
    (C) African warriors of the Sudan
    (D) Celtic druids
    (E) None of the above

108. Wovoka (1858–1932), a Paiute prophet, taught that pacifism and the sacred dance would cause the whites to disappear and would free all Native Americans from death, disease, and misery. What was his dance called?

    (A) Gavotte
    (B) Sun Dance
    (C) Ghost Dance
    (D) Eagle Dance
    (E) None of the above

109. A circle dance with lively, skipping steps used by Lully in court ballets and by Couperin and Bach in their keyboard suites was the

    (A) jig
    (B) waltz
    (C) tango
    (D) gavotte
    (E) flamenco

110. A musical about youth and love that incorporated dance and song and that was based on a Shakespearean play from an Italian tale was

    (A) *Hair*
    (B) *My Fair Lady*
    (C) *West Side Story*
    (D) *Grease*
    (E) *Annie*

111. A musical, speechless entertainment that involves the actor in dance, movement, exaggerated gestures, and sometimes face paint is called

    (A) ballet
    (B) pantomime
    (C) burlesque
    (D) vaudeville
    (E) None of the above

112 A summer season held in an outdoor theater built in 1968 that presents half a dozen operas yearly is the

    (A) Spoleto Festival
    (B) Newport Jazz Festival
    (C) Sante Fe Opera
    (D) Berkshires Festival
    (E) Aspen Music Festival

113. It is written for the aristocracy, involves music, dance, and highly stylized gesture and costume, and is full of religious and supernatural elements. Its earliest known playwright was Bhasa (ca. third-century C.E.). This is a description of

(A) Chinese drama
(B) Japanese drama
(C) Sanskrit drama
(D) Arabian drama
(E) Greek drama

114. Of the three major Asian dramas, which of the following is the oldest?

(A) Japanese
(B) Chinese
(C) Sanskrit
(D) Korean
(E) None of the above

115. Japan produced a writer who won the Nobel Prize for literature in 1968. Who was this writer?

(A) Murasaki Shikibu
(B) Kawabata Yusunari
(C) Mishima Yukio
(D) Ihara Saikaku
(E) Akutagawa Ryunosuke

Questions 116–118 refer to the following picture.

116. The picture above shows the

(A) Kremlin
(B) Houses of Parliament
(C) Citadel
(D) Louvre
(E) Vatican

117. The structure in the picture above was designed by

(A) Frank Lloyd Wright
(B) I. M. Pei
(C) E. E. Viollet-le-Duc
(D) Sir Charles Barry and A. W. Pugin
(E) John Nash

118. The structure in the picture above was built

(A) in 1812
(B) From 1873 to 1901
(C) From 1836 to 1864
(D) From 1732 to 1747
(E) From 1932 to 1939

119. Which of the following do the architects Brunelleschi and Alberti have in common with the sculptor Donatello?

I. Renaissance
II. Were among the first to visit Rome to study ancient ruins
III. Incorporated classical principles into their work
IV. Worked during the Gothic period
V. Shared a growing esteem and enthusiasm for physical nature, the individual, and classical antiquity

(A) IV and V
(B) I, IV, and V
(C) II, III, and V
(D) I, II, III, and V
(E) II, III, IV, and V

120. The High Renaissance encompassed which of the following years?

(A) 1300–1500
(B) 1350–1450
(C) 1400–1500
(D) 1490–1520
(E) 1600–1700

121. Which artist was exposed to the Medici circle of Neoplatonic thought in Florence because he lived with the family in their palace?

(A) Michelangelo Buonarotti
(B) Leonardo da Vinci
(C) Raphael
(D) Brunelleschi
(E) All of the above

GO ON TO THE NEXT PAGE

122. By the beginning of the sixteenth century, which artist brought glory to Venetian art?

(A) Titian
(B) Tintoretto
(C) Giorgione
(D) All of the above
(E) None of the above

123. In the Low Countries in Europe during the 1420s, who developed oil painting and, with it, the ability to achieve subtle variations in light and color?

(A) Fra Filippo Lippi
(B) Titian
(C) Jan Van Eyck
(D) Vincent van Gogh
(E) Paul Gauguin

124. Among Hieronymous Bosch, Pieter Brueghel, Regier van der Weyden, Martin Schongauer, and Albrecht Dürer, who made the first and greatest contributions in woodcuts and engravings?

(A) Bosch and Bruegal
(B) Weyden and Bosch
(C) Schongauer and Dürer
(D) Brueghel and Weyden
(E) Bosch and Weyden

125. Why was there a marked decline in artistic activity after 1348?

(A) There was no interest.
(B) War broke out.
(C) The Black Death hit Europe.
(D) No one bought art then.
(E) None of the above

126. Ballet dancers were a favorite subject of

(A) Titian
(B) Paul Gauguin
(C) Edgar Degas
(D) Pablo Picasso
(E) Claude Monet

127. Applying pigment to wet plaster is called

(A) fresco painting
(B) frieze
(C) balustrade
(D) mural
(E) panorama

128. A likeness of a person is called a(n)

(A) impression
(B) portrait
(C) oil
(D) picture
(E) glaze

129. The twentieth-century artist known for the *artworks* movement—enclosing large outdoor areas with plastic, cloth, or nylon sheets—is

(A) Louise Nevelson
(B) Christo
(C) George Segal
(D) Georgia O'Keeffe
(E) Elsworth Kelly

130. The principal movement involving all the arts that flourished in Europe in the first half of the nineteenth century that stood for the emotive and intuitive outlook was

(A) Neoclassical
(B) Expressionism
(C) Romanticism
(D) Renaissance
(E) None of the above

131. A period in which artists preferred the unidealized scenes of modern life was known as

(A) Romanticism
(B) Impressionism
(C) Neoclassical
(D) Realism
(E) None of the above

132.

The painting above represents what movement?

(A) Realism
(B) Impressionism
(C) Cubism
(D) Romanticism
(E) None of the above

133.

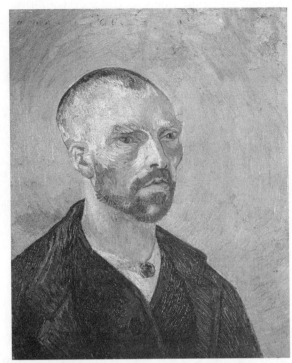

This is a self-portrait of

(A) Paul Gauguin
(B) Claude Monet
(C) Vincent van Gogh
(D) Edouard Manet
(E) None of the above

134. Who was the famous contemporary sculptor responsible for the Mount Rushmore memorial?

(A) Auguste Rodin
(B) Henry Moore
(C) Claude Monet
(D) Robyn Denny
(E) Gutzon Borglum

135. Which artist studied with Peter Paul Rubens in Antwerp, Belgium, and went on to paint Charles I, the King of England?

(A) Jan van Eyck
(B) Sir Anthony Van Dyck
(C) Michelangelo da Caravaggio
(D) Hans Holbein
(E) Thomas Gainsborough

136. The name applied to the painters of the early twentieth century who used vivid color and abbreviated form was

(A) Cubists
(B) Fauvists
(C) Impressionists
(D) Expressionists
(E) Symbolists

137. The movement that used elements of other movements as an escape from the mundane and the intolerably boring world of practicality was

(A) Fauvism
(B) Impressionism
(C) Expressionism
(D) Symbolism
(E) Cubism

138. Drama in the medieval period

(A) was created by the clergy
(B) made fun of the pope
(C) was written with music
(D) was written by the peasants
(E) parodied life within the church

139. The line *My love is like a red, red rose,* by Robert Burns, is an example of

(A) a soliloquy
(B) a simile
(C) malapropism
(D) litotes
(E) ottava rima

140. A form of narrative in which the characters, places, and actions represent abstract ideas while, at the same time, operating as part of the story, is known as

(A) literary license
(B) biography
(C) autobiography
(D) allegory
(E) fable

141. Which of the following is NOT a type of dance?

(A) Courante
(B) Sarabande
(C) Gigue
(D) Allemande
(E) Fugue

142. The Baroque period flourished during the seventeenth century. Of the following, who was NOT representative of this era?

(A) John Milton
(B) Francis Bacon
(C) Johann Pachelbel
(D) Peter Paul Rubens
(E) Domenico Scarlatti

GO ON TO THE NEXT PAGE

143. Of the following, who was NOT considered a Surrealist?

    (A) Max Ernst
    (B) Piet Mondrian
    (C) André Breton
    (D) Salvador Dalí
    (E) Marc Chagall

144. In classical styles of architecture, columnar types fall into how many classical orders?

    (A) Two
    (B) Three
    (C) Four
    (D) Five
    (E) Six

145. Which order, largely Asiatic in origin, had a scroll-shaped capital above a slender, fluted column? In Greece, the only major example is the Erechtheum.

    (A) Doric
    (B) Ionic
    (C) Corinthian
    (D) Composite
    (E) Tuscan

146. A Muslim building of worship is a

    (A) parthenon
    (B) temple
    (C) cathedral
    (D) mosque
    (E) minaret

147. A form of temple common to the Sumerians, Babylonians, and Assyrians was a(n)

    (A) mosque
    (B) mihrab
    (C) minaret
    (D) ziggurat
    (E) erechtheum

148. A painting by Salvador Dalí of melting watches in a deserted landscape is an example of

    (A) Abstraction
    (B) Impressionism
    (C) Cubism
    (D) Surrealism
    (E) Expressionism

149.

What is this famous building?

    (A) Louvre museum
    (B) Chartres cathedral
    (C) Castel de Monte
    (D) Notre Dame cathedral
    (E) None of the above

150.

This representation of a Gothic structural detail is a(n)

    (A) arch
    (B) facade
    (C) frieze
    (D) flying buttress
    (E) entablature

STOP If you finish before the time is up, you may check your work on this section only. Do not turn to any other section in the test.

POSTTEST ANSWER KEY AND EXPLANATIONS

PART I

1. B	16. A	31. A	46. E	61. C
2. B	17. B	32. C	47. D	62. C
3. A	18. B	33. D	48. D	63. C
4. D	19. C	34. C	49. C	64. C
5. A	20. B	35. D	50. C	65. C
6. E	21. A	36. B	51. C	66. A
7. D	22. C	37. C	52. C	67. A
8. A	23. D	38. C	53. A	68. D
9. A	24. E	39. D	54. B	69. E
10. C	25. A	40. D	55. C	70. C
11. C	26. B	41. B	56. B	71. C
12. A	27. C	42. C	57. E	72. C
13. B	28. D	43. B	58. C	73. C
14. E	29. D	44. C	59. B	74. B
15. D	30. B	45. C	60. A	75. B

PART II

76. A	91. E	106. D	121. A	136. B
77. C	92. C	107. B	122. D	137. D
78. D	93. D	108. C	123. C	138. A
79. A	94. D	109. D	124. C	139. B
80. C	95. E	110. C	125. C	140. D
81. D	96. B	111. B	126. C	141. E
82. C	97. D	112. C	127. A	142. E
83. A	98. A	113. C	128. B	143. B
84. C	99. E	114. C	129. B	144. D
85. E	100. D	115. B	130. C	145. B
86. B	101. D	116. B	131. D	146. D
87. C	102. B	117. D	132. B	147. D
88. A	103. E	118. C	133. C	148. D
89. B	104. D	119. D	134. E	149. D
90. C	105. E	120. D	135. B	150. D

PART I

1. **The correct answer is (B).** The correct order (with dates) is:
   6. Laws of Solon (590 B.C.E.—establishment of democracy in Athens)
   3. Edict of Milan (313 C.E.—religious freedom for Christians)
   4. Koran (640—Muhammad's teachings)
   5. Magna Carta (1215—King John's guarantee of the rule of law)
   10. *Martin Luther's Theses* (1517—Protestant Reformation begins)
   2. The Mayflower Compact (1620—Pilgrims' first "constitution")
   8. U.S. Constitution (1787—democratic government begins)
   1. Bill of Rights (1791—first ten amendments to U.S. Constitution)
   7. Code Napoleon (1804—French civil law)
   9. *Communist Manifesto* (1848—communist philosophy—Marx/Engels).

2. **The correct answer is (B).** While Jay Gatsby was a larger-than-life character, his flawed and naive view of love and success was a tragic story, not an epic.

3. **The correct answer is (A).** These essays are important in the study of literary criticism.

4. **The correct answer is (D).** In a letter to John Taylor, dated February 27, 1818, Keats expressed this idea, which, with its romantic tone, could not easily fit the other poets listed.

5. **The correct answer is (A).** Houseman is known for composing poems about pastoral scenes and the glory of youth.

6. **The correct answer is (E).** The use of *silent summer* repeats the "s" sound. Alliteration is the repeating of initial sounds in successive words.

7. **The correct answer is (D).** The use of a human activity—"sleeps" and "waken"—personifies the representatives of nature to argue how "natural" it is for the addressed to awaken with the poem's speaker.

8. **The correct answer is (A).** These lines are from *Paradise Lost*.

9. **The correct answer is (A).** Tennyson wrote both choice (D) and choice (E). The former is from *The Princess*; the latter is from *The Revenge*.

10. **The correct answer is (C).** Carlyle wrote this not as poetry, but it appeared in *Critical and Miscellaneous Essays*. While not intended to be poetry, it has elements of poetic language such as repetition.

11. **The correct answer is (C).** The quote translates to "The Fifth Column." The general was referring to an internal group within Madrid that was secretly working to defeat the city, while four columns of rebels marched on the city. It has become a term referring to anyone working on the inside to undermine an organization. Ernest Hemingway wrote a short story with the same title.

12. **The correct answer is (A).** Hamlet is referring to his anger for his uncle's causing harm to Laertes.

13. **The correct answer is (B).** Caesar makes this statement in response to Calpurnia's expressing her fear.

14. **The correct answer is (E).** While all of these writers write in various styles, the only thing they have in common is that they are essayists.

15. **The correct answer is (D).** All of these writers won the Pulitzer Prize, which is given by a fund established by an American publisher. Only William Faulkner won the Nobel Prize.

16. **The correct answer is (A).** The others are all fictional characters. Nellie Bly was a reporter who broke the fictional record of Jules Verne's protagonist Phileas Fogg. Fogg took eighty days to travel around the world, and Bly did it in $72\frac{1}{2}$ days.

17. **The correct answer is (B).** The others are all real people. Dan McGrew was a character from the poem "The Shooting of Dan McGrew," by Robert Service.

18. **The correct answer is (B).** Pele lived in the Kilauea Crater in Hawaii and erupted when angered.

19. **The correct answer is (C).** Singer wrote of his Jewish heritage and of American life from his insight as a person of such heritage.

20. **The correct answer is (B).** Of those listed, only Alcott wrote for youth. Buck wrote of struggles in China. Crane wrote novels of stark realism. Buntline wrote "dime novels" about the West. Burroughs wrote about Tarzan.

21. **The correct answer is (A).** None of the others is British. Sand is French, Martinson is Swedish, Fuentes is Spanish, and Simon is French.

22. **The correct answer is (C).** "Old Mother Hubbard/ went to her cupboard/to fetch her poor dog a bone."

23. **The correct answer is (D).** "Old King Cole was a merry old soul/and a merry old soul was he."

24. **The correct answer is (E).** "Simple Simon met a pieman/going to the fair."

25. **The correct answer is (A).** "Bobby Shafto's gone to sea/Silver buckles at his knee."

26. **The correct answer is (B).** "Little Jack Horner/sat in a corner/eating a Christmas pie."

27. **The correct answer is (C).** All of these writers have written science fiction as well as other types of stories.

28. **The correct answer is (D).**

29. **The correct answer is (D).** Hemingway wrote stories about testing the limits of what it means to be a man.

30. **The correct answer is (B).** There are three main variations, but all have the same five feet of iambs (unstressed and stressed syllable pairs).

31. **The correct answer is (A).** There is one other variation (abba abba cd cd cd).

32. **The correct answer is (C).**

33. **The correct answer is (D).**

34. **The correct answer is (C).** Pan, the half-man, half-goat, Greek god of nature, calls in the ritual of renewing spring, even in an urban setting.

35. **The correct answer is (D).** Free verse depends on the organization of sounds to create the cadence rather than on rhyme or rhythm.

36. **The correct answer is (B).** The exuberance of the lines is expressed by the assonance of the vowel sounds and the echoing d's and l's.

37. **The correct answer is (C).** The repeating l's create, through alliteration, a cadence.

38. **The correct answer is (C).** The games the children play set the poem in an urban area.

39. **The correct answer is (D).** Metonymy is the use of a part of the whole for the action of the whole.

40. **The correct answer is (D).** The rhyming of the ends of these lines and the preceding *rend* and *befriend* create a rhyming couplet. Other lines rhyme, but not as couplets.

41. **The correct answer is (B).**

42. **The correct answer is (C).** The keys to the title are in *route of evanescence*, and *rush of cochineal*, which, along with the other images of flowers and wings, lend credence to this title.

43. **The correct answer is (B).** *Adjusts* is the only predication that connects the static nouns in the first part with the mysteries of the ending.

44. **The correct answer is (C).** These are part of the whole that is the unnamed being.

45. **The correct answer is (C).** This is the substitution of one sense for another. *Resonance* is an auditory phenomenon that is attributed to sight or color, while *rush* implies the sensation of motion and is applied to another visual phenomenon, the color, *cochineal*.

46. **The correct answer is (E).** The exaggeration that any postman could deliver the mail in such a short time creates the image of extreme swiftness to emphasize the magic of the hummingbird.

47. **The correct answer is (D).** These plays were written before 1970 about the Black experience and were written especially for the younger generation of Black people.

48. **The correct answer is (D).**

49. **The correct answer is (C).** The nearly perfect character, Billy Budd, was a victim of jealousy and of his own frustration; when accused of mutiny, he accidentally killed his tormentor.

50. **The correct answer is (C).** Jealous of Billy's goodwill with the crew, the master-at-arms sought to falsely accuse Billy of mutiny.

51. **The correct answer is (C).** The name was ironic for Billy, whose last words were, "God bless Captain Vere." Also ironic was the fact that despite his original innocence, Billy's hanging secured the authority of the crown at sea.

52. **The correct answer is (C).** Herman Melville had won his fame with *Moby Dick*, another tale of the sea. *Billy Budd* was not published until 1924, thirty-four years after Melville's death.

53. **The correct answer is (A).** K., a young man seeking entrance to the castle, is both puzzled and irritated by his inability to get to the castle, where he had thought himself needed as a land surveyor.

54. **The correct answer is (B).** Kant investigated the process by which we possess knowledge without experience.

55. **The correct answer is (C).** Cyrano was well known for his wit and his skill in duels as well as for possessing a large nose.

56. **The correct answer is (B).** The plot is simple. It concerns the hero's scheme to buy, from landlords, serfs who have died since the last census, in order to perpetuate the hero's own real estate deal in eastern Russia.

57. **The correct answer is (E).**

58. **The correct answer is (C).** Cather wrote honestly of her material, never twisting it to her own end, to produce an epic, yet personal, saga.

59. **The correct answer is (B).** Plato wrote of the lessons he learned from Socrates, and Socrates would be an unknown teacher if not for the writings of Plato.

60. **The correct answer is (A).** Lord Byron used the vehicle of the epic poem to digress in order to give his views on wealth, power, chastity, poets, diplomats, and England.

61. **The correct answer is (C).** Christian was a character in *Cyrano de Bergerac*.

62. **The correct answer is (C).** This story is a regional chronicle of the Salinas valley, yet it carries a heavy echo of the Cain-and-Abel story.

63. **The correct answer is (C).** This novel is the most critically acclaimed and popular of Edith Wharton's works.

64. **The correct answer is (C).** The main character, Everyman, is called by Death to answer to God. The journey with other allegorical characters presents a morality play for mankind.

65. **The correct answer is (C).** The sound that a word makes that sounds like its meaning is onomatopoeia.

66. **The correct answer is (A).** Alliteration is the reccurrence of sounds at the beginnings of successive words.

67. **The correct answer is (A).** Assonance is the repetition of vowel sounds.

68. **The correct answer is (D).**

69. **The correct answer is (E).**

70. **The correct answer is (C).**

71. **The correct answer is (C).**

72. **The correct answer is (C).** F. Scott Fitzgerald, Ernest Hemingway, and William Faulkner were also members of this group.

73. **The correct answer is (C).**

74. **The correct answer is (B).**

75. **The correct answer is (B).** St. Thomas Aquinas listed these sins.

PART II

76. **The correct answer is (A).** *The Rite of Spring* caused a riot in its first performance, given in Paris in 1913. This was strange, since the rehearsal had gone off without a problem. However, yelling and catcalls could be heard from the audience throughout the entire performance.

77. **The correct answer is (C).** Polyphonic music consists of several instruments or voices performing contrapuntally (several voices of melody occurring simultaneously). While this type of composition was most popular during the thirteenth through sixteenth centuries, polyphony occurred well past the seventeenth century.

78. **The correct answer is (D).** Polytonal music is the concurrent use of more than one key in a piece of music. Should there be only two keys used, the piece would then become bitonal.

79. **The correct answer is (A).** The performance of a single musician or instrument, such as a song with or without accompaniment, is known as a solo.

80. **The correct answer is (C).** The polonaise is a Polish dance of moderate tempo in simple triple time usually characterized as a grand ceremonial procession. Chopin composed thirteen such dances.

81. **The correct answer is (D).** The slur is the marking used in musical notation above or below several notes that are to be played smoothly.

82. **The correct answer is (C).** Aaron Copland composed these three ballets using popular tunes. *Appalachian Spring* is possibly his most well known ballet.

83. **The correct answer is (A).** Nationalism is characterized by the use of folk songs, folk dances, and rhythms and the use of historically or culturally relevant themes peculiar to one's birthplace.

84. **The correct answer is (C).** The troubadour, or minstrel, traveled alone or in small groups from village to village, earning a living by singing songs (usually about love), playing instruments, performing antics, and displaying trained animals.

85. **The correct answer is (E).** The staff is the system of parallel lines and spaces upon which notes are written. Pitch is determined both by the clef sign and the position of the note on the staff.

86. **The correct answer is (B).** Treble is the upper part of a composition opposite to the bass. The treble clef is used to denote higher-pitched voices or instrumentation.

87. **The correct answer is (C).** The tonic, or keynote, is the first note of a major or minor scale and the note from which the key gets its name.

88. **The correct answer is (A).** Transposing changes the pitch of an entire composition without other change—for example, the raising or lowering of the pitch of a piece in the key of C to that of the key of D or B.

89. **The correct answer is (B).** Magadizing refers to a performance in which the vocalists sing in octaves.

90. **The correct answer is (C).** Pitch is the position of a sound in the tonal scale that depends on the frequency of vibrations from the origin of the sound. More frequent vibrations produce a higher pitch, while less frequent vibrations produce a lower pitch.

91. **The correct answer is (E).** Moderato does NOT describe the quality of a musical tone; rather, it describes the pace at which a piece of music is performed.

92. **The correct answer is (C).** A canon is a musical form in which a melody is imitated at timed intervals note for note.

93. **The correct answer is (D).** Amati, Guarneri, Strainer, and Stradivari were all famous violin makers. Stradivari, the maker of the Stradivarius, is the best known today.

94. **The correct answer is (D).** The tuba is a brass instrument. The woodwinds get their name from instruments that were usually made of wood and played with or without the use of a reed. Brass instruments were generally made of brass, although today they are often made of other types of metal, but never of wood.

95. **The correct answer is (E).** Score does not pertain to pitch. A score is a complete copy of music that shows all parts appropriate to various instruments or performers.

96. **The correct answer is (B).** A scale is a series of individual notes progressing up or down stepwise within an octave.

97. **The correct answer is (D).** A sharp, when placed beside a note, raises the pitch of the note one half-step, or a semitone.

98. **The correct answer is (A).** The common tone linking together a succession of chords within a progression is called a connecting tone.

99. **The correct answer is (E).** The flat lowers the pitch of a note by one half-step, or semitone.

100. **The correct answer is (D).** The chromatic scale consists of twelve ascending or descending semitones.

101. **The correct answer is (D).** The contra-bassoon is NOT a member of the stringed instruments. The contra-bassoon is a member of the woodwinds, because it is usually made of wood and is played by blowing into a mouthpiece that has a double reed.

102. **The correct answer is (B).** The clarinet does NOT belong to the percussion section. The clarinet is a woodwind instrument.

103. **The correct answer is (E).** Franz Schubert composed six *Moments Musicale* from 1823 to 1828.

104. **The correct answer is (D).** Franz Joseph Haydn composed the *Clock Symphony* (No. 101 in D Major) in London in 1794. The symphony is so named because of the "ticktock" accompaniment at the beginning of the second movement.

105. **The correct answer is (E).** Maurice Ravel composed the three-scene ballet *Daphnis et Chloë* in 1909-1911.

106. The correct answer is (D). Aaron Copland does NOT belong to the Romantic period of music. The Romantic period lasted from ca. 1830 to 1900. Copland was born in 1900 and belongs with the twentieth-century group of composers.

107. The correct answer is (B). The rites were discouraged by missionaries and the U.S. government to such an extent that they are now almost forgotten, and their true meaning has been lost.

108. The correct answer is (C). After his supernatural "bulletproof" ghost failed tragically at Wounded Knee, the appeal of his religion waned.

109. The correct answer is (D). This was originally a peasant dance of the Gavots, in upper Dauphine, France.

110. The correct answer is (C). The plot of this musical about rival New York street gangs was loosely based on the story of Romeo and Juliet.

111. The correct answer is (B). Pantomime makes use of facial and body gestures without props to allow the viewer's imagination to supply the other elements.

112. The correct answer is (C). This world-famous opera season has been held in Sante Fe, New Mexico, since 1957.

113. The correct answer is (C). Love and heroism are the most common sources of emotion, unlike the Chinese and Japanese dramas.

114. The correct answer is (C). It dates from 1500 B.C.E.

115. The correct answer is (B). Written in a lyrical, impressionistic style, his novels are distinguished by a masterful use of imagery. His novels include *Snow Country* (tr. 1956) and *The Sound of the Mountain* (tr. 1970).

116. The correct answer is (B). The Houses of Parliament were built in London on the site of the Palace of Westminster, where Edward I presided over the Model Parliament in 1295.

117. The correct answer is (D). Sir Charles Barry designed the building, and A. W. Pugin designed the intricate decoration.

118. The correct answer is (C). The structure was completed in twenty-eight years.

119. The correct answer is (D). These artists, along with many others, broke away from the medieval Gothic tradition and were inspired by classical values in all of the arts.

120. The correct answer is (D). The major figures in High Renaissance art were Leonardo da Vinci, Michelangelo Buonarotti, and Raphael.

121. The correct answer is (A). Michelangelo was invited by Lorenzo de' Medici to live in the palace when he was about fourteen years old.

122. The correct answer is (D). Along with the Bellini family and Veronese, these artists were known as the Venetian colorists.

123. The correct answer is (C). Brothers Hubert and Jan Van Eyck painted with rich details in this new medium. Though they did not practice geometric perspective or show any interest in accurate anatomy, their use of color and precision inspired Italian artists.

124. The correct answer is (C). These artists made graphic arts a popular medium throughout Europe.

125. The correct answer is (C). The Black Death, or Bubonic Plague, had a profound effect on all activity in Europe as thousands of city inhabitants died a painful death.

126. The correct answer is (C). Degas was intrigued by the movements of the dancers. He painted and sketched them stretching, rehearsing, and, sometimes, performing.

127. The correct answer is (A). Meaning "fresh" in Italian, the medium involved applying colors to wet plaster in sections.

128. The correct answer is (B).

129. The correct answer is (B). Christo Javacheff, known as Christo, is well known for such works of art as *Running Fence*, which consisted of 24 miles of nylon sheeting running through the hills of California. His objective is to create a harmony of art with nature.

130. The correct answer is (C). As opposed to the rational movement, this movement emphasized the subjective and fantastic.

131. The correct answer is (D). The unofficial leader was Courbet.

132. The correct answer is (B). This painting, titled *Impression: Sunrise*, by Claude Monet, 1872, was in a show that was dubbed by critic Louis Leroy as "the Exhibition of Impressionism."

133. The correct answer is (C). Vincent van Gogh painted himself at various times in his life, and the works reveal his passion and intensity.

134. The correct answer is (E). Gutzon Borglum began the sculptures of Washington, Jefferson, Lincoln, and Theodore Roosevelt at Mount Rushmore in 1930. The final details were finished after his death, in 1941, by his son, Lincoln Borglum.

135. The correct answer is (B). Van Dyck was knighted by Charles I and was named Principal Painter to the King of England.

136. The correct answer is (B). *Fauves*—meaning *wild beasts*—is said to have been coined by the French critic Louis Vauxcelles.

137. The correct answer is (D).

138. The correct answer is (A). Drama was created for the general public rather than courtly audiences, and was created by local priests. These plays consisted of both mystery plays and morality plays.

139. The correct answer is (B). The use of the words *like* or *as* are indicative of a simile, which is a comparison of unlike things with similar traits (i.e., *my love* and a *rose*).

140. **The correct answer is (D).** In an allegory, for example, characters may stand for good or bad traits in mankind; a road may represent the right or wrong way in life, and so on.

141. **The correct answer is (E).** A fugue is a form of music, normally monothematic, and was composed in all media, including choral ensembles. It was composed as an independent piece or as movements in larger works.

142. **The correct answer is (E).** Scarlatti, who spent most of his adult life in Spain, was considered part of the classical movement. The Baroque movement was replaced by this newer form of music, in which counterpoint disappeared and was replaced by homophonic textures and the use of new instruments.

143. **The correct answer is (B).** Mondrian developed a theory of art called Neoplasticism, which was an outgrowth of Cubism. His paintings consisted of horizontal and vertical lines and rectangular shapes in primary colors as well as in black-and-white.

144. **The correct answer is (D).** The orders are: Doric, Ionic, Corinthian, Composite, and Tuscan.

145. **The correct answer is (B).**

146. **The correct answer is (D).** The mosque's basic elements are space to assemble and some orientation so that the faithful may pray facing toward Mecca. This direction is marked by a mihrab, usually a decorated niche.

147. **The correct answer is (D).** It was a pyramidal brick structure with receding tiers, set on a rectangular, square, or oval platform, with a shrine at the summit.

148. **The correct answer is (D).** Dalí used common objects to create a feeling of reality taken to some extreme.

149. **The correct answer is (D).** Notre Dame is an example of Gothic architecture built in the twelfth and thirteenth centuries.

150. **The correct answer is (D).** These double-stage flying buttresses create a fantastic landscape as well as support the cathedral walls of Winchester Cathedral in England. In many constructions, the walls were replaced by glass.

Part V
SOCIAL SCIENCES AND HISTORY

Chapter 11
PRETEST

PART I

Directions: Each of the questions or incomplete statements below is followed by five suggested answers or completions. Select the one that is best in each case.

1. What was the name given to the basic document in English constitutional law granted by King John at Runnymede, Surrey, in 1215 and whose main purpose was to confirm the privileges of the feudal barons and limit the king's powers over them?

   (A) Magnum Opus
   (B) Magna Carta
   (C) Bill of Rights
   (D) Papal Bull
   (E) Writ of Mandamus

2. When the English took New Amsterdam in 1664, they changed its name. Which one of the following was the new name?

   (A) New England
   (B) New Jersey
   (C) New Hampshire
   (D) Newark
   (E) New York

3. What was the name of the first direct tax levied by the Crown on the American colonies in 1765?

   (A) Estate duty
   (B) Income tax
   (C) Wealth tax
   (D) Sales tax
   (E) Stamp tax

4. Where did the Pilgrim fathers found their colony when they arrived from England on the *Mayflower* in 1620?

   (A) Plymouth, Massachusetts
   (B) Salem, Massachusetts
   (C) Trenton, New Jersey
   (D) Rochester, New York
   (E) Baltimore, Maryland

5. Which one of the following treaties fixed the terms of peace after World War I and was signed on June 28, 1919?

   (A) Treaty of Versailles
   (B) Treaty of Westphalia
   (C) Treaty of Utrecht
   (D) Treaty of Vienna
   (E) Treaty of Ghent

6. To what well-known English dynasty did the following monarchs belong: King Henry VII, King Henry VIII, King Edward VI, Queen Mary, and Queen Elizabeth I?

   (A) Victorian
   (B) Stuart
   (C) Tudor
   (D) Georgian
   (E) Somerset

7. The first African blacks who were brought to English North America were sold at which location?

   (A) Jamestown, Virginia
   (B) New York City
   (C) Plymouth Colony, Massachusetts
   (D) Philadelphia, Pennsylvania
   (E) Washington, D.C.

GO ON TO THE NEXT PAGE

8. Which one of the following refers to the pontifical palace, the largest palace in the world and the resident home of Catholic popes since 1377?

   (A) Palace of Versailles
   (B) Buckingham Palace
   (C) The Hague
   (D) Rome
   (E) The Vatican

9. How many English colonies of the eastern seaboard declared their independence in 1776 when they formed the original United States of America?

   (A) 13
   (B) 17
   (C) 28
   (D) 45
   (E) 48

10. What famous revolution of 1789 is commonly associated with the storming of the Bastille?

    (A) Industrial Revolution
    (B) Bolshevik Revolution
    (C) Glorious Revolution
    (D) Bloodless Revolution
    (E) French Revolution

11. What was the approximate population of the United States when the first census was recorded in 1790?

    (A) 3.9 million
    (B) 8.7 million
    (C) 50 million
    (D) 75 million
    (E) 100 million

12. The St. Valentine's Day massacre in Chicago in 1929 marked the

    (A) peak of gangster wars
    (B) overnight dismissal of Herbert Hoover's cabinet
    (C) crash of a domestic airliner with 250 passengers aboard
    (D) mass murder of convicted prisoners on a single day in a Chicago jail
    (E) beginning of the heroin drug war

13. Before it moved to its permanent home in New York City in 1946, the United Nations had been originally established in another U.S. city in 1945. Which city was it?

    (A) San Francisco
    (B) Los Angeles
    (C) San Diego
    (D) Honolulu
    (E) Phoenix

14. The Truman Doctrine of 1947, which held out United States economic and military assistance to Greece and Turkey, was part of a policy aimed at

    (A) denationalizing state-owned enterprises
    (B) encouraging freedom of the press
    (C) obtaining military and naval bases in reciprocity
    (D) regulating the economies of aid-receiving countries
    (E) containing communism

15. The first nonstop solo flight from New York City to Paris was made in 1927 by

    (A) Amelia Earhart
    (B) Freddie Laker
    (C) George C. Marshall
    (D) Charles A. Lindbergh
    (E) Wilbur Wright

16. In 1607, the English founded their first permanent settlement in America under the leadership of John Smith. In which of the following cities was this settlement located?

    (A) Plymouth
    (B) Jamestown
    (C) Boston
    (D) Yorktown
    (E) Bunker Hill

17. Modern Great Britain is composed of

    (A) England, Wales, Scotland, and Northern Ireland
    (B) England, Republic of Ireland, and Scotland
    (C) England and Northern Ireland
    (D) England, Republic of Ireland, and Wales
    (E) England, Scotland, and Wales

18. The U.S. Declaration of Independence was signed in 1776. Which one of the following cities was the venue for the signing?

    (A) New York City
    (B) Philadelphia
    (C) Boston
    (D) Lexington
    (E) Washington, D.C.

19. The Russo-Japanese peace treaty was signed at Portsmouth, New Hampshire, in 1905. The American president who played the role of mediator was eventually awarded the Nobel Peace Prize in 1906 for his efforts. Who was this president?

    (A) Theodore Roosevelt
    (B) William McKinley
    (C) William Howard Taft
    (D) Franklin Delano Roosevelt
    (E) Woodrow Wilson

20. The first attempt of the British working classes to capture power was made in 1838. By what name was this movement popularly known?

    (A) Suffragette movement
    (B) Reform movement
    (C) Proletariat movement
    (D) Socialist movement
    (E) Chartist movement

21. The event that sparked the beginning of World War I took place in Sarajevo, Austria, in 1914. Which of the following events was it?

    (A) The signing of the Entente Cordiale by France and England
    (B) The announcement by Austria of its annexation of Bosnia and Herzegovina
    (C) The assassination of Archduke Francis Ferdinand
    (D) The abdication of Archduke Francis Ferdinand
    (E) The declaration of a policy of neutrality by Austria

22. The American Revolution began with the Battle of Lexington and Concord in 1775. It ended with the British surrender at Yorktown. In what year did the British surrender?

    (A) 1775
    (B) 1776
    (C) 1781
    (D) 1787
    (E) 1789

23. What was the name given to the famous nationalist movement led by the middle classes and nobility for the political unification of Italy from 1859 to 1870?

    (A) Reformation
    (B) Risorgimento
    (C) Red Purge
    (D) Chartism
    (E) Balkanization

24. The first communist state in the world was established in 1922. Which of the following was it?

    (A) Union of Soviet Socialist Republics
    (B) Ukrainian Soviet Socialist Republic
    (C) Byelorussia
    (D) Czechoslovakia
    (E) Hungary

25. The U.S. Declaration of Independence is usually attributed to the work of one person. Who was he?

    (A) Thomas Jefferson
    (B) George Washington
    (C) Benjamin Franklin
    (D) Abraham Lincoln
    (E) Thomas Paine

26. The Indian Mutiny of 1857–1858 was engineered by sepoy troops against colonial rule in India. Although it was ruthlessly suppressed, it went down in Indian history as a major political event of that century. The mutiny was directed against the

    (A) Americans
    (B) Japanese
    (C) Portuguese
    (D) Dutch
    (E) British

27. Between 1847 and 1854, several million immigrants came to America, with the majority originating from what two countries?

    (A) Italy and France
    (B) England and Spain
    (C) Ireland and Germany
    (D) Norway and Denmark
    (E) Japan and Austria

28. Until September 2002, which country had refused to join the United Nations because it felt that membership in the world body would contravene its neutrality?

    (A) Austria
    (B) West Germany
    (C) Japan
    (D) Finland
    (E) Switzerland

29. The ancestors of American Indians are said to have migrated in prehistoric times. From what continent did they migrate?

    (A) Asia
    (B) Africa
    (C) Australia
    (D) Europe
    (E) The Americas

GO ON TO THE NEXT PAGE

30. What was the name given to the conflict between Great Britain and thirteen of its colonies on the Atlantic coast of North America?

   (A) Battle of Waterloo
   (B) Battle of Bunker Hill
   (C) Civil War
   (D) Battle of Yorktown
   (E) American War of Independence

31. In January 1776, Thomas Paine published what is considered the most influential American revolutionary tract, in which he called for independence and vigorously attacked the venerated institutions of royalty and the English Constitution. What is the name of this famous treatise?

   (A) *Uncle Tom's Cabin*
   (B) *Age of Reason*
   (C) *Common Sense*
   (D) *Rights of Man*
   (E) *Crisis*

32. Which of the following is the explorer whose name commemorates America?

   (A) Christopher Columbus
   (B) Vasco de Gama
   (C) Amerigo Vespucci
   (D) Prince Henry the Navigator
   (E) Marco Polo

33. Which one of the following treaties, signed in 1648, ended the Thirty Years' War in Europe?

   (A) Treaty of Westphalia
   (B) Treaty of Versailles
   (C) Treaty of Vienna
   (D) Treaty of Utrecht
   (E) Treaty of Brandenburg

34. What is the common term used to describe a measure of the market value of all commodities and services produced by a nation during a given period of time (usually a year)?

   (A) Per capita income
   (B) National income
   (C) Gross national product
   (D) Balance of payments
   (E) Collective wages

35. The flood of certain foreign consumer goods like television sets and automobiles into the American market has recently focused attention on the practice of foreign countries selling their products in the United States below the price at which they are sold at home. Which one of the following terms best describes this practice?

   (A) Monopoly
   (B) Oligopoly
   (C) Undercutting
   (D) Competition
   (E) Dumping

36. Which one of the following is the primary function of the Washington-based World Bank?

   (A) Finance industrial projects in wealthy countries
   (B) Make long-term loans for development projects in developing countries
   (C) Give economic aid to Latin American countries
   (D) Make short-term loans to Western European countries
   (E) Provide international security assistance

37. If Nation A erects high tariffs and creates many nontariff barriers in order to restrict the flow of imports from other nations, Nation A is following the economic policy of

   (A) free trade
   (B) comparative advantage
   (C) protectionism
   (D) positive trade balances
   (E) laissez-faire

38. What is the term used to describe the lowering of the par value of a nation's currency relative to gold or to the currency of other countries?

   (A) Depreciation
   (B) Devaluation
   (C) Depletion
   (D) Digression
   (E) Revaluation

39. What is the most common statistic used to measure the average change in prices of goods and services purchased by urban consumers?

   (A) Per capita income
   (B) Real wages
   (C) Consumer price index
   (D) Unemployment insurance
   (E) Social Security

40. What economic and political system, developed in the late eighteenth century in England—currently in existence in modified form in most of Western Europe and the United States—was inspired by Adam Smith's *Wealth of Nations* (1776) and the English classical school of economics?

    (A) Capitalism
    (B) Authoritarianism
    (C) Fabian socialism
    (D) McCarthyism
    (E) Conservatism

41. What was the name given to the post–World War II foreign-aid plan to restore the economic stability of Western Europe?

    (A) New Deal
    (B) Eisenhower Doctrine
    (C) Marshall Plan
    (D) de Gaulle Plan
    (E) Kennedy Round

42. In modern economic jargon, the poor countries of the world are officially designated l.d.c.'s. What does "l.d.c." stand for?

    (A) Less developed countries
    (B) Late developing countries
    (C) Little developed countries
    (D) Least demanding countries
    (E) Least developed countries

43. The surplus-value theory of labor, which is considered one of the most significant contributions to economic theory, holds that capitalist profit is the value of labor minus the amount paid to the laborer. Who was the best-known proponent of this theory?

    (A) Charles Darwin
    (B) John Stuart Mill
    (C) Thomas Malthus
    (D) Friedrich Engels
    (E) Karl Marx

44. A rise in the general level of prices is usually the same thing as a fall in the value of money. What is the economic term used to describe such a state of affairs?

    (A) Devaluation
    (B) Deflation
    (C) Depression
    (D) Inflation
    (E) Slump

45. In 1971, international monetary actions taken by the United States spelled an end to the Bretton Woods system and created a new global monetary system based upon

    (A) the gold standard
    (B) the metric system
    (C) floating exchange rates
    (D) sterling, or the pound system
    (E) the "basket of currencies" concept

46. In a private-enterprise economy, government regulation is generally at a minimum. This doctrine of "noninterference by the state" was developed in Herbert Spencer's social Darwinism in late nineteenth-century England. What is the more popular term to describe this?

    (A) Capitalistic socialism
    (B) Free-wheeling economy
    (C) Laissez-faire
    (D) Mixed economy
    (E) Socialistic capitalism

47. According to the laws of supply and demand, if the supply of a product is scarce or declines and demand for that product goes up substantially, then the price of that product will most likely

    (A) drop
    (B) increase
    (C) neither increase nor decrease
    (D) suffer a small drop, followed by a small increase, then return to its original level
    (E) not matter, since consumers will lose interest due to the short supply

48. "The natural price of labor is that which is sufficient to keep the laborer alive on a subsistence level and, that in an economic system regulated by the law of supply and demand, the market price of labor tends to approximate this natural price." Which one of the following does this statement represent?

    (A) Iron law of wages
    (B) Labor theory of value
    (C) Wage-price spiral
    (D) Law of diminishing returns
    (E) Market equilibrium

GO ON TO THE NEXT PAGE

49. What do the following dates have in common: 1819, 1837, 1857, 1873, 1893, 1907, and 1929?

   (A) They were years in which the U.S. economy suffered financial crashes.
   (B) They were years in which incumbent presidents introduced far-reaching legislation in the field of trade and business.
   (C) They were years in which the seven major U.S. corporations launched into business.
   (D) They were years in which new denominations of currency were introduced in the United States.
   (E) They were years in which the U.S. economy was hit by hyperinflation.

50. If any significant factor is to be singled out, what was the most striking effect of the Great Depression of 1929 that resulted in a major postwar economic slump in the United States?

   (A) Food shortages
   (B) Emergence of monopoly capital
   (C) Artificial scarcity of television sets
   (D) Unemployment
   (E) Increase in Japanese consumer products in the U.S. market

51. What is the term commonly used to describe duties or customs fees charged on merchandise entering competition?

   (A) Tariffs
   (B) Treaties
   (C) Taxes
   (D) Exemptions
   (E) Capital levies

52. Which one of the following statements is factually INCORRECT?

   (A) The growth of industry after the Civil War and the beginning of mass immigration to the United States increased the child labor force, and, by 1900, more than 2 million children were working.
   (B) Capital is that part of money and wealth used in production: the more production, the more capital.
   (C) The cause of inflation is too much money purchasing too many goods.
   (D) The United States depends on developing countries for more than two thirds of its demand for bauxite, tin, natural rubber, and other strategic raw materials.
   (E) Capitalists believe that a free-market economy works best when external forces do not interfere.

53. In a 1912 speech, President William Howard Taft coined a phrase that signified the use of American investments to stabilize strategic underdeveloped areas, primarily in Latin America. What was this foreign policy called?

   (A) Dollar diplomacy
   (B) New international economic order
   (C) Double-taxation agreement
   (D) Multilateral aid
   (E) Aid without strings

54. What is the name given to a government restriction on trade, usually ordered during wartime?

   (A) Embargo
   (B) Boycott
   (C) Apartheid
   (D) Censure
   (E) Penalty

55. American trade policy does not discriminate between the products of foreign nations in tariff rates as long as those nations do not discriminate against U.S. trade. What is the name given to this nondiscriminatory trade policy?

   (A) Antidumping
   (B) Economic opportunity act
   (C) Most-favored-nation policy
   (D) Free-enterprise system
   (E) Hands-off policy

56. The basic responsibility of the Federal Reserve System is to set

   (A) banking policy
   (B) monetary policy
   (C) trade policy
   (D) wage policy
   (E) tax policy

57. Which one of the following can best be described as one of the primary functions of the Washington-based International Monetary Fund?

   (A) It advances military credits.
   (B) It doles out food aid to developing countries.
   (C) It controls the world's money supply.
   (D) It advances emergency monetary aid to countries affected by floods, earthquakes, typhoons, and so on.
   (E) It promotes international monetary cooperation and makes loans to tide countries over during temporary payment problems.

58. Which of the following statements is true regarding a strong U.S. dollar and its impact upon exports, imports, foreign consumers, or foreign businesses?

   (A) A strong dollar makes imports more expensive.

   (B) A strong dollar usually means that Americans will buy fewer imports.

   (C) A stronger dollar makes American goods and services less expensive for foreign customers to buy.

   (D) A stronger dollar is generally bad for American exports.

   (E) A stronger dollar is bad for foreign businesses.

59. What is the name given to the international commercial and financial transactions of a country's citizens and government, including the total payments made to foreign nations and the total receipts from foreign nations?

   (A) Balance of payments

   (B) Terms of trade

   (C) Balance of trade

   (D) Invisible earnings

   (E) Kickbacks

60. What is the stock market term for someone who buys commodities or securities in anticipation of a rise in prices or who tries, through speculative purchases, to effect such a rise in order to sell later at a profit?

   (A) Gambler

   (B) High roller

   (C) Optimist

   (D) Numbers runner

   (E) Bull

STOP   If you finish before the time is up, you may check your work on this section only. Do not turn to any other section in the test.

TIME—45 MINUTES   65 QUESTIONS

PART II

Directions: Each of the questions or incomplete statements below is followed by five suggested answers or completions. Select the one that is best in each case.

61. SDR is the paper gold created by the International Monetary Fund and distributed to its member countries. The creditworthiness of a country in the IMF depends on the strength of its SDRs. What does "SDR" stand for?

    (A) Special deflationary rates
    (B) Special distribution rights
    (C) Special demand rights
    (D) Special drawing rights
    (E) Special drawing rates

62. The Egyptian pharaoh Akhenaton was most noted for

    (A) constructing the Great Pyramid and the Sphinx
    (B) driving the Israelites out of Egypt
    (C) creating a single deity for Egyptians to worship
    (D) defeating Egypt's enemies through a series of brilliant military battles
    (E) marrying Cleopatra

63. The Fahrenheit thermometer scale is being gradually replaced in most countries with the centigrade scale devised by a Swedish astronomer. What is the name of this measuring scale?

    (A) Celsius
    (B) Richter
    (C) Vesuvius
    (D) Avoirdupois
    (E) Metronome

64. Which one of the following does the Dow Jones Industrial Average measure?

    (A) Cost-of-living index
    (B) Gasoline prices
    (C) Interest rates
    (D) Stock market
    (E) Windchill factor

65. The symbol pictured below is the universally recognized logo of what famous world body?

    (A) World Bank
    (B) United Nations
    (C) U.S. Congress
    (D) Red Cross
    (E) Amnesty International

66. In 1996, the nation whose GDP in billions of dollars ranked second in the world behind that of the United States was

    (A) Japan
    (B) Russia
    (C) Brazil
    (D) Germany
    (E) Canada

67. Yoga is a Hindu discipline aimed at training the consciousness for a state of perfect spiritual insight and includes a system of exercises practiced as part of this discipline. With which of the following countries is yoga commonly associated?

    (A) Nepal
    (B) Bangladesh
    (C) Pakistan
    (D) Turkey
    (E) India

68. The Nobel Peace Prize for 1978 was shared by two political leaders for their efforts toward creating peace in the Middle East. Who were these two leaders?

    (A) Gamal Abdel Nasser and David Ben-Gurion
    (B) Anwar as-Sadat and Menachem Begin
    (C) Moshe Dayan and King Hussein
    (D) Abba Eban and Yassir Arafat
    (E) James Callaghan and Helmut Schmidt

69. When inflation is at its extreme, money becomes so worthless that the whole economic system breaks down. In 1923, one of the countries in Western Europe suffered what economists called "galloping inflation," a condition in which a loaf of bread was paid for with a wheelbarrow full of money. What was the country that underwent this experience?

(A) United Kingdom
(B) France
(C) Belgium
(D) The Netherlands
(E) Germany

70. In 1997, the People's Republic of China absorbed which former British colony?

(A) Macao
(B) Hong Kong
(C) Taiwan
(D) Thailand
(E) Vietnam

71. Monrovia, which was named after President James Monroe, is the capital of

(A) Nigeria
(B) Liberia
(C) Mauritania
(D) Tunisia
(E) Niger

72. During the mid-1990s, Russia fought a brutal war against a secessionist province known as

(A) Georgia
(B) the Ukraine
(C) Armenia
(D) Chechnya
(E) Uzbekistan

73. The Philippines, a country in Southeast Asia that was once under the control of the United States, was named after

(A) Philip Marlowe
(B) Philadelphia
(C) King Philip II of Spain
(D) the Philistines
(E) John Philip Sousa

74. In Great Britain, the prime minister is actually selected by

(A) the voters of the nation
(B) the Queen
(C) the majority party in the House of Commons
(D) both parties in the House of Commons
(E) the British cabinet

75. In the American political system, "separation of powers" refers to the

(A) division of governmental functions into three distinct branches, namely executive, legislative, and judicial
(B) division of state, church, and the press
(C) division of political power in the hands of the president, the Senate, and the House of Representatives
(D) army, navy, and air force
(E) newspapers, radio, and television networks

76. An "executive order" is a

(A) piece of legislation passed by Congress
(B) presidential directive
(C) presidential pardon staying the execution of a convicted murderer
(D) directive that prevents congressional committees from interrogating executive officials
(E) congressional decree announcing the declaration of war

77. When the president rejects a bill sent to him by both houses, he writes which of the following words across it?

(A) Hold
(B) Veto
(C) Disapproved
(D) Rejected
(E) Suspended

78. In Congress, a "whip" is

(A) a member of the legislature who serves as his or her party's assistant floor leader
(B) a piece of legislation banning corporal punishment in schools
(C) a disciplinary committee of the House
(D) another name for the Speaker of the House
(E) using strong-arm tactics to ensure the passing of a bill

79. The Bill of Rights is

(A) the first ten amendments to the Constitution, ratified in 1791
(B) the right of minorities to employment
(C) a piece of legislation ensuring freedom of the press
(D) the first five amendments to the Constitution, guaranteeing citizenship to immigrants
(E) legislation that provides for the protection of the rights of resident aliens

GO ON TO THE NEXT PAGE

80. A meeting of political party leaders gathered together to agree on a candidate, position, or program is a(n)

    (A) convention
    (B) assembly
    (C) ad hoc committee
    (D) caucus
    (E) committee of the whole

81. A presidential candidate with little support beyond his or her state delegation at the national convention is called a

    (A) lame duck
    (B) favorite son
    (C) presidential hopeful
    (D) dark horse
    (E) president-elect

82. A delegate is a

    (A) representative to a party convention
    (B) senator representing a Midwestern state
    (C) member of the credentials committee at a national convention
    (D) presidential candidate carrying his or her party's nomination
    (E) member of Congress

83. On election day, the Democratic candidate for president wins 60 percent of the popular vote in California, compared to the Republican candidate's 40 percent. If California has 54 electoral votes, how many of that state's electoral votes are awarded to the Democratic candidate?

    (A) Slightly more than 32
    (B) 28
    (C) 52
    (D) 54
    (E) None of the above

84. "Double jeopardy," prohibited by the Fifth Amendment, is a constitutional immunity ensuring that no person can be tried for

    (A) the same crime twice
    (B) two different crimes simultaneously
    (C) two different crimes at two different times
    (D) the same crime in two different states
    (E) a crime committed outside the United States

85. The requirement that all competing candidates at an election receive equal amounts of broadcasting time is

    (A) the run-off
    (B) the nonpartisan ballot
    (C) the equal-time provision
    (D) equity
    (E) the Equal Rights Amendment

86. The obstruction of a legislative act or program through prolonged speechmaking is

    (A) featherbedding
    (B) logrolling
    (C) impeachment
    (D) filibustering
    (E) roll call

87. The Department of Defense is housed in the

    (A) Pentagon
    (B) White House
    (C) Smithsonian Institution
    (D) Watergate complex
    (E) Kennedy Center for the Performing Arts

88. The term commonly used to denote heads of the executive departments of government is

    (A) FBI
    (B) CIA
    (C) Pentagon
    (D) Cabinet
    (E) Oval Office

89. A trial by jury consists of laypeople selected from the community and supervised by a judge to ensure a fair trial according to the laws applicable to the case. How many jurors most typically comprise such a panel?

    (A) 6
    (B) 8
    (C) 12
    (D) 19
    (E) 33

90. The U.S. Congress, which is the legislative branch of the federal government, consists of the Senate and the

    (A) president
    (B) Supreme Court
    (C) Pentagon
    (D) CIA
    (E) House of Representatives

91. The term of a U.S. senator is _____ years. He or she is elected by voters within his or her _____. Which choice accurately fills in both blanks?

    (A) two; district
    (B) two; state
    (C) four; state
    (D) six; district
    (E) six; state

92. *Brown v. Board of Education of Topeka* was a landmark Supreme Court ruling in 1954 because it

    (A) extended the Truman Doctrine to the Middle East
    (B) ended segregation in the armed forces
    (C) approved the North Atlantic Treaty Organization
    (D) outlawed racial segregation in public schools as inherently unjust
    (E) ensured the admission of the first African-American student to the University of Mississippi

93. The Twenty-second Amendment to the Constitution affecting the executive branch was ratified in 1951. This amendment limited

    (A) the president's military power
    (B) the president to two consecutive terms in office
    (C) the president's power of pardon
    (D) the president's executive privileges
    (E) limited the president's veto power

94. The type of jury that issues "indictments" is called a

    (A) petit jury
    (B) trial jury
    (C) jury of one's peers
    (D) traverse jury
    (E) grand jury

95. John Jay (1745–1829), Charles Evans Hughes (1862–1948), John Marshall (1755–1835), and Harlan Fiske Stone (1872–1946) all had one thing in common. They were

    (A) newspaper publishers
    (B) vice presidents
    (C) senators
    (D) chief justices of the Supreme Court
    (E) Hollywood movie producers

96. What is the term commonly used to describe the means by which a defendant is notified of civil action and by which the court asserts control over the defendant, thereby obtaining common-law jurisdiction over the person?

    (A) Summons
    (B) Subpoena
    (C) Tort
    (D) Unicameralism
    (E) Veto

97. When an accused civilian refuses to answer in a court of law for an alleged crime on the grounds that he or she could incriminate himself or herself by doing so, he or she usually seeks refuge in the

    (A) Third Amendment
    (B) Fifth Amendment
    (C) Sixth Amendment
    (D) neighboring church
    (E) Constitution

98. The bill that President Lyndon B. Johnson signed in 1967 to give the public greater access to government records was the

    (A) Freedom of Press Act
    (B) Foreign Service Act
    (C) Administrative Procedure Act
    (D) Disclosure of Information Act
    (E) Freedom of Information Act

99. Evidence that is improperly obtained cannot be used as evidence in a court of law. This rule of law is known as the

    (A) exclusionary rule
    (B) rule of four
    (C) rule of probable cause
    (D) cruel and unusual punishment rule
    (E) Miranda rule

100. In 1966, the Warren Court reached a landmark decision on a controversial ruling that guaranteed suspects the right to counsel before questioning. What was this case?

    (A) *Miranda v. Arizona*
    (B) *Plessy v. Ferguson*
    (C) *Gitlow v. New York*
    (D) *Griswold v. Connecticut*
    (E) *Perez v. Brownell*

101. During the Cold War era, the term "Second World" referred to the

    (A) affluent industrialized democracies
    (B) underdeveloped countries
    (C) communist states
    (D) nations of Asia only
    (E) nations of Latin America only

GO ON TO THE NEXT PAGE

102. Islam is the religion founded by Prophet Muhammad. It is, next to Christianity, the largest religion in the world. The Arabic word "Islam" means "submission to the will of Allah" (God). The followers of this religion are called

   (A) Buddhists
   (B) Zoroastrians
   (C) Hindus
   (D) Shintoists
   (E) Muslims

103. The wealthy, oil-rich nation in the Middle East that was invaded by Saddam Hussein in 1990 and then liberated by the United States and its allies during the ensuing Gulf War in 1991 was

   (A) Saudi Arabia
   (B) Bahrain
   (C) Oman
   (D) Kuwait
   (E) Qatar

104. Serious accidents at Three Mile Island in 1979 and Chernobyl in 1986 generated major concerns about the safety of

   (A) nuclear power
   (B) coal-burning power plants
   (C) military storage facilities containing nuclear weapons
   (D) solar power technology
   (E) oil tankers

105. Yellow journalism is journalism that exploits, distorts, or exaggerates the news to create sensations and attract readers. A person commonly associated with this brand of journalism is

   (A) Adolph Ochs
   (B) Katharine Graham
   (C) Edward W. Scripps
   (D) William Randolph Hearst
   (E) Edward R. Murrow

106. Which of the following past or present leaders is incorrectly matched with the nation he or she led (leads)?

   (A) Fidel Castro . . . Haiti
   (B) Mao Tse-Tung . . . China
   (C) Nikita Khrushchev . . . Russia
   (D) Golda Meir . . . Israel
   (E) Nelson Mandela . . . South Africa

107. Which of the following wars occurred before the other four?

   (A) Vietnam War
   (B) Korean War
   (C) World War II
   (D) Iran-Iraq War
   (E) Falkland Islands War

108. A dead language is a language no longer used in day-to-day life by any major group in the world. Such a language is

   (A) Amharic
   (B) Hindi
   (C) Urdu
   (D) Sinhalese
   (E) Sanskrit

109. All of the following made major discoveries in medicine EXCEPT

   (A) Zacharias Janssen
   (B) Casimir Funk
   (C) Michael de Bakey
   (D) Wilhelm Roentgen
   (E) David Livingstone

110. International crimes like drug trafficking and political terrorism are usually investigated and tracked down by an organization founded in Vienna in 1923. Currently headquartered in Paris, this organization is named

   (A) Sureté Générale
   (B) Scotland Yard
   (C) Royal Canadian Mounted Police
   (D) International Criminal Police Organization (INTERPOL)
   (E) International Court of Justice (ICJ)

111. Thomas R. Malthus (1766–1834), the English economic and social philosopher, propounded a philosophy called Malthusian doctrine, currently applicable to most developing countries. Which one of the following is nearest to his doctrine?

   (A) The best way to keep population down is to create artificial food shortages.
   (B) While food production increases arithmetically, population increases geometrically.
   (C) In a country where population is in plenty, food should necessarily be scarce.
   (D) Population growth can be curbed only by reducing infant mortality.
   (E) A country's food production can be increased domestically only by banning imports.

112. John Tyler, James Buchanan, William H. Harrison, Millard Fillmore, and James Abram Garfield were all

(A) House speakers
(B) United States presidents
(C) movie stars
(D) New York City mayors
(E) newspaper publishers

113. Which one of the following statements is INCORRECT?

(A) Socialism developed in Europe in reaction to deplorable industrial conditions.
(B) India and China have the two largest human populations in the world.
(C) The potato blight of Ireland resulted in the deaths of about 1 million people from starvation and disease by the year 1851.
(D) Iran is one of the largest oil-producing countries in the Arab world.
(E) Miss Marple is a famous detective in fiction created by well-known mystery writer Agatha Christie.

114. Utopia is an imaginary island that serves as the subject and title of a book written by an English humanist. The fictitious island is represented as a seat of perfection in moral, social, and political life. The author of *Utopia* was

(A) Rudyard Kipling
(B) William Shakespeare
(C) Alfred Lord Tennyson
(D) Sir Thomas More
(E) T. S. Eliot

115. Epicurus (341 B.C.E.–270 B.C.E.) was the Greek philosopher who lent his name to an English word that signifies a person with refined taste in food and wine. This word is

(A) epicarp
(B) epicure
(C) epicene
(D) epiboly
(E) epicotyl

116. Which one of the following statements is factually INCORRECT?

(A) Trygve Li of Norway was the first secretary general of the United Nations, holding office from 1946 to 1951.
(B) The American Revolution began in 1775 with the Battle of Lexington and Concord, and it ended with the British surrender at Yorktown in 1781.
(C) The French Revolution began when a Paris mob stormed the Bastille in 1789.
(D) Karl Marx was a political philosopher who advocated the merits of capitalism and private property.
(E) Risorgimento was a nationalist movement led by the middle classes and nobility for the political unification of Italy between 1859 and 1870.

117. The sales tax is criticized by some because such a tax is considered

(A) progressive
(B) regressive
(C) proportional
(D) incomprehensible
(E) ineffective

118. The "greatest happiness of the greatest number" was the philosophy of utilitarianism founded by an English philosopher who lived from 1748 to 1832. His name was

(A) Roger Bacon
(B) Jeremy Bentham
(C) John Locke
(D) Thomas Hobbes
(E) John Knox

119. Alfred B. Nobel (1833–1896), the Swedish chemist who established the prestigious annual Nobel Prizes for physics, chemistry, literature, physiology or medicine, and peace, was also an inventor. He invented

(A) the stethoscope
(B) the kidney machine
(C) the microscope
(D) dynamite
(E) the X-ray machine

GO ON TO THE NEXT PAGE

120. The first transplant of a human heart was considered a miracle of modern medicine when it was performed by a South African surgeon in 1967. His name was

(A) Michael de Bakey
(B) Christian Fletcher
(C) William Beaumont
(D) Bernard Lee
(E) Christiaan Barnard

121. "Mahatma" is a Hindu title of respect for a man renowned for spirituality and high-mindedness. It was applied to an internationally renowned Indian spiritual leader, best known for preaching the concept of civil disobedience and nonviolent protest, and whose teachings influenced civil rights leader, Martin Luther King Jr. He was

(A) Jawaharlal Nehru
(B) Mohandas Gandhi
(C) Morarji Desai
(D) Indira Gandhi
(E) Swami Vivokanada

122. Napoléon Bonaparte, the one-time invincible emperor of France, was eventually defeated by an Englishman at the famous Battle of Waterloo in 1815. This Englishman was

(A) Lord Nelson
(B) Sir Warren Hastings
(C) the Duke of Wellington
(D) Lord Mountbatten
(E) Sir Alec Guinness

123. The religion of the Jewish people is the world's oldest great monotheistic faith and the parent religion of both Christianity and Islam. The name of this religion is

(A) Taoism
(B) Zionism
(C) Polytheism
(D) Judaism
(E) Zoroastrianism

124. The Soviet Union launched the world's first artificial satellite in 1957, initiating the Space Age. The satellite was called

(A) *Pravda*
(B) *Betamax*
(C) *Sputnik*
(D) *Soyuz*
(E) *Vostok I*

125. The Treaty of Versailles, which ended World War I, was negotiated in 1919 by four leaders of the time: Georges Clemenceau (France), Lloyd George (England), Virrotio Orlando (Italy), and

(A) Warren G. Harding
(B) Richard M. Nixon
(C) Woodrow Wilson
(D) Thomas Jefferson
(E) Calvin Coolidge

STOP If you finish before the time is up, you may check your work on this section only. Do not turn to any other section in the test.

PRETEST ANSWER KEY AND EXPLANATIONS

PART I

1. B	13. A	25. A	37. C	49. A
2. E	14. E	26. E	38. B	50. D
3. E	15. D	27. C	39. C	51. A
4. A	16. B	28. E	40. A	52. C
5. A	17. A	29. A	41. C	53. A
6. C	18. B	30. E	42. A	54. A
7. A	19. A	31. C	43. E	55. C
8. E	20. E	32. C	44. D	56. B
9. A	21. C	33. A	45. C	57. E
10. E	22. C	34. C	46. C	58. D
11. A	23. B	35. E	47. B	59. A
12. A	24. A	36. B	48. A	60. E

PART II

61. D	74. C	87. A	100. A	113. D
62. C	75. A	88. D	101. C	114. D
63. A	76. B	89. C	102. E	115. B
64. D	77. B	90. E	103. D	116. D
65. B	78. A	91. E	104. A	117. B
66. A	79. A	92. D	105. D	118. B
67. E	80. D	93. B	106. A	119. D
68. B	81. B	94. E	107. C	120. E
69. E	82. A	95. D	108. E	121. B
70. B	83. D	96. A	109. E	122. C
71. B	84. A	97. B	110. D	123. D
72. D	85. C	98. E	111. B	124. C
73. C	86. D	99. A	112. B	125. C

PART I

1. **The correct answer is (B).** Repeatedly reissued and modified by John's successors, the Magna Carta became a symbol of superiority of the law over the king and his prerogatives. In later history, some of the features essential to democratic governments have been traced to the Magna Carta.

2. **The correct answer is (E).** The name "New York" derives from the English monarch Charles II, granting his brother James, the Duke of York, all territory between what is now known as Connecticut and Maryland. Interestingly enough, the Duke did not interfere with Dutch life in the area. Dutch settlers eventually adjusted to English rule.

3. **The correct answer is (E).** The stamp tax was "direct" in that it was obviously a "public" tax (stamps were attached to all kinds of public documents and publications), not a "hidden" tax, such as trade duties. The purpose of the stamp tax was to raise revenue for the British Empire, i.e., to ask Americans to help in meeting the costs of the empire's administration.

4. **The correct answer is (A).** The Pilgrims originally intended to settle in Virginia territory but actually made landfall on the northern tip of Cape Cod. This new location encouraged them to develop a plan of self-government.

5. **The correct answer is (A).** It contained fifteen parts, ranging in subject from territorial dispositions to restrictions on armaments.

6. **The correct answer is (C).** The Tudor rulers named in the question ruled from 1485 through 1603.

7. **The correct answer is (A).** Institutionalized slavery in America began in the South.

8. **The correct answer is (E).** "Vatican City," which houses the Vatican, is actually a small sovereign state of slightly more than 100 acres.

9. **The correct answer is (A).** The thirteen colonies were: New Hampshire, Massachusetts, Rhode Island, Connecticut, New York, New Jersey, Pennsylvania, Maryland, Delaware, Virginia, North Carolina, South Carolina, and Georgia.

10. **The correct answer is (E).** The Bastille was the notorious prison in Paris. The storming of the Bastille symbolized the collapse of the old order in France. The French Revolution was followed by the rise of Napoléon Bonaparte as emperor of France in 1804.

11. **The correct answer is (A).** By 1820, the population had grown to nearly 10 million. By 1840, the American population had reached 17 million.

12. **The correct answer is (A).** Infamous gangsters such as "Scarface" Al Capone of Chicago were further symbols of these Prohibition-era massacres.

13. **The correct answer is (A).** Since the United Nations moved to New York City, its membership has grown significantly over the years. By 2002, the total membership of the United Nations approached 191.

14. **The correct answer is (E).** The Truman Doctrine also committed the United States to supporting all free people who were "resisting attempted subjugation by armed minorities or outside pressures."

15. **The correct answer is (D).** Lindbergh's flight took 33 hours and transformed him into an American hero. Lindbergh's success also hastened the era of civilian passenger flights.

16. **The correct answer is (B).** The Jamestown, Virginia, settlers would probably have perished if not for the leadership of Smith, who understood the need to build shelter, grow food, and trade with the Indians.

17. **The correct answer is (A).** The Republic of Ireland is a separate nation. Note that in recent years, nationalists in both Wales and Scotland have argued for independence.

18. **The correct answer is (B).** Philadelphia was where the Continental Congress met, so it was natural that the Declaration of Independence would be written and eventually signed in that city.

19. **The correct answer is (A).** Theodore Roosevelt believed a president could transform America into a global police officer and that the world could progress much as America had. His ability to mediate an end to the Russo–Japanese War won him a Nobel Peace Prize.

20. **The correct answer is (E).** Even though Parliament refused the Chartist (workers) demands, virtually all eventually became law. Those original demands included universal manhood suffrage, the secret ballot, and annually elected Parliaments, among others.

21. **The correct answer is (C).** The Archduke (heir to the throne of Austria-Hungary) and his wife were assassinated by a Serbian nationalist, Gavrilo Princip. Austria-Hungary delivered an ultimatum to Serbia. When Serbia refused to comply, Austria-Hungary declared war on Serbia, and soon the other great states of Europe became involved, thus ushering in the devastating conflict known as World War I.

22. **The correct answer is (C).** The British General Cornwallis was trapped at Yorktown and forced to surrender due to the cooperation between American land troops and French naval forces.

23. **The correct answer is (B).** The nationalist movement called Risorgimento was spearheaded by leaders such as Mazzini, Count Cavour, and Garibaldi.

24. **The correct answer is (A).** The Union of Soviet Socialist Republics (USSR) would endure until its breakup in 1991.

25. **The correct answer is (A).** Jefferson was a member of the committee appointed by the Continental Congress on July 2, 1776, to write the Declaration of Independence. The Declaration was adopted by the Congress two days later.

26. **The correct answer is (E).** The British were the colonial rulers of India. The Indian Mutiny symbolized one of the first attempts to openly resist British rule in India.

27. **The correct answer is (C).** The Irish potato blight and crop failures in Germany compelled these immigrants to flee to America.

28. **The correct answer is (E).** Even though Geneva, Switzerland, is the home of many United Nations agencies, successive Swiss governments had in the past refused to join the United Nations on the grounds that it would contravene their neutrality. However, on September 10, 2002, Switzerland changed its policy and joined the United Nations.

29. **The correct answer is (A).** A land bridge (of ice) existed between Asia and North America some 75,000 years ago in the area of the Bering Strait. Ancestors of the Indians used this bridge to enter the New World.

30. **The correct answer is (E).** The American War of Independence was the climax to the conflict between Great Britain and thirteen of its colonies.

31. **The correct answer is (C).** Thomas Paine convinced many that separation was not only inevitable but right and just.

32. **The correct answer is (C).** Amerigo Vespucci (1454–1512) is the correct answer. The name *America* is said to be derived from *Amerigo*.

33. **The correct answer is (A).** The Treaty of Westphalia established the principle of state sovereignty while also allowing each German prince to determine the religious beliefs of his subjects.

34. **The correct answer is (C).** The market value is measured only once, at the point of final sale. The value of inventories at the end of the period is included, but these inventories are subtracted from the subsequent period's product. GNP figures in the United States are prepared by the Department of Commerce.

35. **The correct answer is (E).** Nations often retaliate against the practice. For example, Mexico found that China was "dumping" Chinese shoes onto its national market, and so the Mexican government promptly placed an added duty of 1,105 percent on those shoes, thus making their cost so high that Mexican consumers would not buy them.

36. **The correct answer is (B).** In 1993, the Bank defined *developing countries* as those whose GNP per capita averaged less than $8,600 annually. In that year, the U.S. figure was nearly $25,000.

37. **The correct answer is (C).** Protectionism is usually designed to protect a nation's own industries from international competition.

38. **The correct answer is (B).** Countries that are members of the International Monetary Fund register the value of their currency in terms of gold or the United States dollar and agree to maintain the value, plus or minus 1 percent. They also agree not to devalue their currency by more than 10 percent without agreement of the board of directors of the International Monetary Fund.

39. **The correct answer is (C).** As implied in the question, the consumer price index, or CPI, is used mainly to calculate the annual inflation rate each year. The recent prices of goods and services are compared to an earlier base period, thereby showing the percentage change in overall cost.

40. **The correct answer is (A).** Two broad economic principles underlie capitalism: a nation's welfare should be measured by its total annual production and each individual, if left in freedom, will do everything possible to maximize his or her own property.

41. **The correct answer is (C).** The plan lasted from 1948 to 1952 under a $13-billion appropriation by the Congress. Basically, the United States supplied materials, technical advice, and money, while the participating countries were responsible for planning the details of recovery.

42. **The correct answer is (A).** Compared to the "developed" nations of the world, where there is usually adequate health care, a decent standard of living, and pervasive literacy, many of the less developed countries suffer from poor health care, extensive poverty, and pervasive illiteracy.

43. **The correct answer is (E).** Karl Marx argued that workers were exploited by their capitalist employers, since the amount of value they produced was deserving of much higher wages, not the incredibly low wages that they were actually paid.

44. **The correct answer is (D).** In the United States, inflation is commonly measured in terms of the wholesale price index or the consumer price index, both prepared by the Bureau of Labor Statistics.

45. **The correct answer is (C).** Floating exchange rates meant that a nation's currency would find its true international value based upon global supply-and-demand relationships.

46. **The correct answer is (C).** The laissez-faire doctrine is most frequently traced to the writings of Adam Smith.

47. **The correct answer is (B).** When supply drops and demand increases substantially, the price goes up. If the reverse occurred, then the price would go down.

48. **The correct answer is (A).** The "iron law of wages" implied that wage levels would keep workers mired in perpetual poverty. However, in reality, American workers' wages have increased to the point that the vast majority of workers enjoy a decent, middle-class standard of living.

49. **The correct answer is (A).** Other terms used for "financial crashes" have been "panics" or "depressions." A depression is a lengthier and far more serious economic condition than a recession.

50. **The correct answer is (D).** At one time during the Great Depression, nearly one fourth of the workforce was unemployed.

51. **The correct answer is (A).** Tariff relations between the United States and other countries are overseen by the Tariff Commission.

52. **The correct answer is (C).** The cause of inflation is too much money purchasing too few goods. When money supply increases, people tend to use their excess funds to bid up the price of goods, which is also called demand-pull inflation. This phenomenon usually occurs during wars and when the government is creating large quantities of money to meet its growing expenditures. Inflation can also occur when governments operate deficit budgets.

53. **The correct answer is (A).** Taft not only believed in using dollars instead of bullets to ensure stability, but he also wanted American investments to replace European capital in Latin America, thus enhancing American influence in that region.

54. **The correct answer is (A).** Under an embargo, ships of the embargoed country are either detained in port or banned from entering the port.

55. **The correct answer is (C).** The most-favored-nation (MFN) principle promotes free trade among nations in that tariff preferences granted to one state must be given to all others that export the same product.

56. **The correct answer is (B).** The Federal Reserve System is responsible for monetary policy within an economy with relatively full employment, stable prices, and economic growth.

57. **The correct answer is (E).** The International Monetary Fund was founded in Washington, D.C., in December 1945. Membership in the Fund is a prerequisite to membership in the World Bank.

58. **The correct answer is (D).** A stronger dollar makes American exports more expensive, so sales of those exports may go down along with profits of American manufacturers.

59. **The correct answer is (A).** The balance of payments is computed by figuring the difference between total payments and total receipts during a specific period of time.

60. **The correct answer is (E).** A "bull market" investor expects stocks or other securities to increase in value (a "bull" butts upward). A "bear" (a "bear" claws downward) investor expects prices to go down.

PART II

61. **The correct answer is (D).** SDRs encourage the growth of international liquidity by means other than increasing the outflow of dollars from the United States.

62. **The correct answer is (C).** Akhenaton (also called Amenhotep IV) decreed that Egyptians should worship only the solar deity Aton. He closed down the temples of other local gods. Akhenaton's conception of Aton was that of a universal god rather than that of an exclusively Egyptian deity.

63. **The correct answer is (A).** Anders Celsius (1701–1744) devised the thermometric scale used by most scientists today. In this scale, the temperature interval between the freezing and boiling points of water is divided into 100 degrees. The "centigrade scale" is now usually called the Celsius scale (abbreviated as "C").

64. **The correct answer is (D).** The Dow Jones Industrial Average uses the average prices of thirty major stocks. Any changes are expressed in terms of "points" rather than "dollars" (each point is equivalent to one dollar).

65. **The correct answer is (B).** The United Nations logo shows the various world continents surrounded by olive branches, the symbols of peace.

66. **The correct answer is (A).** Germany ranked third.

67. **The correct answer is (E).** Yoga has also become an attractive method of self-relaxation to many Americans.

68. **The correct answer is (B).** With the help of President Jimmy Carter, Sadat and Begin signed the Camp David Accords, an agreement that formally established peace between Egypt and Israel.

69. **The correct answer is (E).** Inflation in Germany during the 1920s was a contributing factor to the rise of Hitler and Nazism.

70. **The correct answer is (B).** Residents of Hong Kong feared that the new Chinese government would interfere with their thriving system of capitalism and civil liberties.

71. **The correct answer is (B).** Liberia is Africa's oldest independent republic, founded by freed Negro slaves from the United States in the early 1880s.

72. **The correct answer is (D).** Russia feared that if Chechnya was successful in its independence bid, then other regions in the Russian federation might try to secede.

73. **The correct answer is (C).** The Philippines was discovered in 1521 by Magellan. By 1571, the Spanish assumed control and ruled it as a colony for the next 300 years. The country was ceded to the United States following the Spanish–American War in 1898.

74. **The correct answer is (C).** If the same procedure were followed in the United States, it would be roughly analogous to Congress choosing the president. Voters in America not only choose the president directly but also cast separate votes for their senator or representative. In Great Britain, a new majority party in the House of Commons means a new prime minister.

75. **The correct answer is (A).** The framers of the Constitution believed that justice could best be served and tyranny avoided if the functions of government were parceled out among three branches of government, namely executive, legislative, and judicial.

76. **The correct answer is (B).** Congress allows the president to issue executive orders to establish or modify the practices of administrative agencies, to enforce legislative statutes, and to enforce the Constitution or treaties with foreign powers. As a point of fact, the privilege of issuing executive orders increases the legislative power of the president.

77. **The correct answer is (B).** The veto provides the president with considerable powers over legislative programs. It is rare for Congress to override a presidential veto, owing to the difficulty of getting a two-thirds majority.

78. **The correct answer is (A).** The whip is expected to maintain a close liaison with his or her party's representatives, sound them out on various issues before the House, and make sure they are present during voting time.

79. **The correct answer is (A).** The first ten amendments to the Constitution, which constitute the Bill of Rights, protect certain liberties of the people against encroachment by the national government.

80. **The correct answer is (D).** In the early nineteenth century, members of Congress caucused to choose their party's nominee for the presidency. Currently, the caucus is used by Democratic members of both houses of Congress to choose party leaders and make decisions on pending issues. The Republicans use the word *conferences* to call similar meetings.

81. **The correct answer is (B).** It is the name commonly used to describe the practice of state delegations nominating for the presidency their own political leaders, usually their governors, at the national convention.

82. **The correct answer is (A).** Delegates to national nominating conventions are "won" by presidential candidates through two major avenues—caucuses and the more numerous presidential primaries.

83. **The correct answer is (D).** The candidate who receives the greatest number of popular votes in a state wins all of that state's electoral votes.

84. **The correct answer is (A).** Double jeopardy prevents the state from trying someone over and over again in order to obtain a conviction. However, an individual who committed a crime that broke both state and federal laws could be tried in a state court and, if found innocent, then be tried for the offense in a federal court.

85. **The correct answer is (C).** In broadcasting, "equal-time provision" is a law embodied in the Federal Communications Act of 1934 requiring a station that allots free time to a particular candidate to allot the same amount of free time to all candidates for the same office.

86. **The correct answer is (D).** A filibuster can occur only in the U.S. Senate. Filibusters are usually employed by a minority of senators who wish to prevent the entire Senate from voting on a bill. Filibusters can be ended through a cloture vote by three fifths of the Senate.

87. **The correct answer is (A).** The name is derived from the five-sided structure that has become synonymous with the United States military establishment.

88. **The correct answer is (D).** The fifteen departments are state, treasury, defense, justice, interior, agriculture, commerce, labor, health and human services, housing and urban development, transportation, energy, homeland security, education, and veterans' affairs.

89. **The correct answer is (C).** The jury system was considered so essential to liberty that it was guaranteed by the Seventh Amendment and the state constitutions.

90. **The correct answer is (E).** Congress is a bicameral, or two-house, national legislature.

91. **The correct answer is (E).** Members of the House are elected for two-year terms from congressional districts.

92. **The correct answer is (D).** The Brown decision finally overturned the doctrine of "separate but equal," enunciated in the 1896 ruling of *Plessy v. Ferguson*.

93. **The correct answer is (B).** This amendment was initiated by Republicans in Congress who felt that President Roosevelt's twelve years in office (elected to four terms) had constituted too much time in the Oval Office.

94. **The correct answer is (E).** A grand jury's indictment means that this jury feels there is enough evidence to warrant a trial jury. Typically, a grand jury consists of twenty-three people.

95. **The correct answer is (D).** Recent chief justices have included Earl Warren (1953-1969), Warren E. Burger (1969-1986), and William H. Rehnquist (1986 to the present).

96. **The correct answer is (A).** Generally, the summons must be personally delivered to the defendant.

97. **The correct answer is (B).** The Fifth Amendment ensures that no person shall be compelled in any criminal case to be a witness against himself or herself.

98. **The correct answer is (E).** The act superseded the Disclosure of Information Act (1966). The new act made exemptions in the following areas: national defense, confidential financial information, law enforcement files, and certain personnel files, in addition to information whose disclosure was prohibited by statute. The act has been criticized on the grounds that government agencies circumvented the law by reclassifying their policies under the permitted exemptions.

99. **The correct answer is (A).** The exclusionary rule is controversial, with opponents claiming that it can interfere with the prosecution and conviction of truly guilty people. In recent years, the Supreme Court has relaxed this rule, allowing "good faith" exceptions to be made by the police.

100. **The correct answer is (A).** In the 1966 decision, the majority in the Warren Court declared that henceforth the suspect should be immediately informed of his or her right to a court-appointed lawyer, his or her right to remain silent under questioning, and right to be informed that anything he or she does say may be used as evidence against him or her during the trial. The minority complained that the majority was distorting the Constitution by placing the rights of the individual criminal suspect above the rights of society as a whole.

101. **The correct answer is (C).** During the Cold War, the First World referred to affluent industrialized countries such as the United States, France, and Great Britain. The Second World referred to the socialist bloc of China, the Soviet Union, and Eastern Europe. The Third World referred to the poorer, developing countries of Asia, Africa, and Latin America.

102. **The correct answer is (E).** Followers of Islam today number more than one billion worldwide.

103. **The correct answer is (D).** Forced to leave Kuwait, Iraqi forces set the Kuwaiti oil fields afire. It took months for those fires to be extinguished.

104. **The correct answer is (A).** Three Mile Island is in Pennsylvania, and an accident at the nuclear power plant there did release radioactive contamination. Chernobyl (in the former Soviet Union) was a true disaster, with released radioactivity killing thousands and spreading fallout to Europe.

105. **The correct answer is (D).** The kind of journalism promoted by Hearst involved reporting scandals, violence, and disasters of various sorts. It even contributed to the Spanish–American War's outbreak in 1898. The term "yellow journalism" may have come from the inexpensive yellow paper used by Hearst publications.

106. **The correct answer is (A).** Castro is the leader of Cuba and has been in power since 1959.

107. **The correct answer is (C).** World War II occurred from 1939-1945. The four other wars all came after 1945.

108. **The correct answer is (E).** An ancient language of India belonging to the Indic branch of the Indo-Iranian subfamily of Indo-European languages, Sanskrit was the language of the Vedas, the Hindu sacred writings.

109. The correct answer is (E). David Livingstone (1813–1873) was a Scottish medical missionary-explorer in Central Africa. The others were all inventors or discoverers: Janssen (microscope), Funk (vitamins), de Bakey (first use of artificial heart for circulating blood during heart surgery), and Roentgen (X-rays).

110. The correct answer is (D). Sureté Générale relates to France, Scotland Yard is the famed British law enforcement unit, the Mounted Police is Canadian, and the International Court is not a police organization.

111. The correct answer is (B). In plain English, Malthus predicted that the growth in population would eventually outstrip the supply of food. Famine would result.

112. The correct answer is (B). These men were all presidents during the nineteenth century.

113. The correct answer is (D). Iran is not Arab but Persian.

114. The correct answer is (D). The others were famous poets, playwrights, or novelists who never wrote a utopian treatise.

115. The correct answer is (B). Epicurus also advanced a philosophy that advocated freedom from pain and emotional strife.

116. The correct answer is (D). Karl Marx was a German philosopher and political economist who predicted the historical victory of communism, the abolition of the concept of private property, and the destruction of capitalism.

117. The correct answer is (B). A sales tax is considered regressive because high-income persons usually spend a smaller share of their income than is the case with poorer people.

118. The correct answer is (B). This ethical theory is also associated with the English philosopher John Stuart Mill. Utilitarianism also states that if something is useful, then it has essential goodness or value.

119. The correct answer is (D). Nobel's invention was obviously destructive, so his way of reconciling that invention was to establish a reward for creativity that would benefit, and not harm, humanity.

120. The correct answer is (E). Since 1967, heart transplants have become accepted medical practice, with such operations saving, or at least extending, the lives of people who otherwise would have died.

121. The correct answer is (B). Gandhi's doctrine of nonviolent resistance eventually forced the British out of India; Martin Luther King Jr. employed similar tactics in the American South during the turbulent era of civil rights demonstrations.

122. The correct answer is (C). The Battle of Waterloo in Belgium ended any chance of Napoléon's regaining power, and he was eventually sent into exile on the tiny south Atlantic Ocean island of St. Helena. He died there in 1821.

123. The correct answer is (D). Today, the United States has the world's largest Jewish population, with approximately 6 million Jews living in the country.

124. The correct answer is (C). In Russian, the word sputnik meant "fellow traveler of Earth." Concerned about Russian space advances, the United States began spending more money on rocket research and educational programs in science and mathematics.

125. The correct answer is (C). Woodrow Wilson, the American president, was forced to make concessions regarding the Treaty of Versailles' provisions in order to ensure acceptance of his League of Nations. Unfortunately, the U.S. Senate rejected the treaty and U.S. membership in the League.

Chapter 12
OVERVIEW

ECONOMICS
MACROECONOMICS

Macroeconomics is the branch of economics that deals with the whole economy. It is chiefly concerned with aggregates—aggregate or total demand by households, aggregate or total supply of output by businesses, aggregate or total income earned by households and businesses, and aggregate or total employment in the economy.

CIRCULAR FLOW OF INCOME

The circular flow of income is the number of times a dollar flows from households to businesses or expenditures on output, which is goods produced by the economy. Business returns dollars to households in the form of income, which is payments for services rendered. Following is an illustration of the circular flow of income, showing the relationship between households and businesses.

GROSS NATIONAL PRODUCT

The Gross National Product (GNP) is the market value of all final goods and services produced in the economy in one year.

GROSS NATIONAL INCOME

Gross National Income is the total monetary value of all incomes earned in producing a year's Gross National Product. The GNP includes

1. wages and salaries

2. corporate profits before taxes
3. income from unincorporated enterprises or proprietor's income
4. interest paid by businesses for bonds, mortgages, and insurance
5. rental income

FOUR-SECTOR ECONOMY

The American economy consists of four sectors:

$$C + I + G + X = \text{Gross National Product}$$

C = Personal Consumption Expenditures by Households or Consumers

Households may be defined as persons living alone and families. They purchase (1) nondurable goods (food, clothing, beverages), (2) durable goods (appliances, automobiles, etc.), and (3) services (health, education, transportation, and legal).

I = Investment Expenditures by Businesses

Economists define investment expenditures by businesses as: (1) new plant and equipment; (2) new residential construction; and (3) additions to business inventories.

G = Government Purchases of Goods and Services

The government offers collective goods and services that benefit all citizens in a society (e.g., roads, schools, and defense). It hires private firms to produce these goods. The government also hires individuals to perform services to the community (e.g., president, members of Congress, postal clerks, secretaries, judges, police, fire fighters, and teachers).

X = Exports

Exports are goods produced in the United States, the demand for which comes from citizens of other nations. Imports are foreign-made goods demanded by Americans.

$$C + I = \text{the private sector of the economy}$$
$$G = \text{the public sector of the economy}$$
$$X = \text{the foreign sector or international trade}$$

The Gross National Product is measured in monetary terms. The selling price of every final good and service is recorded in the year's GNP. This is why the GNP is often referred to as the nation's cash register.

FISCAL POLICY

Fiscal policy is action taken by the government to affect employment and prices. An important objective of national economic policy is to achieve full employment with price stability. Fiscal policy includes the raising and lowering of taxes, money borrowed from the public through the sale of bonds, and government expenditures on goods and services.

To lower unemployment, the government would:

1. increase government expenditures
2. lower taxes
3. increase borrowing

To reduce inflation, the government would:

1. decrease government expenditures
2. increase taxes
3. decrease borrowing

GOVERNMENT TRANSFER PAYMENT

This is a payment that is made by the government to an individual for which no good or service is returned (e.g., pension benefits, welfare-assistance payments, and Social Security payments to retired persons). A transfer payment differs from a government purchase in that a transfer payment is not a payment for a good or a service, whereas a government purchase is a payment made in return for a good or a service.

MONEY

What is money? Money is a means by which individuals exchange goods and services. It places a value on products produced in the economy.

What kinds of money exist in the American economy?

1. fractional currency (coins)
2. paper money (Federal Reserve notes)
3. demand deposits (checking and savings accounts)
4. near money (stocks, bonds, insurance policies). Near money cannot be used for purchase of goods and services. It can be converted into coins and paper money for the purpose of purchase transactions.

What is meant by the "money supply"? The most common definition of "money supply" is currency (coins and paper money) and demand deposits (checking accounts).

What is the difference between government money and demand deposits? Federal reserve notes and coins are created by the government. A demand deposit is bank-created money. A depositor who has opened a checking account with a bank can demand coins and paper money up to and including the amount deposited in the account.

What is "monetary policy"? Monetary policy deals with the supply of money in circulation during a given period of time.

Who determines the amount of money in circulation during any given period of time? Essentially, the public (households and businesses) does this by making a decision whether to hold money in its savings or checking accounts or to draw down on savings or checking accounts. The government cannot legally or morally affect the supply of money by use of a printing press.

What is the function of the Federal Reserve Bank? The Federal Reserve Bank is a semi-independent institution created in 1913 to regulate the supply of money in circulation. The chairman of the Federal Reserve Board is appointed by the president of the United States, with the consent of the Senate. There are twelve Federal Reserve Banks, and the Federal Reserve Bank has jurisdiction over commercial banks in its district. Commercial banks earn their profits through the loans they make to households and businesses, but the Federal Reserve Bank limits their lending potential (their ability to write checks) to the amount they hold in their checking accounts, so the commercial banks must have enough money in reserves with the local Federal Reserve Bank to cover their checks for loans. The U.S. Treasury Department holds its deposits with the Federal Reserve Board, which is also the central bank of the United States.

How does the Federal Reserve Board regulate a commercial bank's lending potential? The objective of the monetary policy is to make sure there is the right amount of money in the economy to ensure full employment with price stability. No one is certain as to what amount constitutes the "right amount of money" in the economy at a given time. However, the Federal Reserve Board makes use of three tools to regulate the supply of money in the economy:

1. Buy or sell securities. The Federal Reserve Banks enter the market to buy securities in order to increase the supply of money. The Bank will sell securities if the Board wishes to reduce the supply of money in the economy.

2. Raise or lower the *reserve ratio*. Every bank that is a member of the Federal Reserve System must keep a percentage of its demand deposits on hand with a Federal Reserve Bank. No bank is permitted by law to dip into these reserves. Suppose the reserve ratio is 20 percent. Therefore, with a $100 demand deposit, the bank must keep $20 as required reserve (20 percent of $100). Should the reserve ratio be raised to 25 percent, then the required reserve is $25. With a 20 percent reserve ratio, the bank is able to lend $80. This represents the bank's excess reserve. With a reserve ratio of 25 percent, the bank's excess reserve is $75.

3. Raise or lower the *discount rate*. Very often a member bank is short of excess reserves. In that case, it may be forced to borrow money from the Federal Reserve Bank. In return for the loan to the commercial bank, the Federal Reserve Bank will charge it "interest." The interest on a loan by a bank from the Federal Reserve is called the "discount rate."

MONETARY POLICY

To increase demand, which might lower the rate of unemployment, the Federal Reserve would:

1. buy securities
2. lower the reserve ratio
3. lower the discount rate

To reduce demand to lower the rate of inflation, the Federal Reserve would:

1. sell securities
2. raise the reserve ratio
3. raise the discount rate

ECONOMIC GROWTH

Economic growth refers to the annual rate of increase in output and income. The rate of economic growth is dependent on the rate of investment spending (purchases of machines, tools, tractors, transportation, etc.) and technology.

The rate of growth is also dependent upon political and social conditions and upon the attitude of society toward increased industrial expansion.

ECONOMIC EFFICIENCY

An economic system is efficient when it obtains the maximum amount of output at the least possible cost. It attempts to avoid the unemployment and underemployment of resources.

UNEMPLOYMENT OF RESOURCES

This refers to resources that are not utilized in production. Resources are also referred to as *factors of production*. The factors of production include:

1. land
2. labor
3. capital (machines, tools)
4. managerial ability (the manager or employer combines and organizes his or her factors of production in such a way as to get maximum output from each and every factor of production)

UNDEREMPLOYMENT OF RESOURCES

This refers to resources that are not employed in their best possible uses; for example, land suitable for cotton production is used for growing wheat, or a skilled machinist is put to work on a drill press.

DIMINISHING RETURNS

This condition is reached when each additional resource, such as labor put to work on a fixed parcel of land, tends to produce less and less output or when each additional worker employed on a machine in a factory adds less and less to the total production.

ECONOMICS OF SCALE OR INCREASING RETURNS TO SCALE

If all factors of production were doubled, then output would more than double. Finding new sources of energy, buying additional plants and equipment, and promoting a change in the level of technology are some examples of putting economies of scale into practice.

ECONOMICS

Economics is generally defined as the study of the method by which a society uses its available resources to satisfy society's wants and needs. This would also include a citizen's interest in finding employment, taxes, and the amount of income available to buy those goods and services that would satisfy an individual citizen's needs.

BUSINESS CYCLES

Business cycles are patterns of expansion and contraction in business activity. There are four phases of the business cycle.

1. Recovery

This occurs after an economy has reached its lowest point. Inventories are low; interest rates on bank loans are low; costs of production are down. Businesspeople are encouraged to expand their plants and equipment. They hire more employees, and the resulting rise in employment encourages more spending.

2. Prosperity

The economy is at full employment. Spending by households and businesses is at a record high. There is also an increased demand for credit. Profits are also high.

3. Recession

Businesspeople cut back on production and tend to lay off more workers. Inventories begin to accumulate, which is a signal that consumers are buying cautiously. Profit margins begin to decline, while interest rates on loans begin to increase.

4. Depression

There is a widespread unemployment of people and machines. Profits are low. Demands for loans decrease. Many firms are forced either to cut back on operations or shut down completely.

INFLATION

What is inflation? Inflation refers to rising prices. Historically, prices have risen since the American Revolution. Up until recently, prices have risen gently by 2 percent or 3 percent each year. In the 1960s, the inflation rate was about 10 percent. (Things cost 10 percent more than they had the year before.)

What causes inflation? Demand-pull inflation occurs when the demand for goods is in excess of their supply. Firms may already be working to plant capacity and have no means to meet the excessive demand. Another explanation for inflation may be cost-push, whereby the cost of hiring resources is excessively high. Wages, for example, may be high, relative to the productivity of the worker. Costs of plant and equipment and raw materials may also rise sharply.

What are the results of inflation? Inflation, generally speaking, hurts everyone. Wages and salaries do not always keep pace with the rise in prices. This tends to reduce the purchasing power of the dollar. Last year's dollar, for example, may have enabled a consumer to purchase four items. To purchase the same four items in the current year, the consumer might pay $1.50. In other words, *real income* has declined. Real income is defined as the number of goods and services an individual can purchase with a dollar. People on fixed incomes are especially hurt by inflation, although Social Security payments to retired persons have managed to keep in line with rising prices.

How do we measure the overall change in prices? The *Consumer Price Index* measures the change in prices from year to year. It compares current prices paid for goods and services with those purchased in a year in which prices were considered to be stable. The price index for the base year is said to be 100. Suppose that, during the current year, the consumer paid $120 for the same number of items he purchased for $100 in the base year. The Consumer Price Index is said to have risen by 20 percent.

SUPPLY AND DEMAND

SUPPLY

Supply refers to the amounts or quantities of goods that firms or producers are willing and able to produce during a given period of time.

DEMAND

Demand refers to the amounts or quantities of goods consumers are willing and able to purchase at each and every price during a given period of time.

MICROECONOMICS

Microeconomics refers to economic decisions made by an individual consumer and an individual producer.

PRICE ELASTICITY OF DEMAND

This refers to the response of consumers to a change in price. Suppose a price is reduced by 20 percent, and the volume of sales increases by 40 percent; then, the firm knows consumers were responsive to a change in the price. Assume now that price goes up by 20 percent, and the volume of sales increases by only 10 percent; then, the firm also knows that consumers were responsive to a change in price.

REVENUE

Revenue refers to the selling price of an item. To a consumer, the amount paid for goods is the price. To a businessperson, the money received from the consumer is revenue.

PROFIT

Profit represents money that is left to the firm after costs of production have been deducted. Or:

Total Revenue minus Total Costs = Total Profit

PERFECT COMPETITION

This refers to a market in which there are many firms in an industry. It assumes that there is no interference by government or labor unions with pricing decisions. Prices and resource allocations are determined by the interaction of supply and demand. Since there are so many firms in an industry, no one firm has control over the price and the supply of output in a particular market. All firms within an industry, acting interdependently, determine price and output.

IMPERFECT COMPETITION

This refers to a market in which a single firm does have a large degree of control over price and output. The firm may be a monopoly—the only producer of the commodity. Or three or four firms may dominate an industry—such as automobile, steel, and detergent—to such an extent that they are in a position to determine price and output. This market condition is called an oligopoly.

SINGLE OWNERSHIP

An individual owns the enterprise. He or she alone is responsible for making decisions concerning the firm. A single owner is also liable for all debts incurred.

PARTNERSHIP

Two or more persons may enter into a partnership in order to make more money available for expansion. Each partner is liable for debts incurred by the firm. In some cases, the partnership may dissolve when one partner leaves the firm or is deceased.

CORPORATION

There is a separation of ownership and management. The owners of the firm's assets are the stockholders. Management operates the business and makes decisions as to price and output. More money is made available for research and development. Best of all, there is limited liability for all debts incurred by the firm.

TAXES

Taxes are revenue received by local, state, and federal governments to pay for collective goods and services.

TYPES OF TAXES

CAPITAL GAINS TAX

Tax on profits generated by selling property, including bonds, common stocks, and real estate.

DIRECT TAXES

Direct taxes are those that tax individuals. These include personal income tax, corporate income tax, gift and estate taxes, and inheritance taxes. *Indirect taxes* are those that tax specific goods. These include sales and excise taxes. A *sales tax* is a tax on the total amount of goods purchased. An *excise tax* is a tax on a specific commodity, such as luggage or jewelry.

FLAT TAX

This is a system of taxation where all income groups pay the same percentage of their income in taxes.

PROGRESSIVE TAX

This is a tax that is gradually increased as income increases. Personal and corporate income taxes are examples of progressive taxes.

PROPORTIONAL TAX

A proportional tax is one that taxes individuals at the same rate regardless of income. If the tax rate is 10 percent, then all incomes are taxed at the same rate. This type of tax tends to hurt individuals at lower rates of income.

REGRESSIVE TAX

A regressive tax is one whose rate declines as taxable income rises. Sales, payroll, and cigarette taxes are considered to be regressive. A person with a lower rate of income usually spends all of his or her income. Thus, all of his or her income is subject to the regressive sales tax, whereas a person at a higher level of income does not necessarily spend all of his or her income, therefore subjecting to the tax only what is spent.

INTERNATIONAL TRADE

Balance of Trade. Total of exports and imports of physical merchandise.

Favorable Balance of Trade. Exports of physical merchandise exceed imports of physical merchandise.

Balance of Payments. Monetary payments made by the United States to foreign countries and monetary payments made by foreign countries to the United States.

Foreign Exchange Rate. This refers to the price of foreign currency.

Floating or *Flexible Exchange Rate.* The price of foreign currency is determined by supply and demand.

Balance-of-Payments Deficit. A nation incurs a deficit in its balance of payments when it does not receive enough foreign currency to pay for its imports.

Visible Items. Visible items on a balance-of-payment statement refer to actual physical goods.

Invisible Items. Items such as purchases of securities, loans, shipping charges, and tourism are invisible items because they are not physical goods.

Appreciation. This refers to the increase in purchasing power of a currency relative to other currencies.

Depreciation. This refers to a decline in the purchasing power of a particular currency relative to other currencies.

Devaluation. Whereas appreciation and depreciation of currency are determined by supply and demand, devaluation is an official act of the government to depreciate its currency to attract foreign customers to its goods.

Free Trade. The international movement of goods free from tariff or non-tariff restrictions.

Protectionism. The use of tariffs (taxes on imports) and non-tariff barriers by a nation in order to restrict the flow of imports into the nation or to raise the price of those imports so as to make them non-competitive with comparable domestic products.

GATT, General Agreement on Tariffs and Trade. The world's primary organization that is dedicated to the expansion of free trade. The World Trade Organization superseded GATT in 1995.

WTO, World Trade Organization. The organization that replaced the GATT organization as the body that implements GATT, the treaty.

NAFTA. The North American Free Trade Agreement, consisting of a common market among the United States, Canada, and Mexico.

GEOGRAPHY

Geography is the study of our physical environment and our relation to it. It includes the study of climate and topography, natural resources, and bodies of water and examines how the natural environment affects where people, plants, and animals live.

What is meant by *natural environment*? The natural environment includes all the natural agents and processes in the world and can be broken down into the following elements:

1. landforms
2. minerals
3. native plant life
4. native animal life
5. oceans
6. coastal zones
7. soils
8. weather and climate
9. size of areas
10. size of regions

How does geography affect our way of life? The natural environment affects our patterns of living in the following ways:

1. transportation
2. dietary habits
3. occupations
4. clothing and housing patterns
5. political and social attitudes, values, and customs

MAJOR LANDFORMS

Mountain Range. A mountain range refers to a series or chain of mountains that extends over a large area, such as the Rocky and Sierra-Nevada Mountain Ranges in the United States or the Vosges and Jura Mountains in Europe.

Plains. A plains area is usually a flat area of low elevation. Most plains areas throughout the world are characterized by the types of vegetation found on them. Different kinds of plains areas are prairie, savanna, steppe, and pampas.

Plateau. A plateau rises well above sea level and is flat.

Escarpment. An escarpment is characterized by a steep slope at the edge of a plateau.

Island. This landform is surrounded on all sides by water and is smaller than a continental land mass.

Archipelago. An archipelago is a chain of islands within a larger body of water.

Peninsula. A peninsula is a landform that is surrounded on three sides by water. Italy and Korea are peninsulas.

WATER BODIES

Ocean. An ocean is a large body of water between continents.

Sea. Seas are bodies of salt water wholly or partly enclosed by land.

River. Rivers usually begin in areas of high land elevation and flow to lower-level areas. They are formed by fresh water from rain and snow and, in some areas, from melting glaciers.

CLIMATE

Climate and Weather. Climate refers to average weather conditions over a long period of time. Weather refers to a condition of the atmosphere for a specific period of time.

Tropical Rain Forest. Usually located in the equatorial regions of the world, it is typically characterized by a single season—very hot and very rainy, although there may be a "dry" season. Vegetation is abundant.

Tropical Desert. This is characterized by very long, hot summers, short winters, and very little rainfall. When rains do come, it is only for a short period of time. There is very little native animal or plant life in a tropical desert.

Tropical Steppe. In this climate, it is generally very hot throughout the year, and there is very little rainfall.

Tropical Savanna. This climate has two seasons: one hot and rainy, the other hot and dry. The land is characterized by tall grasses, few trees, and various types of wildlife.

Polar Ice Cap. This climate is found at the polar regions. The northern polar ice cap is located in an ocean region, while the southern polar ice cap extends over a broad continental land area. Temperatures are extremely low.

Tundra. The tundra regions are characterized by very long winters with large quantities of snow and short, cool summers.

Taiga. These are the northern forest lands, characterized by four seasons. Winters last for seven months, during which time temperatures are extremely low. Summers last for three months, and temperatures are moderate. Spring and autumn each last one month. Coniferous (cone-producing) trees grow here.

Humid Continental. This is usually located in the middle latitudes and is characterized by four seasons, with cold winters and hot summers. Precipitation occurs throughout the year. The world's most important agricultural areas are found in this region.

Humid Subtropical. This climate is characterized by heavy rainfall, extremely hot summers, and mild winters. During the winter, rainfall is generally light.

Marine. A marine climate has four seasons, with moderate temperatures throughout the year. Regions with a

POPULATION
Land Areas of the World

Area	Population (est.)	Percentage of Total Land Area	Approximate Land Area in Square Miles
Asia (includes Philippines, Indonesia, and Turkey)	3,403,451,000	18.2	10,644,000
Africa	721,472,000	20.0	11,707,000
North America (includes Central America and Caribbean region)	454,187,000	16.0	9,360,000
South America	319,553,000	11.8	6,883,000
Antarctica		10.3	6,000,000
Europe	509,254,000	3.3	1,905,000
Oceania (Australia, New Zealand, Polynesia)	28,680,000	5.6	3,284,000
Russia (and new independent republics)	297,508,000	14.8	8,647,000

PRINCIPAL OCEANS

Name	Area (Square Miles)
Pacific Ocean	64,000,000
Atlantic Ocean	31,815,000
Indian Ocean	25,300,000
Arctic Ocean	5,440,200

marine climate are usually located near large bodies of water. Rain falls throughout the year.

Mediterranean. This climate is usually found in the coastal areas of Europe, northwest Africa, and parts of southern California. It is characterized by two seasons: warm, dry summers and mild winters with heavy rainfall.

MAPS

What is a map? A map is a flattened rendering of the world. Mapmakers are known as cartographers.

Map Legend. A map legend, or key, is used to locate areas of interest in a particular area. It usually includes symbols for types of roads (e.g., multi-lane highways, paved or unpaved roads, state and U.S. highways, etc.), as well as other points of interest, such as lakes, campgrounds, and national parks.

Map Scale. A map is not an accurate picture of the area it represents. Therefore, a scale helps to measure distances and compare sizes and distances. All maps are drawn to scale, which means that an inch might represent 50, 75, 100, or even 1,000 miles. Measurements may be given in miles, nautical miles, kilometers, or other scales that are necessary for the type of map being used.

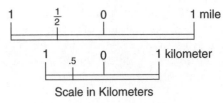

Scale in Miles

Scale in Kilometers

One inch equals 1 mile or 1.6093 kilometers

Latitude Lines. Latitude lines are imaginary lines that run in an east-west direction parallel to the equator. A line that is drawn from the North Pole to the equator (see longitude lines) forms a 90-degree angle with the equator. This north-south line also forms angles with other latitude lines. If the angle is 50 degrees, the latitude is said to be 50 degrees; if the angle is 40 degrees, the latitude is said to be 40 degrees.

Longitude Lines. Lines of longitude, also measured in degrees, are lines that run perpendicular to the equator, from the North Pole to the South Pole. The distance between longitudinal degrees is greatest at the equator and decreases as the lines approach the poles. Zero degrees longitude passes through Greenwich, a suburb of London, England, and is known as the Greenwich Meridian. West longitude is measured west of the Greenwich Meridian to 180 degrees longitude. East longitude is measured east from Greenwich, also to 180 degrees. Longitude is used to measure time all over the world. Earth rotates 15 degrees of longitude every hour, which amounts to a total of 360 degrees every 24 hours.

To interpret a map, follow these simple rules:

1. Read the title located at the bottom of the map.
2. Check the source of the map, e.g., U.S. Geological Survey.
3. Study the legend to determine the location of the points of interest.
4. Check the scale of miles to compare distances and areas.

POLITICAL SCIENCE

Political science studies the functioning of government in order to determine and understand the principles responsible for efficient government. The study of political science deals with such subjects as the Constitution; administration of laws; police activities; governments at local, state, and national levels; elections; political parties; minorities; taxation; finance; and international relations.

Since this is not a textbook, we are more concerned with the basic understanding of political science and how it relates to us. The easiest way to begin an overview of the United States's political direction is to look at our own Constitution.

THE U.S. CONSTITUTION
HISTORICAL BACKGROUND
The Constitutional Convention convened in Philadelphia in 1787. The purposes of the Convention are summarized in the Preamble to the document.

"We the People of the United States, in Order to form a more perfect Union, establish Justice, insure domestic Tranquility, provide for the common defence, promote the general Welfare, and secure the Blessings of Liberty to ourselves and our Posterity, do ordain and establish this Constitution for the United States of America."

There was general agreement that the government previously established under the Articles of Confederation was not wholly satisfactory. Many historians referred to this government as "government by supplication" since it did not delegate enough power to the central government. Under the Articles, all power resided with the states. Therefore, the central government could not regulate commerce, raise revenue through levying taxes, raise armies for national defense, formulate domestic and foreign policy, or coin money for economic stability without first seeking approval from the states.

In 1787, Alexander Hamilton, ever mindful of the deficiencies of the Articles, called for a meeting of the states in Annapolis, Maryland. At this meeting, Hamilton hoped to begin a revision of the Articles of Confederation, and it was generally agreed to hold another meeting in Philadelphia for the purpose of revising the existing government.

The 55 delegates who met in Philadelphia created a new government under the Constitution. Their objective was to create a republican form of government whose powers would be shared by the national government and the states. The new Constitution was also designed to give the central government more authority without encroaching on the political freedom of the states.

THE CONSTITUTION—
"A Bundle of Compromises"
Each of the 55 delegates at the Constitutional Convention represented different areas or sections of the United States. To reach agreement on the Constitution, it was necessary to compromise on the demands made by each group of delegates. The following plans illustrate why the Constitution has been called "a bundle of compromises."

VIRGINIA PLAN
Virginia, representing the large states, proposed that the population of each state should determine the number of representatives sent to Congress.

NEW JERSEY PLAN

New Jersey, representing the small states, proposed that each state should have equal representation in Congress.

CONNECTICUT COMPROMISE— GREAT COMPROMISE

Connecticut proposed the establishment of a two-house legislature. Each state would send two representatives to the Senate. This would guarantee that each state, large or small, would have equal power. The size of population would determine the number of representatives sent to the House of Representatives.

THREE-FIFTHS COMPROMISE

A question arose as to whether to include slaves as part of a state's population to determine its actual size for taxation and apportionment of representative purposes. The Southern delegates insisted that slaves be counted as part of the population for purposes of representation but not taxation. The Northern delegates, however, wanted slaves to be counted for taxation purposes but not for representation.

The dispute was resolved when the South agreed to count three fifths of its slaves for both taxation and representation. If a state had 50,000 free men and 50,000 slaves, the state would be entitled to declare a population of 80,000 for taxation and representation.

COMMERCE COMPROMISE

Congress was assigned the power to regulate interstate and foreign commerce, including the authority to levy tariffs on imported goods. In return for this concession, Congress was denied the power to levy taxes on exports.

RATIFICATION

Article VII of the Constitution, which states specifically that a vote by the conventions of nine states was needed for ratification, was officially ratified in 1789. Delaware was the first state to vote for approval, and Rhode Island was the last.

DIVISION OF POWERS

POWERS OF CONGRESS UNDER THE FEDERAL FORM OF GOVERNMENT

The federal system of government calls for a division of powers between the central government and the states. Article IV, Section 4, of the Constitution specifically states that the federal government "shall guarantee to every State in this Union a republican form of government."

Powers explicitly assigned to the federal government under the Constitution are:

1. to levy and collect taxes
2. to borrow money
3. to regulate interstate and foreign commerce
4. to establish uniform citizenship and bankruptcy laws
5. to coin money
6. to establish post offices
7. to establish patents and copyrights
8. to declare war
9. to raise and support armies and navies

IMPLIED POWERS

Article I, Section 8, Clause 18, states: "To make all laws which shall be necessary and proper for carrying into execution the foregoing powers, and all other powers vested by this Constitution in the government of the United States, or in any department or office thereof."

This clause is often referred to as the "implied powers" or "elastic" clause. For example, Congress has been delegated the right to regulate interstate commerce. On the basis of this delegated power, Congress is able to pass laws regarding regulation of railroads, airlines, radio, and TV. It has established commissions such as the Civil Aeronautics Board and the Federal Communications Commission to enforce these regulations.

RESERVED OR RESIDUAL POWERS

The Tenth Amendment to the Constitution states that "powers not delegated to the United States by the Constitution nor prohibited by it to the States, are reserved to the States respectively, or to the people."

This gives the states a broad range of authority to legislate on matters of divorce, marriage, education, health standards, gambling, wages, and other matters.

CONCURRENT POWERS

These are powers shared by both national and state governments. The right to tax is an example of a concurrent power.

SEPARATION OF POWERS

There are three branches of government: executive, legislative, and judicial. To ensure that no one branch attempts to gain all the power for itself, the Constitution has a built-in checks-and-balances system.

The president, for example, cannot declare war without the approval of Congress. Congress can check the war-making powers of the president by holding back financial appropriations for defense.

The president checks the powers of Congress by using his veto power. If a bill passed by Congress is not to the president's liking, he can refuse to sign it (veto), and he sends it back, with an explanation, to the house in which it originated.

The Supreme Court checks the powers of both Congress and the president by judging whether or not a law is constitutional.

POWERS OF THE PRESIDENT

1. To act as commander-in-chief of the army and navy

2. To make treaties with the advice and consent of two thirds of the Senate

3. To appoint ambassadors, public ministers, justices of the Supreme Court, and heads of departments with the advice and consent of the Senate

POWERS OF THE SUPREME COURT

ORIGINAL JURISDICTION—CASES THE SUPREME COURT IS THE FIRST TO HEAR

1. cases involving one of the states
2. cases involving foreign diplomats

APPELLATE JURISDICTION—CASES APPEALED TO THE SUPREME COURT FROM ANOTHER COURT

1. cases from other federal courts
2. cases from state courts, provided they have some relevance to federal matters

QUALIFICATIONS FOR CONGRESS

	House of Representatives	Senate
Number of Members	435	100
Term of Office	2 years	6 years
Minimum Age	25	30
U.S. Citizenship	7 years	9 years
Residency	Must be resident of the state	
Miscellaneous	May not hold any other U.S. government office	

LAW MAKING

Step 1: Bill introduced in Senate
Step 2: Bill sent to Senate committee to discuss details
Step 3: Bill scheduled on calendar for debate and vote
Step 4: Debate and vote in Senate
Step 5: Bill sent to House
Step 6: Bill sent to House committee for discussion
Step 7: Debate and vote in House
Step 8: Bill sent back to Senate
Step 9: Bill sent to Senate committee to discuss differences between House and Senate versions
Step 10: Bill sent to House, then Senate, for debate and vote
Step 11: Bill signed by Speaker of the House and by vice president
Step 12: Bill signed by president

BILL BECOMES LAW

It should be noted that the president may either sign the bill or veto it. The president's veto may be overridden by a two-thirds vote in each house. Another alternative is for the president to take no action at all on the bill. If the bill is on the president's desk for ten days (not including Sundays) without being signed, and if Congress is still in session, the bill becomes a law. However, if the president does not sign the bill and Congress adjourns before the ten-day limit is over, the bill is "killed." This is referred to as a "pocket veto."

AMENDING THE CONSTITUTION

Proposal	Ratification
Two-thirds of both houses of Congress may propose an amendment	Upon the approval of three-quarters of the state legislature
Or	Or
Two-thirds of the state legislatures may request a national convention, which may propose an amendment	Upon the approval of special conventions in three-quarters of the states

SUMMARY OF AMENDMENTS TO THE CONSTITUTION

Amendment 1.	Freedom of religion, speech, press, assembly, and petition
Amendment 2.	Right to bear arms
Amendment 3.	Quartering of troops
Amendment 4.	Search and seizure: warrants
Amendment 5.	Rights of accused persons
Amendment 6.	Right to speedy trial
Amendment 7.	Jury trial in civil cases
Amendment 8.	Bail, fines, and punishment
Amendment 9.	Powers reserved to the people
Amendment 10.	Powers reserved to the states
Amendment 11.	Suits against states
Amendment 12.	Election of president and vice president
Amendment 13.	Slavery abolished
Amendment 14.	Powers prohibited the states; apportionment of members of House of Representatives
Amendment 15.	Right of citizens to vote
Amendment 16.	Income tax
Amendment 17.	Direct election of senators
Amendment 18.	National prohibition
Amendment 19.	Women's suffrage
Amendment 20.	"Lame Duck" amendment
Amendment 21.	Repeal of prohibition
Amendment 22.	Two-term limit for president

Amendment 23. Presidential electors for District of Columbia

Amendment 24. Poll tax banned in national elections

Amendment 25. Presidential succession

Amendment 26. Gives 18-year-olds the right to vote

Amendment 27. Congressional pay raises

PRESIDENTIAL SELECTION

Step One: The Democratic and Republican parties each hold a National Convention to nominate their respective candidates for president and vice president.

Step Two: The Democratic and Republican parties each choose electors who promise to vote for the respective nominees for president and vice president.

Step Three: In November (Election Day), the voters vote for the candidates of their choice.

Step Four: The electors of the victorious party convene in the state capital and vote for their party's presidential and vice presidential candidates separately. This is the electoral vote.

Step Five: The president of the Senate receives certified copies of these electoral votes.

Step Six: On January 20, the president of the Senate counts the electoral votes in the presence of the Senate and the House of Representatives. A candidate must receive a majority of electoral votes to be elected.

President	Vice President
Term of office: 4 years	Term of office: 4 years
May serve no more than 8 years by virtue of the Twenty-second Amendment to the Constitution	May serve no more than 8 years by virtue of the Twenty-second Amendment to the Consitituion
Qualifications: Natural-born citizen of the U.S. and a resident of the U.S. for at least 14 years	Qualifications: Natural-born citizen of the U.S. and a resident of the U.S. for at least 14 years
Minimum Age: 35 years	Minimum Age: 35 years

PRESIDENTIAL SUCCESSION

The Twenty-fifth Amendment to the Constitution states that if the president becomes disabled and cannot carry out the responsibilities of the office, the vice president will assume the role of president. The amendment also empowers the president to select a vice president whenever the office is vacant. This amendment was put into effect when President Nixon nominated Gerald Ford to the vice presidency at the time of Spiro Agnew's resignation. Gerald Ford became president when President Nixon resigned. Upon taking the oath of office, President Ford then designated Nelson Rockefeller as his vice president with the advice and consent of Congress.

AMERICAN HISTORY

History is the documented story of the past. It includes all written material as well as other forms of documentation, such as buildings, artifacts, and monuments.

History is constantly being rewritten as new discoveries come to light. Because certain physical pieces of evidence, such as artifacts, may be interpreted differently by different people, various historical schools of thought have sprung up throughout the ages. In the twentieth century, historians took a new direction and began to consider history as encompassing larger areas of study. What follows is a time line of sorts, suggesting relationships between the United States and the rest of the world, taking into account the political and international situations of the day.

AMERICAN FOREIGN POLICY

1793

Proclamation of Neutrality. George Washington publicly announced that America would remain neutral in the war between France and England.

1796

Washington's Farewell Address: "It is our true policy to steer clear of permanent alliances with any portion of the foreign world." He added, however, the United States could "safely trust to temporary alliances for extraordinary emergencies."

1803

Thomas Jefferson purchased the Louisiana Territory for $15,000,000; it more than doubled the size of our nation.

1807–1812

Jefferson and Madison attempted in vain to involve the United States in a war with either France or England.

1812

The United States declared war against England. Prime cause: impressment of American seamen into the British Navy. "War Hawks," such as Henry Clay and John C. Calhoun, saw an opportunity to annex Canada to the United States.

1823

The Monroe Doctrine: President Monroe responded to the threat of European intervention in Latin America. With England's support, Monroe stated simply:

1. The Western Hemisphere is closed to further colonization.

2. There will be no intervention in the internal affairs of the Western Hemisphere.

The Monroe Doctrine was invoked as recently as 1962, the time of the Cuban Missile Crisis. President Kennedy ordered Premier Khrushchev to dismantle all missile sites, which were considered to be a threat to the safety of the United States, in Cuba.

1894–1914

The United States concentrated on protecting its interests in Central America, particularly the safeguarding of the Panama Canal, to ensure that it would share in trade with China.

1900–1901

The Open Door Policy. This policy, proposed by Secretary of State John Hay, recognized the spheres of influence established in China by Great Britain, Germany, and Japan but declared that trade with China should be open to all. It also stated that each nation should respect the territorial integrity of China. In 1900, the United States came to the aid of China during the Boxer Rebellion.

The defeat of Spain. The defeat of Spain in the Spanish-American War (1898) brought about the nominal independence of Cuba. The Philippine Islands were annexed to the United States. Guam, an important refueling station, became an American possession.

1914–1933

The United States became involved in World War I. To avoid any more commitments, the United States refused to become a member of the League of Nations in 1919. Nevertheless, the United States did participate in a number of disarmament conferences.

1933–1945

The United States, after much debate as to whether or not it should maintain its isolationist stance, entered the war against Germany, Italy, and Japan in 1941. On December 7, 1941, the Japanese bombed the American naval station at Pearl Harbor, which was the immediate cause for the United States to discontinue its isolation policy.

The period is also notable for its Good Neighbor Policy in Latin America. After years of U.S. intervention in Latin

American affairs, the United States pledged not to interfere in the internal affairs of any Latin American nation.

1945–1960

The post–World War II days were marked by a "Cold War" between the United States and the Soviet Union. In a question of democracy vs. communism, each nation tried to advertise itself as the better way of life for all.

The United States and the Soviet Union confronted each other over the Berlin Wall (1961) and the Korean War (1950).

During this period, the United States made many military and financial aid commitments. This was the start of the North Atlantic Treaty Organization (NATO) in which the United States, Western European nations, Greece, and Turkey declared that an attack on one is an attack on all. It has been estimated that the United States, foreign aid bill totaled $150 billion during this period.

1961–1975

This period is marked by our stand in Vietnam. The United States believed that it was in its best interest to send American troops to Vietnam. The Vietnam War literally divided this country into two hostile camps. Although peace negotiations had been in progress since 1968, it looked as if peace would never come to that land. In 1973, President Nixon attempted to speed up negotiations through the use of "saturation bombing" of North Vietnamese cities. He seemed to be reviving the concept of "massive retaliation" proposed by President Eisenhower's secretary of state, John Foster Dulles. In 1975, Saigon, the capital of South Vietnam, surrendered to the North Vietnamese.

1971–1978

This was the period (1972) when President Nixon visited Communist China—opening a new door to relations with that country. This time span was also marked by Henry Kissinger's philosophy of détente with the Soviet Union. It was also a time of an Israeli-Arab conflict, when the Middle East flared up once again with the "Yom Kippur" War of 1973.

The oil-producing Arab nationals (Saudi Arabia, Libya, and Kuwait) began their oil embargo, threatening the slowdown of economic growth in the United States, Western Europe, and Japan. The oil-producing countries organized the strongest international cartel (Organization of Petroleum Exporting Countries—OPEC) in the world. They could control the price and output of oil to any and all nations.

1977–1978

In 1977, the world was astounded by historic visits of Anwar as-Sadat (Egypt's president) to Israel and of Menachem Begin (Israel's prime minister) to Egypt in a powerful effort to bring an end to the discord in the

Middle East. The United States often found itself in the role of mediator between the Arabs and Israelis.

In 1978, Sadat and Begin signed the "Framework for Peace" after a thirteen-day conference at Camp David led by President Carter.

1979–1983

Tensions increased. Renewed tension with Soviet Union following Soviet invasion of Afghanistan in 1979. Arms race cranked up again. South Korean Boeing 747 jetliner bound for Seoul shot down by a Soviet SU-15 fighter; all 269 aboard were killed, including 61 Americans (August 1983). Ayatollah Ruholla Khomeini and revolutionary forces took over in Iran. Iranian militants seized the U.S. embassy in Tehran and held hostages (November 1979).

1983–1985

Terrorist activities increased. Benigno S. Aquino Jr., political rival of Philippine President Marcos, slain in Manila (August 1983). Terrorist explosion killed 241 U.S. Marines in Beirut (October 1983). The U.S. and Caribbean allies invaded Grenada (October 1983). Two Shiite Muslim gunmen hijacked a TWA airliner with 133 aboard (June 1985). Palestine Liberation Organization (PLO) terrorists hijacked Italian cruise ship, *Achille Lauro* (October 1985). Terrorists seized Egyptian Boeing 737 airliner after takeoff from Athens (November 1985).

1986–1990

Iran-Contra scandal unfolded. Allegedly, U.S. officials were involved in secretly diverting funds obtained from selling arms to Iran, in order to support the Nicaraguan Contras, in violation of the Boland Amendment.

1990–1991

Persian Gulf War. Iraq's leader, Saddam Hussein, invaded neighboring Kuwait (August 1990). Operation Desert Storm was launched to liberate Kuwait (January 1991).

1991–1993

Closer relations with Russia. In 1991, the Soviet Union ceased to exist. In its place were fifteen separate republics. This drastically affected U.S. foreign policy in these areas. The old goal of containing communism seemed to have been achieved. The new goal would be to nurture democracy and free-market economic structures in Russia and other eastern nations making the transition from communism.

1993–1994

Peaceful relations developed in the Middle East. Israel and members of the PLO opened formal diplomatic talks (1993). Israeli Prime Minister Yitzhak Rabin and PLO leader Yassir Arafat signed a historic accord in Washington, D.C. (September 1993). Jordan became the second Arab nation to declare an end to its state of war with Israel (July 1994).

1995–1997

In one of the worst domestic tragedies in the history of the U.S., a car bomb exploded outside the Oklahoma City federal building, killing 168 people (April 1995). The U.S. opened full diplomatic relations with Vietnam (July 1995). Organized by Nation of Islam leader Louis Farrakhan, the Million Man March brought African-American men to a giant rally in Washington, D.C. (October 1995). Israeli Prime Minister Yitzhak Rabin was assassinated by a religious fanatic (November 1995). The U.S. Senate ratified the second Strategic Arms Reduction Treaty (START II) (February 1996). South Africa adopted a new democratic constitution, eliminating white minority rule (May 1996). William Jefferson Clinton was reelected president of the United States, defeating former senator Robert J. Dole (November 1996). Chinese paramount leader Deng Xiaoping died (February 1997). President Mobutu of Zaire fled the country; rebels renamed the country Democratic Republic of the Congo (May 1997). After an eighteen-year rule, the Tories lost to the Labour Party in Britain's election (May 1997). China assumed control of Hong Kong, ending more than 150 years of British colonial rule (July 1997).

LATE 1997–2000

Some 160 nations signed the Kyoto Protocol that calls on individual nations to reduce emissions of carbon dioxide and other greenhouse gases (December 1997). President Clinton undertook the most extensive trip to Africa of any American President (March 1998). Terrorist Osama bin Laden orchestrated bombing attacks outside U.S. embassies in Kenya and Tanzania, killing 190 people (August 1998). The U.S. mediated an Israeli-Palestinian agreement (October 1998). A U.S.-led NATO launched a 77-day aerial bombardment of Yugoslavia in order to stop the government of Slobodan Milosevich from persecuting ethnic Albanians in the province of Kosovo (March 1999). The U.S. Senate rejected the Comprehensive Test Ban Treaty (October 1999). Boris Yeltsin, the Russian President, resigned and handed power over to his vice president, Vladimir Putin (December 1999), who was overwhelmingly reelected as president of Russia (March 2000). President Clinton normalized relations with China (October 2000). The *USS Cole* was bombed by terrorists in Aden, resulting in the deaths of 17 American military personnel (October 2000). President Clinton visited Vietnam, the first visit by a U.S. president since the end of the War (November 2000).

THE 21ST CENTURY

George W. Bush, son of former president George Bush, took office as the 43rd president of the United States after a controversial election. Bush was declared the victor on the basis of the electoral vote, although losing the popular vote to Vice President Al Gore. The difference was based on an unprecedented recount in several states, but the key to his victory was the 25 electoral votes from Florida, eventually awarded to Bush by the U.S. Supreme Court (January 2001).

Timothy McVeigh, sentenced for the bombing of the Federal Building in Oklahoma City, was executed. Slobodan Milosevic was turned over to the Hague to be tried for war crimes in Yugoslavia (June 2001).

President Bush said he would permit limited federal funding of research, using existing stem cell lines. Scientists believe that stem cell research may be the best hope for finding cures for many diseases, such as Alzheimer's and Parkinson's (August 2001).

One of the deadliest events in U.S. history took place when four passenger planes were hijacked. Two planes were deliberately crashed into the World Trade Center in New York City and one into the Pentagon in Washington, D.C. The fourth plane crashed into the ground as the passengers and crew tried to retake control from the hijackers. As a result almost 3,000 people lost their lives in this terrorist attack, commonly known as 9/11. The blame was directed toward Osama bin Laden, a wealthy Saudi terrorist and leader of the Al Qaida organization, which has ties to the Taliban leadership in Afghanistan (September 2001).

A multination coalition, led by the United States, attacked Afghanistan and removed the Taliban leadership from power (October 2001).

The Republican Party gained control of the Senate and held on to their majority in the House. After four years, U.N. weapons inspectors returned to Iraq after a new U.N. resolution demanded their return. Iraq was required to provide a "currently accurate, full, and complete declaration" of any weapons of mass destruction. Because Iraqi President Saddam Hussein did not comply with the resolution, U.S. and British forces invaded Iraq and toppled the regime (March 2003).

The Democratic Party gained control of the Senate and the House. As a result of the Democratic victory, Nancy Pelosi became the first woman and the first Californian elected Speaker of the House (November 2006).

BEHAVIORAL SCIENCE

Behavioral sciences are receiving increasing recognition and exerting a growing influence on our society. Books, magazines, television, and other forms of mass media have popularized theories of self-awareness, interpersonal relations, better health care, and how to be successful in life. Behavioral scientists discuss such topics as marriage, work, social institutions, ethnic and sexual identity, interpersonal and group conflict, and organizational behavior. The common link in all these areas is behavior. Behavioral science is the study of the behavior of organisms. Behavior covers a wide range of observable events—from the behavior of animals (rats, pigeons, and monkeys) to the conduct of human beings. An important point to remember is that behavior is observable and, therefore, can be measured, analyzed, and developed into theories based on the similarities and differences of behavior patterns. These patterns of behavior can be studied in relationship to individuals, groups, cultures, and social institutions.

The behavioral sciences are divided into four specialized areas: anthropology, psychology, social psychology, and sociology. The methods applied to the study of behavior are shared by all of these sciences, and, frequently, the concerned interests and the application of research findings will overlap from one area to the next. Following is a brief overview of the distinguishing characteristics of each of these areas.

ANTHROPOLOGY

Anthropology is the science of *Homo sapiens*, the only living species of the genus "man." It especially studies male and female humans in relation to the origin of the species, historical classification and relationship of races, physical and environmental characteristics of people, and the social and cultural relationships of men and women as they evolved from prehistoric beings.

EVOLUTION OF PEOPLE (FOUNDATIONS)

To most of us, the knowledge of our family tree may go back only several generations or even several centuries. Anthropologists, however, have traced our common descent back to a creature called the "human ape," which existed more than a million years ago in southern and eastern Africa. Although these animals were not yet human, they were also no longer apes. The distinguishing feature and basis for the evolution of people from their primate ancestors was their ability to capture animals for food, as opposed to being strictly vegetarians. Developmentally, the "human ape" no longer needed arms and hands for mobility and had an upright posture, leaving his upper appendages free for carrying food.

Although some anthropologists believe that it was the enlargement of the brain that led to the ability to make weapons and hunt other animals, it is now believed that tool-making and hunting came first. The existence of this "human ape" has also been cited as the beginning of communicative interrelationships. In order to obtain larger animals for food, these primitive humans needed cooperation from others. This primary group needed to function as an organized hunting unit, preparing together, planning for action, and determining a means for distribution of their capture. In order to accomplish the hunting tasks, social rules emerged. It is believed that these original "human ape" groupings can be viewed as an initial attempt to form a society. It can be inferred, therefore, that societies were formed as a basic means of survival and were the beginnings of the family and kinship units as we know them today.

PSYCHOLOGY

Human beings have never stopped trying to understand their own behavior. It is only within the past hundred years that a scientific model has been applied to the study of human behavior. Psychology was established as a separate science in 1879 when the first psychological laboratories were set up by Wilhelm Wundt. The need to establish standards for defining human behavior has led psychologists to consider a variety of practical problems, from measuring a child's intelligence to designing tests for job placement.

Clinical psychologists specialize in trying to understand how the mind works. They have developed theories of personality to help people who have difficulty coping with problems and functioning in daily life. No two people are alike; every individual exhibits different behavior, and the science of psychology seeks to understand why individuals behave the way they do and to apply its findings to the general population. There are several components of psychology, some of which will be outlined here.

BIOLOGICAL FOUNDATIONS OF BEHAVIOR

This area of study focuses on human biological functions—how and why certain systems operate to produce certain kinds of behavior. This complicated process can be narrowed down to three basic functions relating to different bodily structures or mechanisms:

1. *receptors:* mechanisms that receive information from the environment

2. *nerve cells:* mechanisms that connect the incoming messages to the spinal cord, which then transmits the information to the muscles and glands of the body

3. *effectors:* mechanisms that react to these messages and produce an observable reaction, or behavior

If you burn your hand, for instance, you experience an environmental stimulus (heat) to the skin. The sensory receptors in the skin travel via neurons or sensory fibers (nerve cells) to the spinal cord, where electrical and chemical changes occur. A chemical message is returned through other neuron fibers to the muscles in your arm and hand; the muscles contract, and you withdraw your hand from the source of heat. This process is called sensorimotor reflex, and it is the most basic form of behavior. This reflex behavior can even be found in the lowest forms of life, like the single-celled amoeba. What distinguishes human behavior and responses from those of animals is the physiological development of the brain, helping us to generalize behavior and learn through experience. We can learn that fire will burn, generalize this knowledge, recall the experience, and apply it to other situations so we won't be burned again.

PSYCHOLOGICAL PROCESSES

SENSATION

The sensory psychologist studies an organism's sensitivity to internal and external stimuli. Sensitivity is an organism's ability to respond to and discriminate between various stimuli. The most commonly studied sensory mechanisms are vision and hearing, but taste, touch, and smell also fall into this category. We depend heavily on our senses for everything we do. In order to see the print on this page, you must know how bright a light is needed; or, if you listen to the radio, you have to know the correct volume adjustment. Knowing the physiology of the eye and ear, the psychologist can determine what emotional responses are connected to our senses. For instance, one might want to know which colors are most soothing for hospital patients or factory workers, at what distance a street sign is most visible, or what hazards are caused by the noise of subways or machines.

PERCEPTION

Once an organism is able to detect stimuli in the outside world, it also must be able to perceive it. Perception is the organization of what we see, hear, taste, touch, smell, and feel into recognizable forms. For instance, if you see four lines connected at 90-degree angles, you are able to identify this form as a square. The visual ability to recognize a square as separate from a solid background (figure-ground perception) also helps you distinguish all the other objects in your environment. Other characteristics of perception are nearness, similarity, continuity, and size constancy. When we talk about objects being three-dimensional or having depth, these are also concerns of psychological study. Although psychologists study perception from a scientific perspective, magicians utilize the laws of perception, changing the environment to cause perceptual distortions and thereby create illusions.

LEARNING

Psychologists concerned with the phenomenon of the learning process have tried to reveal fundamental principles that define how we acquire certain behaviors to the exclusion of others. For instance, there are an infinite number of skills, tasks, and concepts that have to be learned before even beginning the process of learning to read.

There are numerous learning theories, but no one theory is conclusive; teaching methods are continually being revised. Most educators and psychologists agree, however, that learning is the result of the interaction between internal organismic systems and the external, environmental systems. Most learning takes place through a process called conditioning. Simplistically, this process has two parts:

1. a behavior is reinforced and therefore, is repeated to obtain that reinforcement again

2. the behavior is not reinforced (or is sometimes punished) to discourage repetition

Of course, the influence of the person who is reinforcing or discouraging the behavior cannot be ignored; factors such as inherited traits, intelligence, motivation, emotions, and environmental conditions also determine how a person will learn.

PERSONALITY DEVELOPMENT

Until now, this discussion has been centered primarily around individual learned behaviors. When these behaviors come together to form a pattern, it can be said that the pattern represents an individual's personality. Personality is the consistent way individuals behave in a range of life situations. The development of an individual's personality takes place over a period of time. As in the other areas of psychology, there is no hard-and-fast rule that determines how personality is developed.

The two types of psychologists who deal with personality development are:

1. those who seek to identify uniformities in the behavior of all people (personality theorists)

2. those who try to predict how an individual person will behave in a particular real-life situation (clinical psychologists)

When we talk about someone's "personality," we describe who that person is by the way he or she behaves in a given situation. Terms such as "shy," "aggressive," "anxious," "autonomous," "honest," "pleasant," or "creative" are a few of the ways of describing these behavior patterns.

There are many schools of thought about how a personality is formed. Some psychologists believe that it is purely through environmental influences, while others conclude that we are born with a basic personality structure that is either brought out or prevented from developing by our experiences. Sigmund Freud, one of the most influential psychological theorists, suggested that personality develops as a result of a person's development during a predetermined sequence of early childhood experiences (infancy to adolescence). He believed that the child's interaction with his or her environment would determine an ability or inability to interact with that environment throughout a lifetime.

Other theorists have expanded or abandoned Freud's theories, depending on their view of the "self," or how a person views oneself and others within a given environment. Personality theories can be charted along a continuum ranging from Freud's psychoanalytical principles, which deal with conscious and unconscious functioning of the mind, to the behaviorist, who believes that personality is developed, like other behaviors, through reinforcement or lack of it. The holistic or eclectic theorist takes a middle ground between Freud and the behaviorist, believing that personality is the total functioning of an individual—including heredity, biological systems, family influence, social development, self-concept, and societal influences.

BEHAVIOR PATHOLOGY OR ABNORMAL PSYCHOLOGY

This branch of psychology deals with mental disorder or behavior that prevents a person from maximizing his or her potential in a given situation. Deciding what is normal or abnormal is a complex matter often based on the background and beliefs of whoever is doing the defining. From the medical point of view, abnormal behavior is the result of a diseased mental state determined by the presence of certain clinically recognized and labeled symptoms (e.g., fears with no apparent cause, delusions, hallucinations, or antisocial behavior). However, if we also consider the cultural viewpoint, a person is described as normal or abnormal in terms of his or her social environment. Customs and attitudes considered normal in one cultural group may be called abnormal in another. Furthermore, what was considered abnormal behavior in one generation might be perfectly acceptable in another. "Normality" is a relative term, and the influence of one's community and age group cannot be ignored in determining one's ability to maintain life functions.

Several traits can be mentioned that are considered characteristic of a healthy personality:

1. a realistic degree of self-awareness and understanding

2. the ability to learn by experience and apply that learning to related situations

3. an ability to make independent decisions and act upon them

4. a sense of social environment

5. the ability to delay gratification and, thereby, control oneself and control changes in one's environment

To varying degrees, we all have difficulty making decisions, coping with stress, and understanding who we are. It would not be healthy to be completely free of problems or conflicts, but a person who is unable to make the necessary changes in his or her behavior to cope with a life situation, or who is destructive to self or society, is in need of the services of a mental health professional (e.g., psychiatrist, psychologist, social worker, or psychiatric nurse).

The definition of "mental health" usually accepted among mental health practitioners is the conformity or adjustment of one's behavior patterns or personality to some socially acceptable standard of conduct. Although this definition lacks recognizable clarity as to the definitions of "adjustment" and "standard of conduct," it also leaves room for a broad definition of the "well-adjusted" person.

PSYCHOLOGICAL DISORDERS

The three major categories of psychological disorders are:

1. psychoneurosis (neurosis)
2. psychosis
3. personality disorder

Some symptoms exhibited by people who are said to have a psychological dysfunction can also be seen in the healthy or well-adjusted individual. The symptoms of severe mental disturbance, however, are exaggerated and out of control.

PSYCHONEUROSIS

The neurotic person admits to being unhappy and unsatisfied with life, behaves irrationally, and can be anxious, highly compulsive, or phobic. A person with neurotic tendencies consistently punishes himself or herself and, since the cause of the problem cannot be pinpointed, conflicts remain unresolved and this person is unable to enjoy life's experiences fully.

PSYCHOSIS

The psychotic suffers from the most severe pathological conditions. Psychotic people are unable to interact realistically with others, often display unusual or bizarre mannerisms, may be harmful to themselves or others, and may be unable to care for themselves. Schizophrenia is the most commonly discussed disorder in this category.

PERSONALITY DISORDERS

At one time, these were called "character disorders." People with disturbances in this category have no internalized sense of right and wrong and are unaware of the needs of others or of societal standards. They rarely feel anxious or guilty about the consequences of their behavior. The chronic criminal offender, alcoholic, drug addict, and sexual deviant would be considered to have personality disorders.

METHODS OF TREATMENT

There is general agreement among those who treat mental disorders that treatment or therapy of any type is designed to help an individual or group of individuals function more effectively in their environment and to create in the individual a sense of well-being and security. The methods used to achieve these therapeutic goals vary according to the therapists' educational training and their theories of personality development. The main types of treatment fall into two categories:

1. psychotherapy, which tries to modify the patient's behavior by communication (verbal and nonverbal) and training procedures

2. somatotherapy, which tries to change behavior through direct physiological intervention with the use of medication, electric shock, or biofeedback

It is important to remember that one doesn't have to be "sick" or "crazy" to seek professional help; people often go to mental health practitioners for guidance during times of crisis, when they might be feeling overwhelmed. Professionals are able to help them sort out their problems and arrive at solutions that will make life easier and more satisfying.

SOCIAL PSYCHOLOGY

Social psychology concentrates on how each of us reacts to other people and to our social environment. There is no clear distinction between social psychology and its allied fields, sociology and anthropology. For our purposes, however, we can assume that sociology and anthropology examine behavior as a collective entity or from the perspective of the whole group, while social psychology has a greater interest in the individuals within any particular group.

The definition covers a wide range of social interactions, including everything from how a child plays with his or her peers on the playground to how a corporate president reacts at a board of directors meeting. Social psychology covers a wide variety of behavior that is learned by parental reinforcement and influenced by relatives, teachers, and the society in which a person is raised. Even the most basic behavior—likes or dislikes for particular foods, for instance—is determined by social customs that exist in our family, culture, or country. The social psychologist investigates that process by which we learn these social behaviors. We cannot cover the broad field of social behavior in this brief overview, so the following will be a discussion of the focal points of social psychology.

SOCIALIZATION

Socialization is the process by which individuals are trained from birth to obtain the particular knowledge, skills, and motivations that make them acceptable members of their society. The three important influences on the socialization process are:

1. culture
2. subculture
3. social dyad

CULTURE

Culture refers to the behavior patterns shared by people of the same society. Historically, it is passed down through arts and sciences, language, religion, and philosophy. In addition, general knowledge is taught through the systems of technology, political ideology, and social customs.

SUBCULTURE

Subculture represents a distinct group within a larger culture. Although every culture has its common traditions, morals, and mores, there are numerous smaller groups who adopt special qualities that identify them as a group. The hundreds of subcultures in any given society are most commonly characterized by: (1) *social class*, in which behavior is based on the acquired or individually perceived economic level (for example, the lifestyle of the jet-setter or the problems of the impoverished); (2) *social role*, which is the pattern of behavior based on social position, such as age, sex, occupation, academic degrees, or marital status; and (3) *ethnic identity*, in which certain behavior is retained because of personal heritage or racial or national differences (e.g., language, physical characteristics, and manners).

SOCIAL DYAD

Social dyad is the simplest interpersonal interaction. It is the relationship between 2 people in which a reciprocal learning process takes place. The primary social dyad between parent and child appears to be a one-way learning process in which the parent teaches and the child learns. However, a closer look reveals that the child teaches the parent when he or she is hungry, cold, or unhappy. There are many social dyads in our society. The initial relationship between parent and child determines that child's ability to form attachments and one-to-one relationships in the future.

SMALL GROUP BEHAVIOR

It is difficult to determine the specific behavioral effect of complex social systems, such as an entire culture. Therefore, the social psychologist narrows down the field by studying the behavior of a small group and determines the effects of this small group on individual behavior. This is achieved by observing behavior as it occurs in a natural group or by creating artificial groups in a controlled setting where basic social processes can occur. By studying the interaction among group members, we can gain an understanding of interpersonal relationships. There are many variables to consider when studying group dynamics, and many psychologists believe that the key to improving human relations is an understanding of the roles people play in such groups. They examine communication patterns, leadership, roles and role conflict, intergroup tensions and prejudice, verbal and nonverbal language, attitudes, perceptions, motivation, and many other external and internal factors that influence group behavior.

EXTERNAL GROUP INFLUENCES

The factors that exist before a group even begins to interact can have an influence on the way members of a group relate to one another. The three key external factors that can influence group functioning are:

1. physical setting
2. group size
3. group composition

The physical environment, or space, in which a group meets is often important in the enhancement or prevention of certain social processes. For instance, we recognize that communication is increased if people meet in a small space, as opposed to a larger one, or if people are seated in a circle, as opposed to rows. The use of space or territory can also work in a negative way, as evidenced by hostile or aggressive behavior in overcrowded situations. Group size and group composition are also factors that influence group interactions. We can predict that people will act and react in a specific way, depending upon the size of the group and the attitudes of its members. You have probably observed that communication is much more relaxed and open among your friends and classmates than it would be if a stranger or an authority figure were present.

INTERNAL INFLUENCES ON THE GROUP

Like external influences, internal factors, such as communication patterns, leadership, and roles play an important part in determining how a group will function.

Communications, the sharing of information and understanding, is primarily facilitated by language. The spoken word, however, is not the only form of communication. We have only to look at the language of the deaf to understand how communication can exist nonverbally. Even among speaking people, gestures, facial expressions, and body postures frequently communicate what one is trying to express and may affect how others relate to us without our even being aware of it. Any attempt to understand or improve communications patterns among group members must take into account communication barriers. For instance, if there is anxiety, tension, or differences in purpose, background, or approaches to problem solving, this will influence the effectiveness of conveying ideas and meanings within the group.

Leadership is an important factor of group interactions, as it affects the group structure. The group will behave in significantly different ways, depending on how the leadership role is defined. An effective leader is one who is able to affect and control a group's efforts toward resolving problems or achieving specific goals. The personality of the leader as well as the personalities of individual group members will determine how efficiently tasks are completed. Social psychologists have determined that there are certain people who more naturally fill the leadership role, just as there are others who usually become the workers or followers in a group. The leader of the group must take on certain functions that go along with that leadership role. Other members of the group fill other roles that are equally important to the group.

The term "role" is usually defined as the position or function one fills in different social settings, such as parent, student, teacher, club member, or politician. Everyone plays different roles at different times, and with each role comes the expectation that certain behavioral or personality traits and certain rights and duties will accompany that role. We expect, for instance, that our parents, friends, or teachers are going to be understanding and supportive or that an employer will deal fairly with us. When someone does not live up to these expectations, however, a role conflict exists. This conflict can exist between people or within an individual and will certainly have an effect on the way that an individual acts within a group.

From studies done by psychologists and social psychologists have come the familiar techniques employed in personal-growth groups. Like sensitivity training, encounter groups, Gestalt groups, or study groups, the purpose of the personal-growth group is designed to teach or train a specific subject or skill. The goals are to provide an intensified experience so that the individuals in the group gradually become more aware of their own feelings and the feelings of others and come to understand their relationships within the group more accurately. These experiences will improve personal attitudes and behaviors, and, subsequently, each individual will be able to relate more effectively to others in daily life.

SOCIOLOGY

Sociology is the systematic study of society, social institutions, and human social relationships. Similar to the social psychologist, the sociologist studies the development, structure, and function of human social behavior in groups. Although sociologists are concerned with the processes and patterns of group influence on individual behavior, they also focus on patterns of collective behavior. Collective behavior, or the behavior of large groups of people, is related to *social stratification*, a form of social differentiation based on the roles of group members; *demographic characterization*, the size, growth, and distribution of populations; and *the econological patterning of communities and societies*, which includes the study of relationships of organisms to their environment. It also includes the study of crowd behavior and organization behavior (as in large business firms, hospitals, or government agencies). The sociologist seeks to develop a body of interrelated knowledge that may be used to generalize or explain social behavior and may, under specified conditions, predict or help in understanding behavior. Sociological studies cover a wide range of factors, often comparing such seemingly different cultures as communal peasant life in Zambia to the lifestyle of a street gang in New York City.

SOCIETAL INFLUENCES

Sociology, as its name implies, is concerned with the socialization process as it relates to our society. It is said that we are influenced by the society of which we are a member as well as by the other factors that go into our development. Most societies tend to socialize their youth by reinforcing conformity to the norms of the culture and basic adherence to the rules set down by that culture. These rules can be written, as in the United States Constitution, or unwritten, as in the rituals and family traditions passed down from generation to generation. This process seems deceptively simple, but it does not necessarily work smoothly or automatically, nor is it always the best situation for the people involved. We are well aware that although certain societies claim that all their citizens are equal and receive equal opportunities for education and employment, this may not be true. Some of the questions a sociologist might ask about a given society are: How well does it work? What type of people live in it? What effects does the society have on its people? What are the benefits? What are the consequences? In which direction is the society headed? The list is endless, but it is the sociologist's job to narrow down the range of commonalities and differences so that a given society can be studied in manageable terms. By nature, society is constantly changing because it is made up of people whose needs are always changing. Similarly, society is a mechanism of social cohesion as well as an arena for conflict when people are not able to work together or have different needs. Any given society must work at solving its problems and dilemmas. The changes in society are influenced by many different factors at any given time: ecological, technological, economic, religious, political, and cultural.

SOCIAL INSTITUTIONS

Some theorists believe that in order for a given society to perpetuate itself, it must be responsive to the physical, psychological, and emotional needs of its individual members. For this reason, people create social institutions to meet the needs of the general population. These social institutions serve to maintain specific standards, to perpetuate the functions of daily life, and to mold socially acceptable behavior. Those most commonly known are your family; school; hospitals; houses of worship; government agencies (including local, state, and federal legislatures and organizations); the police, sanitation, and fire departments; and many other regulatory bodies.

AREAS OF SPECIAL INTEREST IN SOCIOLOGY

A sociologist might choose a specific area of study in which to work. Following is a list of special interest areas and a brief description of each.

OCCUPATIONAL SOCIOLOGY

Occupational sociology is the analysis of professions and vocations, such as the study of career patterns or employment statistics.

MEDICAL SOCIOLOGY

Medical sociology studies issues related to illness—for example, social attitudes toward illness, incidence of illness in particular areas, or the relationship of illness to the organization of society. Also included is the study of the sociological structure of hospitals and doctors, nurses, social workers, attendants, and other medical personnel.

EDUCATIONAL SOCIOLOGY

Educational sociology is the study of educational institutions and their relationship to other social institutions (political, medical, legal, and religious) within a given society.

POLITICAL SOCIOLOGY

Political sociology is the study of political institutions, like political parties or government organizations, and their relationship to other institutions. The political sociologist might be concerned with the phenomena of political movements and ideologies as representative trends in a given society.

RURAL SOCIOLOGY

Rural sociology is the study of rural communities and traditions in agricultural and industrialized societies.

URBAN SOCIOLOGY

Urban sociology is the study of urban social life and organizations. This sociologist might be concerned with race relations, the effects of poverty, or the characteristics of neighborhoods.

THE SOCIOLOGY OF ART

The sociology of art is concerned with the influence of society on art as well as the influence of art upon society. This includes a creation of art by the artist, the evaluation of art by the critics and the public, and the use and distribution of art. For example, in certain periods of history, there has been greater or lesser availability or opportunity to produce works of art.

THE SOCIOLOGY OF LAW

The sociology of law is primarily concerned with legal institutions and their relationship to society. A study of social norms, for instance, would also include understanding the influence of legal codes. Since laws and their enforcement relate to the general structure and function of society, this area is of primary concern to sociologists, particularly in reference to the social roles of lawyers, judges, jurors, and other legislative and enforcement personnel.

THE SOCIOLOGY OF RELIGION

The sociology of religion is viewed in terms of the social interaction created by religious institutions. The role of religious leaders and the characteristics of religious groups in terms of stratification and socialization are of significance to sociologists.

REVIEW QUESTIONS

Read each question carefully, mark your answers, and then check them with the answers and explanations that appear at the end of the Overview section.

1. Following the events of September 11th, the attack by the United States and a multination coalition was directed at

   (A) Afghanistan
   (B) Saudi Arabia
   (C) Iraq
   (D) Israel
   (E) Iran

2. Which of the following happened in the 2000 presidential election?

   (A) The Democrats won the presidency for the third consecutive time.
   (B) The Republican presidential candidate won the popular vote but lost in the Electoral College.
   (C) Neither presidential candidate received an electoral college majority.
   (D) Disputes over voting recounts in Georgia were not resolved until weeks after the election.
   (E) The national popular vote winner lost the election.

3. Who succeeded Boris Yeltsin as the new Russian president at the end of 1999?

   (A) Mikhail Gorbachev
   (B) Vladimir Putin
   (C) Leonid Brezhnev
   (D) Slobodan Milosevich
   (E) Nikita Khrushchev

4. A tax that an individual pays on profits from the sales of stocks, bonds, or property is known as the

   (A) sales tax
   (B) property tax
   (C) personal income tax
   (D) excise tax
   (E) capital gains tax

5. Members of the National Rifle Association would look to which amendment of the U.S. Constitution to support their opposition to comprehensive gun control policies?

   (A) First
   (B) Second
   (C) Sixth
   (D) Eighth
   (E) Twentieth

6. Which country in the Balkans was bombed for 77 days by NATO air forces in 1999?

   (A) Albania
   (B) Bulgaria
   (C) Yugoslavia
   (D) Croatia
   (E) Macedonia

7. Which of the following foreign policy events did NOT occur during the two presidential terms of President Bill Clinton?

   (A) The Persian Gulf War
   (B) Normalization of trade relations with China
   (C) Mediation between the Israelis and Palestinians
   (D) The Kyoto Protocol signing
   (E) The bombing of U.S. embassies in Kenya and Tanzania

8. A state that has five representatives in the U.S. House of Representatives would have how many electoral votes?

   (A) One
   (B) Three
   (C) Five
   (D) Seven
   (E) Nine

9. The last time Congress officially declared war upon another nation or nations was at the start of

   (A) the Korean War
   (B) the Vietnam War
   (C) World War I
   (D) the Persian Gulf War
   (E) World War II

10. What other country besides Iran was involved in the Iran-Contra scandal?

   (A) Cuba
   (B) El Salvador
   (C) Nicaragua
   (D) Mexico
   (E) Guatemala

11. A salaried representative of an interest group is traditionally called a(n)

   (A) "influence provider"
   (B) CEO
   (C) agenda-setter
   (D) lobbyist
   (E) trustee

12. According to a specific compromise at the 1787 Constitutional Convention, a state having 20,000 slaves in its population would actually count how many slaves for purposes of taxation and representation in Congress?

    (A) 1000
    (B) 10,000
    (C) 12,000
    (D) 16,000
    (E) 20,000

13. A tariff is a(n)

    (A) tax placed on a nation's exports
    (B) free-trade device
    (C) national tool that is opposed to the protectionist philosophy
    (D) tax placed on imports coming into a nation
    (E) economic tool no longer used by any nation today

14. NAFTA is an economic alliance consisting of which three nations?

    (A) The United States, Chile, and Honduras
    (B) The United States, Canada, and Mexico
    (C) Canada, Mexico, and Brazil
    (D) Guatemala, Ecuador, and Uruguay
    (E) The United States, Mexico, and Cuba

15. Which of the following is an example of a concurrent power?

    (A) The power to coin money
    (B) The power to tax
    (C) The power to declare war
    (D) The first three choices are all examples of concurrent powers.
    (E) None of the first three choices is an example of a concurrent power.

16. In the field of sociology, using the case study approach, there is a problem with

    (A) matching people who share the same crucial variable
    (B) obtaining random samples
    (C) establishing a control group
    (D) people behaving differently in the experiment
    (E) over-generalization

17. Which of the following demonstrates operant or instrumental conditioning?

    (A) Ordering and then smelling and eating a good meal at a nice restaurant
    (B) A smiling and nodding parent feeds her young child
    (C) A student is praised each time she makes a statement critical of the teacher
    (D) None of the above
    (E) All of the above

18. Our attitudes toward sexual behavior, politics, economics, and religion are generally shaped by

    (A) our own thought processes and determination of what is right
    (B) our personality
    (C) the result of negative conformity
    (D) feedback from reference groups
    (E) All of the above

19. Which of the following does NOT represent a renewable form of energy?

    (A) Wind
    (B) Tide
    (C) Natural gas
    (D) Geothermal
    (E) Hydroelectric

20. In the 2000 political race, one term that was frequently used was "soft money." What does this refer to?

    (A) Money collected at Washington fund-raising events and $1,000 a plate dinners
    (B) Money that is "off the books" and doesn't need to be reported
    (C) Money that comes from federal matching funds so the candidate doesn't have to work hard for it
    (D) Money given to political parties that is not subject to limits in terms of the size of individual or corporate contributions
    (E) Illegal campaign spending

REVIEW ANSWERS AND EXPLANATIONS

1. **The correct answer is (A).** The Taliban movement and Al Qaida were, and continue to be, the principle targets of the war. Although the Al Qaida movement is located throughout the world, Afghanistan was where Osama bin Laden, their leader, was located at the time.

2. **The correct answer is (E).** Voting recount disputes occurred in Florida. Republican George W. Bush won the election with 271 electoral votes, but Gore had 540,000 more popular votes nationwide.

3. **The correct answer is (B).** Putin was officially elected the Russian president in 2000.

4. **The correct answer is (E).** The other choices do not fit the definition covered in the question's stem.

5. **The correct answer is (B).** The Second Amendment deals with the right to bear arms.

6. **The correct answer is (D).** NATO was trying to stop ethnic cleansing in Kosovo.

7. **The correct answer is (A).** The Gulf War occurred during the presidency of George Bush.

8. **The correct answer is (D).** Each state's electoral votes are equal to its total representation in Congress. Thus, this state would have five House members plus two from the U.S. Senate, or seven electoral votes.

9. **The correct answer is (E).** This occurred on December 8, 1941, one day after the Japanese attack upon Pearl Harbor. There was no official congressional war declaration in the other conflicts.

10. **The correct answer is (C).** Funds obtained from selling arms to Iran were diverted to rebels in Nicaragua, (i.e., the Contras). The scandal occurred during the Reagan Administration.

11. **The correct answer is (D).** The term derives from interest group representatives contacting legislators in the "lobby" outside of legislative chambers. None of the other choices is appropriate.

12. **The correct answer is (C).** The compromise was known as the three-fifths compromise, whereby 60 percent of a state's slave population would count for taxation and representation purposes. Sixty percent of 20,000 is 12,000.

13. **The correct answer is (D).** Tariffs are protectionist devices, not free trade tools. They are still used by some nations today.

14. **The correct answer is (B).** NAFTA stands for the North American Free Trade Association.

15. **The correct answer is (B).** A concurrent power is one that can be exercised by more than one level of government in the United States. Coining money and declaring war are only the responsibility of the federal government. But taxes can be administered by federal, state, and local levels of government.

16. **The correct answer is (E).** Sociologists tend to become too focused on the case study itself. They see the case as being a typical of the larger society, perhaps more typical than is warranted, and so tend to over-generalize about the results and the usefulness of their case study. The other answers are difficulties of experimentation.

17. **The correct answer is (E).** Operant conditioning is when a behavior receives a response which is then followed by a reinforcing stimulus. Each of these examples have a behavior, a response, and feedback that is reinforcing of the response.

18. **The correct answer is (D).** According to psychologists, reference groups provide a standard by which one evaluates one's own behavior and by rewarding and punishing conformity to accept beliefs among the reference groups. Reference groups provide one with social norms that one tends to follow.

19. **The correct answer is (C).** Only natural gas is not renewable since it is a byproduct of fossilization. As a result natural gas can not be created or renewed as the other four items are continually.

20. **The correct answer is (D).** There was a considerable amount of discussion in the 2000 political campaign about Campaign Finance Reform, including the issue of "soft money." When the campaign laws were enacted in the 1970s there was tremendous concern for what seemed to be the decline of political parties. So the parties were not made subject to the same limits so that there would be money for party mailings, voter registration, and other party activities. This has proved to be a huge loophole—especially in presidential campaigns.

Chapter 13
POSTTEST

TIME—45 MINUTES   60 QUESTIONS

PART I

Directions: Each of the questions or incomplete statements below is followed by five suggested answers or completions. Select the one that is best in each case.

1. Who was the French artillery officer who rose to become Emperor of France in 1804 and who overcame Austria at Austerlitz (1805), Prussia at Jena (1806), threatened Great Britain with invasion and blockade, and came to terms with Russia in the Treaty of Tilsit (1807)? Finally, he was decisively beaten at the Battle of Waterloo by the Duke of Wellington.

   (A) Ferdinand de Lesseps
   (B) Charles de Gaulle
   (C) Louis XIV
   (D) Napoléon Bonaparte
   (E) Georges Pompidou

2. In the early 1990s, the Serbs, Croats, and Bosnian Muslims fought among themselves on territory that had once been what former communist nation?

   (A) Hungary
   (B) Yugoslavia
   (C) Poland
   (D) Albania
   (E) East Germany

3. What was the name given to the unsuccessful United States–sponsored invasion of Cuba by Cuban refugees organized, trained, and supplied by the Central Intelligence Agency (CIA) in April 1961 in an attempt to overthrow the Castro regime?

   (A) Cuban missile crisis
   (B) Bay of Pigs
   (C) Mayagüez incident
   (D) Christmas bombing of Haiphong Harbor
   (E) Operation Grand Slam

4. As of 1997, who were the five nations who were "permanent" members of the United Nations Security Council?

   (A) Italy, Russia, the United Kingdom, France, and the United States
   (B) Russia, France, Germany, Japan, and the United States
   (C) China, France, Russia, the United Kingdom, and the United States
   (D) China, Japan, Russia, France, and the United States
   (E) Germany, Japan, China, the United Kingdom, and the United States

5. The Democrats and Republicans symbolize the concept of the two-party system in American politics. The two-party system originated and was well established during the administration of George Washington. One of the parties at that time was called the Democratic-Republicans. What was the name of the other party?

   (A) Federalists
   (B) Secessionists
   (C) Jeffersonians
   (D) Conservatives
   (E) Whigs

GO ON TO THE NEXT PAGE

6. One of the states in the Union was acquired from Russia in 1867 for $7.2 million by President Andrew Johnson's Secretary of State, William Henry Seward. The acquisition was popularly known as "Seward's Folly," and no interest was expressed in the faraway possession until gold was discovered in the Yukon in 1896. What is this state?

(A) Arizona
(B) Alaska
(C) Hawaii
(D) New Mexico
(E) Nevada

7. Which one of the following statements about the American Revolutionary War is factually INCORRECT?

(A) An overwhelming majority of Americans fully supported the war effort.
(B) The war, from Lexington and Concord to Yorktown, lasted less than two years.
(C) George Washington, the commander of the American forces, did not lose a battle during the war.
(D) Great Britain and the United States signed a peace treaty a few months after the final battle at Yorktown.
(E) The Americans did not actually win the war, since it was the British decision to end the war that really led to political independence.

8. In the British political system, the "Question Period" refers to

(A) the style of debate that exists between members of the majority and minority parties within Parliament
(B) the reigning monarch's political beliefs about major issues facing the nation
(C) members of the House of Commons interrogating government officials about any issue of concern
(D) the ritual of written questions being submitted to the prime minister by members of the British media
(E) British voters holding town meetings to decide who will represent them in Parliament

9. On what platform was Abraham Lincoln elected president of the United States?

(A) Free trade
(B) Freedom of the press
(C) Antislavery
(D) Independence of the judiciary
(E) A stronger executive branch

10. The French Revolution began when a group of middle-class radicals took over the administration with the help of a Paris mob and tried to set up a constitutional monarchy. In what year did the French Revolution begin?

(A) 1787
(B) 1789
(C) 1848
(D) 1889
(E) 1900

11. NATO, the North Atlantic Treaty Organization, was originally created in 1949 for what purpose?

(A) To hasten political unification among the states of Western Europe
(B) To create a unified Germany
(C) To prevent a Soviet invasion of Europe
(D) To help integrate the economies of France, West Germany, and Great Britain
(E) To create a military force that could be used against communist aggression anywhere in the world

12. In the ten U.S. presidential elections from 1960 to 1996, which of the following men were *all* elected as Republican presidents?

(A) Johnson, Kennedy, and Carter
(B) Nixon, Reagan, and Bush
(C) Clinton, Johnson, and Reagan
(D) Nixon, Bush, and Kennedy
(E) Kennedy, Bush, and Clinton

13. At the height of the Vietnam conflict in 1968, the number of U.S. combat troops in Vietnam was at a peak. Which one of the following is nearest to the approximate figure?

(A) 200,000
(B) 545,000
(C) 1 million
(D) 2 million
(E) 3 million

14. Which currency was replaced by the Euro?

(A) Japanese Yen
(B) Italian Lira
(C) Swedish Kronor
(D) Norwegian Kroner
(E) Australian Dollar

15. What was the name of the Augustinian monk who rebeled against the abuses within the Roman Catholic Church and was the first great inspirer of the Reformation?

   (A) Erasmus
   (B) Pope Leo X
   (C) Martin Luther
   (D) Sir Thomas More
   (E) John Calvin

16. What institution, which was cited as a model among its peers, is called the "mother of Parliaments" because of its rigid historical traditions as a legislative assembly?

   (A) Israeli Knesset
   (B) U.S. House of Representatives
   (C) Japanese Diet
   (D) British House of Commons
   (E) French National Assembly

17. Which one of the following was the famous German field marshall who was also known as the "Desert Fox"? He served in World War I, was prominent in the annexations of Central Europe, and came close to destroying the British Eighth Army before being defeated by it at the Battle of El Alamein.

   (A) Adolf Hitler
   (B) Konrad Adenauer
   (C) Erwin Rommel
   (D) Klemens Metternich
   (E) Napoléon Bonaparte

18. England used the Molasses Act of 1733 to

   (A) prohibit trade between its American colonies and France's West Indian colonies
   (B) ban the export of sugar and confectionery to the United States
   (C) impose a heavy sales tax on sugar in the United States
   (D) ban slavery
   (E) regulate the restricted flow of American consumer goods into Great Britain

19. The Louisiana Territory was purchased in 1803 for 80 million francs from a French emperor. Who was he?

   (A) Charlemagne
   (B) Charles de Gaulle
   (C) Napoléon Bonaparte
   (D) Nero
   (E) Francis Ferdinand

20. November 11, 1918, is a famous date in history because an armistice was signed, bringing a major war to an end. Which war was it?

   (A) World War I
   (B) World War II
   (C) Wars of the Roses
   (D) Battle of Waterloo
   (E) Hundred Years' War

21. The stock market crash was the culmination of the boom market and unrestrained speculation of the Coolidge era, which ushered in prolonged depression followed by increasing unemployment, bank failures, and business disasters. When did the crash of the stock market take place?

   (A) September 1914
   (B) October 1929
   (C) August 1935
   (D) November 1938
   (E) January 1952

22. The atomic bombs that were dropped on Hiroshima and Nagasaki finally ended which war?

   (A) Spanish–American War
   (B) World War I
   (C) World War II
   (D) Korean War
   (E) Russo–Japanese War

23. The U-boat was a submarine used extensively during World War II in the battle of the Atlantic. What does "U" stand for?

   (A) Utility
   (B) Underwater
   (C) Underground
   (D) Undersea
   (E) Untersee

24. What was the name commonly given to anti-allied forces in World War II?

   (A) Axis
   (B) Blitzkrieg
   (C) Triple Alliance
   (D) Enténte Cordiale
   (E) Double Entendre

GO ON TO THE NEXT PAGE

25. The scandal of Watergate, the opening of American relations with the People's Republic of China, the Paris Peace Accords, and the Kent State killing of four college students all occurred during the administration of which American president?

    (A) Lyndon Johnson
    (B) Gerald Ford
    (C) George Bush
    (D) Richard Nixon
    (E) Jimmy Carter

26. When the Suez Canal was nationalized in July 1956, threatening British communications with the East, both France and Great Britain intervened, precipitating a major political crisis. The nationalization also resulted in an Israeli attack against Egypt, which outraged world public opinion. Who was responsible for the nationalization of the canal?

    (A) President Anwar as-Sadat
    (B) King Farouk
    (C) Kemal Ataturk
    (D) Shah of Iran
    (E) President Gamal Abdel Nasser

27. In 1997, at which age were young men in America required to register with Selective Service?

    (A) 17
    (B) 18
    (C) 19
    (D) 20
    (E) 21

28. Which one of the following states resulted from the decisive Battle of San Jacinto on April 21, 1836?

    (A) Arizona
    (B) Pennsylvania
    (C) California
    (D) Texas
    (E) Ohio

29. What common factor linked the following three presidents: Abraham Lincoln, William McKinley, and James Garfield?

    (A) They were responsible for far-reaching legislation against slavery.
    (B) They were signatories to three major peace treaties with Russia.
    (C) They were assassinated.
    (D) They were responsible for vetoing much of the legislation passed by Congress.
    (E) They were the only three presidents to die in office.

30. If both the U.S. president and vice president died at the same time, who would be next in line to become the president?

    (A) Speaker of the House
    (B) President pro tem of the Senate
    (C) Secretary of Defense
    (D) Secretary of State
    (E) Secretary of Commerce

31. President Andrew Jackson, the seventh president of the United States, is credited with having nationalized the practice of basing appointments on party service. What was this practice called?

    (A) Patronage
    (B) Nepotism
    (C) Spoils system
    (D) Parish pump politics
    (E) Pork barrel

32. When the Treaty of Paris was signed with Spain on December 10, 1898, following the Spanish-American War, Spain withdrew from Cuba and ceded to the United States three of its territories, two of which were Puerto Rico and the Philippines. What was the third?

    (A) Hong Kong
    (B) Guam
    (C) Okinawa
    (D) Marshall Islands
    (E) Christmas Island

33. The first U.S. president to be inaugurated in Washington, D.C., the new capital, was settled in office on March 4, 1801. Who was this president?

    (A) Thomas Jefferson
    (B) Theodore Roosevelt
    (C) John Quincy Adams
    (D) James Madison
    (E) Andrew Jackson

34. Which of the following was the controversial and influential British economist who, in seeking to understand the causes of the depression of the 1930s, showed that demand in total was determined by expenditures and that full employment was necessary for recovery?

    (A) John Stuart Mill
    (B) John Maynard Keynes
    (C) Thomas Malthus
    (D) Harold Laski
    (E) Sidney Webb

35. The TVA, formed in 1933 and considered a pacesetter among government-owned corporations, has determined and encouraged a seven-state region with rural electrification; industrialization along the riverfront; land, soil, forest, and strip-mine reclamation; flood damage programs; and demonstration projects in man-made lakes, outdoor recreation, and conservation education. It is also the prime source of power for U.S. atomic and space programs. What does TVA stand for?

(A) Trans Valley Authority
(B) Tennessee Valley Authority
(C) Texas Valley Authority
(D) Territorial Voluntary Authority
(E) Tri-State Viaduct Authority

36. What is the term commonly used to describe the tax on personal and corporate incomes used to finance federal, state, and local government?

(A) Sales tax
(B) Income tax
(C) Value-added tax
(D) Excess-profits tax
(E) Regressive tax

37. Internationally, an important concept is the "most-favored-nation principle," or MFN. MFN deals with the general issue of

(A) military alliances
(B) trade
(C) diplomacy
(D) treaties that end wars
(E) membership in the United Nations

38. Which country must import more than half of its daily supply of petroleum?

(A) United States
(B) Saudi Arabia
(C) Kuwait
(D) Mexico
(E) Dubai

39. What does inflation do to the purchasing power of the American dollar?

(A) It increases purchasing power.
(B) It has no effect upon purchasing power.
(C) It decreases purchasing power.
(D) It both increases and decreases purchasing power.
(E) It increases purchasing power for inexpensive items and increases purchasing power for expensive items.

40. The primary role of a federal reserve bank is to be a(n)

(A) banker's bank
(B) exporter's bank
(C) international trading bank
(D) industrialist's bank
(E) importer's bank

41. What is the stock market term commonly used for an investor or concern that sells shares in the expectation that prices will fall?

(A) Stockbroker
(B) Pessimist
(C) Bear
(D) Dead duck
(E) Stockjobber

42. In Keynesian economics, unemployment compensation, Social Security benefits, food stamps, and farm subsidies are all examples of

(A) multiplier effects
(B) automatic stabilizers
(C) price controls
(D) pump primers
(E) income transfers

43. Basically, the price of any commodity in the market is traditionally governed by the

(A) theory of marginal productivity
(B) labor theory of value
(C) laws of supply and demand
(D) strength of the country's national currency
(E) law of diminishing returns

44. NAFTA is a trade association whose three international members are

(A) Mexico, Canada, and the United States
(B) Great Britain, France, and Italy
(C) Mexico, Costa Rica, and Guatemala
(D) Nigeria, Algeria, and Tunisia
(E) the United States, Great Britain, and Australia

45. The wages that employees receive are generally different from the real purchasing power of such wages. This difference is commonly known as

(A) minimum wages
(B) base rate
(C) featherbedding
(D) piece rate
(E) real wages

GO ON TO THE NEXT PAGE

46. What is the name given to common stock in a company known nationally for the quality and wide acceptance of its products or services and its ability to make money and pay dividends?

   (A) Growth stock
   (B) Round lot
   (C) Blue chip
   (D) Liquid assets
   (E) Common stock

47. What federal executive department, established in 1913, is responsible for the economic and technological growth of the United States?

   (A) Department of Commerce
   (B) Department of Transportation
   (C) Department of the Interior
   (D) Department of the Treasury
   (E) Department of Health, Education, and Welfare

48. Karl Marx (1818–1883) and Friedrich Engels (1820–1895) collaborated to write a famous treatise in which they proclaimed that historical change is caused by class struggle and that the modern struggle is between the owners of economic production (the bourgeoisie) and the workers (the proletariat), who must overthrow the owners and redistribute the wealth. What is the name of this treatise?

   (A) *The Communist Manifesto*
   (B) *Das Kapital*
   (C) *Grammar of Politics*
   (D) *Reflections on the Revolution of Our Time*
   (E) *Arms and the Man*

49. What is the name given to a corporation's accounting year?

   (A) Calendar year
   (B) Leap year
   (C) Financial year
   (D) Fiscal year
   (E) Legal year

50. Third World countries charge that most American multinational corporations are exploiting poor countries by cutting into domestic manufacture, jacking up prices, and withholding technology from consumer countries. Which one of the following best describes multinationals?

   (A) Corporations with worldwide activities either in the field of manufacture or sales or both
   (B) Corporations that deal exclusively with oil purchases
   (C) Corporations that have set up headquarters outside the United States but don't sell to foreign countries
   (D) Corporations that run foreign governments
   (E) Corporations that deal with banana products from Latin American countries

51. The Clayton Anti-Trust Act of 1914 is a law that is applicable to all industries. The act prohibits

   (A) monopoly and collusion
   (B) unrestricted price increases of consumer products
   (C) unfair competitive practices
   (D) shoddy consumer products in the market
   (E) waste and pollution

52. What is the popular name for laws that various states have enacted to protect the public against securities fraud?

   (A) Blue sky laws
   (B) Blue laws
   (C) Civil laws
   (D) Criminal laws
   (E) Ecclesiastical laws

53. Nation A buys $11.9 billion of exports from Nation B. Nation B spends $12 billion purchasing exports from Nation A. Therefore, Nation A has what kind of trade relationship with Nation B?

   (A) A slightly unfavorable balance of trade
   (B) A protectionist trade relationship
   (C) An equivalent or parity trade relationship
   (D) A slightly favorable balance of trade
   (E) A mercantile trade relationship

54. What is the term commonly used to describe a condensed statement showing the nature and amount of a company's assets, liabilities, and capital on a given date?

   (A) Capital gains and losses
   (B) Discretionary account
   (C) Listed stock
   (D) Quotation
   (E) Balance sheet

55. "Centrally planned economies" are usually state-run economies in which private enterprise is virtually nonexistent. Prior to the demise of communism in the early 1990s, which one of the following groups of countries fell into this category?

(A) West European
(B) East European
(C) Southeast Asian
(D) Latin American
(E) Oil-producing countries

56. A "tariff" is essentially a tax on

(A) imports
(B) exports
(C) both imports and exports
(D) corporate profits
(E) individual incomes over $100,000

57. The Bretton Woods international monetary system, which lasted from 1946 through 1973, was a system in which the value of the U.S. dollar was fixed in terms of gold. The international monetary system that replaced Bretton Woods was based upon the fundamental concept of

(A) comparative inflation rates among nations
(B) silver and platinum prices
(C) floating exchange rates
(D) fixed exchange rates
(E) mercantilism

58. Which one of the following best describes a form of government in which the state assumes responsibility for minimum standards of living for all?

(A) Welfare state
(B) Democratic state
(C) Fascist state
(D) Theocratic state
(E) Autocratic state

59. If the U.S. dollar becomes "weaker" or declines in value against the Japanese yen, then an American consumer who wished to purchase a Japanese VCR would find that the VCR's price

(A) remained the same, since currency exchange rates do not affect retail prices
(B) declined, i.e., became less expensive
(C) increased, i.e., became more expensive
(D) would automatically equal the price of all other VCRs (from other countries) currently on the American market
(E) was unimportant, since Japan would pull all of its VCRs out of the American marketplace

60. What federal institution exercises the following functions: (1) determines and collects duties and taxes on merchandise imported to the United States, (2) controls importers and exporters and their goods, and (3) works to control smuggling and revenue fraud?

(A) Bureau of Customs
(B) Department of Commerce
(C) Federal Bureau of Investigation
(D) Internal Revenue Service
(E) Bureau of Labor Statistics

STOP If you finish before the time is up, you may check your work on this section only. Do not turn to any other section in the test.

TIME—45 MINUTES   65 QUESTIONS

PART II

Directions: Each of the questions or incomplete statements below is followed by five suggested answers or completions. Select the one that is best in each case.

61. The Uruguay Round, which eventually led to a new international agreement in 1994, dealt with what major global issue?

    (A) Nuclear nonproliferation
    (B) International antipollution standards
    (C) Biodiversity
    (D) Reduction of tariff and nontariff barriers
    (E) Nonaggression treaties among the nations of South America

62. Which region of the world has suffered the greatest food shortage problem during the last decade?

    (A) Sub-Saharan Africa
    (B) Latin America
    (C) Eastern Europe
    (D) North America
    (E) Middle East

63. The S.P.C.A. is an internationally renowned organization whose primary function is the welfare of animals. What does S.P.C.A. stand for?

    (A) Society for the Propagation of Charity to Animals
    (B) Society for the Promotion of Charitable Acts
    (C) Society for the Prevention of Cruelty to Animals
    (D) Society for the Promotion of Civilizing Animals
    (E) Society for the Prevention of Criminal Acts

64.

The architecture shown in the structure pictured above is characteristic of which one of these East European countries?

    (A) Hungary
    (B) Poland
    (C) Romania
    (D) Bulgaria
    (E) Russia

65. Portuguese is a language of Latin origin spoken in very few countries of the world, with the exception of Portugal and its former colonies, like the Cape Verde Islands, Angola, and Mozambique. However, there is one South American country in which it is a language in everyday use. Which one of the following is it?

    (A) Bolivia
    (B) Chile
    (C) Argentina
    (D) Paraguay
    (E) Brazil

66.

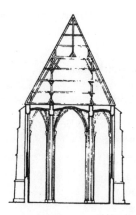

The sketch shown above of the hall church is characteristic of a well-known school of architecture. Which one of the following is it?

(A) Muslim
(B) Byzantine
(C) Gothic
(D) Romanesque
(E) Gupta

67. In international trade, the concept that each nation should specialize in producing those exports that it is most qualified to do so from a cost-efficient basis is known as the

(A) Malthusian law
(B) Law of Comparative Advantage
(C) Free Trade Ideal, or Liberal Trading Order
(D) Law of Supply and Demand (Global Level)
(E) Law of Voluntary Export Restraints

68.

In Roman mythology, what was the name given to the aboriginal spirit of the doorway developed by the Latin people into a double-headed deity who also gave his name to a month of the year?

(A) Zeus
(B) Hercules
(C) Janus
(D) Juno
(E) Julius Caesar

69. The Leaning Tower of Pisa, as its name indicates, is a structure that is permanently tilted and is one of the major tourist attractions of Europe. Where is the Leaning Tower located?

(A) Greece
(B) France
(C) Great Britain
(D) Italy
(E) Belgium

70. Singapore, once an integral part of the Federation of Malaysia, is now an independent city-state located in

(A) southern Asia
(B) eastern Asia
(C) Southeast Asia
(D) the Near East
(E) western Asia

71. Of the following, the only country that has not changed its name is

(A) Gold Coast
(B) Aden
(C) Cambodia
(D) Ceylon
(E) Morocco

72. This nation possesses the strongest industrial base and the largest population of the Arab world. Important leaders of this nation include Sadat and Mubarak. This nation is identified as

(A) Kuwait
(B) Iran
(C) Egypt
(D) Syria
(E) Jordan

73. Australia is an island continent bordering on the Indian Ocean and the Pacific Ocean and has an estimated population of 13.6 million people. Its capital is

(A) Melbourne
(B) Sydney
(C) Wellington
(D) Canberra
(E) Cairo

GO ON TO THE NEXT PAGE

74. Alaska and Hawaii, the last two states to join the Union, were admitted in:

(A) 1947
(B) 1957
(C) 1958
(D) 1959
(E) 1974

75. A secret study commissioned by the Pentagon to analyze U.S. involvement in the Vietnam War and made public in 1971 by The *New York Times* was called the

(A) Valachi papers
(B) Watergate tapes
(C) Pentagon papers
(D) Marshall Plan
(E) French Connection

76. Cooperation among legislators to ensure the passage of laws, particularly those beneficial to their constituencies, is called

(A) filibuster
(B) logrolling
(C) pairing
(D) back-scratching
(E) apportionment

77. The Twenty-sixth Amendment to the U.S. Constitution, ratified in 1971, guarantees

(A) voting rights to 18-year-olds
(B) continuity in case of presidential disability
(C) abolition of the poll tax
(D) voting rights to resident aliens
(E) limiting the presidency to two consecutive terms

78. The "Alliance for Progress," the Peace Corps, and the "New Frontier" are all associated with the administration of which American president?

(A) John F. Kennedy
(B) Richard M. Nixon
(C) Gerald Ford
(D) George Bush
(E) Bill Clinton

79. Executive power is vested in the hands of the

(A) House of Representatives
(B) Senate
(C) President
(D) First Lady
(E) Secretary of Defense

80. All legislative powers are vested in the hands of

(A) Congress
(B) the president
(C) the Speaker of the House
(D) the whip
(E) the Supreme Court

81. The first African American to be appointed to the U.S. Supreme Court was

(A) Thurgood Marshall
(B) Clarence Thomas
(C) Johnny Cochran
(D) Andrew Young
(E) Martin L. King

82. The practice that prevents congressional committees from interrogating executive officials without the express consent of the president is called

(A) executive privilege
(B) executive order
(C) executive agreement
(D) executive authority
(E) extraterritoriality

83. In the 1992 presidential election, the third-party candidate who received 19 million popular votes was

(A) John Anderson
(B) Bob Dole
(C) H. Ross Perot
(D) Steve Forbes
(E) Pat Buchanan

84. Progressive or insurgent members of a political group or institution seeking a voice or control are

(A) young turks
(B) opposition
(C) liberals
(D) radicals
(E) counterculturists

85. Resistance to state authority—particularly military service on the grounds of moral or religious views—is known as

(A) passive resistance
(B) a hunger strike
(C) conscientious objection
(D) the silent majority
(E) passive nonviolence

86. The term "sunset law" refers to a law that

(A) requires legislative hearings to be open to the public

(B) prohibits public officials from accepting gifts from interest-group lobbyists

(C) requires newspaper reporters to reveal their sources of information

(D) mandates the termination of a bureaucracy or agency that is no longer needed

(E) removes a public official from office given the necessary number of voter signatures on a petition

87. The surrender by a state of a person accused or convicted of a crime to the state in which the offense was committed is called

(A) expulsion

(B) expatriation

(C) extradition

(D) exemption

(E) excommunication

88. The type of political system whereby political power is divided or shared between a central government and the states or other local units is termed

(A) unitary

(B) a confederation

(C) federal

(D) a commonwealth

(E) socialist

89. A court order commanding an inferior court, an executive, or an administrative official to perform his or her duty is called

(A) a writ of mandamus

(B) habeas corpus

(C) tempus fugit

(D) pro bono publico

(E) writ of certiorari

90. No one can be compelled to be a witness against himself or herself according to the U.S. Constitution. The more popular statement—"I refuse to answer on the grounds that my answer may tend to incriminate me"—is drawn directly from which constitutional amendment?

(A) First

(B) Fifth

(C) Eighth

(D) Fourteenth

(E) Nineteenth

91. The only federal court that uses a jury trial to try defendants is the

(A) U.S. Supreme Court

(B) U.S. Court of Appeals

(C) U.S. District Court

(D) U.S. Tax Court

(E) U.S. Court of Claims

92. The nation's highest court of law is the

(A) Supreme Court

(B) appellate court

(C) district court

(D) municipal court

(E) probate court

93. In 1993, the gun-control Brady Bill was passed by Congress. One key element of the new law was

(A) severe restrictions upon private gun sales between or among individuals

(B) a waiting period before handguns could be purchased

(C) the outlawing of gun ownership among Americans under the age of eighteen

(D) the banning of all assault rifle sales in America

(E) mandatory gun training for all new owners of handguns

94. The famous 1973 Supreme Court decision of *Roe v. Wade* dealt with what issue?

(A) Segregation in the public schools

(B) A woman's right to an abortion

(C) Unreasonable searches and seizures

(D) Prayer in the public schools

(E) The constitutionality of the death penalty

95. The Civil Rights Act of 1991 passed legislation that allowed lawsuits for those individuals who were victims of discrimination in

(A) private housing sales

(B) voting

(C) the workplace

(D) educational institutions

(E) public accommodations

GO ON TO THE NEXT PAGE

96. The Communist Control Act of 1954
    (A) prevented communists from running for the presidency
    (B) barred communists from leaving the continental United States
    (C) banned the communist party from the U.S. political system
    (D) made it a crime for any American to join the communist party
    (E) exempted the Communist party from the rights accorded to other legally constituted bodies or political parties

97. As final interpreter of the Constitution, the institution that has the power to invalidate presidential actions or congressional statutes that it regards as unconstitutional is the
    (A) Supreme Court
    (B) Senate
    (C) Court of Appeals
    (D) press
    (E) National Security Council

98. The thirty-eighth president is considered unique in American history because he was neither an elected president nor a vice president but, rather, was appointed vice president under a new constitutional amendment. He was
    (A) Richard M. Nixon
    (B) Lyndon B. Johnson
    (C) Gerald R. Ford
    (D) Harry S Truman
    (E) John F. Kennedy

99. In August 1990, the forces of this nation crossed the border into Kuwait, eventually forcing the United States and its allies into the 1991 Gulf War. The aggressor nation was
    (A) Syria
    (B) Egypt
    (C) Iran
    (D) Libya
    (E) Iraq

100. The Monroe Doctrine, enunciated by President James Monroe (1758-1831), was primarily the work of his Secretary of State, John Quincy Adams, and contained elements contributed by Thomas Jefferson and James Madison. Which one of the following can be best described as coming nearest to the Monroe Doctrine?
    (A) The Western Hemisphere was no longer open for European colonization, and the United States would regard any European overture as a threat.
    (B) The United States had the right to intervene in any country threatened by communism.
    (C) The colonization of Latin America was the exclusive preserve of the United States.
    (D) U.S. exports were to be banned from communist countries.
    (E) If one country in Asia fell into the hands of communists, all the others would necessarily follow suit.

101. The World Bank's primary function today is to promote economic development for
    (A) the industrialized democracies of Europe
    (B) the less developed nations
    (C) the wealthier nations of North America
    (D) multinational corporations that wish to invest in less developed nations
    (E) only the former nations of Eastern Europe

102. A Methodist is a member of a Protestant-Christian denomination (the United Methodist Church) with a theology developed in England in the early eighteenth century and characterized by an emphasis on the doctrines of free grace and individual responsibility. The man generally credited as the founder of Methodism is
    (A) John Wesley
    (B) Pope Paul IV
    (C) Martin Luther
    (D) John Stuart Mill
    (E) Francis Bacon

103. Harriet Beecher Stowe (1811-1896) was the American humanitarian whose novel was a factor in bringing about the Civil War. The title of this novel is
    (A) *Soul on Ice*
    (B) *The Autobiography of Malcolm X*
    (C) *Roots*
    (D) *Uncle Tom's Cabin*
    (E) *Alice in Wonderland*

104. *On the Origin of Species*, published in 1859, set forth the idea of the natural selection of living things. The celebrated author was

(A) Bertrand Russell
(B) Albert Einstein
(C) Charles Darwin
(D) Isaac Newton
(E) Sergei Eisenstein

105. Kemal Atatürk introduced sweeping reforms to westernize the modern republic that he founded. This republic is

(A) Syria
(B) Lebanon
(C) Turkey
(D) Iran
(E) Iraq

106. The American army general who pledged that he would return to the Philippines after abandoning those islands to the invading Japanese in December 1941 was

(A) Dwight D. Eisenhower
(B) George S. Patton
(C) Omar Bradley
(D) Mark Clark
(E) Douglas MacArthur

107. In 1945, this nation lay in ruins. Divided by the victors after the war, it would not be politically unified again until 1990. This nation is

(A) Korea
(B) Ireland
(C) Germany
(D) Japan
(E) Czechoslovakia

108. The eating of beef is taboo among the followers of one of the world's best-known religions, which considers the cow a sacred animal. This religion is

(A) Islam
(B) Zen Buddhism
(C) Taoism
(D) Shintoism
(E) Hinduism

109. The United Nations is a world body made up entirely of independent states in pursuit of peace and the betterment of mankind. The United Nations headquarters is located in

(A) Geneva
(B) New York City
(C) Vienna
(D) Nairobi
(E) London

110. According to Karl Marx, one of the founders of communism, working-class control over society is called

(A) survival of the fittest
(B) dictatorship of the proletariat
(C) from each according to his means, and to each according to his needs
(D) the liberation of mankind
(E) the greatest happiness of the greatest number

111. All of the following are spoken languages of Asia EXCEPT

(A) Urdu in Pakistan and India
(B) Chinese in Hong Kong
(C) Tagalog in the Philippines
(D) Sinhalese in Sri Lanka
(E) Xhosa in Nepal

112. Avicenna (980–1037), physician and philosopher, wrote the *Canon of Medicine*, the most famous textbook of medicine until the seventeenth century. What nationality was he?

(A) Greek
(B) Turkish
(C) Polish
(D) Persian
(E) Indian

113. The ancient concept connoting the usurpation of legitimate political authority by a single individual is

(A) fascism
(B) despotism
(C) communism
(D) Nazism
(E) Marxism

GO ON TO THE NEXT PAGE

114. In 1950, Joseph McCarthy (1909–1957), U.S. senator from Wisconsin, set off a raging controversy with an accusation that visibly jolted political life in the United States. The main thrust of his accusation was that

    (A) the Supreme Court was packed with pro-Soviet judges
    (B) Congress was dominated by members of the communist party
    (C) the CIA was teeming with double agents
    (D) the State Department was infiltrated by communists
    (E) the press was making unwarranted exposures of the United States intelligence services

115. On December 7, 1941, there was a surprise attack on Pearl Harbor in Honolulu, which subsequently forced Congress to declare war. Which group was responsible for the attack?

    (A) Chinese
    (B) Japanese
    (C) Russians
    (D) Cubans
    (E) Communists

116. Which of the following statements is factually INCORRECT?

    (A) William Harvey discovered the principle of color photography in 1628.
    (B) The United States purchased Alaska from Russia in 1867.
    (C) Albert Einstein formulated his theory of relativity in 1905.
    (D) The Russian astronaut Yuri Gagarin was the first man to orbit Earth.
    (E) The British unit of currency is called the English dollar.

117. A well-known seventeenth-century English philosopher, regarded during his time as the prophet of reason, expounded the thesis that every human's mind is at birth a blank page on which experience makes its impressions, which are gradually formed into general ideas. Who was this philosopher?

    (A) John Locke
    (B) Thomas Hobbes
    (C) Adam Smith
    (D) Bertrand Russell
    (E) Sir Carol Reed

118. What do the following people have in common: Baruch Spinoza, Arthur Schopenhauer, Socrates, Seneca, and Blaise Pascal?

    (A) They were scientists.
    (B) They were mathematicians.
    (C) They were dramatists.
    (D) They were philosophers.
    (E) They were army generals.

119. The General Assembly is the name given to the main policy-making body of a well-known international organization that represents practically all independent states. Which of the following is it?

    (A) World Bank
    (B) United Nations
    (C) International Court of Justice
    (D) European Common Market
    (E) North Atlantic Treaty Organization

120. Dialectical materialism is a philosophy signifying that everything in this world is material and that change takes place through the conflict of opposites. Which of the following is nearest to this philosophy?

    (A) Fascism
    (B) Communism
    (C) Nazism
    (D) Fabian socialism
    (E) Zionism

121. The most populous nation on Earth is

    (A) India
    (B) Indonesia
    (C) Japan
    (D) China
    (E) Russia

122. In politics, one who espouses or exemplifies ideas fundamentally at variance with a given social, political, or economic order is a

    (A) radical
    (B) liberal
    (C) reformist
    (D) rightist
    (E) fanatic

123. Article 1, Section 8, of the U.S. Constitution promotes the progress of science and arts by securing authors and inventors the exclusive right to their writings and discoveries. This protection is called

   (A) exclusivity
   (B) royalties
   (C) patronage
   (D) copyright
   (E) patent

124. The theory developed by Einstein based on the hypothesis that velocity is the same as measured by any one of a set of observers moving with constant relative velocity is the

   (A) law of supply and demand
   (B) marginal productivity theory
   (C) law of gravity
   (D) theory of relativity
   (E) theory of relative growth

125. Richard M. Nixon resigned from office in 1974 before being impeached by the House of Representatives. The only American president actually to be impeached by the House and then to stand trial in the U.S. Senate was

   (A) Harry S Truman
   (B) James K. Polk
   (C) Ulysses S. Grant
   (D) Woodrow Wilson
   (E) Andrew Johnson

STOP If you finish before the time is up, you may check your work on this section only. Do not turn to any other section in the test.

POSTTEST ANSWER KEY AND EXPLANATIONS

PART I

1. D	13. B	25. D	37. B	49. D
2. B	14. B	26. E	38. A	50. A
3. B	15. C	27. B	39. C	51. A
4. C	16. D	28. D	40. A	52. A
5. A	17. C	29. C	41. C	53. D
6. B	18. A	30. A	42. B	54. E
7. A	19. C	31. C	43. C	55. B
8. C	20. A	32. B	44. A	56. A
9. C	21. B	33. A	45. E	57. C
10. B	22. C	34. B	46. C	58. A
11. C	23. E	35. B	47. A	59. C
12. B	24. A	36. B	48. A	60. A

PART II

61. D	74. D	87. C	100. A	113. B
62. A	75. C	88. C	101. B	114. D
63. C	76. B	89. A	102. A	115. B
64. E	77. A	90. B	103. D	116. E
65. E	78. A	91. C	104. C	117. A
66. C	79. C	92. A	105. C	118. D
67. B	80. A	93. B	106. E	119. B
68. C	81. A	94. B	107. C	120. B
69. D	82. A	95. C	108. E	121. D
70. C	83. C	96. E	109. B	122. A
71. E	84. A	97. A	110. B	123. D
72. C	85. C	98. C	111. E	124. D
73. D	86. D	99. E	112. D	125. E

PART I

1. **The correct answer is (D).** Napoléon's defeat at the hands of Wellington meant his permanent exile to the south Atlantic Ocean isle of St. Helena. He died there in 1821.

2. **The correct answer is (B).** After the demise of communism, Yugoslavia became an ethnic battleground. Eventually, United Nations troops and then American troops occupied the region and managed to establish a shaky peace among the warring peoples.

3. **The correct answer is (B).** The refugees, organized, trained, and paid for by the Central Intelligence Agency, numbered about 1,200 to 1,400. They landed about 90 miles south of Havana on April 7, 1961, in an attempt to overthrow the Castro regime. However, they were defeated and imprisoned within three days.

Air cover that had apparently been planned for the refugees' invasion was withdrawn, and the refugees were left unaided.

4. **The correct answer is (C).** A veto by any one of the five permanent members prevents the Security Council from taking a particular action. These vetoes were especially common during the Cold War, when the two superpowers—the Soviet Union and the United States—used the veto to block Council actions that they opposed. Note that in 1996, both Japan and Germany suggested that they should also become permanent members of the Security Council.

290

5. **The correct answer is (A).** The Federalists, led by Alexander Hamilton, represented the northern commercial and manufacturing interests, supported a strong central government, and believed in a ruling national aristocracy. The Democratic-Republicans, led by Thomas Jefferson, spoke for agriculture, a limited federal role, and a belief in the wisdom of the common man.

6. **The correct answer is (B).** Seward dreamed of an American empire overseas, and, in addition to purchasing Alaska from Russia, he acquired the Virgin Islands from Denmark and the Midway Islands in the Pacific.

7. **The correct answer is (A).** Historians estimate that only about one third of the population supported the war. Another one third was loyal to the Crown, and about one third of the population was neutral or indifferent.

8. **The correct answer is (C).**

9. **The correct answer is (C).** While Lincoln opposed slavery, he also deemed secession by the South to be an unconstitutional action. In short, Lincoln felt that war was preferable to a perpetual North-South division of the country.

10. **The correct answer is (B).** The French Revolution erupted due to oppressive taxes upon the peasants and middle class, animosity among the social classes, high prices for food, and the intellectual appeal of the ideals of liberty.

11. **The correct answer is (C).** NATO's original fifteen members pledged that they would come to the aid of one another if the Soviet Union attacked. Ironically, in 1997, a non-Communist Russia entered into a new, cooperative arrangement with NATO.

12. **The correct answer is (B).** Nixon was elected in 1968 and 1972, Reagan in 1980 and 1984, and Bush in 1988.

13. **The correct answer is (B).** The United States would eventually suffer more than 58,000 deaths during the duration of the war.

14. **The correct answer is (B).** Japan and Australia are not part of the European continent. There were twelve European countries—Austria, Belgium, Finland, France, Germany, Greece, Holland, Ireland, Italy, Luxembourg, Portugal, and Spain—who adopted the Euro. Sweden and Norway did not choose to adopt the Euro as their currency.

15. **The correct answer is (C).** Martin Luther's fame began in 1517 when he posted a set of ninety-five theses, or statements, on the door of Wittenberg Church, attacking the practices of the Catholic Church.

16. **The correct answer is (D).** The British Parliament consists of two houses: the House of Commons, which comprises elected representatives, and the House of Lords, which consists of hereditary peers.

17. **The correct answer is (C).** Field Marshal Erwin Rommel's eventual defeat in North Africa paved the way for the subsequent Allied invasion of Italy and the overthrow of Benito Mussolini in 1943.

18. **The correct answer is (A).** The Molasses Act of 1733, passed by Parliament, had placed a tax upon all foreign molasses (especially French West Indian molasses) entering British America. The importing of molasses from the British West Indies was duty-free. The idea was to make the colonists buy only British molasses.

19. **The correct answer is (C).** Napoléon sold the Louisiana Territory to the United States in order to finance his impending war against Great Britain.

20. **The correct answer is (A).** World War I ended less than four months after Allied counteroffensives employing hundreds of thousands of American troops pushed German forces back from their advanced positions in France.

21. **The correct answer is (B).** The "crash" was caused by wild speculation in stocks and the extensive use of credit (buying on "margin"). By November 1929, the loss in the market value of stocks totaled $30 billion.

22. **The correct answer is (C).** The two atomic bombs dropped on Japanese cities by the United States forced Japan's surrender in September 1945. Germany had surrendered in April of that year.

23. **The correct answer is (E).** Unterseeboot was the German name for the submarine. The German U-boat figured prominently in fighting World War II.

24. **The correct answer is (A).** The Rome–Berlin Axis was formed in 1936 during the Italian invasion of Abyssinia and became a full military alliance in 1939. The term was expanded to include Japan (September 1940) and then Hungary, Bulgaria, and Romania. The Axis collapsed when Italy surrendered in 1943.

25. **The correct answer is (D).** All those events occurred between 1970 and 1974, covering the first and second Nixon administrations. Nixon was forced to resign the presidency in 1974.

26. **The correct answer is (E).** Nasser nationalized the Suez Canal in response to the United States' withdrawing a loan for the Aswan Dam. Great Britain depended on the canal for more than half its oil imports. Israel saw Nasser as a threat to its security. France resented Nasser's appeal to Arabs in Algeria (a French colony at the time).

27. **The correct answer is (B).** Registration did not mean being inducted into the armed forces. No draft existed in 1997. The military services relied upon volunteers.

28. **The correct answer is (D).** Sam Houston's forces defeated General Santa Anna's forces on a prairie near the San Jacinto River in April 1836. Santa Anna was forced to sign a treaty that recognized the independence of Texas.

29. **The correct answer is (C).** Lincoln was assassinated by John Wilkes Booth in 1865, Garfield by Charles J. Guiteau in 1881, and McKinley by Leon Czolgosz in 1901.

30. **The correct answer is (A).** After the Speaker would come the Senate pro tem. The Secretary of State would follow, and then down through the cabinet by order of departmental creation.

31. **The correct answer is (C).** The practice of rewarding supporters, even when they may have lacked qualifications for the job, was eventually challenged with the introduction of the merit, or civil service, system in 1883.

32. **The correct answer is (B).** These new overseas possessions gave America important military bases and new trade routes in the Caribbean and Asia.

33. **The correct answer is (A).** Previous presidents had been inaugurated in New York City and Philadelphia.

34. **The correct answer is (B).** Keynes's most significant work, *The General Theory of Employment, Interest, and Money* (1936), divided economists into two political camps and had a profound effect on the economic policies of Franklin D. Roosevelt and war financing, both in the United States and in Great Britain.

35. **The correct answer is (B).** The Tennessee Valley Authority provided electricity to tens of thousands of farm families; it was electricity that private utility companies had refused to furnish, claiming that such service to rural areas would be too costly.

36. **The correct answer is (B).** The income tax is designed to be a progressive tax, i.e., the more one earns, the more (in theory) one is supposed to pay in actual taxes.

37. **The correct answer is (B).** MFN states that the tariff preferences granted to one state must be granted to all other states exporting the same product.

38. **The correct answer is (A).** Since American domestic oil reserves are dwindling, the United States has had to rely on oil imports to meet its needs. The other countries mentioned in the question have ample oil supplies.

39. **The correct answer is (C).** Inflation means that the dollar can buy less over time. If inflation is extremely severe, then the dollar's purchasing power is reduced substantially.

40. **The correct answer is (A).** Services provided by federal reserve banks include furnishing currency for circulation, supervising member banks, acting as fiscal agent for the government, clearing and collecting checks, and holding member bank reserves.

41. **The correct answer is (C).** A bear has claws that tear "down." Conversely, a "bull" market means that investors think prices will go up (a bull butts "up" with its horns).

42. **The correct answer is (B).** Automatic stabilizers increase spending (tax revenues decrease) when the economy slumps and decrease expenditures (tax revenues increase) when the economy booms.

43. **The correct answer is (C).** Fundamentally, when supply goes up and demand drops, prices go down. When supply drops and demand increases, prices go up.

44. **The correct answer is (A).** NAFTA stands for the North American Free Trade Association. The agreement, which went into effect in 1994, pledged removal of all tariff barriers among the three nations by the year 2009.

45. **The correct answer is (E).** If inflation is high, wages will buy proportionally less. If wages of workers increase at a lower rate than the rate of inflation, their "real wages" in terms of purchasing power are actually decreasing, not increasing.

46. **The correct answer is (C).** Good examples of "blue chip" stocks today include Coca-Cola and McDonald's, among many others.

47. **The correct answer is (A).** The department assists the states and industry, doles out financial aid to areas with a sluggish economy, and promotes the export of U.S. products and travel to the United States.

48. **The correct answer is (A).** The work predicted that communism would inevitably replace capitalism and, in so doing, would create a "utopian" existence with no class warfare or private property.

49. **The correct answer is (D).** A fiscal year for a corporation typically ends on a date other than December 31.

50. **The correct answer is (A).** Typical multinational corporations include Exxon and General Motors.

51. **The correct answer is (A).** A monopoly means that a certain product or service is controlled by one supplier or perhaps two. Without competition, prices may be artificially high and hurt the consumer.

52. **The correct answer is (A).** The term is believed to have originated when a judge ruled that a particular stock had about the same value as a patch of blue sky.

53. **The correct answer is (D).** Nation A has spent $11.9 billion on Nation B's exports, but received $12 billion from Nation B from the sale of its exports to that nation, hence a slightly favorable balance of $100 million. A favorable balance of trade between two nations means that one nation takes in more money from the sale of its exports to another nation than it spends on imports from that same nation.

54. **The correct answer is (E).** In dollar amounts, the balance sheet shows what the company owed and what it owned and the ownership interest in the company of its stockholders.

55. **The correct answer is (B).** East European nations, such as Poland, Hungary, and Czechoslovakia, were forced to copy Soviet-style "centrally planned" economies after World War II. With the demise of the Soviet Union in 1991 and the region's political liberation, most of the East European states moved toward the free-market model.

56. **The correct answer is (A).** Tariffs are taxes that are added to the price of imports, thereby making those products more expensive vis-a-vis domestically produced equivalent products.

57. **The correct answer is (C).** Floating exchange rates meant that the link between the dollar and gold was cut, with market forces being relied upon to adjust the relative value of international currencies.

58. **The correct answer is (A).** The main areas with which the welfare state concerns itself are unemployment, housing, education, health, and old age.

292

59. **The correct answer is (C).** A weaker dollar against the Japanese yen means that it will take more dollars to equal the value of the Japanese yen, upon which the price of the VCR is based. Hence, the product is more costly for the American consumer.

60. **The correct answer is (A).** Individuals who try to smuggle illegal goods into the country or try to avoid paying duties or import taxes face stiff fines or even imprisonment in some cases.

PART II

61. **The correct answer is (D).** The Uruguay Round, part of the GATT movement (General Agreement on Tariffs and Trade), was the latest set of negotiations (begun in 1986 and ratified in 1994) to reduce trade obstacles. Overall, the countries that signed the agreement consented to at least a one-third reduction in tariffs over a ten-year period.

62. **The correct answer is (A).** Per capita food production in the region has declined dramatically, with some nations in the region experiencing a 25 percent (or even more) decrease.

63. **The correct answer is (C).** Humane treatment of animals has become a more visible issue in recent years.

64. **The correct answer is (E).** The cathedral is St. Basil's in Moscow. The architecture reflects the influence of the Russian Orthodox Church.

65. **The correct answer is (E).** The first Portuguese arrived in Brazil in 1500 when the explorer Pedro Alvares Cabral claimed the land for the King of Portugal.

66. **The correct answer is (C).** The illustration shows a section through the nave of a typical late–German Gothic hall church.

67. **The correct answer is (B).** In theory, the law predicts that if all nations produce and export those items best suited to their own economies, then international prices will be fair, and free trade among all nations should be facilitated.

68. **The correct answer is (C).** The month of January was named after him.

69. **The correct answer is (D).** Recently, the Italian government has taken steps to reinforce the tower and prevent further leaning. Otherwise, the tower would someday crash to the ground.

70. **The correct answer is (C).** Singapore is located at the southern tip of the Malaysian peninsula and is in proximity to the Indonesian archipelago.

71. **The correct answer is (E).** Gold Coast is now known as Ghana. Aden is the People's Republic of Yemen. Cambodia is Kampuchea. Ceylon is known as Sri Lanka.

72. **The correct answer is (C).** As of 1997, Egypt's leader was Hosni Mubarek. The United States provides more than $2 billion in foreign aid to Egypt each year, reflecting the American belief that Egypt's stability is vital to peace in the Middle East.

73. **The correct answer is (D).** Canberra is located in New South Wales province between Sydney and Melbourne.

74. **The correct answer is (D).** One reason for the two states being admitted in the same year was the political balance being achieved, with Hawaii becoming a traditional supporter of the Democratic party and Alaska seen as a supporter of the Republican party.

75. **The correct answer is (C).** The Nixon administration sought to enjoin The *New York Times* and other newspapers from publishing the documents, but the courts upheld the principle of freedom of the press, in part on the grounds that publication of the rationale behind the 1968 policy decisions did not impair current national security. The *Times* later won the Pulitzer Prize for its reporting.

76. **The correct answer is (B).** In simple language, logrolling means that "I'll vote for your bill, if you'll vote for mine."

77. **The correct answer is (A).** The Twenty-fifth Amendment was continuity in the event of presidential disability, and the Twenty-fourth Amendment was the abolition of poll tax.

78. **The correct answer is (A).** The "Alliance" concerned aid to Latin America, the Peace Corps dealt with Americans serving as volunteers in other nations, and the "New Frontier" was a Kennedy slogan calling for Americans to confront new challenges.

79. **The correct answer is (C).** This power was created by Article II of the U.S. Constitution.

80. **The correct answer is (A).** This power was created by Article I of the U.S. Constitution.

81. **The correct answer is (A).** Justice Marshall was appointed to the Supreme Court by Lyndon Johnson in 1967.

82. **The correct answer is (A).** One should note that "executive privilege" is not an absolute power. For example, President Nixon's invoking of executive privilege regarding the infamous Watergate tapes was not upheld by the Supreme Court in 1974.

83. **The correct answer is (C).** Perot, a businessman, also ran unsuccessfully for the presidency in 1996.

84. **The correct answer is (A).** Originally, *young Turks* referred to a member of a revolutionary party in Turkey in the early twentieth century.

85. **The correct answer is (C).** Conscientious objection to military service dates from the Civil War, when the Quakers refused to fight.

86. **The correct answer is (D).** Sunset laws are used almost exclusively at the state level.

87. **The correct answer is (C).** Extradition is provided for in Article IV, Section 2, of the U.S. Constitution.

88. **The correct answer is (C).** Unitary governments concentrate power in the central authority, where confederations grant most of the political power to the states or provinces.

89. **The correct answer is (A).** The order is not applicable if the official has the discretion to act. It merely compels action when that is the official's duty, which he or she is not performing.

90. **The correct answer is (B).** Invoking the Fifth Amendment is not necessarily a confession of guilt. Rather, no citizen is obligated to say anything that might create an impression of guilt.

91. **The correct answer is (C).** The U.S. District Courts are also the only federal courts to have grand juries that issue indictments (there is enough evidence to justify a trial). Federal crimes such as bank robbery, treason, mail tampering, etc., are heard in the District Courts, of which there are more than ninety across the nation.

92. **The correct answer is (A).** The Supreme Court heads the judicial branch of the American government. It also performs a political function of tremendous significance as the official interpreter and expounder of the Constitution.

93. **The correct answer is (B).** The Brady Bill established a five-day waiting period. During that time, a background check of the prospective buyer could be run.

94. **The correct answer is (B).** Although attacked over the years, the decision has not been overturned. In general, a woman still has the basic right to an abortion in the first trimester of pregnancy.

95. **The correct answer is (C).** The law was aimed at countering a series of Supreme Court rulings that had made it more difficult for workers to bring and win job discrimination lawsuits.

96. **The correct answer is (E).** The act does not make it illegal to be a communist but refers individual liability to the Internal Security Act. Membership in a communist organization is determined, subject to court appeal, by the Subversive Activities Control Board. Considered unconstitutional by some, the act has not been enforced or strictly tested in the courts but has prevented the communist party from appearing on the ballot.

97. **The correct answer is (A).** The Supreme Court's power is known as judicial review and was first applied in the 1803 case of *Marbury v. Madison.*

98. **The correct answer is (C).** Ford was appointed vice president by Richard Nixon, replacing Spiro Agnew, who was forced to resign due to a personal scandal. When Nixon himself resigned the presidency after Watergate, Ford became president in 1974.

99. **The correct answer is (E).** Saddam Hussein's forces invaded Kuwait for a variety of reasons. First, Hussein considered Kuwait's oil a valuable prize. Second, he thought of Kuwait as rightfully belonging to Iraq. Third, he believed the United States would not respond to the invasion.

100. **The correct answer is (A).**

101. **The correct answer is (B).** Poorer nations in Africa, Asia, and Latin America require infusions of outside aid in order to develop viable economies.

102. **The correct answer is (A).** Wesley (1703–1791) delivered more than 40,000 sermons in his lifetime and traveled extensively throughout England to recruit those who found the established churches of the day irrelevant to their spiritual needs.

103. **The correct answer is (D).** Stowe's novel fueled the abolitionist cause by depicting the evils of owning slaves and harm inflicted upon the slaves themselves.

104. **The correct answer is (C).** Darwin's work advocated the theory of evolution, meaning that all species had evolved from lower forms.

105. **The correct answer is (C).** Atatürk (1881–1938) created a Turkish republic with a Western-style constitution and implemented numerous social changes, including introduction of the Western calendar and alphabet, voting for women, banning of polygamy, and the replacement of Turkish law with European codes.

106. **The correct answer is (E).** MacArthur did return in 1944.

107. **The correct answer is (C).** East Germany was reabsorbed by West Germany in October 1990. One Germany was now a political reality.

108. **The correct answer is (E).** This religious taboo remains strong, as evidenced by contemporary conditions in India.

109. **The correct answer is (B).** New York City was seen as a logical location since the drive to establish the United Nations was led by the United States after World War II.

110. **The correct answer is (B).** The dictatorship of the proletariat meant that the proletariat would be led by a "vanguard" who would hasten the transition to full utopian communism in the future.

111. **The correct answer is (E).** Xhosa is a language spoken in South Africa. Nepali is spoken in Nepal.

112. **The correct answer is (D).** Avicenna combined the knowledge of both classical and Islamic medical knowledge. His work appeared in a Latin translation by the twelfth century.

113. **The correct answer is (B).** Despotism would be comparable to rule by a supreme dictator.

114. **The correct answer is (D).** It also spawned the concept of McCarthyism, coined by opponents of Senator McCarthy, to define the political practice of publicizing accusations of disloyalty or subversion with insufficient regard to evidence. It was also used to define methods of investigation and accusation regarded as unfair in order to suppress opposition.

115. **The correct answer is (B).** Japan's sneak attack on Pearl Harbor was probably designed both to destroy the core of the American navy and to ensure Japanese control of and consolidation over its Pacific empire.

116. **The correct answer is (E).** The British unit of currency is called the pound sterling. All of the other statements are factually correct.

117. **The correct answer is (A).** Locke called this blank slate the tabula rasa. Experience through careful education would lead to the mind's ultimate development.

118. The correct answer is (D). All of these men were proponents of philosophical values, ideas, or systems. Their time spans range from the ancient Greeks to the nineteenth century.

119. The correct answer is (B). The General Assembly comprised 189 nations in 2003.

120. The correct answer is (B). The idea of dialectical materialism influenced Karl Marx, who saw the clash between the thesis and its antithesis producing a new synthesis. This clash was repeated throughout history, ending with the final synthesis, communism.

121. The correct answer is (D). The estimate in 2003 was that China had a population of almost 1.3 billion people.

122. The correct answer is (A). Radicals usually advocate a fundamental transformation of society. Their advocacy is listened to by others when the current society has major problems and is no longer viewed as legitimate by key segments of the population.

123. The correct answer is (D). Federal law allows copyrights on books, works of art, lectures, musical compositions, motion pictures, and photographs. A copyright is different from a patent in that a patent is a temporary exclusive right of invention covering a period of seventeen years.

124. The correct answer is (D). The theory of relativity is expressed by the formula $E=mc^2$ (E equals mc squared). In short, energy equals mass times the velocity of light squared. Matter and energy are freely convertible into each other.

125. The correct answer is (E). Johnson's impeachment in the House almost led to his conviction in the Senate in 1867. The conviction was denied by one vote, thus preserving the independence of the executive branch.

Part VI

NATURAL SCIENCES

Chapter 14
PRETEST

TIME—45 MINUTES	60 QUESTIONS

PART I
BIOLOGICAL SCIENCE

Directions: Each of the questions or incomplete statements below is followed by five suggested answers or completions. Select the one that is best in each case.

1. Which of these is NOT a development commonly seen in plant evolution as plants moved to land?

   (A) Vertical growth
   (B) Development of vascular tissue
   (C) Structures to reach underground water
   (D) Reduction in the number of essential minerals
   (E) Structures to take advantage of plentiful light

2. As an action potential is propagated along a neuronal membrane, which of these events comes first?

   (A) Influx of K+
   (B) Influx of Na+
   (C) Outflow of Na+
   (D) Outflow of K+
   (E) Refractory period

3. Which of the following is NOT a mechanoreceptor?

   (A) Statocysts
   (B) Pacinian corpuscles
   (C) Meissner's corpuscles
   (D) Semicircular canals
   (E) Ommatidia

4. The portion of the mammalian brain that is most highly developed and that is used in the processing of thought is the

   (A) cerebellum
   (B) spinal cord
   (C) cerebrum
   (D) optic lobe
   (E) neuron

5. If the cells are separated at the two-cell stage in the normal development of a human embryo, the result will be

   (A) death for each cell
   (B) identical twins
   (C) fraternal twins
   (D) one male child, one female child
   (E) one cell lives, the other dies

6. Ignoring the environmental influences and genetic background of the father, if the ovaries of a rat that continually produces black offspring (and whose ancestors have also always produced black offspring) are removed and replaced with the ovaries of a rat, which, along with her ancestors, has always produced white offspring, that rat will now produce

   (A) brown offspring—a combination of the black and white colorings
   (B) some black and some white offspring
   (C) black offspring, as she did prior to the operation
   (D) offspring that are part black and part white
   (E) white offspring

7. If the pancreas of a dog is surgically removed, the dog will die shortly thereafter because

 (A) it will be unable to properly regulate its sugar levels, and it will be unable to adequately digest certain food materials
 (B) it will contract diabetes
 (C) it will starve
 (D) it will go into shock from the surgery
 (E) too much sugar will enter its bloodstream, thereby overloading the kidneys and resulting in kidney failure

8. Blood that passes through the liver gets to the heart via the hepatic vein. Blood in the hepatic vein has a high amount of

 (A) red blood cells
 (B) white blood cells
 (C) carbon dioxide
 (D) urea
 (E) bile

9. The rate that it takes water to travel from the roots of a plant into its stem (or trunk) and out the leaves is controlled by the

 (A) mitochondria
 (B) xylem
 (C) phloem
 (D) stomata
 (E) resin ducts

10. In order to maintain a normal life, freshwater fish must maintain certain levels of sodium in their systems. In order to do this, they actively transport sodium

 (A) out through the kidneys and in through the gills
 (B) out of the blood through the gills and into the blood through the kidneys
 (C) into the blood both through the kidneys and gills
 (D) into the digestive system without the use of gills or kidneys
 (E) through the skin

Questions 11–13 refer to the following diagram.

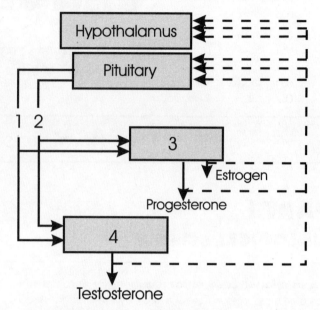

11. Number 3 in the diagram is the

 (A) uterus
 (B) testes
 (C) ovary
 (D) follicle-stimulating hormone
 (E) thyroid gland

12. The broken lines that connect several structures in the diagram are representative of pathways for hormones that function as

 (A) inhibitors
 (B) follicles
 (C) stimulators
 (D) luteinizers
 (E) testosterone

13. The production of sex hormones is controlled by

 (A) the testes and ovaries
 (B) the hypothalamus and FSH
 (C) the pituitary and ovaries
 (D) estrogens and progesterones
 (E) a negative feedback system

14. "The Pill" interferes with the normal hormonal cycle of the ovaries. In doing so, it inhibits ovulation by "shutting off"

 (A) luteinizing hormone (LH)
 (B) estrogen
 (C) progesterone
 (D) androgen
 (E) testosterone

15. Photosynthesis utilizes light energy from the sun to manufacture an energy-storage product that is one of the:

    (A) proteins
    (B) sugars
    (C) nucleic acids
    (D) amino acids
    (E) gases we breathe

16. During the developmental process of a chick embryo, numerous cell movements occur that result in the cells originally near the front end of the embryo being at the rear of the animal at hatching. A simple way to follow those movements would be to

    (A) make histological sections of the embryo at various stages of development
    (B) take movies of the entire process of development
    (C) color the cell with a vital stain
    (D) put a hole in the cell wall of the cell you wish to follow, thereby making it visible
    (E) There is no simple way this can be done.

17. A new ultramicroscopic organelle (cell structure) is reported by a microscopist. Another biologist challenges the report, claiming that the organelle is an artifact caused by the chemicals used in preparing the cells for electron microscopy. How would you go about testing which biologist is correct?

    (A) Do a chemical analysis of the cells to determine if they contain the chemical compound in question.
    (B) Look at living cells with a phase-contrast microscope.
    (C) See if any other report of the organelle exists in previous literature.
    (D) Use different electron microscopic preparation procedures on similar cells and see if the organelle is present.
    (E) Use the same procedure as the electron microscopist used on many different cells to see if they have the organelle.

Questions 18–21 refer to the following passage. Read the passage and then mark the letter of the description that best fits each statement.

The problem of the actual attachment of the spindle fibers to the centromere is an important point in this discussion. This has been confirmed by electron microscopy, and it has been postulated that the chromosomal spindle fibers are developed from the centromeres of each chromosome and grow toward the poles of the cell. The fact that chromosomal fragments without a centromere do not undergo anaphase movements confirms the importance of these spindle fibers in chromosomal movements.

    (A) A fact or restatement of a fact about mitosis presented in the passage
    (B) A fact or true statement not presented in the passage
    (C) A hypothesis or assumption presented in the passage
    (D) A hypothesis or deduction not presented in the passage but that is logical and directly deducible from material in the passage
    (E) A false statement or illogical conclusion

18. Chromosomal fibers extend from the centromeres toward the poles.

19. Astral fibers are associated with mitosis in certain cells.

20. Separation and migration of centrioles toward opposite poles begin during prophase.

21. A chromosomal fragment lacking a centromere will not be included within a daughter cell nucleus.

22. Cells are able to make ATP in two different ways. One, called substrate level photophosphorylation, forms ATP by transferring a phosphate group to ADP. The second way is by

    (A) catabolism of proteins into amino acids
    (B) production of lactic acid during anaerobic respiration
    (C) production of alcohol during anaerobic respiration
    (D) harvesting electrons and transferring them along the electron transport chain
    (E) production of triglycerides from three fatty-acid molecules and one glycerol molecule

GO ON TO THE NEXT PAGE

23. A difference between T-lymphocytes and B-lymphocytes is that

    (A) T-lymphocytes are produced in the thymus and B-lymphocytes are produced in the bone marrow
    (B) T-lymphocytes mature in the thymus after being produced in the bone marrow, while B-lymphocytes do not migrate after their production in the bone marrow
    (C) B-lymphocytes mature in the bone marrow after their production in the thymus, while T-lymphocytes do not migrate after their production in the thymus
    (D) T-lymphocytes are temporary phagocytes, while B-lymphocytes are permanent
    (E) There is no difference between B-lymphocytes and T-lymphocytes.

24. The nitrogen base present in RNA but not in DNA is

    (A) uracil
    (B) udenine
    (C) thymine
    (D) guanine
    (E) cytosine

25. The Earth's early atmosphere contained virtually no free oxygen. Our modern-day atmosphere contains about 20 percent free oxygen (O_2). Where did it come from?

    (A) A by-product of aerobic respiration
    (B) Breakdown of O_2
    (C) Photosynthesis
    (D) Oxidation of metals
    (E) Splitting of water by sunlight

26. A current theory of species formation specifies the need for isolation in the formation of a species. This isolation can be generated by differences in

    (A) environmental requirements
    (B) geographical distribution
    (C) seasonal or physiological aspects of sexual reproduction
    (D) sexual apparatus
    (E) All of the above

27. Within relatively recent times, two groups of birds have become extinct. The dodo and passenger pigeon had a common cause of extinction, mainly

    (A) snakes that ate their eggs
    (B) a viral infection
    (C) human predation
    (D) malarial-type disease
    (E) lack of gravel for their digestive systems

28. That radiation can significantly increase the rate of mutation in humans is best shown by studies that point out a higher rate of birth defects among children of

    (A) radio technicians
    (B) "ham" radio operators
    (C) TV announcers
    (D) radiologists
    (E) astronomers

29. Which of the following theories was suggested by its early proponents in an effort to explain the tendency of populations of organisms to grow to a nonsustainable size?

    (A) Modern synthetic theory of evolution
    (B) Theory of natural selection
    (C) Autogenic theory
    (D) Mutation theory
    (E) Theory of inheritance of acquired characteristics

30. The tissue type that contributed most to the success and wide distribution of land plants is

    (A) meristematic
    (B) vascular
    (C) sporogenous
    (D) fruiting body
    (E) parenchymatous

31. Sea squirts and lampreys share several characteristics, such as a notochord at some stage in development, a ventrally located heart, and a perforated pharynx. The similarities of these two different animals can be explained by postulating

    (A) similar adaptations to the same predators
    (B) similar eating habits
    (C) similar environmental pressures
    (D) the same type of embryonic cleavage pattern
    (E) common ancestry

32. In a population in Hardy-Weinberg equilibrium, the recessive allele has a .2 frequency. What percentage of the population will be heterozygous?

    (A) 8 percent
    (B) 16 percent
    (C) 20 percent
    (D) 32 percent
    (E) 80 percent

Questions 33–36 consist of *statements* and a *conclusion*. The statements are identified by Roman numeral I and the conclusions by Roman numeral II. The statements may be true or false, and the conclusions may or may not be logical. To be logical, the statements must lead directly to the conclusions. If the statements are postulates or principles of the theory of evolution, then select your answer from (A)–(D) in the key; if the statements are from some other theory, such as molecular biology, Mendelian genetics, or some other nonbiological or nonevolutionary topic, then select (E).

(A) The deduction from statement to conclusion is logical, and the conclusion is true.

(B) The deduction from statement to conclusion is illogical, but the conclusion is nevertheless true.

(C) The deduction from statement to conclusion is logical, but the conclusion is not true.

(D) The deduction from statement to conclusion is illogical, and the conclusion is not true.

(E) The statements are neither postulates nor principles of evolutionary theory.

33. I. The greater the adaptive value of a genetic trait, the greater will be the probability of its frequency increasing in successive generations. II. In malarial-endemic centers, the heterozygote for sickle-cell anemia has a greater adaptive value than it does in the normal heterozygote.

34. I. The beneficial characteristics acquired during the life of an individual are transmitted by heredity to successive generations. II. The transmission of new characteristics to successive generations results in the gradual formation of new taxa.

35. I. Most gametes are haploid cells. II. Meiosis produces haploid cells.

36. I. The geographical distributions of the species that comprise a genus are restricted to a particular geographical region. II. The geographical regions occupied by most species are circumscribed by other geographically distinct regions with effective geographical barriers.

37. Intelligent animal life on another planet is more likely to be aerobic rather than anaerobic because

(A) all planets have O_2 atmospheres

(B) aerobes are about twenty times more efficient in extracting energy from foodstuffs than are anaerobes

(C) life has never existed in an O_2-free environment

(D) breathing deeply enhances brain functions and intelligence

(E) all anaerobes are fungi

38. Plants convert solar energy to chemical energy through pigments such as chlorophyll, the electrons of which are "excited" by exposure to sunlight. A red-orange pigment that functions similarly is

(A) biliverdin

(B) NADP

(C) cytochrome

(D) carotenoid

(E) ubiquinone

39. The dark reaction of photosynthesis involves

(A) hydrolysis of glucose

(B) production of ATP

(C) fixation of CO_2

(D) activation of photopigments

(E) synthesis of new photopigments

40. A compound that is split during photosynthesis is

(A) H_2O

(B) CO_2

(C) NADP

(D) ADP

(E) DNA

41. Grana of chloroplasts, cristae of mitochondria, villi of the intestines, and brush borders of some kidney cells share the function of

(A) protecting the structure from damage

(B) providing a large membrane surface area for chemical reaction

(C) increasing osmotic pressure

(D) exerting control over cellular metabolism

(E) stimulating cellular reproduction

GO ON TO THE NEXT PAGE

Questions 42–44 refer to the following passage and graph.

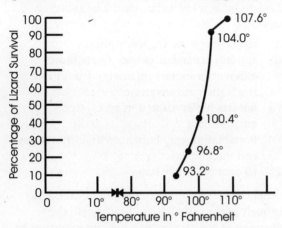

Lizards are poikilotherms and can adjust their body temperatures only by changing their environments. Scientists observing lizards in a terrarium noted that when a lizard became sick, it positioned itself close to a lightbulb, which served as a source of heat. The scientists then performed the following experiment: A large number of lizards were infected with a bacterial agent. Some lizards were placed in each of five separate terrariums, each set at a different temperature around the range preferred by healthy lizards. The graph above indicates the survival rate at various temperatures. The survival rate was high only for lizards kept at temperatures above those temperatures usually selected by healthy lizards (which might be called their normal body temperature).

42. From the passage and data above, one can conclude that the highest temperature that can be called the normal or preferred body temperature of healthy lizards is

(A) 93.2°F
(B) 96.8°F
(C) 100.4°F
(D) 104.0°F
(E) 107.6°F

43. The passage indicates that

(A) lizards are healthier at higher temperatures
(B) bacteria must be prevented from reproducing at higher temperatures
(C) the lizards' white cells have greater immunological activity at higher temperatures
(D) the preferred body temperature for these lizards is below that of normal human temperature
(E) the lizards' ability to withstand infection is enhanced at higher temperatures

44. An implication of the experiment for the treatment of humans with microbial infections and accompanying fever is that

(A) very high fevers can lead to convulsions and brain damage
(B) antipyretic drugs such as aspirin should be used routinely to lower fever for the patient's comfort
(C) fever may interfere with the patient's sleep
(D) low-grade fevers may play a role in fighting infection, and, perhaps, they should be allowed to run their course
(E) persistent fever can cause dehydration in humans

Questions 45–46 refer to the following graph.

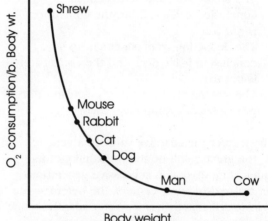

45. O_2 consumption per gram body weight gives a measure here of each animal's approximate

(A) metabolic rate
(B) life span
(C) environmental temperature preference
(D) intelligence
(E) number of inspirations per minute

46. Where would you expect an elephant to be on this graph?

(A) Higher than man on the vertical axis, and somewhat to the left of man horizontally
(B) Well above the shrew on the vertical axis, and to the left of the cow horizontally
(C) Below the cow on the vertical axis, and even farther to the right horizontally
(D) Below the x-axis and to the right of the cow on the horizontal axis
(E) The graph does not provide any information that can be extrapolated to an elephant.

47. One of the recent diet fads was a high-protein, high-fat, low-carbohydrate diet. Among the metabolic changes it caused were increased production of ketoacids, acetone breath, and acidic urine. These duplicate some of the symptoms of which metabolic disease?

    (A) PKU
    (B) Lactose deficiency
    (C) Tay-Sachs disease
    (D) Diabetes mellitus
    (E) Diabetes insipidis

48. Those molecules used to cut DNA at specific locations based on recognition sequences are

    (A) RFLPs
    (B) restriction enzymes
    (C) inducers
    (D) promoters
    (E) plasmids

49. Competition for light, space, and food is probably most severe between two

    (A) closely related species occupying the same niche
    (B) closely related species occupying different niches
    (C) unrelated species occupying the same niche
    (D) unrelated species occupying different niches
    (E) species in different but adjacent overlapping ecosystems

50. Arctic penguins are much larger than penguins living in more temperate regions. An explanation of this would most likely involve which one of the following factors?

    (A) In Antarctica, breeding seasons are short; as a result, penguins there lay fewer and larger eggs than penguins in warmer climates.
    (B) The fishes on which penguins feed are larger in cold water than in warmer water.
    (C) Cold air contains a larger percentage of oxygen than warm air.
    (D) Large bodies have a smaller surface-to-volume ratio than do small bodies.
    (E) Fewer parasites live in Antarctic regions than in temperate regions.

51. Fossil spores of magnolias have been found in Scotland. These trees are not native to Scotland today. The most likely reason for this discrepancy is that

    (A) the magnolias had all been cut down for firewood
    (B) the Scotch pine is more resistant to insect infestation than the magnolia
    (C) glaciers uprooted all the magnolias during the Ice Age
    (D) magnolias cannot survive the salt spray that sweeps across Scotland
    (E) at one time, the environment in Scotland was much warmer than it is now

52. Although populations remain relatively constant over long periods of time, they oscillate around a mean or average. The regulation of populations has been called a form of homeostasis. Which of the following responses best describes the relation of the oscillations to homeostasis?

    (A) The larger the oscillations, the more efficient the homeostatic mechanism.
    (B) The smaller the oscillations, the more efficient the homeostatic mechanism.
    (C) The more frequent the oscillations, the more efficient the homeostatic mechanism.
    (D) The less frequent the oscillations, the more efficient the homeostatic mechanism.
    (E) There is no relation between oscillations and homeostasis.

53. Which of the following was MOST influential upon Darwin's formulation of the theory of natural selection?

    (A) DeVries's concept of mutations
    (B) Lamarck's ideas on inheritance of acquired characteristics
    (C) Malthus's essay on population
    (D) Mendel's genetic studies on peas
    (E) Wallace's paper on survival

54. The BEST reason for using mathematics in a study of populations is that it allows us to

    (A) define the limits of a population
    (B) quantify and predict growth in a population
    (C) regulate population
    (D) determine when we are working with a population
    (E) isolate populations

GO ON TO THE NEXT PAGE

55. Which of the following does NOT represent a way in which a single white oak tree is like a population of white oaks?

(A) It may increase in mass with time.
(B) It is subject to genetic drift.
(C) It is sensitive to temperature changes in the environment.
(D) It is subject to parasitism.
(E) It may have a cyclical pattern of growth.

56. It is hypothesized that hawk species, *H*, is a major factor in controlling squirrel species, *S*. The best preliminary step in a study of this might be to determine

(A) if the squirrels are first-order consumers and the hawks are second-order consumers
(B) if the hawks eat the squirrels
(C) what kind of diseases the squirrels can contract
(D) the type of food the squirrels eat
(E) the habitats occupied by the hawks and the squirrels

57. The most workable and valid procedure for an investigator to use to attack the situation in question 56 would be to study

(A) examples of all species of squirrels and hawks
(B) samples of representative populations of hawk *H* and squirrel *S*
(C) all individuals of a representative population of hawk *H* and squirrel *S*
(D) representative individuals of squirrel *S*
(E) samples of all major ecosystems

58. If the hypothesis that the hawks are controlling the squirrels is correct, then

(A) a decrease in the population of owls should decrease the squirrel population
(B) a decrease in the population of squirrels should increase the hawk population
(C) an increase of squirrel diseases should not affect the hawk population
(D) an increase in food for squirrels should not change the hawk population
(E) an increase in hawks should decrease the population of squirrels

Questions 59–60 refer to the following passage.

Each year, farmers buy 5 million tons of steel and about 320 million pounds of rubber, enough to put tires on nearly 6 million automobiles. Farmers use more petroleum than any other single industry and more electricity than all the people and industries in Chicago, Detroit, Boston, Baltimore, Houston, and Washington, D.C., combined. Each year, trucks carry about 375 million tons of food off the farms.

By the time food has reached the table, more energy has been expended on transportation and distribution than is contained in the food. Without the energy input from fossil fuels, modern food chains could not survive. And fossil fuels, except coal, may be expended within fifty to 100 years. At that time, we may have to use atomic energy to support our modern food chains.

(A) Fact presented in the passage
(B) Fact or true statement not presented in the passage
(C) Hypothesis or assumption that is presented in the passage
(D) Hypothesis or deduction that is not presented in the passage, but that is logical and directly deducible from material in the passage
(E) False statement or illogical conclusion

59. Unless alternate sources to energy beyond fossil fuels are developed within 100 years, there is every possibility of a worldwide famine, resulting in a large number of deaths.

60. People and industries in Chicago, Detroit, Boston, Baltimore, Houston, and Washington, D.C., utilize about the same amount of electricity as it takes the farmers in the United States to produce some 375 million tons of food.

STOP If you finish before the time is up, you may check your work on this section only. Do not turn to any other section in the test.

TIME—45 MINUTES	60 QUESTIONS

PART II
PHYSICAL SCIENCE

Directions: Each of the questions or incomplete statements below is followed by five suggested answers or completions. Select the one that is best in each case.

1. There are three major types of natural radioactive decay: alpha radiation, beta radiation, and gamma radiation. Which, if any, is the most penetrating radiation?

   (A) Alpha rays
   (B) Beta rays
   (C) Gamma rays
   (D) Alpha and beta rays are more penetrating than gamma rays.
   (E) They are all equally penetrating.

2. Which of the following, if any, is an example of nuclear fusion?

   (A) $^{235}_{92}U + ^{1}_{0}n \rightarrow ^{139}_{56}Ba + ^{94}_{36}Kr + ^{1}_{0}n$
   (B) $^{2}_{1}H + ^{3}_{1}H \rightarrow ^{4}_{2}He + ^{1}_{0}n$
   (C) $^{234}_{92}U \rightarrow ^{4}_{2}He + ^{230}_{90}Th$
   (D) All of the above
   (E) None of the above

PERIODIC TABLE OF ELEMENTS

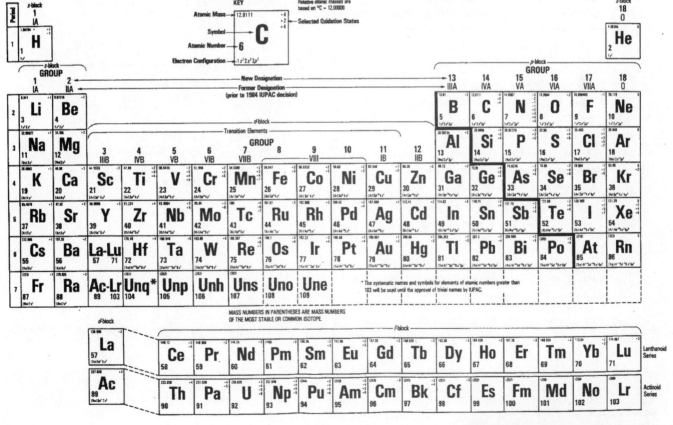

GO ON TO THE NEXT PAGE

3. Which of the following statements is least correct concerning the fact that the half-life of carbon-14 is 5,770 years?

(A) Half of a gram sample of carbon-14 will decay in 5,770 years.

(B) Given two atoms of carbon-14, one of them will decay in 5,770 years.

(C) Half of the carbon-14 on Earth will decay in 5,770 years.

(D) Carbon-14 is a long-lived radioactive isotope.

(E) The age of organic matter can be determined by using this fact.

4. Radioactive decay will occur no matter what is the chemical nature of the atom involved. How it is bonded and how reactive it is are immaterial to how dangerous it may be, since the decay of its nucleus is the factor that determines penetrating power. Therefore, which of the following statements requires further investigation?

(A) Strontium-90 is dangerous since it reacts, chemically, the same as nonradioactive strontium.

(B) Carbon dioxide in the air contains a certain percentage of radioactive carbon-14.

(C) Radon is in Group VIII and is, therefore, an inert gas as harmless as helium.

(D) All of these statements are above suspicion.

(E) None of these statements is strictly true, and all require further investigation.

5. The following elements are all in Period IV (see the Periodic Table of Elements): C, Si, Ge, and Sn. Which of these has the largest atomic radius?

(A) C

(B) Sn

(C) Ge

(D) Si

(E) They are all the same size.

6. An examination of the Periodic Table, with some knowledge of the nature of elements, would indicate which of the following?

(A) There are more metals than nonmetals.

(B) There are more nonmetals than metals.

(C) The number of metals and nonmetals is about the same.

(D) All metals are elements with heavy masses, and all nonmetals are elements with light masses.

(E) There is no way of distinguishing metals and nonmetals by examining the Periodic Table of Elements.

7. Most metals are solids, and most common nonmetals are gases. Which of the following pairs of metals and nonmetals are exceptions (i.e., metal is a liquid and nonmetal is a solid)?

(A) Gold and nitrogen

(B) Mercury and sulfur

(C) Sodium and sulfur

(D) Mercury and nitrogen

(E) Gold and sulfur

8. How many atoms of each element are in the compound ammonium dichromate $((NH_4)_2Cr_2O_7)$?

(A) 1 nitrogen, 4 hydrogens, 2 chromiums, 7 oxygens

(B) 1 nitrogen, 8 hydrogens, 2 chromiums, 7 oxygens

(C) 2 nitrogens, 4 hydrogens, 2 chromiums, 7 oxygens

(E) 2 nitrogens, 8 hydrogens, 14 chromiums, 7 oxygens

(D) 2 nitrogens, 8 hydrogens, 2 chromiums, 7 oxygens

9. Which of the following is NOT a properly balanced chemical equation?

(A) $SO_3 + H_2O \rightarrow H_2SO_4$

(B) $H + O_2 \rightarrow H_2O$

(C) $BaO + H_2O \rightarrow Ba(OH)2$

(D) $CH_4 + 2O_2 \rightarrow CO_2 + 2H_2O$

(E) They are all balanced equations.

10. In which of the following reactions would the rate of the forward reaction (left to right) be increased by raising the temperature?

(A) $2Hg + O_2 \longleftrightarrow 2HgO$

(B) $SO_3 + H_2O \longleftrightarrow H_2SO_4$

(C) $2 KClO_3 \longleftrightarrow 2 KCl + 3 O_2$

(D) $N_2O_5 + H_2O \longleftrightarrow 2 HNO_3$

(E) None of the above

Questions 11–14 refer to the following pairs of substances.

    I.   CO and CO_2

    II. O_2 and O_3

    III. $^{12}_{6}C$ and $^{14}_{6}C$

    IV. CH_3-CH_2-CH_2-CH_3 and CH_3-CH-CH_3

                                CH_3

11. Which of these pairs of substances are isotopes?

(A) I only

(B) II only

(C) III only

(D) IV only

(E) II and IV only

12. Which of these pairs of substances are isomers?

(A) I only

(B) II only

(C) III only

(D) IV only

(E) II and IV only

13. Which of these substances are allotropes?

(A) I only

(B) II only

(C) III only

(D) IV only

(E) II and IV only

14. Which of these substances illustrates the law of multiple composition?

(A) I only

(B) II only

(C) III only

(D) IV only

(E) None of the above

Questions 15–18 refer to the following compounds.

    I. $MgCl_2$

    II. CH_4

    III. HCN

    IV. H_2O

15. Which compound(s) illustrate(s) ionic bonding?

(A) I only

(B) IV only

(C) I and III only

(D) I and IV only

(E) II and III only

16. Which compound(s) illustrate(s) covalent bonding (sharing of electrons)?

(A) I only

(B) I and IV only

(C) II and III only

(D) I, II, and IV only

(E) II, III, and IV only

17. Which compound(s) illustrate(s) multiple covalent bonding (sharing of more than one pair of electrons between two atoms)?

(A) I only

(B) II only

(C) III only

(D) IV only

(E) II, III, and IV only

18. Which compound has very strong intermolecular forces (binding molecules together by hydrogen bonding)?

(A) I only

(B) II only

(C) III only

(D) IV only

(E) None of the above

19. A person is sitting in the bathtub relaxing with an alcoholic drink, a powdered-sugar donut, and an electric hair dryer. Which of the following is a contributing cause of his or her electrocution when the dryer slips and falls into the tub?

(A) Alcohol from the drink has dissolved in the water.

(B) Salt from the perspiration of the body has dissolved in the water.

(C) Sugar from the donut has dissolved in the water.

(D) The water has nothing dissolved in it from any source.

(E) None of these is a contributing cause.

GO ON TO THE NEXT PAGE

20. The most common reaction known to chemists is the neutralization of an acid by a base. Which of the following statements is (are) true?

    I.   Water is always a product.
    II. Salt and water are products.
    III. A gas is always a product.
    IV. The pH increases when the base is added to the acid.

    (A) III only
    (B) I and II only
    (C) I and III only
    (D) I, II, and IV only
    (E) I, III, and IV only

21. The quantity of heat required to change the temperature of a unit amount of a substance by 1°C is its

    (A) specific heat capacity
    (B) heat of fusion
    (C) heat of vaporization
    (D) mechanical equivalent of heat
    (E) thermal conductivity

22. When a vapor condenses into a liquid

    (A) it absorbs heat
    (B) it generates heat
    (C) its temperature rises
    (D) its temperature drops
    (E) no heat is transferred

23. Two elements cannot be combined chemically to make

    (A) a compound
    (B) another element
    (C) a gas
    (D) a liquid
    (E) a solid

24. A pinch of salt is added to a glass of water. The result is a(n)

    (A) element
    (B) compound
    (C) solution
    (D) heterogeneous substance
    (E) crystal

25. The smallest subdivision of a compound that exhibits its characteristic properties is a(n)

    (A) elementary particle
    (B) atom
    (C) molecule
    (D) element
    (E) cell

26. The first law of thermodynamics is the same as the

    (A) second law of thermodynamics
    (B) law of conservation of energy
    (C) law of conservation of momentum
    (D) first law of motion
    (E) second law of motion

27. Electromagnetic radiation is emitted

    (A) only by radio and television antennas
    (B) only by bodies at higher temperatures than their surroundings
    (C) only by bodies at lower temperatures than their surroundings
    (D) by all bodies
    (E) by no bodies

28. A refrigerator

    (A) produces cold
    (B) removes heat from a region and transports it elsewhere
    (C) causes heat to vanish
    (D) changes heat to cold
    (E) produces energy

29. Which atom is the heaviest?

    (A) Hydrogen
    (B) Iron
    (C) Lead
    (D) Uranium
    (E) Helium

30. A dam is thicker at the bottom than at the top because

    (A) pressure is greater with increasing depth
    (B) surface tension exists only at the surface of liquids
    (C) a dam would not look right with a thin bottom
    (D) water is denser at deeper levels and therefore exerts greater pressure at the bottom of the dam
    (E) the dam itself is enormous

31. The reason a life jacket helps you float is that it

    (A) makes you lighter
    (B) and you together have less density than you alone
    (C) is made about as dense as the average human
    (D) repels water
    (E) is filled with gas

32. If an automobile tire explodes, the air that was contained in that tire

(A) increases in temperature
(B) decreases in temperature
(C) remains the same
(D) increases in pressure
(E) None of the above

33.

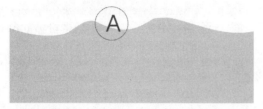

Water weighs 64 pounds per cubic foot. The ball shown above, A, has a volume of 2 cubic feet and floats with half its volume extending out of the water. How much does the ball weigh?

(A) 16 pounds
(B) 32 pounds
(C) 64 pounds
(D) 128 pounds
(E) It is impossible to calculate.

34. The silver coating on the glass surface of a thermos cuts down on

(A) conduction of heat energy
(B) convection of heat energy
(C) radiation of heat energy
(D) germs
(E) breakage

35. Evaporation is a cooling process because

(A) more energetic molecules evaporate, leaving less energetic ones behind
(B) the remaining liquid undergoes a decrease in temperature
(C) heat is radiated away
(D) of conduction and convection
(E) of conduction only

36. The needle of a magnetic compass

(A) is affected only by permanent magnets
(B) rotates continuously in the magnetic field of an electric current
(C) aligns itself parallel to a magnetic field
(D) aligns itself perpendicular to a magnetic field
(E) is not magnetized

37. Which of the following are not electromagnetic in nature?

(A) Infrared rays
(B) Ultraviolet rays
(C) Radar waves
(D) Sound waves
(E) X-rays

38. The property of light waves that leads to the phenomenon of color is their

(A) amplitude
(B) velocity
(C) wavelength
(D) momentum density
(E) intensity

39. In a vacuum, the velocity of an electromagnetic wave

(A) depends upon its frequency
(B) depends upon its wavelength
(C) depends upon its amplitude
(D) is a universal constant
(E) varies with the type of wave

40. The bending of a beam of light when it passes from one medium to another is known as

(A) refraction
(B) reflection
(C) diffraction
(D) dispersion
(E) polarization

41. People have seen photos of "weightless" astronauts orbiting Earth in the Skylab satellite. The "weightless" astronauts are actually

(A) shielded from Earth's gravitational field
(B) beyond the pull of gravity
(C) pulled only by gravitation to the ship itself, which cancels to zero
(D) like the craft, pulled by Earth's gravity
(E) floating

GO ON TO THE NEXT PAGE

42.

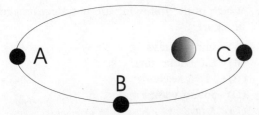

A satellite describes an elliptical orbit around a planet, as shown above. At which position is the satellite traveling fastest?

(A) A
(B) B
(C) C
(D) The speed is the same at all points.
(E) None of the above

43. The theory of relativity shows that Newtonian mechanics are

(A) wholly incorrect
(B) correct only for velocities up to the velocity of light
(C) approximately correct for all velocities
(D) approximately correct only for velocities much smaller than that of light
(E) completely correct

44. According to the equation $E = mc^2$

(A) mass and energy, when combined, travel at twice the speed of light
(B) mass and energy, when combined, travel at the speed of light squared
(C) energy is actually mass traveling at the speed of light squared
(D) energy and mass are related
(E) energy and time are related

45. An object traveling at a relativistic speed past a stationary observer appears to

(A) have a shorter life
(B) expand
(C) be more massive
(D) move at the velocity of light
(E) All of the above

46 According to Kepler, the paths of planets around the sun are

(A) straight lines
(B) squares
(C) circles
(D) ellipses
(E) parabolas

47. According to Einstein's theory of relativity

(A) space and time are aspects of each other
(B) energy and mass are aspects of each other
(C) light moves in curved paths
(D) Only (A) and (B)
(E) None of the above

48. Which of the following statements about the moon's tangential velocity is true?

I. The moon is beyond the main pull of the Earth's gravity.
II. The net force on the moon is zero.
III. The moon is being pulled by the Sun and planets, as well as the Earth.
IV. The moon is falling toward the Earth.

(A) I only
(B) II only
(C) III only
(D) IV only
(E) I, II, III, and IV

49. The three most common minerals found in the rocks of Earth are

(A) quartz, chlorite, and talc
(B) apatite, pyrite, and calcite
(C) calcite, quartz, and feldspar
(D) magnetite, graphite, and calcite
(E) copper, graphite, and quartz

50. It is obvious that, to measure time accurately, you must have either an invariable point of reference or a reference point that varies with predictability. One of the most obvious reference points is the sun, but it is also clearly variable. Which of the following procedures would best predict the variable location of the sun?

(A) Visually follow the path of the sun each day, taking the proper precautions to protect the eyes.
(B) Set up a series of observation stations in a straight line running from the North Pole to the South Pole and keep records of the sure location.
(C) Set up a station in the ocean right on the equator and measure the intensity of sunlight throughout the day.
(D) Take the elapsed time from sunrise to sunset each day, divide it into equal periods, and average those equal periods for many days.
(E) Construct a pinhole camera at a set location. When the sun is at its highest point, open the lens and mark the spot. Do this until the cycle of the sun's movements returns to the mark where it began.

51. The process by which a fossil is formed when the minerals of the groundwater replace the original molecules and produce a mineralized copy of the dead organism is called

    (A) mold formation
    (B) petrification
    (C) cast formation
    (D) microfossilization
    (E) chemical fossilization

52. The nitrogen in the air we breathe

    (A) is not inhaled
    (B) is inhaled and exhaled
    (C) behaves just like oxygen
    (D) behaves just like carbon dioxide
    (E) is "fixed" in the body

53. Groundwater is important in fossil formation because of its content of

    (A) tiny fossilizing organisms
    (B) calcium carbonate
    (C) amber
    (D) silicon dioxide
    (E) sodium chloride

54. Climate is controlled by which of the following?

    (A) Many factors, including nearness to various landforms, latitude, and altitude
    (B) Mainly the location of high- and low-pressure areas
    (C) Average yearly temperature
    (D) The type of soil
    (E) The yearly rainfall

55. Prevailing wind patterns have northern and southern directions mainly because of the

    (A) rotation of Earth about its axis
    (B) revolution of Earth in its orbit
    (C) uneven heating of Earth's surface by the sun
    (D) varying nature of weather
    (E) high heat capacity of the seas

56. Continental drift via floor spreading may be explained by

    (A) paleomagnetism
    (B) saltwater currents
    (C) volcanic activity
    (D) convection currents in rock
    (E) convection currents in water

57. A tall, jagged mountain is younger than a smooth, rounded mountain because it has not had time to

    (A) metamorphose
    (B) crystallize
    (C) sink
    (D) fossilize
    (E) erode

58. As water freezes, it is destructive to rock because it

    (A) reacts
    (B) expands
    (C) decomposes
    (D) evaporates
    (E) is so cold

59. Weathering and erosion can take place through the action of

    (A) water
    (B) wind
    (C) ice
    (D) Both (A) and (C)
    (E) All of the above

60. The electromagnetic spectrum is made up of

    (A) only visible radiation
    (B) all possible wavelengths
    (C) mostly radio waves
    (D) waves detected by telescope
    (E) only magnetic and electronic waves

STOP If you finish before the time is up, you may check your work on this section only. Do not turn to any other section in the test.

PRETEST ANSWER KEY AND EXPLANATIONS

PART I BIOLOGICAL SCIENCE

1. D	13. E	25. C	37. B	49. A
2. B	14. A	26. E	38. D	50. D
3. E	15. B	27. C	39. C	51. E
4. C	16. E	28. D	40. A	52. B
5. B	17. D	29. B	41. B	53. C
6. E	18. A	30. B	42. C	54. B
7. A	19. B	31. E	43. E	55. B
8. D	20. B	32. D	44. D	56. B
9. D	21. D	33. A	45. A	57. B
10. C	22. D	34. C	46. C	58. E
11. C	23. B	35. E	47. D	59. D
12. A	24. A	36. A	48. B	60. A

PART II PHYSICAL SCIENCE

1. C	13. B	25. C	37. D	49. C
2. B	14. A	26. B	38. C	50. E
3. B	15. A	27. D	39. D	51. B
4. C	16. E	28. B	40. A	52. B
5. B	17. C	29. D	41. D	53. B
6. A	18. D	30. A	42. C	54. A
7. B	19. B	31. B	43. D	55. A
8. D	20. D	32. B	44. D	56. D
9. B	21. A	33. C	45. C	57. E
10. C	22. B	34. C	46. D	58. B
11. C	23. B	35. A	47. D	59. E
12. D	24. C	36. C	48. D	60. B

PART I

BIOLOGICAL SCIENCE

1. **The correct answer is (D).** Without knowing the correct answer, one should be able to derive it by applying the test of logic to each choice. There is no rationale for choice (D), since there are as many diverse minerals available on land as in the sea.

2. **The correct answer is (B).** The influx of sodium depolarizes the membrane, which in turn allows a greater influx via a positive feedback mechanism. This culminates in an action potential. These events repeat themselves as the sodium spreads along the membrane, with other events all following.

3. **The correct answer is (E).** A mechanoreceptor is sensitive to physical displacement or pressure. An ommatidium is a segmented eye and, therefore, a light receptor.

4. **The correct answer is (C).** Choice (B) is not a part of the brain. Choice (E) is a nerve cell, and effectively, all nerve cells are similar regardless of location. Choice (D) could easily be recognized as a specialized portion of the brain having to do with optics or vision. The choice is then left for choices (A) or (C), both portions of the brain. Knowledge of the role of the cerebellum in balance could help indicate the role of the cerebrum in thinking and point to its identification as the correct response.

5. **The correct answer is (B).** The candidate must have general knowledge of twinning. There would be no reason for choices (A) or (E) to happen, since normal development was pointed out in the question. Choices (C) and (D) are similar possibilities, and the candidate must recognize that once development is initiated, the resulting cells, particularly early in development, are identical; thus, the correct response is choice (B).

6. **The correct answer is (E).** While subject to the influence of environment and genetic makeup, both of which were discounted in the question, the ovaries produce their eggs with a genotype peculiar to them. The physical characteristics of the mother have little, if any, actual effect on the resultant offspring and, thus, are not appropriate responses.

7. **The correct answer is (A).** The candidate must be aware of the role of the pancreas both in regulation of sugar in the body and as a producer of digestive juices. Only choice (A) covers both of those functions. Choices (B) and (E) cover one or the other.

8. **The correct answer is (D).** The candidate may reach the correct response by either being aware of liver functions or eliminating choices (A) and (B) by knowledge of spleen and bone marrow functions. Choice (C) is incorrect because all blood entering the heart, save that from the lungs, is high in CO_2. Choice (E) is not correct because the liver does not store bile; this is done by the gallbladder.

9. **The correct answer is (D).** Choice (A) is a supplier of energy but primarily for active processes. Water movement in plants is passive. Choices (B), (C), and (E) are ducts or tubes through which water might be expected to flow, but none has any regulatory devices by which to regulate movement. Only stomata are found on the leaf surface and have the ability to open or close due to their guard cells changing shape.

10. **The correct answer is (C).** This is logically correct because a fish gets sodium into the body via the blood through the two structures that allow penetration of water. Choice (E) is eliminated because the thick scales make the skin impervious in contact with the outside. Choices (A) and (B) are incorrect because each misstates one function of an organ. Choice (D) is incorrect because it specifically eliminates the use of gills or kidneys, which are involved in maintaining levels of materials in body fluids.

11. **The correct answer is (C).** Choice (E) should be eliminated, as it is not involved with the reproductive system. Choice (B) secretes a male hormone. Choices (A), (C), and (D) are left as possibilities. Choice (D) is eliminated because it is a hormone, not an organ, and the shaded boxes in the diagram represent organs. Choice (A) is eliminated because it is not a gland and therefore does not secrete hormones. Choice (C) releases the hormones estrogen and progesterone.

12. **The correct answer is (A).** The endocrine system works via a series of feedback loops. This knowledge allows only choices (A) and (C) as possibilities. Choice (C) is eliminated because the reproductive system that is diagrammed here is a negative feedback system, which means that the dotted lines going to the hypothalamus and pituitary would be used to shut off or inhibit the production of more hormones (testosterone, progesterone, and estrogen).

13. **The correct answer is (E).** The manufacture of sex hormones involves a variety of interactions. Choices (A), (B), (C), and (D) are components of some of the interactions, but choice (E) is all-encompassing and supersedes the others.

14. **The correct answer is (A).** Choices (D) and (E) are male hormones and, therefore, are not involved. Choices (B) and (C) are hormones of the ovary, and shutting them off would be almost "after the fact of ovulation." Furthermore, general knowledge has it that LH is essential for ovulation and, therefore, is the logical response.

15. **The correct answer is (B).** Candidates who know photosynthesis might select choice (E), but the gases we breathe are not an energy-storage product. None of the other responses, choices (A), (C), or (D), is an energy-storage product, nor are they directly involved in photosynthesis.

16. **The correct answer is (E).** Choice (A) doesn't allow for the resolution to follow a single cell. Choice (B) is not at all simple, nor does it offer a way to identify a specific cell. Choice (C), which, indeed, is a standard cytological procedure, is incorrect in light of choice (E) being a very real possibility. Choice (D) has a hint of possibility, but the hole would probably heal, and the cell would again become indistinguishable from the rest.

17. **The correct answer is (D).** Choice (D) is the only one that tests the same cells using a different procedure. Choice (A) would surely find the chemical present since it was used in preparing the cell. Choice (B) would give no pertinent data, given the size of the organelle. Choice (C) generates no data, and choice (E) does not test the cell in question but tests different cells.

18. **The correct answer is (A).** Aside from being a generally well-known fact, this is also stated in the paragraph, "chromosomal spindle fibers are developed from the centromeres of each chromosome and grow toward the poles of the cell."

19. **The correct answer is (B).** It is commonly known that asters are involved in mitosis of plants even though this fact is not discussed in the statement.

20. **The correct answer is (B).** This is not presented in the statement, but it is a well-known biological fact.

21. **The correct answer is (D).** Since chromosomal fragments lacking a centromere do not undergo anaphase movements toward the poles, when the nuclear membrane reforms at the conclusion of mitosis, it is logical to assume that the fragment will not be included within this membrane.

22. **The correct answer is (D).** This is the only other way of making ATP. While choices (A), (B), (C), and (E) are true, they do not make ATP.

23. **The correct answer is (B).** The other four statements are incorrect.

24. **The correct answer is (A).** Uracil in RNA replaces choice (C), thymine, in DNA. Choices (B), (D), and (E) are all present in both DNA and RNA.

25. **The correct answer is (C).** Photosynthesis is and has been the major source of O_2 in the atmosphere. While it is possible that choices (A), (B), (D), and (E) could release small amounts of oxygen, none gives off large amounts.

26. **The correct answer is (E).** All items—choices (A), (B), (C), and (D)—can result in isolation for reproduction.

27. **The correct answer is (C).** All evidence points to human predation as the major cause. While each of the other factors, with the possible exception of choice (E), may have affected some of the birds, none could have been severe enough to wipe out an entire population. As far as choice (E) is concerned, it is a rare bird indeed that is unable to find gravel to ingest so that the gizzard can grind food.

28. **The correct answer is (D).** Radiologists are physicians who use X-rays. Candidates should know this. Some of the other choices can cause extensive exposure to radioactive materials.

29. **The correct answer is (B).** Choices (A) and (B) are the only theories listed that deal with population. Choice (B) involves areas such as genetic and differential reproduction. Several of the other theories are modern and unrelated to the question.

30. **The correct answer is (B).** Vascular tissue allows water, minerals, and foodstuffs to be carried throughout the plant. The other choices are involved in growth, reproduction, and support, which could occur without the materials carried by the vascular system.

31. **The correct answer is (E).** The similarities involved are not ones that choices (A), (B), (C), and (D) could have caused. Given the structures involved, a common ancestry is more likely.

32. **The correct answer is (D).** Hardy-Weinberg equation is $p^2 + 2pq + q^2$, with p being the dominant allele and q the recessive allele. $2pq$ is the heterozygote. If $q = .2$, then $p = .8$ (since $p + q = 1$), so, $2pq = 2(.8)(.2) = .32$ or 32 percent.

33. **The correct answer is (A).** In successive generations, the gene for the lethal sickle cell, a homozygote, will probably increase in frequency in malarial-endemic centers. It is logical to assume that if the heterozygote is adaptive, the gene will increase in frequency and confer an immunity to malaria.

34. **The correct answer is (C).** The beneficial characteristics acquired during life by an individual result in the gradual formation during successive generations of new taxa. The acquisition of new and beneficial characteristics will not necessarily result in the formation of new taxa.

35. **The correct answer is (E).** Most gametes are produced by meiosis. These statements and the conclusion, while true and logical, are not principles of evolutionary theory.

36. **The correct answer is (A).** The geographical distributions of the species that comprise a genus are restricted from other geographically distinct regions by effective geographical barriers. The statement logically arrives at the correct conclusion that species are separated one from the other by geographical barriers.

37. **The correct answer is (B).** This is another interdisciplinary question that measures your ability to reason and apply what you know. Choice (B) is correct as intelligent animal life is assumed to require a great deal of energy. We know that brain tissue consumes large amounts of energy. You can reason this from knowing that a few minutes without O_2 can destroy the human brain before any other organ. Anaerobes cannot break down molecules completely and, therefore, extract little of their energy. All the other answers are incorrect. Mars has no oxygen in its atmosphere, nor did Earth in the days when living cells first appeared. Intelligence cannot be changed by breathing deeply. There are many anaerobic organisms other than fungi.

38. **The correct answer is (D).** Once again, a careful perusal of the answer choices yields a clue to the correct answer even if you know nothing of the subject matter. The pigment we seek is red-orange, like a carrot, and choice (D), carotenoid, is the answer.

39. **The correct answer is (C).** Photosynthesis involves two processes. The sun's energy in the light reaction activates photopigments. This energy is stored as ATP. In the dark reaction, glucose is synthesized, using the energy yielded by breakdown of ATP. Thus, all answers are incorrect except choice (C). Fixation or reduction of CO_2 is the process by which hydrogen is bound to CO_2 as a first step in glucose synthesis.

40. **The correct answer is (A).** The source of the hydrogen mentioned above is H_2O. None of the other molecules is split in photosynthesis.

41. **The correct answer is (B).** If you know that all of these structures are elaborately folded membranes, you can reason that choice (B), providing a large membrane surface area for chemical reaction, is correct. Membranes contain vital enzymes and serve as interfaces where many chemical reactions occur. They cannot perform the other functions mentioned.

42. **The correct answer is (C).** The graph shows high survival rates only at 104°F and 107.6°F. The passage indicates these to be higher than the temperature healthy lizards select. The answer must therefore be choice (C), 100.4°F.

43. **The correct answer is (E).** Choice (A) conflicts with the article's implication that healthy lizards choose somewhat lower temperatures. Choices (B) and (C) both are speculations as to the mechanism by which fever helps. The passage mentions neither, since the actual mechanism is not yet known. Choice (D) is incorrect since the normal body temperature for humans is 98.6°F, which is lower than the temperature preferred by these lizards.

44. **The correct answer is (D).** The answer choices include a number of true statements, but choices (A), (C), and (E) are not implications of the passage presented. Choice (B) is a common medical practice called into question by the experiment. Therefore, choice (D) is the only choice implied by the experiment. (Please note: this idea is controversial in medical circles.)

45. **The correct answer is (A).** Oxygen consumption is a measure of metabolic rate in animals. Choices (B), (C), and (D) are obviously wrong, while choice (E) can be reasoned to be wrong since an organism breathing slowly and deeply can be supplied with abundant oxygen.

46. **The correct answer is (C).** Since the animals are arranged from left to right by increasing body weight, the heaviest, the elephant belongs to the right of the cow. The implication of the graph is that metabolic rate is inversely proportional to size. Thus, the elephant would be expected to have the lowest metabolic rate, closest to the x-axis. Choice (E) is incorrect, as this number cannot be negative, and choices (A) and (B) are obviously wrong. Choice (D) is incorrect since there is nothing in the information to indicate that it cannot be generalized to include all mammals.

47. **The correct answer is (D).** Diabetes mellitus is a disease in which, due to endocrine problems involving a lack of active insulin, sugar cannot enter the cells to be metabolized. The result is an abnormally high blood sugar, with sugar unavailable to most body cells. Therefore, these cells must metabolize fat and protein. Choices (A), (B), and (C) are metabolic diseases, but none has these particular symptoms. Choice (E) is another endocrine disease in which a lack of the hormone ADH causes production of large amounts of dilute urine.

48. **The correct answer is (B).** Choice (A) is cut pieces. Choices (C) and (D) are parts of an operon. Choice (E) is a piece of extrachromosomal DNA found in prokaryotes.

49. **The correct answer is (A).** The student must be aware that species occupying the same niche would be competitors, particularly if they were closely related. Choices (B), (D), and (E) are eliminated because different niches are occupied. Choice (C) offers possibility for competition, but not as severe as is the potential in choice (A).

50. **The correct answer is (D).** The student should be aware that the important factor is maintaining a constant body temperature. Body size, choice (D), is critical in this respect. None of the other responses would have any direct effect on body size.

51. **The correct answer is (E).** If choice (A) occurred, they could have grown back. Choice (C), while possible, is not as encompassing an answer as is choice (E).

52. **The correct answer is (B).** It shows that homeostasis allows for only slight changes in population numbers, which is efficient. Choice (E) contradicts logic, and choices (A), (C), and (D) cannot be used in defining efficiency because they are either large, choice (A), or do not give a level of oscillation, choices (C) and (D).

53. **The correct answer is (C).** The student must be aware of Malthus's great impact on Darwin. Darwin knew nothing of genetics, so choices (A) and (D) are eliminated. Choice (B) does not deal in terms of natural selection. Choice (E), Wallace, shared the discovery of the phenomenon of natural selection with Darwin. Indeed, Darwin was greatly surprised by Wallace's work.

54. **The correct answer is (B).** It is the only response involving quantification.

55. **The correct answer is (B).** Choices (A), (C), (D), and (E) are all situations that could reasonably be expected to affect a single individual. Choice (B) is a population phenomenon.

56. **The correct answer is (B).** It is the most parsimonious and the easiest way to start. Choices (C) and (D) have nothing to do with hawk-squirrel interaction. Choices (A) and (E) are good procedures, but only after choice (B) has been ascertained.

57. **The correct answer is (B).** To study the interaction of populations of organisms, the groups involved must be represented by sample individuals from those groups.

58. **The correct answer is (E).** In choice (E), more hawks would require squirrels for food. Thus, there would be a decrease in the population of squirrels, as originally hypothesized. Choices (A) and (B) are false. In both cases, the opposite would occur. The effect of choice (C) would be the same as in choice (B). If food for squirrels increased, as in choice (D), then one could expect the squirrel population to increase. One could reasonably expect the hawks to increase because of the additional supply of squirrels for food.

59. **The correct answer is (D).** Paragraph 2 clearly states that we are subsidizing food output with fossil fuels, and that there are 100 years left to go before running out (except for coal). One could logically expect a famine and death if energy is not available for food production and distribution.

60. **The correct answer is (A).** Paragraph 1 states this in a slightly altered manner.

PART II
PHYSICAL SCIENCE

1. **The correct answer is (C).** Alpha particles (helium nuclei) and beta particles (high-energy electrons) are stopped by paper or thin sheets of metal. Gamma rays are electromagnetic rays and are the most dangerous and penetrating—lead shielding of substantial thickness is required as protection from them.

2. **The correct answer is (B).** Fusion is the combining of smaller nuclei to produce larger ones. Choices (A) and (C) are examples of fission, the breaking down of a large nucleus into smaller ones.

3. **The correct answer is (B).** Half-life is a statistical measurement that makes for statements equivalent to "the life span of the American male is sixty-nine years." Hence, a half-life of 5,770 years is most accurate when the sample is large. A half-life of 5,770 years between two atoms means nothing, just as does deciding if Sam or Frank will live to be 69 years old. It is a nonsensical prediction.

4. **The correct answer is (C).** Radon gas may be in the same "inert" group as He, Ne, Ar, Kr, and so on, but its nuclear activity is unrelated to this fact.

5. **The correct answer is (B).** The "lowest" member of a chemical group has more shells (energy levels). Hence, it has a larger atomic radius.

6. **The correct answer is (A).** Metals generally have fewer than four valence electrons in their outer shell. (They are to the left of Group IV in the table.)

7. **The correct answer is (B).** Experience should indicate that all metals are solids except mercury, which is a liquid. This eliminates choices (A), (C), and (E). Also, from common knowledge, we know that nitrogen is a common gaseous component of air.

8. **The correct answer is (D).** A subscript after a parenthesis in a formula multiplies all atoms within the parentheses. So, $(NH_4)_2$ means 2 N atoms and 8 H atoms.

9. **The correct answer is (B).** In a balanced equation, the number of each type of atom on either side of the arrow must be the same. The only equation that is not balanced is choice (B)—there is one H atom on the left and two on the right, and two O atoms are on the left and only one on the right.

10. **The correct answer is (C).** Heat (increased temperature) will release a gas from a reaction mixture. The only equation showing a gas on the right side (product side) of the arrow is choice (C). Raising the temperature will increase the rate of this reaction from left to right, producing more oxygen.

11. **The correct answer is (C).** Isotopes are atoms of the same element that differ only in mass. Pair I is oxides of carbon, pair II is molecules of oxygen, and pair IV is two hydrocarbons.

12. **The correct answer is (D).** Isomers are compounds having the same formula (same numbers of each kind of atom) but a different arrangement of them in their bonded structures. In pair IV, each structure has four carbon atoms and ten hydrogen atoms; the formula for each isomer is C_4H_{10}.

13. **The correct answer is (B).** Allotropes are two or more different forms of the same element. In pair II, we see the element oxygen as oxygen gas (O_2) and as ozone (O_3).

14. **The correct answer is (A).** The law of multiple composition, as its name implies, refers to the same elements forming two or more different compounds with different formulas. The correct answer is pair I. It shows carbon and oxygen as carbon monoxide (CO) and carbon dioxide (CO_2).

15. **The correct answer is (A).** This is the only compound composed of a metal and a nonmetal. An ionic bond is formed when electrons are transferred from a metal atom (Mg, in this case) to a nonmetal atom (Cl, in this case). This produces a salt with metallic positively charged ions and nonmetallic negatively charged ions in a geometrical crystal structure. The other three compounds are composed of only nonmetals. Nonmetals bond by sharing electrons (covalent bonding).

16. **The correct answer is (E).** From the previous criteria, the student can see that CH_4, HCN, and H_2O are all covalent compounds.

17. **The correct answer is (C).** Obviously, only CH_4, HCN, and H_2O are covalent and are possibilities. From the position of C, H, N, and O in the periodic table, the student can determine how many valence (bonding) electrons each atom has: C in Group IV (four valence electrons), N in Group V (five valence electrons), O in Group VI (six valence electrons), and H, the simplest atom (one valence electron). Putting the formulas of the compounds together to make eight shared electrons for each atom (except H, which can have only two), we get:

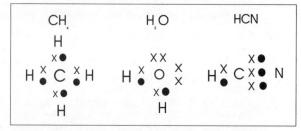

Hence, the answer is HCN (it has a triple bond).

18. **The correct answer is (D).** Water molecules have strong forces of attraction. Any time H is bonded to O, there is set up a dipolar structure. Hydrogen bonding is the name given to this intermolecular attraction.

19. **The correct answer is (B).** Pure water cannot conduct electricity—it is covalent, and no ions are present to act as conductors. Even though sugar and alcohol dissolve in water, these compounds do so when hydrogen bonds with water, and no ions are produced. Hence, choices (A) and (C) are incorrect. Salt is ionic, however, and water dissolves salt, pulling the ions apart. So, positive and negative ions are free in the water to help conduct the electric current.

20. **The correct answer is (D).** A neutralization reaction always produces a salt and water (e.g., HCl + NaOH = NaCl + H_2O). Certainly, a gas is not necessarily a product, so choice (C) is incorrect. The pH of an acid is lower than 7. Adding a base in the neutralization process increases the pH value toward 7. Therefore, there are three correct statements: I, II, and IV.

21. **The correct answer is (A).** The statement given is the definition of specific heat capacity. Choices (B) and (C) refer to heat flows for a change of phase of a material. The mechanical equivalent of heat relates motion to heat, and thermal conductivity involves, as the name indicates, its ability to conduct heat.

22. **The correct answer is (B).** When a vapor condenses into a liquid, heat must be lowered. The temperature will remain constant during the transition. By releasing heat, the particles can come together, or condense.

23. **The correct answer is (B).** An element cannot be subdivided into more basic elements by chemical means. They can be combined in a nuclear fusion to make another element (and vice-versa), but not chemically.

24. **The correct answer is (C).** Salt added to water will dissolve. The salt is the solute and the water is the solvent, the combination of which is a solution.

25. **The correct answer is (C).** A compound is a chemical combination of two or more atoms. A molecule, made up of two or more atoms, is the definition of the smallest unit of a compound.

26. **The correct answer is (B).** The first law of thermodynamics is the same as the law of conservation of energy; namely, we can neither create nor destroy matter.

27. **The correct answer is (D).** Electromagnetic radiation is emitted by all bodies and includes such radiation as infrared radiation.

28. **The correct answer is (B).** A refrigerator transports heat from within to the outside. Heat is energy; it cannot vanish.

29. **The correct answer is (D).** Uranium has the largest atomic weight, or a greater number of neutrons and protons, than any of the other elements listed.

30. **The correct answer is (A).** A dam is thicker at the bottom than at the top because water pressure increases with increasing depth of water. Water is practically incompressible, and, therefore, not denser at deeper levels.

31. **The correct answer is (B).** A life jacket is made of material that is much less dense than the human body. Hence, the combined density of a life jacket and you is less than that of you alone, enabling you to float on water. Some life jackets do not contain a gas or do not inflate with a gas.

32. **The correct answer is (B).** Air contained in an exploding automobile tire undergoes a rapid explosion or release of air, and a decrease in pressure results, contributing to a lowering in temperature.

33. **The correct answer is (C).** Half the volume of ball A is one cubic foot, which is submerged under water. Since an object floats because its weight is supported by the amount of water displaced, we must conclude that 1 cubic foot, or 64 pounds, of displaced water must equal the weight of the floating object.

34. **The correct answer is (C).** The silver coating in a thermos bottle reflects radiation, which reduces the amount of radiant heat energy transfer, both into and out of the thermos. For example, if the thermos contained ice, it would melt slowly as heat from the outside was reflected back outside.

35. **The correct answer is (A).** During evaporation, the remaining liquid undergoes a decrease in temperature, but it does so because the more energetic molecules leave and less energetic ones stay. Therefore, choice (A) is a more fundamental answer than choice (B).

36. **The correct answer is (C).** The needle of a magnetic compass aligns itself parallel to a magnetic field. It is affected not only by permanent magnets, but also by electromagnets.

37. **The correct answer is (D).** Electromagnetic waves are undulations of electric and magnetic fields. Sound waves are elastic mechanical vibrations of a material having nothing to do with electric and magnetic fields.

38. **The correct answer is (C).** The wavelength of a light wave is related to the spectral color it exhibits. Amplitude affects its intensity. Choices (B) and (D) do not lead to color.

39. **The correct answer is (D).** In a vacuum, all electromagnetic waves have the same velocity, namely the velocity of light, making it a universal constant, which makes it independent of the other choices.

40. **The correct answer is (A).** When a beam of light passes from one medium to another, its velocity changes, leading to a change in direction of the beam. This phenomenon is known as refraction.

41. **The correct answer is (D).** The astronauts are not weightless at all. They and the craft are similarly accelerated by Earth's gravitation, and, therefore, fall at the same rate as their spacecraft, making them appear, inside the craft, as not falling.

42. **The correct answer is (C).** In an elliptical orbit around a planet, a satellite will be closest to the planet at an extreme of its orbit (the planet resides at one of the focuses of the ellipse). This is also the position of strongest gravitational pull. Hence, at point C, the acceleration will have reached its maximum, giving the satellite its highest velocity.

43. **The correct answer is (D).** The theory of relativity shows that Newtonian mechanics are approximately correct only for velocities much smaller than that of light. As velocity approaches the speed of light, changes in Newtonian mechanics begin to be evidenced.

44. **The correct answer is (D).** The equation $E = mc^2$ relates mass and energy. It says nothing about the speed of travel for either the mass or the energy, as the other choices indicate.

45. **The correct answer is (C).** To an observer in an inertial frame of reference, an object moving at a speed close to that of light would appear to be more massive. It would also appear to have a longer life and would seem to be contracted.

46. **The correct answer is (D).** Kepler discovered that the planets move in elliptical paths around the sun. They cannot be straight lines, and their motion confirms they are not circular. A parabola is open-ended.

47. **The correct answer is (D).** In relativistic theory, both space and time and mass and energy are aspects of one another.

48. **The correct answer is (D).** The moon does fall to Earth. It never gets any closer because it also has a tangential velocity that moves it away from Earth by the same amount. The "falling" to Earth is caused by the gravitational pull of Earth on the moon.

49. **The correct answer is (C).** The minerals listed in choice (C) are more abundant than any other of the listed combinations.

50. **The correct answer is (E).** This is the only option that has a fixed point and a fixed instant at which to take a measurement. All of the other choices have too many variables. The result of the procedure in choice (E) is a figure-eight-looking structure called an analemma, which is seen on globes and maps.

51. **The correct answer is (B).** This process is *petrification*, or turning to stone. Mold or cast formation refers to phenomen such as footprints or worm holes. The phenomenon described in the question is not confined to microfossilization and is also not chemical fossilization.

52. **The correct answer is (B).** Nitrogen comprises 78 percent of the atmosphere, but we cannot use it in its gaseous form.

53. **The correct answer is (B).** The calcium carbonate precipitates out of the groundwater to help form fossils.

54. **The correct answer is (A).** Climate has numerous controlling factors, and choice (A) includes most factors. The other choices are too narrow to control climate.

55. **The correct answer is (A).** Earth's rotation causes the Coriolis effect, which moves the air around. Air moves from regions of high to low pressure. Low pressure is found near the poles and equator, and high pressure falls between these.

56. **The correct answer is (D).** Choice (A) shows that drifting has occurred. It is the currents in choice (D) that appear to have moved the continental plates. Volcanic activity shows activity but not in a pattern that would show drift.

57. **The correct answer is (E).** When mountains form, they are tall and jagged. As time goes on, weather and plant growth eat away at the mountains and round and smooth them off.

58. **The correct answer is (B).** As water freezes, it expands, thus, pushing against cracks in the rock. The pressure may be great enough to further crack the rock.

59. **The correct answer is (E).** All are very effective in weathering and erosion.

60. **The correct answer is (B).** The spectrum includes all possible waves. All other responses are included in choice (B).

Chapter 15
OVERVIEW

This section will provide an overview of the basic scientific concepts that you will need to know and understand before you take the Natural Sciences General Examination of the CLEP. This test consists of two major sections, Biological Sciences and Physical Sciences.

The major sections here are broken into smaller units that include biology, chemistry, physics, and earth and space science. Since this examination does not require you to be a science major, only to have a basic understanding of scientific concepts, a review of this material will be extremely helpful.

Keep in mind that you do not need to remember facts, merely to understand the concepts that will be part of the knowledge that an adult with a liberal arts education should have. Many colleges may grant you up to 6 semester hours of credit if you achieve satisfactory scores on this portion of the exam.

BIOLOGY
LIFE FUNCTIONS
All living things carry out certain activities or functions in order to maintain life.

NUTRITION
Nutrition is the process of ingesting and absorbing food to provide the energy for life, promote growth, and repair or replace worn or damaged tissues.

TRANSPORT
Transport involves movement of nutrients, water, ions, and other materials into and out of the various cells and tissues of organisms. This process includes absorption of small molecules across cell membranes and secretion of biochemicals, such as enzymes, mucous, and hormones. In many species, the circulatory system plays an important role in transport.

METABOLISM
Metabolism includes the process by which nutrients and simple molecules are used to form more complex molecules for growth, repair, and reproduction (anabolism). Metabolism also includes the process of breaking down complex molecules to release energy from chemical bonds (catabolism) and to provide small molecules, such as simple sugars and amino acids, as building blocks for more complex molecules (anabolism).

HOMEOSTASIS
An internal balance in all aspects of metabolism and biological function is called homeostasis.

DIGESTION
Digestion is a special form of catabolism that breaks down food into smaller molecules and releases energy.

ABSORPTION
Absorption allows small molecules to pass through cell membranes throughout the body tissues. This allows for gas exchange, and, in some species, such as plants and fungi, nutrients are obtained by absorption from soil and water.

STIMULI
The behavior of living things is a response to stimuli in the environment. These stimuli may include things such as light, chemical signals, noise, or a change in the seasons.

EXCRETION
Excretion is the elimination of waste products.

REPRODUCTION
Reproduction is the creation of offspring. Living things reproduce sexually, asexually, or both. Life comes from other living things.

CHEMISTRY OF LIFE
All living things are made up of the same elements, with the most abundant being:

1. carbon
2. hydrogen
3. nitrogen
4. oxygen
5. phosphorous
6. sulfur

Trace elements and minerals are also essential components of all living things.

All species consume or absorb nutrients to carry out essential biological activities. Catabolic activities, such as digestion, provide the energy and building blocks for biosynthetic (anabolic) activities, such as growth, repair, and reproduction.

Digestion in some species includes both a mechanical breakdown of food or nutrients (chewing) and absorption. In animals such as humans, the digestive tract is a system that is complex in both structure and function. In more primitive organisms, digestion may occur in a less specialized fashion. For example, some protozoa can absorb nutrients, then digest them within membrane-bound vacuoles that contain digestive enzymes. Some bivalves, such as clams and oysters, have gills within a mantle cavity that are used for gas exchange.

Regardless of their specific metabolic processes, all living things use enzymes to catalyze the chemical reactions of life. Whether consuming energy or releasing it, these chemical reactions are essential to all living things.

RESPIRATION AND PHOTOSYNTHESIS

CELLULAR RESPIRATION

Cellular respiration is a catabolic activity that breaks down carbohydrates, fats, and proteins to produce energy in the form of adenosine triphosphate (ATP). This process consumes oxygen and produces carbon dioxide and water as by-products. In eukaryotic cells, cellular respiration takes place in the mitochondria. In prokaryotic cells—bacteria—this process takes place on the cell membrane, since bacteria do not contain mitochondria.

Respiration includes several metabolic pathways:

1. glycolysis
2. the Krebs cycle
3. the electron transport chain

These pathways can work together to completely oxidize one molecule of glucose, producing up to thirty-eight molecules of ATP in the process. Synthesis of ATP is an anabolic process.

PHOTOSYNTHESIS

Photosynthesis occurs in plants and some other organisms, such as algae. These organisms use sunlight as a source of energy to synthesize carbohydrates, lipids, proteins, and other organic substances. Photosynthetic organisms are the producers of the biosphere.

CHLOROPLASTS

Chloroplasts are the site of photosynthesis in plants and eukaryotic algae. Photosynthesis includes two separate processes. One stage of photosynthesis is the "light reactions" that convert solar energy to chemical energy.

The second stage is the Calvin cycle, which consumes carbon dioxide from the environment. This cycle uses ATP produced in the light reactions as a source of energy to produce carbohydrates from CO_2.

GENETICS AND REPRODUCTION

CHROMOSOMES

Humans have twenty-three pairs of chromosomes in each cell. Each person has one pair of sex chromosomes, coded XX for females and XY for males. The sex chromosomes contain the genes that determine sex, as well as some other characteristics. The remaining twenty-two pairs of chromosomes are called autosomes. Other species have different numbers of chromosomes.

Each pair of chromosomes is a homologous pair. For each of the twenty-three pairs in humans, one chromosome of each pair is from the mother, and one is from the father. The gametes, or sex cells, contain twenty-three single chromosomes each. When fertilization occurs, the fertilized egg, or zygote, then contains twenty-three pairs of chromosomes.

DNA—deoxyribonucleic acid

Chromosomes are made up primarily of DNA. DNA occurs as a double-stranded molecule in cells. The subunits of DNA are bases called adenine (A), cytosine (C), guanine (G), and thymine (T). They always occur in pairs in DNA. The pairing is specific: A-T or T-A and G-C or C-G. These are called complementary base pairs. When the bases bond to each other, they hold the two strands of DNA together. The DNA then coils to form a double helix.

When the strands of DNA separate to reproduce, the base pairs split apart. Each strand then binds to new complementary bases to form two identical daughter strands. Each new double strand of DNA contains one of the original strands and one new strand. This is called semiconservative replication.

GENES

Chromosomes are made up of subunits called genes. Individual genes code for various traits or characteristics of all living things. Pairs of genes that have the same position on each member of a pair of chromosomes, and which can take alternate forms, are called alleles. Allele codes for dominant traits are assigned uppercase letters, and recessive traits are assigned the same letter but in lowercase form.

Dominant genes control the phenotype (appearance) of the individual. For example, assume that red flowers (R) are dominant, and white flowers (r) are a recessive trait of peas. An individual with one dominant gene from one parent and one recessive gene from the other parent will have a genotype of Rr. The individual will express the dominant gene and, therefore, will have red flowers. Individuals with a genotype of RR will also produce red flowers. In order to produce white flowers, the individual must inherit two recessive genes and have a genotype of rr.

RNA—ribonucleic acid

RNA helps transcribe the genetic code in DNA and translates it into proteins. RNA, a single-stranded molecule, is also made up of nitrogen bases, except that it contains uracil (U) instead of thymine (T). If RNA were being produced using DNA as the template or code, the messenger RNA (mRNA) would contain a U instead of a T, and that U would be opposite or complementary to an A on the DNA strand. All other complementary pairs are the same as with two strands of DNA.

There are three types of RNA: (1) messenger RNA (mRNA), (2) transfer RNA (tRNA), and (3) ribosomal RNA (rRNA). These three work together in the cell cytoplasm to carry out protein synthesis. The mRNA carries the "message" or genetic code from the DNA. Ribosomes, made up of rRNA, serve as the site of protein synthesis. Ribosomes and tRNA work together to "translate" the message. The tRNA carries amino acids to the site of protein synthesis. The tRNA anticodon pairs with the codon on the mRNA to make sure that the correct amino acid is added to the protein being synthesized.

CODONS

Codons are triplets of nucleotide bases (A, T, U, G, and C) that code for specific amino acids. For example, UGU and UGC are both codons for the amino acid cysteine. There are sixty-four codons, but there are only twenty amino acids. Having more than one codon for most amino acids allows for some variation in the genetic code. Amino acids are the building blocks of proteins.

MITOSIS

Mitosis is an asexual process whereby cells divide for the purpose of growth and repair. Two identical daughter cells are produced. Occasional differences may occur due to mutations. Each daughter cell contains the same number of chromosomes as the parent cells. Other types of asexual reproduction are budding and binary fission.

MEIOSIS

Meiosis is a process of cell division that produces gametes for sexual reproduction. Sexual reproduction combines genes from two different parents to produce offspring that are genetically diverse.

MOLECULAR GENETICS AND MOLECULAR BIOLOGY

Rapid advances in technology have greatly increased our knowledge of genetics at the molecular level. This has opened exciting new fields of study in genetic engineering and biotechnology. The technology can be applied to many disciplines, including agriculture, medicine, pharmaceuticals, consumer science, biology, forensic medicine and criminology, and biochemistry.

Genes can be manipulated to correct genetic defects. Genes can be transferred from one organism to another. Transgenic plants, bacteria, and animals containing genes from other species are being developed routinely.

Human gene products such as insulin and tissue plasminogen activator are now produced by inserting the genes into bacteria or yeast cells. These microbes are then grown in huge quantities, and the genes produce the desired "product" as the organisms grow. Many other therapeutic and industrial products are produced in a similar manner.

Animals and plants are genetically engineered (modified) to improve productivity, yield, nutrient content, appearance, and conceivably almost any trait one could imagine. This may become essential to increasing the food supply as populations increase and as farmland disappears. This technology is rapidly changing our ability to fight disease and genetic disorders.

The human genome project is being conducted to "map" the location and function of every gene on all of the human chromosomes. It is estimated that humans have approximately 100,000 genes.

There are many social and ethical issues relating to biotechnology, genetic engineering, and molecular biology. It will become increasingly important for the general public to be educated about these issues.

BIOREMEDIATION

Bioremediation is a special area of biotechnology that uses microorganisms to destroy harmful materials in the environment, leaving harmless molecules as byproducts. Some of these organisms are genetically engineered to perform certain tasks. They can clean up oil spills or toxic chemicals by breaking them down into harmless substances.

EVOLUTION

Charles Darwin traveled throughout the Southern Hemisphere in the 1830s aboard the HMS *Beagle* in order to observe the abundant and unique life forms. He gathered evidence supporting the hypothesis of common descent— that all living things have a common ancestry. He also made observations and documented evidence that species adapt to changes in their environment, and these adaptations result in biological diversity.

Darwin, along with Alfred Russel Wallace, presented a joint paper hypothesizing that natural selection accounts for the origin of new biological species. The theory of natural selection proposes that adaptations occur due to a constantly changing environment.

The theory of natural selection essentially states that:

1. Members of a species have different traits, which can be inherited.
2. All species produce more offspring than can reproduce or survive (survival of the fittest).
3. Some individuals adapt to change, and they survive and reproduce more successfully than those that cannot adapt.
4. The offspring of subsequent generations inherit the adaptive characteristics.
5. Natural selection produces populations adapted to their particular environment.

Random mutations or changes also occur. In both cases, advances in molecular biology are making it possible to analyze the genetic relatedness of various species and to identify mutations that did not arise through adaptive change.

Humans and higher primates, such as apes and chimpanzees, are closely related genetically. This supports the hypothesis of common descent.

Adaptations may produce similarities or differences based on the environment. Some animals have developed similar features, such as hooves or claws. However, there are different types of hooves for running, claws for defense or climbing, and so on.

ECOLOGY

Ecology is the study of the interactions of organisms with their environment, both living (biotic) and nonliving (abiotic). That environment and all organisms and things within it are collectively called an ecosystem.

The biotic potential of a population is the maximum rate of growth that will occur under ideal conditions (food, space, etc.).

The carrying capacity of the environment limits the size of a given population. Variables such as the change of seasons may cause fluctuations in population size due to different capacities over time.

Communities contain a variety of populations. They interact in many ways, including competition, symbiosis, and predation. Competition for food, space, and other things limits population size. Natural predators help keep populations in balance within a community. Symbiosis is the close association of two species. It may be beneficial to one species (commensalism) or to both (mutualism). It may also harm one species while benefiting the other (parasitism).

A balanced ecosystem recycles dead and used materials, has an energy source, and includes producers (green plants), consumers (herbivores, carnivores, and omnivores), decomposers (bacteria and fungi), and abiotic components.

Succession is a sequence of communities evolving from simple to complex in a particular environment. Each community is a seral stage, and the entire sequence is a sere. The first seral stage is a pioneer community. Climax communities are final seral stages. Succession from sand dunes to mature deciduous forests represents a sere typical of the mid-Atlantic coastal region of the United States.

Humans create waste and pollution that endanger the balance of ecosystems. Depletion of the ozone layer, for example, could increase the amount of ultraviolet light reaching the earth, which may cause mutations, and possibly extinction, of many species. Some scientists hypothesize that global warming is occurring due to the build-up of carbon dioxide (CO_2) from combustion of fossil fuels and the depletion of oxygen caused by deforestation. An increase in global temperature of just a few degrees centigrade could cause a substantial increase in sea levels as well as a marked change in the variety and numbers of various species.

Proper disposal and recycling of wastes, sustainable use of natural resources, and development of alternative energy sources (other than fossil fuels and wood) are but a few things needed to maintain life as we know it.

THE CELL

All living things are made of cells. Surrounded by a cell membrane, each cell contains the genetic material that codes for the structure and function of the entire organism. Some organisms are unicellular, while most organisms are multicellular. Cells are surrounded by cell membranes. Some cells also have cell walls.

Cell membranes are selectively permeable, in that they control which molecules enter or leave the cell. This may include gases, nutrients, water, and wastes.

The cell membrane is a bilayer of phospholipids (a type of fat). Proteins imbedded in this bilayer sometimes help transport molecules across the bilayer by forming channels. These are called carrier proteins.

Although each cell of an individual contains all the genetic information for its form and function, not every cell expresses all the information. In multicellular organisms, cells develop in different ways as the embryo develops. This unique ability for cellular differentiation allows the development of specialized cellular organelles, cells, tissues, organs, and systems that make each member of a species unique.

The expression and the composition of the genetic material within each cell contribute to both the unity and diversity of living things.

EUKARYOTES

Some cells contain a nucleus—eukaryotes. The nucleus is surrounded by a porous membrane, and it contains chromosomes. The nucleus is the control center of the cell because it contains all the genetic information. Some cells (prokaryotes) have no nucleus. Bacteria are prokaryotes. They have only one chromosome, which is located in an area of their cytoplasm called a nucleoid.

All eukaryotic cells contain mitochondria. Mitochondria are the site of ATP production. They are the powerhouse of the cell. Prokaryotes produce ATP using cytochromes imbedded in their cell membrane.

CYTOPLASM

Cytoplasm is a semifluid liquid that fills the cell and holds the components of a cell. It also holds dissolved nutrients, such as amino acids and sugars.

ER—ENDOPLASMIC RETICULUM

ER is a network of folded membranes that carry materials from the nucleus to the cytoplasm. The rough ER is studded with ribosomes, which are the site of protein synthesis. The smooth ER produces lipids and hormones. Ribosomes are also found free in the cytoplasm.

LYSOSOMES

Lysosomes are membrane-bound vacuoles in the cytoplasm. They contain hydrolytic enzymes that digest materials that enter the cell. The enzymes are in vacuoles so that they don't destroy the cell itself.

GOLGI

The Golgi apparatus is another series of folded membranes and has several functions. It receives materials from the endoplasmic reticulum for processing (modification), packaging (putting a membrane around a molecule), or secretion (leaving the cell).

BIOLOGY: REVIEW QUESTIONS

The following questions will give you a chance to practice. Read each question carefully, mark your answers, and then check them with the answers and explanations that appear at the end of the Overview section.

1. All the following illustrate homeostasis EXCEPT
   (A) breaking down food into smaller particles
   (B) putting amino acids together to make proteins
   (C) sleeping
   (D) staying in one place
   (E) fighting off a virus

2. Which of the following characteristics CANNOT be used to describe life functions?
   (A) Sexual reproduction
   (B) Asexual reproduction
   (C) Osmosis
   (D) Absorption of materials dissolved in water
   (E) Anabolism

3. The byproducts of cellular respiration are
   (A) water, oxygen, and carbon monoxide
   (B) water, carbon dioxide, and oxygen
   (C) water and oxygen
   (D) water and carbon dioxide
   (E) water, carbon dioxide, and sugars

4. Only one of the following statements about respiration is true. Which one is it?
   (A) Thirty-eight molecules of ATP can be produced from one molecule of glucose.
   (B) Bacteria oxidize sugars in their mitochondria.
   (C) The Krebs cycle produces sugars from carbon dioxide and water.
   (D) Most of the ATP produced in the mitochondria is produced in the Krebs cycle.
   (E) Pyruvate is produced in the electron transport chain.

5. Photosynthesis involves two separate processes, the light reactions and the Calvin cycle. The products of the light reactions are _____ / and the products of the Calvin cycle are _____.
   (A) carbon dioxide and water / sugars
   (B) light and water / sugars
   (C) oxygen and ATP / sugars
   (D) sugars and oxygen / ATP
   (E) sugars / ATP

6. In pea plants, axial flowers are dominant to terminal flowers. If I crossed an axial flowered plant and a terminal flowered plant and got half terminal and half axial, I would know that
   (A) the axial flowered parent plant was heterozygous
   (B) the axial flowered parent plant was homozygous
   (C) the terminal flowered parent plant was heterozygous
   (D) all the offspring were hybrids
   (E) the terminal offspring were heterozygous

7. Which of the following is the correct base pairing in DNA?

   (A) Adenine with guanine
   (B) Adenine with thymine
   (C) Guanine and thymine
   (D) Thymine and uracil
   (E) Adenine and uracil

8. Which of the following statements about protein synthesis is TRUE?

   (A) Proteins are assembled from amino acids at the ribosome.
   (B) The ribosome contains both the mRNA and the DNA.
   (C) Amino acids are carried to the site of protein synthesis by rRNA.
   (D) Only (A) and (B) are true.
   (E) All of the above are true.

9. A fruit fly has 4 pair of chromosomes in each nucleated cell. Which one of the following statements is correct?

   (A) The haploid number of the fruit fly is 4 and each gamete will contain 4 chromosomes.
   (B) The diploid number of the fruit fly is 4 and each gamete will contain 8 chromosomes.
   (C) The haploid number of the fruit fly is 8 and each gamete will contain 8 chromosomes.
   (D) The haploid number of the fruit fly is 4 and each will contain 8 chromosomes.
   (E) Only females have the diploid number of chromosomes in the fruit fly.

10. Scientists have used recombinant DNA technology to do all the following EXCEPT

   (A) clone a sheep
   (B) have bacteria produce human insulin
   (C) replace a dysfunctional immune system
   (D) keep strawberries from freezing
   (E) clean up oil spills

11. The theory of natural selection proposed by Charles Darwin is based on all of the following EXCEPT:

   (A) Members of a species are different and varied.
   (B) Organisms pass along characteristics they achieved during their lifetime.
   (C) Some individuals are more adapted to their environment than others of their species.
   (D) Natural selection produces populations that are adapted to their environment at any particular time.
   (E) Some organisms produce more offspring than others of their species.

12. The symbiotic relationship that describes benefit to one party and neither benefit nor harm to the other is

   (A) parasitism
   (B) competition
   (C) mutualism
   (D) nihilism
   (E) commensalism

13. The carrying capacity of a population could be described as

   (A) a number on a graph that shows the organisms that exist in a population over time
   (B) the maximum number of organisms that can be supported in an environment at any one time
   (C) being affected by humans
   (D) variable according to both abiotic and biotic factors
   (E) All of the above

14. The organelle most closely associated with the production of energy in a cell is the

   (A) nucleus
   (B) endoplasmic reticulum
   (C) mitochondria
   (D) golgi apparatus
   (E) vacuole

15. Proteins are modified in the

   (A) nucleus
   (B) endoplasmic reticulum
   (C) mitochondria
   (D) golgi apparatus
   (E) vacuole

16. The cell membrane may be described as

   (A) a layer that is made of lipids
   (B) the boundary of a cell containing proteins
   (C) a regulatory organelle
   (D) Only (A) and (B)
   (E) All of the above

17. A balanced ecosystem contains

   (A) an energy source
   (B) abiotic and biotic factors
   (C) producers and consumers
   (D) Only (B) and (C)
   (E) All of the above

18. A student using a compound microscope with a 10× ocular lens and a 4× objective lens measured his field of view with a plastic ruler to be 4 mm. He then placed some of his cheek cells on a slide, found them using the 4× objective lens and switched to the 40× objective lens. He counted twelve cells, side by side, that stretched from one side of the field of view to the other. What is the best estimate for the diameter of a cheek cell?

    (A) 0.0033 mm
    (B) 0.0132 mm
    (C) 0.033 mm
    (D) 0.132 mm
    (E) 1.32 mm

19. Predators in an ecosystem

    (A) help the community by keeping the number of prey from outstripping their resources
    (B) help the prey population by removing the sick and less fit individuals
    (C) enhance species diversity
    (D) reduce the possibility of competitive exclusion
    (E) All of the above

20. The stage of mitosis when the chromosomes break apart and move to the opposite poles is called

    (A) interphase
    (B) prophase
    (C) metaphase
    (D) anaphase
    (E) telophase

CHEMISTRY

BASIC CONCEPTS

Chemistry can be described as being concerned with the composition of matter and the changes that it can undergo. There are several main "branches" of chemistry. Organic chemistry is mostly concerned with the study of chemicals containing the element carbon. Inorganic chemistry is the study of all elements and compounds other than organic compounds. Analytical chemistry is the study of qualitative (what is present?) and quantitative (how much is present?) analysis of elements and compounds. Physical chemistry is the study of reaction rates, mechanisms, bonding and structure, and thermodynamics. Biochemistry is the study of the chemical reactions that happen within the biological process.

Matter is defined as anything that has mass and occupies space. Mass is the quantity of matter in a particular body. Weight is the gravitational force of attraction between that body's mass and the mass of the planet (usually Earth) on which it is weighed.

Chemists are often concerned with energy as well as matter, since energy is either required for some reactions or is given off in other reactions. Energy is defined as the capacity to do work or to transfer heat. Early chemists understood that while matter and energy may change form, they are always conserved. By the Laws of Conservation of Mass and of Energy, neither mass nor energy is created or destroyed in the transformation of matter. There are three commonly employed temperature scales that measure energy: Fahrenheit, Celsius, and Kelvin; only Celsius and Kelvin are accepted universally. The Kelvin and Celsius scales have identical degree increments but different zeros. In particular, °Kelvin = °Celsius + 273, or °Celsius = °Kelvin − 273. The calorie (cal), a unit of measurement for heat energy, is defined as the amount of heat required to raise the temperature of 1.00 g of water from 14.5°C to 15.5°C. The calories that people count when dieting are actually kilocalories, or Calories. The joule (J) is the unit of energy preferred in the international system of units (SI); 1 joule = 0.234 cal. Specific heat is defined in the metric system as the number of calories required to raise the temperature of 1.00 g of a substance 1°C. Different matter has different characteristic properties, like specific heat. Water has a high specific heat (1 cal/°C), while copper's specific heat is about 0.1cal/°C. That means, of course, that it's 10 times easier to raise the temperature of 1 gram of copper one degree than to raise 1 gram of water one degree.

Matter also varies by its density, defined as the mass of a substance occupying a unit volume, i.e.,

$$\text{Density} = \text{Mass} / \text{Volume}$$

There are three physical states of matter—solids, liquids, and gases—although many chemists now recognize a fourth state, a plasma. All gases, at standard temperature and pressure, STP, occupy the same volume. Matter is further divided into two major subdivisions: homogeneous and heterogenous. Homogenous matter is uniform throughout, and no differing parts can be discerned. Heterogeneous matter is not uniform throughout, and differing parts can be distinguished, such as in muddy water.

Homogeneous matter, or pure substances, are divided into two groups: compounds and elements. A compound is a pure substance that can be broken down by various chemical means into two or more different substances. An element is a pure substance that cannot be decomposed into simpler substances by ordinary chemical means. Mixtures, or heterogeneous substances, can be separated by physical means, such as distillation. The basic building block of a compound is a molecule. The basic building block of an element is an atom. As such, atoms make up molecules and molecules make up compounds. When we write $3H_2O$ we're conveying the idea that 3 molecules of water are present, each made of two hydrogen atoms and an oxygen atom.

ATOMS AND ATOMIC THEORY

The atom is a complex unit composed of various subatomic particles, including electrons, protons, and neutrons. Protons have a relative mass of 1 (atomic mass unit) and carry a positive electric charge. Like the proton, the neutron also has a relative mass of 1 (atomic mass unit), but the neutron carries no electric charge. Electrons carry a negative electric charge and have almost negligible mass. The basic "shape" of an atom consists of a dense nucleus, composed of neutrons and protons, and a "cloud" of orbiting electrons. The electrons orbit around the nucleus at various energy levels called quantum levels. The average path that an electron takes while traveling around the nucleus is known as its orbital. Orbitals vary in size, shape, and spacial orientation. Each electron occupies an orbital, and orbitals can hold no more than two electrons (Pauli Exclusion Principle). When a pair of electrons occupies a single orbital, they must have opposite "spin." The electrons in the outermost principal energy level of an atom are known as the valence electrons. Each electron can be described by 4 quantum numbers. The first quantum number, n, designates the main energy level of the electron and has integral values of 1, 2, 3, etc. The second quantum number designates the shape of the orbital, the first two being s, spherical, and p, dumbell shaped. One can glean much information by using the principal quantum number. For example, if $n = 2$, the number of sublevels = 2. The number of orbitals is n^2 or 4, and the number of electrons required to fill the second main energy level is $2n^2$ or 8. Electrons can "jump" from one energy level to another but cannot exist in between levels. Electrons absorb energy in order to move to higher levels, and emit energy upon moving to lower levels. The energy that is lost or gained is done so in discrete quantities known as quanta. Elements may be identified by examining the spectral lines produced by the energy radiated or absorbed by electrons moving from one quantum level to another. Each element has its own identifying "finger-print" of spectral lines.

Atoms of different elements have a different combination of electrons, protons, and neutrons. Although a proton in a gold nucleus would "look like" a proton in a silver nucleus, the difference between gold and silver is in the *number* of protons found in the nuclei of these atoms. The nucleus of a gold atom contains 79 protons, and the nucleus of a silver atom contains 47 protons.

The mass of an atom is measured in atomic mass units (amu). The mass is almost entirely contained in the nucleus, but the atomic volume is almost completely outside the nucleus (defined by the orbiting electrons). The atomic *number* of an element is the number of protons in the nucleus. Since only protons and neutrons have significant mass, the atomic *mass* of an element is the sum of the number of protons and neutrons. For example, if an atom of gold has an atomic number of 79 and an atomic mass of 197 (amu), its nucleus must contain 79 protons and 118 neutrons. Atomic mass numbers are based on the standard mass of 12.000 for a carbon atom. The actual atomic mass found on the Periodic Table is the average for the natural abundance of the atomic masses of the known isotopes.

Most elements exist as isotopes. An isotope of an element necessarily has the same number of protons but a different number of neutrons. Some elements exist as radioactive isotopes, others have one or more radioactive isotopes, and still others have none.

Radiation is the disintegration of the nucleus of an atom with emission from its nuclear particles. Nuclear disintegration may produce alpha particles, beta particles, gamma rays, or a combination of these three. Alpha particles are heavy, with a structure similar to a helium nucleus carrying a +2 charge. Beta particles are essentially high-speed electrons, and gamma rays are not particles but high-energy X-rays. The time used to measure the disintegration of the atom is its half-life, which is the time required for one half of the nuclei in a microscopic sample to disintegrate.

PERIODIC CLASSIFICATION OF ELEMENTS

The modern Periodic Table is the evolution of work begun by a German chemist, Lothar Meyer (1830–1895), and a Russian chemist, Dmitri Mendeleev (1834–1906). Mendeleev is credited with much of the successes of the table, since he purposely left gaps in its construction to allow for the discovery of elements that had not yet been found but had "predictable properties."

The table is arranged in an order consistent with increasing atomic number (number of protons). Elements with metallic properties are found on the left side of the table, while nonmetals are found on the right side of the table. Metals tend to lose electrons (and form positive ions), while nonmetals tend to gain electrons (and form negative ions), or they can often share electrons with other nonmetals. Vertical columns in the Periodic Table are called *groups* or *families*, and they are elements with similar electron arrangements and similar chemical properties.

There are eight nonmetals that form homonuclear diatomic molecules when found naturally in the environment. An easy method to remember them is the phrase: *hydrogen + "the magic seven!"* Hydrogen, of course, is diatomic, existing as H_2 in the environment. To find the

PERIODIC TABLE OF ELEMENTS

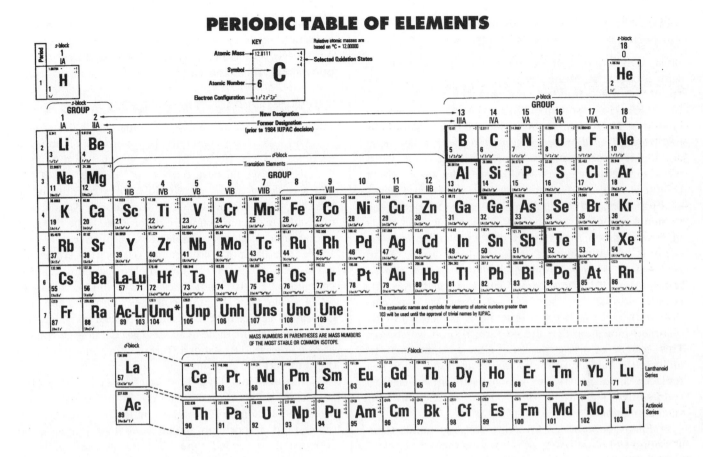

other seven diatomic elements, look at a Periodic Table. Find element number 7 (nitrogen), and, beginning with nitrogen, note that number 7 is formed on the table with the remaining diatomic elements! They are (forming the number 7) nitrogen, oxygen, fluorine, chlorine, bromine, iodine, and astatine! Their formulas would be written as $N_2 - O_2 - F_2 - Cl_2 - Br_2 - I_2 - At_2$, respectively. All other elements exist in nature as monatomic elements.

The elements in the vertical column headed by lithium (on many periodic tables hydrogen is placed here for "graphic balance") are known as *alkali metals.* Column II (headed by beryllium) contains the *alkaline earth metals.* On the right side of the table, the column headed by oxygen is often called the *chalcogen* family, while the column of elements headed by fluorine is known as the *halogens.* All of the elements in the final column are very unreactive elements previously know as the inert gases; they now are called the *noble gases.*

The Periodic Table can be used to predict the number of valence electrons (and resulting oxidation number), which is helpful in writing chemical formulas. For example, in a chemical bonding situation, all of the alkaline metals carry a charge of +1, the alkaline earth metals +2, and the halogens −1.

A chemical bond forms by the transfer of an electron from one atom to another, or by the sharing of an electron of an electron pair.

Ionic bonds are formed when electrons are completely transferred. Ionic bonds are often formed when a metal from the left side of the Periodic Table transfers an electron to a nonmetal from the right side of the table. The number of electrons that transfer dictates the nature of the ionic bond and can be used to predict the formula of the compound. Examples: sodium (with one available valence electron to transfer) combines with chlorine ("looking" for a valence electron) and forms the compound NaCl (sodium chloride). Magnesium (with two available valence electrons to transfer), then, would need to combine with two chlorine atoms (each atom "looking" for one valence electron) to form the compound $MgCl_2$ (magnesium chloride).

Covalent bonds, found in chemicals such as carbon dioxide (CO_2) and sulfur trioxide (SO_3), involve the sharing of electrons rather than the transfer of electrons. Ionic bonds are usually stronger, forming chemicals with higher melting and boiling points.

When energy is absorbed, chemical bonds can be broken. When chemical bonds are formed, energy is released. During these rearrangements of atoms or molecules the Laws of Conservation of Mass and Conservation of Energy still apply.

CHEMICAL NOMENCLATURE OF INORGANIC COMPOUNDS

Binary compounds result from the combination of a metal with a nonmetal. Name the metal first, followed by the "root" of the nonmetal, and add the ending "ide." Examples: NaCl (sodium chloride), $MgCl_2$ (magnesium chloride), Al_2O_3 (aluminum oxide). Binary compounds involving a transition metal combining with a nonmetal are slightly more complex. Transition metals can exist with different valences (oxidation numbers), which produces compounds with different chemical and physical properties, and this difference must be included in the nomenclature of the compound. For example, iron exists in two common forms (with different oxidation numbers). It can combine with chlorine, for example, as an Fe^{+2} ion or as an Fe^{+3} ion, producing $FeCl_2$ and $FeCl_3$, respectively. The first compound is named iron (II) chloride (indicating that the +2 form of iron was involved), and the latter compound is named iron (III) chloride (indicating that the +3 form of iron was used). This system of using numbers (Roman numerals) to indicate the valence of the metal involved in a bond has replaced an older system, which used (inconsistently) Latin suffixes such as "ic" and "ous" to correspond with valence numbers.

Binary compounds involving covalent bonds (usually nonmetals combining with nonmetals) use a series of prefixes to indicate how many atoms of each molecule are involved in the compound. Examples: sulfur can combine with oxygen in at least three different ways, depending on laboratory or environmental conditions. The compound SO is named sulfur monoxide, while SO_2 is named sulfur dioxide, and SO_3 is named sulfur trioxide. Correspondingly, the chemical P_2O_5 is named *diphosphorous pentoxide*. Note: these prefixes are used only in nonmetal-nonmetal bonded chemicals.

A knowledge of *radicals* is essential in understanding the nomenclature of inorganic chemicals. Radicals are molecular fragment elements with a specific oxidation number. Radicals enter into chemical reactions without internal change in their own bonding. Examples: The hydroxide radical (OH^{-1}) "behaves" like a halogen when forming compounds. Combining a metal with hydroxide, such as Na, produces a compound with the formula NaOH, which is named sodium hydroxide. Magnesium combining with hydroxide produces the compound $Mg(OH)_2$, named magnesium hydroxide. Note that the parentheses around the (OH) in this case indicate there are two individual hydroxide radicals involved in the formation of this compound. The same Roman numeral "rules" for transition metals combining with radicals continue to apply. Thus, $Fe(OH)_3$ is named iron (III) hydroxide. One should also consult a chemistry text to memorize polyatomic ions and their oxidation or valence numbers. For example, the nitrate ion, NO_3, has an oxidation state of -1 and sodium nitrate would be written $NaNO_3$. Other important ions would be sulfate, phosphate, and ammonium.

STOICHIOMETRY CALCULATIONS

The basic unit for all chemical calculations is the *mole.*

A mole of *anything* contains Avogadro's number of particles (6.02×10^{23}). Therefore, if you had a mole of pencils, you would have 6.02×10^{23} pencils, but if you had a mole of gold, you would have a quantity of an element that contained 6.02×10^{23} atoms. Atomic and molecular masses in grams are determined to be the mass at one mole of atoms or molecules, respectively. For example: one mole of gold contains 6.02×10^{23} atoms and has a mass of 196.967 g. One mole of sodium chloride contains 6.02×10^{23} molecules of NaCl and has a mass of 58.44 g (one adds the atomic masses of both sodium and chlorine together for this result). A special consideration for gases only: one mole of an ideal gas occupies a volume of 22.4 liters at STP (Standard Temperature and Pressure—0°C and 760 mm pressure).

In problems involving stoichiometric ratios, the balancing numbers (coefficients) in an equation are *moles*. Stoichiometry problems must be calculated in moles, and a thorough understanding of gram-to-mole conversions is needed. One can calculate the number of moles by this important formula:

$$moles = \frac{grams}{molecular\ mass}$$

For example:

65.8 grams of sodium chloride = how many moles?

moles = (65.8 grams, given in the problem) divided by (58.4 grams/mole—the molecular mass)

moles = 1.1

All stoichiometry problems assume a *correctly balanced equation.*

For example:

Based on this correctly balanced equation, $N_2 + 3H_2 \rightarrow 2NH_3$, how many moles of nitrogen are needed to react completely with 6 moles of hydrogen?

The solution is based on the ratio of the moles of nitrogen (1) and hydrogen (3) from the correctly balanced equation. Since 1 mole of nitrogen reacts with 3 moles of hydrogen, twice as many moles $\left(\frac{6}{3} \text{ or } 2\right)$ of nitrogen are needed. How many moles of nitrogen are required to make 6 moles of ammonia?

The answer is 3.

The *molarity* of a solution is the number of moles of solute contained in 1 liter of solution. Other methods of calculating the concentration of solutions include *normality* and *molality*. The molality calculation is the number of moles of solute per kilogram of solvent.

SOLUTIONS, ACIDS, AND BASES

Electrolytes are substances that dissolve in water to form solutions that will conduct an electric current. Dissolved ions conduct current. Solutions that donate protons or accept protons are called acids and bases, respectively.

Acids have the following properties: acid solutions conduct electricity (i.e., acids are electrolytes); acids react with many active metals to liberate hydrogen gas; acids turn litmus paper red; acids form a salt and water when reacting with bases; acids have a sour taste; acids, when measured on the pH scale, have pH < 7. An acid, as defined by Arrhenius in 1884, is a substance that yields a hydrogen ion H^+ when dissolved in water. Arrhenius's definition has since been expanded to include its producing a hydronium H_3O^+ ion.

Bases have the following properties: basic solutions conduct electricity (i.e., bases are electrolytes); basic solutions react with acids to form salts and water; bases turn litmus paper blue; bases have a bitter taste; bases feel "slippery" (caustic properties); bases, when measured on the pH scale, have pH > 7. Most common bases contain the OH^- ion.

Some chemicals, such as water, are *amphiprotic*—that is, they can be either proton donors or acceptors (and, thus, can be considered as either an acid or a base).

A salt results from the combination of an acid and a base. A salt is formed from the negative ion (anion) of the acid and the positive ion (cation) of the base. Neutralization is the reaction by which equivalent quantities of an acid and a base react to form a salt and water. In the laboratory, titration is the procedure that is used to quantitatively mix acids and bases to measure the strengths of acids, bases, or quantities of various ions.

pH is a measure of the concentration of an acid or base. By definition, it is the negative of the common logarithm ($-\log_{base\ 10}$) of the hydrogen ion (actually the hydronium ion) concentration. On a practical basis, it is a scale from 0 to 14, with the number 7 being considered neutral. Water that is neutral, with a pH of 7, has a concentration of hydrogen ions that is 1.0×10^{-7} moles/liter. Acids have a pH < 7, and bases have a pH > 7. The scale is designed to measure the concentration of dilute acids and bases. Concentrated acids can have a pH *below* 0, and concentrated bases can have a pH *above* 14. A reciprocal scale, the pOH scale, is a measure of the concentration of OH^- ions in solution. In pH calculations, it is important to remember that pH + pOH = 14.

ELECTROCHEMISTRY

A knowledge of oxidation numbers is important in the understanding of electrochemistry and also in balancing complex oxidation/reduction (redox) equations. An oxidation number is a "label" assigned to atoms that indicates the extent to which they have either lost or gained electrons. Assigning oxidation numbers is based on many complex considerations involving the type of bonding involved.

Following are some general rules for assigning these numbers to atoms and some examples:

The oxidation number for an element that is not in a multicompound element is always zero.

N_2 (each nitrogen has an oxidation number of zero)

The oxidation number of an atom that is a monatomic ion in a compound is the same as the electrical charge of the ion (its valence).

$MgBr_2$: This compound is formed from Mg^{+2} ions and Br^- ions, so the oxidation numbers are identical to the electrical ion charges.

Mg = (+2)   Br = (−1)

Al_2O_3: This compound is formed from Al^{+3} ions and O^{-2} ions, so the oxidation numbers are identical to the electrical ion charges.

Al = (+3) O = (−2)

The oxidation number of H (hydrogen) is always +1 (except in salts, where hydrogen is bonded to a metal).

The oxidation number of O (oxygen) is almost always −2 (except in peroxides and superoxides).

The sum of all oxidation numbers in a compound must be ZERO. The sum of oxidation numbers in an ion must equal the charge of the ion.

Example 1

H_3PO_4: The sum of the oxidation numbers must total zero. Using the rules above, hydrogen always carries a charge of +1, but there are 3 hydrogen atoms in the compound, resulting in an overall charge of +3. Oxygen always carries a charge of −2, but there are 4 oxygen atoms in the compound, resulting in an overall charge of −8. To balance the +3 (from the hydrogen) and the −8 (from the oxygen), an oxidation number must be assigned to phosphorus (P) to make the total equal zero. The number +5 results from phosphorus. (+3) + (+5) + (−8) = (0)

Example 2

SO_3^{-2} (sulfite ion): In this case, the sum of the oxidation numbers must equal the assigned charge on the ion (−2). The oxidation number of oxygen is −2, but there are 3 oxygen atoms in the ion's formula, giving an overall charge of −6. A number (+4) must then be assigned to the sulfur atom to make the overall charge equal −2. (+4) + (−6) = (−2), the charge on the sulfite ion.

In an oxidation/reduction (redox) reaction, the electrons lost by one compound always equal the electrons gained by another. The term *oxidation* describes a reaction in which the oxidation number increases (as you examine the reaction from the reactant to the product side). In other words, when an ion is oxidized, it loses electrons and becomes more positive. For example, $Fe^{+2} \rightarrow Fe^{+3} + e^-$ iron is changing from the +2 ion to the +3 ion. Its oxidation number is increasing; therefore, by definition, it is being oxidized.

The term *reduction* describes a reaction in which the oxidation number decreases. In other words, when an ion is reduced, it gains electrons and becomes more negative. For example, $Br_2 + 2e^- \rightarrow 2Br^-$ bromine is changing from an oxidation state of zero (by definition, all "free" elements have an oxidation number of zero), to a charge of −1 (of course, there are 2 bromine ions, so the overall charge is −2). To accomplish this change, molecular bromine needed to *gain* 2 electrons; thus, it is *reduced*.

In all *redox* reactions, the oxidation and reduction occur simultaneously. There is always a conservation of both mass and charge. The particle that is being oxidized is also known as the *reducing agent;* conversely, the particle that is being reduced is known as the *oxidizing agent.* In an electrolytic cell (a battery), oxidation takes place at the positive electrode (called the cathode), while reduction takes place at the negative electrode (called the anode).

CHEMICAL EQUILIBRIUM

Chemical reactions may either release heat (exothermic) or absorb heat (endothermic). The minimum amount of energy needed to initiate a chemical reaction is known as the *activation energy.* The total amount of heat released or absorbed is known as the *heat of reaction.* While catalysts can lower the activation energy, the heat of the reaction will be unaffected. The heat of reaction is usually measured in kJ/mol and is given the symbol ΔH (Delta *H*) in heat of reaction expressions. A negative value for a ΔH measurement is assigned to exothermic reactions, while a positive ΔH value is assigned to endothermic reactions.

The rate of a chemical reaction as well as the equilibrium between reactants and products is based on numerous factors, including temperature, concentration of reactants, pressure, and the presence of catalysts and/or inhibitors. A knowledge of Le Châtelier's Principles is important in understanding equilibrium situations. He found that systems in equilibrium under stress will act to relieve that stress. Chemical equilibrium represents a state of balance between reactants and products. Altering any of the experimental conditions forces the system to shift and establish a new equilibrium.

CHEMISTRY: REVIEW QUESTIONS

The following questions will give you a chance to practice. Read each question carefully, mark your answers, and then check them with the answers and explanations that appear at the end of the Overview section.

1. An element has an atomic number of 3 and an atomic mass of 6.94. The number of protons in each nucleus of that element is

   (A) 3
   (B) 3.94
   (C) 6.94
   (D) 9.94
   (E) It is impossible to tell from the given data.

2. The isotopes of an element have mass numbers of 35 and 37. If the atomic number of this element is 17 and its average atomic mass is 35.453, the most common isotope has how many neutrons?

   (A) 17
   (B) 18
   (C) 35
   (D) 37
   (E) 72

3. An element has the following electron structure: $1s^2\ 2s^2,\ 2p^5$. The total number of electrons is

   (A) 2
   (B) 4
   (C) 5
   (D) 7
   (E) 9

4. The number of protons for the above element (with $1s^2\ 2s^2,\ 2p^5$) is

   (A) 2
   (B) 5
   (C) 7
   (D) 9
   (E) 14

5. If the freezing temperature of a substance is 300 degrees Kelvin, the freezing temperature in degrees Celsius would be

(A) 27
(B) 100
(C) 300
(D) 327
(E) 408

6. A certain element has a half-life of 200 days. If one had 10 grams of this substance today, how much would be left in 800 days?

(A) 0 grams
(B) 0.625 grams
(C) 1.25 grams
(D) 5 grams
(E) 10 grams

7. Which of the following does NOT form naturally diatomic molecules?

(A) Hydrogen
(B) Helium
(C) Nitrogen
(D) Oxygen
(E) Chlorine

8. Which of the following is the correct chemical formula for magnesium oxide based on oxidation numbers (or valence electrons)?

(A) MgO
(B) Mg_2O
(C) MgO_2
(D) Mg_2O_3
(E) None of the above

9. Iron (III) oxide is correctly written as

(A) Fe3O
(B) 3FeO
(C) Fe_3O_2
(D) Fe_2O_3
(E) None of the above

10. How many moles of water exist if one has 93 g of water?

(A) 1
(B) 5.2
(C) 5.8
(D) 7.75
(E) 9.3

11. Calcium chloride and iron (III) sulfate combine to yield calcium sulfate and iron (III) chloride according to the following unbalanced formula:

$$CaCl_2 + Fe_2(SO_4)_3 \qquad CaSO_4 + FeCl_3$$

In a balanced equation, the numbers before calcium sulfate and iron (III) chloride would be:

(A) 1 and 2
(B) 2 and 1
(C) 2 and 3
(D) 3 and 2
(E) 3 and 3

12. Calculate the mass of iron (Fe) formed when 1.6g of iron (III) oxide reacts with carbon monoxide to yield iron and carbon dioxide according to the following formula:

$$Fe_2O_3 + 3CO \qquad 2Fe + 3CO_2$$

(A) 0.8 g
(B) 1.1 g
(C) 1.6 g
(D) 3.2 g
(E) 5.5 g

13. Analysis of a compound shows that it is composed of 0.14 g Fe (iron) and 0.18 g Cl_2 (chlorine). The best empirical formula according to that data would be

(A) FeCl
(B) Fe_2Cl_3
(C) Fe_2Cl_5
(D) Fe_2Cl
(E) $FeCl_2$

14. What is the molarity of a solution that has 13.9 g of magnesium iodide (MgI_2) dissolved in enough water to make 500 ml of solution?

(A) 0.05 M
(B) 0.10 M
(C) 0.18 M
(D) 0.36 M
(E) MgI_2 will not dissolve in water.

15. Which of the following properties is INCORRECT for acids?

(A) Acid solutions coduct electricity.
(B) Acids react with many active metals to produce hydrogen gas.
(C) Acids have a sour taste.
(D) Acids when measured on the pH scale have pH$>$7.
(E) Acids turn litmus paper red.

16. When a solution of copper chloride is subjected to electrolysis by a direct current, electrons enter the solution at the _____ and are taken up by the _____.

    (A) interface, water
    (B) cathode, ray tube
    (C) anode, cathode
    (D) cathode, cations
    (E) anode, anions

17. Hydrochloric acid and zinc react to give hydrogen gas and zinc chloride according to the following formula:

    $$2HCl + Zn \quad H_2 + ZnCl_2$$

    How many liters of hydrogen gas at STP can be produced from the reaction of 65.4 g of zinc with hydrochloric acid?

    (A) $2.92 \, \ell$
    (B) $5.84 \, \ell$
    (C) $22.4 \, \ell$
    (D) $65.4 \, \ell$
    (E) $130.8 \, \ell$

18. The most electronegative element is

    (A) F
    (B) Ne
    (C) He
    (D) Cl
    (E) O

19. What is the oxidation number of S in the compound H_2SO_4?

    (A) +1
    (B) +2
    (C) +4
    (D) +6
    (E) −2

20. The Haber process is used to produce ammonia according to the following reaction:

    $$N_2 + 3H_2 \quad 2NH_3 + heat$$

    Which of the following actions will NOT favor the forward reaction?

    (A) An increase of nitrogen concentration
    (B) An increase in ammonia concentration
    (C) An increase in pressure
    (D) An decrease in temperature
    (E) An increase in the hydrogen concentration

PHYSICS

UNITS OF MEASURE

The metric system:

giga-	1,000,000,000	10^9
mega-	1,000,000	10^6
kilo-	1,000	10^3
centi-	0.01	10^{-2}
milli-	0.001	10^{-3}
micro-	0.000001	10^{-6}
nano-	0.000000001	10^{-9}

Basic units of measurement:

	Metric System	English System
length	meter	foot
mass	kilogram	slug
time	second	second
volume	liter	quart
charge	coulomb	—

UNIT CONVERSIONS

1 inch = 2.54 centimeters

1 meter = 39.37 inches

1 slug = 14.6 kilograms

1 liter = 1.06 quarts

1 gallon = 3.78 liters

DERIVED UNITS

newton (N) = 1 kg • m/s^2 The force necessary to accelerate one kilogram of mass at the rate of one meter per second squared.

joule (J) = 1 N • *m* The energy required to exert one newton of force through a distance of one meter.

watt (W) = 1 J/*s* The power corresponding to energy being expended at the rate of one joule per second.

pascal (Pa) = 1 N/m^2 Pressure corresponding to one newton of force being exerted over one square meter of area.

volt (V) = 1 J/C The potential difference equal to a change in potential energy of one joule for one coulomb of charge.

ampere (A) = 1 C/*s* A measure of electric current equal to one coulomb of charge per second.

ohm (Ohm) = 1 V/A The electric resistance in a conductor such that a potential difference of one volt is required to produce a current of one ampere.

MECHANICS

Velocity. Velocity is the time rate of change of the position of an object. It is a vector with both magnitude and direction. The magnitude of the velocity vector is the *speed*.

Acceleration. Acceleration is the time rate of change of the velocity vector. Even if the speed is constant the acceleration will not be zero if the direction of the velocity is changing.

Mass. Mass is the quantity of matter in a body.

Momentum. This quantity, equal to the product of mass and velocity, characterizes how difficult it is to change the motion of a body.

Force. Force causes a body to change its state of motion, i.e., to accelerate. Acceleration is proportional to force.

Gravity. Gravity is the force of attraction between masses. The force between two masses is proportional to the product of the two masses divided by the square of the distance between them.

Kinetic energy. This is the energy of motion, equal to one half its mass times the square of its velocity

Potential energy. This is the energy of an object which depends on the object's position. For example, a gravitational force field causes the energy of all masses in it to depend on their position.

Newton's three laws of motion.
1. First law: *Inertia.* An object will continue with the same speed and direction unless acted upon by an outside force.
2. Second law: *Force.* When a force acts on a body, the acceleration is proportional to the force and inversely proportional to the mass.
3. Third law: *Reaction.* When one body exerts a force that acts upon another body, the second body exerts an equal and opposite force back on the first.

Time dilation. Time dilation is the slowing of clocks in a reference frame moving at speeds comparable to the speed of light with respect to an observer, as seen by that observer.

Lorentz contraction. The Lorentz contraction is the reduction of lengths in the direction of motion of a reference frame moving at speeds comparable to the speed of light with respect to an observer, as seen by that observer.

WAVE MOTION

Transverse waves. The medium through which the waves travel oscillates in a direction perpendicular to the direction of propagation of a transverse wave (e.g., radio waves and light).

Longitudinal waves. The medium through which the waves travel oscillates in a direction parallel to the direction of propagation of a longitudinal wave (e.g., sound waves).

Wavelength. The wavelength is the distance from one crest of a wave to the next crest.

Frequency. The frequency is the number of complete cycles per unit time of a wave or oscillation.

Phase velocity. The phase velocity of a wave is the speed of motion of a wave crest through a medium, equal to the wave's frequency times its wavelength.

LIGHT AND SOUND

Visible light. Light is electromagnetic radiation that can be perceived by the eye. This includes the colors of the rainbow that are, in order of increasing frequency, red, orange, yellow, green, blue, indigo, and violet.

Electromagnetic spectrum. The electromagnetic spectrum is the continuous spectrum of all forms of electromagnetic radiation. These are, in order of increasing frequency, radio waves, microwaves, infrared, visible light, ultraviolet, X-rays, and gamma rays.

The law of reflection. When light impinges on a reflecting surface, the angle of incidence is equal to the angle of reflection.

Refraction. Refraction is the bending of light when it travels from one medium into another. The refracted angle, measured from the normal, is smaller if the new medium has a higher refractive index and larger if the new medium has a lower index.

Dispersion. As light travels through a prism, each frequency (or color) is refracted by a slightly different amount because the refractive index depends on wavelength. Each color emerges from the prism at a slightly different angle and is separated from the others.

Photon. The photon is the quantum of light. The energy of a photon is proportional to its frequency.

Sound waves. As sound waves travel through a medium, they cause a compression and rarefaction of the medium. The speed of sound through a gas depends on its temperature and molecular weight.

ELECTRICITY AND MAGNETISM

Charge. A charge can be positive or negative. Like charges repel, opposite charges attract.

Electric current. Electric current is the flow of electric charge. Current produces a magnetic field.

Magnet. A magnet is a body, usually made of iron or an alloy, that contains a permanent magnetic field. The magnetic field has two poles: north and south. Each atom in the magnet produces a tiny magnetic field due to the motion of it electrons. In certain substances, such as iron, these atoms can be aligned in response to an external magnetic field, producing a magnet that is stable unless disrupted by outside influences, such as excessive heat or shock.

Magnetic force. Whenever a charge moves through a magnetic field, it experiences a force perpendicular to both the velocity of the charge and the magnetic field. If the charge moves parallel to the field, then no force is experienced.

ATOMIC AND NUCLEAR STRUCTURE

Atom. Atoms are the smallest units of matter that are identifiable as a chemical element. They are composed of a core (the nucleus) of protons and neutrons surrounded by a cloud of electrons.

Proton. Protons are positively-charged elementary particles that make up, along with neutrons, the nucleus of atoms. All atoms of a given chemical element have the same number of protons.

Neutron. Neutrons are neutral elementary particles, also found in atomic nuclei. They have approximately the same mass as protons.

Electron. Electrons are negatively-charged elementary particles that surround the nuclei of atoms. They are responsible for the chemical properties of atoms.

Isotope. Atoms of a given chemical element with different numbers of neutrons are isotopes of the element.

PHYSICS: REVIEW QUESTIONS

The following questions will give you a chance to practice. Read each question carefully, mark your answers, and then check them with the answers and explanations that appear at the end of the Overview section.

1. If a planet has an orbital period of 8 years, what is its distance from the Sun in Astronomical Units?

   (A) 2
   (B) 4
   (C) 8
   (D) 64
   (E) There is not enough information.

2. Star A has an apparent magnitude of −1 and Star B has an apparent magnitude of +4. Which of the following statements is true?

   (A) Star B is 5 times brighter than Star A.
   (B) Star A is 5 times brighter than Star B.
   (C) Star B must be more massive than Star A.
   (D) Only (A) and (C)
   (E) None of the above

3. A star of spectral type M might have a surface temperature of

   (A) 3000°K
   (B) 6000°K
   (C) 9000°K
   (D) 12,000°K
   (E) 50,000°K

4. Which planet does not have at least one moon?

   (A) Pluto
   (B) Venus
   (C) Mars
   (D) Only (A) and (B)
   (E) Only (B) and (C)

5. Which of the following represents the greatest distance?

   (A) 10 Astronomical Units
   (B) 20 parsecs
   (C) 30 light years
   (D) 4.5×10^8 kilometers
   (E) 4.5×10^8 miles

6. The diffraction angles of light through an aperture are greater if

   (A) the aperture is larger
   (B) the wavelength is shorter
   (C) the aperture is smaller
   (D) the frequency is higher
   (E) None of the above

7. Which of the following is true when traveling at speeds near the speed of light with respect to an observer?

   (A) Objects are contracted in all directions.
   (B) Objects are contracted only perpendicular to the direction of motion.
   (C) Objects are lengthened in all directions.
   (D) Clocks tick more slowly.
   (E) Only (A) and (C)

8. An electric charge is initially at rest in a static magnetic field. The charge

   (A) accelerates uniformly
   (B) accelerates asymptotically to a constant speed
   (C) accelerates at an increasing rate
   (D) remains at rest
   (E) moves with a constant velocity

9. Which of the follow is true of sound but not light?

   (A) It is a longitudinal wave.
   (B) It is a transverse wave.
   (C) It requires a medium through which to propagate.
   (D) It exhibits interference and diffraction.
   (E) Only (A) and (C)

10. Ice and water are in thermal equilibrium in an insulated container. When heat is slowly added

    (A) the temperature in the container rises
    (B) some ice melts
    (C) the entropy falls
    (D) Only (A) and (B)
    (E) Only (B) and (C)

11. A neutron is composed of

    (A) three quarks
    (B) a proton and an electron
    (C) a positron and an electron
    (D) two protons
    (E) None of the above

12. The speed of sound in an ideal gas increases when

    (A) the pressure increases
    (B) the pressure decreases
    (C) the temperature increases
    (D) the density increases
    (E) the volume increases

13. What happens when a gamma ray photon scatters from an electron (Compton scattering)?

    (A) The electron annihilates.
    (B) The electron decays to a neutrino.
    (C) The gamma photon energy increases.
    (D) The gamma photon wavelength increases.
    (E) The gamma photon energy remains the same.

14. A car accelerates uniformly from rest to 20 *m/s* in 2 seconds. How far does it travel?

    (A) 5 m
    (B) 10 m
    (C) 20 m
    (D) 40 m
    (E) 80 m

15. Doubling the mass of a pendulum

    (A) doubles the period
    (B) quadruples the period
    (C) leaves the period unchanged
    (D) halves the period
    (E) increases or decreases the period, depending on the pendulum's length

16. Two masses collide inelastically. Which of the following is not conserved?

    (A) Energy
    (B) Momentum
    (C) Velocity
    (D) Mass
    (E) Only (A) and (C)

17. A mass rests on a frictionless surface. When a constant force is applied

    (A) the mass moves at constant speed
    (B) the mass accelerates at a constant rate
    (C) its kinetic energy increases at a constant rate
    (D) its momentum is conserved
    (E) Only (B) and (C)

18. Two equal electric charges are placed one meter apart. When the distance is increased to 2 meters, the force

    (A) quadruples
    (B) doubles
    (C) is reduced to $\frac{1}{2}$
    (D) is reduced to $\frac{1}{4}$
    (E) remains the same

19. An ideal gas expands into a vacuum. Which of the following remains constant?

    (A) Pressure
    (B) Temperature
    (C) Volume
    (D) Density
    (E) Only (A) and (B)

20. The occupant of a moving car drops a heavy object out the window. If air resistance is neglected, the path of the object as seen by an observer on the sidewalk

    (A) is a straight line
    (B) is a circular arc
    (C) is a parabola
    (D) is a hyperbola
    (E) It cannot be determined from the data given.

EARTH AND SPACE SCIENCE

Earth science encompasses all of the scientific disciplines that seek to understand the Earth and the surrounding space. Earth science is usually broken down into geology, oceanography, meteorology, and astronomy. Geology is the study of the solid Earth and the dynamic processes that occur on and under the surface. Oceanography is the integrated use of scientific inquiry for the study of the oceans. Oceanography combines physics, chemistry, geology, and biology to ocean processes. Meteorology is the study of atmospheric processes, weather, and climate. Astronomy is the study of the universe and Earth's relationship within it. Earth scientists study the rocks that make up the Earth; the atmosphere, water, and the oceans; climate and meteorology; the history of life; how the Earth formed and its evolution; and the Earth's place in the solar system.

GEOLOGY

Geology is often divided into physical geology and historical geology. Physical geologists study the composition of the Earth and the processes on and within the planet. Historical geologists study the origins of the Earth and seek to piece together development of the Earth from its origins to the present time. This study of the past includes the establishment of major geologic events, the inhabitants of the Earth, and major climactic changes.

CRUST

The Earth is a zoned or layered body, with each layer having characteristic physical and chemical properties. The outermost layer is the crust; it is the thinnest layer, with a thickness of 5 to 45 km. It is composed of rocks made up predominantly of silicate (silicon and oxygen) minerals. It is also the least dense layer, with a density of 2.5 to 3.0 g/cm^3. There are two types of crust. Continental crust is less dense (about 2.7 g/cm^3) than oceanic crust (3.0 g/cm^3).

MANTLE

Below the crust is the mantle; it extends about halfway to the center of the Earth (approximately 2285 km.) and is also composed of silicate minerals rich in magnesium and iron. It is denser than the crust, with a density of 3.3 to 5.0 g/cm^3.

CORES

The third layer from the surface is the outer core, which is liquid, and is composed mostly of iron and nickel. The outer core is approximately 2270 km thick. The inner core is also mostly iron and nickel but is solid, with a density of 12.6 to 13.0 g/cm^3. The inner core has a radius of approximately 1216 km.

ALTERNATE ZONING

An alternate zoning method separates the crust and mantle slightly differently. The term lithosphere refers to the solid crust and that portion of the upper mantle that is also solid. The lithosphere, while made up of both the crust and a portion of the mantle, often functions as a unit when examining tectonic motions and events. Below the lithosphere is the asthenosphere, a plastic region of the upper mantle on which the lithosphere glides.

MINERALS

Minerals are the building blocks of the Earth. A material is defined as a mineral if it is naturally occurring, inorganic, solid, and has a definite chemical structure. Rocks are aggregates of different minerals.

Rocks can be classified into three basic types: igneous, sedimentary, and metamorphic. This classification categorizes rocks based on the process by which they are formed. The rock cycle defines the relationships, by process, between the three basic types of rocks.

IGNEOUS

Igneous rock is formed as a result of the cooling and crystallization of lava or magma. Magma is molten minerals located under the Earth's surface. When magma reaches the surface through eruption from volcanoes, the molten minerals are called lava. Igneous rocks formed from magma typically cool very slowly, producing plutonic igneous rocks, which have a coarser texture (with larger crystal size) than volcanic rocks. Granite is the most common type of plutonic rock. Lava, which cools much more quickly, produces igneous rocks that have a fine-grained texture. Basalt is such a volcanic rock.

SEDIMENTARY

Sedimentary rocks form as rocks, exposed at the surface, undergo the processes of weathering and erosion, producing small rock fragments called sediments. Sediments of gravel, sand, silt, and clay particles are deposited in layers, and with time and great pressure the process of compaction and cementation transforms sediments into sedimentary rocks. Plants and animals that were living at the time can be buried in the sediment, and parts of their anatomy can be preserved as fossils. Sedimentary rocks and any included fossils can yield information about the past depositional environment.

Weathering is the process whereby rocks break down into smaller and smaller pieces. This process occurs either as a result of mechanical action, such as water freezing and thawing in the cracks of rocks, breaking them apart, or by chemical changes of the minerals, such as the formation of clay by the weathering of the mineral feldspar. The process of erosion occurs when water or wind transports the weathered material. An important product of weathered rocks is soil. Almost all life on land is dependent upon soil, directly or indirectly. Soils are a mixture of weathering residues (primarily sand, silt, and clay), decaying organic matter, living creatures (bacteria, fungi, worms, and insects), air, and moisture. The thickness of soils can vary from a few centimeters to many meters thick. Factors that affect the type of soil that is formed are primarily the rock material from which it forms, the climate (temperature and moisture), and the terrain. Soils may take hundreds to thousands of years to form and are very susceptible to degradation through poor management and human use. Once severely damaged, a soil is virtually lost to any productive use. Desertification is the process, mostly from human use, whereby a productive soil in a semiarid area becomes unproductive and desert conditions prevail.

METAMORPHIC

Metamorphic rocks form from existing rock. When rocks undergo heating and pressurization, metamorphic rock results. The pressure and heat cause the mineral structure of the existing rocks to realign, forming a new rock from the old. Metamorphic rocks can form from igneous, sedimentary, and even other metamorphic rocks. For example, the sedimentary rock shale will become slate, while sandstone will become quartzite.

PLATE TECTONICS

Plate tectonics is the theory currently used to explain the interrelationship of Earth processes and is a unifying theory of geology. It explains the formation of mountains and their location as well as the shape and locations of the present continents. The outer shell (lithosphere) of the Earth is relatively brittle and cold. It is broken into about nine major and many minor semirigid plates. Processes within the Earth cause these plates to move, sometimes against each other. Most geologic activity, earthquakes, igneous activity (volcanoes), and mountain building, occurs along plate boundaries. At the boundaries, plates spread apart, collide, or slide past each other. The Pacific Ring of Fire, a volcanically and seismically active region, corresponds to the boundary of the Pacific tectonic plate.

FAULTS

Faults are extensive cracks in rocks where they slip or slide past each other. This motion is not steady but occurs in sudden jolts. The result of one of these "slips" causes large vibrations and tremors at the surface of the Earth, producing an earthquake. Faults may or may not correspond to tectonic plate boundaries. The San Andreas Fault is an example of a fault following a plate boundary.

OCEANOGRAPHY

Earth is often called the "Blue Planet" for good reason. The oceans cover approximately 71 percent of the Earth's surface. More than 80 percent of the Southern Hemisphere is ocean. Approximately $360,000,000 \text{ km}^2$ of the Earth is covered with oceans. Worldwide, the salinity of the oceans averages 3.5 percent. The primary salt in ocean water is sodium chloride (NaCl), common table salt. Ocean water circulates worldwide following clearly defined currents. These currents help regulate temperature extremes in the oceans and within the atmosphere as well. Tides are daily, cyclical changes in the elevation of the ocean surface. Tides are primarily caused by the gravitational pull on the oceans by the moon.

CONTINENTAL

The continents are all ringed by continental margins, which are regions where the continents meet the oceans. The continental margins are, in turn, made up of a gently dipping continental shelf, a more steeply inclined continental slope, and (in some locations) a more gently dipping continental rise. The continental shelf extends outward from the coast to a depth of about 100 meters. The continental shelf is a region that, in the past, may have been dry land when the oceans were smaller. The continental shelf gives way to the continental slope. The continental slope is the true edge of the continents, as the sea actually extends up onto the continents. The continental slope plunges steeply towards the ocean bottom, often to the Abyssal plains, which are regions of ocean bottom with a relatively constant depth of about 4 to 5 km. In areas where the continental slope gradually decreases in slope as it approaches the ocean bottom, a continental rise is said to exist. The continental rise is the transitional area between continental slope and ocean bottom.

Other common features on the sea floor include sea mounts, ridges, and plateaus. Sea mounts are usually submarine volcanic peaks. When they reach above sea level, they form islands. Mid-ocean ridges form the longest linear feature on the planet surface. Typically, mid-ocean ridges rise about 2.5 km above the surrounding ocean floor and are 2,000 km wide. The best known mid-ocean ridge exists in the mid-Atlantic and defines the boundary between the North American/Caribbean and South American plates and the Eurasian and African plates. They are a location of intense seismic and volcanic activity. It is here that new ocean crust is created as the sea floor spreads apart.

Ocean trenches are features where the depth reaches 11,000 meters (averaging about 8,000 meters). Trenches are long and relatively narrow (about 100 km). They may be found along a continental margin—the Peru-Chile Trench extends along western South

America—or they may be found away from the margins as, for example, the Marianas Trench in the western Pacific Ocean. Trenches form when two plates of the Earth's crust come together, and one (always oceanic crust) descends back into the mantle.

HYDROLOGY

Hydrology is the study of water at the Earth's surface and in the ground. The hydrologic cycle describes the movement of water on and within the Earth. Ninety-eight percent of the water on Earth is found in the oceans. Most water that falls as precipitation comes ultimately from oceans. Water is taken into the atmosphere by evaporation in the form of water vapor. Condensation occurs when the air is saturated, causing the vapor to condense into water or freeze into ice crystals. Precipitation occurs when the droplets or ice crystals become too heavy to stay suspended in the atmosphere, and they fall toward the surface. Some water will stay above ground, where it collects together to form runoff. Runoff follows gravitational forces and can feed river systems or collect in low areas. Standing water most often evaporates into the atmosphere. Other runoff collects to form streams; these, in turn, feed rivers. Some runoff may go into lakes.

Water can also soak into the ground by infiltration and become groundwater. The level below which water in the ground is saturated is termed the water table. The depth of the water table depends on the climate of the area as well as the terrain and the nature of the rocks. In general, groundwater flows from areas of higher topography to areas of lower topography, and flows toward the oceans—as do rivers. The movement of groundwater is much slower than that of surface water. From the soil, some water evaporates into the atmosphere again. Evapotranspiration (evaporation plus transpiration) is the term describing the collective transfer of water back into the atmosphere over the land surface.

Layers of rock and sediment that contain water and allow it to be pumped out are called aquifers. A common aquifer material is poorly cemented sandstone. An aquiclude is a rock through which water is unable to flow. Examples of an aquiclude are shale and granite. Because the movement of groundwater is so slow, aquifers are very susceptible to contamination from pollutants. Contamination of groundwater makes it unusable and very difficult to clean up. Most efforts to address groundwater contamination involve monitoring the movement of the contaminant and trying to control its spread by studying the effects of pumping nearby wells.

THE SOLAR SYSTEM

The sun is the largest body of our solar system and is also its center. Its diameter is 109 Earth diameters, or 135 million km. Yet, because of the gaseous nature of the sun, its density is less than the solid Earth's, very closely approximating the density of water. The sun's composition is 90 percent hydrogen, almost 10 percent helium, and minor amounts of other heavier elements. The sun has a surface temperature of 6,000°C and an interior temperature estimated at 15×10^{6}°C. The source of the sun's energy is nuclear fusion. In the interior of the sun, a nuclear reaction occurs, converting four hydrogen nuclei (protons) into a nucleus of helium. In this nuclear reaction, some of the mass of the hydrogen nuclei is converted into energy. This results in a tremendous amount of energy being released.

The formation of our solar system occurred approximately 5 billion years ago. The most accepted theory of the origin of the sun and planets of our solar system is the nebular hypothesis. This hypothesis holds that a nebula or cloud of gas existed, consisting of approximately 80 percent hydrogen, 15 percent helium, and a few percent of the heavier elements. This cloud began to collapse or condense together under the influence of its own gravity. At the same time, the cloud had a rotational component to it, and, as its collapse continued, the rotational velocity became faster. This rotation caused the nebula to form a disklike structure, and, within the disk, small nuclei developed from which the planets would eventually form. Most of the matter, however, became concentrated in the center, where eventually the sun formed. As more and more matter collapsed inward, the temperature of this central mass began to rise due to compression of the gases. As the collapse continued, gravitational attraction got stronger, resulting in the compression of the hydrogen gas with the consequence of heating it. Eventually, the temperature became hot enough to begin nuclear fusion. The sun contains 99.85 percent of the mass of our solar system. The rest is found within the planets, moons, asteroids, and comets.

There are nine planets in the solar system. They are, in order of increasing distance from the sun, Mercury, Venus, Earth, Mars, Jupiter, Saturn, Uranus, Neptune, and Pluto. Based upon their gross physical characteristics, the planets fall within two groups: the terrestrial planets (Mercury, Venus, Earth, and Mars) and the Jovian (Jupiter-like) planets (Jupiter, Saturn, Uranus, and Neptune). Pluto is not included in either category because its position at the far edge of the solar system and its small size make its true nature a mystery. The terrestrial planets are so called because of their Earth-like characteristics; all four are composed primarily of solid, rocky material. Size is the most obvious difference between the two groups. Earth, the largest terrestrial planet, at a diameter of 12,751 km, is only one quarter the size of the smallest Jovian planet, Neptune, at 46,500 km. Mercury is the smallest planet, with a diameter of 4,854 km. The largest planet, Jupiter, has a diameter of 143,000 km.

Other characteristics in which the two groups markedly differ include mass, density, and composition. The Jovian planets are much more massive compared to the terrestrial planets. Earth is the most massive terrestrial planet. Venus is about 0.8 as massive. Mercury is the least massive planet at about 0.06 times the mass of Earth. Jupiter is the most massive planet at 318 times the Earth's mass. Uranus is the least massive Jovian planet at 14.6 times the mass of Earth. The densities of the terrestrial planets average about 5 g/cm^3, or five times the density of water. The Jovian planets, despite their large masses, have an average density of about 1.5 g/cm^3. Compositional variations are responsible for the differences in densities.

The materials of which both groups are composed can be divided into three groups. They are gases, rocks, and ices and are based upon their melting points. Gases are those materials with melting points close to absolute zero or −273°C (Absolute zero is the lowest theoretical temperature). Hydrogen and helium are the gases. The rocky materials are made primarily of silicate minerals and iron and have melting points greater than 700°C. The ices have intermediate melting points and include ammonia (NH_4), carbon dioxide (CO_2), methane (CH_4), and water (H_2O).

The terrestrial planets consist mainly of rocky and metallic material with minor amounts of gases and ices. The Jovian planets consist of a large percentage of hydrogen and helium with varying amounts of ices. This composition accounts for their low densities. All the Jovian planets are thought to contain a core of rocky and metallic material, much as the terrestrial planets do.

Finally, the atmospheres are the last major difference. The Jovian planets have thick, dense atmospheres of hydrogen and helium, while the terrestrial planets have comparatively thin atmospheres. Gravity on the Jovian planets is much greater than on the terrestrial planets, so they have been able to hold on to the abundant hydrogen and helium. The terrestrial planets, however, have much weaker gravity fields and probably lost all their original hydrogen-helium atmospheres early in their history to the solar winds. On Earth, a second atmosphere formed from outgassing (loss of gases during volcanic activity).

THE ATMOSPHERE

Study of the Earth's atmosphere is a very important part of the earth sciences. All life on Earth is dependent on the atmosphere. The composition of the atmosphere is fairly simple. Nitrogen gas (N_2) comprises about 78 percent, oxygen (O_2) makes up about 21 percent, and argon (Ar) about 0.93 percent. One gas that forms a very small component in terms of abundance but has a big impact on weather and climate is carbon dioxide (CO_2). Its abundance is about 0.035 percent.

Carbon dioxide, along with some other gases, absorbs infrared radiation going from the Earth's surface out into space, resulting in the trapping of heat in the atmosphere. This process is known as the greenhouse effect. This is natural process and is an important aspect of our atmosphere. Without it, our atmosphere would not be warm enough to sustain life as we know it, and our planet would probably be too cold for liquid water to exist.

Human activity over the past century is increasing the amount of carbon dioxide in the atmosphere. Over the last fifty years, carbon dioxide levels have been rising. Extensive use of fossil fuels in cars, factories, and homes, and the burning of rain forests, have each helped to increase the level of carbon dioxide in the atmosphere. The threat is that this increase may cause the atmosphere to become warmer, perhaps too warm. The burning of the rain forests is a double threat because the burning releases additional carbon dioxide while destroying trees, a user of carbon dioxide. This effect is termed global warming. If global warming is occurring, the changes could have significant consequences to human culture. Currently, it appears that the temperature of the atmosphere is rising. Increasing carbon dioxide levels are not exclusively responsible for this rise in temperature. As more and more regions of the earth are paved over and developed, increased industrialization is thought to play a role in the amount of solar energy reflected back into the atmosphere.

Another way human activities have an impact upon the atmosphere concerns ozone (O_3). Ozone is a gas found in the upper atmosphere, where it functions as a filter of harmful ultraviolet radiation from the sun. Without it, life could not exist on the surface of our planet. The use of several chemicals has had a detrimental effect on the ozone layer. The best known group of chemicals affecting the ozone layer are chloroflourocarbons (CFCs), used as refrigerants and as propellants for aerosol sprays. CFCs go into the stratosphere and cause the breakdown of ozone, thereby reducing its concentration. There have already been international treaties signed limiting the use of CFCs to reduce the threat to the ozone layer.

TROPOSPHERE

The Earth's atmosphere is divided into four layers based on temperature gradient. The bottom layer is known as the troposphere. The troposphere extends to an altitude of approximately 8 to 18 km and is characterized by an average decrease in temperature of 6.5°C per kilometer increase in altitude. It contains approximately 80 percent of the mass of the atmosphere. Virtually all clouds and precipitation form in and are restricted to this layer. The vertical mixing of this layer is extensive and is the layer in which "weather" occurs.

STRATOSPHERE

Above the troposphere and extending to about 50 km is the stratosphere. Here, the temperature remains constant with increasing altitude to about 20 km, then begins to increase with altitude. The stratosphere is important because it contains ozone (O_3), the gas that absorbs most ultraviolet light, keeping it from reaching the Earth's surface, and thus protecting life on the surface.

MESOSPHERE

The mesosphere lies above the stratosphere, and, here again, temperatures decrease with increasing altitude. At about 80 km, the temperature is approximately −90°C.

THERMOSPHERE

The layer above, with no well-defined upper limit, is the thermosphere. Here, temperatures rise again, to 1,000°C, due to the absorption of short-wave radiation by air molecules. Even though temperatures are very high, it would not feel hot if you were exposed to this air. Temperature is defined as the average kinetic energy of the atoms present in what is being measured. Molecules of air here are moving very fast with a high kinetic energy and, therefore, have a high temperature. The air is so thin, however, that anything exposed to it has very few molecules striking it, resulting in little transfer of energy.

ENERGY

Energy from the sun has the most important control over the weather and climate of the Earth. Solar radiation accounts for virtually all the energy that heats the surface of the Earth and drives the ocean currents and creates winds. Several factors affecting the amount of solar radiation Earth receives influence basic atmospheric processes.

ROTATION

The Earth, in space, has two principal motions: rotation and revolution. Rotation is the spinning of the Earth about its axis, the line running through the poles. The Earth rotates once every 24 hours, producing the daily cycle of daylight and darkness. Half the Earth is always experiencing daylight, and the other half is always experiencing darkness.

REVOLUTION

Revolution is the motion of the Earth orbiting around the sun. The distance between the Earth and sun averages about 150 million km. The Earth's orbit is not circular but slightly elliptical. Each year on about January 3, the Earth is 147 million km from the sun, closer than any other time of the year. On about July 4, the Earth is 152 million km from the sun, farther away than any other time of the year. Even though the distance from the sun varies during the course of the year, this results in only a slight variation in the amount of energy received from the sun, and has little consequence when explaining major seasonal temperature variations. Consider that the Earth is closer to the sun during the Northern Hemisphere winter. The angle of exposure is much more important in determining atmospheric heating and therefore weather.

Probably the most noticeable aspect of seasonal variation is the difference in the length of daylight. Days are longest during the summer and shortest during the winter. However, this fact does not account fully for the seasons. Another factor that may not be as noticeable is the height of the sun above the horizon at noon. On the summer solstice, the sun is highest overhead at noon. It gradually retreats lower and lower in the sky from this day through the fall, until, on the winter solstice, it is at its lowest noon position in the sky. It then begins daily to get higher and higher in the sky again, repeating the cycle. This altitude of the sun affects the angle at which the sun's rays strike the surface of the Earth, resulting in a difference in the intensity of solar radiation received from the sun. This results in a seasonal variation in solar heating. The more direct rays of summer result in more energy being received on the Earth's surface in the hemisphere experiencing summer. In winter, when the rays are less direct, less energy is received in the winter hemisphere, for, as the rays of the sun become less direct, the energy is spread over a greater area. Also, the oblique rays must travel through more atmosphere before reaching the Earth's surface, which means that they have more chance of being filtered, scattered, or reflected before reaching the Earth's surface.

The revolution of Earth in its orbit around the sun causes this yearly fluctuation in the angle of the sun. As Earth travels along its orbit, there is a result of the continual change in orientation of the Earth with respect to the sun. The Earth's axis is not perpendicular to the ecliptic (the plane of orbit around the sun) but is inclined at an angle of about 23° from the perpendicular. As the Earth orbits around the sun, the axis of the Earth remains pointed in the same direction (toward the North Star). As a result, the angle at which the sun's rays strike a given location on the Earth is continually changing. On one day during the year (the summer solstice), the Northern Hemisphere is leaning 23° toward the sun, and vertical rays of the noon sun strike the Tropic of Cancer, 23° north latitude. Six months later (the winter solstice), it is leaning 23° away from the sun, and vertical rays of the noon sun strike the Earth at the Tropic of Capricorn, 23° south latitude. At the vernal and autumnal equinoxes (first day of spring and autumn, respectively), vertical rays of the noon sun strike at the equator.

WEATHER

Weather occurs as a result of the unequal heating of the Earth's surface. The strongest radiation from the sun is received around the equator, and the poles receive the least. There is also a difference resulting from the fact that the oceans and continents do not heat up equally. The atmosphere is constantly acting to redistribute this energy from the equator toward the poles.

Winds also result from the unequal heating of the surface, moving from areas of higher atmospheric pressure (and lower temperature) to areas of lower atmospheric pressure (and higher temperatures). Both localized winds and global winds follow this basic pattern. High-pressure centers occur when cool air sinks toward the surface and spreads laterally outward. In low pressure centers, air is warmer and rises upward in the troposphere. Fronts form at the boundaries of air masses that have different temperature and moisture characteristics; fronts are generally sites of active weather, such as storms and precipitation.

All air contains at least some water vapor. Humidity is a measure of the amount of water vapor in the air. Relative humidity gauges the amount of water in the air in terms of the saturation point. In order for the water vapor to condense, it must become saturated in the air. Saturation occurs mainly as a result of air cooling in some way. Dew point is the temperature at which a given volume of water vapor causes saturation. Warm air can hold more moisture than can cold air.

The cooling of air is accomplished mainly along fronts where warm air is pushed upward over cooler air, or cool air is shoved under warmer air. As air rises, it expands due to the decrease in pressure. As air expands, it also cools. If there is enough moisture, or the temperature drops enough, condensation will occur, and clouds will form. Clouds are formed of tiny ice crystals or of water droplets suspended in the air. If the ice crystals or water droplets become large and heavy enough to fall through the air, precipitation may occur. Since most clouds form high in the atmosphere, most precipitation begins as snow, even in the summer.

Cooling of air can also occur along mountain ranges where the air is forced upward to get over the mountain. Orographic lifting occurs when elevated terrain (e.g., mountains) forms a barrier to the flow of air currents, causing vertical air movement. This results in the windward side of the mountains receiving a greater amount of precipitation than the leeward side. The leeward, or desert side, is referred to as being in a rain shadow.

EARTH AND SPACE SCIENCE: REVIEW QUESTIONS

The following questions will give you a chance to practice. Read each questions carefully, mark your answers, and then check them with the answers and explanations that appear at the end of the Overview section.

1. Runoff and erosion would probably have the least effect on a land area that is

   (A) sloping and contour plowed
   (B) sloping and barren of vegetation
   (C) gently sloping and covered with grass
   (D) flat-lying and highly-covered with vegetation
   (E) above sea level

2. A line on a weather map connecting points of equal pressure is called an

   (A) isobar
   (B) isotem
   (C) isohyet
   (D) isotherm
   (E) isodyne

3. Astronomers believe a black hole can be identified by its

   (A) high luminosity and small angular size
   (B) emission of X-rays
   (C) large redshift
   (D) emission of pulsed radio signals
   (E) surrounding nebulae

4. Which of the following is the best evidence of continental drift?

   (A) A buried lava flow
   (B) Tropical fossils in arctic soil samples
   (C) Tilted sedimentary rocks
   (D) Sediments below sea level
   (E) Metamorphic pyroxenes

5. Cooler air tends to sink through warmer air because

   (A) it weighs more
   (B) it is more dense
   (C) heat transfer increases
   (D) a convection cell is set up
   (E) heat transfer decreases

6. What gas in the atmosphere is responsible for limiting the amount of ultraviolet radiation reaching the earth?

(A) Argon
(B) Oxygen
(C) Nitrogen
(D) Carbon dioxide
(E) Ozone

7. Which of the following stars would have the highest surface temperature?

(A) Red dwarf
(B) Red giant
(C) Yellow main sequence star
(D) Blue giant
(E) There is not enough information.

8. If Mars has an orbit approximately 1.52 AU from the Sun, how long will it take to orbit the Sun?

(A) 1.52 years
(B) 1.88 years
(C) 2.25 years
(D) 3.50 years
(E) There is not enough information.

9.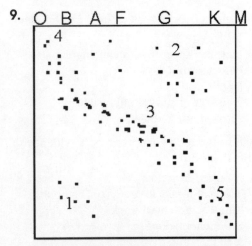

In the Hertzsprung-Russell (H-R) diagram above, what number might represent a Red dwarf?

(A) 1
(B) 2
(C) 3
(D) 4
(E) 5

10. Sedimentary rocks can be formed

(A) only from molten silicates
(B) at temperatures above 1000°C
(C) below the crust of the earth, under pressure
(D) only with volcanic activity
(E) in layers at the bottom of a body of water

11. Kepler's second law states that

(A) force equals mass times acceleration
(B) the square of the period of a planet's obit is proportional to the cube of its mean distance from the Sun
(C) the orbit of each planet is an ellipse, and the Sun is at a focus
(D) each planet orbits the Sun in such a way that an imaginary line connecting the planet and the Sun will sweep out equal areas in equal times
(E) None of the above

12. What type of sedimentary rock can be classified as either organic, clastic or chemical?

(A) Conglomerate
(B) Obsidian
(C) Salt
(D) Limestone
(E) Gneiss

13. What is the most common group of rock-forming minerals in the earth's crust?

(A) Sulfates
(B) Halides
(C) Silicates
(D) Oxides
(E) Carbonates

14. Calcite will scratch gypsum. This is an example of the physical characteristic called

(A) streak
(B) hardness
(C) fracture
(D) cleavage
(E) specific gravity

15. All of the following are minerals EXCEPT

(A) salt
(B) gold
(C) sugar
(D) quartz
(E) feldspar

16. The process by which nutrients seep from one soil horizon to another is called

(A) leaching
(B) sheeting
(C) deflation
(D) rilling
(E) abrasion

17. What is the plastic region of the mantle on which the rest of the mantle and crust float?

    (A) Asthenosphere
    (B) Lithosphere
    (C) Laccolith
    (D) Batholith
    (E) Plutonic

18. An ocean plate being pushed under an adjacent continental plate would occur at what type of tectonic boundary?

    (A) Transverse
    (B) Rift zone
    (C) Divergent
    (D) Subduction zone
    (E) Mid-ocean ridge

19. The ocean floor is most comparable to what dry land ecosystem?

    (A) Plains
    (B) Deserts
    (C) Mountains
    (D) Plateaus
    (E) Marshes

20. The geologic law states that in geologic strata, the oldest layer of rock on the bottom is called

    (A) Superposition
    (B) Discontinuities
    (C) Unconformities
    (D) Relative position
    (E) Indexing

REVIEW ANSWERS AND EXPLANATIONS

BIOLOGY

1. **The correct answer is (D).** Homeostasis requires a balance of biological functions such as metabolism and disease prevention. Staying in one place offers no advantage to many organisms.

2. **The correct answer is (C).** Osmosis is the diffusion of water, and it need not take place in living organisms.

3. **The correct answer is (D).** Water is created when the final electron acceptor, oxygen, combines with the protons that have been transferred from higher to lower energy compounds in the electron transport chain. Sugars broken down in glycolysis supply some of the carbon compounds that will be broken down in the mitochondria.

4. **The correct answer is (A).** Bacteria, as all prokaryotes, lack any membrane-bound organelles such as mitochondria. Most of the ATP is produced by the electron transport chain. Pyruvate, a 3 carbon compound, is an intermediate compound in respiration.

5. **The correct answer is (C).** Oxygen is produced from the breakdown of water by energy supplied by radiant energy of the sun. ATP is also produced in the light reactions and is used in the Calvin cycle.

6. **The correct answer is (A).** Since terminal is recessive, the only genotype that it can be is homozygous (aa). If the axial parent was homozygous, then all the offspring would have been axial.

7. **The correct answer is (B).** Adenine (A) always hydrogen bonds to thymine (T) and guanine to cytosine. Uracil is the nucleotide that replaces thymine in RNA.

8. **The correct answer is (A).** DNA never leaves the nucleus and amino acids are ferried about by tRNA (transfer RNA).

9. **The correct answer is (A).** Gametes have the haploid (N) number of chromosomes, while somatic (body) cells have the diploid number (2N). In flies, 2N = 8; therefore, N = 4.

10. **The correct answer is (A).** Sheep are cloned by using the DNA of a somatic cell of one organism and inserting it into the egg of another organism. No DNA is cut and then recombined with another's DNA.

11. **The correct answer is (B).** The idea expressed in (B) is Lamarkian, and contrary to Darwinism. Darwin believed the reproductive success of certain individuals who were best adapted to their environment is the driving force of evolution.

12. **The correct answer is (E).** Commensalistic relationships do not affect one party. For example, a rhino with a small bird on his back doesn't care that the bird is there, but the bird enjoys a free ride. Note: If the bird were eating parasites off the rhino's back it would be mutualism.

13. **The correct answer is (E).** The carrying capacity is a real, although variable, number.

14. **The correct answer is (C).** The mitochondria has been described as the "powerhouse of the cell." Most of the production of ATP takes place here.

15. **The correct answer is (D).** The golgi apparatus modifies proteins by adding sugars and lipids to certain proteins and frequently marks them for transport either out of the cell or to be used in the cell.

16. **The correct answer is (E).** By using transport (carrier) proteins, cells can gain molecules that are too large to diffuse through the membrane. The phospholipid bilayer nature of the membrane serves to make it a boundary between the cell and the environment.

17. **The correct answer is (E).** All ecosystems must have an energy source, even those deep-sea vent ecosystems miles under the ocean surface. (Down there the producers are bacteria which use hydrogen sulfide as their energy source.)

18. **The correct answer is (C).** The magnification is the product of the ocular and objective lenses. Since the student is looking at 400 magnifications rather than 40, he's seeing one-tenth as much, or 0.4 mm. If 12 cells spanned 0.4 mm, each is about 0.033 mm.

19. **The correct answer is (E).** While many people view predators with distaste, they are an integral part of any community for all the reasons given.

20. **The correct answer is (D).** During interphase (G1, S, and G2 in the cell cycle) the chromosomes are not visible. They become condensed at prophase and the nuclear membrane disintegrates. At metaphase the chromosomes move to the middle on the spindle fibers. At anaphase they are pulled apart as they move to the opposite poles.

CHEMISTRY

1. **The correct answer is (A).** The atomic number of an element gives both its number of protons and electrons.

2. **The correct answer is (B).** Isotopes are different forms of an element. Isotopes of the same element have the same number of protons, but diffent numbers of neutrons. Since protons and neutrons combine to give the element its atomic mass, and since the average of all isotopes is 35.453, by subtraction 18 neutrons exist in the most common form.

3. **The correct answer is (E).** The electron configuration contains both main levels (2) and sublevels, s and p. The superscript shows the number of electrons in each sublevel. By adding the superscripts, we get 9 electrons total.

4. **The correct answer is (D).** The number of protons and the number of electrons are equal and are the atomic number of an element.

5. **The correct answer is (A).** Degrees Kelvin = degrees Celsius + 273, or degrees Celsius = degrees Kelvin − 273.

6. **The correct answer is (B).** Half of the substance decays every 200 days. After the first 200 days there would be 5 grams. After 400 days, 2.5 grams, 1.25 grams at 600 days, and 0.625 grams after 800 days.

7. **The correct answer is (B).** The eight atoms that form diatomic molecules as their natural state are hydrogen, nitrogen, oxygen, fluorine, chlorine, bromine, and iodine.

8. **The correct answer is (A).** Magnesium is in Column II of the periodic chart (and the Alkali Earth Metals) and has an oxidation number of +2. Oxygen is in Column VIA and has an oxidation number of −2. Therefore, one magnesium atom will give up or share 2 electrons with one oxygen.

9. **The correct answer is (D).** The Roman numeral after a metal gives the oxidation state. Since iron is +3 and oxygen is −2, the common denominator is 6, so there will be 2 irons for each 3 oxygens.

10. **The correct answer is (B).** The number of moles is calculated by dividing the number of grams (93) by the molecular mass (18).

11. **The correct answer is (D).** Start with metals in balancing equations. Since there are two iron atoms on the left, there need to be two on the right. Since one cannot change subscripts, the coefficient must be added before the compound. By adding a 2 there however, we now have 6 chlorine atoms on the right. By adding a 3 before calcium chloride, we can get 6 on the left side. Since there are now 3 calcium atoms on the left, we add a 3 before calcium sulfate. Checking, the number of types of atoms are the same on both sides of the equation.

12. **The correct answer is (B).** Conversion to moles are required to do stoichiometry problems. 1.6 g of iron (III) oxide is 0.01 moles of iron (III) oxide (1.6 g/160 g/mole). By the equation, for each mole of Fe_2O_3 one gets 2 moles of Fe. Therefore, 0.02 moles of Fe is 1.1 g (0.02 moles/55.8 g/mole).

13. **The correct answer is (E).** By changing both masses to number of moles (0.0025 and 0.005), we see that there are twice as many chlorine atoms as iron.

14. **The correct answer is (B).** Molarity is a concentration expression defined as moles/liter. 13.9 g of MgI_2 is 0.05 moles. However, we didn't dissolve it to make 1 liter. It's twice as strong because we have only half a liter.

15. **The correct answer is (D).** The pH scale is the negative log of hydrogen ions in a solution. This means that as the number of hydrogen ions gets larger (more acidic), the pH will go down.

16. **The correct answer is (D).** The cathode is the negative pole to which the positively charged copper ions are attracted. Positive ions are called cations.

17. **The correct answer is (E).** Changing the mass of zinc to moles, we have 1 mole of Zn. For every mole of Zn present, 1 mole of hydrogen will be formed. One mole of any gas at STP occupies 22.4 liters.

18. **The correct answer is (A).** Pauling's electronegativity scale assigns an arbitrary number of 4 to fluorine, the most electronegative.

19. **The correct answer is (D).** In a neutral compound the oxidation numbers must sum to 0. The oxidation number of hydrogen is +1. The oxidation number of oxygen (except in peroxides) is −2. Therefore, +2 for hydrogen and −8 for oxygen requires +6 for sulfur to make the sum 0.

20. **The correct answer is (B).** LeChatelier's principle is that stress applied to a system will cause the system to react to reduce that stress. Increasing either reactant will make more moles and to reduce the number of collisions, more ammonia will be formed. Increasing the pressure also causes more collisions. If one treats heat as a product, reducing either product will favor the forward reaction. Only by increasing heat or concentration of ammonia can we drive the reaction to the left.

PHYSICS

1. **The correct answer is (B).** Using Kepler's third law, which states that the square of the period of revolution in years is proportional to the cube of the average distance between the Sun and planet in Astronomical Units.

2. **The correct answer is (E).** The smaller the number, the brighter the star. Each five magnitudes means a star appears 100 times brighter or dimmer, so Star A is 100 times brighter than Star B.

3. **The correct answer is (A).** M Stars have surface temperatures below 3900°K.

4. **The correct answer is (E).** Venus and Mercury are the only planets in the Solar System with no moons. Mars has two (Phobos and Deimos) and Pluto has one (Charon).

5. **The correct answer is (B).** One parsec is equal to 3.26 light years. One light year is equal to 63,240 Astronomical Units, and one A.U. is equal to 93 million miles or 149.6 million kilometers.

6. **The correct answer is (C).** Diffraction angles are proportional to the wavelength divided by the aperture size. For the angles to be larger, either the wavelength must be longer or the aperture must be smaller. Higher frequency is equivalent to shorter wavelength.

7. **The correct answer is (D).** Time slows and lengths contract in the direction of motion at relativistic speeds.

8. **The correct answer is (D).** Static magnetic fields only exert force on moving charges.

9. **The correct answer is (E).** All waves exhibit interference and diffraction, but light is not longitudinal and can propagate through the vacuum.

10. **The correct answer is (B).** The added heat melts some ice. Temperature remains constant during melting and the entropy rises.

11. **The correct answer is (A).** Neutrons, like protons, are composed of three quarks.

12. **The correct answer is (C).** The speed of sound in an ideal gas depends only on temperature.

13. **The correct answer is (D).** Compton scattering results in a loss of photon energy with a corresponding increase in wavelength. The electron remains intact.

14. **The correct answer is (C).** The acceleration (a) is equal to 20m/s divided by $t = 2s$. $a = 10$m/s^2. The distance traveled is $\left(\frac{1}{2}\right)a\,t^2 = \left(\frac{10}{2}\right)(2^2) = 20$m.

15. **The correct answer is (C).** The period of a pendulum is independent of mass.

16. **The correct answer is (E).** Momentum and mass are always conserved, but energy and velocity change in an inelastic collision.

17. **The correct answer is (E).** Constant force implies constant acceleration. Therefore, the velocity changes. Since the kinetic energy is proportional to the square of velocity, its rate of increase is not constant.

18. **The correct answer is (D).** The electrostatic force is inversely proportional to the square of the distance. Double the distance implies $\left(\frac{1}{2}\right)^2 = \frac{1}{4}$ the force.

19. **The correct answer is (B).** Only the temperature remains constant when an ideal gas expands into a vacuum since the internal energy remains constant.

20. **The correct answer is (C).** The trajectory is a parabola or a straight line for any object acted upon only by gravity. Since the object has an initial horizontal velocity with respect the observer, it is a parabola.

EARTH AND SPACE SCIENCE

1. **The correct answer is (D).** Erosion occurs easiest on steep, barren hillsides. Choice (D) has no slope and, with vegetation, encourages absorption of the water.

2. **The correct answer is (A).** Isobars connect areas of the same atmospheric (iso-) pressure (-bar) on a weather map.

3. **The correct answer is (B).** Astronomers believe that black holes cannot be seen directly because of their exceedingly small size and exceptional gravitational field. What can be seen is the evidence of matter being trapped in the gravitational well and X-ray emissions.

4. **The correct answer is (B).** Given that there is no dramatic evidence that the polar regions of Earth were once equatorial, the only logical argument for tropical fossils to exist in places like Antarctica is that the land mass was not always located in the polar region.

5. **The correct answer is (B).** Sinking and rising air is a matter of density, not weight. A finite number of gas molecules will become less active and take up less space when cooler and therefore travel toward the surface.

6. **The correct answer is (E).** Argon, nitrogen and oxygen (O_2) have no effect on ultraviolet (UV) radiation. Ozone has the ability to absorb UV energy.

7. **The correct answer is (D).** Temperature is a big clue to the surface temperature of stars. Blue stars are hottest, (30,000°K) followed by Yellow stars (~5500°K) and Red stars are coolest (3000°K).

8. **The correct answer is (B).** Kepler's third law states that the square of the period of revolution in years is proportional to the cube of the average distance between the Sun and planet in Astronomical Units.

9. **The correct answer is (E).** Region 1 on the H-R diagram represents white dwarfs. Region 2 is home to the Supergiants. Region 3 is the main sequence where you would find our sun. Region 4 is the locale of the super hot blue stars. Region 5 is where you would find the cooler red stars.

10. **The correct answer is (E).** Choices (A), (B), and (D) are associated with igneous rocks. Choice (C) refers to metamorphic rocks. Sedimentary rocks often form as the result of the compaction of layer upon layer of silt/sediment brought to a location by running water.

11. **The correct answer is (D).** Choice (A) is Newton's second law; choice (B) is Kepler's third law; choice (C) is Kepler's first law, and choice (D) is Kepler's second law.

12. **The correct answer is (D).** Calcite ($CaCo_3$), the chief mineral in limestone, is also the chief mineral in shells. Limestone rocks can form also from calcite fragments or the calcite can precipitate directly from water. The most common forms of biochemical limestones are coquina and chalk. Inorganic limestone can form from calcium carbonate precipitates in places like caverns. A common inorganic limestone is tavertine.

13. **The correct answer is (C).** The majority of all minerals in the crust are forms of silicates. One single type of silicate, feldspars, comprises more than 50 percent of Earth's crust.

14. **The correct answer is (B).** Using the Moh's scale, geologists use a standardized system to rank mineral hardness from 1 (softest) to 10 (hardest). One criteria of hardness is that any harder mineral scratches the softer mineral. Calcite is rated 3 and gypsum is rated at 2.

15. **The correct answer is (C).** One of the criteria for designation as a mineral is that it is inorganic. Sugar, choice (C), is organic in origin.

16. **The correct answer is (A).** Leaching involves the depletion of soluble minerals from higher horizons of soil by rain or other downward percolating water. All other choices refer to erosional or weathering processes.

17. **The correct answer is (A).** Choice (B) refers to the rigid upper mantle and crust layer. Choice (C) (laccolith) is a massive igneous intrusion between existing strata. Choice (D) (batholith) is a larger mass of igneous rock formed from cooling magma that is exposed by erosion. Choice (E) (plutonic) is a class of igneous rock.

18. **The correct answer is (D).** Transverse boundaries, choice (A), show lateral motion with shearing forces. Choices (B), (C), and (E) refer variously to types of divergent boundaries.

19. **The correct answer is (B).** Ocean floors are very barren places with little biological activity. Most biological activity in the ocean is either along coastlines or just under the surface of the ocean.

20. **The correct answer is (A).** As long as no deformations exist, geologists argue that deeper layers of sediment will always be older. Unconformities, choice (C), and discontinuities, choice (B), are breaks in the geologic record. Relative position, choice (D), is a technique used to order fossil records based on depth. Indexing, choice (E), is technique to assign age to a geologic strata or fossil by comparing it with other strata or fossil of known age, based on position in the geologic record.

Chapter 16
POSTTEST

TIME—45 MINUTES	60 QUESTIONS

PART I
BIOLOGICAL SCIENCE

Directions: Each of the questions or incomplete statements below is followed by five suggested answers or completions. Select the one that is best in each case.

1. Sickle-cell anemia is a disease that is often fatal before the victim reaches puberty. About one in ten African Americans is a carrier of the trait. This paradoxically high frequency of carriers can be explained by which of the following?

    (A) An epidemic of contagious disease in Africa during the eighteenth century caused widespread genetic damage.
    (B) The heterozygote had a selective advantage over the noncarrier—greater resistance to malaria.
    (C) There is genetic deterioration of ova among women who give birth late in life.
    (D) The disease is linked to those genes determining racial characteristics.
    (E) The concept of natural selection fails to account for this phenomenon.

2. Which of the following genetic abnormalities can be currently detected by the technique of amniocentesis (prenatal diagnosis)?

    (A) Down syndrome
    (B) Muscular dystrophy
    (C) Manic depression
    (D) Albinism
    (E) Diabetes

3. A male fruit fly with white eyes mates with a female with wild type. White eyes are a sex-linked recessive in the heterozygote. What will be the expectation regarding their offspring?

    (A) Males will have white eyes, females will have wild type.
    (B) Females will have white eyes, males will have wild type.
    (C) Half the females will have white eyes; all the males will have wild type.
    (D) Half the males will have white eyes, and all the females will have wild type.
    (E) All males and females will have wild-type eye coloring.

4. In birds, the sex chromosomes are reversed in terms of the sexes. The male has two Z sex chromosomes, whereas the female has one Z and a small w and is therefore hemizygous for sex-linked genes. A sex-linked recessive trait will be inherited in which of the following ways?

    (A) The father, who is a carrier but does not show the trait, will pass it on to daughters, with a 100 percent probability of them showing the trait.
    (B) The mother, who is a carrier, will pass it on to her sons, with a 50 percent probability of them showing the trait.
    (C) The father, who is a carrier, will pass it on to his daughters, with a 50 percent probability of them showing the trait.
    (D) The mother, who is a carrier, will pass it on to her sons, with a 50 percent probability of them showing the trait.
    (E) The mother, who is a carrier, will pass it on to her daughters, with a 50 percent probability of them showing the trait.

GO ON TO THE NEXT PAGE

5. Which of the following is due to aneuploidy of an autosome?

(A) Turner's syndrome
(B) Klinefelter's syndrome
(C) Down syndrome
(D) XYY syndrome
(E) XXX syndrome

6.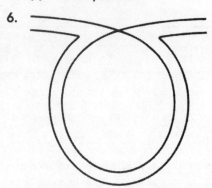

If homologous chromosomes form the pattern illustrated above during synapsis, the anomaly is a(n)

(A) deletion
(B) inversion
(C) duplication
(D) translocation
(E) transcription

7. Of the purebred organisms below, which would best serve as the P generation to begin an experiment illustrating Mendel's principle of random assortment?

(A) In *Drosophila:* winged x wingless
(B) In corn: yellow x purple
(C) In peas: yellow x green
(D) In peas: round x wrinkled
(E) In *Drosophila:* black body with normal wings x wild-type body with curled wings

8. Which of the following is an example of a trait involving multiple alleles?

(A) Color of pea seeds
(B) Shape of pea seeds
(C) Human blood types
(D) Human widow's peak
(E) Height of pea plants

9. The nonallelic gene interaction in which the effect of one pair of alleles can override the effect of a second pair (at a second locus) is

(A) penetrance
(B) pleiotrophy
(C) incomplete dominance
(D) epistasis
(E) concordance

10. The ratio of F2 phenotypes expected in a typical dihybrid cross is

(A) 1:2:1
(B) 3:1
(C) 9:3:3:1
(D) 15:1
(E) 12:4

11. In fowl, comb shape is determined by two pairs of genes at different loci. P_rr gives a pea shape; ppR_ gives a rose shape; pprr gives a single comb; and P_R_ gives a walnut-shaped comb. In the cross Pprr × ppRr, what phenotypic ratio is expected in the first generation?

(A) 1:1:1:1
(B) 9:3:3:1
(C) 9:6:1
(D) 9:7
(E) 15:1

12. How many different kinds of gametes can be produced by an individual with the genotype Aa Bb Cc?

(A) 6
(B) 8
(C) 10
(D) 12
(E) 15

13. An animal has 14 chromosomes in its somatic cells. Twelve different loci are known for this organism. Of these, five of the gene pairs are in one linkage group and four in another. None of the remaining pairs is linked to each other. How many chromosome pairs are there for which there are no marker genes?

(A) 1
(B) 2
(C) 4
(D) 6
(E) 9

14. If one parent has type-AB blood and the other has type-O, what is the probability that their first child will be a type-B boy?

(A) 1 in 8
(B) 1 in 4
(C) 1 in 2
(D) 3 in 4
(E) 1

15.

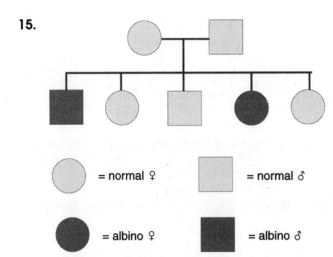

The pedigree above indicates that albinism is inherited as a(n)

(A) sex-linked recessive
(B) sex-linked dominant
(C) autosomal recessive
(D) autosomal dominant
(E) codominant gene

Question 16 is based on the following information.

$$x^2 = \sum \frac{d^2 o}{e}$$

where

x^2 = chi-square

d^2 = deviations

o = *observed minus expected for each class*

e = expected value for that class

Σ = sum of

This formula for the "chi-square test" is used to evaluate results of experiments, such as breeding experiments in genetics. The value of chi-square is calculated and then used to determine how well the experimental data fit the model or expected results. This is done by locating the x^2 value in the table in column 2 in that row with the number of degrees of freedom (df) appropriate to the experiment. (Degrees of freedom = the number of classes minus one.) Purebred green pod peas (yy) are crossed with purebred yellow pod peas (YY). The F2 generation consists of 78 yellow and 22 green pea pods.

16. The x^2 value for these results is

(A) 0.16
(B) 0.18
(C) 0.24
(D) 0.48
(E) 1.43

Question 17 is based on the following table.

PROBABILITY OF GETTING THESE DEVIATIONS PURELY BY CHANCE
Possibility of Chance Occurrence in Percentage
(5 percent or less considered significant)

Degrees of Freedom	90%	80%	70%	50%	30%	20%	10%	5%
1	0.016	0.064	0.148	0.455	1.074	1.642	2.706	3.841
2	0.211	0.446	0.713	1.386	2.408	3.219	4.605	5.991
3	0.584	1.005	1.424	2.366	3.665	4.642	6.251	7.815

17. Using the table above, determine the probability that deviations of this size could be obtained purely by chance. P equals

(A) 90 percent
(B) between 80 percent and 90 percent
(C) between 70 percent and 80 percent
(D) between 30 percent and 50 percent
(E) between 20 percent and 30 percent

18. In the haploid fungus *Neurospora crassa*, fertilization of one mating type by another yields a diploid nucleus that undergoes meiosis to yield four haploid nuclei, lined up single file in the ascus. These then undergo mitosis to yield eight haploid spores still lined up single file in the ascus as follows:

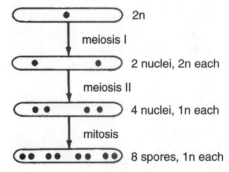

If the two mating types differ in the alleles for color, one producing an albino or white mold (W) and the other a normal pink mold (P), which arrangement of spores in the ascus is both possible and the result of crossing over?

(A) PP PP WW WW
(B) PP PW WW PW
(C) PP WP WW WP
(D) WW WW PP PP
(E) PP WW PP WW

GO ON TO THE NEXT PAGE

19. Chromosome maps can be constructed by test crosses between organisms with three or more pairs of alleles in the same linkage group. This is based on the observation that

(A) the map distance between two sets of alleles is proportional to the frequency of crossover between them

(B) the genes for related functions are always grouped together

(C) crossovers occur most commonly during mitosis

(D) there is never crossing over in the production of gametes in male *Drosophila*

(E) female *Drosophila* are always heterozygotes

20.

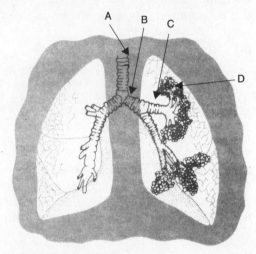

In the diagram of human lungs and respiratory passages above, the actual gas exchange occurs in the structures marked

(A) A

(B) B

(C) C

(D) D

(E) All of the above

21. In cnidarians, the function of specialized cells called nematocysts is to

(A) sting and paralyze prey

(B) produce digestive juices

(C) provide a rudimentary nervous system

(D) rid indigestible waste

(E) produce a swimming motion

22. The French dish beefsteak tartar is chopped raw beef topped with a raw egg. Though delicious to some palates, it presents a danger of illness because

(A) uncooked beef commonly has a dangerous amount of bacteria

(B) these foods are a common source of amoebic dysentery

(C) uncooked beef may have tapeworm cysts, and uncooked eggs may carry salmonella

(D) uncooked eggs present no danger, but uncooked beef may carry tapeworm

(E) uncooked beef presents no danger, but uncooked eggs may carry salmonella

23.

The drawing above illustrates

(A) cloning

(B) conjugation

(C) digestion

(D) iysogeny

(E) symbiosis

24.

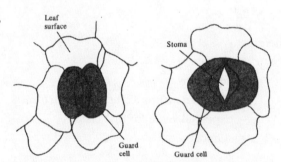

The function of the guard cells above is to

(A) transport nutrients stored in plant roots

(B) produce gametes for sexual reproduction

(C) make chlorophyll to trap light energy

(D) bring water upward from the roots

(E) prevent water loss from leaves while allowing gas exchange

Questions 25–27 are based on the following information regarding three new species of animals that fit into our present classification system.

	I	II	III
Habitat	terrestrial	marine	terrestrial
Location of embryo development	water	mother	egg
Location of mating	in water	in water	on land
Type of skeleton	internal	internal	internal
Type of epidermis	slime or mucus	hair	scales

25. If we arrange the animals according to the proportion of yolk in their eggs, the most likely sequence (least to most yolk) is

(A) I, II, III
(B) I, III, II
(C) II, I, III
(D) II, III, I
(E) III, II, I

26. Which of the following most likely has gills at some time after birth or hatching?

(A) Species I only
(B) Species II only
(C) Species III only
(D) Species I and II only
(E) Species I and III only

27. Which animal(s) is (are) probably dormant when the air temperature is below freezing?

(A) Species I only
(B) Species II only
(C) Species I and II only
(D) Species I and III only
(E) None of the above

28. An adaptive radiation is characterized by

(A) high levels of radioactivity
(B) a variety of closely related organisms making use of a great diversity of habitats
(C) numerous different organisms coming together to occupy a similar environment
(D) a single organism being capable of withstanding a wide variety of different environmental situations
(E) a population moving from one region to another

29. One of the most critical evolutionary events was the arrival of amphibians onto land many millions of years ago. Amphibians evolved from a group of fish characterized by lobed fins. A most critical process during this transformation of the amphibian must have been

(A) the loss of scales by the fish
(B) the loss of gills by the fish and the evolution of lungs in amphibians
(C) its new ability to use fins for locomotion on land
(D) its new ability to reproduce on land
(E) its new nervous system, including eyes and ears for receiving airborne stimuli

30. In order for a mutation to have an evolutionary effect, it must occur in

(A) germplasm DNA
(B) a centriole
(C) the endoplasmic reticulum
(D) somatoplasm RNA
(E) proteins

31. Which cellular organelles are the site of protein synthesis?

(A) Mitochondria
(B) Chromosomes
(C) Ribosomes
(D) lysosomes
(E) Golgi bodies

32.

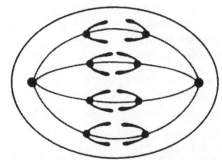

In an organism in which the diploid number is 4, what stage of cell division is indicated in the figure above?

(A) Metaphase of meiosis I
(B) Metaphase of mitosis
(C) Anaphase of meiosis I
(D) Anaphase of meiosis II
(E) Anaphase of mitosis

GO ON TO THE NEXT PAGE

33. One function of the NASA landing probe sent to Mars was to look for "animal life," which was defined as living organisms whose metabolism is similar to that of earthly animals. Of the following choices, select the best way to test for animal life by noting changes in chemical compounds that the Martian surroundings might make on reactants supplied by the lander.

    (A) Starting with C_{14} and labeled CO_2, look for the incorporation of C_{14} into glucose.
    (B) Look for the production of CO_2 (with C_{14} glucose).
    (C) Look for the production of labeled nitrates from labeled NH_3.
    (D) Look for the incorporation of labeled nitrogen from nitrates into amino acids.
    (E) Look for the release of labeled H_2 gas from the breakdown of glucose with labeled hydrogen.

34. The process of creating mRNA from the DNA template in the nucleus is

    (A) translation
    (B) transcription
    (C) translocation
    (D) polymerization
    (E) initiation

35. In human males, meiosis occurs in the

    (A) penis
    (B) Cowper's gland
    (C) seminiferous tubules
    (D) nephron tubules
    (E) prostate gland

36. DNA replication takes place during what portion of the cell cycle?

    (A) Prophase
    (B) Interphase
    (C) Telophase
    (D) Anaphase
    (E) Metaphase

37.

The tubular structure indicated in the diagram above is what cellular structure?

    (A) Ribosomes
    (B) Nuclear membrane
    (C) Centrioles
    (D) Endoplasmic reticulum
    (E) Vesicles

38. A major component of cell membranes that is water soluble and can thus participate in reactions with the cell's watery internal and external environments is

    (A) phospholipid
    (B) polysaccharide
    (C) sterol
    (D) neutral fat
    (E) protein

39. The function of the Golgi apparatus or complex is to

    (A) break up ingested food particles
    (B) prepare cell products for secretion
    (C) provide energy to the cell
    (D) enclose waste products
    (E) transport materials to the nucleus

40. When cells break down compounds to yield energy, this energy is stored by synthesis of another compound with a high-energy bond whose energy is readily available. This compound is

    (A) ATP
    (B) NAD
    (C) glucose
    (D) glycogen
    (E) ADP

41. Glycolysis can take place in the cytoplasm of a eukaryotic cell, but the Krebs cycle (or citric acid cycle) and the electron transport systems (or respiratory assemblies) exist only in

    (A) nuclei
    (B) ribosomes
    (C) mitochondria
    (D) desmosomes
    (E) nucleoli

42. Which of the following elements is present in all amino acids but not in sugars?

(A) Carbon
(B) Hydrogen
(C) Nitrogen
(D) Oxygen
(E) Phosphorus

Questions 43–44 refer to the following graph, which gives some information about a group of organisms coming in to inhabit a new place.

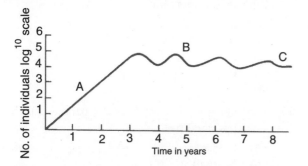

43. Region B of the graph shows that

(A) groups of organisms vary in numbers
(B) this particular population is having difficulty with its new environment
(C) the population is about to decline
(D) the population is about to increase
(E) the numbers in the population are leveling off, perhaps seeking a level that is in concert with the environment

44. Region A of the graph indicates that

(A) there is the potential for unlimited growth to the population
(B) it takes three years for any population to reach about 10,000
(C) there were ample environmental circumstances for the first three years to allow for a rapid population increase
(D) populations increase logarithmically
(E) All of the above statements are true.

45. In a certain ecosystem, rabbits are preyed upon by owls, hawks, and snakes. Wild dogs enter the system, and this factor adds another predator for the rabbits. From the following choices, what is the most likely short-term outcome of the addition of the wild dogs?

(A) An increase in snake population
(B) A tendency for owls and hawks to prey on the dogs
(C) The extinction of either the owls, the hawks, or the snakes
(D) A greater depletion of the rabbits
(E) The migration of snakes, hawks, or owls to another ecosystem

46. Which of the following is an ecological principle?

(A) Evolution is irreversible.
(B) Double links are mirror images of each other.
(C) Ontogeny recapitulates phylogeny.
(D) All life arises from preexisting life.
(E) Animals living in colder climates have relatively smaller appendages than those living in warmer climates.

Questions 47–49 are to be interpreted in relation to the following graphs. For each item, select the graph that best represents the data presented in the item.

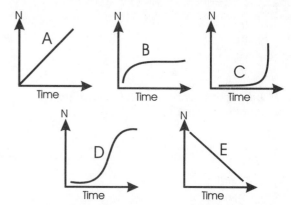

47. Which graph best represents the population growth (total number for an organism that reproduces by splitting in constant-time intervals without any death)? (*x*-axis represents time; *y*-axis represents population numbers on an exponential scale)

48. Which graph best represents actual population growth (total number) of flies kept in a closed environment well stocked with food, air, and water?

49. Which graph indicates a serious deficiency in the environment of the population (total numbers)?

GO ON TO THE NEXT PAGE

Questions 50–54 are concerned with a high grassland area located in the mountains. The grassland has a slight slope, and there are forests above it. Five elements are found: grass; rodents and herbivores that feed on the grass; small meat-eating forms, such as fox and weasel, that feed on rodents; large carnivorous forms, such as pumas and wolves, that feed on the herbivores; and soil that contains bacteria, bugs, worms, etc.

We assume in the beginning that the area is in balance and that the five elements can be represented by a food pyramid, as in Fig. I. Fig. II is divided into five parts and shows a growth curve for an animal population. These figures must be used in answering the questions.

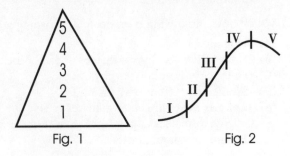

Fig. 1   Fig. 2

50. Under normal conditions of balance, the populations could be represented by what part of the growth curve?

(A) I
(B) II
(C) III
(D) IV
(E) V

51. If a drought occurred, which animal group would be affected first?

(A) 2
(B) 3
(C) 5
(D) 2 and 3
(E) 4 and 5

52. Which group would be least affected if a drought accurred?

(A) 3
(B) 4
(C) 5
(D) 3 and 4
(E) 4 and 5

53. Which part of the curve represents the effect of the drought?

(A) I
(B) II
(C) III
(D) IV
(E) V

54. Suppose a larger carnivore appears on the scene, preying only on the large carnivores that eat the herbivores. The part of the growth curve that best represents the short-range effect on the herbivore population is

(A) I
(B) II
(C) III
(D) IV
(E) V

55. Unicellular animals such as the paramecium were first described by

(A) Linnaeus
(B) Malpighi
(C) Hooke
(D) Leewenhoek
(E) Swammerdan

56. A tentative statement or supposition adopted provisionally as a working tool to explain certain facts and to guide investigations of the problem is a

(A) law
(B) conclusion
(C) hypothesis
(D) purpose
(E) principle

57. It is not advisable to keep a large number of plants in the hospital room of a patient with respiratory problems because

(A) the moisture they release makes breathing more difficult
(B) the plants can cause CO_2 poisoning
(C) the plants will reduce the O_2 concentration at night
(D) the plants will produce too high an O_2 concentration level
(E) many patients are allergic to house plants

58. Which of the following factors can cause variations in the thickness of the annual rings produced by a tree?

    (A) The amount of sunlight
    (B) The amount of rain
    (C) The richness of the soil
    (D) Caterpillars eating many of the tree's leaves
    (E) All of the above

59. The primary nutrient-absorptive organ of the digestive system is the

    (A) pancreas
    (B) stomach
    (C) liver
    (D) small intestine
    (E) large intestine

60. Cartilage serves as flexible support and as a shock absorber. It is found in all of the following locations EXCEPT

    (A) the nose
    (B) the ends of long bones
    (C) the walls of the trachea
    (D) between vertebrae
    (E) All of these places contain cartilage.

STOP   If you finish before the time is up, you may check your work on this section only. Do not turn to any other section in the test.

TIME—45 MINUTES   60 QUESTIONS

PART II
PHYSICAL SCIENCE

Directions: Each of the questions or incomplete statements below is followed by five suggested answers or completions. Select the one that is best in each case.

61. Carbon has an atomic number of 6. It therefore has how many principal energy levels?

   (A) 1
   (B) 2
   (C) 3
   (D) 4
   (E) 5

62. Copper (Cu) has an atomic number of 29 and a mass number of 64. One copper atom, therefore, has how many protons?

   (A) 27
   (B) 29
   (C) 31
   (D) 35
   (E) 64

63. One copper atom has how many neutrons?

   (A) 27
   (B) 29
   (C) 31
   (D) 35
   (E) 64

PERIODIC TABLE OF ELEMENTS

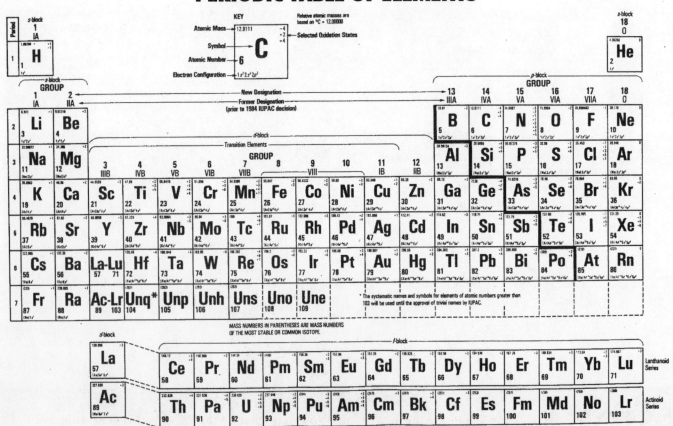

64. One copper atom has how many electrons?

(A) 27
(B) 29
(C) 31
(D) 35
(E) 64

65. One copper ion (symbol Cu++) has how many electrons?

(A) 27
(B) 29
(C) 31
(D) 35
(E) 64

66. Since Dalton put forth the modern atomic theory, there have been a number of models proposed for the nature of the atom. Historically, the sequential progression of the types of models envisioned is

(A) solid sphere model, solar system model, quantum mechanical model
(B) solar system model, solid sphere model, quantum mechanical model
(C) solid sphere model, quantum mechanical model, solar system model
(D) quantum mechanical model, solid sphere model, solar system model
(E) quantum mechanical model, solar system model, solid sphere model

67. Which of the following statements concerning the difference between nuclear properties and electronic properties of an atom is true?

(A) The nucleus is negligible in weight, whereas the mass of electrons is significant in contributing to the mass of the atom.
(B) Changes in the nucleus of an atom are unrelated to chemical bonding.
(C) Radioactivity involves the motion and distribution of electrons and not the central, stationary nucleus.
(D) Both the nucleus and the electrons are involved in bonding between atoms.
(E) The nucleus always has twice the mass of the electrons around it.

68. The following represents a nuclear change with one of the products missing:

$$^9_4Be + ^4_2He \rightarrow \underline{\quad} + ^1_0n$$

The missing product is

(A) ^4_2He
(B) $^{12}_6C$
(C) $^{14}_7N$
(D) $^{16}_8O$
(E) ^8_4Be

69. The following balanced equation represents a reaction taking place in water containing dissolved silver nitrate:

$$Cu + 2\,AgNO_3 \rightarrow 2\,Ag + Cu(NO_3)_2$$

Which of the following statements about this reaction is FALSE?

(A) The symbol Cu may represent a piece of copper wire placed in the solution.
(B) Silver metal is plated out in this reaction.
(C) Silver is a more reactive metal than copper.
(D) There is no change in the nitrate ion in this reaction.
(E) Both copper nitrate and silver nitrate are salts.

Questions 70–72 pertain to the following reactions.

$$Fe + H_2O \xrightarrow{cold} \text{no reaction}$$
$$Fe + H_2O \xrightarrow{steam} FeO + H_2$$
$$2Na + 2H_2O \xrightarrow{cold} 2NaOH + H_2$$
$$Cu + HCl \rightarrow \text{no reaction}$$
$$Pb + H_2O \xrightarrow{cold\ or\ steam} \text{no reaction}$$
$$Pb + 2HCl \rightarrow PbCl_2 + H_2$$

70. The most reactive metal is

(A) Fe
(B) Na
(C) Cu
(D) Pb
(E) H

71. The least reactive metal is

(A) Fe
(B) Na
(C) Cu
(D) Pb
(E) H

GO ON TO THE NEXT PAGE

72. Which of the following is a TRUE statement?

    (A) Iron (Fe) is less reactive than sodium (Na) but more reactive than lead (Pb).
    (B) Sodium (Na) is less reactive than iron (Fe) but more reactive than copper (Cu).
    (C) Copper (Cu) is less reactive than iron (Fe) but more reactive than lead (Pb).
    (D) Iron (Fe) is less reactive than copper (Cu) but more reactive than lead (Pb).
    (E) Lead (Pb) is more reactive than sodium (Na) but less reactive than copper (Cu).

Questions 73–76 refer to the following reactions.

   I. $SO_3 + H_2O \rightarrow H_2SO_4$
  II. $H_2 + O_2 \rightarrow H_2O$
 III. $BaO + H_2O \rightarrow Ba(OH)_2$
 IV. $CH_4 + 2O_2 \rightarrow CO_2 + 2H_2O$

73. Which of the reactions represents the combustion of a hydrocarbon?

    (A) I
    (B) II
    (C) III
    (D) IV
    (E) None of the above

74. Which of the reactions represents the direct combination of two elements?

    (A) I
    (B) II
    (C) III
    (D) IV
    (E) None of the above

75. Which of the reactions represents the generalization that an oxide of a nonmetal reacting with water will form an acid?

    (A) I
    (B) II
    (C) III
    (D) IV
    (E) Only I and III

76. Which of the reactions represents the generalization that an oxide of a metal reacting with water will form a base?

    (A) I only
    (B) II only
    (C) III only
    (D) IV only
    (E) Only I and III

77. One of the more serious problems confronting tourism today is the deterioration of ancient statues and buildings, e.g., the Parthenon in Greece. A common chemical reaction is the reaction of acid with carbonate salts to break down the salts, producing carbon dioxide. The substance most likely to cause statue and building corrosion is

    (A) carbon dioxide, a natural component of air
    (B) oxides of sulfur produced by the burning of fossil fuels
    (C) hydrocarbons produced by inefficient gasoline combustion
    (D) ozone produced by electrical discharge
    (E) particulate matter produced by industrial furnaces

78. Under which of the following conditions would the carbonation in an open bottle of soda be retained the longest?

    (A) Low temperature and low pressure
    (B) Low temperature and high pressure
    (C) High temperature and low pressure
    (D) High temperature and high pressure
    (E) All of the above

Questions 79–80 are based on the graph shown below, which represents the pressure/volume relationship of a gas at constant temperature (Boyle's law).

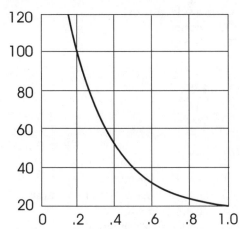

79. If the pressure of the gas is one half of an atmosphere, what is the approximate volume?

    (A) 30 liters
    (B) 40 liters
    (C) 50 liters
    (D) 60 liters
    (E) 80 liters

80. The product of the pressure and the volume of a given amount of gas at a constant temperature equals a constant. From the graph, the constant can be determined to be

    (A) 0.083
    (B) 8.30
    (C) 20
    (D) 22.4
    (E) 120

81. A body with constant velocity has

    (A) a positive acceleration
    (B) a negative acceleration
    (C) zero acceleration
    (D) a constant acceleration
    (E) All of the above

82. A body undergoing acceleration must

    (A) be moving
    (B) have an increasing velocity
    (C) have a changing velocity
    (D) have a changing direction
    (E) have a decreasing velocity

83. An airplane travels 250 miles in half an hour at constant velocity. Its speed is

    (A) 125 miles per hour
    (B) 250 miles per hour
    (C) 500 miles per hour
    (D) 1000 miles per hour
    (E) 2000 miles per hour

84. The acceleration of a stone thrown upward is

    (A) greater than that of a stone thrown downward
    (B) the same as that of a stone thrown downward
    (C) smaller than that of a stone thrown downward
    (D) zero until it reaches the highest point in its motion
    (E) always zero

85. A force acts on a body that is free to move. If we know the magnitude and direction of the force and the mass of the body, Newton's second law of motion enables us to determine the body's

    (A) weight
    (B) position
    (C) velocity
    (D) acceleration
    (E) momentum

86. The weight of a body

    (A) is the quantity of matter it contains
    (B) refers to its inertia
    (C) is basically the same quantity as its mass but expressed in different units
    (D) is the force with which it is attracted to another body
    (E) is its acceleration

87. When a horse pulls a wagon, the force that causes the horse to move forward is the force

    (A) the horse exerts on the wagon
    (B) the wagon exerts on the horse
    (C) the horse exerts on the ground
    (D) the ground exerts on the horse
    (E) None of the above

88. A body undergoes acceleration only when

    (A) its mass increases
    (B) its velocity increases
    (C) its velocity decreases
    (D) it falls toward the Earth
    (E) a force acts upon it

GO ON TO THE NEXT PAGE

89. The action and reaction forces referred to in Newton's third law of motion

    (A) act upon a body
    (B) do not act in the same line
    (C) need not be equal in magnitude, but must have the same line of action
    (D) must be equal in magnitude, but need not have the same line of action
    (E) None of the above

90. The proper use of lubricants CANNOT reduce

    (A) inertia
    (B) sliding friction
    (C) static friction
    (D) rolling friction
    (E) None of the above

91. According to the principle of conservation of energy, energy can be

    (A) created but not destroyed
    (B) destroyed but not created
    (C) both created and destroyed
    (D) neither created nor destroyed
    (E) transformed to momentum

92. A golf ball and a Ping-Pong ball are dropped in a vacuum chamber. When they have fallen halfway down, they have the same

    (A) velocity
    (B) potential energy
    (C) kinetic energy
    (D) rest energy
    (E) momentum

93. If a shell fired from a cannon explodes in midair, its total

    (A) momentum increases
    (B) momentum decreases
    (C) kinetic energy increases.
    (D) kinetic energy decreases
    (E) kinetic energy and momentum change

94. The action of all cutting tools is based on the

    (A) wheel and axle
    (B) fulcrum
    (C) lever
    (D) inclined plane
    (E) screw

95. Heat is a physical quantity most closely related to

    (A) temperature
    (B) friction
    (C) energy
    (D) momentum
    (E) force

96. Waves transmit _____ from one place to another.

    (A) mass
    (B) amplitude
    (C) wavelength
    (D) energy
    (E) frequency

97. Sound waves do not travel through

    (A) solids
    (B) liquids
    (C) gases
    (D) a vacuum
    (E) lead

98. The nucleus of an atom CANNOT be said to

    (A) contain most of the atom's mass
    (B) be small in size
    (C) be electrically neutral
    (D) deflect incident alpha particles
    (E) contain protons

99. An object has a positive electric charge whenever

    (A) it contains an excess of electrons
    (B) it contains a deficiency of electrons
    (C) the nuclei of its atoms are positively charged
    (D) the electrons of its atoms are positively charged
    (E) the object moves

100. A permanent magnet

    (A) attracts all substances
    (B) attracts only ferromagnetic substances
    (C) attracts ferromagnetic substances and repels all others
    (D) attracts some substances and repels others
    (E) None of the above

101. The sun's energy comes from

    (A) nuclear fission
    (B) radioactivity
    (C) the conversion of hydrogen to helium
    (D) the conversion of helium to hydrogen
    (E) cosmic radiation

102. Sun spots appear dark because they

    (A) are coronal holes
    (B) are cooler than the surrounding surface
    (C) are hotter than the surrounding surface
    (D) have a different chemical composition than the surrounding surface
    (E) move on the sun's surface

103. A new scientific theory will be most widely accepted if it can

    (A) explain known results
    (B) be adjusted to agree with new results
    (C) predict new results
    (D) be incomparable with new results
    (E) produce equations

104. Two different isotopes of the same element have the same

    (A) number of neutrons
    (B) number of protons
    (C) mass
    (D) number of alpha particles
    (E) nucleus

105. The moon rises at midnight. Its phase is

    (A) new
    (B) first quarter
    (C) full
    (D) third quarter
    (E) unidentifiable

106. The tail of a comet is generally directed

    (A) in the same direction of motion as the comet
    (B) opposite to the direction of motion of the comet
    (C) away from the sun
    (D) away from the Earth
    (E) None of the above

107. When we see the Milky Way, we are looking at

    (A) the center of our galaxy
    (B) stars in the plane of the galaxy
    (C) companion galaxies to our own
    (D) the combined light of distant galaxies
    (E) hot distant gas clouds

108. The gravitational field near a black hole is enormous, mainly because of the

    (A) enormous mass of the black hole
    (B) extensive shrinkage of space-time
    (C) closeness to the great compacted mass concentration of the black hole
    (D) great attraction for everything, including light itself
    (E) All of the above

109. Assume that a method is developed to remove continuous cores 1 foot in diameter and 2,000 feet long from the Earth. Examination of thousands of cores would probably reveal that as one goes from top (surface) to bottom (inward), the

    (A) species of fossils decrease
    (B) species of fossils remain constant
    (C) species of fossils increase
    (D) number of fossils decreases but the kinds increase
    (E) number of fossils increases but the kinds decrease

110. Miller, in his famous series of experiments on the origin of life, used an electrical discharge as a source of energy because

    (A) electricity breaks water into oxygen and hydrogen
    (B) electricity is commonly used in chemical experiments
    (C) electrical storms were thought to have been common in the early atmosphere
    (D) electrical storms commonly occur today in the atmospheres of Earth and Venus
    (E) ultraviolet light or radioactivity could not be used

111. If carbon deposits in rocks were produced by living organisms and if such carbon deposits occur in rocks that are calculated to be older than known fossil-bearing rocks, *then life existed upon the Earth prior to the time that any now-known fossil-bearing rocks were formed.*

    How would the italicized portion of the above statement be categorized?

    (A) It is an assumption upon which the validity of the concept of evolution depends.
    (B) It is a deduction from postulates or premises.
    (C) It is a generalization based upon empirical observation.
    (D) It is a conclusion that is not supported by empirical evidence.
    (E) It is an analogy comparing an unknown with something that is known.

112. The Doppler effect could be used to determine the

    (A) temperature of a star
    (B) age of a star
    (C) diameter of a star
    (D) speed of a star
    (E) composition of a star

GO ON TO THE NEXT PAGE

Questions 113–116 present a term followed by a choice of five words, lettered (A) through (E). From these words, select the one most closely related to the first term.

113. Magma

    (A) Lava
    (B) Pumice
    (C) Shale
    (D) Limestone
    (E) Salt

114. Plateau

    (A) Valley
    (B) Hill
    (C) Slope
    (D) Horizontal
    (E) Cliff

115. Geosyncline

    (A) Volcano
    (B) Dike
    (C) Trough
    (D) Primary wave
    (E) Earthquake

116. Seamount

    (A) Granite
    (B) Primary wave
    (C) Seismic wave
    (D) Salt
    (E) Volcano

117. Serious pollution problems in the sea are caused by

    (A) rotting hulls of sunken ships
    (B) oil
    (C) magnesium
    (D) carbon monoxide
    (E) algae

Questions 118–120 refer to the following diagram, a partially completed cycle of the rocks on Earth. The boxes describe processes that connect the substances in the filled spaces. In some cases, the same process connects different items.

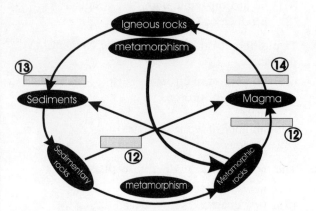

118. Name the process (number 12) by which sedimentary and metamorphic rocks become magma.

    (A) Erosion
    (B) Sedimentation
    (C) Crystallization
    (D) Melting
    (E) Metamorphism

119. Name the process (number 13) by which rocks become sediments.

    (A) Crystallization
    (B) Melting
    (C) Fossilization
    (D) Erosion
    (E) Petrification

120. Name the process (number 14) by which magma becomes igneous rock.

    (A) Crystallization
    (B) Fossilization
    (C) Erosion
    (D) Metamorphism
    (E) Melting

STOP If you finish before the time is up, you may check your work on this section only. Do not turn to any other section in the test.

POSTTEST ANSWER KEY AND EXPLANATIONS

PART I BIOLOGICAL SCIENCE

1.	B	13.	B	25.	C	37.	D	49.	E
2.	A	14.	B	26.	A	38.	E	50.	D
3.	E	15.	C	27.	D	39.	B	51.	B
4.	C	16.	D	28.	B	40.	A	52.	C
5.	C	17.	D	29.	C	41.	C	53.	E
6.	B	18.	E	30.	A	42.	C	54.	B
7.	E	19.	A	31.	C	43.	E	55.	D
8.	C	20.	D	32.	E	44.	C	56.	C
9.	D	21.	A	33.	B	45.	D	57.	C
10.	C	22.	C	34.	B	46.	E	58.	E
11.	A	23.	B	35.	C	47.	C	59.	D
12.	B	24.	E	36.	B	48.	D	60.	E

PART II PHYSICAL SCIENCE

61.	B	73.	D	85.	D	97.	D	109.	A
62.	B	74.	B	86.	D	98.	C	110.	C
63.	D	75.	A	87.	D	99.	B	111.	B
64.	B	76.	C	88.	E	100.	D	112.	D
65.	A	77.	B	89.	A	101.	C	113.	A
66.	A	78.	B	90.	A	102.	B	114.	D
67.	B	79.	B	91.	D	103.	C	115.	C
68.	B	80.	C	92.	A	104.	B	116.	E
69.	C	81.	C	93.	C	105.	D	117.	B
70.	B	82.	C	94.	D	106.	C	118.	D
71.	C	83.	C	95.	C	107.	B	119.	D
72.	A	84.	B	96.	D	108.	C	120.	A

PART I BIOLOGICAL SCIENCE

1. **The correct answer is (B).** This gene has flourished, due to heterozygote advantage, in populations originating in tropical climates that have had a resistance to malaria. Choices (A) and (D) are incorrect, as natural selection would have worked to lower the frequency. Choice (C) is a factual but irrelevant statement. Choice (E) is simply incorrect.

2. **The correct answer is (A).** Down syndrome (formerly called Mongolism) is caused by the presence of an extra chromosome and, thus, can be detected from a karyotype (photographic examination of stained chromosomes) made from any cultured fetal cells. The other diseases involve visually imperceptible mutations in one or more pairs of alleles and cannot yet be chemically assayed.

3. **The correct answer is (E).** As in humans, male drosophila have only one X chromosome and a small y. They are hemizygous for genes on the X and, therefore, show the trait of any single recessive genes they have on the X. Since the male passes his X only to daughters, no sons will carry or show the trait. In the case discussed, all daughters will carry the trait but not show it, as it is recessive. To solve genetic problems such as this, one should write out the genotypes (and in this case, also the chromosomes) involved:

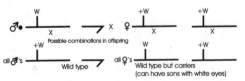

4. The correct answer is (C). This case is the reverse of the previous one. The father, who is a carrier, will have the gene on his Z chromosome and will be a carrier. His Z is passed to his daughters, and there is a 50 percent chance that they will show the trait since they have only one Z chromosome.

5. The correct answer is (C). Down syndrome is most often caused by an entire extra autosome. All of the other choices are aneuploids of sex chromosomes.

6. The correct answer is (B). During meiosis, homologous chromosomes come together and line up point by point (allele by allele). In the case of an inversion, such pairing can only be accomplished by the following configuration:

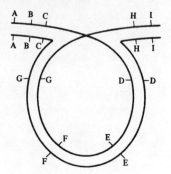

The lower chromosome has the inversion: A B C G F E D H I, instead of the normal A B C D E F G H I sequence of genes.

7. The correct answer is (E). Mendel's principle of random assortment must be demonstrated with a dihybrid cross, of which choice (E) is the only example. The principle simply means that traits associated in the parents assort randomly in the offspring, thus forming new combinations.

8. The correct answer is (C). Human blood types involve more than two possible alleles, as the types include genes for either A, B, O, or some combination of the three. The other possible answers involve only two alleles each.

9. The correct answer is (D). Epistasis is a case of nonallelic genes interacting. All of the other terms involve entirely different concepts.

10. The correct answer is (C). A typical dihybrid cross involves two unlinked pairs of alleles, both on autosomes and both exhibiting simple dominance. Such a question may be simplified by choosing an example such as AABB times aabb and working it through. The F1 would all be AaBb, and the F2 can be found either by multiplying fractions or by filling in a Punnett square, such as the one below:

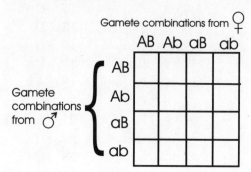

All that is necessary is to fill in the boxes and then categorize and count them as one of these four possible phenotypes:

9 A_B_
3 A_bb
3 aaB_
1 aabb

Since a dihybrid cross is two monohybrid crosses performed simultaneously, an alternate method of calculation is to multiply the ratios expected for each monohybrid cross:

$A\_ = \dfrac{3}{4}$ $B\_ = \dfrac{3}{4}$

$aa = \dfrac{1}{4}$ $bb = \dfrac{1}{4}$

Therefore, A_B_ together $= \dfrac{3}{4} \times \dfrac{3}{4} = \dfrac{6}{16}$.

11. The correct answer is (A). This dihybrid cross involves an epistatic reaction, not simple dominance, but it can be calculated in the same manner as above.

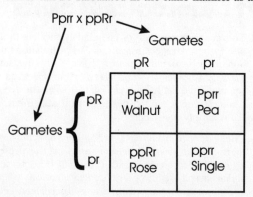

12. The correct answer is (B). The number of possibilities can be found by using the rule that it equals $2n$ where n = number of pairs of alleles. It can also be worked out (as can most genetic problems) by the forked-line method, as illustrated below:

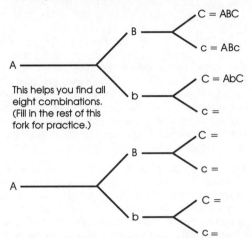

This helps you find all eight combinations. (Fill in the rest of this fork for practice.)

13. The correct answer is (B). An animal with 14 chromosomes has 7 pairs or linkage groups. Of the 12 marker loci, 5 are on one chromosome pair, 4 on another, and the remaining 3 are on separate pairs. So 5 pairs are marked, leaving 2 unmarked. The correct answer is (B). Choices (A), (C), and (D) are incorrect, as is choice (E), the answer you would have gotten had you forgotten that chromosomes are paired.

14. The correct answer is (B). These two parents can expect that their children will have a 50 percent probability of having either type-A or type-B blood. This 50 percent is multiplied by the 50 percent probability of a boy to give 25 percent.

15. The correct answer is (C). Since neither parent has the trait but the children do, it is recessive. Since both a son and a daughter have it, it cannot be sex-linked.

16. The correct answer is (D). $x^2 = 0.48$. You need not be familiar with the concept of x^2 to solve this problem, but you do need to know that the expected results of a typical monohybrid cross with simple dominance are 3 dominant, 1 recessive, for the F2. Of 100 offspring, 75 should be yellow (Y = dominant), and 25 should be green (yy = recessive). These are the expected values for the two classes of data. The solution follows:

Classes of Data	Yellow	Green
$d \times (ob - e)$	3	−3
d^2	9	9
$\dfrac{d^2}{e}$	$\dfrac{9}{75}$	$\dfrac{9}{25}$

$$x^2 = \frac{9}{75} + \frac{9}{25} = \frac{36}{75} = 0.48$$

17. The correct answer is (D). Checking for 0.48 in the first row (1 degree of freedom) of the table provided, we find that it falls between the columns, indicating 30 percent to 50 percent probability that such deviations are due to chance. Thus, the data fit the model well.

18. The correct answer is (E). Crossing over occurs during meiosis I. With no crossover, the spores would be arranged like this:

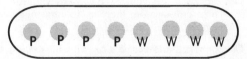

Or it can occur in reverse order. If crossing over occurs, the 4 chromatics of the tetrad can end up in any order. As each forms a separate nucleus before duplicating itself in mitosis, each makes an identical pair of nuclei. So, the possible results after crossing over are equal numbers of pairs of P and W in any order so long as each pair is together, as shown below:

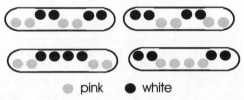

⬤ pink　● white

19. The correct answer is (A). The example below illustrates further:

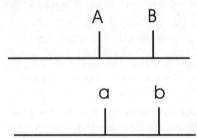

Here are homologous chromosomes: one has A and B linked, the other has alleles to these, a and b. The likelihood that a break and crossover will occur somewhere between A and B (giving recombinations Ab on one and aB on the other) is greater as the distance between A and B increases. If A and B were very close, the likelihood of a random crossover between them would be small. Choices (B), (D), and (E) are incorrect and demonstrate an important point to keep in mind when you take the exam: beware of any answer that has absolute words such as "always" or "never." Choice (C) is incorrect, as this event is rare in mitosis.

20. The correct answer is (D). Alveoli and the tiny ducts leading to them are the only structures thin enough to allow the passage of gas. The other structures—the trachea, bronchial tubes, and bronchioles—are multiple cell-layers thick and are referred to as "respiratory dead space."

21. The correct answer is (A). The nematocysts uncoil to sting and ensnare prey for the cnidarians.

22. **The correct answer is (C).** Warnings are often sounded about undercooked pork, but raw beef may also be infected with tapeworms. Likewise, the bacterium salmonella is often found in chicken eggs. Choices (A) and (B) are incorrect. The clue here is the word *commonly*. It is not that common to find beef tainted as in (A) and still palatable; amoebic dysentery is rare in general and is not contracted in this manner.

23. **The correct answer is (B).** Spirogyra, the alga, is shown in conjugation, literally "joining together." The other answers are unrelated.

24. **The correct answer is (E).** The illustration gives a clue. When guard cells (and the plant in general) have plenty of water, the cells swell, leaving a stoma or opening for transpiration (water loss) and gas exchange. When the plant needs to conserve water, the cells are somewhat shrunken, and the opening is sealed. Though choices (A) and (D) are a result of stomata opening and transpiration, they are not direct functions of guard cells. Choices (B) and (C) are not their specialized functions either.

25. **The correct answer is (C).** Since organism II develops in the mother, who nourishes it, it would not need much yolk. Organism I lives on land but mates in water and does not have dry skin. It is obviously an amphibian that develops rapidly and, while containing yolk, could not be expected to have very much. Organism III develops from an egg, is highly terrestrial, mates and lives on land, and has scales. It is obviously a reptile, which is well known to be closely related to birds, both groups having large amounts of yolk.

26. **The correct answer is (A).** Species I lives on land that is close to water. It is an amphibian and, like a tadpole, has gills. Species II lives in water but has hair, making it a mammal, which does not have gills. Species III has no contact with water at all.

27. **The correct answer is (D).** Species II has the hair and internal developmental characteristics of a mammal that is warm-blooded (a homeotherm), so it would not be greatly affected by a decrease in temperature. Species I and III are not mammals, and Species III could not be a bird because birds lack scales. Therefore, Species III is a reptile. Species I and III could potentially go into shock at temperatures below freezing.

28. **The correct answer is (B).** This represents the best answer. Choice (A) is absurd. Choice (C) does not at all represent radiation. Choices (D) and (E) do not involve a variety of organisms as do radiations.

29. **The correct answer is (C).** Choices (A) and (E) are superfluous. Choice (D) is inaccurate, as amphibians require water for reproduction. Choice (B) could be a factor, but lobe-finned fish already had a lung structure, and many amphibians retain gills, flawing this response.

30. **The correct answer is (A).** Only germplasm DNA is passed from parent to offspring in a constant manner. Unless this process occurs, there is no means for a mutation to be carried into a lineage.

31. **The correct answer is (C).** This is a straightforward factual question to which choice (C), ribosomes, is the answer. They are made in part of ribonucleic acid, hence their name.

32. **The correct answer is (E).** This interpretive question is based on a diagram of a cell with four pairs of chromosomes moving to opposite poles in the process of anaphase, eliminating choices (A) and (B). The question also states that the diploid number is 4. Thus, the cells being produced will both be diploid, eliminating choice (D), which would produce a haploid cell. To choose between choices (C) and (E), you must know that the homologous chromosomes are synapsed (paired together) in meiosis I. This is not what the diagram shows, so the answer must be choice (E), anaphase of mitosis.

33. **The correct answer is (B).** This is a multidisciplinary question that you may answer based on knowledge from news reports of the Mars mission, or you may simply derive the answer knowing that the basis of animal or heterotrophic life on Earth is the consumption of sugars, fats, and proteins and oxidation of these to CO_2 and H_2O. Thus, choice (B) is the only answer that would differentiate animals from other organisms. Choice (A) is a function only of plants. Choice (E) is clearly wrong and does not occur in living systems.

34. **The correct answer is (B).** Choice (A), translation, is the process of making a protein from the mRNA molecule. Choice (C), translocation, is the exchange of chromosome segments between nonhomologous chromosomes. Choice (D) is the process of creating a large molecule out of identical small units, and choice (E) has no relevant meaning.

35. **The correct answer is (C).** Semen includes sperm produced by meiosis. Of the answers given, choice (C), seminiferous tubules, is correct. This can be derived by reading the answers with care. The name seminiferous indicates some relation to semen production. It is true of many scientific terms that the name, often from Latin or Greek prefixes or suffixes, indicates the function.

36. **The correct answer is (B).** The already duplicated chromosomes separate in mitosis; hence, choice (B), interphase, is the correct answer.

37. **The correct answer is (D).** The membranous infoldings within the cell are choice (D), endoplasmic reticulum. Choice (B) is incorrect, as it would have to surround the nucleus. The other choices mentioned are small "bodies" within the cell or other types of organell.

38. **The correct answer is (E).** Three of the choices offered are not water soluble; only choices (A) and (E) are. Of these two, only choice (E), protein, is a major component (with phospholipid) of all cell membranes. Many of these proteins serve as enzymes for cellular reactions.

39. **The correct answer is (B).** The Golgi apparatus is thought to prepare cell products, such as hormones, for secretion by the cell. Lysosomes, which lyse or break up organic molecules, break up ingested food particles; mitochondria provide energy to the cell; vacuoles enclose waste products; and the endoplasmic reticulum may transport materials to the nucleus.

40. The correct answer is (A). ATP is the energy "currency" of all living cells. Energy from breakdown of glycogen, glucose, fats, proteins, etc., is used to form the high-energy phosphate bond converting low-energy ADP to ATP. NAD functions in electron transfer reactions.

41. The correct answer is (C). Mitochondria perform these energy-producing functions for the cell. The nuclei, with their nucleoli and chromosomes, perform genetic and control functions. Ribosomes synthesize protein, and desmosomes are membranous connections between cells.

42. The correct answer is (C). All organic compounds have C, H, and O. The correct answer is choice (C): nitrogen forms the amino group of all amino acids. Phosphorus, choice (E), is common to certain lipids and nucleic acids.

43. The correct answer is (E). Choice (A) is incorrect because this graph does not have enough information to extrapolate to all populations. There is no evidence that choice (B) is in effect, particularly when choices (C) and (D) of the graph cannot be predicted from the data given.

44. The correct answer is (C). Candidates must be aware that populations cannot grow without limitation, thus eliminating choice (A). Choice (B) is not correct because there is no evidence that this graph can be applied to all populations, nor is there evidence that choice (D) is a basis for all populations. Since choice (C) is obvious from the graph, choice (E) is eliminated.

45. The correct answer is (D). The candidate must keep in mind that we are looking for a short-term outcome. Choices (A), (C), and (E) are long-term. Given relative sizes of the organisms involved and the facts that owls and hawks prey on small organisms, there is no logical reason to expect choice (B) to occur.

46. The correct answer is (E). Choices (A), (B), (C), and (D) have little, if anything, to do with the relationship of an organism to its environment.

47. The correct answer is (C). Choices (B) and (D) do not show constancy. Choice (A) is not exponential, and choice (E) shows a decrease.

48. The correct answer is (D). It is a normal growth curve depicting rapid population growth and then a leveling off due to increased population needs for space as well as problems associated with an accumulation of waste products.

49. The correct answer is (E). It is the only graph in which there is a rapid decrease in numbers. Choices (A) and (C) are increasing, while choices (B) and (D) are leveling off but not decreasing.

50. The correct answer is (D). It is almost level—a sign of equilibrium. All other responses are either increasing or decreasing.

51. The correct answer is (B). It includes the herbivores and rodents that feed on grass. They would lose the grass in a drought. Also, given the rodents' small body size, they would probably not have much food and water reserves in their bodies with respect to their activity level.

52. The correct answer is (C). It includes larger forms that prey on a wide variety of choices, making the effects of a drought on them minimal. They could also extract liquid for themselves from the body fluids of their prey.

53. The correct answer is (E). It is the only part of the curve that shows a decrease in number.

54. The correct answer is (B). It shows a rapid increase in numbers of the herbivores as the obvious immediate result of the larger carnivores being preyed upon.

55. The correct answer is (D). Leeuwenhoek is well known for inventing the microscope and seeing unicellular microscopic forms.

56. The correct answer is (C). The candidate must be aware of commonly known definitions involved in scientific methodology.

57. The correct answer is (C). Moisture promotes gas exchange across the lung surface so that choice (A) cannot be correct. At night, plants metabolize the sugar they make during the day; therefore, they use O_2 and produce CO_2, possibly reducing the O_2 concentration in a closed room. CO_2 is not a poison; in fact, it is a respiratory stimulant. Choice (D) is incorrect, as it is well known that patients are often administered gas with high concentrations of O_2. Choice (E) must be incorrect because of the word "many."

58. The correct answer is (E). Any factor that can alter the rate of growth of a tree in a given year will also alter the thickness of the annual ring produced.

59. The correct answer is (D). The pancreas, choice (A), and liver, choice (C), are secretory organs. The stomach, choice (B), functions for food storage and protein digestion. The large intestine, choice (E), absorbs water and minerals but no nutrients.

60. The correct answer is (E). All of these places contain cartilage.

PART II PHYSICAL SCIENCE

61. The correct answer is (B). The number of electrons for a neutral carbon atom (atomic number 6) is six. Two electrons are maximum for the first shell or level, and eight electrons are maximum for the second. Since carbon has six electrons (two in the first shell and four in the second), it can have only two shells or energy levels.

62. The correct answer is (B). The atomic number of an element has been set as the number of protons. Hence, copper has 29 protons.

63. **The correct answer is (D).** $64 - 29 = 35$ neutrons. The mass number of an element is equal to the number of protons and neutrons. Since copper has 29 protons, the difference between 64 and 29 equals 35 neutrons.

64. **The correct answer is (B).** The number of electrons equals the number of protons in an atom.

65. **The correct answer is (A).** Twenty-seven electrons (the atom has lost two negative electrons, producing a +2 copper ion). The atomic number is always the number of protons in the nucleus of the atom. Since the number of protons is the same as the number of electrons in an atom, the atomic number also represents the number of electrons (protons are positively charged, and electrons are negatively charged; in an atom, the two must balance). In the ion Cu++, there are two fewer negative electrons; the number of protons is still the same—29. The mass number is the sum of protons and neutrons in the nucleus. The number of neutrons can be determined by subtracting the number of protons (atomic number) from the mass number (protons and neutrons).

66. **The correct answer is (A).** Before Dalton introduced the modern atomic theory, atoms were thought of as hard, impenetrable spheres locked adjacent to one another in compounds. Then, after the electrical nature of atoms was observed and after certain experiments of Rutherford's yielded evidence that there was relatively great space between a positively charged nucleus and negatively charged electrons surrounding the nucleus, the solar system model emerged (the nucleus as "sun" and electrons as "planets"). Then it was seen that there cannot be a negatively charged "planet" orbiting a positively charged "sun" without the electrons falling into the nucleus. Hence, the most recent model admits an uncertainty for the placement of electrons; they are not the particles of ordinary existence but rather a combination of matter and energy that is treated in the mathematics of quantum/wave mechanics.

67. **The correct answer is (B).** Since chemical bonding is a property of electronic structure, it has nothing to do with the nucleus, except that the nucleus defines the particular protons and neutrons. Choices (A), (C), and (D) are incorrect. Electronic structure influences chemical properties, and the nature of the nucleus determines radioactivity.

68. **The correct answer is (B).** The sum of the atomic numbers (subscripts) on both sides of the arrow must be the same ($4 + 2 = 6 + 0$). This represents the number of protons in total. Likewise, the mass number (superscripts) on both sides of the arrow must be the same ($9 + 4 = 12 + 1$). This represents the number of protons and neutrons in total. So, the missing product must have a subscript of 6 and a superscript of 12. This is the normal isotope of carbon.

69. **The correct answer is (C).** Recognizing that the symbol for copper is Cu, silver is Ag, and a nitrate ion is NO_3 will allow the student to see that choices (A), (B), and (D) are true. The correct answer is a FALSE statement. If the student knows that what is occurring in the reaction is the displacement of silver (Ag) from a solution of silver salt by copper (Cu) and recalls the generalization that a more reactive metal will displace a less reactive metal from its salt in solution, the required answer will be seen as a false statement immediately. Finally, copper nitrate and silver nitrate are both salts.

70. **The correct answer is (B).** Na is seen to react with cold water. Fe and Pb do not, and Cu does not even react with acid. Hydrogen is not a metal.

71. **The correct answer is (C).** Cu, copper, is the least reactive, as it does not even react with cold water. Hydrogen is not a metal.

72. **The correct answer is (A).** Fe, iron (by reasoning similar to that used in question 10), is the correct choice. Once again, sodium reacts with cold water, iron reacts only with steam, and lead reacts with neither cold nor hot water.

73. **The correct answer is (D).** Combustion is a reaction with oxygen, and a hydrocarbon is a compound containing only hydrogen and carbon.

74. **The correct answer is (B).** This is the only reaction involving the reaction of two elements—hydrogen and oxygen—combining to form water. It is also called a synthesis reaction.

75. **The correct answer is (A).** The student must recognize sulfuric acid (H_2SO_4) and SO_3 (as an oxide of the nonmetal, sulfur). Combined with water, SO_3 forms an acid, H_2SO_4.

76. **The correct answer is (C).** Barium hydroxide [$Ba(OH)_2$] is a base, and BaO is an oxide of the metal barium. Combined with water, BaO forms the base $Ba(OH)_2$.

77. **The correct answer is (B).** The correct answer cannot be choices (C) or (D), since the statement in the question implies a reaction of building materials with acid. From the generalization in question 76, the student is told that oxides of nonmetals form acids when placed in water. Both CO_2 and SO_3 are oxides of nonmetals. Carbon dioxide forms a very weak acid, carbonic acid, so the best answer is choice (B); oxides of sulfur in the air come down as "acid rain" and do considerable damage to stone materials, but only locally and not as globally as CO_2.

78. **The correct answer is (B).** All gases have limited solubility in water. Carbon dioxide in carbonated beverages is no exception. Experience should tell the student that more gas will stay in the solution at low temperature; heating will generate more gas. Also, when the cap is opened on a bottle of soda or beer, the gas is released, since pressure is lessened. Hence, maximum solubility occurs at low temperature and high pressure.

79. **The correct answer is (B).** Locating 0.5 atmosphere halfway between 0.4 atmosphere and 0.6 atmosphere on the horizontal axis and following in a straight line up to the curve, the student will see that this corresponds to about 40 liters on the vertical axis.

80. **The correct answer is (C).** Multiplying any two matching volume/pressure points on the curve will give the value of 20. For example, 0.2 atm × 100 liters, 0.5 atm × 40 liters, and so on.

81. **The correct answer is (C).** Since acceleration demands a change in velocity, constant velocity can occur only with zero acceleration. Choices (A), (B), (D), and (E) demand a changing velocity.

82. **The correct answer is (C).** Since acceleration demands a change in velocity a body undergoing acceleration must have a changing velocity. Choice (B) is incorrect because acceleration can also be a decreasing velocity.

83. **The correct answer is (C).** The calculation of speed is displacement per time. In this case, we have 250 mph divided by $\frac{1}{2}$ hour. The result is 500 mph.

84. **The correct answer is (B).** The acceleration of any object in free flight on the surface of the Earth is the acceleration due to gravity. All the other statements imply some other kind of acceleration.

85. **The correct answer is (D).** Newton's second law relates the net force acting on a body to the product of its mass and acceleration. Knowing the force and mass of a body enables one to calculate its acceleration.

86. **The correct answer is (D).** The weight of a body is the force of the object's gravitational attraction acting on that body. All the other choices refer to mass, which is a different property.

87. **The correct answer is (D).** The only force causing the horse to move forward is the force that the ground exerts on the horse. Choices (A) and (C) are not forces on the horse, and choice (B) is a force on the horse against the motion.

88. **The correct answer is (E).** Choices (B) and (C) are special-case accelerations. Choice (A) does not tell us what is happening to the force, and choice (D) is too exclusive.

89. **The correct answer is (A).** Action and reaction are the forces acting upon a body. They are equal in magnitude and opposite in direction.

90. **The correct answer is (A).** The proper use of lubricants always reduces friction, but has nothing to do with inertia, which is related to mass.

91. **The correct answer is (D).** The most fundamental principle of science is that of conservation of energy, by which energy can neither be created nor destroyed.

92. **The correct answer is (A).** Since both objects would have the same acceleration, they must have the same velocity. The other answers are incorrect, since the masses of the objects are different.

93. **The correct answer is (C).** An explosion is a release of energy. Although the fragments may have increased velocities, the total momentum will remain the same. But the explosion of the shell adds motion to the particles by the release of energy from the explosions.

94. **The correct answer is (D).** To cut a material, it is necessary to wedge a tool between two parts of the material. This action takes advantage of the inclined plane. With some, but not all tools, the wedging is aided by lever action. Work is done when one cuts, but, again, the action is via leverage.

95. **The correct answer is (C).** Heat is a form of energy. Its transfer is dependent upon temperature differences, and friction produces heat, but heat, itself, is energy.

96. **The correct answer is (D).** Waves transmit energy but not particles. Particles in the medium bump one another and, thus, move the energy but not the particles.

97. **The correct answer is (D).** Sound waves do not travel through a vacuum. They need a material medium for support and are passed along by particles of the medium hitting one another.

98. **The correct answer is (C).** The nucleus of an atom cannot be said to be electrically neutral. It contains protons that are positively charged. It is certainly small in size, contains most of the atom's mass, and can, and does, deflect alpha particles.

99. **The correct answer is (B).** An object has a positive electric charge whenever it contains a deficiency of electrons. The nuclei of atoms are positively charged, and atoms in a substance are neutral, since they contain an equal number of negative charges via their electrons. If you remove some electrons, the substance will exhibit a positive charge.

100. **The correct answer is (D).** A permanent magnet attracts some substances and repels others. Any object having a magnetic field, be it ferromagnetic or electromagnetic, will be attracted or repelled by a permanent magnet depending upon the orientation of the field.

101. **The correct answer is (C).** The sun's energy is released through fusion, a process whereby hydrogen is converted to helium.

102. **The correct answer is (B).** Sun spots are areas on the sun that are cooler than their surroundings and, hence, radiate less energy, thus appearing darker.

103. **The correct answer is (C).** A scientific theory is useful because it can predict new results. Although choices (A) and (B) are also correct, choice (C) is more important and more correct.

104. **The correct answer is (B).** Isotopes are atoms of the same element differing only in their number of neutrons, i.e., atomic weight. Since they are the same atom, their proton number is the same.

105. **The correct answer is (D).** When the moon rises at midnight, it is approximately $\frac{3}{4}$ of a day behind the sun in rising. This puts the moon in its third quarter.

106. **The correct answer is (C).** The tail of a comet is composed of very fine particles. As it nears the sun, radiation pressure from the sun pushes the tail away from the sun.

107. **The correct answer is (B).** The Earth sits about $\frac{1}{3}$ of the way in along the diameter of our galaxy, the Milky Way. When we see the Milky Way, we are looking through the long plane of the rest of the galaxy.

108. **The correct answer is (C).** A black hole is an extremely compacted mass concentration. Therefore, if you are close to it, you are in an enormous gravitational field. The key word is *compacted*. Choice (A) does not tell us if the field is compacted or dispersed.

109. **The correct answer is (A).** The number of species greatly decreases in older rocks, which would be near the bottom of the core sample.

110. **The correct answer is (C).** An experiment of this sort should try to mimic the original situation and best available evidence.

111. **The correct answer is (B).** Choice (A) has nothing to do with evolution, choices (C) and (D) are unfounded, and choice (E) is illogical. Choice (B) follows a logical deduction.

112. **The correct answer is (D).** The Doppler effect has to do with wave motion. The pitch of an automobile hum as a car passes is a Doppler-effect situation. In astronomy, the color wavelength shifts are used to determine the speed of the stars.

113. **The correct answer is (A).** A molten material called magma is found deep within the Earth. During an earthquake, the lava, which is magma-like, pushes to the surface.

114. **The correct answer is (D).** A plateau is a horizontal surface found on tops of hills.

115. **The correct answer is (C).** Ocean troughs, or depressions, are structures called geosynclines. Choices (A) and (B) have to do with liquid rock, and choices (D) and (E) have to do with earthquakes.

116. **The correct answer is (E).** Seamounts are underwater mountains formed by volcanoes.

117. **The correct answer is (B).** The student must be aware of problems created by oil spills from ships or drilling. Oil kills birds and fish.

118. **The correct answer is (D).** Rocks may become magma by melting, a process that involves great pressure.

119. **The correct answer is (D).** The process of erosion chips away bits and pieces of rocks, which are then reunited to become sedimentary rocks by settling most often in a body of water.

120. **The correct answer is (A).** Via crystallization, the molten magma becomes igneous rock.

Appendix

The CLEP Subject Exams

The CLEP Subject Exams offer the highly motivated, well-qualified student an opportunity to get greater value from each education dollar by starting right at an advanced level, thereby learning more. If the college grants actual college credits, the student with a qualifying score can save both time and money. Actual college credits substitute for actual college courses; they can shorten the time you must spend in college and reduce the number of terms for which you must pay tuition.

Even at colleges that accept CLEP scores but that do not grant credits, a qualifying CLEP score can help get distribution requirements out of the way or may fulfill introductory course prerequisites. By bypassing the introductory prerequisite, you can start right away with advanced courses in the subject area and progress farther during your undergraduate career.

OVERVIEW OF THE CLEP SUBJECT EXAMS

Some CLEP Subject Exams presuppose that you have received formal training, even if not in a degree-granting program, in the area being tested. Other CLEP Subject Exams allow for the possibility that you are self-taught through a combination of work experience, life experience, and self-directed reading. Still other such exams lend themselves to individuals with generally good work and test-taking habits.

The college-level Foreign Language exams fall into this last category. The most popular of all the CLEP Subject Exams is the College Spanish, Levels 1 and 2 exam. This is strictly an exam of language competency; it is in no way based upon familiarity with literature and makes no reference to authors or to their works. While native speakers of Spanish tend to have a rich cultural background related to their country of origin or that of their parents, the Spanish exam presupposes neither any knowledge of the variety of Spanish-speaking cultures nor any outside reading in that language. What all three foreign-language exams do require are reading ability, listening comprehension, and an understanding of the structure of the language.

Obviously, success with a Foreign Language CLEP Exam requires true familiarity with the language—its vocabulary, idioms, grammar, and structure. This familiarity may have been gained through study, through experience living in a foreign country, or through use of the language at home. The source of the knowledge, as with all CLEP Subject Exams, is irrelevant; the sole requirement is that you demonstrate competence.

More than 2,300 colleges accept CLEP scores in some subjects for credit or placement or both. Since the Spanish exam is taken by so many test-takers, it obviously has a high acceptance rate. It gives a leg up to the many native Spanish speakers in this country. Even so, we must reiterate the advice given to you earlier in this book: Unless you are taking a CLEP exam just to satisfy yourself that your mastery of the subject matter is of college quality, ask questions before you register. This advice holds especially true for the Foreign Language exams. Many colleges prepare their own internal exams for exemption from language requirements or for placement in upper-level language or foreign-language literature courses. Usually the internal exams are free. If there is an internal exam, be sure that you can gain a real advantage from taking the CLEP exam, that is, that you can earn actual college credits with a qualifying CLEP score.

AREAS OF DIFFERENCE AMONG CLEP EXAMS

Most of the CLEP Subject Exams are decidedly verbal, but in the subject groups of Science, Mathematics, and Business, there is a mathematical component as well. In general, the test-taker must "do" the math. On multiple-choice exams, you need not show your work, but you must arrive at and choose the correct answer. The use of a non-graphing, non-programmable calculator is permitted but not required during the Calculus, College Algebra, General Chemistry, and Introductory Accounting exams. Being allowed to use a calculator may be a plus or a minus depending on your personal computational skills. The calculator is a factor to consider in choosing to take a particular CLEP subject exam in the realms of Science, Mathematics, and Business.

The optional free-response or essay exam comprises another area of variation among CLEP Subject Exams. Optional 90-minute free-response sections are available for the four Subject Exams in Composition and Literature. These sections are required by some—but not all—institutions. It is up to you to find out whether your college requires the essay section and to register for it if necessary.

THE EXAMS— ONE BY ONE

HISTORY AND SOCIAL SCIENCES

The catch-all category of Social Sciences and History includes eleven exams and covers a broad range of subject matter. All of the exams in this category presuppose extensive reading, though not necessarily of specific works, and factual knowledge. These exams call for an understanding of cause and effect, of the interrelationships among events. In addition, they require logical reasoning and plain common sense. Some of the exams include questions that require you to recall names of personalities and theories; others are less narrowly focused.

On each of the exams, the bulk of the questions are based upon a statement or on a short quoted excerpt. Nearly all of the exams include some questions based on charts, graphs, tables, photos, cartoons, diagrams, or maps.

Most of the questions follow the familiar (A)-to-(E) format. Some of the questions, however, are of a two-step construction. These offer three, four, or five statements and five combinations of these statements from which to choose your answer. An example of this question style is as follows:

> During the late nineteenth century, Congress enacted laws to regulate
>
> I.   railroad practices.
> II. the creation of trusts.
> III. child labor in mines and factories.
> IV. women's wages and work hours.
>
> (A) I and II
> (B) II and IV
> (C) I, II, and III
> (D) II, III, and IV
> (E) I, II, III, and IV

The correct answer is (A). ICC regulations of the railroads were enacted in 1887; the Sherman Antitrust Act dates to 1890. Labor, if regulated at all, was regulated only by the states in the nineteenth century.

All of the Social Sciences and History exams are divided into two separately timed 45-minute sections. The number of questions varies from exam to exam.

AMERICAN GOVERNMENT—100 multiple-choice questions based upon subject matter typically covered in a one-semester course.

Topics covered by this exam include, but are by no means limited to, the historical development and current operation of the Constitution and our government institutions; patterns and workings of the political process; the courts; parties and pressure groups; and elections and voting behaviors. Questions may refer to court cases, departments and agencies in the Executive Branch, and published expositions of philosophy of government. Some questions ask the test-taker to speculate as to the outcome of certain governmental manipulations. This speculation requires not only understanding of relationships but also careful reasoning based upon pragmatic observations of human behavior.

HISTORY OF THE UNITED STATES I: EARLY COLONIZATIONS TO 1877—120 multiple-choice questions based upon material covered in the first semester of a full-year course.

This examination asks questions beginning with the French, Spanish, and English colonies, moving through the forces and pressures that led to the formation of the nation, and on through the dynamics of the Civil War and reconstruction. The greatest proportion of the questions concern the period from 1790 to 1877. Exam questions are not sequential through time, but rather are mingled in no particular order.

By virtue of the period covered, there is overlap between this exam and that of American Government. The History of the United States I exam does hinge on specifics, such as names of people, legislative actions, literary works, philosophies, and movements. With reference to these specifics, the exam requires identification, chronology, and understanding of interplay. Success with this exam involves ability to analyze, interpret, explain, and evaluate.

HISTORY OF THE UNITED STATES II: 1865 TO THE PRESENT—120 multiple-choice questions based on material covered in the second semester of a full-year course.

Aside from the period covered, this exam mirrors the History of the United States I exam. Again the questions are mingled through time, and again emphasis is on the second half of the time period, from 1915 to the present.

HUMAN GROWTH AND DEVELOPMENT (Infancy, Childhood, Adolescence, Adulthood, and Aging)—90 multiple-choice questions based on material taught in a typical one-semester introductory course in child psychology, child development, or developmental psychology.

This exam does presuppose sufficient reading to make the test-taker thoroughly conversant with psychologists and their theories, with terminology, and with design and results of experiments. However, it also relies much more heavily than most CLEP Subject Exams on plain common sense. The Human Growth and Development exam is close behind the two most popular CLEP Subject Exams, College Spanish and College Composition. Its popularity probably stems from the possibility of scoring well simply by drawing on experience and reasoning applied to some reading.

INTRODUCTION TO EDUCATIONAL PSYCHOLOGY—95 multiple-choice questions based on material taught in a one-semester course.

As is the case with the other psychology-related exams, the Educational Psychology exam requires familiarity with psychologists and their theories, with terminology, with specific methods, and with statistics. It also includes many questions that draw upon common sense in applying theories to situations and to speculating on results.

PRINCIPLES OF MACROECONOMICS—80 multiple-choice questions based upon material taught in a one-semester course.

This exam does not require recall of the names of economists, but it does require familiarity with theories and terminology. About 20 percent of the exam covers general economics—that is, concepts familiar to both macroeconomics and microeconomics. Within the realm of macroeconomics—money and banking, taxation, business fluctuations, income distribution, etc.—questions require understanding concepts, interpreting diagrams, evaluating data, and understanding interactions and workings of monetary systems.

PRINCIPLES OF MICROECONOMICS—80 multiple-choice questions based on material taught in a one-semester course.

This exam is similar to that of macroeconomics except that 80 percent of the exam is based on microeconomics. The exam requires test-takers to interpret diagrams and to reason on the basis of understanding the interrelationships and true workings of systems, markets, etc.

INTRODUCTORY PSYCHOLOGY—95 multiple-choice questions based on the material presented in a one-semester survey course.

This exam touches upon a little bit of everything. The areas covered include physiological psychology, learning theories, development, behavior, personality models and disorders, social psychology, statistics, and others. Questions require knowledge and understanding of terminology, psychologists' names, and specific theories.

INTRODUCTORY SOCIOLOGY—100 multiple-choice questions based on material taught in a one-semester introductory course.

Questions on the Sociology exam rely heavily on knowledge of terminology and the names of theorists and their beliefs. The questions test understanding of statistics, institutions, processes and patterns, and the interpretation of data. Answering the questions calls for application of common sense to a thorough grasp of meanings in the "language" of the discipline.

WESTERN CIVILIZATION I: ANCIENT NEAR EAST TO 1649—120 multiple-choice questions based on material taught in the first semester of a full-year course on western civilization.

The Western Civilization I exam is an extremely comprehensive exam beginning in Ancient Greece and following through into the mid-seventeenth century. It requires knowledge of facts and events and of the causes and effects of events, as well as an understanding of graphs and maps. The exam requires familiarity with civilizations by name, with people, and with places, and it requires placement of events in time.

WESTERN CIVILIZATION II: 1649 TO THE PRESENT—120 multiple-choice questions based on material taught in the second semester of a full-year course on western civilization.

This exam closely resembles the one given in the first semester. It requires a strong background in names, events, causes and effects, and interrelationships. Test questions involve interpreting ideas and include maps, pictures, and other graphic materials.

COMPOSITION AND LITERATURE

Four separate examinations fall into the broad category of Composition and Literature. These, in turn, may be divided into two groups: those based heavily upon the reading of specific works and those based upon a more global understanding of works written in the English language, their interpretation, and their structure.

All four exams present excerpts from poetry, drama, fiction, and critical essays. The American and English Literature exams require interpretation of these excerpts in relation to specific authors, their styles, and their works. The other two exams require interpretation based upon overall knowledge of literature and literary analysis without specific reference to known works. The composition-related exam tests both writing skill and analytical ability.

The American Literature and English Literature exams cover ground that is very familiar to most well-educated people. However, since they are predicated on one's having read specific works on an unpublished reading list, they frighten away many test-takers and are among the least frequently taken of CLEP Subject Exams. Conversely, the other two exams in the Composition and Literature category are among the most popular, probably because people who consider themselves educated and intelligent are quite confident in their own powers of analysis and self-expression.

AMERICAN LITERATURE—100 multiple-choice questions based on material covered in a full-year survey course.

The American Literature exam asks questions concerning American literature from colonial through modern times, with emphasis on fiction and poetry. The exam includes questions on particular works, their authors, and their meanings. There are questions on characters and events, on historical settings, and on social import, and you may even be asked who wrote a specific work, what character spoke a certain line, or from what work a passage is excerpted. In addition, many questions require interpretation of poetry and short prose selections reprinted in the exam.

The free-response option entails writing two essays. The first is on an assigned topic, a critical generalization that must be discussed and supported. The second essay is a discussion on your choice of one of two topics, prose or poetry, printed in the test booklet.

ENGLISH LITERATURE—105 multiple-choice questions based on material covered in a full-year survey course.

As with the American Literature exam, the English Literature exam relies heavily on knowledge of specific works from *Beowulf* to the present. Test-takers must know authors and their works, styles, literary periods, and literary references. The exam requires heavy analysis of reprinted excerpts and poetry for meanings, moods, andáforms.

The free-response option entails two essays. The first essay is based on an excerpt printed in the test booklet. The second essay is to be a discussion of one of two general statements with the test-taker's point of view supported by examples from English literature.

ANALYZING AND INTERPRETING LITERATURE—80 multiple-choice questions based on material taught in a two-semester course on general literature.

Like the examinations in American and English literature, this exam presupposes wide reading with ability to analyze and interpret. Unlike the other two literature exams, it does not require familiarity with specific works. The scope of the exam includes poetry, fiction, nonfiction, and drama; British works, American works, and works in translation; and the Classical period through the twentieth century. The questions are all based on reprinted excerpts and are designed to measure understanding, analysis of elements, interpretation of metaphors, and response to nuances of meaning and style.

The free-response option requires two assigned essays. The first is based on a poem printed in the test booklet; the second requires application of a general literary statement to a work of the test-taker's choice.

FRESHMAN COLLEGE COMPOSITION——90 multiple-choice questions based on material taught in a one-year course on expository writing.

This is a General Exam requiring recognition and application of the fundamentals of standard written English, recognition of styles and techniques, logical development, and use of resource materials. Some questions closely resemble questions on routine tests of English usage and grammar; others are questions based on short passages reprinted in the test booklet.

The free-response option requires a 35-to-40-minute expository essay on a required topic and, in the remaining time, a second essay on one of two topics.

FOREIGN LANGUAGES

The three Foreign Language exams measure knowledge and language skills that a student might be expected to have gained in two years of college study. The material on the exams is so structured that a lower score may signify achievement at the one-year-of-study level. Colleges may, therefore, on the basis of score attained, grant two, three, or four semesters' credit.

Each Foreign Language exam consists of two components. One of these components, called the reading section, is a multiple-choice section consisting of written questions, some short and self-contained, others based on reading passages. The other component is a listening section. In this section, the test-taker answers multiple-choice questions on the basis of spoken (taped) statements, conversations, and narratives. The tapes have been prepared by native speakers, some men and some women. In some instances, even the questions are spoken, and the student must choose from the answer choices on the printed page.

The two parts, reading and listening, are scored separately, yielding a reading subscore and a listening subscore. A single total score is also reported. Many colleges will require a certain total score to qualify for credit and a qualifying score on both subtests as indication of overall mastery of the language.

The Foreign Language exams weigh each part as 50 percent of the score. Where the two parts have unequal numbers of questions, all questions on the exam do not have equal value. In this respect, the Foreign Language exams differ from all other CLEP Subject Exams on which all multiple-choice questions carry the same weight.

FRENCH LANGUAGE—LEVELS 1 AND 2—Reading part: 60 minutes, 90 questions; Listening part: 30 minutes, 55 questions.

The reading part measures vocabulary mastery by means of sentence-completion questions requiring the correct word or idiomatic phrase; grammar via sentence-completion questions requiring the correct grammatical form; grammar and vocabulary via word substitutions within a sentence; and reading comprehension with questions about content, meaning, and the effects of structural forms in a passage.

The listening part becomes progressively more difficult. First, the test-taker must choose the picture best represented by a spoken statement. Then come short conversations with printed questions about locale of the conversation, identity of speakers, and subject of the conversation. Finally, there are longer conversations or narratives followed by spoken questions. In this instance, only the answer choices are printed. Conversations, questions, and choices are all in French; directions are in English.

GERMAN LANGUAGE—LEVELS 1 AND 2—Reading part: 60 minutes, 80 questions; Listening part: 30 minutes, 55 questions.

The reading part includes sentence completions both in single sentences and within a short paragraph. The sentence completions are designed to measure vocabulary, mastery of grammatical forms, and manipulation of idiomatic expressions. The reading comprehension questions based on reading passages include questions on content, meaning, structure, and writing style.

The listening part begins with a choice of a picture represented by a spoken statement. The second type of question on the German listening part consists of short conversations. The task of the test-taker is to complete the conversation by choosing the most appropriate next statement. Finally, the test-taker must listen to a lengthy conversation and answer spoken questions based upon it. Of course, conversations, questions, and answer choices are all in German; directions, however, are in English.

SPANISH LANGUAGE—LEVELS 1 AND 2—Reading part: 45 minutes, 70 questions; Listening part: 45 minutes, 70 questions.

The reading part comprises sentence-completion questions and reading comprehension. Some sentence-completion questions are designed to measure vocabulary mastery, and others measure ability to choose the correct grammatical form. Some of the grammar questions include a vocabulary and idiom choice component as well. The reading comprehension questions are based on reading passages. The questions cover content, interpretation, and recognition of the purposes served by certain constructions and figures of speech.

As with the French and German exams, the listening part begins with the task of choosing the picture represented by a spoken sentence. The second segment of the listening part consists of short conversations followed by printed questions and printed choices. The questions seek to determine comprehension of the situation. The third question style in the listening part consists of a fairly long narrative followed by a spoken question. The final question style of the Spanish listening part appears only on the tape. First, directions are given orally on the tape. Then comes a single spoken question followed by four spoken answer choices. The test-taker must note which of the four spoken answer choices is most appropriate and mark that letter on the answer sheet. If the test-taker has a reasonable grasp of spoken Spanish, the answers to the questions are fairly obvious. The difficulty lies in concentrating on both the correct answer itself and the letter of that answer.

SCIENCE AND MATHEMATICS

The six exams in the Science and Mathematics family are precise, technical examinations of specific knowledge and understanding. These exams do not rely on the test-taker's having studied any particular texts or sources but demand true mastery of the full scope of the subject matter and ability to manipulate and reason with this knowledge. It is unlikely that a candidate could be successful with any of the science and mathematics exams without concerted study and guided experience or exposure. Common sense has no part in answering the science and mathematics questions, but creative thinking is an important component of success.

The use of a non-graphing, non-programmable scientific calculator is permitted during the Calculus, College Algebra, and General Chemistry exams.

CALCULUS WITH ELEMENTARY FUNCTIONS—45 multiple-choice questions based on concepts and skills taught in a one-year course.

The Calculus exam presupposes a solid background in basic mathematics, algebra, plane and solid geometry, trigonometry, and analytic geometry. It seeks to gauge understanding of calculus and experience with methods and applications. About 10 percent of the Calculus exam is devoted to elementary functions—algebraic, trigonometric, exponential, and logarithmic. The remainder of the exam is divided about equally into differential calculus and integral calculus.

COLLEGE ALGEBRA—60 multiple-choice questions based on material taught in a one-semester college algebra course.

This is a test of knowledge of basic algebra. It covers topics such as linear and quadratic equations, inequalities, and graphs and includes topics such as the theory of equations and exponential and logarithmic functions. Understanding of algebraic vocabulary, symbols, and notation is taken for granted. About half of the exam is devoted to routine problems to measure algebraic skills; the other half consists of nonroutine problems that require understanding of concepts and application of those concepts and skills.

COLLEGE ALGEBRA—TRIGONOMETRY—63 multiple-choice questions. Part One: 45 minutes, 30 algebra questions; Part Two: 15 minutes, 13 trigonometry questions; Part Three: 30 minutes, 20 trigonometry questions.

This exam is designed to cover material taught in a one-semester course that includes both algebra and trigonometry. The questions within each part reflect the same goals and emphases as those on the separate Algebra and Trigonometry exams. While the two parts are of equal length in both time and number of questions, they are not scored separately. Only a total score is reported; there are no subscores.

TRIGONOMETRY—80 multiple-choice questions based on material taught in a one-semester college trigonometry course.

This exam assumes that a one-semester college trigonometry course concentrates mainly on analytical trigonometry. It further assumes familiarity with both radian and degree measurement and with trigonometric vocabulary and notation. The topics covered include trigonometric functions and their relationships, evaluation of trigonometric functions of positive and negative angles, trigonometric equations and inequalities, graphs of trigonometric functions, and trigonometry of the angle. The greater part of the exam presents routine problems in which students demonstrate basic trigonometric skills. The remaining questions involve nonroutine problems that require an understanding of concepts and their application.

GENERAL BIOLOGY—120 multiple-choice questions based on material taught in a typical one-year college biology course.

The Biology exam gives about equal coverage to the three major broad fields of biology: molecular and cellular biology, organismal biology, and populational biology. The exam is not, however, divided into three sections; questions in these three areas are randomly mingled throughout the examination. The function of the exam is to determine knowledge of facts, principles, and processes as they relate to both plants and animals. The exam also seeks to establish that the test-taker is competent in the lab-science aspects of biology—that is, information gathering, hypothesis construction and measurement, experimental design, and interpretation and generalization of data. To this end, a number of questions are based on experiments and on graphic presentations. There are also questions related to the environment and ecology and to the ethical implications of biological advancements.

GENERAL CHEMISTRY—80 multiple-choice questions based on the material taught in a full-year introductory general chemistry course.

The person who has mastered introductory general chemistry should be able to answer questions showing that he or she knows facts, can apply concepts, and can interpret data relative to the structure and states of matter, reaction types, equations, stoichiometry, equilibrium, kinetics, thermodynamics, descriptive chemistry, and experimental chemistry. Questions on this exam are designed to measure such knowledge through diagrams, equations, and descriptions of experiments and their results. Use of a calculator is permitted for the solving of equations.

BUSINESS

The five business-related exams cover an eclectic range of topics from computers through management, accounting, business law, and marketing. Some of these exams clearly presuppose training or work experience in the field being tested. Computer and accounting expertise, for example, can hardly be gained through reading alone; some hands-on experience is required. The other exams can be passed by drawing on knowledge that combines outside reading, some sort of related training or work experience, and a good portion of careful reasoning and common sense.

Many of the questions on the Business exams are of the two-step format, as presented below:

> The Federal Fair Housing Act specifically prohibits discrimination in residential sales on the basis of
>
> I.   age.
> II. sexual orientation.
> III. marital status.
> IV. religion.
>
> (A) I only
> (B) IV only
> (C) I and IV
> (D) I, III, and IV
> (E) I, II, III, and IV

The correct answer is (B). The Federal Fair Housing Act prohibits discrimination in sales on the basis of race, color, religion, sex, or national origin.

INFORMATION SYSTEMS AND COMPUTER APPLICATIONS—100 multiple-choice questions based on material taught in a typical introductory college-level business course.

This is not a computer exam as such. While the exam does take as a given a general familiarity with information systems and computer applications, it does not raise questions based on specific languages, packages, or products. Questions on the exam are about equally divided between those measuring knowledge of terminology and basic concepts and those testing application of knowledge. Topics covered, without reference to specific products, include hardware, software, systems, programming, user support, information processing, and issues such as intellectual property and privacy rights. The questions clearly presuppose computer literacy and previous experience in computer use.

PRINCIPLES OF MANAGEMENT—100 multiple-choice questions based on material taught in a one-term introductory management course.

The focus of this examination is on the functional aspects of management, though it also asks questions related to the operational aspects of management and to human resources. The examination asks questions requiring knowledge of purposes, functions, and techniques of management; terminology related to management ideas, processes, and techniques; theory and underlying assumptions of concepts of management; and application of knowledge to specific problems. A person who has had experience in the business world, who has done some independent reading, and who reasons clearly should be able to succeed on this examination without formal course work. An in-service course would give an additional advantage.

PRINCIPLES OF ACCOUNTING—78 multiple-choice questions based on content of two semesters of college accounting courses.

Questions on the Accounting exam measure knowledge of both financial accounting and managerial accounting in about the proportion of two thirds to one third. A college may grant one or two semesters of credit depending on the configuration of courses at that college. Answering the accounting questions requires familiarity with accounting concepts and terminology, skill at preparation and use of financial reports, ability to apply accounting techniques to problem situations, and understanding the rationale behind principles and procedures in accounting. Some of the accounting questions involve computations.

Experience, training, or both are needed as qualifying background for success with this exam. The use of a calculator is permitted during this exam.

INTRODUCTORY BUSINESS LAW—100 multiple-choice questions based on content of a one-semester college course.

The bulk of this exam concerns business contracts, their formation, their meaning and applications, and the laws specific to their enforcement. Other questions concern American legal history, legal systems and procedures, and specific laws pertaining to agency and employment, torts, consumer protection, and other areas. About one third of the questions deal with knowledge of basic facts and terms, one third with understanding of concepts and principles, and one third with application of knowledge to specific case problems.

Background for this exam should include reading, experience, and, perhaps, a noncredit course in a subject such as real estate. Common sense and judgment also enter into qualifications for this exam.

PRINCIPLES OF MARKETING—100 multiple-choice questions based on material taught in a one-semester introductory marketing course.

This exam requires basic understanding of markets and marketing. It includes questions on demographics, consumer behavior, the effects and interactions of government regulation, economic trends, effects of advertising, transportation, billing procedures, and related areas. The successful candidate will have a good grasp of the structure of various marketing institutions and will fully comprehend just how the marketing function fits into the business firm and how marketing actions have an impact on the activities and profits of the firm.

Reading, experience, and logical reasoning should all contribute to success on this examination.

NOTES

NOTES

Peterson's
Book Satisfaction Survey

Give Us Your Feedback

Thank you for choosing Peterson's as your source for personalized solutions for your education and career achievement. Please take a few minutes to answer the following questions. Your answers will go a long way in helping us to produce the most user-friendly and comprehensive resources to meet your individual needs.

When completed, please tear out this page and mail it to us at:

> Publishing Department
> Peterson's, a Nelnet company
> 2000 Lenox Drive
> Lawrenceville, NJ 08648

You can also complete this survey online at **www.petersons.com/booksurvey.**

1. **What is the ISBN of the book you have purchased? (The ISBN can be found on the book's back cover in the lower right-hand corner.)** _____

2. **Where did you purchase this book?**
   - ❑ Retailer, such as Barnes & Noble
   - ❑ Online reseller, such as Amazon.com
   - ❑ Petersons.com
   - ❑ Other (please specify) _____

3. **If you purchased this book on Petersons.com, please rate the following aspects of your online purchasing experience on a scale of 4 to 1 (4 = Excellent and 1 = Poor).**

	4	3	2	1
Comprehensiveness of Peterson's Online Bookstore page	❑	❑	❑	❑
Overall online customer experience	❑	❑	❑	❑

4. **Which category best describes you?**
   - ❑ High school student
   - ❑ Parent of high school student
   - ❑ College student
   - ❑ Graduate/professional student
   - ❑ Returning adult student
   - ❑ Teacher
   - ❑ Counselor
   - ❑ Working professional/military
   - ❑ Other (please specify) _____

5. **Rate your overall satisfaction with this book.**

Extremely Satisfied	Satisfied	Not Satisfied
❑	❑	❑

6. **Rate each of the following aspects of this book on a scale of 4 to 1 (4 = Excellent and 1 = Poor).**

	4	3	2	1
Comprehensiveness of the information	❏	❏	❏	❏
Accuracy of the information	❏	❏	❏	❏
Usability	❏	❏	❏	❏
Cover design	❏	❏	❏	❏
Book layout	❏	❏	❏	❏
Special features (e.g., CD, flashcards, charts, etc.)	❏	❏	❏	❏
Value for the money	❏	❏	❏	❏

7. **This book was recommended by:**
   - ❏ Guidance counselor
   - ❏ Parent/guardian
   - ❏ Family member/relative
   - ❏ Friend
   - ❏ Teacher
   - ❏ Not recommended by anyone—I found the book on my own
   - ❏ Other (please specify) _____

8. **Would you recommend this book to others?**

Yes	Not Sure	No
❏	❏	❏

9. **Please provide any additional comments.**

_____

_____

_____

_____

_____

Remember, you can tear out this page and mail it to us at:

Publishing Department
Peterson's, a Nelnet company
2000 Lenox Drive
Lawrenceville, NJ 08648

or you can complete the survey online at **www.petersons.com/booksurvey.**

Your feedback is important to us at Peterson's, and we thank you for your time!

If you would like us to keep in touch with you about new products and services, please include your e-mail address here: _____